The Years Before School

THE YEARS BEFORE SCHOOL

Guiding Preschool Children

SECOND EDITION

Vivian Edmiston Todd
Curriculum Specialist

Helen Heffernan
Formerly Chief, Bureau of Elementary Education
State of California

THE MACMILLAN COMPANY
COLLIER-MACMILLAN LIMITED, LONDON

THE MACMILLAN COMPANY
COLLIER-MACMILLAN CANADA, LTD., TORONTO, ONTARIO

Printed in the United States of America

Preface

Parents and grandparents like to know effective ways of working with a child, or with a child and his playmates, when the children are two, three, four, or five years old and are eager learners. Pediatricians, social workers, librarians, and others who work with families use information about pre-school children and like to have it in written form to show to and discuss with parents. Those who work with groups of children in day- or child-care centers, religious centers, parent-cooperative play groups, nurseries, and kindergartens also like to use a book which brings together under one cover the breadth of thought about teaching preschool children. *The Years Before School* is planned for use in all these ways for the betterment of children when they are two, three, four, and five years old.

The first edition of this book focused on good practice in any preschool group and left to each group those adaptations that the local situation and the individuality of people require. The present edition is occasioned by the great increase in preschool groups for children from families that par-ticipate in preschool education when it is available but do not arrange such education on their own initiative. Government funds, especially at the state and national levels, now make it possible for such children to have rich preschool years. This edition, therefore, supplements good practice in general with practice especially suitable for children from families with limited incomes. The second edition elaborates the essential elements of the first edition and includes specific suggestions for working with frag-mented and other families from ghetto, slum, and impoverished rural areas.

The decade of the 1960s involved not only a tremendous expansion in preschool education, but also the demonstration that the early environment of a child is of great importance. Awareness of the rapidity of early de-

v

velopment has led to increasing research and experimentation to determine limits within which development should be encouraged. By presenting the principles and practices of preschool groups today, *The Years Before School* establishes a bench mark helpful in further research.

Great as the development of preschool education has been, it is yet only a beginning. "Child Care Arrangements of Working Mothers in the United States," a 1968 joint report of the U.S. Department of Health, Education, and Welfare and the U.S. Department of Labor, shows that there are over 2.5 million working mothers with one or more children under six years of age. Only a little over 2 per cent of all mothers who work arrange for their children to be in a group-care center; over 8 per cent expect their children to look after themselves. When the numbers of children participating in preschool groups are compared with the numbers of children left unattended while their mothers are at work, the challenge to extend preschool education must be recognized. The challenge is intensified by noting that over 8 per cent of the group-care situations and almost 10 per cent of the self-care ones are reported to be unsatisfactory. More adequate provisions for education of children and for parent education are imperative.

The primary purpose of this edition is the same as that of the first, to provide teachers, parents, and others who work with preschool children a picture of what is done that is based on sound research findings and well-established principles of behavioral science. This purpose is set within a broader purpose of helping to enrich preschool years as a step toward attaining a better world. As every child enjoys the best possible opportunity for finding suitable outlets for his talents, community life will be improved and families will have neighbors with whom they can live and work.

A book such as *The Years Before School* requires wide observation of children of preschool age as a means of validating hypotheses about them formulated on the basis of professional reading and actual experience as a parent, teacher, and consultant in preschool groups. This breadth of observation must be supplemented by the depth of observation possible only through making case studies of children throughout their preschool years. Because the kind of case material obtainable is of interest to the student learning about preschool children, a variety of anecdotes about "Neal" are given in the book to illustrate the wide range of behavior of a preschool child.

To observe preschool children is a time-consuming process requiring much patience, because each child is only beginning to learn to relate to people outside his family, and each individual relationship must be built slowly and carefully if it is to lead to valid observations and interpretations of the child's behavior. Much significant behavior is observable and interpretable only by mothers of the children. For instance, feedback for an event at school in the morning may occur spontaneously as a child is helped to get ready for bed, and may be couched in terms that are understood only by the person who has guided his language development since its beginning. Yet these mothers are so occupied with the physical care of the preschool child and the other members of his family that they find it difficult to record what they observe in their busy lives.

Other problems of study include the usual ones, such as finding and training observers who are on location with children of the age range under consideration, who are sufficiently interested to observe and record over the period of time required for even a cross-sectional study, let alone a longitudinal one, and who are sensitive to what constitutes significant behavior.

The intensive study for *The Years Before School* was made possible primarily because of the cooperation of neighbors and friends who shared the authors' interest in the preschool field. Furthermore, Susan Todd, during the years that she was in kindergarten and first grade, not only provided her mother with an interval of time for writing but also with the opportunity for observing her younger friends—especially Neal, whose mother was an excellent and continuing observer. To the Clyde Osborne family, the Bertram McGarrity family, and the many other families who contributed their insightful observations as parents, we express our sincere appreciation.

The illustrations of this edition are evidence of the numerous excellent provisions made for preschool children across the United States and Canada. Pictures were contributed by individuals, schools, colleges, governmental agencies, and other groups interested in fostering improved practices in preschool education. From the pictures showing outstanding preschool situations were selected those with photographic excellence. Mariam M. Cook and Walter Jay Cook served as technical advisors. These professional contributions are gratefully acknowledged.

Acknowledgment is also made to those who directly and indirectly contributed to the preparation of this edition of *The Years Before School*. Organizations whose contribution has been continuing and extensive include the following:

Long Beach Unified School District
Long Beach Public Library, Boys and Girls Department
California State College at Long Beach
Long Beach Council of Parent Nursery Schools
Long Beach Day Nursery

Friends and colleagues in the field of early childhood education and adult education have been most generous in sharing the breadth of their experience and the depth of their insight.

V. E. T.
H. H.

Contents

PART ONE
Groups for American Preschool Children

1 Preschool Education in America Today 3
2 Understanding Preschool Children 29
3 Arranging for the Preschool Group 73
4 Getting the School Ready 106
5 A Preschool Group 145

PART TWO
The Curriculum for the Group

6 Health and Safety 193
7 Furthering Physical Development 240
8 Learning to Participate in the Culture 263
9 Building Science Concepts 306
10 Exploring Time, Space, and Numbers 353
11 Developing Verbal Communication 386
12 Stories for Preschool Children 420
13 Arts and Crafts for a Preschool Group 451
14 Enjoying Musical Sounds 478
15 Guiding Emotional Development 504

PART THREE
Participation in the Preschool Group

16 Parent Education 547
17 The Preschool Group as a School Laboratory 588
18 Participation in Teaching Preschool Groups 621
Index 659

List of Tables

1-1   Preschool Groups Auxiliary to Other Schools   11
2-1   Report of Observation   34
2-2   Aspects of Development of Preschool Children   36
2-3   Developmental Tasks in Ten Categories of Behavior   45
2-4   Behavior of Gifted and Handicapped Preschool Children   58
4-1   Physical Needs of Children Are Met
      Through the Physical Plant   108
4-2   The Physical Plant Helps to Develop a Healthy Personality   109
4-3   The Physical Plant Facilitates the Work of Adults   109
5-1   Behavior Expected in Preschool Children   164
7-1   Physical Development as an Integral
      Part of Preschool Activities   244
16-1   Master Schedule for a Preschool Group   573
18-1   Schedule of Community Cooperative Nursery   641

The Years Before School

Part One
GROUPS FOR AMERICAN PRESCHOOL CHILDREN

CHAPTER 1

Preschool Education in America Today

An exciting social change has been occurring in the United States. For many years the accepted age for entrance into an organized school group has been six years. First-grade classes have been made up of all the children in the community who had attained their sixth birthday. But in October of 1966, 3,674,000 children, about 30 per cent of the children between the ages of three and five, were enrolled in private or public preschool groups.[1] Furthermore, a rationale about the importance of preschool education is now widely accepted throughout the nation. The American public is rapidly developing the belief that it cannot afford to delay entrance to school if the best interests of the society are to be served, crime and juvenile delinquency are to be kept in check, and children are to grow into adults who have realized their potential.

Since the first public kindergarten opened in Saint Louis in 1873, development of preschool groups in the United States has been continuous.[2] Especially in the last decade, during which we have experienced greatly expanded arrangements for preschool children from less advantaged families, the United States has moved a considerable distance in providing all preschool children with constructive experience. The Economic Opportunity Program acted like a pump primer in developing community organizations,

[1] Samuel Schloss, Office of Education, U.S. Department of Health, Education, and Welfare, "Nursery-Kindergarten Enrollment of Children Under Six" (Washington, D.C.: U.S. Government Printing Office, 1967), pp. 6–7.

[2] Sarah Hammond Leeper, "Nursery School and Kindergarten," *What Research Says to the Teacher* (Washington, D.C.: National Education Association, 1968), pp. 3–4.

frequently entitled Project Head Start, which brought together families not taking advantage of other preschool arrangements. Parents who had not dreamed of bus trips, playmates, and teachers for their preschool children began thinking about what these children should do before entering school; they thus started growing into new roles of helping to plan for preschool children. These parents, who have experienced the fellowship of common concern about their children, will continue to be in favor of community arrangements for preschool children.

Middle-class families take satisfaction in providing for their preschool children through various groups. Sometimes these groups are organized cooperatively; sometimes through such community institutions as schools, churches, and recreation programs; and sometimes on a private-enterprise basis. What they value for their own children, they realize more and more, is desirable for future classmates of their children. An elementary school class can progress no faster than can the majority of its pupils, unless increased taxes make additional resources available to provide smaller classes and fuller programs.

State legislatures are taking a close look into the proportion of tax money to be spent for welfare and for education and are deciding that money for preschool programs may be money well spent. Money for widening the lives of preschool children may obviate some later expenditures for juvenile delinquents and criminals.

Responsible citizens realize that they need to be informed about how to develop programs for preschool children, how to maintain such programs at a satisfactory level, and how to provide programs that have educational features for both parents and their children. Teachers and parents who have known the benefits of nursery schools and kindergartens take on new responsibility as they serve as resource persons for newly forming preschool groups. Forward-looking states recognize the importance of trained leadership for such groups and enact laws and develop guide lines to facilitate their development and safeguard preschool children.[3]

Laws and other provisions to facilitate education of preschool children have been based on a growing body of knowledge about the importance of the early environment for such children. Benjamin S. Bloom, in discussing *Stability and Change in Human Characteristics,* interprets and summarizes research findings as follows:

We believe that the early environment is of crucial importance for three reasons. The first is based on the very rapid growth of selected characteristics in the early years and conceives of the variations in the early environment as

---

[3] National Council of State Consultants in Elementary Education, *Education for Children Under Six* (1968). (Available from Elementary Education, Wyoming State Department of Education, Cheyenne, Wyoming.)

so important because they shape these characteristics in their most rapid periods of formation.

. . . another way of viewing the importance of the early environment has to do with the sequential nature of much of human development. . . . the developments that take place in the early years are crucial for all that follows.

A third reason for the crucial importance of the early environment and early experiences stems from learning theory. It is much easier to learn something new than it is to stamp out one set of learned behaviors and replace them by a new set. . . .

. . . all three tend to confirm the tremendous power of early learning and its resistance to later alteration or extinction.[4]

Provisions for preschool groups across the nation are increasingly important as the nation rapidly develops a population half of which is under age twenty-five. Implicit in the mobility of youth is the fact that the impoverished young husband and wife with few marketable skills but with preschool children are of concern not only to the community in which

The essence of nursery school is another parent who loves you. (Courtesy of Montgomery County Head Start Program, Maryland.)

[4] Benjamin S. Bloom, *Stability and Change in Human Characteristics* (New York: John Wiley and Sons, Inc., 1964), pp. 215–216.

they grew up but also to the communities to which they migrate in search of opportunity. If their time and energy are so consumed that they have little to give to their children and if they have not yet learned much about helping their children develop, they need to have the provisions they do make for their children augmented by preschool group experience.

The older part of the population is also concerned with the preschool population. The threat of new generations of ignorant youth with responsibility for community affairs, or with the power to interfere with smooth functioning of municipalities and rural areas, concerns people. Out of fear for their own future at the hands of poorly informed and irresponsible youth, the older members of the population see the advantages of maximizing the development of preschool children. Values, beliefs, and interests in the better aspects of life should begin early. Preschool children need to be gradually initiated into command of the learning processes. To cope with explosions of knowledge, they need to grow up with experienced-filled hours as an important part of their lives.

In a statement of policy and proposed action regarding prekindergarten education, the New York State Board of Regents summarizes current thinking about the desirability of early provisions for schooling.[5] Such provisions are a "means of fully developing the talents of our citizens" and a "key component to the solution of social problems." They assure that future generations are able to cope with society's demands. Such beliefs are based on both experience and research with and about children during their preschool years. "These are the years when growth must be most carefully nurtured; the time when schooling must begin."

RESPONSIBILITY OF PARENTS

Responsibility for raising young children is today, as it always has been, primarily that of parents and the home. Parents are the first and foremost teachers, but they need not carry this important task alone . . . resources in addition to those of the home . . . can be used. A prekindergarten is such a resource.[6]

This quotation from a position paper by the New York State Board of Regents of the University of the State of New York defines the preschool group as a supplement to the home, not a substitute for it. The preschool group promotes more even and more complete development of the child than the home can easily provide. Most parents are limited in what they can give in the way of space, variety of equipment, educational materials, and experiences for their children. Many parents are so burdened with

[5] The State Education Department, University of the State of New York, "Prekindergarten Education" (Albany, N.Y.: University of the State of New York, December, 1967).
[6] Ibid., p. 5.

their own concerns that they are unable to provide the guidance that a child needs as he faces problems and frustrations. Especially where mothers are the sole support of the family, children may be left in the care of untrained and unhealthy people, in a crowded apartment devoid of playthings and playmates that children need. Early intervention with provision of preschool experience helps families cope with problems of urban living.

If the child's preschool years are characterized by neglect and deprivation, his growth will suffer, and severe and lasting effects of such deprivation will result. If, however, the formative years are characterized by exposure to a wide variety of learning activities and social contacts, skilled teaching, and intelligent guidance, then healthy growth and adjustment occurs.[7]

In nursery school or kindergarten, preschool children have a group experience which extends the values of family life, giving them a total experience in democratic living in which cooperation is strengthened and competition minimized. Both at home and in a preschool group the children experience the kind of life desirable in the present scientific age—life in which health, comfort, and safety are furthered; life in which it is important to find out what is not yet known and to develop more abundant and more satisfying living; life in which goals are set, plans made, and decisions reached in terms of fundamental values.

In order for preschool children to have a continuous environment characterized by democratic family values, "close parent collaboration and involvement are absolutely essential"[8] to the preschool program. Parents as well as children develop when preschool children attend nursery school or kindergarten, especially when the eldest child of a family is in a preschool group. The whole family, present and future, benefits from the parent education that is an integral part of the program. A parent who learns to listen carefully to what a preschool child is trying to communicate, for instance, is more apt to listen carefully to what others of the children are trying to communicate. In addition, improved human relationships with preschool children often lead to improved adult relationships as well.

WHAT FAMILIES BENEFIT FROM PRESCHOOL GROUPS?
The preschool groups which meet regularly throughout the school year are attended primarily by children whose families find it convenient to get them to the group. The family that lives near a preschool group or has an adult going past it each morning is the more likely to have its child attend. The location of a preschool group is an important factor in determining what families it will serve. The parent education groups available to fam-

[7] Ibid., p. 6.
[8] Ibid., p. 7.

ilies in socially concerned communities are largely attended by children whose families find it geographically convenient for them to do so.

Preschool groups may be classified according to the age level of the children they serve, according to whether they are laboratory schools, and according to the kind of family need they meet. Kindergartens are for five-year-old children; nursery groups are for three- and four-year-old children (although some include two-year-old children). A children's center typically cares for nursery children throughout the day, and for kindergarten and older children after their school hours. A laboratory school set up to benefit students in a high school, college, or adult education program may be either a nursery school or a kindergarten. Parent-cooperative groups are usually nursery groups in communities that offer kindergarten as part of the public school system, but nursery groups and kindergartens in communities that do not.

Private schools are owned and operated as a business enterprise; day or children's centers are operated as community welfare projects. In parent-cooperative groups, however, the business—and even some of the teaching—is the direct responsibility of the parents. Private schools, Head Start projects, day-care centers, and parent-cooperative groups developed independently to serve different kinds of family needs, but their personnel now work together in professional organizations to further the interests of all preschool children. Their differences in origin, operation, and function are less important than their common goal: to serve preschool children and their families.

As the number of preschool groups continues to expand, so does their variety. The needs of the families in particular communities have given rise to the formation of preschool groups for children of working or absent mothers, for future parents and teachers who wish to learn about children through observation and participation in preschool groups, and for families who wish to enrich the lives of both parents and children.

DAY NURSERIES

The day nurseries of a city are supported by the community chest, endowments and donations, and fees based on the size of the family, its income, and its ability to pay. The aim of the day nurseries is "to provide a happy, healthy, and understanding environment in which a child may grow and develop during the time his own parents, for some reason or other, are unable to care for him . . . 70 per cent of the children . . . are from homes broken by death, divorce, or desertion. They are cared for during the day while the 'breadwinner' of the family is away working, with the knowledge that his or her child is safe and happy."[9]

---

[9] *Some Facts About the Long Beach Day Nursery* (Long Beach, Calif.: Long Beach Day Nursery, 1956).

The day nurseries endeavor to reach the low-income families and other families who need their services. Referrals are made to them by the juvenile authorities and other social agencies of the city. Parents apply to them directly for admission of their preschool children. Yet many eligible families have not heard of the nurseries and many other eligible families feel that the nurseries are not for them. Although the nurseries make no distinctions of race or religion, eligible families are not always willing or able to find this out for themselves. Meanwhile, the newspapers of the city continue to carry accounts of preschool children who are left in locked automobiles while their parents work or who are hurt while playing under the inadequate care of a neighbor or of an elderly or adolescent member of the family.

Probably it is accurate to say that the children from broken homes in the city attend a nursery group when someone responsible for them makes arrangements for them to attend. In addition, children in many families under financial stress are enrolled by their parents in the day nursery and children's centers available through welfare channels.

CHILDREN'S CENTERS AND HEAD START PROJECTS

Wide community concern with provisions for educating preschool children usually results in formation of preschool groups which may be an integral part of the school system or may benefit at least from sharing some of its resources. To finance such groups, government funds, at both state and national levels, are supplemented by local contributions, and professional and nonprofessional people are encouraged to donate their skills to promote the effectiveness of the group. A government pamphlet about Project Head Start describes the child development center as follows:

The Child Development Center is both a concept and a community facility. In concept it represents the drawing together of all those resources—family, community and professional—which can contribute to the child's total development. . . .

As a community facility the Child Development Center is organized around its classroom and outdoor play areas. Ideally it should also provide a program for health services, parent interviews and counseling, feeding of the children, and meetings of parents and other residents of the community.[10]

A survey of Head Start programs offered during the summer by public school systems enrolling 300 or more pupils showed that such programs were operated in whole or in part by 63 per cent of the systems. The remaining 37 per cent of the public school systems cooperated in such pro-

[10] Office of Economic Opportunity, "Project Head Start, Daily Program I for a Child Development Center" (Washington, D.C.: U.S. Government Printing Office, 1967), p. 1.

grams by providing facilities; helping to recruit teachers, volunteers, or teacher aides; providing consultant services; and providing professional services such as testing.[11]

The preschool programs of school systems constitute the main thrust toward extending school entrance downward for all the children of the community. In the foreseeable future every family may be able to plan on early group experience for its children regardless of the size of the family income.

SCHOOL-AFFILIATED PRESCHOOL GROUPS

An increasing number of preschool groups is organized within high school, college, and adult education programs. The present social order is unique in having many educators sensitive to the characteristics of the social order and to parental—actual and prospective—responsibilities to it. Through adult education programs, these educators provide the insight and leadership that families need to arrange group experiences for their preschool children. Through the regular school program, and especially through child-development laboratories auxiliary to schools, these educators teach the parents of the future the skills and ideas necessary for raising a family as well as the pleasures and satisfactions it is possible to realize with a family. In college undergraduate and graduate programs, they prepare teachers for the preschool groups that further family life.

School systems which recognize the importance of the family as a social unit have preschool groups tied into their programs at several points. In some communities, schooling begins with three- and four-year-old children. In many communities, kindergarten is the first school experience. High school home economics programs which prepare students for family living and care of children operate nursery schools as laboratories in which the students observe and participate. Adult education programs provide an opportunity for parents to observe their children in group situations, then to discuss their observations; to participate in parent discussions and lecture forums under able leadership; and to participate in educational courses of their choice while their children are in a preschool group.

The preschool groups that are an integral part of high schools and colleges designed to prepare future parents, or accommodate actual parents, are selective and have limited enrollments. They are attended by children of families who are willing to assist the school or college in achieving its educational goals. Often parents are members of the school faculty or students in the college. Some schools and colleges give preference to the preschool children of their faculty members or students. In general, schools and colleges do not publicize their preschool groups. They have a steady

---

[11] National Education Association, Research Division, "Head Start in the Public Schools, 1966–67," *NEA Research Bulletin*, Vol. 46, No. 1 (March 1968).

flow of applicants who are sympathetic to the objectives of the school and are interested in having their preschool children participate in a school-sponsored program.

Preschool groups in adult education programs are primarily for the education of the parents, and are generally available to the families of all preschool children. The groups are attended by children and parents of families who are sufficiently interested in their children to make the effort to come regularly as often as the group meets.

Colleges and universities which prepare nursery, elementary, and high school teachers and leaders for home economics, child development, and adult education programs also make nursery school or kindergarten observation and participation available to their students. They recognize that those who are to work with families need to have experience with preschool children.

The fact that schools and colleges provide schools for preschool children is incidental to their accomplishment of other objectives. In educating citizens for contemporary living, the schools are at the same time educating prospective parents who will have a key part in preparing the next generation of citizens. Increasing realization of this relationship will lead to further increases in the number of preschool groups within schools and colleges. Preschool groups typically connected with each of the several types of school, and the major purposes of each connection, are set forth in Table 1-1.

TABLE 1-1.   Preschool Groups Auxiliary to Other Schools

SCHOOL CONNECTION OF PRESCHOOL GROUP	EDUCATIONAL PURPOSE OF THE PRESCHOOL GROUP
Elementary school	To provide education and care for preschool children in families of working parents, in disadvantaged families, and in families wanting to enroll. To help parents guide children.
Adult education program	To help parents in observing and guiding their children.
Elementary school; Junior high school	To give upper-grade pupils experience with small children.
Junior college; College; University	To give babysitters and prospective and actual parents an opportunity to understand and guide children. To provide observation and laboratory experience for students in behavioral studies. To prepare students for teaching and other work with children. To further development of teachers and others in service with children. To provide care for preschool children of married students.

PRIVATE NURSERY SCHOOLS AND KINDERGARTENS

Families at the higher end of the economic scale in a city enroll their children in private preschool groups supported entirely by fees. These groups are convenient for families in which the mother has professional responsibility, club or social activities, or other personal interests. From the time her preschool child is picked up by the school bus until he is delivered at home, the mother feels free to think about other matters. Meanwhile, the child participates in a social situation supervised each day by the same teacher—an experience more suited to his age than that provided by a succession of babysitters.

CHURCH-SPONSORED GROUPS FOR PRESCHOOL CHILDREN

In addition to the nursery groups and kindergartens operated to make a profit for their owners, a city has several nonprofit preschool groups operated by religious organizations which charge fees that compare favorably with those charged by babysitters in the community. The children attend half-day sessions two or three times a week. If a large number of families in the neighborhood of a church desire to enroll their children, preference is sometimes given to those families who are members of the church.

The policies of a church-sponsored preschool group determine what and how many families it will serve, and are subject to review by the governing board of the church. At worst, the board may oppose the use of church facilities by preschool children; at best, it may supplement fees with funds to be used to improve equipment and to increase the amount of teaching time in relation to the number of children in the school.

Increasingly, churches favor use of their premises by a preschool group of their own, a parent-cooperative school, or a group operated by a community organization—such as an association of university women. The church governing board recognizes that the preschool group fosters values important in a Christian society; helps children at an age critical in their development; benefits the community; and benefits the church directly by sharing, with the Sunday school, equipment needed by both groups. In the future, more and more families can look to their synagogue or church to provide weekday as well as day-of-worship group experience for their preschool children.

OTHER AFFILIATED PRESCHOOL GROUPS

Other community agencies provide for children by enriching family living. Recreation commissions provide activities for preschool children as well as for people of other ages. Libraries recognize the preschool audience by scheduling a weekly storytelling hour for them. Parent-Teacher Associations, the American Association of University Women, the Young Women's Christian Association, and similar groups provide group experience for preschool children, often at the same time that they have meetings for parents.

PARENT-COOPERATIVE GROUPS

Families who wish to share the preschool experience of their children form parent-cooperative groups. They meet in the city park, in church, or in community centers. The mothers take turns in assisting the teacher whom they select. Each children's group meets two, three, or four mornings a week—depending upon the age of the children and the planning of their parents and teacher. The program of parent-cooperatives is described as follows:

Cooperative nurseries help children develop through democratic and constructive play situations. Mothers cooperate in providing regular supervised play for their preschool children, planned and carried out with professional help. This cooperative experience aids in the education, growth, and better adjustment of not only the children but also the mothers. The entire family and the community benefit from the cooperative nursery. . . . In the urbanized culture of today, cooperative nurseries help to develop the group feelings and relationships of the large family and the small neighborhood community of yesteryear. . . .

What the parent gets:

1. Better understanding of her own child and of children in general.
2. A supervised play group for her child . . . including a wealth of educational activities, companionable playmates, and the use of more equipment than the usual home can easily provide.
3. Each month ten or more free mornings for her own interests. . . .
4. A voice in determining how the cooperative nursery operates.

What the parent gives:

1. Two hours one evening each week (for one semester) . . . attending a class.
2. Two mornings each month assisting the nursery group teacher with the children.
3. Five dollars entrance fee plus —— dollars each month.
4. One evening each month for the monthly business and educational meeting of parents.[12]

With the mothers assisting her, the teacher is able to plan a program which includes activities that the mothers suggest and provide. Furthermore, the teacher knows that she can help a child with a temper tantrum, or a cut, or some other problem, while assistants help the other children to carry on any activity that requires careful supervision. Thus the parent-

[12] Vivian Edmiston Todd, ed., *Cooperative Nursery School Handbook* (Long Beach, Calif.: Long Beach Council of Parent Nursery Schools, 1957).

cooperative preschool group is characterized by a rich program for the children. It adds to the family life of professional people, educators, and others actively interested in cooperating with each other to further the development of their children.

BACKYARD PLAY GROUPS

Backyard groups form when several neighborhood families with pre-school children find it useful to have their children play together regularly. The mothers work out whatever arrangements seem most agreeable to them. Usually the mothers take turns in supervising the children, so that the other mothers have time for housekeeping and personal interests. The quality of care thus depends on the standards accepted by all the mothers and upon their individual talents for handling a group of preschool children. When these informal groups meet in a backyard well equipped for children, or at a playground area, the number of conflict situations among the children is less than when they are expected to play in an environment that has little to stimulate constructive activities.

Backyard groups differ from the organized groups already described in that they do not have one mother figure but a succession of them. For the children, this discontinuity in their experience is much like having a series of babysitters who reappear from time to time.

Backyard groups sometimes suffer because parents lack information about children and their needs, but the groups which make use of the licensing and advisory services available through such agencies as the State Department of Social Welfare are helpful both to children and their mothers. Backyard play groups, like other preschool groups, make it possible for the children to have group experience.

The Basic Element of a Preschool Group

Fundamental both to family and to preschool group is an atmosphere of love. The importance of love is only now being recognized as the factor which makes the difference between a play group and a preschool group in which children happily learn at an optimum rate.

The element of love is essential to life at every age level. The physiological and biological aspects of love which loom as overwhelmingly important during the mating period are seen as less important than the aspects of love which are basic to human relationships at all age periods. Educators who had thought love extraneous to the classroom now recognize it as an element conducive to learning.

WHAT IS LOVE?

Daniel A. Prescott, an educator concerned with child development, recognizes the presence of love in the educative process and defines it realistically in terms of human relations appropriate throughout the life span. He says that love "is a valuing to the degree that one achieves empathy with the loved one and a willingness to make one's resources available to promote his self-realization."[13]

The definition of love, applied in the preschool group experience, emphasizes several attributes:

- Valuing each child.
- Making all of one's resources available to the child as needed.
- Having a high degree of empathy with him, with confidence that he will achieve his potential.
- Guiding him in recognizing alternatives, making choices, and finding satisfaction in decisions.
- Helping him to reach goals with awareness of what he has done.

Here indeed is a challenge to teachers of preschool children, to put into action this concept of love.

Consider the implications of this definition for the relationships between adults and children. "Valuing each child" is a basic concept in democracy. Respect for the individual implies respect for the child as an individual. Each child has the right to express his feelings, both positive and negative, and his preferences and his desires with the expectation that the adults who are present will listen respectfully and attentively. Listening does not always imply a granting of these wishes, but it does imply their careful consideration in realistic terms. "I want a doll," says the little girl, wanting attention rather than another doll. The adult to whom she addresses her remark is interested and responds, "You want a doll?" After the adult has listened further to just what kind of a doll the girl wants, she may share her wishes with the little girl: "You want a doll. Do you know what I want?"—and then go on to explain that she is not going to get what she wants because it is not something she really needs. "You and I don't always get what we want. But we always get the food and things that we need," the adult concludes with a hug. She knows that the little girl will be much older before she really understands that abstract verbal distinction.

Such a conversation based on love can be contrasted with the more usual brief conversation in which the adult does not value the child to the point of recognizing his wants of equal importance to the adults:

[13] Daniel A. Prescott, *The Child in the Educative Process* (New York: McGraw-Hill Book Company, Inc., 1957), p. 410.

CHILD   I want a doll.
ADULT   You have enough dolls.

Valuing a child is one way in which the adult encourages the child to realize his own importance as an individual and to value others in turn.

Evidence of a loving relation between adult and child is found in their empathy. This is more than the adult's ability to see things from the standpoint of the child; it implies laughing when the child laughs, having confidence that he will create what should be, sympathizing when he meets with unhappiness, sharing his satisfaction in achievement—and at all times throughout this pacing, thoroughly appreciating and respecting him as a person. When empathy is broken by an evaluative remark, such as, "You have enough dolls," the love relationship is temporarily impaired. The sensitive adult then reassures the child of her love and, at the same time, helps the child cope with reality. Her calm reassurance is in sharp contrast to the unhappy argument between child and adult when love is absent. Where there is empathy, there is love.

Willingness to make one's resources available is also a test of love. Certain adults are willing to buy a child whatever he wants but are not willing to spend time with him. Other adults use their energy to prepare activities for children and then are unhappy when the children prefer activities of their own choosing. They insist on having the children with them constantly. But the adult who really loves children is able to adapt the timing of activities to the children's rhythm of activity and rest, to introduce new activities only at transition points in the play of children, and to say, "Okay," when the children respond negatively to the question: "Would you like to do this now?"

An adult who loves children wishes to promote their self-realization. She tries to help preschool children realize their importance as individuals. She does this, for instance, by expressing her love for the child, and by helping each child to do what he wants to do—within the limits of physical safety. As the recipient of such love, the child feels secure, happy, and loving, and is able to profit from the resources available to him. Such a foundation is essential if the child is to grow into a person who can go on to realize his potentialities.

Erich Fromm writes, "The most fundamental kind of love, which underlies all types of love, is *brotherly love*. By this I mean the sense of responsibility, care, respect, knowledge of any other human being, the wish to further his life. This is the kind of love the Bible speaks of when it says, 'Love thy neighbor as thyself.' "[14]

Such a statement enlarges on earlier statements, such as that made by Pestalozzi during the latter part of the eighteenth century: "Love is the

[14] Erich Fromm, *The Art of Loving* (New York: Harper & Row, Publishers, 1956), p. 47.

sole and everlasting foundation on which our nature can be trained to humaneness."[15]

Through love, children develop the ability to be humane. By receiving love, they become able to love others. The parents and the teachers who love the children also benefit. As Montagu says in his definition of love, "Love is reciprocal in its effects, and is as beneficial to the giver as it is to the recipient."[16]

Montagu concludes "that the most important function of education is to draw out and develop the potentialities of the child for being a loving human being."[17] Certainly this is the most important function in the preschool group: to help each child to be a loving human being.

THE PLACE OF LOVE IN PRESCHOOL AND IN SCHOOL

The place of love in preschool differs from that in school because the function of preschool is different from that of school. Preschool goals are in terms of children developing each at his own pace; school goals are in terms of adult expectations for future citizens. Competent preschool teachers develop simple dialogue with each preschool child, using body and oral language, and valuing him as a person. Competent school teachers, on the other hand, must go beyond these learning bridges which are an integral part of what is termed love. A school teacher is expected to guide the learning of children in such a way that they develop defined skills, beliefs, and concepts. Her success as a school teacher is tied in with the successful learning of the children. She is apt under that circumstance to equate "love" with "a way of binding and controlling children,"[18] and find it difficult to "love" thirty or more pupils or students.

With genuine love it is possible for both school teacher and preschool teacher to accomplish the "major task of the teacher," namely, "not to lose her credibility and authenticity as a person."[19] With love, the kindergarten teacher helps five-year-old children develop an understanding of what a rule is and an interest in setting up and following rules. Because "it is probable that what children seek from teachers and vice versa is a relationship of respect and agreement on rules by which both can plan the game of learning with zest and satisfaction,"[20] the preschool teacher, through love, lays a foundation on which the school teacher can subsequently guide children in learning what is expected of them as future citizens, and, at the same time, retain her identity as a person.

[15] M. F. A. Montagu, *The Direction of Human Development* (New York: Harper & Row, Publishers, 1955), p. 304.
[16] Ibid.
[17] Ibid.
[18] Eli M. Bower, "Fostering Maximum Growth in Children" (Washington, D.C.: National Education Association, 1965), p. 37.
[19] Ibid., p. 38.
[20] Ibid., p. 37.

The Role of the Preschool Teacher

The teacher in the preschool group, like the mother in the home, is the person responsible for creating an atmosphere of love. As she is, so will the preschool group be. The love that she radiates to those who participate in the school is reflected from person to person and back to her. When parents and students participate as assistant teachers, they—like the children—feel the teacher's love and, through their own love, increase its radiance. The empathy of the teacher with each person, and the empathy among persons is a measure of the love that permeates the preschool group.

A BALANCED CURRICULUM

Although love is the *sine qua non* of a preschool group, it is not enough in itself. The teacher must create a physical as well as a social environment favorable to the development of children. Love must have a physical environment in which the children are safe, happy, and learning at an optimum rate. And love must be supplemented with an understanding of children and a curriculum suited to their needs.

It is the responsibility of the teacher to see that the children have the apparatus and activities required for well-rounded physical development. Three- and four-year-old children are just beginning to develop control of their large muscles; none must be neglected. The teacher also should help the children to develop an understanding of the various roles they have and will have in the society—being a child now and an adult later, being a city dweller or a rural one, being feminine or masculine, becoming a mother or a daddy—and she should help them to understand, to appreciate, and to use the artifacts associated with these roles. She should encourage them to explore the physical environment in which they live. She should introduce them to quantitative as well as qualitative relationships.

The teacher must recognize the value of verbal as well as empathetic communication as she encourages the children to express themselves in words. She should introduce them to the wealth of children's literature and help them to dramatize their favorite stories. She should also encourage them to get acquainted with various art media and to express themselves through these media. She should provide them with a wealth of musical experience as an integral part of each day. As she plans and provides a well-balanced curriculum for the children, she must always be aware of the importance of helping them to relate to her and to each other in socially acceptable ways.

DEVELOPMENT OF PARENTS

The teacher who creates an atmosphere of love in which the children develop socially, emotionally, physically, and intellectually, also creates an atmosphere favorable to the development of the parents and prospective parents who observe or participate in the preschool group. As they experience the comfortable feeling of the children's group, they can become aware of the combination of love, democratic procedure, and educational technique, which produces it.

Prospective parents free actual parents and teachers to observe and guide preschool children. (Courtesy of San Marcos Parent Child Workshop, San Marcos High School, Santa Barbara, California.)

When the teacher participates in the discussions of high school or college students, or of parents, she should contribute to the discussion as one of the resource people, and also as a person who furthers love and democracy, family life and preschool group experience.

DEVELOPMENT OF STAFF MEMBERS

The effective preschool teacher enjoys working with adults as well as preschool children. She should have such interest in guiding learning of young children that her enthusiasm attracts and holds others who share her interest—parents, grandparents, and other volunteers; teen-age students; and aides serving as teacher assistants. As she works with them and with the preschool children, the teacher expresses appreciation of their helpfulness, observes what each does and does not do in guiding the children, interprets his behavior as feedback on what he needs to learn, and makes constructive suggestions about how to provide learning activities for the children. She furthers his awareness of how preschool children learn and of what changes in the social and physical environment of a child contribute to changes in his behavior. She encourages colleagues and assistants in exploring alternative procedures and observing resulting changes in the development of children. She helps them in obtaining feedback as they guide learning, and in planning more effective means for accomplishing their objectives. In short, the preschool teacher is sensitive to her role in augmenting the professional development of her colleagues and assistants. Her role as a master teacher working with apprentices is so important that it is discussed in detail in Chapter 18.

INTERPRETATION OF THE PRESCHOOL GROUP TO THE COMMUNITY

Realizing the importance of preschool group experience, the teacher should help other members of the community to appreciate how the preschool group strengthens and enriches family life. The teacher who is aware of the various types of preschool groups can advise families who are looking for the group especially suited for their family.

Through membership in such professional organizations as the National Association for Education of Young Children and the Association for Childhood Education International, the teacher has the opportunity to work with others who are interested in preschool children. She must put aside her vested interests in the particular type of preschool education with which she is associated—private nursery school, children's center, parent-cooperative play group, or school-sponsored preschool group. The good of preschool children in general is more important than loyalty to any type of administrative organization—no matter how significant in the history and development of preschool groups. The teacher should be primarily concerned that preschool groups be planned in terms of children of preschool age, and in terms of families as they are today. With this wider purpose, she should strive to help people to understand the desirability of a full, rich life for young children and the importance of a preschool group experience in love and democracy as a bridge between the home and the elementary school.

Ways Children Develop in a Preschool Group

EXPECTED CHANGES

Preschool group experience is expected to influence the behavior of children who have it. Such children should develop values and interests they have not had, should acquire mental and motor skills in greater number than children lacking such experience, and should have a fund of information beyond what they would have had otherwise. Such aims and expectations have been defined in some detail for the use of Head Start projects as follows:

To help children
  learn to work and play independently, at ease about being away from home, and able to accept help and direction from adults;
  learn to live effectively with other children, and to value one's own rights and the rights of others;
  develop self-identity and a view of themselves as having competence and worth;
  realize many opportunities to strive and to succeed—physically, intellectually and socially;
  sharpen and widen language skills, both listening and speaking;
  be curious—that is, to wonder, to seek answers to questions;
  strengthen physical skills, using large and small muscles;
  grow in ability to express inner, creative impulses—dancing, making up songs, painting, handicrafts, etc.;
  grow in ability to channel inner, destructive impulses—to turn aggression into hard work, talk instead of hit, understand the difference between feeling angry and acting angry, feel sympathy for the troubles of others.[21]

It is logical to expect that children who have preschool group experience will gain from that experience. Fears of being in a group should be replaced by familiar pleasures of group participation. Successful and happy days in a preschool group not only make for self-confidence and a favorable stance toward group experience in school later, but also may well result in a "net gain in years of education," as the New York State Board of Regents believe. This gain is especially important for children because "the impact of school at this early time may well have far stronger consequences than the impact at any other age."[22]

Whether expected changes actually occur is a challenge to research workers. Currently researchers are concerned about early experience in relation to cognitive development,[23] and the U.S. Office of Education has an additional concern with development of a National Laboratory in Early Childhood Education. Furthermore, progress reports by Head Start projects include evaluation of the project and study of its accomplishments. Out of

[21] Office of Economic Opportunity, "Project Head Start, Daily Program I, For a Child Development Center" (Washington, D.C.: U.S. Government Printing Office, 1967), p. 8.
[22] New York State Education Department, The University of the State of New York, "Prekindergarten Education," op. cit., p. 10.
[23] Susan W. Gray and James O. Miller, "Early Experience in Relation to Cognitive Development," *Review of Educational Research*, Vol. XXXVII, No. 5 (December 1967), pp. 475–493.

these beginnings should come understanding of what is reasonable to expect of preschool children from different styles of life and evidence as to its attainment under various preschool programs.

The starting point: a first day at preschool. (Milwaukee Journal Photo. Courtesy of University of Wisconsin at Milwaukee.)

Meanwhile experienced kindergarten and first-grade teachers report on their experience with children who have had previous group experience much as did Mrs. Anne McKee, a kindergarten teacher in Trenton, New Jersey, who said, "In September, the class got off to a much better start because half of the children already had school experiences. . . . There was a happier and better adjustment at once because the inexperienced children watched and followed those who felt secure."[24]

Mrs. McKee described the behavior of children who had had prior nursery school experience, as follows:

They were more willing to enter into and take part in physical activities during rhythm periods.

[24] New Jersey State Department of Education, "Alice and Her Wonderful World of Discovery," Progress Report I, Trenton Junior Five Project (Trenton, N.J.: State Department of Education, 1966), p. 33.

They were interested in many activities and always kept busy. They did not ask, "What can I do now?"

They enjoyed the different interest centers in the room.

They worked independently and did not demand that the teacher help them or want to show their work constantly.

They had more definite ideas in working with blocks.

Only one child with nursery-school experience cried and had difficulty adjusting to the group. About six children without nursery-school background made slow adjustment. The child with nursery-school experience adjusted after two days. When she entered nursery-school the previous year, she cried many days before she was willing to stay.

Most of the children from the nursery-school carried on conversations more fluently. They listened to stories in an interested manner and enjoyed looking at books.[25]

DEVELOPMENT AS A PERSON

The child's experience in a preschool group should foster his development in every way. This development may be described as having four aspects: social, intellectual, physical, and emotional. These categories are used only for convenience in looking at a child's development so as to obtain a fuller understanding of his nature. They need not obscure the fact that the child is an integrated personality and a delightful little person who, above all, has fun in his preschool group with children of his age range. In fact, this is a primary objective of a preschool group because it is a basic axiom that he who enjoys life fully at one age is most apt to enjoy life fully at succeeding ages.

The fun, of course, is always within the bounds of safety and the expectations of the society. It merges in adulthood into family life and vocational and community responsibility. The child who learned to have fun in a preschool group learns to go on having fun constructively with members of his family, his work group, his neighborhood, and the larger society of the nation and the world.

SOCIAL DEVELOPMENT

When parents consider a preschool group for their child, they are apt to think of its social benefits for him:

There aren't any children on our block the age of Timmy. He just doesn't have anybody to play with in our neighborhood.

When the older children go off to school. Mary cries and seems lost without them.

Johnny needs someone to play with. He wants me to watch what he's doing instead of letting me get the housework done.

[25] Ibid., p. 34.

Certainly the nursery group is an ideal situation for furthering social development. There the child finds a wealth of things to play with by himself while other children play nearby. Presently, he finds that he can ride a tricycle while his friend rides a tricycle, or make a picture while another friend is making a picture, or drink juice with other friends. This individual and parallel play has brief interludes of cooperative play as the child comes to share in a group sandbox project or in a bit of dramatic action. Progress in playing with others is social progress, readily observed as a benefit of preschool group experience.

Preschool furthers social, intellectual, physical, and emotional development. (Courtesy of Jacksonville Schools and Florida State Department of Education, Tallahassee, Florida.)

As a child goes from his home into a nursery group, into kindergarten, and on into the primary grades of the elementary school, he moves into atmospheres of gradually increasing formality and more rigidly structured programs of activities. This increase in structuring parallels his social development. As he learns to be part of a group, he is able to participate in group activities for longer periods of time. His first nursery experiences are essentially individual ones, with increasing exploration of group activities. By the time he is in the first grade, he should be ready for a preponderance of group activities.

INTELLECTUAL DEVELOPMENT

Parents of nursery children sometimes say with surprise, "And Mary learned things, too," as if intellectual development were an unexpected but appreciated by-product of the preschool group. Actually, growth toward an understanding of the world he lives in is a most important objective of a good preschool group, and one that has been pointed out by such pioneers of preschool education as Pestalozzi.

Today it is evident that all aspects of the elementary school curriculum have their roots in the nursery group and kindergarten. The child takes on essential attitudes, develops the beginnings of skills, and builds concepts basic to all fields of knowledge. He learns at his age level what will be a foundation for his later learning about health, social studies, science, mathematics, language, literature, art, and music. He starts joyously into the whole world of knowledge when he has experience in a well-planned curriculum.

PHYSICAL DEVELOPMENT

A preschool group should also be an aid to the well-rounded physical development of children. Apparatus helps them learn how to climb and how to handle their bodies in different positions. The good teacher analyzes the kind of play children have in their community and plans activities designed to supplement their play. For instance, if the children play only on level ground at home, the teacher plans experience in getting over uneven ground. Realizing that few children are encouraged in rhythmic activities at home, the good teachers include these in the group program. Keeping in mind that preschool children are very active, she plans a minimum of sedentary activities and provides daily opportunities for vigorous, large-muscle activities. Thus she sees to it that the well-rounded physical development of children is furthered in her preschool group.

EMOTIONAL DEVELOPMENT

The importance of the emotional development of children during their preschool years is apparent in such expressions as, "As the twig is bent, so is the tree inclined," or, "Set his feet upon the path, and in later years he will not depart therefrom." Yet, although psychoanalysts and religious workers have long recognized that basic emotional patterns are developed in the early years of life, comparatively little attention has been given to identifying the ways in which children may be helped to develop an emotional foundation to stand them in good stead throughout their lives.

Teachers of nursery groups and kindergartens must be aware of the importance of making daily provision for helping children to find suitable emotional outlets, to find pleasure in socially acceptable behavior, and to experience and reflect genuine love. Only the home is more important in furthering desirable emotional development.

CREATIVE DEVELOPMENT

In the preschool group a child is free to develop creatively. The preschool group is carefully planned and administered to provide an atmosphere of love and a rich environment in which a child is free to develop unique aspects of his personality and to create, in words and in space, expressions of his thoughts and feelings. The preschool is an environment which makes optimal the self-development of each child.

Situations for Discussion

A preschool teacher is apt to find herself in situations similar to the four described here. As you think of what to do in each situation, consider whether each course of action suggested is desirable or not. Use points brought out in the chapter as well as ideas from your own experience to justify your views. Suggest alternative courses of action to supplement those given.

SITUATION 1   You have moved to a new community and are interested in making an informal survey of the nursery group situations in it. You should

- Talk with the principal of a nearby elementary school.
- Watch for nursery school announcements in the local paper.
- Use the classified section of the telephone directory.
- Talk with the librarian in charge of the books for boys and girls.
- Inquire of the adult education office.

SITUATION 2   You are a member of a panel, considering the nursery group as an institution related to the present social order in the United States. You suggest that the panel discuss

- Importance of early environment.
- Growth of cities.
- Mobility of young parents.
- Education for parenthood.
- Women in industry.

SITUATION 3   A family in your neighborhood asks you about their only child, a four-year-old girl. Do you think she should go to nursery school? In talking with them, you see that they understand that

- Families make their own decisions.
- Nursery school experience prepares children for school experience.
- An only child needs playmates of his own age.
- The choice of a nursery school depends on how the parents wish to participate in it.

SITUATION 4   A parent group is discussing the topic: "The Nursery School Strengthens the Family." As a member of the group, you help to bring out that nursery school

- Is built on love.
- Helps the preschool child be more cooperative.
- Gives the family a rest from the preschool child.
- Provides early discovery of talents and special interests.
- Is an experience in democracy.

Current Professional Books and Pamphlets

AMETJIAN, ARMISTRE. *The Effect of a Preschool Program upon the Intellectual Development and Social Competency of Lower-Class Children.* Palo Alto, Calif.: Stanford University Library, 1966. [Reports a full-day six-month nursery-school program for disadvantaged children. Scores on mental age, social competency, and language ability were significantly higher for the experimental than for the control group.]

BLOOM, BENJAMIN S. *Stability and Change in Human Characteristics.* New York: John Wiley and Sons, Inc., 1964. [Verifies importance and influence of early environment and experience.]

BOSSARD, JAMES, and ELEANOR BOLL. *The Sociology of Child Development.* New York: Harper & Row, Publishers, 1966. [Child development is within family life.]

BURGESS, EVANGELINE. *Values in Early Childhood Education.* Washington, D.C.: National Education Association, 1963. [A booklet of the Department of Elementary-Kindergarten-Nursery Education.]

CHRISTIANSON, HELEN M., MARY M. ROGERS, and BLANCHE A. LUDLUM. *Nursery School: Adventure in Living and Learning.* Boston: Houghton Mifflin Company, 1961. [Chapter 7 discusses "Nursery School Education— Twentieth Century Development."]

Encyclopedia of Educational Research. New York: The Macmillan Company, 1960. ["Early Childhood Education" is discussed by Elizabeth Mechem Fuller, pp. 385–398 in this work produced by American Educational Research Association.]

GRAY, SUSAN W., RUPERT KLAUS, JAMES O. MILLER, and BETTYE J. FORESTER. *Before First Grade.* New York: Teachers College Press, Columbia University, 1966. [Describes the experimental testing of an intervention program designed to improve the educability of young deprived children.]

HAMLIN, RUTH, ROSE MUKERJI, and MARGARET YONEMURA. *Schools for Young Disadvantaged Children.* New York: Teachers College Press, Columbia University, 1967. [A school for disadvantaged children involves cooperation of many people.]

HAMMOND, SARAH L., and others. *Good Schools for Young Children.* New York: The Macmillan Company, 1968. [Part I discusses "Why Schools for Young Children?"]

HEADLEY, NEITH. *The Kindergarten: Its Place in the Program of Education.* New York: The Center for Applied Research in Education, Inc., 1965.

[Historical backgrounds, status of the kindergarten in the United States, value, curriculum, relation to elementary school, current trends and issues.]

HECHINGER, FRED M. *Pre-School Education Today.* Garden City, N.Y.: Doubleday and Company, Inc., 1966. [Background readings on new developments in preschool education, especially provisions for disadvantaged children.]

HEFFERNAN, HELEN, ed. *Guiding the Young Child.* Boston: D. C. Heath & Company, 1958. [Chapter I deals with "The Young Child in a Democratic Society."]

HEFFERNAN, HELEN, and VIVIAN EDMISTON TODD. *The Kindergarten Teacher.* Boston: D. C. Heath & Company, 1960. [Discusses kindergarten in relation to elementary school, and provides a guide to appropriate experiences for kindergarten personnel.]

HYMES, JAMES L. *Public Kindergartens.* Washington, D.C.: National Education Association, 1966. [A useful leaflet to encourage downward extension of the elementary school.]

LEEPER, SARAH HAMMOND. *Nursery School and Kindergarten.* Washington, D.C.: National Education Association, 1968. [Types of services, standards, objectives, curriculum are considered in this Number 22 of What-Research-Says-to-the-Teacher.]

National Education Association. *Kindergarten Education.* Washington, D.C.: National Education Association, 1968. [Each of several authors discusses an important aspect of kindergarten education.]

TAYLOR, KATHARINE WHITESIDE. *Parents and Children Learn Together.* New York: Bureau of Publications, Teachers College, Columbia University, 1968. [In parent cooperative preschool groups both parents and children learn.]

UNESCO. *Preschool Education.* Paris, France: United Nations Educational, Scientific and Cultural Organization, 1963.

U.S. Office of Education. *Educating Children in Nursery School and Kindergarten.* Washington, D.C.: U.S. Government Printing Office. 1966. [Lillian S. Gore and Rose Koury prepared this government bulletin, Bulletin No. 11 Mackintosh, Gore, and Lewis prepared *Educating Disadvantaged Children Under Six.*]

Wage and Labor Standards Administration, United States Department of Labor. *Working Mothers and the Need for Child Care Services.* Washington, D.C.: U.S. Government Printing Office, 1968. [A study of how children of working mothers are cared for showed 2 per cent of the children in group care and 8 per cent looking after themselves.]

CHAPTER 2

Understanding Preschool Children

Increasingly, teachers and parents are recognizing that preschool years are the golden age for learning. By capitalizing on the child's social sensitivity and on his many interests at these ages, adults help him prepare for meeting the developmental problems that lie ahead. A full life at three and four years of age is one of the best guarantees that a child will enjoy a full life in succeeding years.

The question most often asked and answered by those working with preschool children is, "What is good for the children?" Administrative procedure, each phase of the curriculum, and the day-to-day operations of the school are all decided in terms of this basic question. Even in those situations in which the school is a laboratory for students or parents, the basic question is still, "What is best for the children?"

What is best for the children is also best for those who work with them, and for observers of the children as well. For instance, those who come at rest time to see the physical activity of children observe, not activity, but something fundamental to activity—namely, the necessary alternation with it of rest. While their needs are respected by the continuance of their usual daily routine, the children are observable as fascinating little people. Their teacher needs to explain, but not to apologize for, what the children do. Each child is doing whatever seems best for him under the circumstances. The wise teacher helps observers understand children from the point of view of the child, a point of view to be distinguished from that of adults.

THE POINT OF VIEW OF A CHILD

To understand that adults and children look at things from two different points of view, an adult need only get down to the eye level of the child

29

and see what is visible from there. A child may see only the fence when an adult, looking over it, is enjoying the sight of a beautiful flower garden beyond.

The parents who were eager to take their child with them to the zoo waited until he was almost three to show him the big animals that fascinated them. At the zoo they took their son to cage after cage. "Look at the bear! *Look,* David! He's doing a trick! He's standing up on his hind legs!" The child obligingly watched, but without his parents' enthusiasm. He seemed more interested in the little chickens wandering along on the paths with the people. Suddenly he was alert, interested in something ahead. His parents followed him as he ran as fast as his short legs could carry him to a door they had not noticed, and happily set about turning the knob back and forth.

On the way home the father and mother realized that their almost-three-year-old son was as interested in a chicken as in a monkey because of his limited experience with animals—he had seen each of them only once or twice. They realized, too, that of the many kinds of animals in the zoo it was the unusual ones that interested them, and to a little boy getting acquainted with all kinds of doorknobs, the unusual doorknobs at the zoo were the interesting thing. They were learning what all parents and teachers need to know—the point of view of the child.

The way that David's parents learned the point of view of their son at the zoo is a good way to learn a child's point of view: observe what he does and does not do. What interests the child? With what events, localities, or people is each interest associated? Knowing the interests of a child, and the factors associated with his interests, the parent or teacher is in a position to capitalize on these interests, expand them, and guide them toward the adult world.

CHARACTERISTIC BEHAVIOR

Gesell and Ilg[1] emphasize the facts that all children of a given age level have certain aspects of behavior in common and that there is a sequence in patterns of behavior. These sequences are to be noted within four fields:

1. Motor Behavior (posture, locomotion, prehension, and postural sets).
2. Adaptive Behavior (capacity to perceive significant elements in a situation, and to use present and past experience to adapt to new situations).
3. Language Behavior (all forms of communications and comprehension by gestures, sounds, words).
4. Personal-Social Behavior (personal reactions to other persons and to the social culture).[2]

[1] Arnold Gesell and Frances L. Ilg, *Child Development* (New York: Harper & Row, Publishers, 1949). This single volume contains *The Infant and Child in the Culture of Today* and *The Child From Five to Ten.*
[2] Ibid., p. 62.

In the field of personal-social behavior, a sequence is observable, for instance, in the way a child reacts to the toys he possesses. Gesell and Ilg reported the sequence of such behavior as follows:

Two Years Old
Strong feeling of ownership in toys. "It's mine" is a constant refrain.
Difficulty in sharing toys; hoards them.
May bring small token such as marble, orange section, etc., to school and hold onto it all morning, objecting to anyone's taking it.[3]
Three Years Old
Beginning to share toys; less hoarding.
Brings possessions to school to share with others; books, for instance.[4]
Four Years Old
Is more apt to share possessions with special friends than with others.
This is an age of barter and swapping of possessions.[5]

Parents and teachers find such descriptions of behavior sequences useful because they constitute a basis for planning how to work effectively with children at a given age level.

Recording and studying their observations of children, Gesell and Ilg developed awareness of outgoing periods followed by withdrawal periods. Outgoing ages, characterized by activity in many directions at once, are followed by nodal ages at which the child seems to be especially in tune with himself and his social order:

OUTGOING AGES	NODAL AGES
Two and one half years of age	Three years of age
Four years of age	
Six years of age	Five years of age

Pediatricians and others who see a child only a few times a year are especially aware of these behavioral swings, and take them into account as they note the physical development of the child. They know that the child reacts to the routine of the physical examination differently when he is in an outgoing phase of development than when he is in a more balanced nodal period.

Grandparents and other relatives who see children only at intervals also need to be aware of the alternation of outgoing exploring periods with nodal periods during which the child consolidates his gains and may seem comparatively withdrawn. In fact, since nodal-age behaviors are the more compatible with the expectations of adults, relatives who prefer quiet and order do well to time their visits when the children are at such ages.

[3] Ibid., p. 169.
[4] Ibid., pp. 213–214.
[5] Ibid., p. 236.

CHILDREN FROM LESS ADVANTAGED ENVIRONMENTS

Currently it is realized that preschool children differ according to their home environments. The style of life that a child has known, for instance, has much to do with his ways of expressing emotions. If he has grown up in an upper-middle-class home, he probably has known security in getting food when he was hungry and has been cared for by people who were able to control the environment for his benefit. Observation of his behavior shows him to be confident and ready for new experiences in a preschool group. But if the child has grown up in a family that has little control of its environment, he may have known deprivation and even undernourishment, and he may consequently have felt frustrated and afraid. Observation of his behavior may show him to be underdeveloped, withdrawn, and in need of learning in a preschool group that the world can be a place of security and freedom from fear and want.

When he enters a preschool group, the child from an upper-middle-class home may already have had hours with a parent trained as a teacher. His interest in hearing stories and looking at picture books is easily observable. So are his mastery of basic concepts; his sense of his own worth; his pleasant emotional outlook; and his ability to observe, interpret, and control his environment. In contrast, observation of the child who enrolls in a program for less advantaged children may show behavior indicating his need to be considered as an individual and his need to develop self-confidence and a happy identity in the preschool group.

Depending upon the style of life of their families, preschool children may have known controlled emotions or a wide range of emotional expression, with adults playing fear-inspiring games with them. Some children may have been understimulated because adults confined them and prevented their exploration of their environment. Other children may have been overstimulated, when, for example, parent unemployment led to families sharing meager quarters. But no matter what style of life a child comes from, he should find in his preschool group adults who take a genuine interest in him and endeavor to observe and understand his point of view and provide an environment with dependable routine, adequate nourishment, predictable events, stimulating intellectual experiences, opportunity to use a variety of materials, and secure affection.

How to Observe Children

The first step in understanding children is learning to observe them, not only from the standpoint of adult behavior, but, more important, from the standpoint of themselves. What is this child doing? What is he trying to do? How is his behavior related to his physical environment? How is his behavior related to the other people near him? The observer of a child should first watch the child's behavior, recording what he observes. He looks for the relationships which will help him understand what the child's world is and how it fits in with the world around him.

Those who work with children should understand the child's picture of himself and his world. It is easy for the adult to lose sight of this in his eagerness to have the child grow into the adult world. A parent, for instance, intent on accomplishing an errand, may hurry his preschool children through stores filled with objects fascinating to a curious child and along streets filled with interesting people and their intriguing accessories. The parent will do better to plan a child-centered excursion through the shopping center and a separate trip for doing his errands.

The teacher who lessens her observations of children can immediately notice the result of trying to have them primarily in her world rather than theirs. Her rapport with individual children is strained to the point where empathy is lost with some children. She must, then, spend time with each child, following his lead until he again is confident that she is trying to help him do what he really wants to do.

It is clear that observations of children must first record exactly what the child does—what he says in his own words, and his overt behavior. Later, on the basis of the written record and the memory of the incident, the observer may make interpretations of what he observed. But such interpretations are definitely a second, separate step. To make interpretations while observing is to mix the adult world too much into that of the child. Such mixing results only in distortion, and is to be avoided.

Table 2-1 shows an observation form that is appropriate for use in many instances. It consists of two parts: a brief statement describing the observation situation by answering the questions "When?" "Whom?" "What?" and a blank for recording what the children do.

Only after an observer is competent in recording what the children say and do is he ready to move on to more precise recording which will give him a feeling of the time elapsing as he observes. Then, a column entitled "Time" may be added at the left edge of the page to be used for recording the time of day for successive observations.

Observations are made in order to have a basis for an objective discussion about what children do. The quality of observations improves rapidly when observers come together to discuss their observations. Trivialities soon drop out of their recordings, and the detailed accuracy of their observations improves. Observers learn from each other, as well as from the teacher and other resource people meeting with the discussion group.

Observations of children may serve many different purposes, and observers need to be aware of the use to be made of their observations. Initial observations may be a means of acquainting students or parents with the individual children in a group. Further observations may stimulate study of age level characteristics of children. Observers note in the column

TABLE 2-1. Report of Observation

Observer_____ Observations for _____

                                                                           kindergarten

Observation of _____ group in _____ nursery group

Date _____ Time of Day _____

Situation: _____

_____

_____

Children observed _____ _____

                    Name   Age   Name   Age

Behavior Observed* (What each child says; and overt behavior of each)	*Comments* (To be made later)

* Experienced observers often add another column at the left for recording the minute at which the observation was made.

for comments those behaviors which are typical of the age level of the child.

What observers focus their attention on depends on their reason for observing children. Prospective swimming teachers observing a group of children at a swimming pool may notice the body build of each child and the behavior associated with it (for example, the plump girl floats well, the thin child's teeth chatter). Medical students preparing to be pediatricians may notice, for example, how a child's use of his feet is related to his bone formation. Future parents may observe a child's use of different toys and thus be better prepared to select toys appropriate in terms of age levels that will remain useful for play over a period of time. Prospective teachers may be interested in noticing when a child plays alone, in parallel to another, and in cooperation with others. Observers need guidance as to what to observe. Students instructed repeatedly to "observe children" find themselves observing the same kinds of things and lose interest in being with children. But students are eager to observe when they are guided into increasing awareness of new facets of child development through discussions of what they record.

How to Interpret Child Behavior

Those who work with preschool children generally find it desirable to observe children from the standpoint of two questions:

● How does the child's present status compare with that of others in his age group?
● How does the child's present status compare with his past?

A parent wants to know:

● Is my child normal?
● Is he continuing to develop?

In order to plan her work, a teacher needs to know:

● Is each child mature for his age?
● Is he developing as rapidly as most children of his age?

To answer these questions, parents and teachers can make use of writing such as that by Spock,[6] or of the original work done at the Clinic of Child Development at Yale University. There Gesell and Ilg and their coworkers made "periodic, longitudinal studies of groups of normal children,"[7] and were able to describe in detail the kind of behavior commonly

[6] Benjamin Spock, *Baby and Child Care* (New York: Pocket Books, 1967).
[7] Op. cit., p. ix.

TABLE 2-2 Aspects of Development of Preschool Children

AGE LEVEL

Aspect of Development	TWO YEARS		THREE YEARS		FOUR YEARS		FIVE YEARS	
	Abilities	*Implications*	*Abilities*	*Implications*	*Abilities*	*Implications*	*Abilities*	*Implications*
PHYSICAL	Balances forward	Hits forehead in falling	Balances erect	Fall may break a tooth	Climbs easily	Learns to use a fireman's pole	Has more motor control	Able to sit longer
	Can kick object	Kicks big ball	Alternates feet Stands on one foot	Climbs stairs Learns to hop	Actively runs jumps, hops	Covers more ground	Crosses street safely	Explores neighborhood Does simple errands
	Steps in place	Climbs by restepping	Developing coordination	Jumps, walks and runs with music	Has more motor control	Learns to skip Saws Cuts on a line Throws over-hand	Has more eye-hand control	Learns to lace shoes Learns to use overhead ladder Learns left from right
	Pats, pokes	Enjoys clay Enjoys action toys		Unbuttons buttons Rolls ball				
	Runs, lugs	Pulls or carries a load		Throws underhand				
	Pushes, pulls	Likes to fit pieces		Toilets self during day	Has more coordination	Talks and eats Talks and plays	Self-sufficient in personal care	Uses bathroom by himself
	Rotates fore-arm	Opens doors Fills and empties		Talks, or eats, or plays				
	Voluntary muscle control	Learns to toilet self Likes water play						
SOCIAL	Must possess	Holds and hoards Does not share	Learning to share	Shares toys Not able to share Brings posses-sions to share	Continuing sensitivity to people	Quotes parents as authorities Dislikes isolation from group Learns to express sympathy	Is social	Has more co-operative play Likes to play house and baby Gets along well in small group
	Slow in re-lating to new adults	Wants familiar adult	Sensitive to people	Tries to please and conform Feels sympathetic Likes simple guessing Enjoys dressing up		Likes to dress up and play dramatically Talks about inviting, not inviting someone		Conforms to adult ideas Asks adult help as needed
	Does not cooperate in play	Prefers solitary play Watches others			Likes birth-day parties			
					More coopera-tive	Plays with small group May not take others into group		

36

EMOTIONAL	Likes to touch Likes people Dependent on mother	Can be moved to new location Watches others Imitates Understands: "He needs it" Plays with baby doll Plays house	Shows self-control Proud of what he makes Developing independence	Rests for ten minutes Waits until it is time Takes turns Likes to take it home but often forgets to Leaves mother for nursery school Plays by himself	Goes out of bounds Is learning limits	Likes to brag Likes freehand drawing (not coloring books) Likes to go on excursions Runs ahead, but waits on corner Interested in rules Plans ahead with adults Acts silly if tired	Poised and in control Proud of what he has and does Likes to have rules	Learns what is right to do and say
INTELLECTUAL	Increases his control language Has short attention span Attends to words spoken a few at a time	Learns words easily Talks as part of play Has brief snatches of play Responds to brief commands	Is attentive to words Compares two objects Counts to three Uses words more Participates in planning	Responds to adult suggestions Likes to talk with adults Listens longer to stories Enjoys praise and simple humor Builds a three-block bridge Points out three objects in a picture Talks about proposed study trip Tries out words dramatically	Experiments with words Asks "Why?" and "How?" Likes to imagine Has fluid thought	Makes up words and rhymes Likes new words, big ones Listens to stories longer Runs a topic to the ground Likes to have explanations Does much dramatic play Learns to distinguish fact and fancy Interested in death Changes title of his drawing as he draws	Interests widen Thinks correctly Has purpose Is flexible	Recognizes some numbers and letters Interested in the clock and time Asks "What?" and "How?" Learns his address and telephone number Draws what he has in mind at the moment Is not concerned with inconsistencies

37

found at each of a series of age levels. The age-level descriptions include those of special interest to the preschool teacher:

Two Years Old   Four Years Old
Two and a Half Years Old   Five Years Old and Older
Three Years Old

These descriptions are especially useful for adults working with groups of children from families selected by socioeconomic factors and such other factors as interest in children, research, and education. Adults working with children selected by other factors—for instance, on the basis of family need—may find it desirable to distinguish descriptions of behaviors that are due primarily to maturation or that are due primarily to environmental factors.

OBSERVING MATURITY

When an adult starts to get acquainted with a child, almost immediately he asks, "How old is he?" Knowing how far along a child is in his development is the basis for understanding the child and planning experiences to further his development. But adults differ in how they interpret age. One adult may remark, "My, he's big for his age!" Another may observe, "Well, from the way he talks, I'd say he was about five, but from the way he carries himself I can tell he's a three-year-old." Another may say, "You know, my children were always small for their age."

To know the maturity of a child, the adult should use information such as that given in Table 2-2, and observations that he has made of the child's physical development and his social, emotional, and intellectual behavior. Then the adult is in a position to comment meaningfully about the physical, social, emotional, and intellectual maturity of the child. Furthermore, knowing the maturity of a child, an adult is in a position to plan activities that will further the child's development.

Table 2-2, which uses material reported by Gesell and Ilg and by others, is a summary of important aspects of development at significant age levels of the preschool child. Abilities of children at each age level are grouped under four headings: Physical, Social, Emotional, and Intellectual. Other groups could be used (Gesell and Ilg used others), but the four given here are the most commonly understood and frequently used.

Basic Concepts Concerning Children

Those who work with individual preschool children or groups of them find it desirable to make several kinds of observations about the children for use in planning activities and programs for them. In doing so, they make fundamental assumptions about children, as follows:

ASSUMPTION	IMPLICATION
Children of a given chronological age have certain behavior in common.	Plan individual and group activities in terms of age level. Interpret the behavior of children in relation to behavior characteristic of their age level.
Children often go through certain stages in their development, some outgoing and exploratory, others nodal consolidation intervals.	Identify developmental stages of concern to the family and to the physician. Guide children through developmental stages.
As a child grows up in this social order, he faces a series of problems.	Identify the developmental problems of concern to each child. Help each child solve his current problems.
When he is physically, socially, emotionally, and intellectually ready, a child learns.	Planning of activities should be based on observations of readiness. Each child is a unique individual who has his own timing in learning.

It is interesting to consider examples of how these four points of view affect the work of those who work with preschool children.

Knowing the Level of Development

A teacher or parent must know the age level of a child. An adult making a batch of dough or clay for a group of four-year-old children wonders how much to make. If she makes as much as she would for as many three-year-old children, it will not be enough. She will be besieged with requests for more clay and will have to resort to dividing the children into two groups, one working with clay and the other with a second activity, or in some other way provide each of them with the large mass of clay a four-year-old likes for modeling. If the adult, however, had taken time to review the characteristics of four-year-old children, she would not have made this mistake.

IMPORTANCE FOR TEACHERS

At the beginning of the school year, the kindergarten teacher who answers the room telephone and finds out that she is wanted in the office, replies in terms of the age level of five-year-old children, "I am introducing a new activity now. If I come in ten minutes, will that be soon enough?" When she gets to the office, she should calmly explain to the principal, "I was sorry not to come at once, but, as you know, with five-year-olds a new activity has to be introduced to the point where they can go ahead with it by themselves."

In planning activities for the children, the teacher must take into account the age level of the children, as well as their immediate interests. She should avoid craft projects suitable for primary grade children, but provide materials the children need for exploring, pasting, painting or other craft processes. She should avoid stories about abstractions and experiences of interest to older children and, for the most part, choose simple, realistic stories. For the three-year-old children she should arrange simple and brief

Play with a toy guides learning. (Courtesy of The Merrill-Palmer Institute and Donna J. Harris, Detroit, Michigan.)

excursions within the neighborhood, and for the four-year-old children, somewhat more extended trips. Her planning for the three year olds is essentially a day-by-day program; for the four year olds, a program which includes projects extending over several days.

Each day the adult must be constantly aware of the age level of the children as well as the needs and interests of each individual child. When four-year-old Jimmy hits his friend Mike on the nose, she should help the boys solve their problem and also help Jimmy sympathize with his injured friend. But when three-year-old children hit each other, she should center the attention only on the problem that led to the hitting. The development of expressions of sympathy requires more attention than the children are likely to give at that time.

A four-year-old goes over the top while a three-year-old climbs to the middle. (Courtesy of California State College at Long Beach and Mariam M. Cook, Long Beach, California.)

IMPORTANCE FOR PARENTS

If parents are to avoid expecting too much of their children, they must know what may reasonably be expected of a child at a given age level. The parent who buys a two-wheel bicycle for a nursery school child must know that compliance with rules for safety cannot be expected of preschool children. The parent who asks a young child to keep his room picked up consistently exerts so much pressure on the child with this untimely expectation that he will sooner or later have a child with undesirable behavior. The parent who interferes with a child's urge to talk at the age level for learning to talk may later be disturbed by the child's lack of facility and fluency in the use of language. But the parent who knows what can and cannot be expected of a child at each age level can take pride in the continued progress of the child and wait patiently for the problems and the accomplishments of older age levels.

IDENTIFYING STAGES OF DEVELOPMENT

As children grow, their characteristic behavior for a period of time is sometimes in contrast to earlier behavior. This difference may be associated with a new awareness of the child, or a new relationship to some facets of the social or physical environment. His parents and teachers may become aware of new behavior—expressions of fear, frequent shyness with people, great exuberance and enthusiasm for activities, for instance. Noticing that these intervals of unusual behavior are followed by other intervals characterized by quite different behavior, they speak of "stages" in the development of a child. For instance, outgoing two-and-a-half-year-old behavior is followed by nodal three-year-old behavior, and then by outgoing four-year-old behavior and subsequent nodal five-year-old behavior.

Sometimes adults who do not recognize the phase a child is in may complicate the child's learning. For instance, the parent of a possessive two-year-old may attempt to have his child learn to share before the child is ready for that advanced learning. His premature insistence on sharing may result in undesirable emotional reactions. But a parent who understands that a child must have a full experience with possession before he can go on to the subsequent step of learning to share guides the child's development more gently and more surely.

Eating is another area of behavior in which it is important to know what stage a child is in. The adult who is unaware of a child's new discernments may interpret a child's "I won't eat!" as stubbornness. But perhaps the child has suddenly noticed a color, texture, or shape in his food and needs guidance in understanding factors associated with that characteristic. Or perhaps the child is experimenting with making choices and needs help in making more appropriate choices, perhaps choices among kinds of cereal rather than the choice of eating or not eating. The adult who is aware of stages in development is more apt to be helpful to the children, and less apt to interpret their remarks as a personal insult. Adults should realize that undesirable behavior drops out of use through lack of repetition and, recognizing stages of child behavior, be confident that a stage characterized by behavior socially undesirable in the adult world will pass.

Dr. Benjamin Spock, a pediatrician writing for parents, finds it useful to encourage parents in thinking of certain more specific stages that a child is apt to go through and others that he may go through. He writes:

> Boys and girls around three have reached a stage in their emotional development when they feel that their fathers and mothers are wonderful people[8] . . .

[8] Benjamin Spock, *Baby and Child Care* (New York: Pocket Books, Inc., 1967), p. 357.

At any age there are a few children who handle their genitals a great deal, sometimes in public.[9] . . . Like compulsions, tics occur most commonly around the age of 9, but they can come at any age after 2.[10]

This emphasis on certain aspects of behavior is useful to adults working with children. The adults are alert as they observe children, and are quick to notice behavior which suggests that a child needs medical assistance.

Parents and teachers who think of children as going through different stages of development sometimes think of a "stage" as something that happens to a child, something he will live through, and something that they can only tolerate. They sigh and say, "This stage will pass." A more constructive attitude is to identify the beginning phases of the stage and to provide the experiences and guidance that will help a child successfully move through the stage at a rate suitable to his total development. The experienced teacher or parent often anticipates a stage a child goes through, prepares for it in advance, and capitalizes on it to further the over-all development of the child. The inexperienced teacher, recognizing the early phases of a stage, seeks help from her supervisor on how best to guide a child through it.

DEVELOPMENTAL PROBLEMS

Another concept useful to those who work with preschool children is that the child growing to adulthood in this social order must face and solve a series of developmental problems. As an infant grows into a child, the child into an adolescent, and then into an adult, he must solve the problems through which he develops into a full-fledged member of the society. These problems challenge him physically, intellectually, socially, and emotionally. How he solves them determines how he functions in the social order.

Consider the series of developmental problems centering around loco-motion. Within his first year the infant will solve the problems of sitting erect, crawling, and perhaps even walking upright. The one-year-old is so intent on walking that he is in constant motion when he is awake. His parents may fasten him in his high chair or run after him with a spoon in order to feed him. His urge to walk is irrepressible. By three years of age he has solved problems of walking, running, and tip-toeing, and is busy with the problem of hopping. By five years of age he has solved the problem of walking a rail unassisted and is working on the problem of skipping. Meanwhile he has mastered a tricycle and is becoming interested in a bicycle. As a child in the elementary school, he will solve the problem of how to ride the bicycle safely; in high school, of how to drive a car safely. If he has solved each problem in locomotion successfully, he will be

---

[9] Ibid., p. 370.
[10] Ibid., p. 391.

able to get around as he needs to as an adult. But whether he does go safely where he needs to go depends also on concomitant solving of other developmental problems. If he has not been successful in his solution of problems in emotional development, he may be prone to have accidents. If problems of his intellectual development have not been completely solved, he may not be able accurately to judge the speed appropriate to unusual road conditions. If his social development has not included solving the variety of problems important in the social order, he may not have sufficient sense of social responsibility to drive a car so that others on the highway are also safe. To be a full-fledged adult, he must have solved thoroughly the problems of physical, intellectual, social, and emotional development.

The problem-solving approach to understanding children is useful to teachers and parents because it focuses adult attention on those aspects of child development at which adults may be especially helpful. The adult who is skillful in identifying the problem that a child is most concerned with on a particular day is the adult who can realistically praise his accomplishments or tactfully phrase a question.

The problem-solving approach is better understood by teachers than by parents. A parent may say, "My child is all right. He doesn't have any problems," or, "I'm worried. My child has so many problems." Parents need guidance in understanding that all children develop through the process of solving the problems of their age level. The question to be asked is not, "Does this child have problems?" but, "What problems is this child now concerned with?" and "What will help him in solving these developmental problems?"

Evelyn Duvall, writing about family development,[11] presents the developmental problems that are important for family members at different ages in their lives. The problems for the early years of life are summarized in Table 2-3.

READINESS FOR LEARNING

Another basic concept useful to teachers and parents is that of readiness for learning: a child will learn when he is ready. Only when a child has matured sufficiently and has sufficient related experience is he ready for a new facet of the culture. The teacher or parent who understands this concept of readiness does not waste time and energy attempting to teach what a child is not ready to learn. Instead, she waits for evidences of maturity and provides a wealth of related experiences at the child's level. In this way neither the child nor the teacher is frustrated by undue expectations of achievement. The patient parent takes into account the concept of readi-

[11] Evelyn M. Duvall, *Family Development* (Philadelphia: J. B. Lippincott Company, 1957).

TABLE 2-3.   Developmental Tasks in Ten Categories of Behavior

BEHAVIOR CATEGORY	INFANCY (BIRTH 1 OR 2)	EARLY CHILDHOOD (2–3 TO 5–7)
1. Achieving an appropriate dependence-independence pattern	Establishing one's self as a very dependent being Beginning the establishment of self-awareness	Adjusting to less private attention; becoming independent physically (while remaining strongly dependent emotionally)
2. Achieving an appropriate giving-receiving pattern of affection	Developing a feeling for affection	Developing the ability to give affection Learning to share affection
3. Relating to changing social groups	Becoming aware of the alive as against the inanimate, and the familiar as against the unfamiliar Developing rudimentary social interaction	Beginning to develop the ability to interact with age-mates Adjusting in the family to expectations it has for the child as a member of the social unit
4. Developing a conscience	Beginning to adjust to the expectations of others	Developing the ability to take directions and to be obedient in the presence of authority Developing the ability to be obedient in the absence of authority where conscience substitutes for authority
5. Learning one's psycho-socio-biological sex role		Learning to identify with male and female adult roles
6. Accepting and adjusting to a changing body	Adjusting to adult feeding demands Adjusting to adult cleanliness demands Adjusting to adult attitudes toward genital manipulation	Adjusting to expectations resulting from one's improving muscular abilities Developing sex modesty
7. Managing a changing body and learning new motor patterns	Developing physiological equilibrium Developing eye-hand coordination Establishing satisfactory rhythms of rest and activity	Developing large-muscle control; learning to coordinate large muscles and small muscles
8. Learning to understand and control the physical world.	Exploring the physical world	Meeting adult expectations for restrictive exploration and manipulation of an expanding environment

TABLE 2-3—*continued*

BEHAVIOR CATEGORY	INFANCY (BIRTH 1 OR 2)	EARLY CHILDHOOD (2–3 TO 5–7)
9. Developing an appropriate symbol system and conceptual abilities	Developing preverbal communication Developing verbal communication Rudimentary concept formation	Improving one's use of the symbol system Enormous elaboration of the concept pattern
10. Relating one's self to the cosmos		Developing a genuine, though uncritical, notion about one's place in the cosmos

SOURCE: Evelyn M. Duvall, *Family Development* (Philadelphia: J. B. Lippincott Co., 1957), p. 108–109.

ness, and is confident that his child will learn in time what is expected of him.

Attention to readiness for learning leads to recognition of individual differences, and to understanding that each child has his own schedule of development. The nursery school, dealing as it does with children who are in a period of widespread development, takes into account the importance of dealing with children as individuals and of helping each child develop skills and concepts as rapidly as he is ready to undertake them.

Parents utilize the concept of readiness when they feed their infants on demand, let them sleep as needed, and toilet train them when they are sufficiently mature. A mother listening to the new baby soon learns to know when the baby is hungry and should be fed. She responds to his demands for food. Both the baby and the mother find satisfaction in that response. The mother learns, too, how the baby behaves when he is tired. Identifying the cues of readiness for sleep, she rocks the baby and helps him get to sleep.

The procedure of identifying the behavior which signifies readiness for an activity, then helping the child with the activity, is the essence of being a parent and teacher. Consider, for instance, how the parent helps the child take responsibility for going to the toilet. When the child is about two-and-a-half years old, the mother observes that the child is ready to assume some responsibility for himself. Perhaps she finds him urinating outdoors, or taking off his clothes in the bathroom, or attentively watching another child urinate, or clutching himself in the genital area, or showing other evidence that the nerve endings in the genital area are sufficiently mature that he can interpret sensations there. Mother helps the child respond to his body feelings by going to the bathroom and using the toilet. She helps him learn first one aspect then another of the toileting process— how to manage his clothes, self, and the toilet. Each time she observes behavior similar to that of an adult she praises the accomplishment and helps the child take satisfaction in it. With her four-year-old child, she rushes for the bathroom, with relief sighs, "We made it!" She then helps him flush the toilet and wave "bye-bye" to the BM as it is flushed away.

The teacher becomes expert in observing a child's readiness to modify a familiar skill, adapt it to a new situation, or to learn some new skill. She watches for signs of the child's interest in the skill—watching others exercise it, awkward attempts to try out some aspect of the skill, persistent questioning about it. She encourages the child in his attempts—guiding his behavior with praise about the successful aspects of it, providing him with interesting situations in which to practice it, helping him relate the new skill to his other interests and activities.

In her eagerness to be helpful, the teacher or parent must be careful to guide, not push, the child in learning the new skill. Always the adult takes her cues from the child. Only as the child evidences interest and need for help does the adult enter into the child's play. The child learns by doing, and the adult paces what the child does, not interfering with it either by over-direction or by lagging too far behind in providing help. The following descriptive account of four-year-old Jimmy illustrates the feelings of a sensitive teacher gently guiding a shy and sensitive child in being a member of the group during his second year at nursery school.

OCTOBER   Jimmy has become so independent, no longer needs mama at school. He's so easy and lovable and helpful. So well adjusted. His mother was so patient and wise in weaning him from her.

NOVEMBER   Alas, Jim has returned to wanting his mother at school. She suggests he has been intimidated a bit by the aggressiveness of John and Mike and others. When we can minimize that, we may restore Jim's security. He's not a noisy protester but he wants his mother. At lunch at our house (with his mother, too), he played nicely with our girls. He seemed comfortable and contented. Some other time we'll try it alone.

JANUARY   Jim has gone into a dependency on mother. Today she left him anyway, after a short while. I had agreed to hold him lovingly when she left. He cried only briefly and quietly and presently was very happy. (This departure technique has also been successful with David.)

APRIL   Jim comes each morning the past month or so, yelping loudly. He sings his favorite song with unbelievable volume. He rides a trike with gay abandon with the boys, but plays happily with almost everyone, it seems. He doesn't need much direction—finds his own amusements mostly. His moods are pleasant. He is sometimes playful and giggly. He is sensitive to the attitudes and whims of others. He needs tenderness then. (Don't we all!) Jim enjoys and wants his mother's attention on her working days. If Jim were mine, I'd be like his mother. He has such a lovable, appealing way about him that ministering to his needs is a lovely emotional experience. I think many people will love Jimmy.

THE PRINCIPLE OF READINESS

Readiness for reading or mathematical experiences has been studied by research workers in child development and in education. Primary-grade teachers study the research findings to learn how to work most effectively with different children. All children are not ready for these experiences at six, or seven, or even eight years of age. Premature insistence on early learning of the skills may create psychological blocks to their achievement when the child has the visual, psychological, and experiential readiness to master them.

The watcher is getting ready to try a new activity. (*Courtesy of Montgomery County Head Start Program, Maryland.*)

Nursery school and kindergarten teachers are also concerned about the principle of readiness. They must be able to ask and answer questions about the many kinds of activities for which the preschool child becomes ready.

The teacher of three-year-old children is prepared, for instance, to list questions and their answers regarding "taking turns":

QUESTIONS	ANSWERS
At what age is readiness for taking turns especially evident?	Three years of age.
What kinds of child behavior indicate readiness?	Brings a toy or book to school "to share." Likes to be in line with other children who want to go down the slide. In the sandbox, tries to hold several toys, more than he can play with.
How can the adult further readiness?	When a child brings a toy, ask him if he wants to share it for play, or to put it away until he goes home. Praise the taking of turns whenever it occurs. Explain to children in the sand box that each child takes only as many toys as he can use. With pictures and flannel board, show children taking turns and sharing.

The teacher of four-year-old children is prepared to answer the same kinds of questions about behavior important for the four-year-old child to learn, for instance, expressing sympathy:

QUESTIONS	ANSWERS
At what age is readiness for being sympathetic especially evident?	Four years of age.
What kinds of child behavior indicate readiness?	Has empathy with mother and with his teacher. Enjoys being with other children. Is aware of a child crying. Sees relationship in two events.
How can the teacher further readiness?	Talk sympathetically with individuals as well as groups. In a conflict between two children, help each child see how the other feels. Act out favorite stories with sympathetic feeling.

It is easy to identify the school or home in which the concept of readiness is understood and appreciated. It is characterized by remarks such as: "When you are ready, you will try it," and, "When you are ready, you will do it by yourself," as well as by praise and reward of accomplishment. In contrast is the teacher or mother who frequently says, "Why didn't you do it?" "You do what I say!" blaming a child for not performing up to her expectations, or withdrawing his privileges as a means of trying to teach him something he is not ready to learn. The happy home and the happy preschool group take into account the child's readiness for new experiences.

Adult Reactions to Age Characteristics

Adults react to children of a given age in terms of the behaviors characteristic of that age. For instance, many nursery-group teachers find great satisfaction in helping children learn to share, or to notice different facets of the world around them. Such teachers are sensitive to the changes which occur in the children they teach. Many parents enjoy the preschool years of their children because they like to help the children begin to be self-sufficient.

Other parents and teachers do not care for behavior that characterizes preschool children. For instance, they may dislike the heavy breathing that is typical of a child intent on some activity—even if they realize that adenoidal tissue does not recede until later years, the heavy breathing irritates them nonetheless. Adults may be irritated by toileting incidents, noise, running noses, spilled liquids, and the like. Such adults and those who react only at a fast tempo are not compatible with small children. Such adults must choose to think through the reasons for their irritation and to replace it with behavior conducive to good rapport with the children, or else find ways of working with people of a different age range.

But adults who delight in the warm response of small children—their frankness and sincerity, their pleasure in exploring the world around them —enjoy nursery school children and enjoy spending many hours of the day with them. Such adults focus their attention on the many changes in children as they react to new experiences. The adults see the new skills a child develops and the improvements he makes in familiar skills. They see evidence of change in his attitudes toward his world and toward the adult world around him. They see him gain new concepts and start making use of them. It is thrilling to such adults to watch these changes in young children and to realize their contributions toward these learnings.

The adult working with a preschool group must appreciate the difference between the sensitivities of adults and those of children. The adult world has concepts which do not exist in the child's world. For instance, the adult concept of stealing does not beset children endeavoring to build an understanding of ownership and property rights. Children do not think of noise as they learn how to produce different sounds; they need much experience before achieving the ability to distinguish precisely among different tones. An adult should not think of a preschool child's casual interest in exploring sensations as masturbation, an interest easily guided into more socially acceptable explorations.

The child is a learner; the adult, a skillful performer. Consequently, there is a marked contrast between the pace of the child and that of the adult. As a beginner, the child moves slowly. He is easily diverted by some new, perhaps unrelated aspect of a skill. He takes time to move awkwardly through some feat of physical skill, and he takes time to find the words for an idea not yet clarified in his thinking. His time consumption requires patience from the adults around him. The adults need to remember that they too were learners. They must give the child the courtesy they would like to have if they were trying out new activities. They must be confident of the final attainment, and must praise the steps that mark intermediate attainment.

PRESCHOOL AND ADULT STANDARDS DIFFER

At his level of development, an adult may find it difficult to be tolerant of the immature level of development of the preschool child. It is especially difficult for adults to be tolerant of the child who makes errors as he learns to take responsibility for toileting himself. Adults, depending upon the part of the social order to which they belong, have been thoroughly indoctrinated about proper toileting behavior, appropriate modesty, and choice of words regarding private matters. From the time she was a small child, a mother or a teacher has experienced the reprimands of society for mentioning the excretory processes. Now, with preschool children, parents and teachers must put aside their adult intolerance, appreciate the point of view of the child, and lay a sound basis on which preschool children may grow to adulthood.

What is the child's point of view? When the nerve endings in the genital area mature to the point where he can gain control over his excretory processes, he is delighted with each phase of his success. He shares his delight with the people around him. "Come see!" exclaims the two-and-one-half to three-year-old, and the whole family gathers around to admire the bowel movement or the urination made into the toilet. The child has demonstrated considerable muscular control. He recognizes the signs of what was about to happen, got hmself to the right place at the right time, removed any clothing that might get in the way, and controlled the performance. He has much indeed of which to be proud. The adults who shared the child's pleasure in his success also can be proud. They demonstrated their ability to see the child's behavior from his, rather than their, point of view.

Knowing that modesty is learned in a community by six-year-old children, the adults working with preschool children feel free to let each child develop toileting routines at his own pace, and with other children as he wishes. Boys and girls are free to use the bathroom alone or with friends of their choosing, either boys or girls. Thus they come casually to understand that people are of two kinds, a wholesome foundation for the lessons of modesty and manners which are appropriate at older ages.

The teacher and the parent of the preschool child recognize the difference between the child's point of view and that of the adult world, and help other adults understand this difference. For instance, the teacher who talked with a woman professor of English who had never married explained the two points of view in the following manner.

PROFESSOR   I think a faculty wife should maintain standards in her home.

TEACHER   What standards are you thinking of?

PROFESSOR   Well, I shouldn't mention it, but let me tell you the incident that occurred the last time I visited the home of a professor in our department. I stopped by one afternoon and, while I was there, their little youngster deliberately went to the bathroom right on the living-room rug! I watched him, and could just see him deciding to do it.

TEACHER   How old is their youngster now?

PROFESSOR   I don't know. But, let me see, I can figure it out.

TEACHER   Is he somewhat over two years of age?

PROFESSOR   Yes, I think so. How did you know?

TEACHER   Because the incident you describe is an example of readiness for self-toileting, and that kind of readiness occurs when a child is in the neighborhood of two-and-one-half years of age. But you are probably more familiar with readiness for reading, which occurs in many children at about six-and-one-half years of age.

PROFESSOR   Hmmm. I had not thought about different kinds of readiness.

TEACHER   Each is important. As you know, the readiness phase is the entrance to a period of fast learning. Probably, when you visit the professor's family again, their youngster will be toileting himself in the bathroom.

ADULTS NEED TO UNDERSTAND NEGATIVE BEHAVIOR

Adults who work with children as teachers, parents, or in some other role, need help in understanding certain aspects of child behavior. The continued existence of the nursery group, or at least their happiness within it, depends on whether they identify the resistance behavior of the children and interpret it correctly. Sooner or later a child is apt to express feelings and emotions through biting, hitting, and other overt actions, or by saying, "I don't like you!" "Go'way!" "I don't want to!" rather than through compliance and obedience.

An interesting progression occurs as a child learns to handle negation and to express the resistance he feels. As a toddler he encounters the word *no* and realizes its restrictions. He presently explores with this tool of language. *No* is an easy word for the child to say, so he enjoys repeating it. By using the word where it applies and where it does not apply, he learns how others react to it. Many a loving parent or teacher has carried a resistant two-year-old inside for his rest as a means of helping him realize that saying *no* was not appropriate behavior at that point. But later, that same adult has interpreted the *no* literally when the child momentarily refused the ride he wanted to take.

Nursery children are not far removed from the period in which their most-used word was *no.* To every suggestion they replied "No." Three-year-olds are still apt to respond negatively to a firm command. For instance, Marilyn, age three-and-one-half, used such a response whenever a sudden, firm command interrupted what she was intent on doing:

ADULT You'd better go back now.
MARILYN *(to adult)* No! *(Pause, then to playmate)* You'd better go back.

Through such experiences, child and adult arrive at a mutual understanding of the areas of living in which the adult makes decisions, and those in which the child is free to agree or resist.

When a child is frustrated and feels resistant in a situation, he often expresses his feelings in actions, perhaps in grabbing, biting, hitting, or kicking. For instance, a child who has been at home with adults who created for him a favorable environment may find companions in the nursery group less agreeable about giving him what he wants. When he reaches for an interesting toy, he suddenly encounters not an encouraging adult, but a possessive child who wants to keep the toy. Here, then, is an opportunity for him to learn about other people. Until he has enough language to express himself verbally, he explores expression of resistance through various actions. Adults need to understand such a child's shift from docility to self-assertion through biting, hitting, and other aggressive behavior for what it is—an important step in socialization and in learning how to get along with other people.

Adults encourage self-assertion as they help children learn to express their resistance to a situation through words rather than through actions that might hurt others. In doing this they may experience having a child say, "I don't like you," to them. They need to recognize this as a higher level of *no,* the child's earlier expression of resistance, and to treat it in the same way. Instead of interpreting it literally or taking it personally, they help the child toward a more precise statement of his resistance. For instance:

MARY *(to an adult serving tomato juice)* Go 'way.
ADULT Don't you want tomato juice today?
MARY No.
ADULT I'll bring you a glass of water, then.

Or, when the teacher returns to the nursery group after being absent for several days:

SUSAN I don't like you. I'm going to chop you up.
ADULT *(putting her arms around Susan)* You missed me! I wanted to be with you, but I had to stay in bed and keep away from you children so you would not get sick. Now I'm back, and I want to help you swing

away up in the air. (*Talks while she and Susan walk over to the swing that is not occupied.*) I'll give you a start and let's see how high you can pump.

When a child says he does not want to go to nursery school, both parents and teachers may require weeks to find out what he is trying to say. He may be resistant to leaving home for fear of missing something going on there, or of having father or someone he especially likes come while he is away. He may feel that mother does not want him to go, and so says he does not want to go for fear of displeasing the person who looks after him. He may be unwilling to go to nursery school because he does not yet feel at home, or does not have an intimate friend there. He may be afraid of a child who hits and may want mother to go with him to protect him from the hitter until he can learn what to do himself. Or, as is often the case for a four- or five-year-old, he may simply be trying out a new phrase to see what effect it has on the people around him—in which situations it gets attention, and in which it does not.

Adults, parents, and others who work with preschool children must be prepared for negative expressions and must be ready to interpret them in terms of the needs of the child. Negative expressions are one of the signs of readiness to learn some new technique or idea about getting along with others. The wise adult recognizes negative behavior as a child's call for help in meeting a new situation or a familiar situation which the growing child now sees in a different light.

Adults Appreciate Rapid Changes in the Preschool Child

Dr. Benjamin S. Bloom has collected evidence on which he makes the statement that, for certain characteristics other than school achievement, "the most rapid period for the development . . . is in the first five years of life."[12] He further states that he believes additional research will reveal that the rapidity of the development during these early years has probably been underestimated.

The rapid growth of the preschool child makes parents and teacher eager to capitalize on each part of it. To do this requires constant sensitivity to change and willingness to provide enlarging experience in keeping with the changes. Those who work with preschool children realize that they must know what characterizes each age level, and how to note the developmental patterns of each child. They realize, too, that the rates of development in preschool children are higher than those in older children and much higher than those in adults.

A teacher talking with a group of parents reported the following instance of changed behavior which she had been slow in detecting.

[12] Benjamin S. Bloom, *Stability and Change in Human Characteristics* (New York: John Wiley and Sons, Inc., 1964), pp. 204–205.

Chris seemed so independent at first, so contented and capable that I know now I overestimated him. And when his mother called my attention to a change in him—a new and greater need for direction and help and attention—I realized how watchful one must be even of those who seem so resourceful.

One day I found Chris crying quietly by the drinking fountain because, as it turned out, he couldn't turn it on. But he wouldn't howl in protest, as some children do. The next day I gave him almost constant attention and as much as possible since then. He literally sparkles in response.

This experience with Chris is a good reminder to be alert to the many changes in one year in one child.

Individual Differences

The most important fact about a child is not his age, the stages he is in, his developmental problems, or any other grouping which describes him; it is the fact that he is *himself,* a unique personality. He will go through a succession of ages and stages and will solve a succession of developmental problems, each in his own way and with his own timing. Sometimes he may take the succession so slowly that he seems to be making little or no progress in what others consider important; sometimes rapidly; sometimes more evenly than unevenly. He develops as an individual at his own rate. His springs will unwind smoothly, or jerkily. As he grows through the ages and stages of development and solves his developmental problems, a major factor in his success will be the confidence adults who work with him express that, "He will do it when he is ready."

Appreciating each child for himself, adults help the child appreciate himself, and help him appreciate others as individuals too. A person must accept the fact that his own eyes are a certain color, that John's eyes are brown, that Tommy's eyes can't see very well. Adults working with children help them understand differences and accept them. Differences are recognized, but evaluative comparisons are not made. Susy is short, so she stands on the stool to reach the washbasin; Mary is tall, and stands on the floor. Tommy walks on the walking board without holding on to anyone; Jimmy walks on the board while he holds onto an adult's hand. Both Tommy and Jimmy know that when Jimmy is ready he will walk on the walking board without holding on to anyone.

The adult working with preschool children needs to be very much aware of individual differences among children and of factors associated with these differences. She knows that the position a child holds in his family influences his behavior. The first child in the family is different from other members of his family because of his experience as a center of interest for his two parents, and because of his older-age abilities that make him more able to take responsibilities than are his younger siblings. The youngest child of a family is different from other members of his family because his lesser abilities and greater dependence on those around him make him well able to elicit attention. Middle children are apt to be rebellious or crushed as they compete with their more successful older and younger siblings for the attention and affection of the people around them. Recognizing a child's place in his family, the teacher is in a better position to work effectively with him.

The teacher also is aware of other factors associated with individual differences. She recognizes that each child has a unique family background. Families have individual patterns of TV watching. Some families stay very much to themselves; others enrich their lives with excursions and social events. Within each family affectional relationships are unique. The preschool child is affected by the characteristics of his home and family, and he brings his individuality to school with him. His teacher is challenged to work with him as an individual, a unique member of his family and of the preschool group.

Progress Versus Attaining Standards

Recognition of individual differences is the essence of the preschool philosophy. Elementary school personnel, while deeply concerned with total development of each child, must focus their attention on skills to be learned—reading, writing, and arithmetic, and work habits expected of every citizen. Personnel of a preschool group, on the other hand, focus their attentions on the children and take it for granted that each child will learn the skills and ideas that he needs as he grows and develops. Adults working with preschool children are delighted with the progress that a child makes and share his enthusiasm about it, but they do not press him for performance for which he is unready. Confident that he will learn, the adults provide activities to further his readiness and are pleased with the learning when it does occur.

Characteristics the Teacher Identifies

As the initial educational institution for children, the nursery group or kindergarten is the logical place for identifying children with special talents or problems that will influence their subsequent schooling. The preschool teacher is alert to identify each child who

- Is creative.
- Learns easily.
- Is musical.
- Is artistic.
- Has difficulty in hearing.
- Has difficulty in seeing.
- Has difficulty in speaking.
- Has difficulty in understanding.

The experienced teacher also notices differences in dexterity and body

A musically gifted child picks out a piece on a musical instrument. (Courtesy of The Merrill-Palmer Institute and Donna J. Harris, Detroit, Michigan.)

build, and differences between boys and girls because awareness of such differences helps her to work effectively with individual children.

As the school term proceeds, the preschool teacher becomes increasingly aware of the children who are gifted, the children who are physically handicapped, and the children who seem to have low ability. By identifying such children at the nursery school or kindergarten level, she is of great benefit to their parents or guardian, who may help them have the special experiences or services they need, and to their prospective teachers who, informed about such children, can immediately start to help them with their individual problems.

The adult who works with preschool children identifies those who are talented by observing the presence or absence of certain kinds of behavior. In Table 2-4 are given some of the more easily observable kinds of behavior the adult can look for within the nursery school situation. Whether she is able to observe these behaviors depends, of course, on whether the home or school situation gives opportunity for such behavior to occur. For instance, a preschool child who has absolute pitch is apt to be musically talented, but until he knows the names of the notes he cannot give much evidence of this talent.

Parents and teachers are interested in identifying those talented children

TABLE 2-4. Behavior of Gifted and Handicapped Preschool Children

MUSICAL	ARTISTIC
Enjoys musical experience—likes to play phonograph and listen to music	Likes to work with art media—often paints at easels; eager to join craft groups
Picks out a little tune on the piano or autoharp	Is dexterous—pastes neatly; handles brushes and tools skillfully; finishes project early, or elaborately
Sings reasonably in tune	Makes paintings pleasing in color and composition
Enjoys rhythmic activities—likes to conduct; dances; plays drum or other simple instrument	Arranges similar items in patterns—arranges flowers in playhouse

SCHOLASTIC	CREATIVE
Likes to talk with adults—asks questions	Wants to "do-it-himself"
Likes to hear stories	Is confident about what he can do
Likes words as words—rhymes words; savors words	Enjoys humor
Interested in letters and books	Imaginative in what he says
Notices similarities	Makes unique craft products
Sensitive to differences	Notices differences
Notices relationships of place and event	Sees unusual relationships among things
Follows directions	Does things his own way, but with some relation to directions given

VISUALLY HANDICAPPED	AURALLY HANDICAPPED
Rubs eyes—may say eyes hurt	Does not heed what is said
Holds a picture or other object very close	Turns head to listen—watches face of someone talking
Squints	Has difficulty in speaking clearly
	Often has earaches and colds
	Avoids group activities—is restless in listening to stories
	Often is tired
	Overly aggressive; or overly timid

SPEECH HANDICAPPED	MENTALLY RETARDED
Does not express himself with words	Is not able to take care of himself as others do at his age
Withdraws	Does not want to learn
	Is bothered by new or unusual situations
	Remembers very little
	Does not see obvious relationships, similarities or differences
	Does not understand abstractions
	Pays attention only very briefly

who will profit from increased opportunity for the exercise and development of their talents. But they are also interested in identifying any child in need of attention because of some handicap of vision, speech, hearing, or mentality. By getting in touch early with the Bureau of Special Education in the State Department of Education, parents of a handicapped child may provide special education to minimize or offset the handicap and may prevent the development of complicating emotional problems. One of the services the preschool teacher is able to render is observation of, and discussion with parents about, child behaviors such as are listed in Table 2-4.

DIFFERENCES IN DEXTERITY

About one child in ten is gifted with coordination and dexterity which enable him to work with small items as well as large ones. Such a child needs both the usual preschool program, aimed at developing the large muscles, and a supplementary program to meet his individual interests. The teacher recognizes the individuality of the child and encourages him in his solitary pursuits. If he wishes to use in tiny bits art materials that other children use in masses, she is as pleased with what he does as she is with what any other child does. When he brings in miniatures, she shares his enthusiasm about them. In short, she appreciates his unusual talents and encourages him in them at the same time that she encourages his interests in other activities appropriate to his age level.

The child who moves with great deliberateness is also noted by the teacher. She appreciates his need for doing things at his own rate of speed. When she wishes the whole group to move from one activity to another, she is careful to forewarn him of the change. She helps him in getting his belongings together if he must be ready when the others are; otherwise, she gives him only the help needed by a child of his age level and sex. Understanding his needs, she is not irritated by his slowness. She knows that, annoyed with his slow rate of motion, asking him to hurry would be meaningless to a child of his age. She therefore appreciates him as he is and helps him build the self-confidence which will help him attain whatever speed he needs in moving himself through space.

DIFFERENCES IN BODY BUILD

Several different body builds are noticeable in young children. The teacher observes these differences and takes them into account in planning activities for the children. She notices, for instance, the child who is built like a solid chunk and has a greater supply of energy than the usual child. When other children need to rest, he is interested in keeping on with play. In the course of a morning he is constantly active, and his teacher is constantly challenged to help him channel his energies for the good of the other children. As early as possible she helps him to recognize when he needs to blow off steam and to find a suitable outlet for his energy—helping her get out or put away equipment, or using the punching bag, carpentry tools, or art materials.

The teacher also recognizes the child who has small bones and an appearance almost of being fragile. She knows that such a child may tire quickly, and suddenly be in need of rest and refreshment. She is alert for signs of fatigue and helps the child learn to recognize the signs for himself. She arranges a quiet place where he may lie down when he needs to. Swimming teachers realize that for preschool children even a half-hour in the water may be too much for the child with a slight frame. Other nursery school teachers find it necessary to plan a curtailed school program with the parents of the slight child.

DIFFERENCES BETWEEN BOYS AND GIRLS

Differences from individual to individual are of a high order of magnitude compared with differences between boys and girls. Yet those who work with children are aware of differences between the sexes, differences associated with the roles of each sex in the social order.

Immediately at birth the sex of the infant is a factor in how people react to the baby. The social order associates certain colors with boys and other colors with girls. As the children grow, their dress will be more and more differentiated. By the time the children are a year old, the boys may be expected to have short hair, the girls to have long hair. Parents pride themselves on their children as friends comment favorably on the way the child is fitting into expectations of the ways boys behave and the ways girls behave. "Isn't he all boy, though!" "What a dear little girl!" Girls of preschool age are encouraged to be a little mother to dolls, or a little housewife; boys are encouraged in carpentry and driving vehicles.

Children respond to praise by repeating behavior that pleases those around them. Getting praise for behavior in accord with what people expect of boys and girls encourages children to play the role appropriate to their sex. When parents and preschool teachers encourage children to explore both masculine and feminine activities, they do this with an awareness of the boy and girl differences in the social order. The teacher thinks it important for boys to play in the playhouse and for girls to be carpenters because they need a common background out of which to develop within their future families the divisions of responsibility appropriate to the widening range of careers for both men and women. Changing family patterns make it possible for fathers to play a new role involving tenderness and loving care of children, and for mothers to have careers in engineering, finance, and other fields previously reserved largely for men.

Parents and teachers notice that girls are more mature than boys of equal age. Three-year-old girls unbutton their clothing earlier than three-year-old boys do; four- and five-year-old girls are ready to sit still for story- or talking-time, but boys of the same age are not ready for such control. A well-coordinated and dexterous boy is apt to play with girls because boys of his age generally do not have the coordination and dexterity that he has. A girl who is emotionally disturbed by relationships within her family may regress to immature play and find the play of boys especially congenial.

Such hypotheses as yet are not substantiated in research literature. Benjamin S. Bloom, in his study of *Stability and Change in Human Characteristics,* does point out, however, that "aggression is discouraged in females, whereas dependence is discouraged in males."[13] He determined that one half of the criterion variance for aggressiveness in males can be predicted by age three, and for dependence in females, by age four. Intellectuality and general intelligence in both males and females can be predicted similarly by age four.[14]

MAKING A MINI-CASE STUDY

Awareness of individual differences leads into making mini-case studies of individual children in order to gain a more complete understanding of how each behaves and of factors associated with different kinds of behavior. The adult who observes a child who is especially talented is intrigued by what abilities constitute the talent and by what factors are associated with the talent in this particular child. As she continues to observe the child she finds herself asking further questions about the child, answering them by observing what the child does. The questions the adult is most apt to ask about a child are:

QUESTIONS OF PARENTS	QUESTIONS OF TEACHERS
How old is the child?	How old is the child?
How does the child behave throughout his day?	How does the child behave in school?
How does this behavior compare with that expected for this age?	How does this behavior compare with that expected for this age?

The most important part of making a mini-case study is to record one or two brief anecdotes which show the behavior of the child related to each question. Each anecdote gives what the child said and did, and is free from interpretations about what he did and how he felt.

At a later date, perhaps a month later, the recording of anecdotes to answer each question is repeated. After that, the mini-case study is continued by noting the differences between the two sets of answers and interpreting them. The two sets of answers may show progress of the child, no appreciable development in his behavior, or problems on which he needs help.

[13] Benjamin S. Bloom. *Stability and Change in Human Characteristics* (New York: John Wiley and Sons, Inc., 1964), p. 156.
[14] Ibid., p. 205.

A full case study uses published tests. (Courtesy of Minneapolis Public Schools and Mrs. Mary Jane Higley, Minneapolis, Minnesota.)

Mini-case studies may be simple studies considering only one or two aspects of the child's behavior. As adults become increasingly competent in making mini-case studies, their studies become more elaborate, and the scope of the questions more inclusive. Scores on published tests are obtained. An experienced teacher may not be satisfied until she has made at least one comprehensive case study, and is more likely to go on to making one or even two comprehensive case studies each year.

A parent starting to make a mini-case study of his own or another's child may want to consider one or more of the following questions and, on two or more different occasions, to record anecdotes relating to each of them.

- What are favorite activities of the child?
- What is especially interesting to the child?
- How does he think about himself?
- How does he approach a new situation?
- How does he meet a person new to him?
- What developmental problems is the child working on?
- How does he approach each problem?

The parent who has observed the behavior of his child is in a much better position for guiding his development. If he notices that the child is shy in meeting adult friends who come to call, the parent can arrange for a series of friends to call and can talk with his child in advance about the friend who is coming and about what to show the friends. The parent who observes a child to be eager to explore new environments may realize that the child is ready for trips to parks and public buildings.

A teacher making a mini-case study of a child records on two or more different occasions anecdotes which give her answers to such questions as the following:

- How does the child relate himself to other children?
- How does the child play?
- With what does he play by himself?
- What does he play with others?
- With whom does he play?
- What activities does he watch?
- How does he relate himself to the teacher?
- How does he relate himself to other adults?

The teacher who has observed the behavior of a child is much better able to guide his development. If the child is primarily a watcher of activities, she may encourage his mother in having some school playmate play with him at home, and in bringing him to school to explore the equipment when the other children are not there. If the child is eager to be with adults but not children, she may personally guide him into group situations until he feels more at home with some of the other children.

The experienced preschool teacher finds pleasure in starting a case study of one or two children each year. She deepens her understanding of all children through intensive study of individual children. Over the years she accumulates both a file of published and unpublished case studies and a considerable understanding of people. She thinks of each child as an individual person and is eager to follow him in school and out so as to understand him fully.

Meeting the Needs of the Preschool Child

Study of the characteristics of children at different age levels is basic to planning the program activities for the preschool group. Awareness of the fundamental needs of children is essential to planning their daily program and suitable methods of working with them. If the child's needs are met, he will be a happy, healthy person, able to learn and develop at an optimum rate. In addition to his need for a curricular program of activities appropriate to his age level, what other needs does the preschool child have?

PHYSICAL NEEDS

The physical needs of the preschool child must be met within his daily program. These needs include the following:

- Eating when hungry.
- Getting a drink when thirsty.
- Going to the bathroom as necessary.
- Having a rhythm of activity and rest.
- Having one or more physical outlets for emotions.

The experienced teacher knows that if any of these needs are not met within each school day, children will be out of control or unhappy and will interfere with the learning situation for both themselves and others.

NEEDS FOR A HEALTHY PERSONALITY

It is the function of the nursery school to develop healthy personalities in children, especially by furthering the sense of trust, the sense of

At rest time a child who needs to rest will learn to do so. (Courtesy of West-ern Washington State College, Bellingham, Washington.)

Eating, resting, and thinking. (Courtesy of Minneapolis Public Schools and Mrs. Mary Jane Higley, Minneapolis, Minnesota.)

autonomy, the sense of initiative, and conscience. The adult working with preschool children should be a person they can trust. She should be consistent and able to be depended on to react reassuringly even under unusual circumstances. She should also be eager to help them explore, pointing out limits of safety that become necessary. The children need to trust her judgment and appreciate her brief explanations about such matters as, say, keeping in the center of what you stand on, testing a rock to be sure it will not roll under your foot when you step on it, and so on. Children build trust by being with grownups they can trust.

The adult also should further a sense of autonomy in each child, respecting their "do-it-myself" requests and giving them the freedom necessary for developing self-discipline as they are ready for it. With Erik H. Erikson,[15] she should realize that shame and doubt are in direct opposition

---

[15] Erik H. Erikson, *Childhood and Society* (New York: W. W. Norton & Company, Inc., 1964).

to a sense of autonomy. She should avoid saying, "Aren't you ashamed of yourself?" or, "You made a mistake." Instead she may say, "Wasn't that funny? We won't do that again, will we?" or, "Let's try it this way," or, "Let's talk it over."

In guiding older preschool children as they reach for limits and explore the social order and the physical world around them, the wise and sensitive adult helps the children develop a sense of initiative and responsibility. She is careful that the children have a large proportion of success in what they attempt to do. When failures do occur, she helps them understand the objective reason for the failure and to plan for a better trial the next time. Always she avoids making the child feel guilty about what he has or has not done. She says, "Look what Tommy did!" in praise of Tommy's accomplishment, and never in disgust at the mess he has created. When a child hits another, she helps the hitter feel sympathy for the struck child, not guilt for his action. Instead of saying, "You naughty boy! You hurt Mary!" she says, "Mary is crying. How can you help her be happy again?" In this way the adult helps the child focus his attention on what needs to be done. Constructively he is led to help others instead of wasting time and energy feeling guilty about past events. Thus he develops a healthy sense of initiative and a conscience.

Prescott also points out the need for everyone to develop a healthy self-concept. He says, "A healthy self-concept should involve . . . feelings of safety, security, belonging, adequacy, self-realization, and integrity."[16] How does the preschool group help each child develop such feelings and such a healthy concept of himself?

SAFETY

Parents who have been alert and watchful to be sure that their child was safe at home must be sure that the nursery group and kindergarten continue to protect their child at the same time that he is learning to protect himself. The preschool teacher should ever be alert to make sure that the children are safe. They need to feel safe as part of feeling at home at the school. Furthermore, they learn ways of being safe by imitating her ways of keeping safe. On nature walks, she should be careful to remind them of how to cross the street: "Look up the street and down the street. Be sure no car is going to use the street while you go across it." On the ladder up to the slide she should remind them to keep out of the way of each other's feet. She must teach them the importance of always having air to breathe, and of getting help when they need it. In every possible way she should help them learn as rapidly as they are able how to control their world and keep themselves safe.

[16] Daniel A. Prescott, *The Child in the Educative Process* (New York: McGraw-Hill Book Company, Inc., 1957), p. 404.

SECURITY

Apropos of security, Prescott points out that:

Every child has a need for emotional security based on the assurance that he is loved and valued by those who are responsible for him. If this need is met, his feelings of security can carry him through many difficulties and failures. Lacking it, he has a persistent adjustment problem that gives rise to continuing anxiety and self-doubt or to hostility and aggressive demands for notice.[17]

Children feel secure when the adults who work with them value them to the point of empathy with them. Appreciating each child as an interesting and important person is the first step in working effectively with him. When children feel secure in their relationships with people around them, they develop rapidly, and learning takes place at an optimum rate.

BELONGING

Whether a child continues coming to a nursery group depends in large part on whether he feels that he really belongs to the group. The teacher who is aware of this does not leave to chance the relationships of the children. Daily she builds a "we-feeling" as she works with the children in group situations. "Aren't we having fun?" she may say. She is quick to notice the child who has little relationship to other children, and to talk with his mother about having a classmate visit him at times when school does not meet. At some time in the course of each school day, she establishes rapport warmly and appreciatively with each child. If she must restrain a child for his own safety, she makes sure that she soon is with him again so that he feels her love and appreciation.

ADEQUACY

A child has security by virtue of being himself; he has adequacy by virtue of what he can do. Adults further his sense of adequacy as they give him opportunities to be successful, and at older ages, to be successful as the challenge increases. The experienced preschool teacher has a mental list of ways to help the group. Each item is well within the abilities of the children in her group. For instance, when the teacher thanks the children for having brought chairs quietly into a circle around her, her appreciation gives the children a sense of adequacy as well as a sense of belonging through participating in a group activity. Earned praise is not only an excellent means for teaching desirable behavior, it is also a means for meeting the need of children to feel adequate.

[17] Ibid.

A small-group cooking project helps to meet a child's needs for adequacy, be-longing, self-realization—and eating when hungry. (Courtesy of The Merrill-Palmer Institute and Donna J. Harris, Detroit, Michigan.)

SELF-REALIZATION

The principal objective of the family and the preschool group is to have each child appreciate himself as an individual, a unique person of importance. Several situations that the preschool group provides each day help the child achieve self-realization. He is given simple choices, and he comes to understand that what he wants is given due consideration by those around him. He is free to play in a rich environment, and in the knowledge that the adults around him are available to help him do whatever is beyond him. He asks, and he receives either what he asks for or a simple explanation supplemented perhaps by a reasonable substitution for what he wants. As he develops an awareness of his self-importance, he begins to develop an appreciation of the importance of others. Through experience he comes to understand the desirability of differences between himself and others as a means of enriching group activities. Today Mary is passing the napkins at juice time because her mother is present in the nursery school; tomorrow Joe will pass the napkins when his mother is at nursery school. Both know it is an important role to play.

Integrity

By the time he is ready to enter first grade, a child should have developed feelings of safety and security, a sense of belonging and a sense of adequacy, and should have begun to realize his importance as a person. Thus he will be able to capitalize on his preschool experience and develop, during his elementary school years, a sense of integrity. In the preschool group he lays a foundation for a healthy personality throughout school and throughout life.

Meeting the Needs of Less Advantaged Children

Preschool children from less advantaged families often are in need of education to compensate for characteristics of their family style of life. A child surrounded by self-centered adults may not even know his own name. In fact, he may not know that he has a name and that he exists as an individual important in himself. His primary need may be the development of a healthy self-concept.

In contrast to the middle-class child whose mother is used to working with words and concepts, a less advantaged child is apt to have an impoverished environment without verbal affluence and with a mother who has little inclination to help him sort out concepts.[18] His life space may be geographically restricted to a very small area, and his experience may encompass so little that alternatives seldom occur to him. To offset the influence of a restrictive home environment, he greatly needs the preschool group experience such as has become increasingly available through the help of government funds and community sensitivity.

Important objectives for less advantaged preschool children include:

- To develop a healthy self-concept.
- To increase use of words and sentences.
- To expand understanding and use of concepts.
- To widen life space and extend experience firsthand.
- To explore alternatives and make choices.

Such objectives are appropriate in working with any preschool child or group of children, but they are essential in compensatory education of children whose home life has contributed little to their cognitive development.

Situations for Discussion

A preschool teacher is apt to find herself in situations similar to the four described here. As you think of what to do in each situation, consider whether

[18] Robert D. Hess and Roberta M. Bear, *Early Education: Current Theory, Research, and Practice* (Chicago: Aldine Publishing Company, 1967).

each course of action suggested is desirable, or not. Use points brought out in the chapter as well as ideas from your own experience to justify your views. Suggest alternative courses of action to supplement those given.

SITUATION 1   When you return to the nursery center after a week of absence, four-year-old Philip runs up to you and starts hitting you. As the adult in the situation, you should

- Hold Philip's arms so that he cannot hit you.
- Help him pound the punching bag, or the clay.
- Tell him you know how he feels.
- Divert his attention to something else.
- Tell him to stop and to sit on the bench until you can talk with him.

SITUATION 2   Theresa is a sweet three-year-old child. When you read stories to her group, she often looks around the room instead of at the pictures. From the beginning of school about two months ago, she said little or nothing. When you greet her each morning, she smiles at you, watching your face closely. As her teacher, you should

- Ask her parents if her hearing has been tested.
- Plan some time for getting better acquainted with Theresa by herself.
- Talk directly to Theresa when you are giving directions to the children.
- Show the children your watch and notice at what distance Theresa can just hear it tick.
- Observe how Theresa responds to your verbal directions.

SITUATION 3   Mrs. Jones is sensitive about Elisa, her daughter, who is one of the older children in the Head Start group of four-year-old children. Elisa does not yet use some of the toys that the youngest children enjoy. When Mrs. Jones talks with you, she often asks whether you think Elisa can go to kindergarten next year. You should say

- Let's look at the list of what a kindergarten child does.
- I don't think she will be ready.
- I like Elisa very much.
- Would you like to observe a kindergarten group?
- Each child is placed in whatever group seems best for him.

SITUATION 4   You are working with a group of teachers and aides for Head Start projects. They have been recording their observations of children for two weeks and are interested in learning more about how to observe children. In talking with them, you should suggest that they

- Record only what the child says and does.
- Observe the same child several weeks later.
- Look for something specific (e.g., solitary, parallel, or cooperative play).
- Record anecdotes as one of the best ways to learn about children.
- Use observations as a basis for planning activities for the children.

Current Professional Books and Pamphlets

ALMY, MILLIE, and others. *Young Children's Thinking.* New York: Teachers College Press, Columbia University, 1966. [Studies some aspects of Piaget's theory.]

"Arden House Conference on Pre-School Enrichment," *Merrill Palmer Quarterly,* Vol. 10, No. 3, 1966. [Contains presentations by Martin Deutsch, M. D., and J. McV. Hunt on using preschool enrichment as an antidote for cultural deprivation.]

BALDWIN, ALFRED L. *Theories of Child Development.* New York: John Wiley and Sons, Inc., 1967. [One of the college textbooks on child development.]

BLOOM, BENJAMIN S. *Stability and Change in Human Characteristics.* New York: John Wiley and Sons, Inc., 1964. [Identifies aspects of development during preschool years and documents the importance of that part of life.]

COOK, M., tr. *The Origins of Intelligence in Children.* New York: W. W. Norton and Company, Inc., 1963. [Writings of Jean Piaget are translated and published in inexpensive editions.]

DITTMANN, LAURA L., ed. *Early Child Care.* New York: Atherton Press, 1968. [New ways of looking at care of infants, toddlers and preschool children are discussed by leaders in pediatrics, child psychiatry, psychology, anthropology, education, and child-development research.]

Early Childhood—Crucial Years for Learning. Washington, D.C.: Association for Childhood Education International, 1966. [Twenty-two significant articles published originally in *Childhood Education.*]

Encyclopedia of Child Care and Guidance, twelve volumes. Garden City, N.Y.: Doubleday & Company, Inc., 1967. [Sidonie Matsner Gruenberg edited contributions from authorities in all disciplines concerned with human growth and development.]

HARTUP, WILLARD W., and SMOTHERGILL, NANCY L. *The Young Child—Reviews of Research.* Washington, D.C.: National Association for the Education of Young Children, 1968. [Eighteen reviews of research about such topics as development of conscience, racial awareness, and peer acceptance were published originally in *Young Children.*]

HEFFERNAN, HELEN, and VIVIAN EDMISTON TODD. *The Kindergarten Teacher.* Boston: D. C. Heath & Company, 1960. [Chapter 2 discusses kindergarten children and their needs.]

HILL, JOHN P., ed. *Minnesota Symposia on Child Psychology.* Minneapolis: University of Minnesota Press, 1967. [An annual volume of the Institute of Child Psychology presents outstanding papers from the annual symposium of child psychologists invited to present their research studies.]

HOFFMAN, LOIS W., and MARTIN L. *Review of Child Development Research.* New York: Russell Sage Foundation, 1966. [Volume 1 includes a summary of research about effects of early group experience. The initial chapter of Vol. 2 deals with family structure, socialization, and personality.]

HYMES, JAMES L., JR. *The Child Under Six.* Englewood Cliffs, N.J.: Prentice-Hall, Inc., 1963. [An insightful and readable treatment of the early years of life.]

JANIS, MARJORIE G. *A Two-Year-Old Goes to Nursery School: A Case Study of Separation Reactions.* New York: National Association for the Education of Young Children, 1965. [From the master's program at Bank Street College of Education.]

JENKINS, GLADYS G., HELEN SCHACTER, and WILLIAM W. BAUER. *These Are Your Children.* Chicago: Scott, Foresman & Co., 1966. [Characteristics of children's growth.]

KAGAN, J., and H. MOSS. *Birth to Maturity: A Study in Psychological Development.* New York: John Wiley and Sons, Inc., 1962. [The preschool years are set within the total life span from birth to maturity.]

LANDRETH, CATHERINE. *Early Childhood: Behavior and Learning.* New York: Alfred A. Knopf, Inc., 1967. [Psychology of early childhood.]

MURPHY, LOUIS BARCLAY, and associates. *Personality in Young Children.* New York: Basic Books, Inc., 1966. [Volume I, 1956, discusses methods for measuring the inner life of the child, his perception of his environment, and his relation to it. Volume II is a study of *Colin—A Normal Child* from his entrance to nursery school at two years and nine months of age until he is six years and two months of age.]

MURPHY, LOIS. *The Widening World of Childhood.* New York: Basic Books, Inc., 1962. [A twelve-year study of thirty-two normal children coping with daily and stress situations from infancy to adolescence.]

MUSSEN, P., J. CONGER, and J. KAGAN. *Child Development and Personality,* 2nd ed. New York: Harper & Row, Publishers, 1963. [A comprehensive book on all aspects of childhood and their relationship to emergence of individuality.]

PIAGET, JEAN. *Origins of Intelligence in Children.* New York: W. W. Norton & Co., Inc., 1963. [Preschool behavior leads into behavior in which thought processes are more readily apparent.]

SMART, MOLLIE S., and C. RUSSELL. *Children—Development and Relationships.* New York: The Macmillan Company, 1967. [Uses Erikson's concept of development in recognizable stages, and Piaget's analyses of intellectual development.]

SPOCK, BENJAMIN. *Baby and Child Care.* New York: Pocket Books, 1967. [Current printing of the development of a child as seen by a medical practitioner.]

WANN, KENNETH D., MIRIAM S. DORN, and ELIZABETH ANN LIDDLE. *Fostering Intellectual Development in Young Children.* New York: Bureau of Publications, Teachers College, Columbia University, 1962. [Focuses on intellectual aspects of child development.]

WARING, ETHEL B. *Principles of Child Guidance,* Bulletin 420. Ithaca, N.Y.: Cornell University, 1966. [This reprint identifies four underlying principles of child guidance: affection, respect, help, and approval.]

CHAPTER 3

Arranging for the Preschool Group

Adults make it possible for children to have preschool group experience. They provide the facilities and equipment for the school or center. They plan and operate the program. They are responsible for the policies of the preschool group and for the attitudes that underlie its emotional climate. They spend many hours of their time and much of their energy to make possible for preschool children a rich environment suitable for their optimum development.

The Adults

The adults who are associated with a preschool group are the teachers, aides, and assistant teachers, the director and his business, housekeeping, and social work assistants, and student observers and participants. The parent who is associated with the group in any of these capacities functions in the same way as a person who is not a parent—he must carry out his parental responsibilities so that they do not interfere with his responsibilities to the preschool group as a whole.

A small school, meeting part of the day, may have only a teacher, usually with an assistant. A large center in session throughout the working day may need a director and several staff members to carry on the business, housekeeping, and parental functions auxiliary to the teaching functions of the school. A school or center of any size, whether it is in session for part or all of the working day, may have student teachers acting as observers or as participants in the teaching of the children; often parents or other volunteers assist the teacher.

The administrative organization of a preschool group determines the adult roles essential to its functioning. If the preschool group is under the aegis of some welfare or educational agency, it will have an adult acting in a liaison capacity between the school or center and the agency. But if the preschool group is an independent organization, it will have owners and employees taking care of financial and other business functions. If the preschool group is operated as a parent-cooperative group, those functions will be assumed by the parents of the children and the adults they employ.

The adults associated with a preschool group teach the children and carry out the other professional, business, and housekeeping functions related to teaching the children. These functions vary from group to group, each of which has its unique arrangements. Yet the following responsibilities are to be looked for in getting acquainted with the organization of a preschool group.

Adult teamwork makes a preschool group function smoothly. (Courtesy of Lincoln Public Schools and Nebraska Association for Childhood Education.)

Professional responsibilities:

- Planning and administering an educational program for the children.
- Keeping health, family, and attendance records as needed.
- Selecting teaching personnel and defining personnel policies.
- Planning and administering a program of in-service teacher development.
- Attending and participating in professional conferences, lectures, and workshops.
- Studying and writing about preschool children and their education.
- Planning and administering a parent education program.
- Studying and writing about parents and their development.

Business responsibilities:

- Maintaining liaison with city and state departments concerned with preschool groups.
- Conforming to regulations regarding safety, licensing, and zoning.
- Interpreting the preschool group to its constituents and to the community.
- Maintaining liaison with supporting agencies, if any.
- Defining policies of admission, attendance, and so on.

Discussing the supply of sheets. (Courtesy of Long Beach Day Nursery and Mariam M. Cook, Long Beach, California.)

- Planning a budget.
- Bookkeeping and accounting.
- Selecting personnel and defining personnel policies.
- Selecting and maintaining facilities.
- Selecting and repairing equipment.
- Arranging for transportation of children to and from the preschool group.
- Providing perishable supplies as needed.

Housekeeping responsibilities:

- Preparing and serving food each day.
- Regular cleaning of the school rooms and patio or other outdoor areas.
- Regular laundering of such items as sheets, towels, and paint smocks.

PARENT FUNCTIONS IN A PRESCHOOL GROUP

In a parent-cooperative preschool group, the parents have responsibility for all the adult functions of the program, including the selection and employment of a teacher. The following excerpt from a handbook for parents in such a group describes how various functions are distributed among the parents so that each parent has an important role to play in the operation of the preschool group, as well as in assisting the teacher with the children. The list is useful to any group interested in having adults develop through assumption of responsibility.

The following list of responsibilities is suggested for a cooperative nursery having eighteen participating mothers. For a smaller group, the lesser responsibilities may be combined as seems desirable. Often the positions of greatest responsibility, such as Chairman of Mothers, or the Equipment Chairman, or the Chairman of Business, are held by more experienced mothers, sometimes with the help of a second mother as assistant.

1. *Supervisor of Children* or *Teacher:* . . . Gives the cooperative nursery continuity by being with the children every day. The Supervisor of Children is a qualified person, not necessarily one of the mothers. At the monthly meeting of mothers, she leads discussion concerning daily operation of the children's group.
2. *Chairman of Mothers:* . . . Inducts new mothers into the group and maintains a waiting list of mothers awaiting entrance. Helps mothers with their problems through individual conferences and through group meetings. Arranges for continuous educational programs for mothers, leading such discussion at monthly meeting of mothers.
3. *Chairman of Business* or *President:* Presides at all meetings, and coordinates the business activities for the cooperative nursery; countersigns checks issued by the Treasurer.
4. *Secretary:* Keeps the minutes . . . maintains a record of attendance . . . carries on correspondence for the group.

5. *Treasurer:* Collects entrance fees . . . monthly fees . . . takes care of bills . . . maintains records and reports monthly to the members on the finances.
6. *Equipment Chairman:* Assembles and inventories all equipment and sees about replacements and repairs.
7. *Schedule Chairman:* Posts a monthly schedule of days for each mother to assist at the nursery.
8. *Council Liaison:* Gets herself and other parents to the monthly meetings of the Council of Cooperative Nurseries . . . reports the activities of the Council . . . at the monthly meeting of her cooperative nursery; reports the activities and opinions of her cooperative nursery to the Council.
9. *Arts and Crafts Chairman:* Takes charge of craft supplies (e.g., clay, paper, paints) and their replenishment.
10. *Supplies Chairman:* Takes charge of supplies for morning refreshment for the children (e.g., juice, paper cups, paper napkins) and their replenishment.
11. *Music Chairman:* Takes charge of rhythm band instruments, music books, and other materials for the children's music activities.
12. *Story Book Chairman:* Takes charge of story books and materials related to the stories for the children; keeps in touch with a children's librarian.
13. *Housekeeping Chairman:* Sees that the smocks children wear for painting, their blankets, and so on, are washed as often as necessary; takes charge of any other housekeeping problem that arises.
14. *Health Chairman:* Advises the group on safety measures, health inspections, checkups, and so on, and maintains health records for each family.
15. *Social Chairman:* Arranges for places for monthly meetings and for refreshments; acts as chairman of committees for social affairs which include all members of families.
16. *Publicity Chairman:* Sees that activities of the cooperative nursery are announced and reported in the community newspaper.
17. *Librarian:* Acts as Librarian for the books and pamphlets of the cooperative nursery; reviews new books concerning children and nurseries and makes recommendations for desirable purchases.
18. *Telephone Chairman:* Sees that each mother is called regarding meetings, social events, and any other important events.[1]

Depending upon the talents and interests of members of the parent group, other roles may be substituted for those listed, or may be added to the list. For instance, an Excursion Chairman could be useful to the group in finding out about study trips suitable for the children and available in the immediate community, and in arranging for the visit and the transportation of the children. An Educational Chairman could take charge of the educational program, an important part of the monthly meeting of

[1] *Cooperative Nursery School Handbook,* Vivian Edmiston Todd, ed. (Long Beach, Calif.: Long Beach Council of Parent Participation Nursery Schools, 1957), pp. 7–8.

Daddy makes a new experience at nursery school. (Courtesy of The Merrill-Palmer Institute and Donna J. Harris, Detroit, Michigan.)

the mothers. Having a separate Educational Chairman relieves the Chairman of Mothers of part of her responsibilities and serves to emphasize the importance of the educational program.

ROLE OF FATHERS IN A PRESCHOOL GROUP

The father of a family takes part in the activities of a preschool group according to his interests and abilities. His participation depends also on the type of school that his child attends.

Day-Care and Other Welfare Groups. The father may be a child's only parent, and therefore the one who gets the child to and from school. Paying fees, reading bulletins and bulletin boards, and talking briefly with school personnel is as much participation as is likely to fit easily into the full day of such a father. Fathers in a two-parent family may be interested in participating more fully in accord with whatever the school suggests.

Private Preschool Groups. Paying school expenses and receiving reports of the progress of his preschool child is minimum participation for fathers. With encouragement, they become interested in studying such related subjects as child growth and development, and mental health, and in arranging for a variety of experiences to help their young children acquire accurate concepts about their scientific and social world.

Parent-Cooperative Groups. In addition to paying expenses, fathers often participate by repairing and making equipment. At least one of the parent meetings each year is especially for fathers, and such topics as "Being a Father" and "Children's Problems Made and Solved by Parents" are then discussed. Business of the preschool group is carried on by parents, including fathers. In some parent-cooperative groups, the office of president is held mutually by a father and mother working as a team. Participation by any parent is usually a matter of what he wants to volunteer to do.

All Groups. In many preschool groups the children meet at least once a year on a day, often a Saturday, when fathers may come to visit. This visit gives the fathers an opportunity to share with their children an experience of great importance. Fathers sometimes say that after visiting day their children talked with them more about their preschool group. Fathers also appreciate seeing the methods by which the teacher works with the children. Such observations often suggest to fathers ways in which they may work effectively with their children.

NUMBER OF ADULTS

The number of adults associated with a preschool group may be numerous or may be limited to the minimum required by the local licensing agency. The number of responsible adults depends upon the number of children and the type of preschool group. For instance, in California except in parent-cooperative nursery schools, a full-time teacher works with a group of six to ten children, depending on their ages. Another adult is immediately available in case of emergencies. In addition, of course, there is a staff responsible for housekeeping, maintenance, and administration. In parent cooperatives the ratio is one adult, including the director, to five children and also an assistant teacher when there are twenty-five or more children.

The specified intent of these requirements is to make sure that, "No group of children shall be left without adult supervision at any time."[2] It is important to have enough qualified adults to administer the program for the children, with at least one adult available to substitute for the adult in charge of the children in case of emergency.

The program for the children is a fuller one when the talents of more adults are available to enrich it. The program is usually a broad one when it makes use of the special interests and skills of parents and volunteers. The teacher in charge of the children's groups helps plan the contributor's work with the children so that it is suitable to the level of development of the children and is not overly stimulating.

The day-care centers, private schools, and laboratory schools usually capitalize on the fact that experienced preschool teachers are skillful in

[2] Department of Social Welfare, State of California, "Guide to Establishment of Group Day Care Programs for Young Children" (Sacramento: California State Department of Social Welfare, 1959), p. 6.

An adult to answer a question can be a teacher, parent, student, or volunteer.
(Courtesy of Ontario-Montclair School District, Ontario, California.)

adapting to the needs of children in a relatively short interval of time. Often the director of the school or center is available to take over work with a group of children or an individual child when the teacher for the group needs help. The director plans her day so that she is with the children at the times they are most apt to show signs of fatigue—just before their resting and eating times. She also plans to be with the children more frequently when new members are added to the group or when new activities are being introduced.

The number of responsible adults required is determined by the needs of the children. All groups of children need more adult help at the beginning of the year, when they are learning to function as a group. Depending upon their age and emotional development, some groups of children require more guidance than do others. For instance, a group of children needs more adult attention if one of its members is from a home in which an imminent divorce gives the child an inconsistent emotional support fluctuating between rejection of and demand for affection.

When the number of children is too large, it is not possible for the teacher to revitalize her rapport with each individual child within the scope of the morning. The experienced preschool teacher knows that with too many children two and one half hours is not long enough to satisfy the emotional needs of a child who is learning to relate to an adult other than his parents. One parent-cooperative nursery school attempted to reduce its per child costs by adding more children. Within one month the parents saw the need for reducing the ratio of the number of children to the teacher. The mothers reported their children returning from nursery school more fatigued and more often out of control. On the days they assisted the teacher, the mothers noted more frequent conflict situations and felt less successful in their work. The teacher felt frustrated because she could not listen to each child and give him the attention he needed each morning. The mothers and teacher recognized that the children were not experiencing a real preschool group if they did not have daily interaction with a teacher who loved them. Instead of reducing its costs by adding another child or two, the parent-cooperative group in doing so had to increase its costs by adding a second full-time teacher.

In planning a preschool group for children from less advantaged families, it is well to keep in mind the following statement from the Office of Economic Opportunity:

The climate of discipline that fosters learning can only be created if there is a small number of children for each adult, and if the total number in each group is kept small.. To have any group larger than fifteen, and to have any less than two adults for fifteen children (a teacher and a teacher aide) is to court disaster. . . .[3]

PERSONNEL IN INITIATING HEAD START PROGRAMS

How to develop personnel quickly was demonstrated when the numerous preschool programs initiated by community councils under the provisions of the Economic Opportunity Act of 1964 were confronted with a serious shortage of qualified personnel. Care for preschool children was a vigorous but relatively recent development in the United States. Preschool groups which were sponsored by public school systems, by colleges and universities

[3] Office of Economic Opportunity, "Project Head Start Daily Program I for a Child Development Center" (Washington, D.C.: U.S. Government Printing Office, 1967), p. 28.

as laboratories for child study, by cooperating groups of parents, by churches, and by private individuals and institutions were not attracting the enrollment of large numbers of persons needed in professional education programs leading to careers in preschool education.

When Head Start programs were launched in the summer of 1965, many kindergarten and primary teachers made themselves available to staff the projects. Others who had previous preparation for preschool education were intrigued by the opportunities the program offered to enlist in the President's War on Poverty. Instructional materials for them to use were quickly prepared by specialists recruited for the purpose by the Office of Economic Opportunity. Preliminary workshops, conferences, and other types of training sessions were held for prospective directors, teachers, aides, and other personnel. Plans were projected for continuing in-service education.

The first summer of the program more than 500,000 preschool children were enrolled from disadvantaged homes. The results of the program were so gratifying and public enthusiasm was so great that school systems made plans for the continuation of programs through the school year. Colleges and universities cooperated in providing extension and other courses as part of well-designed on-the-job training. The preschool teachers who had been out of service were encouraged to up-grade their professional preparation. Gradually increasing numbers of young people began to be interested in courses leading to paraprofessional or professional service in the field of preschool education.

Many of the aides in the Head Start programs were selected from unemployed persons in the socioeconomically disadvantaged segment of the population. Aides were frequently mothers or relatives of children enrolled in the program. Their participation resulted in restored aspirations, improved child-rearing practices, and understanding of the importance of the nurture and education of young children. The aides became agents of diffusion in spreading these new learnings in their communities. They were excellent interpreters of the program to their neighbors and were recruiters for it.

Adults and Child Development

The responsibility of the adults associated with a preschool group is to create an environment favorable to the development of the children. Policies of the preschool group, whether established by a private owner, a school or welfare bureau, a community council, or a group of parents, must be in terms of what is good for the children. Those who teach or assist the teacher should work always for the optimum development of the children.

THE TEACHER

The teacher, together with her assistants in the classroom, creates the emotional climate for the preschool group. Her personality will determine whether children and the guiding adults move through the day only conscientiously and dutifully, or joyously and pleasantly as well. Her capacity to enjoy life can make a preschool group a delightful experience for everyone concerned.

Effective ways of working with children should be an integral part of the personality of the good teacher. Habitually the good teacher emphasizes what is accomplished, and keeps to herself her awareness of shortcomings and that which is not yet done. Negative criticism has no place in her comments. She makes positive suggestions and is constructive and confident. As a general rule she uses *do* rather than *don't;* sometimes she uses *do* with *don't*. She is kind, but firm. She makes it a pleasure for four-year-olds to recognize a limit and for five-year-olds to follow a rule. "Let's walk around the puddles so our shoes stay dry," says the experienced teacher when the novice might make the mistake of saying, "Don't get your feet wet in the puddles," and wonder why the children went right into the puddles.

There are several techniques that the teacher consciously uses to contribute to the pleasant emotional climate of her preschool group:

1. She works with each child as an individual, and appreciates him as a unique personality. She respects his wishes and his suggestions. She treats him as a real person, and values his autonomy as well as his trust.
2. She keeps written records of her observations of each child, making note of physical growth and development, social achievement, emotional control, and relationships he understands. She writes down anecdotes which reveal his initiative, his interests, his approach to new people and new situations, his sense of his own importance, his confidence in himself and in people around him. She adds these anecdotal records to the folder of other materials about the child—a description of his family background, interview notes regarding parental interest in and thinking about the child, health records, and attendance records. She considers the records in relation to each other and plans how to work effectively with the child.
3. Realizing that all behavior is caused, she looks for factors in the nursery school situation which may be related to the behavior she observes in each child. She keeps in mind the needs of the children to feel they belong to the group and to feel safe, adequate, and secure. She uses the relationships she identifies as a basis for planning.
4. She understands democratic group processes and works with the group in terms of them. She helps the group to see and appreciate the contri-

bution of each child. She helps each child develop, understand, and make use of a few basic social and physical limits.

5. She knows the age level of the children with whom she works, and plans activities for the children in terms of their interests, abilities, and their developmental problems.

6. She provides a permissive atmosphere which encourages each child to develop his competencies and his self-discipline. She gives him opportunity to make choices suitable to his maturity, and helps him find pleasure in the results of his choices and activities.

7. She has a real affection for and appreciation of each child. Her love for each child is apparent in the empathy that pervades her interaction with him.

THE EMPLOYER

Whoever employs the teacher—agency, school, owner, or parent group—can contribute to the emotional climate of the preschool group through their relationship to the teacher. If her employers show consideration for the teacher and express appreciation of her work, they contribute to her feelings about herself as a teacher. She should teach better if she has a written contract well in advance of the school year, accompanied by a letter pointing out realistically aspects of her work which make the employer eager to have her continue her work with the children. Her contract should provide for

- Sick leave.
- Teacher retirement benefits.
- Liability insurance while teaching.
- Professional development through attendance at professional conferences or visitation of other preschool groups.

Thus she can be assured that the children will be provided for in the event she becomes ill; that she will have an income when she retires from active service; that she has financial protection in the event of an accident beyond her control; and that she will have opportunity for continuing professional development. These assurances give her a sense of security; the fact that her employer was considerate enough to make them available gives her a feeling of personal rapport with him. She is thus able to go ahead with her teaching without being burdened by problems of personal security. She can think about the children rather than about herself.

PARENTS

Parents also contribute to the emotional climate of the preschool group: directly, when they participate in the classroom as assistants to the teacher; indirectly, as they play their role as parents. If parents talk about the teacher appreciatively, their children are favorably oriented toward her and toward the preschool group. Parental interest in the preschool group and pleasant home conversation about what goes on at school are indispensable factors in a happy experience for the children. Genuine friendship between parents and teacher, particularly if the teacher is a frequent guest in his home, enriches the child's preschool experience further.

Attributes of the Preschool Teacher

Because she is the key person creating the emotional climate for the children, selection of a teacher is a critical factor in the success of a preschool group: What are her attributes as a person? As a teacher? Evaluation of attributes enables a person interested in becoming a teacher to decide if she is suited to such teaching; it enables employers of preschool teachers to improve their selection.

Among the desirable personality characteristics for individuals who wish to work in the preschool field are pleasure and interest in working with young children, flexible personality, concern for the welfare of others regardless of ethnic or religious differences or economic status, good health, enthusiasm, verbal facility, warmth, sense of humor, imagination, sense of responsibility, good appearance, initiative, reliability, and patience. In addition to these important personal qualities, the preschool teacher should have an excellent foundation in general education as a basis for an appropriate professional curriculum including child growth and development, child nutrition and health care, social problems, mental health, community relations, and family relationships. The prospective teacher should have many experiences in observing and recording child behavior. Her specialization should include studying and using modern methods and teaching materials suitable for the preschool curriculum, including music and rhythmical activities, creative art experiences, children's literature, physical education, science and mathematics, and social studies. Her preparation should also include experiences in holding conferences with parents concerning problems and development of children.

LOVE

Appreciating the importance of love in the preschool group leads to recognition that a capacity for love is an essential attribute in the preschool teacher. Only a loving person can help young children develop senses of trust, security, and autonomy. Only a loving person can guide them toward love of their fellowmen, an essential ingredient of our democracy. At preschool age levels, when children learn rapidly through imitation of those about them, it is important that they have a loving teacher as their pattern to imitate.

Prescott describes the behavior of a person who loves, the kind of behavior one finds in the good preschool teacher.

1. . . . A person who loves actually enters into the feelings of and shares intimately the experiences of the loved one and the effects of these experiences upon the love one.
2. One who loves is deeply concerned for the welfare, happiness and development of the beloved. . . .
3. One who loves finds pleasure in making his resources available to the loved one, to be used by the other to enhance his welfare, happiness, and development. . . .
4. . . . he also *accepts fully the uniqueness and individuality of the beloved and,* to the degree implied by the beloved's maturity level, *accords to the latter full freedom to experience, to act, and to become what he desires* to become. . . .[4]

MATURITY

Whether the teacher is a mature person is not a matter of her chronological age but of her capacity to think through the problems of relationship to other people—to each member of her own family, especially her mother, and to other mothers and fathers. The mature person who teaches preschool children has thought about why she teaches them, and appreciates the difference between the satisfactions of guiding developing personalities and other, more crass satisfactions. Although most persons in our society must have compensation for their work in order to live, the preschool teacher is committed to her work with young children and recognizes the social significance of her service.

UNDERSTANDING HOW TO TEACH CHILDREN

A person may be mature and love children without knowing how to guide them effectively in the preschool group situation. The teacher must also study the theory of child development and of education and combine it with laboratory experience in handling children individually and in groups. She must know

- How children grow and develop during the preschool years.
- The needs and the developmental problems of preschool children.
- The behavior of children at the age level she will work with.
- How school facilities, equipment, and curriculum further child development.

---

[4] Daniel A. Prescott, *The Child in the Educative Process* (New York: McGraw-Hill Book Company, Inc., 1957), p. 358.

If the teacher loves children, she should be interested in guiding them effectively and in taking course work to further her understanding of children and of teaching. If she does not love children for themselves, she may enroll for courses about children and practice in teaching them, but for her own sake and for that of the children she should be guided into a more suitable vocation than that of teaching preschool children.

Relations Among Adults

When many adults are participating in the management and operation of a preschool group, it is necessary that they all work together for the good of the children. Cooperation among the adults cannot be left to chance—they must communicate with each other to clarify preschool group policies and ways of working in terms of the policies. When each adult understands her role and her relation to others, she helps insure smooth operation of the preschool group, and benefits the children in it. Professional relations between teacher and volunteer or paid assistants are discussed in Chapter 18.

RESPONSIBILITIES OF PARENTS

Parents take on certain responsibilities when they enroll a child in a preschool group. Having entered their child in a new situation, they are re-

Observers and participants share experience of the children's group. (Courtesy of California State College at Long Beach and Mariam M. Cook, Long Beach, California.)

sponsible for helping him get the most out of that situation. They need to encourage him as he adjusts to it, and to help him develop favorable attitudes toward the group.

Parents also take on the responsibility of helping their child as he participates in the group. If it is the custom to have parents visit the preschool group so that the children can share the group experience with them, it is the responsibility of every parent to cooperate.

Teachers have responsibility for helping parents to be informed about the group's customs, and in encouraging them to develop a cooperative school spirit in their family. When a child's birthday approaches, the good teacher gets in touch with the parents and works with them in arranging for whatever celebration the child is to have. When a visiting day is scheduled, the good teacher takes the responsibility of seeing that parents have the day clearly in mind and have fitted the occasion into their planning for that day.

In many private schools, the parents arrange for a school bus to transport children to and from the preschool group. In most parent-cooperative groups, parents retain this responsibility and arrange for car pools. The mother assisting the teacher with the group for the day may stop for three or four children of other families who live in her neighborhood. After the school session, she returns the children to their homes. The next day the group meets, the mother of another child in the car pool will pick up the same group of children. In this way the mothers take turns seeing that the children have experience in the small car pool group as it is transported to and from the larger nursery group. The parents should be careful drivers; they should carry liability insurance to protect both their friends and themselves.

When the preschool group is housed in a nearby school building or in another facility in the neighborhood, parents usually bring their preschool children or arrange for older siblings to do so on their way to school. But when the preschool center serves a large community and is state or federally supported, it usually takes responsibility for transporting large numbers of children by bus, making arrangements with the school district or with a reliable commercial company that is a subcontractor of the district. By appropriate scheduling of transportation, young children will not be using the bus when it is needed for older children. In addition to the driver of the bus, provision is always made for a number of adults to ride in the bus with preschool children.

IMPLEMENTING BASIC POLICY OF A PRESCHOOL GROUP

Each rule, regulation, and procedure of a preschool group should be reviewed from time to time to be sure that it is in the best interests of the children. The adults who decide on policies and those who implement them must not be tempted to put their own interests ahead of those of the children. What is good for the children is also for the good of the adults working with them.

Consider, for example, a question which sometimes arises in a parent-cooperative nursery group: May a mother bring a younger sibling on the day she works assisting the teacher? This question must be thought over in terms of the good of the children enrolled in the nursery group. Can a child have his mother come only if she brings his younger siblings? If an assisting mother brings a younger sibling, will she be able to give the teacher the help that she needs with the nursery school children? Will the adult attention given the younger visitor divert attention from the nursery children? Will the child whose sibling visits be better off because of the visit, will his efforts to achieve autonomy and self-sufficiency be hampered or will his self-concept as a helper of others be enhanced? Such questions as

*Taking care of a younger sibling can give a preschool child importance. (**Courtesy of Decatur Public Schools, Decatur, Illinois.**)*

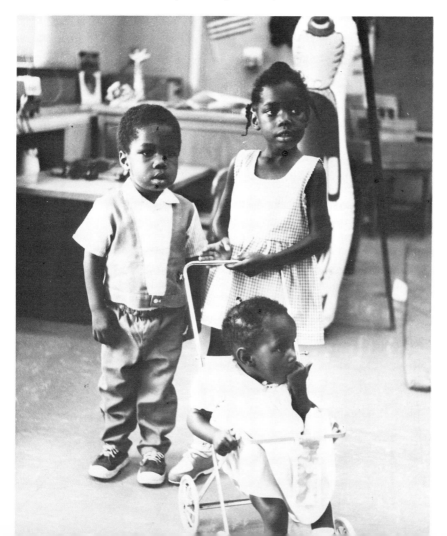

these must be considered in arriving at a policy concerning younger siblings. Questions which are interesting but irrelevant must be recognized as such; for instance, "Is it better for the younger sibling to play with the younger sibling of a mother who is not working that day?" "Does visiting the nursery group prepare a sibling for entering it when he is sufficiently mature?" Any question of nursery school policy must be answered in terms of what is best for the children in the nursery group.

RELATIONS BETWEEN TEACHER AND PARENT

It is especially important that the teacher have good rapport with the parents of the children. In any preschool the children respond to the teacher in terms of their parents' attitudes. If their parents like the teacher, the children will respond to the pleasant tones of voice their parents use in talking about her. "I think you have the loveliest teacher," says the mother; "I like my teacher," thinks the child. The child who is thus oriented favorably to his teacher is ready to learn a great deal from her and enjoys being in the preschool group.

If the parents and the teacher are not in sympathy, the preschool group is apt to pose conflicts to the child—he does not know whether he is supposed to be friendly with the teacher or with his parents. Furthermore, parents not reached by the friendliness of the director and teacher will, sooner or later, find some reason for withdrawing their child.

In a preschool group both mothers who help and the teacher must work smoothly together for the good of the children. The teacher should appreciate what each mother can do, and expect from her only the help that she is able to give. At the same time, each mother should respect the ability of the teacher and give heed to her suggestions. If their views differ, mother and teacher should find some time for talking together when neither must give her attention to children.

Mutual understanding and appreciation between director and mothers is so important to the parent-cooperative school that the mothers should select their own teacher. One group of parents may select a teacher who is highly congenial to them but is of little or no interest to groups of parents from other neighborhoods. Through the selection process the teacher comes to work with families who have basic values and, often, backgrounds and interests that are similar to her own.

Parents must recognize the teacher as an expert in working with a group of preschool children, a person who has studied and continues to study how to handle them. They also must recognize themselves as the persons most intimately acquainted with their own children. Their expertness as the parent of one child is combined with the expertness of the teacher with a group of children to provide the kind of preschool group especially valuable for their children.

RELATIONS BETWEEN TEACHER AND DIRECTOR

In the private or laboratory school, the children's center, and the day-care center, the teacher may have responsibility for a children's group, with the director of the school or center responsible for relationships to parents and business relationships. As the teacher and director work together for the good of the children, they share relationships to parents. Sometimes a parent may speak with the teacher about a problem which the teacher feels is of sufficient importance to the child's family or to the school to warrant further consideration. After the teacher confers with the director, the director arranges for whatever further conferences and discussions with parents seem appropriate. More frequently, parents bring their problems first to the director. If a problem involves the child's relationship to the teacher or to the children's group, the director and the child's teacher both confer with the parents.

Throughout all their relations, teacher and director must keep in mind their joint responsibility for the children's development. They need to be mutually loyal—the director backing up the teacher in her work with the children, the teacher supporting the school and its director.

In some instances a teacher and the director may have divergent views about what is best for the children. One nursery school teacher felt that the children needed study trips to acquaint themselves with aspects of the community they might not otherwise come to know. Her director intellectually understood the teacher's repeated suggestion that study trips be arranged, but he was unwilling to run the risk of an accident which might involve the school financially. The following year the teacher took every opportunity to acquaint the parents and her colleagues with the desirability of excursions, pointing out at the same time the problem of school liability. When she met a parent at the market or on the street, the teacher would stop for a brief conversation which included mention of how well the children were doing at school as well as their need for stimulating excursions. By the next year, the parents were not only asking the director to provide study trips for the children, they were volunteering to use their weekends and public transportation to accomplish them. Study trips for the children became a reality through the persistent and professional action of the teacher, working with the parents while keeping the director informed of her action.

The teacher and director should work together cooperatively as they keep in mind their fundamental responsibility to the children. Because the interests of the children are best served by a teacher who continues to develop as she teaches, the director should encourage teachers to attend professional conferences and to visit other preschool groups. Instead of attending professional conferences every time herself, the good director arranges for her teachers each in turn to represent the preschool group at, and bring back to the entire staff ideas gleaned from, conferences. The director who appreciates the worth of teachers works with them democratically in such a way that both director and teachers develop in service.

RELATIONS BETWEEN TEACHER AND STUDENTS

When the preschool group has students observing or participating in the program, the teacher should keep in mind her primary responsibility to the preschool children—the students are the responsibility of their own teacher. Because they are interested in the preschool group, the good teacher is glad to have students visit and is eager to have them understand what they observe. Especially she wants them to understand what is good for the children, and to realize how every aspect of the preschool group is developed toward that end.

The director should make it possible for the teacher to meet with prospective visitors so that she can help them plan their visit to be most profitable for them, yet be no hindrance to what the children do. The teacher should tell them about the preschool group and show them pictures of it so they can anticipate where they will be. Thus they can plan where to sit or work so as to leave a maximum play area for the children. She should further their sensitivities so that they can observe more fully. She should introduce them to the behaviors of individual children and of groups of children. She describes what she may do and explains how her own behavior contributes to the development of the children. By the conclusion of the planning session, the prospective visitors should know what they will do and what they will look for during their school visit.

The morning of the visit, the teacher should give her attention to the preschool children, as usual. Only when all the children are happily occupied with familiar activities does she have opportunity to speak briefly to some visitor near her. She should, however, observe the children closely in terms of points brought out in the planning session with the visitors. Thus she is prepared to contribute to a followup conference with the visitors at their next class meeting.

Characteristics of Successful Preschool Teachers

The person who loves preschool children and is interested in spending part of each day with them should seriously consider being a teacher of a preschool group. She may study toward that end until she feels she is sufficiently prepared and sufficiently mature to become a teacher. Whether she marries or not, she may continue in preschool education. She should work with groups of young children, study about them, and acquire a liberal arts education. At appropriate intervals she may qualify for certification by the state department of education, and for academic degrees available in the teaching field of her selection.

LOOKING AHEAD IN SCHOOL

The student who is considering a career that involves working with young children can find opportunities for preparatory study and for try-out experiences. For instance, a senior student in a high school in Long Beach, California, can enroll in a home economics course which has classroom activities, followed by two or three laboratory situations serving as an aide to a preschool or primary grade teacher. The practice situations are accompanied by weekly discussions for each original classroom group. Because the course is arranged so that each student participates in it for half a day each day of the week, it provides each student with aide experience in a preschool group during all the time that it meets, and enables its graduates to qualify for employment as an education aide.

A student who feels that he must have employment and feels that working with preschool children is attractive can qualify for a position such as that described below:

Applications for Education Aide

Salary Range: $1.96 an hour to start; $2.30 an hour after 2½ years

Liberal vacation, sick leave, holiday, paid health insurance, retirement, and other benefits

The Position: An Education Aide assists a classroom teacher in an elementary school by performing routine clerical and housekeeping duties. Work is during the time that school is in session.

Entrance Requirements: You must have education equal to completion of the eighth grade and have some experience working with children in group activities such as playground, religious or youth group activities. Full or part-time paid experience within the past 5 years working with children in preschool educational programs may be substituted for the required education on a year-for-year basis.

The Examination: You may be examined for ability to do simple clerical work; to learn and do varied classroom duties; knowledge of how students should behave; how to speak good English; knowledge of problems in your neighborhood; ability to enforce rules; ability to understand and follow written and spoken instructions.[5]

If the student returns to, or remains in, school through the first two years of college, she may qualify for a position such as that described below:

[5] The announcement from which these excerpts are taken was posted in the spring of 1968 by Long Beach Unified School District.

Applications for Parent Education Assistant

Salary Range: $2.64 – $2.80 – $2.93 an hour

Desirable Qualifications:

Education: High school graduation or the equivalent; plus completion of a two-year Preschool Education Curriculum such as that offered by City College General Adult Division, or the equivalent.

Experience: Recent experience in observing and studying young children, such as: (1) a semester college course involving participation with preschool children; or (2) at least one year recent experience in assuming direct responsibility for the guidance of a group of preschool children. Some equivalent combination of education and experience.

The Position:

A Parent Education Assistant works under the supervision of a certificated teacher and is responsible for activities carried on in a group of preschool children. She organizes the daily schedule, keeps attendance records, and assists in preparation of reports; attends teacher's meetings; takes major responsibility for keeping rooms and play space in orderly condition, and for preparing materials for use; guides children's play; supervises children's music; directs parent participants; assists in parent conferences jointly with the Director; participates in the evening orientation program for new parents; assists student observers.

The Examination: Candidates may be examined for knowledge of child psychology, child development, children's games and activities; ability to work effectively with preschool children, parents, and teachers.[6]

TEACHING A PRESCHOOL GROUP FITS INTO MARRIED LIFE

The married woman can find a useful career with preschool children, whether or not she has children. Except for periods of child-bearing, a woman may participate in preschool education according to her interests and according to the opportunities available in the community.

The wife who has children is well occupied with their care when they are infants. But as soon as the oldest child is of nursery age, she can participate in the nursery group as a mother, perhaps as a mother assistant to the teacher. By the time her youngest child is in a nursery group, she may have acquired considerable experience as an assistant teacher; she may even have taken several courses in child development, preschool education, or related fields. As her children go on into elementary and higher schools, she has more time for pursuing a career as a teacher of small children, perhaps teaching part time and studying part time. When her youngest child is in elementary school all day, she may become regularly employed as a

[6] Ibid.

full-time teacher in nursery school, kindergarten, or the primary grades; or as a teacher in a preschool group which is a laboratory group for parents, homemaking students in junior or senior high school, home economics students in junior college or in college, or prospective preschool teachers in college.

The series of courses which prepares teachers specifically for preschool work may be undertaken by an adult at any stage in her life. She may follow her high school studies with junior college courses about young children as well as courses in the liberal arts. If she decides on specialization in preschool education during senior college years, she may enroll in courses which include participation in and study about preschool groups. At any time in her adult life she may enroll in adult education courses about guiding and teaching preschool children, observing and participating in preschool groups at the same time.

Course work and participation in preschool groups soon qualify a woman to begin going up the ladder of professional experience to whatever rung seems most appropriate for her. The rungs of the ladder include:

- Assistant teacher for a preschool group's parent education program
- Teacher responsible for a group of preschool children
- Teacher responsible for children, and working with parents in a children's center or in a parent-cooperative preschool group
- Parent education teacher responsible for a group of parents and their preschool children
- Director or proprietor of a preschool group
- College instructor in preschool education or in parent education

On each rung are to be found women in their twenties or thirties, even their sixties and seventies.

Getting Started in Teaching a Preschool Group

Sometimes a mother who participates in a preschool group discovers that she has an interest in and an aptitude for teaching preschool children. She identifies with the teacher and takes increasing responsibility in the program for the children. By the end of one or two years as an assistant teacher, substituting for the regular teacher when she is absent, this mother will have had sufficient practical experience to become a full-fledged teacher of a preschool group. If she has found time for study of children and preschool education, she is ready to take responsibility as a teacher of a preschool group. Probably people in her own preschool group will help her find a position with another local group; if the waiting list of her own group is a long one, they may help her create a preschool group of her own.

Another access to preschool teaching is through application for the positions advertised by local boards of education. Information about such positions is obtainable at any time from the local board of education. A telephone call to the board will reveal when and how applications for preschool positions are to be made.

The preschool teacher who moves to a new community has several channels through which to obtain information about possible teaching positions. Through the local board of education she can find out what preschool groups are attached to the school system, and what positions are to be filled in the near future. Through the classified section of the telephone directory she can find out what private and church preschool groups are in operation. Usually, by visiting a nursery group and talking with its director, she can find out about day-care centers and other day nurseries, of young children, and about two other sources of information on possible positions: the National Association for Education of Young Children and the local Council of Parent Cooperative Preschools. Both the Association and the Council offer an informal placement service, and both are eager to know the prospective teachers for preschool groups.

TEACHING IN A PRESCHOOL WITH ADULT PARTICIPANTS

Sooner or later a preschool teacher should consider the kind of group in which she would like to teach. If she is comfortable with children but does not enjoy working with adults, she may limit her teaching to private schools, and day-care centers in which she has responsibility only for the children, others taking responsibility for parent and business affairs. She may be able to teach very well in such situations, and become expert in working effectively with children of a given age level. The teacher who aims at perfection finds satisfaction in these situations.

The teacher who is eager to see parents as well as children develop through the preschool group experience should find a place in a group having parents actively cooperating. This teacher can get satisfaction both from her work with the children and from her association with parents. She becomes adept in working with others, giving them responsibility as they are ready to assume it, guiding them with well-timed praise and suggestion. She is as pleased with the successful storytelling of a parent as she is with her own. She realizes that the details of her program for the children are less well worked out when she shares her teaching responsibility with the parents, but she appreciates that the development of the parents is, in the long run, more of a help to their children.

The teacher who especially enjoys working with students of a given age range as well as with preschool children should find a position in a laboratory school used by students of that age range. There she can gain satisfaction from watching and guiding the development not only of the preschool children but also of the high school or college students who observe and learn how to work with them.

Knowing her preferences in human relationships enables a woman who likes preschool children to find a happy responsibility in a congenial preschool situation. The following summary of teacher characteristics distinguishes those characteristics to be found in the preschool group which is a laboratory for students or parents.

TYPE AND DESCRIPTION OF SCHOOL	IMPORTANT CHARACTERISTICS OF CHILDREN'S TEACHER
Day Care Center; Private School Small group of children; no teacher assistants	Is well versed in how to handle groups of children. Has warm appreciation for children; likes to be with them. Is skillful in moving children from one activity to next. Can quiet children or stimulate them.
Parent-Cooperative; Laboratory School Has parent assistants: student or other aides; volunteer helpers	Works with children as individuals and as members of a group. Likes to have others get attention. Is skillful in having assistants lead children in activities. Encourages adults to participate in children's activities. Enjoys both preschool children and adults, singly and in groups.

Selection of Teacher

The individual or group responsible for selecting a preschool teacher should keep in mind the essential qualifications of such a person.

CHARACTERISTICS OF A GOOD PRESCHOOL TEACHER	EVIDENCE OF THE CHARACTERISTICS
Enjoys being with children. Studies how to improve her teaching and better understand children.	Often spends spare time with preschool children. Attends courses and conferences on preschool children.
ADDITIONAL CHARACTERISTICS OF TEACHERS IN A PRESCHOOL HAVING PARENTS OR STUDENTS	
Enjoys being with adults. Studies how to help groups function more effectively.	Actively participates in one or two women's groups. Attends courses, conferences about group dynamics and leadership.

In general, an employing group or individual should select the best preschool teacher available. It should attempt to determine for each candidate her love of children, her ability to develop in service, her maturity, and breadth of education. If the employing agent is filling a position requiring that the teacher work with parents, he should also determine for each candidate her ability to work easily with adults. The employing agent should also take into account the attitudes of the candidate toward her responsibilities as a key member of her own family, and the interests and prejudices commonly held by the community of the preschool group.

IMPORTANCE OF A LIBERAL EDUCATION

Maturity and other outcomes of a liberal education may be acquired either through formal schooling or, less expeditiously, outside of it. Many preschool teachers acquire a liberal education through study in college courses and thus supplement their work with, and study of, preschool children.

The requirement of schooling through some predetermined level is a means of guaranteeing that those who qualify have competence essential for teaching. In the case of preschool teachers, a schooling requirement may not be as essential to success in working with preschool children as is the warm emotional response to them. Until research on this point is more adequate, the question can be asked as to whether the requirement of a specified level of school raises or lowers the quality of preschool teachers. Furthermore, does such a requirement eliminate many excellent teachers who manifest a liberal education but lack the required formal schooling for it?

Out of concern for adequate preparation of those responsible for "Child Care and Guidance," the U.S. Office of Education has suggested a posthigh school curriculum,[7] as follows:

GENERAL EDUCATION COURSES		CHILD CARE AND GUIDANCE COURSES	
Course Title	*Hours*	*Course Title*	*Hours*
English Composition	3	Child Growth and Development	8
Speech	2	Child Nutrition and Health Care	2
Natural Science	3	Community Relationships	2
General Psychology	3	Music for Young Children	3
General Sociology	3	Creative Activities	4
History	3	Literature for Young Children	3
Physical Education	1	Observing and Recording Child Behavior	3
Total	18	Supervised Student Participation	6
		Social Problems	3
		Family Relationships	3
Electives	9		
		Total	37

TEACHING ONE'S OWN CHILD

Fortunate is the child whose mother teaches a preschool group. He has a chance to learn the role of being the teacher's child—all the privileges of that role, as well as all the responsibilities. He can enjoy having his mother say, "Yes, Kenny is my own boy. Of course, *all* the children are 'my' children when we are at nursery school." When his mother is showing the group how to make something, he enjoys helping her with the demonstration, using whatever skills he has to help the others. His role of teacher's helper is an excellent experience for him, and an excellent prototype for the other children to imitate.

[7] Office of Education, "Child Care and Guidance—A Suggested Post High School Curriculum" (Washington, D.C.: U.S. Government Printing Office, 1967).

Some mothers who teach think it better for their children to attend another preschool group. They feel that their children should learn to be one in the group of children, without learning the leadership or helper role. The mother teachers feel too that the children they teach need their complete attention without the distraction of working with a child whose needs may differ markedly from those of the other children. Sometimes mother teachers are self-conscious about their relationship to their own child, and have overexpectations of him, or overprotectiveness toward him. For some mother teachers and their children, it is probably best that they arrange for separate preschool group experiences.

In the parent-cooperative preschool every mother and child has the opportunity to be together in the group when it is the mother's turn to come to assist the teacher. Thus each child has a chance to learn from experience several modes of behavior.

1. The child learns to help mother in serving others. As a three-year-old, he passes out a napkin for each person at juice time; as a four-year-old he is able to give a child a paper cup filled with juice. He can pass the wastebasket so that each child may throw away his used cup and napkin. Mother shares these responsibilities with her child at first, until he is able to do each of them by himself.

2. The child learns to help set up equipment at the beginning of the morning, and to help put it away at the end of the morning. His mother guides him in using his muscles so that he carries heavy objects easily without strain, as she does. Most important is his learning that getting out and putting away are integral parts of an activity.

3. A child learns that when mother is teaching she helps each child, not just him. If her child needs her as his mother, then she comes to be with him. But when she comes as a teacher, her child must share her with the others. This sharing mother with other children at nursery school is as important for the child to learn as to share his mother with a new baby at home.

4. A child learns that mother loves him in the preschool group setting just as she does at home. Although he shares her with others, he has not lessened but enriched his relationship with her. This learning prepares him for understanding later that the affection between any two people is a unique relationship not interfered with but enriched by affectionate relationships to others.

5. A child learns that teachers treat each child alike. The morning that his mother was assisting the teacher and the group made kites, four-year-old Dennis explored the possibility of getting more than the other children. As his mother passed out kite tails to be pasted on, Dennis said, "I want two tails." His mother smiled, "I wish I had two tails to give you, but there is only one for each of us this morning."

SPECIAL QUALIFICATIONS

Whether an exceptional woman or any other woman should teach a preschool group depends on her interest and ability in working with preschool children. A grandmother with physical limitations, for instance, may compensate for them by using her skills in working with people. She may be an excellent teacher for a parent-cooperative school in which her experience is combined with the physical energy of young mothers. At meetings with the mothers, the grandmother-teacher can plan with the mothers what to do with the children individually and as a group. She needs to be skillful in working with the children through their own mothers, and through the mothers as they take turns as her assistants with the preschool group.

If a physically handicapped woman is a mature person who loves children and studies how to work effectively with them, she may develop her own methods of teaching them. When school began in the fall, one teacher quietly slipped off her shoes and stockings to show the children that her feet had fewer than the usual number of toes. She showed them, too, that her hands did not have as many fingers as theirs did. During the year, as she helped each child accomplish his purposes, she taught the children that how a person uses his hands is more important than how they look.

Another teacher used to chuckle appreciatively when the children in her nursery school group would feel the rich warm brown of her skin and ask whether she had had a bath. As a Negro among Caucasians, she taught the children that skins of people differ in color. As a warm, loving person who helped them, she taught them that "pretty is as pretty does."

FITTING INTO THE COMMUNITY

Knowing that attitudes and values are developed during the preschool years, and that identification with adults is one of the important means of aiding the development of desirable attitudes and values, those who select preschool teachers should look for women with the wholesome attitudes admired by the parents of the children, and by the other people of the community. If possible, they should choose two or three qualified teachers and let the parents make the final selection of the teacher they want for their children. The parents' interest in the teacher and their favorable attitudes toward her will carry over into favorable attitudes on the part of the children.

An employer can select a teacher who differs from the people in the community if that difference is sympathetically understood by the community and her worth as a teacher is not interfered with. For instance, one preschool group successfully employed a teacher with a marked accent. The accent constantly reminded people that the teacher's husband had been invited to this country as a specialist much needed by the major industry of the community.

It is especially important that a less advantaged preschool group have a teacher who is acceptable to the parent advisory group but who is also able to recruit children for the group and encourage their families in keeping them in attendance. Often such groups have a local teacher who enjoys being with the children, is eager to increase her preparation for working with them, and is committed to advancing the preschool project. Essentially she is a leader among the preschool families.

INTERVIEWING A PROSPECTIVE TEACHER

When an employer or employing group invites a prospective teacher to visit, he may wish to have on paper a list of questions to be asked and a list of items to use in recording his impressions of the teacher. The Questionnaire for Prospective Preschool Teachers below shows such an interview schedule. The person using it should gain impressions about the prospective teacher, and be able to report the following:

- The percentage of time spent by the prospect on ego building.
- The consistency of the prospect's statements about herself.
- Her interest in children compared with her monetary interest.
- Her appreciation of the role of a mother.

The suggested interview schedule includes the usual questions a prospective teacher expects to be asked: name, address, telephone number, schooling, and experience. It also includes leading questions which should elicit the teacher's interests and lead her to reveal whether her prime interest is herself or the children. A high amount of ego building warns the prospective employer to be wary of employing a neurotic person whose real interests may differ from her expressed interests.

Inconsistency in her reports of her activities and interests reveals a person whose emotional problems may interfere with her success as a teacher. A person who wants to spend most of each day teaching children but has not been with them much may be unrealistic about what she really wants to do. A person who goes out to teach other people's children but leaves her own with a chance succession of babysitters may or may not have more self-interest than child-interest.

Bringing up how much time is needed for work with the preschool group is a way of acquainting the prospective teacher with the requirements of the position. Both employer and employee need to be realistic about what is expected of the teacher in advance of her employment.

The interview questions should reveal the person who really loves children and is eager to be with them in the preschool group. In asking about the teacher's plans for study, the questionnaire gets at the difference between a person who is able to care for children and one who is prepared to teach them.

Questionnaire for Prospective Preschool Teachers

Name _____ Telephone Number _____

Address _____

| Street | City | Zone |

Schools Attended	From	To	Degree or Diploma Received

Experience in teaching in preschool groups:

Name of School	Position Held	From	To

How did you happen to hear of the position for which you are applying? _____

_____

Why are you interested in the position? _____

_____

How much time did you spend and what did you do with preschool children last week?

Day	Activity	Number of Hours
Monday		
Tuesday		
Wednesday		
Thursday		
Friday		
Saturday		
Sunday		

What are you reading or studying about preschool children now? _____

_____

What plans have you for further study? _____

_____

Have you preschool children?____If so, what plans have you for them while you are teaching? _____

TEACHING AND CARING FOR CHILDREN

A good preschool teacher is to be distinguished from a robot designed to help children put on and take off their wraps. She helps the children in ways which are carefully chosen to further the development of each personality, and to contribute to feelings of importance and self-sufficiency.

A good teacher is also to be distinguished from a herdsman who keeps his charges from physical harm. A herdsman provides a safe environment, but a teacher goes further—helping the children to understand their environment and to explore constructive ways of using it. When the teacher provides food for the children, she should guide them in the social relationships that are part of the democratic social order. When she leads them over the hills and valleys, she should lead them also into a fuller appreciation of the world about them.

A good teacher has much in common with a parent, yet she differs from a parent in knowing many variations within what constitutes a particular age level, and in knowing how to help a group of children develop as they tackle the problems appropriate to that age level. The good teacher watches, for instance, how children communicate with adults and with other children. She realizes that communication is a problem of great importance for them at their age level. She realizes also that each child tackles his communication problems in his own way and solves them at his own rate of speed. By observing the child's development and the effects of her guidance on it, she constantly improves her methods of working with a group of children.

The challenge to the preschool teacher is to have each of the children enjoy the group experience in such a way as to develop at a maximum rate physically, mentally, emotionally, and socially. She expects the children to be different at the end of the year as a result of her teaching. She should therefore provide experiences which will awaken new interests and appreciations, seeing new ideas and relationships, and building new and better skills. As she takes care of the children, she should guide them in enjoying the enriched program of activities she provides for them. This is her role as an educator of preschool children.

Situations for Discussion

A preschool teacher is apt to find herself in situations similar to the four described here. As you think of what to do in each situation, consider whether each course of action suggested is desirable, or not. Use points brought out in the chapter as well as ideas from your own experience to justify your views. Suggest alternative courses of action to supplement those given.

SITUATION 1   You are interviewing applicants for the position of director of the nursery center. You have narrowed the choice to two women of about the same age. Mrs. Amos is a calm person who has children in high school and junior college. She has been an assistant teacher in the junior college nursery school during the past year while she took courses there in preschool education. Mrs. Brown is a college graduate, well-groomed, beautifully and expensively dressed. She taught for the past two years in a parent-cooperative nursery school which is now disbanding. On the basis of your interview materials, you should.

- Recommend the employment of Mrs. Amos.
- Recommend the employment of Mrs. Brown.
- Suggest additional interviews with both candidates.
- Suggest the advancement of the most competent teacher now employed.
- Present the information you have without recommendation.

SITUATION 2   The personnel officer in a city school system has been urged to select aides for a preschool program from unemployed members of the minority group from which the enrolment of the preschool is largely drawn. Several other applicants representing the majority group are also eager to work in the preschool program. As the personnel officer you should

- Accept the recommendation to employ minority group representatives and help solve the unemployment problem.
- Invite all applicants to a meeting which discusses the importance of avoiding segregation.
- Review all applications and employ individuals in order of evident competence.
- Request board of education policy statement.
- Announce the selection policy as soon as it is established.

SITUATION 3   For several years you have been participating in a parent-cooperative nursery school with your two children. Now your younger child is in a four-year-olds' nursery group, and you have been invited to become the teacher of that group. You should

- Accept the invitation.
- Wait until your child is out of the group.
- Place your younger child in another nursery school.
- Look for a position in another preschool.
- Decline the invitation.

SITUATION 4   You are a member of a committee considering whether the Department of Education in the state should offer a certificate for teachers of nursery school. You contribute to the meeting of the committee by bringing out the following points:

- Love is the essential attribute of a nursery school teacher.
- Competent preschool teachers differ in the amount of schooling they have had.
- Each preschool should select its own teachers.
- Supply and demand regulates the employment of preschool teachers.
- Some kinds of nursery groups might be unable to pay for certificated teachers.

Current Professional Books and Pamphlets

BURGESS, HELEN STEERS. *How to Choose a Nursery School.* New York: Public Affairs Committee, Inc. 1961. [Public Affairs Pamphlet No. 310, is useful to preschool planners as well as parents.]

DEUTSCH, MARTIN, and ASSOCIATES. *The Disadvantaged Child: Studies of the Social Environment and the Learning Process.* New York: Basic Books, Inc., 1967. [Cognitive and language factors, race and social class, are important for planning and teaching preschool groups for disadvantaged children.]

GARDNER, DOROTHY E., and JOAN E. CASS. *The Role of the Teacher in the Infant and Nursery School.* New York: Pergamon Press, 1965. [Gives a perspective on local practices.]

HEFFERNAN, HELEN, and VIVIAN EDMISTON TODD. *The Kindergarten Teacher.* Boston: D. C. Heath & Company, 1960. [Chapter 3 discusses the social environment of the kindergarten as it is created by the teacher.]

MOUSTAKAS, CLARK E. *Authentic Teacher: Sensitivity and Awareness in the Classroom.* New York: Howard A. Doyle Publishing Co., 1966. [The sensitive teacher is aware of feelings of children in relation to the learning process.]

OSTROVSKY, EVERETT S. *Children Without Men.* New York: Collier, 1965. [The man teacher has a place in preschool and school classrooms.]

PEARL, ARTHUR and FRANK RIESSMAN, *New Careers for the Poor: The Nonprofessional in Human Service.* New York: The Free Press, 1965. [Low-skilled workers can help in service fields like social work, teaching, recreation, and health.]

READ, KATHERINE H. *The Nursery School, a Human Relationships Laboratory.* Philadelphia: W. B. Saunders Co., 1966. [A new edition of an early book in the field.]

RIBBLE, MARGARET A. *Rights of Infants.* New York: Columbia University Press, 1965. [Parents have importance in guiding sexual, emotional, and character development.]

SPIRO, MELFORD E. *Children of the Kibbutz.* Cambridge, Mass: Harvard University Press, 1965. [Relationships between children and nursery teachers, children and nurses, and children and parents are key factors in the development of the children.]

U.S. OFFICE OF EDUCATION. *Child Care and Guidance.* Washington, D.C.: U.S. Government Printing Office, 1967. [One of an increasing number of government bulletins about children.]

WINN, MARIE, and MARY ANN PORCHER. *The Playgroup Book.* New York: The Macmillan Company, 1967. [Contains plans for organizing and carrying on a playgroup for four or five children, with practical suggestions for preschool teachers.]

CHAPTER 4

Getting the School Ready

Before the children come to a preschool group, their age characteristics and their needs are carefully considered as a basis for selecting a location, getting facilities ready, and purchasing necessary equipment and supplies. What children are able to do and are interested in doing determines the kind of place in which they should work and what they need to work with. Planning and preparing the setting for the children in advance results in a more smoothly functioning school and happier children. The wise teacher and the competent people responsible for preschool groups know the importance of location, facilities and equipment, and give adequate time and attention to their preparation.

When a preschool group is developing, a planning committee of professional and lay leaders forms to make the necessary preparations. The prospective parents are an important part of the committee. As soon as possible this committee should include the director of the preschool group. When teachers are added to the staff, one or two of them should meet with the planning committee in order to keep the needs of the children uppermost in the thinking of the group at all times.

In communities planning to launch a year-round program for less advantaged preschool children with assistance of government funds, a survey should be made of available facilities accessible to the homes of the children. Public school facilities are usually available for summer programs of eight or ten weeks duration and sometimes for the entire year. Schools in the downtown areas of cities frequently have experienced enrolment decreases as more affluent families have moved to suburban areas. Rooms in such buildings can be remodeled and refurnished to meet the needs of preschool groups. Many churches have facilities which can be made available at nominal maintenance cost. Other buildings, not currently in use, can be considered in terms of safety, outdoor play space, cost of leasing and re-

106

modeling to create a safe, sanitary, and educationally serviceable preschool environment.

A planning committee can obtain assistance from bulletins published by the Office of Education, Department of Health, Education and Welfare, Washington, D.C., and from many state departments of education. Often the latter can also provide consultation service to local groups seeking to solve difficult problems in housing for preschool groups.

The Planning Committee

The planning committee takes into account the families of the children it serves. Are the parents away from home most of the day, or part of the day? Should facilities for meal preparation be provided, or only facilities for refreshments? Should facilities for resting be adequate for an extended nap, or only for a short period of quiet? Such questions will be answered in terms of the needs of children in the families to be served.

The planning committee also considers the personnel of the school or center. The children, their teachers, and other participants in the school all have needs which must be considered in planning the physical plant. Where will a child who is ill rest until he can be taken home? Where will the director confer with an individual parent or with the members of her staff? What bathroom facilities are needed for the children and for the grownups who work with them? Will observers have a separate room with a one-way screen or will they sit in the room with the children?

The planning committee also considers climate and economic factors. In a cold climate the physical plant will have to have more elaborate indoor facilities to occupy the children on days when it is too cold to go out. In a warm climate, a preschool group will need extensive outdoor facilities. A day-care center may have many of its activities outdoors. A parent-cooperative nursery school may have play groups meet in a public park and store a minimum of equipment there, in accordance with park regulations. A children's center may prefer a location on the grounds of a public school attended by older siblings.

Thus the planning committee must decide on location, facilities, and equipment on the basis of the unique characteristics of the families to be served by the preschool group. However, since preschool children have much in common at each age level, the planning committee must plan primarily in terms of the basic needs of the children.

BASIC NEEDS OF CHILDREN

Inasmuch as all children at a given age level are alike in their basic needs, the committee must constantly check its plans for the physical plant against a list of needs of preschool children. Table 4-1 illustrates the fact that

TABLE 4-1. Physical Needs of Children Are Met Through the Physical Plant

PHYSICAL NEEDS OF CHILDREN	THE PHYSICAL PLANT OF THE SCHOOL		
	Facilities	*Permanent Equipment*	*Perishable Supplies*
Eating when hungry	Kitchen facilities to prepare food and/or refreshments as needed	Cooking equipment Refrigerator Tables, chairs at child height Serving dishes	Foods as required Napkins
Getting a drink when thirsty	Drinking fountain at child height both indoors and outdoors		
A rhythm of rest and activity	A room that can be darkened	Lightweight cots or mattresses, portable and easily stacked for storage	Sheets and/or blankets as temperature and custom require
To be quiet when sick	A separate room A high cupboard	A cot with covers	Quiet toys First-aid supplies Washable cuddle toy
Going to the bath-room as necessary	Child-size toilets and wash basins Bathroom door that opens easily	Steps or large carrying blocks to help child reach adult-size fixtures	Toilet paper Paper towels Soap
Physical outlets	Hard-surfaced and sheltered patio for wheeled toys Sandbox	Tricycles; wagons Step-slide Rocking boat Record player	Clay or dough Punching doll balloon Tin cans to smash

facilities, equipment, and perishable supplies are directly related to the needs of children and should be selected in terms of those needs.

Decisions about what facilities, equipment, and supplies are desirable for the school stem also from knowledge of the age characteristics of young children. A baby-bouncer which is most helpful to the one-year-old as he gains skill in balancing himself is not appropriate for nursery school children who are ready to go on to greater skill in balancing and to the development of new skills. Neither below-age nor over-age items should be purchased. For instance, money should not be spent for books that are excellent for elementary school children but are overly dramatic or frightening to preschool children.

Facilities, equipment, and supplies are selected in terms of what the preschool group attempts to do for children. Table 4-2 illustrates the fact that aspects of a healthy personality are furthered through a suitable selection of items for the physical plant.

TABLE 4-2. The Physical Plant Helps to Develop a Healthy Personality

ASPECTS OF A HEALTHY PERSONALITY	THE PHYSICAL PLANT		
	Facilities	Permanent Equipment	Perishable Supplies
Safety	Fenced play area Playground apparatus set in sand	Magnet for picking up nails Broom, dustpan	Paper towels Sponges Wipe-up cloths
Security	Whatever parents consider important	Plastic apron or smock for painting	Craft items, paintings to take home
Belonging	A locker for each child	Enough duplicate equipment and toys so that each child has a turn without undue waiting	
Adequacy	Sandbox; swings; climbing apparatus; merry-go-round	Equipment and toys appropriate to age level, for satisfying practice with familiar activities	
Self-realization	A variety of playground equipment	Equipment and toys appropriate to age level to widen the skills and interests of each child and to challenge him to further learning	

TABLE 4-3. The Physical Plant Facilitates the Work of Adults

Adult	Responsibility	Facilities	Equipment
Director	Public relations Professional relations	Private office	Desk and chairs Telephone Correspondence file
	Parent relations Staff conference	Bulletin board A room without children	Records file Adult chairs around a table
Teachers	Teach	High shelves out of children's reach Personal desk Personal locker	Files for materials
Nurse	Check on health	Office High cupboard	Desk, chairs Cot
Housekeeper	Order supplies Make an inventory	Storage facilities	Desk Telephone
Janitor	Clean	Janitor's closet	Cleaning equipment
Cook	Order food supplies Prepare food	Storage facilities Kitchen facilities	Telephone Kitchen equipment
Chauffeur	Transport children	Garage	Repair tools
Participants	Assist teachers	Lockers	Student chairs
Observers	Observe children	Lockers	Student chairs

Not only does the planning group consider the needs of the children, it also considers the functions to be performed by the grownups in the school or center and provides the facilities and equipment needed for them. Since grownups are people, they, like children, should have bathroom facilities appropriate to their size, and rest facilities, as well as individual lockers for their personal belongings and outer clothing. Table 4-3 illustrates the fact that the selection of facilities and equipment is related to the work of the adults.

Selection of Location

Those who have responsibility for selecting a location suitable for a group of preschool children should find one that is practical as well as beautiful, comfortable as well as inspirational. They must take into account local zoning regulations and consider the physical features of possible facilities already available in the community. Furthermore, they must see that the school location is convenient for the children to get to because convenience determines attendance to a considerable extent. Mothers of preschool children who live within a block or two of a preschool group are more apt to have their children attend than are mothers living at a greater distance. A working mother finds it convenient to let her child off at the day-care center or private school that is on her way to work. An at-home mother likes to have her trip to the preschool group fit in with her other family activities. She may take her child to nursery school, do the grocery and other shopping or have her hair done, and then pick up her child on the way home for lunch. Many preschool groups benefit from a location convenient to a suburban shopping center.

The planning committee also needs to consider the use to be made of the school or center by parents and by students, and locates the building to facilitate such use. It must keep in mind the importance of the preschool group for high school and college students preparing for parenthood and for other responsibilities of citizenship, and for vocations as homemakers, teachers, pediatricians, nurses, social workers, ministers, and others working with children.

CLIMATE
The climate is an important factor to consider in selecting a location suitable for preschool children. In a warm climate, the children should enjoy the sunshine outdoors much of the time. In a dry climate, such as that of southern California, many parent-cooperative nursery schools meet in city parks and have a program that is primarily an outdoor one. On the few days when it rains, they follow an alternate program arranged in ad-

vance, perhaps with each car pool of children meeting at the home of one of the children.

The parent-cooperative school groups are recognized by the Park and Recreation Department of the city as an important part of its constituency. In one city, the department of recreation has announced its policy for play groups using park or playground facilities as follows:

1. The ———— Recreation Department encourages parents to make use of public recreation facilities for preschool groups when their supervision is adequately provided directly or indirectly by the parents.
2. Cooperative play groups obtain a letter of permit issued by the Recreation Department for specified days and hours for available park and playground facilities.
3. A service charge of one dollar for each day the premises are used is payable monthly by each group.
4. The Recreation Department is continuing its plan for developing fenced enclosures as these capital-outlay items are approved in the annual budgets.
5. Additional help is given groups through providing concrete slabs for play and storage buildings with assistance in locating these structures.[1]

In a climate characterized by high rainfall, considerable snowfall, or other extremes of weather, careful consideration must be given to indoor facilities for the preschool group. Much of the children's program will be carried on indoors and will require space to permit a variety of simultaneous activities if individual differences in children are to be adequately recognized. The children must have sufficient space for activities that contribute to the development of their large muscles. Space is a primary requirement.

In most climates it is important to provide both for indoor and outdoor space adjacent to each other and to the toilet rooms. The early space requirements stipulated for day nurseries in California reflected the thinking of people who work with preschool children.

Indoor Play Space

There must be adequate indoor space for the children's play activities and for dining and napping when these are included in the program.[2]

Rooms to be used for indoor activities must be of suitable size and arrangement to permit:
1. Proper grouping
2. Good program planning
3. Necessary supervision

The indoor playrooms must have sufficient floor space (occupied only by

[1] Vivian Edmiston Todd, ed., *Cooperative Nursery School Handbook* (Long Beach, Calif.: Long Beach Council of Parent Nursery Schools, 1957), p. 10.
[2] *California Administrative Code*, Title 22, Section 34107.

the children's play materials, equipment, and furniture) to provide 35 square feet of floor space per child.[3]

Playground

There must be outdoor play space adequate in size for the group in attendance, properly surfaced and fenced and conveniently located with relation to the indoor facilities.

SIZE: There must be at least 75 square feet per child of outdoor play area. . . . 100 square feet per child would be desirable.[4]

SELECTION OF SUITABLE INDOOR AND OUTDOOR AREAS

Those with responsibility for selecting a location suitable for a preshool group should consider the needs of the children for both indoor and outdoor space. Regarding indoor facilities, they are concerned with four basic questions:

1. Are the physical needs of children adequately provided for?
   - Are toilet facilities adjacent to play facilities and near the entrance?
   - Is there space for installing lockers and other facilities needed for the children?
   - Are drinking fountains of proper height available within the playroom?
   - Can food be prepared and served easily in accord with the children's program?
   - Is there a place where a sick child may be away from the other children?
   - Is the acoustical treatment of the rooms adequate for the number of children using them at one time?
2. Are the premises safe for children?
   - Do local authorities consider the building in accord with all applicable laws, rules, and regulations regarding building safety, sanitation, and fire safety?
   - Are written permits obtainable from the city Fire Department and Health Department for use of the premises by a preschool group?
3. Is the playroom sufficiently large that the children may engage simultaneously in a variety of activities, including activities that promote the development of large muscles?
4. Is there sufficient storage space for the equipment necessary to provide a program of varied activities and of muscle-building activities?
   - Is the storage space conveniently located within the play area?

---

[3] *Manual of Policies and Procedures, Day Nurseries* (Sacramento, Calif.: State of California, Department of Social Welfare, 1964).
[4] Ibid.

Children need opportunity to explore natural environments. (Courtesy of Long Beach Parent Nursery Schools and Mariam M. Cook, Long Beach, California.)

- Is the storage space usable by the children when they help with the equipment?
- Can the storage space for four- and five-year-old children accommodate a continuing construction project?

Regarding outdoor facilities, four comparable questions are of importance:

1. Are the physical needs of children adequately provided for?
   - Are toilet facilities located conveniently?
   - Are there drinking fountains of proper height in convenient locations?
   - Is there sufficient shade and shelter?
2. Is the location safe for the children?
   - Can the children be unloaded from cars in an off-the-street parking area?
   - Is the play area fenced securely? If not, can it be, at a reasonable cost?
   - Is the play area free from broken glass, boards with nails, obstructions children might run into, and other hazards?

113

3. What parts of the landscape can be used in the children's program?
   - Is space sufficient for a variety of vigorous play?
   - Are there trees suitable for climbing as well as for shade?
   - Is there level ground for a grass play area?
   - Is there uneven ground on which children can learn to climb and play?
   - Is a hard-surface area available for tricycle and wagons?
   - Are places of natural interest within walking distance or quickly available by school bus?
   - Is water easily available?
4. Is adequate storage space provided in connection with the play area?
   - Is the storage space usable by the children when they help with the equipment?

After determining what is available in a location, the planning committee should consider the expense involved in providing the other features that are part of the facilities for a preschool group. If the committee decides on substandard accommodations for the school, then the teacher improvises and "makes do" at the same time that she endeavors to acquaint the planning committee with what facilities and equipment are needed for preschool children. The teacher must know what to recommend on an interim basis and what to recommend on a permanent basis. She must know the relative order of importance of different kinds of equipment and of various housing requirements and must be able to explain her preferences, which are based on fundamental concepts of child development. In this way she is of inestimable value to the committee in planning the physical plant for the preschool group.

The planning committee should also avail itself of the experience of other nursery school and kindergarten planning groups. It can visit existing schools or centers most like itself, and also other kinds of schools or centers known to be successful with children and their parents. It can also take advantage of the written materials describing both ideal and actual nursery schools and kindergartens.[5]

It should obtain the written standards for day nurseries in its state, usually from the State Department of Education or of Social Welfare and each member of the planning group should study them carefully so that the preschool group may comply with or exceed accepted standards. It should study its own unique situation and plan what is best for the families to be served. Thus it endeavors to provide a physical plant that takes into account the needs of the children, the director and teachers, other members of the staff, participants, and observers.

[5] Jerome E. Leavitt, ed., *Nursery-Kindergarten Education* (New York: McGraw-Hill Book Company, Inc., 1958). Chapter 12, by Helen Heffernan, contains floor plans for a nursery school as well as for a kindergarten.

Preparation of Facilities

INDOOR FACILITIES

After a location has been selected, the planning group often finds it necessary to use existing buildings until sufficient funds have been collected to construct a building especially designed for the use of preschool children. Whether a new building is constructed at once or other buildings are converted to use, certain items should be provided to enable the children, and their teachers, to work at their best.

Acoustics. Acoustical treatment of walls and ceilings should prevent the tensions caused by noise and should help the children in learning to differentiate between the use of the voice indoors and outdoors. The vigorous activities of children often tend to be noisy. Although children are not readily disturbed by noise, every effort should be made to control the noise so that everyone hears quiet voices and essential noise does not build up into excessive noise.

Wall and window draperies and carpeted areas are an aid to noise control, but not sufficient in themselves. Acoustical tile or surfacing is essential for the ceilings of the children's playrooms. Proper acoustical treatment of the playroom not only prevents outside noise from disturbing inside activities, but also prevents indoor noise from disturbing outside activities.

Bathrooms. Bathrooms should be easily accessible to children from either the indoor or outdoor play areas. They should have either no doors or doors that are easily opened and sufficiently loose-fitting that little fingers are not apt to get pinched by them. The Department of Social Welfare in California[6] required "one toilet and handwashing facility . . . for the first fourteen children; . . . one additional toilet and lavatory . . . added for every ten children, or fractional part thereof in excess of fourteen children" and "one toilet and handwashing facility, separate from the general-use toilets, for isolation, staff, and emergency use," and conveniently located. The bathrooms and their furnishings must be such as can be easily cleaned.

Bulletin Boards. A bulletin board furthers communication between parents and teachers and between the preschool group and its clientele. It can be an effective means of furthering the education of parents about their children and about the importance of a preschool group. A bulletin board can also be used to enhance communication among the teaching personnel of the school, and among the grownups who observe and participate in the program. Bulletin boards should be placed at the entrance to the building where they easily catch the eye of those bringing the children and of the other adults coming into the school or center.

[6] *Manual of Policies and Procedures,* op. cit.

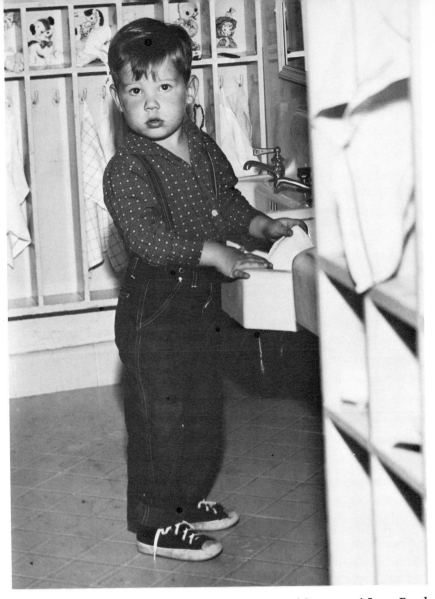

Lockers for each child are near bathroom facilities. (Courtesy of Long Beach Day Nursery and Mariam M. Cook, Long Beach, California.)

Children's Lockers. A locker should be provided for each child for his personal possessions. Having the lockers near the entrance to the street and to the play area helps the children to learn to hang up their outer clothing as they come indoors and to put it on as they go outdoors. Having the lockers near the toilets also helps the children to learn to care for themselves and their personal possessions. A line of lockers may be used to make a passageway, with the backs of the lockers made of cork or fiber board and used for displays of interest to the children.

116

Cleaning Facilities. Adequate provision must be made for regular cleaning of the school or center. Storage space for cleaning equipment must be provided and adequate provision made for the maid or janitor to keep personal belongings and cleaning supplies out of reach of children. A closet containing a utility sink can be kept locked when not in use and can be a convenience which facilitates cleaning.

Drinking Fountain. The children's playroom should have a drinking fountain either at the children's height or with a ramp that makes it easily accessible to them. The nursery child often is learning to incorporate getting a drink into his pattern of daily living. Having water easily available helps him to learn to get a drink when thirsty and prevents his getting out of control because of unsatisfied thirst. It is especially important in warm climates to make it easy for a child to get a drink by himself.

Floors. Since each day the sand from the sandbox is transferred indoors by trouser cuffs and shoes, most floor space needs to be relatively immune to sanding. Hardwood floors soon lose their finish, but linoleum tile and similar surfacing materials resist the sanding process. Furthermore, they are easy to clean and are not usually harmed by spills and messes. Newer floorings are available in a wide choice of color and patterns and at a wide range of costs. Attractive and substantial floor surfacing need not be expensive.

Heating. Proper provisions for heating the building should take into account the fact that children establish controlled metabolic processes in the earliest years of their lives. The bundled-up infant of the last generation has been replaced by the child who is lightly clothed and depends on his bodily functions rather than on added layers of clothing to keep himself warm. Much of the time, nursery children play on the floor and are uncomfortably warm with radiant heating from the floor.

Thermostatically controlled heat and ventilation are desirable as a means of maintaining a uniform temperature with a minimum of teacher attention. In many nursery schools the thermostat is set at 68°F., and the adults who are less active than the children wear sweaters or jackets as they wish.

It is imperative that the heating arrangements be in accord with the regulations of the local fire department. Fireplaces and open-faced heaters must be adequately screened and every precaution taken so that the children do not touch hot surfaces.

Lighting. The children's playroom should be made attractive at all times by having adequate lighting in all parts of the room. This implies that the room must have variable light controls and cheerful colors to beautify it. Of most importance is the avoidance of glare spots which are conducive to tension and fatigue. Direct sunlight and exposed light bulbs are also to be avoided.

Painting. Walls and woodwork need to be both beautiful and easy to clean. Thoughtful selection of light, clear tones of color for walls and ceiling is the first step in beautifying each of the rooms. The second step is the selection of harmonizing furnishings. Whatever paint is selected should be durable, easy to wash, and not conducive to glare or bright reflections of light. A school or center should give preschool children an early experience with harmonious and pleasing surroundings which enhance living. One wall space may have a surface on which the children can paint; another, a surface on which they can use chalk.

Water. The control of water is of such importance to preschool children that provision for its use should be made indoors as well as outdoors. A sink at the working height of the children should have an adjoining working space on which to set things. Open shelves by the sink accommodate a good selection of educational water toys. A laundry tub is also useful for water play.

In learning the proper use of water, the children do not always keep the water in the sink. With floor and adjoining walls and work areas covered with linoleum or some other water-resistant finish, the children—as well as the responsible adults—are comfortable about experimentation with water.

Windows. Standards for Day Nurseries in California emphasized factors to consider in providing adequate lighting and ventilation for centers and schools:

1. Window space must be at least ⅛ of the floor area of the room, and 50 per cent of the required windows must be openable.
2. Windows should be placed to allow maximum desirable light, sunshine, and ventilation, and should be low enough so that the children can see out.
3. Windows should be kept clean so that visibility is not impaired, and those that open should be screened. If plate-glass windows are used, the size of the panes should be kept fairly small as a safety factor in breaking.[7]

OUTDOOR FACILITIES

After the planning group has selected a suitable location for the nursery school or center and given attention to the indoor provisions, it must also consider how to make the outdoor facilities more safe, healthful, and educational.

Fencing. Especially where street traffic is heavy, it is important for the preschool group to have its play areas enclosed with fences. Fences of wire mesh have the advantage of enabling the children to see what is going on in their community—a fire engine or a moving van passing by, street or electrical repair men at work, men providing mail or other services for the community. Fences need not be high if they are only for keeping the preschool children within bounds. But they do need to be high and strong in order to discourage older neighborhood boys who take an interest in preschool play equipment. Older children who do not have satisfactory home

[7] Ibid., pp. 14–15.

relationships may try to express their feelings of aggression by damaging the playhouse. Older children who are not intentionally destructive sometimes cause considerable damage because their weight and force exceed those of preschool children, or their busy fingers pry off shingles and other removable pieces.

Outdoor Furnishings. The children need a place to hang their jackets when they get warm playing in the sun. The clothes hooks or racks should be at their height and close to where they play.

Where the climate makes it possible to have a considerable portion of the nursery school program outdoors each day, a sturdy table suited to outdoor use (for example, a redwood table) makes it possible for children to have craft activities and refreshments outdoors. The table can be made secure by embedding its legs in concrete and attaching the movable benches to it by chains. It should be located at the edge of the grassy play area, and should be of the children's size.

Play Hazards. Facilities which require continuous supervision—for instance, a fish pond, a wading pool, or a swimming pool—should be fenced off when not in use. Incinerators or other physical hazards should be excluded from the children's play area and its approaches. If they cannot be, they should have fencing around them to keep the children away.

The play areas should be so arranged that they are not mutual hazards. For instance, the playhouse may be at the end of the paved patio. If the playhouse door opens into the middle of the paved area, the children emerging from it may be hit by a moving toy vehicle. In the wintertime, the area for sledding and sliding should be separate from the path for returning to the top of the hill.

Selection and Arrangement of Permanent Equipment. Play apparatus and other equipment for the play areas should be selected for the needs and interests of the children as well as for sturdiness. Every preschool group has a large sandbox to stimulate imaginative play, at least one climbing apparatus to develop shoulder muscles as well as leg muscles, and at least one set of swings to help the children in developing rhythm and bodily control. A well-built playhouse serves not only for playing house, store, hospital, firehouse, or fort, but also as a storage place for tricycles, wagons, and other equipment. Sturdy free forms, often made of smooth concrete, are a combination of slide, climber, and tunnel. The simple merry-go-round and the slide from the traditional park playground are useful additions to the nursery school play area. A car body with steering wheel and seats (but neither glass windows or door), a simulated train or bus built to the children's size, an open boat, or an old saddle—these are examples of the kinds of apparatus which encourage skill in handling one's body and in imaginative play.

After selecting equipment appropriate to the children's age range in sufficient quantity to provide a variety of activities for the entire group of children, the planning group needs to consider how to place the equipment. Each item should be placed so that children can use it without interfering with other play groups and can be easily attracted by the next item when their interest in what they are doing lags. Equipment which accommodates only one or two children at a time should be placed at the far edge of the play area so that it is available to those who want to use it but is not apt to become a point of dispute among the children.

Equipment placement stimulates play. Placing the playhouse next to the sandbox will result in sand pies being served in the playhouse, but not always in the sand's being swept out of the playhouse later. Placing the climber sufficiently distant from the sandbox prevents its accessory toys from being carried over to the climber to become a safety hazard to the children using it.

The play area with its apparatus is separate from the paved patio and also from the grassed area used for running play. When a play area is to be used by several groups of children at the same time, the total area may be separated into as many sub-areas as there are groups, with each sub-area fenced off and with the groups rotated among the areas. In this case, a sub-area has a sandbox and a climbing apparatus and one or two other pieces of equipment sufficient to accommodate the number of children in the group.

The arrangement and spacing of permanent equipment depends on the supervision available for it. At least one adult must be present at all times so that the children play safely whether or not other children are being helped in going to the bathroom or in getting first aid. Equipment is also arranged so that entrances and exits are not blocked at any time.

Strength of Materials. All permanent equipment and small buildings should be constructed so that they can be climbed upon and used by adults. This not only permits the grownups to participate freely in the children's play whenever it is desirable to do so, but also prevents destruction of equipment by older children who consider the preschool playground a play place for them as well. Any equipment that is strong enough only for preschool children must be considered portable and stored when not in use.

Sunshine and Shade. The climate and the hours of the day when the preschool group is in session determine the need for increasing or decreasing the natural shade areas. For instance, in a northerly climate a nursery school having outdoor play on the roof of a building during the school year may have potted trees more for educational interest than for shade. The children benefit from whatever sunshine they can have. On the other hand, a nursery school on a California desert may be concerned that at least the sandbox be located so that it is shaded by a building during the school hours.

Surfacing the Play Areas. The outdoor play space has a variety of surfaces to go with the variety of children's activities. Two kinds of surfacing

Arrange indoor, patio, and outdoor facilities to aid supervision. (Courtesy of Ontario-Montclair School District, Ontario, California.)

are essential: a paved patio which dries quickly after rain is necessary for vigorous play with wheeled toys, such as tricycles and wagons; and an apparatus area which has a surface of tanbark, sand, or some other resilient material sufficiently deep to prevent injury from a fall. Also desirable is a grassy area large enough for running; this can also be used for setting up portable equipment such as walking boards and rocking boats, as well as for group activities. If the play area is large enough, it may have natural shrubbery and uneven ground for the children to enjoy. But even a limited area should have some unsurfaced area where the children may dig and garden.

Water. Water play is of such importance to children of nursery school age that water should be provided on every nursery playground in one way or another, unless the climate provides sufficient precipitation for rain puddles, ice, and snow. A summer nursery group benefits particularly from a spray pool. Each nursery school needs a faucet at which the children may fill small buckets to use in molding sand in the sandbox, and where the teacher may fill a large bucket to use for washing hands that have molded clay, sand, or dough. A nursery group is fortunate to have a wee stream winding among stepping stones set firmly in the ground. But any nursery group can have a hose which is regulated to make only a tiny stream when turned on full, and which helps small boys with their personal problem of aiming a tiny stream of water.

Wind. Where the prevailing winds are often strong, or the topographical features cause drafts across the playgrounds, a windbreak may need to be constructed or planted. This will enable the children to make more use of their outdoor play area, especially during the equinoxes.

STORAGE FACILITIES

Both indoors and out it is necessary to have adequate storage facilities for the large variety of equipment and materials used by preschool children. An important part of purchasing equipment and supplies is planning for their storage. How will this contribute to the development of the children? is the first question to consider in the selection of a piece of equipment. The second is: Where will it be stored to facilitate its use? Failure to consider the second question may lead to the equipment's being left out and soon broken, or its being stored in a far corner not often used. The wise teacher, like the wise housewife, is very much aware of the importance of proper storage for equipment and supplies. She knows how to unitize and store materials so as to facilitate their use by the children and by the adults who assist her.

Unitizing. From current studies of cargo handling comes the important concept of unitizing those materials which are to be used together. The concept can be illustrated by thinking about a collection of books which could be organized in several ways: according to color of binding, with all the green books together, all the red books together, and so on; or according to size of the books, with all the large books together, and all the small books together. The first method of organizing the books has the advantage of looking pretty to those who like a monotony of color; the second method has the advantage of convenience in handling a stack of books. But neither of these arrangements facilitates the use of the books with children. When the teacher is helping the children to enlarge their understanding of a caterpillar found in their garden, she needs a small book, *Johnny and the Monarch*[8]; a large book with pictures of different kinds of moths and butterflies in their stages of development; and a glass jar with holes in its cover in which to keep the caterpillar and the leaves it eats. The wise teacher unitizes the caterpillar materials in a shoe box, neatly labels it and arranges it on a shelf along with other science materials. When a child brings in a caterpillar, she is able at once to enlarge the children's understanding of caterpillars without wasting time in locating materials.

Within each unit, materials are of course stored to make the best use of the space available. Within a unit it is helpful to organize the materials according to size, shape, or even color.

Files. In addition to the unitized materials to be used in providing the children with a variety of activities, the teacher has a file of materials. The file accommodates the following:

[8] Margaret Friskey, *Johnny and the Monarch* (Chicago: Children's Press, Inc., 1961).

- Pictures, well mounted and large enough to be seen by a group of children and covered with cellophane if they are to be used by the children as well as by the grownups.
- Flannelboard pictures ready for use.
- Copies of, or references to, songs and poems.
- Brief descriptions of activities for the children.
- References to unitized materials on the cupboard shelves.

The file materials are arranged by topics and are the accumulation of years of working with nursery school children.

Facilitating Movement of Equipment. Because the attention span of young children is not long, a great deal of equipment is moved in and out of storage compartments in the course of a nursery school or kindergarten session. Even grownups who have learned how to use their bodies easily in moving equipment need to have the aid of wheels and pulleys. Furthermore, when the moving of equipment is made easy, the children can take more part in it and can benefit by learning simple generalizations in science; for instance, you can move with wheels something you cannot move without them.

A wheeled dolly is useful in moving the heavy wooden boxes which unitize either the indoor or the outdoor building blocks of the nursery school or kindergarten. However, if only one or two units are heavy ones, it may be less expensive to mount each wooden box on ball-bearing wheeled casters with a rope for a handle than to purchase a dolly.

If wheeled boxes are to be rolled out of storage, or if tricycles and other wheeled vehicles are to come out, the storage unit doors should open along the floor. Even a low lintel means a great deal of extra effort for lifting equipment up and over it each time something is taken out of storage or put back in. The extra effort may mean the difference between the children being able to get or put back equipment themselves and having to have an adult do it.

When the floor space of a storage unit is occupied with wheeled toys, the addition of another heavy wheeled vehicle presents a problem. Shall it be put on top of the other vehicles? Even lifting one tricycle onto and off a wagon each day may make a difference in the eagerness with which adults bring out equipment for the children to use. But an inexpensive pulley with a rope and a hook makes the lifting so easy that the children will enjoy having a turn in lifting the tricycle onto the wagon before it is rolled into the storage unit.

Lifting Equipment. When it is necessary to lift a heavy object, the grownups at nursery school or kindergarten must know how to do it without straining themselves. A trash barrel, for instance, should not be lifted onto a dolly by a direct pull from the shoulders. Instead, the teacher should bend her knees and lift the barrel onto the front part of her thighs with only an easy shoulder pull. This distribution of the lifting over the entire body makes it possible for a comparatively heavy object to be lifted with only a small pull on each of several body parts. Using elbows and knees as fulcrums and the arms and legs as levers often saves the back from undue strain. The adult at nursery school or kindergarten needs to understand the importance of distributed pulls and the use of the levers that are an integral part of the body.

Indoor Storage. Each of the many indoor activities of the preschool group requires storage. If the activities for the children are not to be curtailed, the teacher must give attention to the storing of the materials required for each activity. The teacher must work with carpenters in planning the construction of storage space for the indoor activities she thinks important for the children. She considers such questions as the following and plans shelving and other storage space in terms of her answers:

1. Can the building blocks be stored so that their box can be wheeled easily out of the storage space?
2. Can the heavy crock for keeping clay be kept at the bottom of the storage space, easily accessible to the children? Or should the clay be kept in a plastic or rustproof metal container and stored on a higher shelf?
3. Can the dollhouse be kept on the first shelf where the children can use it? Is the shelf wide enough and deep enough to accommodate it?
4. Can a full-length mirror be hung on the inside of the door of the storage unit, to be used with the dress-up clothes?
5. Is there space for dress-up clothes to be hung attractively within reach of the children? Can they be stored as they are hung? Is there storage space for hats, purses, and other accessories next to the clothes rack?
6. Can the playhouse equipment be stored so that it is immediately available for use?
7. Do the chairs, cots, and rockers need to be stacked and stored? If so, where?
8. Are there shelves to accommodate the materials available only to adults (for example, a first-aid kit; tissues; safetypins, glue, stapler, and other repair items; perishable equipment and supplies for different craft, music and other activities)?
9. Is there shelf space for children's books, puzzles, rhythm instruments, science materials, and accessories used in favorite dramatic play?

Outdoor Storage. Outdoor storage should be provided for several kinds of equipment:

- Sandbox accessories (trucks, trains, cars, shovels, pails, and so on).
- Wheeled vehicles (such as tricycles, wagons, simulated steam rollers, and trains that are big enough to sit on).

- Rocking boats.
- Walking boards and sawhorses.
- Swing seats, and other portable equipment.

The sandbox should be covered so that neighborhood pets will not use it. Lightweight covers can be made from small-mesh wire netting, preferably of aluminum to withstand weathering. Sandbox accessories should be stored adjacent to the sandbox where they will be used. One satisfactory arrangement is a series of low boxes constituting the sides of the sandbox and, also, seats for the children.

If the outdoor facilities include a playhouse, it can accommodate the storage of the swing seats and other portable equipment along with its own equipment. Most of the wheeled vehicles, together with the rocking boats and sawhorses, need their own storage unit—probably a low shed with doors opening outward so that vehicles can be driven in or out easily. The storage unit should be sturdy in construction so that it can serve as a climber, too. A vertical slot along the length of the storage unit accommodates the walking boards.

Equipment and Supplies

Equipment and supplies supplement the facilities of the center or school in implementing the program of activities for the preschool children. The teacher must make decisions about adding to the equipment in order to enrich the program. What, she asks, will the proposed equipment do for the children? Does present equipment provide adequately for such development? Are children of this age level interested in using such equipment? When and how will it be used? Where and how will it be stored?

Preference is given to equipment that will aid development in areas not otherwise provided for, and to equipment especially suitable to the age level of the children. The center or school that is just opening buys equipment that has a wide playing range. A rocking boat that accommodates six or eight children is purchased before a large tricycle that is needed only by the largest boy in the group.

The teacher should keep in mind the number and the ages of children in the preschool group in determining the amounts of equipment and supplies needed. She asks herself, "How many of the children will probably use the equipment at one time?" If the sandbox toys already include a pail and shovel for three out of four children and a variety of well-liked trucks and trains, then the purchase of one sturdy concrete mixer is probably sufficient. But if a parent wants to donate caps that advertise children's merchandise, she advises him to provide at least one for each child and one for the teacher—with extras for the children's brothers and sisters at home.

Another factor to be kept in mind in increasing equipment and supplies is the question of supervision. Adding carpentry equipment to be used during free play probably means adding one grownup to supervise the equipment, or else rotating its use with that of another kind of equipment which also needs continuous supervision. Without supervision, carpentry equipment is a hazard; with supervision, it provides an excellent learning situation. When the purchase of equipment is considered, the teacher must also consider its probable use.

BASIC EQUIPMENT

Meeting the needs of children throughout the school session calls for certain kinds of equipment which are essential to the program; namely, a rug, chairs, tables, open shelves, and cots or mattresses.

A Large Rug. A large rug is a meeting place for all children and their teacher for brief but important discussions of things that concern the entire group. The rug should be large enough to accommodate all the children comfortably. It often is a 9- by 12-foot rug or a section of used carpeting donated or purchased. Because the rug will have spills and messes on it, it should be easily sponged off, or washable.

Chairs. Children learn to sit in a group on a rug and also on chairs arranged around a table. Chairs are available designed to promote good posture, light enough so that each child can carry his own chair, equipped with silencers, and made to stack in a small storage space. If chairs are not stored each day and if the room is to be used by other community groups, the chairs should be selected for their sturdy design and should be strong enough to accommodate an adult's weight.

Chairs are also needed for the grownups who are part of the school group. They too, should promote good posture, have silencers, and be stackable. Because the nursery children will take an interest in the chairs, they should be safe for a child to use also. A folding chair which tips or folds up easily is a hazard to be avoided.

A chair is needed for each child in the preschool groups, and for the largest number of grownups at the center or school at any one time.

Tables. Children learn to sit at tables while they have refreshments or meals, work with craft materials or puzzles, or look at books. Tables should be large enough to accommodate the group of children supervised by one grownup. They should be made with water- and stain-resistant tops, such as linoleum or plastic-coated materials. If the tables are to be used by other community groups, they may be equipped with one set of adult-height legs that fold up and another set of child-height legs that can be screwed into each corner. Removable and foldup legs make it possible to put the tabletops against the wall in order to enlarge the play space for the children.

If space permits, a table can be placed next to a bulletin board and used for seasonal displays of nature objects and related books.

Open Shelves. Shelving, open on both sides and constructed as a movable unit, makes it easy for children to have the toys they need where they need them. With the building blocks on the lowest shelf; the doll-family figures and the community-helper dolls on another shelf; and the cars, trucks, and other accessories on still another shelf, two groups of children— one on either side of the shelves—have everything within reach for a variety of construction projects of their own design.

Cots or Mattresses. The activities and personal relationships in the preschool group are alternated with rest periods to offset fatigue. When lying-down rest is needed, children lie on an individual cot or mattress, and, if the room is cool or custom dictates, a sheet or other washable, light cover is placed over them. Lightweight cots of canvas or plastic material over tubular aluminum can be stacked (or folded and stacked) for storage.

When quilted pads are used in place of cots, they should have washable covers and be piled so that the top side of one is placed against the top side of another.

Equipment for a Variety of Activities

Preschool children need a continuing flow of equipment and materials both during the day and throughout the school year. They have to acquaint themselves with so much of living that they should have its numerous artifacts brought to them in succession. A preschool group can be thought of as a laboratory of living in which the children have a chance to experiment with the important facets of living. Equipment built to their size enables children to parallel in play the life that goes on around them at home and in the community. All the equipment selected for them should be made with nonpoisonous paints and be free from splinters and other sharp protrusions.

What equipment, then, is desirable for preschool groups? The equipment for the five-year-old children in kindergarten is described in several books,[9,10,11] and that for younger children is listed in government and other bulletins.[12,13] The teacher, and others responsible for equiping a preschool group, study such lists and obtain equipment and supplies for those activities the teaching personnel are interested in supervising. The equip-

[9] Helen Heffernan, *Guiding the Young Child* (Boston: D. C. Heath & Company, 1959), Appendix 3.
[10] Helen Heffernan and Vivian Todd, *The Kindergarten Teacher* (Boston: D. C. Heath & Company, 1960), pp. 59–65.
[11] Leavitt, ed., op. cit., pp. 282–293.
[12] Office of Economic Opportunity, "Project Head Start—Equipment and Supplies" (Washington, D.C.: U.S. Government Printing Office), 1966.
[13] U.S. Office of Education, "Child Care and Guidance" (Washington, D.C.: U.S. Government Printing Office, 1967).

ment for each type of activity may be as simple or as elaborate as the teacher wishes. One year she may have a group of girls who enjoy dancing and other music activities, and may add silk scarfs, wrist bells, ballerina skirts, and other costume effects to the music equipment. Another year she may have little use of such equipment if a group has a majority of boys in it. Instead of buying more music equipment, she increases the large-muscle equipment and the carpentry tools.

UNSTRUCTURED MEDIA

The most important equipment for the nursery school are the media which a child can structure, unstructure, and restructure for as long as he likes and in whatever ways he wishes. The child is creative as he tries out and imposes his ideas on an unstructured medium. Whether he will continue to be creative is probably related to whether or not he is encouraged to find satisfaction in his structuring activities.

For the young nursery child, sand is an absorbing medium. The child is completely enthralled with exploring this medium and in finding out what he can do with it. This fascination of the sandbox continues all through nursery school and kindergarten into elementary school. The four-year-old who builds a simple road across the sandbox terrain becomes the fourth-grader who builds an elaborate complex of roads and related structures in

Total involvement in creating a structure. (Courtesy of Child Study Centre, University of British Columbia, Vancouver, Canada.)

a Disneyland of his own creation. No nursery school or center should exist without a large sand area and, for the older preschool children, water to facilitate the molding of the sand.

Water is another unstructured medium over which the young nursery school child is eager to gain control. He learns to spray it out into "rain" and to channel it within "banks." On a warm day he can play for long periods of time with this fascinating medium. Even when he is older, he still enjoys getting right into the water.

As the children become more mature, they are able to structure media which are already somewhat structured in their home living. The playhouse or housekeeping corner is enticing to the four- and five-year-old children, especially the girls, who rework it to create their own patterns of family life. The dollhouse with its doll family often becomes a therapeutic situation in which the child is able to structure models of family living he has not been able to cope with in reality.[14]

The four- and five-year-olds—especially the boys—are sufficiently mature to impose structure on pieces of wood that become the airplanes, boats, and trains of their imagination. The wooden blocks on which Patty Hill builds a kindergarten program for children are an unstructured medium which older preschool children are able to arrange and rearrange as they work together in small groups. Individually and cooperatively, nursery school and kindergarten children delight in using the unstructured media provided for them.

Art and craft activities are also opportunities for the children to structure materials, as well as to explore the use of such tools as paint brushes and scissors. The children put bits upon a plain background to make whatever design they wish. Such structuring is the essence of the art program for nursery children. It can be modified in an infinite number of ways by varying what is arranged and what it is arranged upon.

OUTDOOR EQUIPMENT

Here are suggestions about equipment for different outdoor activities provided for most preschool groups during the warmer months of the year:

Equipment for large-muscle activities:
a. *Essential*
   Large wooden crates
   Wooden ladders with cleats
   Lightweight planks with cleats
   Push-toys, such as wheelbarrows with two front wheels
   Tricycles (e.g., with 16″ front wheel); metal wagons with solid rubber tires
   Large inflated utility balls, beanbags, etc.
   Punching bag (stuffed pillow or jeans hung within child's reach)

---

[14] Virginia Axline. *Dibs: in Search of Self* (Boston: Houghton Mifflin Company, 1964). A study of personality development through play therapy.

Preschool has climbing apparatus not always available at home. (Courtesy of The Merrill-Palmer Institute and Donna J. Harris, Detroit, Michigan.)

b. *Important*
   Low jungle gym (e.g., 5' high)
   Low slide of hardwood (e.g., 5' high)
   Sawhorses (e.g., pairs ranging from 12" to 24" in height)
   Nail kegs
   More boxes, crates, etc.
   Swings with canvas seats
c. *Ideal*
   Barrel with both ends out, screwed or nailed on platform, to climb through
   Rocking boats
   Large cars, trains, airplanes[15]

This list assumes that the children also have access to playground equipment. Some sturdy climbing apparatus is essential for children and must be

[15] Todd, op. cit., p. 14.

A workbench need not be elaborate as long as an adult is at hand. (Courtesy of Riverside Unified School District, Riverside, California. Photo by Jim Henderson.)

available to them on their own playground if possible. The merry-go-round of the small children's playground at the park is also desirable in a well-equipped school or center.

Equipment for sand play:
a. *Essential*
   Sandpile
   Sturdy small shovels (not trowels)
   Large smooth tin cans, old pots and pans
   Large wooden buckets
   Large wooden spoons
   Other kitchen utensils (e.g., mashers, strainers, sifters, jelly molds)
b. *Important*
   Large sandbox (e.g., 6' $\times$ 8')

Dumping buckets
Sifting screens (e.g., $2' \times 1'$)
Collections of cars, boats, trucks, etc., to stimulate dramatic play
c. *Ideal*
   Several large sandboxes, protected from sun[16]

Equipment for water play:
a. *Essential*
   Hose, with turn-off valve permitting only a small stream of water
   Faucet
   Sprinkling cans
b. *Important*
   A second hose
   Bucket, wide rather than deep
   A variety of objects which float
   A variety of bath toys including squeeze toys
c. *Ideal*
   A small stream through the garden
   A spray pool for warm weather
   Lengths of pipe, elbows, and other plumbing fittings

Equipment for carpentry:
a. *Essential*
   Scrap pieces of soft wood, not hardwood
   Large-headed hammers
   Roofing nails (large heads)
   Storage box
b. *Important*
   Short lengths of wood dowels; spools
   Small vise and clamps
   Crosscut saws (e.g., $12''$ and $14''$) that cut well
   Large nuts, bolts, screws that children can easily turn
   Sturdy screwdrivers
   Heavy low table (e.g., old table with legs cut down to $22''$ height)
c. *Ideal*
   Workbench (e.g., $22''$ height)[17]

Equipment for gardening:
a. *Essential*
   Small plot of ground for each child and teacher
   Seeds of plants that grow rapidly (e.g., radish)
   Sprinkling cans (cf., water-play equipment)
b. *Important*
   Real tools, child-size (e.g., rakes, spades, blunt trowels)

INDOOR EQUIPMENT
Indoor equipment and materials can be as diverse as the imagination of

[16] Ibid., p. 14.
[17] Ibid., p. 18.

the teacher permits. They will include those provided for the usual pre-school activities, as follows:

Equipment for large-muscle activities:
a. *Essential*
   Step-platform slide
   Punching-bag balloon
b. *Important*
   Trampoline
   Rocking boat
c. *Ideal*
   Two-child rockers

Equipment for block building:
a. *Essential*
   Small wooden boxes nailed shut and painted or varnished
   Collection of assorted blocks, sanded and painted (cut by lumber company or donated)
   Large wooden boxes for storage
b. *Important*
   Hollow blocks with hand slots in the following sizes:
      $6'' \times 12''$; $12'' \times 12''$; $12'' \times 18''$; $12'' \times 24''$
   A set of 6 each, but some are better than none
c. *Ideal*
   Assorted kindergarten blocks cut in multiple units (e.g., $6'' \times 3'' \times 1\frac{1}{2}''$; $12'' \times 3'' \times 1\frac{1}{2}''$; etc.)
   Basket or chest for storing blocks
   Large wooden trains, cars, and trucks to suggest ideas of building and play
   Hardwood train and track set

Equipment for housekeeping activities:
a. *Essential*
   Rubber (or soft plastic) dolls, doll blankets and doll beds (e.g., boxes); squares of cloth (e.g., $12'' \times 12''$ or larger); simple clothes with ties, zippers, buttons $\frac{1}{2}''$ or more in diameter, big snaps or large hooks and eyes
   Orange-crate furniture which the children can help make—stove, chairs, sink, cupboard, table
   Washtub and soap powder
   Clothesline, clothespins, and toy irons
   Broom and dustpan
   Small-size cooking utensils and a supply of empty food cartons
   Telephones
   Dress-up clothes (e.g., skirts with elastic waistbands, blouses, curtains, lengths of cloth, purses, shoes, gloves, hats)
b. *Important*
   Beds, child-size (e.g., about $48'' \times 24''$) and doll-size
   Carriages, real-baby size, or doll size
   Sturdy tea sets, preferably metal base (aluminum or soft plastic)

Sturdy ironing boards, and more irons

c. *Ideal*

Playhouse with windows, doors, and so on

Old drapes, curtains, bedspreads, blankets, or canvas for making tents

Poles for framework for tents

Chests for keeping dress-up clothes[18]

Full-length mirror

Equipment for library activities:

a. *Essential*

Sturdy hard-covered picture books about transportation, animals, and everyday experiences of children

Simple homemade wooden puzzles (e.g., 3–5 pieces for youngest; 20–30
pieces for oldest)

A mirror may help a child achieve an identity. (*Courtesy of Florida State
Department of Education and Jacksonville Schools.*)

b. *Important*

Copies of recommended children's literature

Shelves for books, or racks like those in a public library

Racks to hold puzzles

Books, pictures borrowed from public library

[18] Ibid., p. 21.

c. *Ideal*

Large attractive pictures hung at child's eye level (e.g., 30″ to 26″ high)
Table and chairs with chair pads, or small rugs to sit on
Attractive shelves, potted plants, curtains, etc.[19]

Equipment for science activities:

a. *Essential*

Space for exhibiting what the children bring
Space for exhibiting seasonal pictures and displays

b. *Important*

Cages for such pets as hamsters, guinea pigs, white mice, or birds
Planting boxes, small pots, or aluminum foil pie dishes for seedlings
Aquaria for turtles and fish

c. *Ideal*

Science equipment, such as magnets, prisms, simple electrical circuits

Equipment for music activities:

a. *Essential*

Phonograph for teacher use
Records brought by children, borrowed from library, or owned by school
Simple rhythm instruments: ankle and wrist rattles; drums; shakers; wood
    blocks

b. *Important*

Phonograph for child use, with old records
Record caddy
Listening Post with head sets for 3 or 4 older children
Enlarged record collection for teacher use
Musical instrument for the teacher to play (e.g., harpsichord, piano)
Rhythm instruments: triangles, music sticks, tomtoms
Music books for use with young children[20]

c. *Ideal*

Extended record collection
Extended collection of music books
Rhythm instruments for children: bells, tambourines, marimbas
Rhythm accessories: hobbyhorses, dance costumes, silk scarves
Listening post additions

Equipment for craft activities:

a. *Essential*

Potter's clay; crock, or galvanized or plastic pail, with cover
Colored dough materials: salt, flour, salad oil, food coloring
Blunt scissors in scissors caddy; papers to be cut; wastebasket
Plain paper; construction paper; paste (not glue); bits to be pasted
Jumbo crayons, one box for every two children (not wax crayons)
Easels (1 for every 8 children); tin cans to fit easel racks; large brushes
    (1″ wide or wider), with long handles (8″ or more); large sheets of

---

[19] Ibid., p. 15.
[20] Heffernan and Todd, *The Kindergarten Teacher,* op. cit., pp. 62–63 and pp. 279–304.

Every day easels are ready for painting. (Courtesy of Ontario-Montclair School District, Ontario, California.)

unprinted newspaper (18″ × 24″ or larger); tempura paints, primary colors; oil of wintergreen; 9 quart jars with covers for mixing tones and tints of colors

Clothesline and clothespins for drying and displaying paintings

Buckets and sponges for cleaning up

Finger painting materials: cornstarch; soap flakes; smooth shelf paper; salt shakers for the tempura paints, or squeeze bottles for food coloring

b. *Important*

Easels (1 for every 5 children), tempura paints in secondary colors and earth colors

Folders in which to keep paintings for each child (e.g., folded newspaper, labeled)

Chalkboards; chalk (individual chalkboards may be made from composition board painted with blackboard paint)

Printing devices (e.g., sponges, toilet-paper rollers)

c. *Ideal*

Bulletin board on which to display paintings

Tagboard frames for paintings

Sets of water colors (semipermeable)

Charcoal; pencils; pens

The amount of any material to be ordered depends on whether the teacher plans to use it with the entire group of children at one time, or with a small group of children during a free-choice period.

USE OF EQUIPMENT

After suitable equipment has been procured, the teacher should plan so that the children have full use of it. Equipment is not obtained in order to occupy shelf space, but in order to help the children learn through play. The teacher should be sensitive to the needs of the children and see that suitable equipment is available for them at all times. She should also be sensitive to her own feelings. Some morning she may feel tired and think, "Oh, let's not put out the paint and easels today. They're so messy!" Recognizing her negative feelings, she is able to be amused by them and go on to plan not in terms of herself but in terms of the children.

Where assistant teachers are in the process of learning to think more about the children than about themselves, their learning includes (1) focusing attention on how the children use equipment, rather than on how the use of it mars its finish, and (2) developing both a casual view of messes as an integral part of the activity and an expertness in cleaning them up at once.

CARE OF EQUIPMENT

Preschool children should be taught the simple rules of respecting equipment and caring for it. The most important rule for their age level is: If you turn it on, then be sure you turn it off when you are through using it. This rule has several variations, each of which is important for the preschool child to understand:

1. If you open the door, close it so that the heat stays in, and, when it is warm, that the flies stay out.
2. If you turn the water on, be sure to turn it off.
3. If you turn on the light, be sure you turn it off when you leave.

Learning such rules in a preschool group is one of the best kinds of training that a teacher can give a child so that at home he will turn off the gas stove or the electric blanket his curiosity has led him to turn on.

ADAPTED EQUIPMENT

Preschool groups often meet in some community building originally built for other purposes. The teacher of such a group should consider her location and the equipment used there by other groups to see if any of the equipment or facilities may also be used for the preschool children. For instance, if the group meets where there is a gymnasium, its program may be enriched from time to time with the following:

- Somersaults on the mats.
- Jumping on the trampoline.
- Ball handling, especially ball rolling.

If the preschool group meets in a recreation center for school children, it may be possible to have the use of the following:

- Large balls.
- Simple ring-toss game.
- Phonograph and records.
- Folding tables (with removable short legs added).

as well as outdoor playground equipment. Or, if the preschool group meets in a church, it may be possible to share with the Sunday school, not materials and perishable supplies, but such facilities and equipment as the following:

- Rocking boats.
- Walking boards and supports.
- Sandbox (but not the accessory toys, shovels and pails).
- Climbing apparatus.
- Tables and chairs.

JUNK

Materials discarded by the community are often educationally useful for the preschool group. The teacher who realizes this encourages parents to bring discarded articles to the school or center. She expresses real appreciation for the cardboard tubes on which toilet tissues are wrapped, knowing that each tube will be a useful printing device when combined with a shallow dish (for example, a discarded aluminum-foil pie plate) of washable paint. She is grateful for an old saddle and mounts it on a low sawhorse for use by the nursery school "cowboys" and "cowgirls" or transforms it into a swing if that kind of equipment is more needed by the children. (A discarded rocking horse also is easily transformed into a swing.) Some of the following are throw-away materials the teacher uses to enhance craft activities:

- Catalogs of mail-order houses.
- Sample books such as those used by a mail-order house, a drapery or yard-goods shop, or an upholstery shop.
- Sample wallpapers.
- Christmas cards received by a family.
- Birthday cards from a birthday party.

Whatever is brought, the teacher should receive gratefully. She must be discriminating, however, about what she makes available for the children to use. She immediately discards any object with rough edges that might scratch or cut, objects with many small parts that are easily lost, toys and other objects so poorly made as to come apart easily or break easily, and objects made for older children but dangerous for preschool children (for instance, bows and arrows and chemistry sets).

The teacher herself can save discarded small plastic bags for the children to use in collecting treasures such as smooth pebbles; milk-bottle tops to use as containers for paste, or as play money, or for making necklaces; discarded waterproof cartons from milk products to make into baskets; bits of colored papers; and so on.

The junk that is especially useful equipment for a preschool group is the discarded boat that can take the children for countless miles on uncharted imagined seas when they go "fishing," or "exploring," or just sit; or the discarded car chassis, devoid of windows and wheels that could move it, but nevertheless able to "transport" children over many imagined miles; or the old airplane fuselage, stripped of hazardous items but equipped with a control wheel to fly the plane into many an adventure.

But when the more realistic equipment of grownups is not available, and sometimes even when it is available, the children are delighted with their own improvisations out of more ordinary junk. Wooden boxes that are big enough for a child to sit in make excellent boats, cars, or airplanes. A wooden box that is big enough for several children to be in is a very good bus, house, train, or ship. The parents who find a discarded piece of furniture or engine crate for the preschool group contribute the opportunity for many hours of imaginative play.

Discarded blocks of soft wood from the local lumber yard provide material for the children's carpentry. Discarded blocks of hard wood, selected in similar and complementary lengths, and sanded smooth, equip the block-building center for the children until the school budget can provide for a better set of blocks.

Discarded school equipment may be the source of tabletops to which may be attached legs to make the table appropriate to the size of the preschool children. Small but sturdy chairs are sometimes discarded by first-grade rooms in sufficient numbers to equip a nursery school.

Parents and teachers who solicit discarded materials are agents for informing the community about its preschool groups. Many a shopkeeper first learns about the group when he has the opportunity of contributing an old sample book. In one community, the people learned of the newly formed nursery school when they opened their evening newspapers and read the fold-in sheet asking them to contribute used equipment such as outgrown tricycles and wagons for the children.

PORTABLE EQUIPMENT

The wise preschool teacher is like the mother who is always prepared for taking her family on a picnic when spring days are warm and the children are eager for new experience. This teacher knows the resources of her community and she arranges for the children to explore and enjoy them. A favorite excursion is to the neighborhood picnic area—a park, beach, meadow, or vacant lot—and the teacher makes a list of the equipment to take to use there.

Here is the list used by a teacher who takes the children once or twice a month to the sandy beach along the lake shore, or to the city park:

Wheeled dolly with rope handle.
Sandbox toys in cardboard box:
    6 shovels (one for every three children)
    4 buckets
    4 trucks
    2 funnels
    4 coffee cans; 6 juice cans (smooth edges)
    6 large pie plates; 4 small pie plates
Large can of juice, can opener, paper cups (to serve juice with sandwich brought by each child).
Bread, butter, and peanut butter for making sandwiches as needed.
Portable flannelboard and pictures for stories.
Scissors caddy, crayon caddy, roll of shelf paper (to use at a picnic table).
Materials for a special activity.

The teacher lists the sandbox toys on the cardboard box to facilitate the return of each item. She considers the cans and aluminum-foil pie plates as either expendable or returnable. She puts the toys and other supplies on the wheeled dolly so that she and the children can easily take them from the car to the picnic place. In this way the teacher provides the children with familiar items in a new setting.

The teacher, too, keeps in mind that the new environment is also equipment for the children to use. Often she selects aspects of the environment as material for science study and does not bring any materials for a special activity. But other times she brings individually wrapped popcorn balls or little bags either of peanuts in shells or of peas in the pod to be hidden for a "treasure hunt."

A city teacher who takes her four- and five-year-old children to a nearby vacant lot brings army surplus shovels, rakes, and watering cans so that the children may dig and garden. A teacher in a seaside community often brings little plastic bags or discarded juice cans so that each child may collect shells or pretty rocks to take home. Thus each teacher plans in terms of the special features of the picnic places to which she takes the children.

RENTAL OF EQUIPMENT

It is the policy among groups meeting only during the school year to make their equipment available to parents on a rental basis for the summer. This arrangement makes it possible for children to continue a favorite activity. For instance, the child who likes to paint at an easel may have opportunity to do so if his family rents an easel for the summer. The shy three-year-old whose family rents a rocking boat returns to nursery school in the fall with greater assurance because he finds familiar equipment in another setting. From the standpoint of the children, the equipment-rental policy has much to commend it.

From the standpoint of the preschool group, the rent for equipment provides extra income. If the rental policy provides for returning the equipment in the same condition in which it was borrowed, the equipment is no worse for the wear and—if a parent is a good repairman—may even be in better condition than it was.

Group Sharing of Equipment

Two groups using the same premises may lessen their capital outlay by sharing the purchase of equipment. For instance, two groups meeting at the same place divided the cost of a climbing apparatus, sandbox, and swing sets, which were installed in the play area used by both groups. Each group had its own set of sandbox toys and canvas swing seats. The chairmen of equipment in each group worked closely together. Whenever either of them noticed the need for some repair, they took turns in arranging for it.

Equipment for the Teacher

The two main equipment items for the teacher to use in presenting ideas to children are a collection of picture books and a flannelboard. (Appropriate picture books for each aspect of the curriculum are listed in bibliographies at the end of Chapters 6–15.) These books and a flannelboard make it possible for the teacher to present new ideas to the children through words and pictures. An idea presented simultaneously through these two media is more apt to be grasped than if presented only through words or only through pictures.

The teacher needs a large flannelboard and a collection of pictures to go with it. She may obtain a piece of wall board of suitable size, substantial but light in weight. Over this, she puts a piece of well-woven flannel which is at least 4 inches larger than the board. Turning the extra material over the edges of the board, she uses upholstering staples to fasten the material into the board, or she uses needle and thread to tie the edges to each other across the back of the board. She is careful to have the material stretched smoothly across the front of the board, as well as fastened securely at the back.

When she uses the flannelboard, the teacher can place it on a painting easel, or improvise an easel which will keep the board from slipping as she uses it. She may place it on the seat of a chair and hold it in place by taping the top of it to the back of the chair with masking tape. Or she may obtain a cardboard box and cut triangular pieces from the two top corners at the back of the box across to the front edges. The sloped top of the box is for the flannelboard. The ledge for holding the board in place is made by cutting along the front side of the box on a line parallel to the bottom of the box but higher than the bottom of the flannelboard. The teacher can carry this cardboard box easel on picnics, using the box as a container for both the flannelboard pictures and the flannelboard, and finding it useful for many outdoor storytelling times.

KEEPING INFORMED

The preschool teacher needs always to be interested in equipment and materials for the children. To keep informed about current books for them, she should regularly talk with the children's librarian at the local public library and borrow for use with the children those books that are appropriate for their age level. She also should patronize regularly the inexpensive bookstands which often have very good stories suitable for young children.

At Christmastime the teacher can visit large department store toy departments and toy stores, and study the catalogs put out by mail-order houses that emphasize purchases for children. Thus she keeps informed about the kinds of toys available and is able to select sturdy and appropriate equipment that complements and supplements what her group already has. For most equipment she depends on catalogs prepared for preschool groups.

Talking with other preschool teachers is an excellent way to learn of useful materials and equipment. The wise teacher welcomes those meetings of teachers which are a round-table exchange about activities for children. At such meetings, she eagerly studies the exhibits which illustrate the reports made by each teacher about her experience in teaching the activity, and asks questions so that she can also obtain the materials and equipment for carrying out the activity if she thinks it desirable for her group of children.

Situations for Discussion

A preschool teacher is apt to find herself in situations similar to the four described here. As you think of what to do in each situation, consider whether each course of action suggested is desirable, or not. Use points brought out in the chapter as well as ideas from your own experience to justify your views. Suggest alternative courses of action to supplement those given.

SITUATION 1 You are on the committee to select a suitable location for a play group to meet during the winter months. In the local community you go to see

- A member of the board of a nearby church.
- The recreation director at the park.

- An elementary school principal.
- A kindergarten teacher at the elementary school.
- A parent-cooperative nursery school.

SITUATION 2 As the teacher for a proposed parent-cooperative nursery, you should help the parents understand what facilities, equipment, and supplies are necessary. You should

- Give a lecture to the parent group on meeting the needs of children.
- Make out a list of facilities, equipment, and supplies you want to use with the children.
- Leave the purchasing of facilities and equipment to the parents.
- Take responsibility for purchasing supplies.
- Make your copy of *The Years Before School* available to the parents.

SITUATION 3 The nursery school is purchasing an aluminum tricycle with an attached wagon, although its present outdoor storage unit is already well filled. As the teacher asking for an additional storage facility, you should

- Leave the design of the storage unit to the carpenter.
- Verbally describe what you want the storage unit for.
- Make a drawing of the desired storage unit.
- Accept whatever storage unit can be donated.
- Insist on sturdy construction.

SITUATION 4 For the three-year-old group you have ordered a rocker which will accommodate two children at a time and supplement the present rocking boat that accommodates five or six children. The morning that the rocker is to be delivered, you should

- Talk with the children about taking turns.
- Have the rocking boat left in storage.
- Tell the children there will be a surprise.
- Plan with the children how to use the new rocker.
- Let the rocker arrive unannounced.

Current Professional Books and Pamphlets

Association for Childhood Education International. *Equipment and Supplies.* Washington, D.C.: Association for Childhood Education International, 1963. [Other ACEI booklets to help equip a preschool group include "Bits and Pieces" (1967), and "A Bibliography of Books for Children."]

California Correctional Industries. *Educational Toys and Instructional Materials."* Sacramento, Calif.: California Department of Corrections, 1965. [This price schedule of items for preschool and school use may have counterparts in other states.]

California State Department of Education. *Kindergarten Education in California.* Sacramento: California State Department of Education, 1960.

Children's Bureau. *Food for Groups of Young Children Cared for During the Day.* Washington, D.C.: U.S. Government Printing Office, 1960. [Other government bulletins of help to preschool groups that feed children include the U.S. Department of Agriculture bulletin entitled, "Food Storage for Schools and Institutions."]

COMSTOCK, N., and E. SPENCER. *McCalls's Just for Fun Book.* New York: McCall Corporation, 1963. [One of the useful books about what children can do and make.]

LADY ELLEN of Hurtwood, and others. *Space for Play.* Holte, Denmark: World Organization for Early Childhood Education (OMEP), 1964.

Equipment Checklist for Preschool, Kindergarten Centers and the Early Grades. Princeton, N.J.: Creative Playthings, Inc. 1967. [An example of catalogs available from commercial enterprises.]

HARTLEY, RUTH E., and ROBERT M. GOLDENSON. *The Complete Book of Children's Play.* New York: Thomas Y. Crowell Co., 1963. [Suggests equipment and supplies needed for children as they develop through play.]

HEFFERNAN, HELEN, ed. *Guiding the Young Child.* Boston: D. C. Heath & Company, 1959. [Appendix III deals with equipment and materials for kindergarten.]

HEFFERNAN, HELEN, and VIVIAN EDMISTON TODD. *The Kindergarten Teacher.* Boston: D. C. Heath & Company, 1960. [Chapter 4 discusses a good physical environment for the kindergarten child.]

MAY, DOROTHY E. *Suggestions for Play Activities for Young Children.* London: The Save the Children Fund, 1967. [Through community contacts, a preschool teacher can get materials to enhance the play of young children.]

Office of Economic Opportunity. *Project Head Start—Equipment and Supplies.* Washington, D.C.: U.S. Government Printing Office, 1966. [Suggests equipment, supplies, and inexpensive materials for a preschool group. Other Project Head Start bulletins deal with such topics as "Nutrition—Better Eating for a Head Start," "Nutrition Guidelines for the Project Head Start Centers Feeding Program," "Parent Education in Nutrition," "Food Buying Guide and Recipes."]

OSBORN, D. KEITH, and DOROTHY HAUPT. *Creative Activities for Young Children.* Detroit Mich.: The Merrill Palmer Institute, 1964. [Useful suggestions about encouraging creative activities.]

U.S. Office of Education. *Child Care and Guidance.* Washington, D.C.: U.S. Government Printing Office, 1967. [Bibliography of professional books, list of films, list of materials, sources of pamphlets, equipment list, program costs, and floor plan are included.]

U.S. Office of Education. *Planning Functional Facilities for Home Economics Education.* Washington, D.C.: U.S. Government Printing Office. Special Publication No. 12, 1965.

Vocational Division, New Jersey State Department of Education. *Resource Materials for the Playschool.* Trenton, N.J.: State of New Jersey, Department of Education, 1965. [Several states have useful publications for preschools.]

WILLIS, CLARICE, and LUCILE LINDBERG. *Kindergarten for Today's Children.* Chicago: Follett Publishing Company, 1967. [Chapter 8 describes "Flexible Settings for Eager Learners."]

CHAPTER 5

A Preschool Group

With the school well equipped and ready for the preschool children, the next steps to be taken include forming the children's group, providing for its maintenance as a group, planning its curriculum, determining ways of helping the group learn, and scheduling its daily activities. Selecting the group participants and providing for their continuance in the group—crucial factors to the success of a preschool group—require cooperation between family and school. Planning a curriculum and daily programs in terms of the needs and characteristics of preschool children is essential to the educational success of the preschool group. Furthermore, appraisal of the children's progress as a basis for continuous improvement is an integral part of curriculum development from its beginning. Indeed, working with the preschool group requires careful thought and preparation on the part of the teacher.

Children for the Group

Nursery school enthusiasts recommend that every child of suitable age be in nursery school. Actually, whether a particular child should go to nursery school is a question to be answered only after careful consideration of family relationships and situation, the abilities of the child, and the offerings of the nursery school. Sometimes the answer is, "No, not for this child at this time." Sometimes it is, "Yes, if there is an opening in the kind of nursery group the family has selected." Sometimes it is unqualified, "Yes, for this child at this age and for his family at this time."

The Doctors Bakwin point out that:

Under proper conditions the nursery school can be a valuable experience for a child. It cannot, however, be taken for granted that every nursery school

145

will benefit every child. The choice of school depends on (1) the maturity of the child and his readiness to be separated from the home, (2) the nature of the home, (3) the qualifications of the staff of the nursery school to understand young children and to handle the special problems which arise when they spend long periods of time together, (4) the physical setup of the nursery school and its health standards, and (5) the question of whether the experience will contribute to the happiness of the child.[1]

Since Congress enacted the Economic Opportunity Act of 1964 and the Elementary and Secondary Schools Act of 1965, community councils, public school systems, and health and welfare agencies working usually in close cooperation have been extending the opportunity for preschool children of socioeconomically disadvantaged families to participate in preschool groups. Such groups are comparable to those provided by excellent private schools, parent cooperative preschools, and other types of children's day-care centers. Previously preschool groups were available only to parents able to pay tuition charges, conduct preschool groups through cooperative parental effort, or, in the case of working mothers, utilize child-care centers provided partially by social welfare or educational agencies and sometimes with fees graduated according to the family's ability to pay. The legislation of 1964 and 1965 initiated a program accessible to many children who could not qualify for membership in any of the organized preschool groups but were in grievous need of the wide variety of experiences such schools provided, including:

Many experiences for speaking and hearing language spoken in functional discussion
Experiences to develop understandings and investigating skills
Informal experiences with number and quantity
Materials to encourage self-expression in art, music and the dance
Many opportunities to deal with information on a firsthand experience level
A chance to use media to reconstruct his perceptions of what he has seen and done
Opportunities for building empathy for people[2]

FAMILY READINESS

Whether a preschool child goes to nursery school or kindergarten often depends on whether or not his family is ready for him to go at that time. The schedules of other members of the family may interfere with his having a preschool group on his schedule. For instance, consider the child who had not had much opportunity for knowing his busy father and was more

[1] Harry Bakwin, M.D., and Ruth M. Bakwin, M.D., *Clinical Management of Behavior Disorders in Children* (Philadelphia: W. B. Saunders Company, 1966), p. 83.
[2] Norma Law, Mary Moffit et al., "Basic Propositions for Early Childhood Education" (Washington, D.C.: Association for Childhood Education International, 1965–66), p. 11.

concerned with his relationships with his father than with relationships and activities of nursery school. When the father's schedule shifted so that he was usually at home in the morning, the child refused to go to nursery school, except on the mornings his father was not home. Another child who had attended nursery school with his older sister the previous year insisted on staying home with her in the morning. When she shifted to a kindergarten group that met in the morning, the child returned happily to his morning nursery school. Such cases make it clear that a child should have no counterattractions at home the mornings that nursery school meets.

The child who is preoccupied with the relationships between himself and the members of his family is a child who is not ready to be in a preschool group. Indeed, if the mother is emotionally dependent on the child, she will avoid enrolling him in, or will remove him from, school. If the child feels insecure about his relation to his mother, he may be unwilling to have her leave him at school. A little girl whose mother had once left her crying in a Sunday school room while she attended a church service refused to have her mother leave her at the nursery school, which met in the same Sunday school room. Children must have a sufficient measure of security in their family relationships before they can go on to explore the relationships of nursery school.

When the family consists of a father and an infant or a one-year-old child, the father is eager for the child's second birthday, at which time the child is eligible to be in a day-care center. The father no longer has to provide a housekeeper. He can care for the child in his after-work hours; the nursery school cares for the child during his working hours.

When the family consists of two parents and one or two small children, the family is not so eager to move its preschool children toward self-sufficiency. The mother probably wishes to continue the children's dependency until they show that they are ready to enlarge their world by entering nursery school. If she has one child, she is apt to enter him in nursery school as a three-year-old. If she has two children close together in age, she may wait until both children are over three years of age. Or, if she thinks the children each need to develop individually, she may provide nursery school for each child in succession.

How a family spends its money may keep some preschool children from school. Parents make choices which may include or exclude nursery school and kindergarten. One mother, when she entered her four-year-old girl in nursery school, remarked, "Last year I gave Janie lovely and expensive clothes to wear. This year I'm giving her nursery school." By the end of the year, the mother realized the greater value of the preschool experience.

Families with an average income and four or more children spaced close together often find that their budget will not permit private nursery schools, and their energy limits make it difficult to participate in parent-cooperative schools. A mother who has been busy with her four or five children needs not more work with children, but a contrasting activity by herself or with adults. She might better join a church circle or a woman's club than a parent-participation nursery school. Often she is able to enroll her preschool children in a church-sponsored nursery school at low cost and with a minimum of parent activity. This arrangement leaves her free to develop herself in roles other than that of mother.

These examples of different family situations make it clear that whether or not a child should belong to a preschool group depends in large measure on his family situation. Realizing this, the preschool teacher should help each family understand what the preschool group offers their child and what responsibilities the group places on the parents, but leave up to the family the decision of whether or not the child should attend. The wise teacher knows that the family which has been overpersuaded to place its child in a preschool group may soon withdraw. The family that is ready for the preschool group experience is the family whose children will remain in the group.

THE TOILETING QUESTION

Whether a particular child should go to a nursery group sometimes is tied in with parental feelings about toilet training. Mothers often think that toileting is a family matter, not one for a nursery group. Mothers talking among themselves may say, "I'm not entering Carol in nursery school this fall. There will be plenty of time for that after she is toilet trained."

In one preschool group a mother enrolled her four-year-old boy, Ned, because she wanted him to have nursery school experience as preparation for kindergarten. Although she seemed pleased with the nursery school, she often kept Ned at home, or, if to do so fitted into her shopping schedule, she brought him for the latter part of the morning. Her expressed eagerness to have her son attend the group seemed to the teacher to be at variance with her behavior. Finally the bewildered teacher learned from another mother that whether or not Ned came to nursery school each morning depended on whether or not he had had his daily bowel movement. Ned's mother felt that such toileting should be done at home. She was not only unwilling to ask the nursery school to help Ned with such a personal problem, she was unwilling even to discuss the matter with the teacher.

Day-care centers often pride themselves on toileting procedures which avoid the problems associated with mother-child competition. Having children from two years of age up, they expect to guide the development of the children in managing themselves. Whether or not a child is toilet trained or has toileting accidents does not bother the nursery teacher.

Many parent-cooperative and other nursery groups accept only children who are mature enough to toilet themselves at least most of the time. They reason that taking responsibility for toileting himself is important to the child. It is one of his problems in development; in solving it, he feels that he is taking a large step forward. His feeling about himself often seems to carry over into his other behavior. Thus, self-toileting is evidence of readiness for the wider environment offered by nursery school. Nursery groups that take this point of view have a primary, well-publicized requirement that toilet training is a condition of entrance.

AGE OF ENTRANCE INTO A NURSERY GROUP

Benjamin Spock, the well-known pediatrician, has this to say about two-, three-, and four-year-old children starting to nursery school:

Two-year-old

A few nursery schools start with 2-year-olds. This may work very well *if* the child is fairly independent and outgoing (many are still quite dependent up to 2½ or 3), *if* the class is small (not more than eight), and *if* the teacher is so warm and understanding that she quickly makes children feel secure. . . .

Three-year-old

Most nursery schools begin with 3-year-olds, and this is a good age to start if your child seems ready for it. . . .

Four-year-olds

Learning how to enjoy other children's company, to cooperate, to think up projects and work them out, and having the freedom to romp and dance and sing, . . . a child needs these experiences at 3 just as much as he needs them at 4. The longer they are postponed, the harder it is to pick them up easily.[3]

THE EXCEPTIONAL CHILD AND THE PRESCHOOL GROUP

The greatest need of the exceptional child is to be treated like other children. Whether he is blind, deaf, crippled, has a speech defect, is gifted, or is mentally handicapped, he needs to play with normal children insofar as he is able. The preschool group is an ideal situation for him, so long as his presence in the group does not alter it. A musically talented child, for instance, fits well into a nursery group. But the brain-damaged child who is hyperactive may find the nursery group too stimulating. For his own good as well as that of the group, he is better off in a situation geared to less activity, greater calm, and a slower pace.

It is important that the group not be adversely affected by the addition of an exceptional child. This implies certain limits. The proportion of exceptional children to the other children must be small, say, one to a group. The key person in the situation, the teacher, must be confident that the needs of each child in the group can be met. If the teacher feels that the exceptional child will affect the group situation adversely, she is apt to work her feelings out in such a way that he does detract. But if, on the other

---

[3] Benjamin Spock, *Baby and Child Care* (New York: Pocket Books, Inc., 1967), pp. 380 and 381.

An exceptional child needs to be with normal children in normal situations.
(Courtesy of Minneapolis Public Schools and Mrs. Mary Jane Higley.)

hand, she feels that the group will go on effectively, her feelings will be reflected in the group situation.

The people responsible for placing an exceptional child in a preschool group are careful to select one with an experienced teacher. They know that the teacher who has learned effective ways of working with children will have confidence in her ability to teach a group of children, and a series of interviews will determine whether she is also willing and eager to work with a child whose ways of learning are out of the ordinary.

Everyone responsible for admitting a child to a preschool group should concur in planning to aid the exceptional child. For instance, the parents should discuss the question of admitting the exceptional child and his family just as they discuss the admission of any other child and his family. Such a discussion prepares the mothers to talk casually with their children about their new friend at school, and to work with the new child in their role of assistant teachers.

Karen had attended a parent-cooperative nursery school for a year. Her mother took her to a pediatrician for an annual examination before the opening of her second school year. The doctor found that a condition of the hip bones made it necessary for her to be in a cast for several months. The cast made it impossible for Karen to sit down as other children did, and limited her ability to run and play. In spite of the cast, Karen kept on thinking about going back to nursery school when it opened in the fall. At the next meeting of the parents, Karen's mother brought up the question of whether Karen should continue in the children's group. She explained that Karen could move around indoors by lying down on a board mounted on wheels, and that she could transport both Karen and the board to and from nursery school each morning. The mothers felt that it was especially important for Karen to be with her friends in nursery school during this period in which her living was modified by the cast. The teacher thought that she could help Karen whenever she needed individual attention. Thus the nursery school made is possible for a child who was temporarily handicapped to be one of a normal group.

Adding New Families

Different policies are in vogue on helping new families come gradually into a preschool group. Teachers who like to have a group that goes on well day after day favor adding new families one or two at a time. With a nucleus of families who know the ways of the school or center, these teachers feel that the basic philosophy will be caught easily by incoming members. The children will learn from the other children while their parents learn from other parents. Furthermore, when families enter one or two at a time, the teacher is able to give each newcomer considerable attention, as it is needed.

Other teachers are willing to have the group fluctuate between periods of fast learning and of ongoing practice. They tolerate the influx of five or six new families at a time, confident that all the newcomers will learn rapidly the ways of a preschool group. A teacher knows that their learning period will involve poor as well as good ways of working with people, but feels that the contrast between poor and effective ways of working will be readily apparent and will be a basis for parent and student education. Learning goes on rapidly when it is part of real experience, and the preschool group soon reaches a satisfactory level of operation.

Maintenance of the Children's Group

Once the children have entered the group, the teacher should do whatever she can to help each child continue his membership. She knows that the child benefits from the group experience according to the length of time he is in it. She knows, too, that separation from the group is a problem both to the child and to the group. Yet she must realize that some families which enroll their preschool children in a group will not be able to maintain them in it. The motives of parents in sending their child to a preschool group are a major factor in whether or not the child will continue to attend. As the Doctors Bakwin have pointed out:

One mother may be motivated by her own feeling of inadequacy, another by the wish to provide the best possible care for the child, and still another by a desire to reduce her own responsibility. These differing motives will affect the child's receptivity to the nursery school experience.[4]

In one family with six children a year or two apart, the mother enrolled one child in a nursery school. A middle child, a girl in a family of five boys, Joan had developed a role of being a sweet and agreeable person, well able to do the same climbing, running, and swinging that her brothers did, adaptable to whatever plans or activities they carried on. Her mother, looking forward to school days for Joan, wanted her to develop a more dominant personality, not the kind that only fitted into the lives of others. When four months of nursery school did not accomplish what her mother had not accomplished in the four years prior to nursery school, she withdrew Joan from the group.

Such a chain of circumstances is not uncommon. A mother immersed in the physical care of children, husband, and house finds it difficult to give each child the individual attention he needs. The oldest and the youngest children are usually able to gain her attention because the oldest child is the most congenial; the youngest, the most dependent. But the middle children are not always able to compete successfully for a fair share of attention. Without the security of evident love on the part of their mother, they develop behavior that gets them unfavorable attention from their parents. Their parents attempt to remedy the situation by enrolling them in a preschool group. But if the unfavorable home situation persists, the child's behavior in the presence of his parents is not apt to be noticeably modified. Soon the parents withdraw the children from the preschool group.

The teacher is challenged by such instances to do several things:

1. Give the quiet child help in relating to other children, and especially in developing a close friendship with another child like himself.

---

[4] Bakwin and Bakwin, op. cit., p. 88.

2. Initiate conferences with parents whose children consistently do not participate in activities.

3. Encourage mothers of quiet children in having their children visit back and forth on nonschool days.

4. Encourage each mother in scheduling half an hour each day with her child, doing what he wants to do, and not being distracted by the housework or other children.

5. Encourage minimum participation by the mother in preschool group activities, with maximum satisfaction in what she does.

6. Refer parents to parent-education classes and events.

Helping Children Develop Self-discipline

Sometimes the home expects immediate obedience and conformity to what mother or father says. The preschool group, on the other hand, endeavors to help children develop self-discipline, encouraging the children to make decisions appropriate to their level of maturity. For instance, at home the child may be expected to come indoors as soon as his mother calls him. At school, the child is free to choose to play outdoors or to come indoors for some group activity. This opportunity to make his own choice is a necessary prelude to having a child learn to move with the group in its succession of activities.

The teacher who is aware of the families in which strict or advanced standards of behavior are upheld must understand points of difference between home and preschool group and be ready to help parents and observers understand them, too. In some families, a preschool child may not have the freedom of choice he needs. For instance, members of the family may have needs which are met at the expense of the child. A family may need the income provided by a grandparent who cannot tolerate movement and noise at variance with his own. A family may have a mother whose energy is not equal to extra washing and cleaning. It may have a wage earner who must sleep during the day. A family may have as the mother a woman who expects behavior from her children too advanced for them, especially at mealtime or when there are visitors.

The teacher must help parents of preschool children to appreciate the importance of having their children in a group situation in which the children are free to develop self-control appropriate to their level of maturity. She should guide the children in appreciating their opportunities for responsibility at school, and the differences in opportunities between home and school. She should guide everyone concerned in realizing that an apparent difference between home and school is not a point of conflict but an extension of opportunity for learning.

The mother who assists with the preschool group may learn to enjoy with her child a different level of freedom from that which they have at home. The mother who has little flexibility may come to see the advantages of greater permissiveness. The mother who has held her family together as a closely knit group may see the advantages of allowing each member of the group opportunity to make his own choices. She should come to appreciate the fact that mothers and teachers are successful in their roles if the children are constantly growing in their independence of them and in their self-control.

PARENTAL RELEASE OF CHILDREN

The teacher should help parents develop skill in releasing their children. When a parent first accompanies his child in coming to the children's center, he helps the child get started in his new surroundings; after staying a little while, he goes on his way. It is not long before the parent merely gets his child to the children's center or to its bus, waits for the child to check in with an adult, waves to him, and leaves. This simple departure procedure is one of the important learnings for the preschool child. The two-and-a-half-year-old may follow the procedure easily. The three-year-old may need a great deal of help with it as he learns to replace feelings of withdrawing by feelings of belonging to the nursery group. The four-year-old soon learns the departure procedure. The usual five-year-old goes into kindergarten with only one or two days of paternal introduction to the fascinating new experience; thereafter he goes and comes by himself. At each age level, the departure procedure must be learned by the child, and the releasing procedure by the parent. The teacher helps both child and parent in learning these roles.

Here are examples of how teachers have helped children and their parents release each other to the nursery situation.

The teacher welcomed three-year-old Debbie and her father to the Sunday school group and helped her father find a chair at the back of the room. During the morning, the teacher observed that the father made no move to help Debbie join the group. He only sat and held Debbie on his lap. Both Debbie and he were onlookers, not participants. As they were leaving, the teacher said, "Thank you for coming, Debbie. Come again next Sunday and I'll show your daddy how to help you go down the slide." Two months later Debbie's daddy sat on a chair next to Debbie's while Debbie enjoyed working at the table with puzzles or crayons. The teacher realized that Debbie and her daddy were not likely to proceed much further in releasing each other. Debbie was more interested in being with her daddy than in entering the nursery school activities. Because Daddy was with her only on Sundays, Debbie did not want to share him with other children. She did not want him to help other children, only herself. The teacher understood that Debbie had to have a real feeling of possessing her daddy before she could share his attentions. The teacher suggested to the father that he continue bringing her to the Sunday school group until the summer vacation. Then, the next fall, when Debbie would be more self-sufficient as a four-year-old, she and her daddy should plan that she would be in Sunday school while he was in church, and that joint projects would be arranged for other times during the day.

Immediately after four-year-old Lorna and her mother arrived at Sunday school, her mother started to leave. Lorna burst into tears and was not easily distracted by the nursery school activities. That morning the teacher helped by saying, "Your mother and the other mothers all come back here after playtime is over. Would you like your mother to leave something with you so you will know that she will be back for you?" Two or three weeks later the teacher helped again by saying to Lorna: "Have you noticed what the children do when their mothers leave for a while? They smile and wave goodbye. Suppose you try that this morning. It's lots of fun because you know your mother will come back soon."

It is important to help children and their parents release each other. Both children and their parents take a step toward maturity as they recognize each other as independent personalities. For the child, release involves such learnings as

- Developing interest in the equipment and activities of the nursery school.
- Feeling at home with the other people at nursery school.
- Understanding that his parent comes back for him.
- Understanding that all parents come and go from nursery school.
- Understanding that a parent and other members of the family must often center their attenion on preparing food, shopping, and so on.
- Developing willingness to let the parent come and go as he needs to.
- Understanding that a parent comes and goes because of his interests, which include many that are different from those of a child.

If mothers are a usual part of a nursery school, a child has further opportunity to explore his relationship to his mother when she comes to help the teacher. He learns that

- Mother and the other mothers take turns helping the teacher at nursery school.
- When Mother is a helper at nursery school, she helps him *and* all the other children, just the way the teacher does.
- When Mother is a visitor at nursery school, she can play with or help him whenever he needs her.
- When Mother is a helper, he is too. Together they do special things, such as passing the napkins for juice, and putting things away.

The teacher should constantly help parents appreciate what their children may learn as a result of the nursery school situation. She points out that both they and the children should take pride in their progress in releasing the children to the nursery group. She encourages the parents to take the responsibility for such release, and complements them on helping their children achieve autonomy and independence. Aware of evidence suggesting need for further release and of evidence that release is fully accomplished, she makes notes such as the following to include in the folder for each child and to mention to parents:

It was almost noon today before Linda started asking about going home.
Today Daisy had a nice dress on. She told me she is afraid to get it soiled.
Priscilla goes at her play with real vim. She is not fastidious about herself when playing in the dirt piles, and there appears to be no notion of cleanliness standing in the way of her fun.

When teacher and mother work together in helping a child bridge the gap between his home and school, they may share his successes and note his progress. Neal's mother was eager to help him achieve a world of his own, independent of his family. But at the same time she was tolerant of his dependency, and understanding about the effort Neal had to make to release her. When he was three years and eight months old, he sometimes had her come with him to nursery school and stay next to him during the time that the teacher and the children talked together, seated in a circle. One morning when Neal was thus seated next to his mother, he whispered to her, "I know this song. You don't." He was proud of recognizing the song he had been learning in his nursery school world, and he was glad to share it with his mother. Both Neal's mother and teacher were pleased with this evidence that he was finding satisfaction in a nursery school activity that was different from his home activities. They recognized his remark as a landmark on his road to self-sufficiency.

Two months later, Neal considered himself "almost four." In this role he was able to do what he and his mother had agreed upon.

MOTHER When will you be able to go to nursery school without me? When you are four?
NEAL Yes.

One day his mother asked, "Now that you are almost four, would you like to go to nursery school by yourself with the other boys and girls?" "Okay," he said, and went willingly along when the nursery school's car stopped for him.

Nursery school personnel—teachers, mothers, observers, and participants—think of releasing children as a major factor in both school and family life. This is shown in the following excerpt from a nursery school handbook for parents:

Can you release your child
—to his own doings
—to play with other children

—to play with the babysitter

—to daddy

—to being one of the nursery group when you are assisting

The point at which your child gives his attention to something or someone else depends on whether he is free to carry out his own wishes, getting help when he passes his own limits, and whether he is respected as a person in his own right.

Following are some situations with suggestions on how we may help our children help themselves and assume responsibility for themselves.

Mrs. C. is assisting at school. Her child, Nancy, needs someone to help her lift the baby-buggy down the step. Mrs. C. goes on with what she is doing as the teacher helps Nancy. The mother does not rush to her daughter's side.

Jean, age 2½, is making a tower with her blocks. Jean cries as the blocks fall. Mother says, "Too bad. How can you put them back again?" Rather than helping Jean put the blocks back, the mother goes on with what she is doing.[5]

Helping Children Leave

When children are getting acquainted with nursery school or are in a period of new awareness with regard to it, they need help in understanding their role in relation to it. The teacher can help them learn that the school and all the toys and equipment will be there when they return to it. She says, "All the things will be here when you come back. The playhouse, Timmy, will be here. Maybe you and Jane can have another tea party there next time." Usually most children are reassured in this way, and are willing to leave.

When one of the children is loathe to leave a favorite toy, the teacher can talk with his mother, "Johnny wants to wear the fire hat home today and bring it back next time. Would you like to have him do that?" The pleasure that the child gets in taking the toy home more than offsets the occasional loss of equipment. Furthermore, children learn responsibility by being trusted.

A child who feels that what he has enjoyed can be enjoyed again is free to leave or go on to other activities. He needs especially to feel secure in the human relations of the situation he is leaving. Saying "goodbye" to his teacher is an important part of his departure. Even more important is his teacher's warm response, "Goodbye, Dan. See you Friday." Dan goes off happily, knowing that his teacher will welcome him back.

Not Going to School

Part of learning to do something is exploring what happens when one does *not* do it. For instance, a child who is learning to go to bed has not really mastered going-to-bed until he has also explored and mastered not-going-to-bed. Adults must help a child with not-doings as well as with doings. One of the most important not-doings is of great concern to

[5] Vivian Edmiston Todd, ed., *Cooperative Nursery School Handbook* (Long Beach, Calif.: Long Beach Council of Cooperative Nurseries, 1957), pp. 36–37.

Adults help with arrivals, departures, and other transitions. (Courtesy of Montgomery County Head Start Program, Maryland.)

teachers, namely, not going to school. As the experienced teacher knows, if a child explores not going to school when he is in nursery school, and if his parents are not well prepared to help him with this exploration, his absence from school may be disquieting to the nursery school group and may lead to other absences by himself and by other children. The experienced nursery school teacher knows that early in the school year, before the novelty of the new experience has worn off, she must acquaint the parents with the fact that most children sooner or later will explore the limits of not going to school. She must help parents, individually and in their group meetings, understand how to interpret Johnny's *no* about going to school, and how to help Johnny quickly and happily make the transition from going to school because of parental insistence to going of his own volition.

When parents help their children with the question of not-going-to-school, they contribute toward the building of the children's conscience. Four- and five-year-old children develop a consciousness of what they should do in terms of the views held by their favorite adults. It helps them to know what their parents think; for instance:

You will be going to kindergarten next year, and this is your only chance to go to nursery school.

I've paid for you to go to school, and you'll have to go.

Daddy has gone to work to earn money so that you can go to school.

Daddy has his job, and you have your job—going to school.

An Innovation in Preschool Grouping

Among the interesting experimental efforts now in progress is a study under the sponsorship of San Francisco State College entitled Nurseries in Cross-Cultural Education.[6] This project, financed by the National Institute for Mental Health for the period from 1965 to 1970, provides an opportunity to study the "effects of cross-cultural education in enhancing the mental health of families in an area of urban redevelopment and slum clearance." In the area, "new construction, low-cost public housing, slum dwellings, middle-income cooperatives, and high-cost housing exist side by side." The area has a cosmopolitan population composed of Negro, Caucasian, and Oriental families, with Negroes outnumbering all other groups.

Under the direction of Dr. Mary B. Lane, School of Education, San Francisco State College, the nurseries included in the project are to provide:

- A family approach to education.
- Opportunity for all to learn through cross-cultural experiences.
- Utilization of community resources for solutions to problems.
- Cooperation and endorsement of major community resources.
- Comprehensive approach to educational problems, including physical, mental, social, and emotional aspects of living.

---

[6] "Nurseries in Cross-Cultural Education" (San Francisco: San Francisco State College, 1967).

e A study of families through a span of three years by using a variety of approaches, including descriptive data, tests, and interviews.

● Opportunity for young children and their families to know male pre-school teachers.

The Curriculum for Preschool Children

The tendency has existed to bring the curriculum down from higher schools without regard to whether the instructional methods and materials of the higher school were appropriate for younger children. Because a child goes from kindergarten into elementary school, for instance, there is a real temptation to overemphasize reading readiness in the kindergarten instead of leaving it primarily to the first grade. Furthermore, there is the tempta-tion to make the nursery school child ready for kindergarten by having him sit still while waiting for the teacher to lead some large-group activity. The absurdity of such expectations is readily apparent to those who work successfully with preschool children.

The curriculum is determined not by anticipation of later curricula, but by the nature of the children at a particular age level. What are the prob-lems a three-year-old child faces in our society? What abilities has he de-veloped by the time he is three years old? What is he especially interested in doing? What limits does he find difficult to penetrate socially, physically, emotionally, intellectually? The answers to these questions must be used in planning the curriculum for the three-year-old; the answers to similar questions, in planning the curricula for the four- and the five-year-old child.

COMPARISON OF PRESCHOOL AND ELEMENTARY SCHOOL CURRICULA

The preschool and elementary school curricula are both child-centered. What the child is able to do at his age level in his community determines what is especially important for the school to do with him at each age. The child's in-school experience reinforces his out-of-school experience, and vice versa. His school experience prepares him for a fuller life out of school, and for a fuller life in later years. Teachers need to know the range in characteristics and the developmental problems of the children at the age level they teach. They need to know the interaction of children with the adults and other children of the community. By giving their attention to the group activities appropriate to the children, as well as to the individ-uality of each child, teachers further the development of the children.

The curriculum for preschool children is an *experience* curriculum. It has to be, for the children are not able to deal with abstractions. The three-year-old moves into simple abstractions, such as thinking of a cat that is not present as well as one that is. The four-year-old can deal with unique past and future events. The five-year-old is able to plan with continual changes in the plans. By the time the child is six and one half years old, he may be able to cope with symbols written on a page and to recall experiences and relate them to the symbols. However, this ability is determined by the maturity of the eye mechanisms of the individual child, his experiential background, his psychological and neurological readiness, among other conditioning factors. The nursery school and kindergarten curricula provide the child with a wealth of sensory experience which constitutes the experiential background for reading, discussions, and the more mature thinking presupposed in the elementary school curriculum.

The nursery school curriculum contributes an important concept to teaching children of all ages; namely, children need to have a full, real experience replete with stimulations for the senses. An experience which is vivid to several of the senses of a child—sight, hearing, smell, taste, touch, and the kinesthetic sense—becomes background for immediate expression through art media, dramatic play, and other verbal expression. The nursery school emphasizes experience that is more vivid to the child because of his greater degree of involvement in it.

The nursery school equipment is replete with real artifacts of the social order and toys that are models or replicas of vehicles, furniture, and other accessories of the social order. These enable the children to think directly about such objects with a minimum of abstraction. They play in a playhouse that has many elements of their own home. Their play in kindergarten brings into ascendancy the blocks which convert from house walls to railroad bridges as rapidly as the more mature thought of the five-year-old flows from one to the other. The first-grade equipment accentuates sheets of paper and books as the children move into word recognition and other reading experiences. In succeeding grades of the elementary school there is an unfortunate tendency to minimize the "real experience" equipment that characterizes all learning from concrete experience and to maximize use of "abstract" materials that assume a background of real experience, which the children may or may not have had. Indeed, the nursery school curriculum has implications for improved teaching in the elementary school, emphasizing the need for actual experience with real situations— bringing facets of the community and home living into the classroom, going out into the community to view those same facets, and other facets related to them, in their original settings.

The range of subjects suitable for a group of preschool children to experience is as broad as that for elementary school children. The experiences of the preschool group, as well as those of the elementary school, may be described under the headings

- Health and Safety
- Physical Education
- Social Studies
- Science
- Geography
- Mathematics
- Language Arts
- Arts and Crafts
- Music
- Social Sensitivity

The curriculum for preschool groups covers the whole range of living. In some areas—for instance, mathematics—only a few simple concepts are of concern to preschool children. But these concepts are so important that they must be developed in a variety of real situations so that they will be available as a foundation for later study.

In one sense, the curriculum of the nursery school is limited because of the slow rate of movement and learning of young children. This slowness is apparent only in contrast to the rates of older children and adults, who are more adept. Actually, the rate of learning seems slower only because of its different quality. Preschool children have greater diffusion in their learning; older people have greater definition. The quality of diffusion characterizes all beginning learning. It provides the learner with a breadth of sensory reaction from which he later gradually extracts what is, for him, of most worth. For instance, the musically talented child extracts from the rhythm experiences of a preschool group those aspects of music which a sensitive ear sorts out. A child who is less attuned to sounds may sort out a succession of movements into the beginnings of dance; a child who is highly verbal may pay attention primarily to the words used in songs. The vivid sensory experience of the preschool curriculum and its slow pace enable each child to gain what he will from each situation.

During their preschool years, children learn to respond to verbal directions. They learn primarily by responding to subliminal cues, and especially to the actions they observe and the tones of voice that they hear. They imitate what the teacher does and what older and more mature or more experienced members of the group do. They learn, to a large extent, by trial and success and by trial and error. Of course, the teacher guiding their learning uses very simple instructions, but she does not depend on it that the children will respond to them until they have had ample opportunity to relate these verbal stimuli to the expected responses. Her verbal instructions first accompany—then, much later, take the place of—other stimuli.

On the other hand, the elementary school teacher, working with more mature children, relies to a considerable extent on purely verbal instruction. She probably should appreciate further what the wise nursery school teacher knows; namely, only after successful practice with materials, examples, and other audiovisual stimuli, can children use the verbal instructions that accompany the practice effectively in place of the concomitant stimuli. The elementary school teacher who profits from nursery school experience depends on a variety of stimuli and on real situations, but not on verbal stimuli alone.

The kindergarten was welcomed by educators as an opportunity for introducing the preschool child to many facets of living, a foundation for subsequent years of schooling. Now educators recognize that many of the concepts, skills, attitudes, and interests of the kindergarten child are more appropriately taught to younger children. When nursery school experience is provided for three- and four-year-old children, the kindergarten is free to provide those experiences especially important for five-year-old children. When kindergarten is available, the first grade can take up problems that interest six-year-old children, without having to recapitulate the preschool experiences. By having schooling at each age level especially planned in terms of the needs and interests of children at that age level, the school furthers the optimal development of children.

Table 5-1 gives some of the skills, attitudes, and concepts which are developed by the curriculum for three-, four-, and five-year-old children. These and other learnings are discussed in detail in Chapters 6 to 15. Presentation of them here gives an overview of the nursery school objectives and shows their relation to the kindergarten objectives. These nursery and kindergarten objectives, developed in terms of the characteristics of children at three, four, and five years of age, are for use in preschool groups whether they are an integral part of a school system or are independent of it; whether they are children's or day-care centers, parent-cooperatives, or privately operated, church-sponsored, or publicly supported nursery schools or kindergartens.

The curriculum developed in terms of the behavior expected of three-, four-, and five-year-old children is built around the succession of seasons in the year. Three-year-old children in nursery school live through the holidays and other activities of each season in succession. Four-year-old children have a fuller experience as they participate again in the seasonal activities of the society in which they live. Kindergarten children are able to anticipate holidays and events associated with each season, as well as to participate in a wide variety of seasonal events.

The program of activities developed for three-year-old children should be simple; the program for four-year-old children, somewhat more concentrated. Programs developed for prekindergarten children are of course simpler and less concentrated than those for kindergarten children. With each succeeding age level, it is possible to have a greater amount of group activity. As the children mature, the highly informal and unstructured program for young nursery children is gradually replaced by a program which still primarily provides for each child individually, but also provides for children who are developing the social skills necessary for working together, especially in small groups.

Each Group Is Unique

Although it is possible to define the preschool curriculum in terms of learning to be expected of children at each age level, it is also to be kept in mind that each group of children is unique in many ways and that the curriculum for the group will be correspondingly unique in many respects. For instance, the weather varies from community to community and the preschool curriculum varies accordingly. A preschool group in the northern part of the United States has extended winter weather, and children learn to take turns with sleds and snow saucers. A preschool group in the south-

TABLE 5-1. Behavior Expected in Preschool Children

CHAPTER	CURRICULUM AREA	EXPECTED BEHAVIOR		
		At Three Years	*At Four Years*	*At Five Years*
6	Health and Safety	Judges how far to climb and return safely Urinates without help unless clothing is complex	Handles blunt scissors safely Knows that blood forms a scab to protect new skin Unzips, unsnaps, and unbuckles	Handles saw and hammer safely Puts away toys and closes cupboard doors Goes to bathroom by himself
7	Physical development	Walks a board holding adult's hand Stops or goes on the slide Likes to swing Climbs a ladder Learns to jump	Walks along a walking board Explores variations on the slide Learns to pump in swinging Goes down fireman's pole Learns to hop	Walks a narrow curb Swings by himself Cuts on the line Learns to skip
8	Social understanding	Enjoys his own birthday Enjoys simple house play and dressing up Learns to move with the group activities	Takes turns Enjoys birthdays and Christmas Extends dramatic play—doctor, store people, delivery man Explores leader or follower role in group activities	Waits for his turn Enjoys birthdays and other holidays Extends dramatic play further Enlarges his feeling of belonging to the group
9	Science	Knows where he came from Knows where his food goes Names several animals Observes what is pointed out	Knows death is part of life Knows sounds, nests, and other things about animals Makes his own observations	Knows how he was conceived Knows what foods different animals eat Reports what he observes
10	Geography	Knows relation of rooms indoors Recognizes his own home	Uses landmarks Can go around the block Recognizes his own neighborhood	Draws and uses a simple map Walks several blocks to school
10	Mathematics	Names a few numbers Lives in the present	Counts a few numbers Deals with the past and the future	Counts to ten Thinks of uses of numbers Uses a wider span of time in planning

TABLE 5-1—continued

CHAPTER	CURRICULUM AREA	At Three Years	EXPECTED BEHAVIOR At Four Years	At Five Years
11	Language development	Learns sounds used in words Uses simple sentences Learns new words	Increases his command of oral sounds Uses compound sentences Increases his vocabulary	Has mastered most word sounds Prints own name Uses adverbial clauses Increases his vocabulary
12	Stories	Likes short picture stories Does short pantomimes with adult	Likes realistic picture stories (e.g., about home) Pantomimes a simple story told by adult	Likes realistic and imaginative stories with little drama and a happy ending Dramatizes simple stories
13	Art	Likes easel painting Scribbles with crayons Enjoys several art media	Likes to use a brush or other tool Paints and draws with some design Enjoys a variety of media and several art tools	Makes designs and realistic portrayals
14	Music	Likes music Distinguishes "indoors" from "outdoors" voice	Creates dance movements to music Enjoys action stories to music Learns short songs by rote	Follows simple dance suggestions Tells high from low, soft from loud, fast music from slow Learns songs by rote Creates song phrases
15	Relating to others	Plays parallel to others	Plays with others or by himself Does dramatic play with others Expresses sympathy Finds his own emotional outlet	Increases his cooperative play Is more sensitive to the needs of others

ern part of the country has little or no winter weather, hence children learn to take turns on tricycles, playground slides, and climbers all through the year.

The needs and interests of preschool children also are somewhat different from year to year, and from group to group. One group may have a preponderance of boys whose great interest is carpentry; another group, a preponderance of girls who enjoy music and dancing; a third group, about an even number of boys and girls all of whom seem unusually mature. Whatever the composition of the group, it affects the planning of activities appropriate for the children.

Another factor that makes the curriculum unique for each preschool group is the personality of the teacher. Each teacher emphasizes different parts of the program, depending on her individual interests and talents. A teacher who enjoys arts and crafts is especially apt to come across interesting variations that will enrich the art and craft activities of her children. A teacher who has a background of science hears the road-grader, the streetsweeper, and other machinery at work in the community and shares her enthusiasm for such phenomena with the children. Each teacher enriches the preschool curriculum according to the activities that she enjoys with the children from day to day throughout the school year.

GUIDING INDIVIDUAL LEARNING

In working with a group of individual children, a teacher is sometimes tempted to adopt a system of teaching for the group instead of working creatively in terms of individual needs. Several such systems have been devised in previous times, usually in a situation where lack of funds or a low ratio of teachers to children made it difficult to provide adequate attention for each individual child. The method devised fifty years ago by Dr. Maria Montessori in Italy is one of the better known systems and is historically an important contribution to early childhood education.

The teacher endeavoring to guide the development of each individual child considers every teaching tactic and every teaching device to guide learning. She may identify a child who often responds eagerly to Montessori materials and methods; another who sometimes is highly creative in his selection and use of playthings; a third who usually likes to work with whatever other children are enjoying; and many other individuals each unique in his approaches to learning. By focusing on diagnosing what a child needs to and is ready to learn at present, the teacher helps each one develop as a unique person, rather than trying to fit him into some teaching system.

THE CURRICULUM FOR PRESCHOOL GROUPS OF A RELIGIOUS NATURE

The curriculum of the preschool group which meets for an hour of worship is essentially that of any other preschool group, but differs from it in having additional expectations of the children. These additional objectives are not in conflict with any of the objectives listed in Table 5-1 or those described in Chapters 6 to 15; they are extensions of them. They may be described as attitudes, beliefs, skills, and concepts to be developed with the children through the experiences of the curriculum. They have points of difference according to the denomination of the church attended, but they usually include the following:

Attitudes:
  Loving
  Friendly
  Cooperative
  Helpful to the teacher and to the group

Beliefs:
  I like you
  You like me
  We like to go to our church (or synagogue)

Skills:
  Saying a simple prayer
  Saying a simple grace
  Sharing what we have
  Giving to others
  Handling great religious books with care

Concepts:
  God
  Oneself as a spiritual being
  Gladness—e.g., We are glad that flowers bloom; that we are growing; that we are learning to take turns; that we have our church (or synagogue).

Some Ways to Help a Preschool Group Learn

Many ways of helping the children learn different subject fields will be discussed subsequently in relation to specific fields, but some methods are of such general use that they may better be discussed here.

The teacher, no matter what subject field she may be emphasizing, is always faced with questions about how to handle the group of children: Should she work with the children as one large, single group, or should she work with them in small groups, or even individually? Should she plan an activity as one of those to be selected while the children play and make their own choice of what to do, or should she plan it to be done under her direct guidance? How the teacher answers such questions each day will have much to do with her success in guiding the children in desirable ways, and in helping them learn optimally with a maximum of pleasant experience.

In planning how to handle a group of children, the teacher should keep in mind the fact that a major task of preschool children is to learn how to be part of a group. Children entering nursery school or kindergarten require a variety of experience in both small and large groups over a considerable period of time before they can be expected to behave easily as part of a group. A preschool child does not automatically move with a group—he learns to do so. The teacher, therefore, must always plan learning activities for the children so that a concomitant learning will be pleasure in the group experience, or at least the avoidance of displeasure in it.

PLANNING FOR FREE CHOICE OF ACTIVITIES

Because preschool children are just learning to participate in group activities, they find it fatiguing to do so for more than a short interval at a time. To conform to a teacher-centered group situation requires a concentration beyond their age level. Often a child held too long, in a group activity recoils from such conformity by excessive or socially undesirable overt behavior. The wise preschool teacher therefore plans primarily to have the children choose their own activities, each continuing an activity only so long as he wishes.

Free-choice activities can be planned for either outdoors or indoors, but in either case they must be primarily activities already familiar to the preschool child. If he is to control his own activity with only an occasional period of direct interaction with the teacher, he must not be learning a new activity in which his trials will yield errors as readily as successes, nor can he be carrying on some dangerous activity, such as hammering or sawing. His teacher therefore should set up for his free-choice activity such outdoor centers of interest as sandbox, playhouse, or wheeled vehicles to supplement the stationary climbing apparatus. Depending on the number of adults available to work with the children, the teacher plans for additional activities under supervision; perhaps, for three-year-old children, a new activity such as blowing soap bubbles or, for a group of four- or five-year-old children, construction activities.

Free-choice activities indoors should be activities which are known to the children and are not dangerous. These include the housekeeping corner, the dress-up corner, blocks, the push-toys for younger children, the rockers, and the quiet-activity table. The extent to which the teacher may supplement these with other activities, perhaps new ones, which require supervision continuously, depends upon the number and training of adults available to help the children.

PLANNING LARGE GROUP ACTIVITIES

Planning primarily for the children to choose their own activities does not preclude large-group activities. The skillful teacher gathers the children into one large group whenever it is appropriate to do so. She knows that one of the ways children learn to enjoy and participate in group experience is to be part of a large group gathered together for some important reason. She does not hesitate, therefore, to ask all the children to meet with her to discuss briefly what will be done on the nature walk or study trip they are about to take, or to listen briefly to some story that is of interest to everyone in the group. Whenever she has something to take up with all the children, she uses a prearranged signal to have them come together. Then she works with the group as a whole, but only for a brief time, the length

Preschool children need brief experiences as part of a large group. (Courtesy of Metropolitan Public Schools, Nashville–Davidson County, Tennessee.)

of which depends on the age level of the children and their experience in being part of a group.

Whenever she is working with the large group of children, the teacher should be careful to see that one or more assistants are available to work with the children who at that moment are not ready for or interested in participation in the large group. She should realize the individual differences among children that affect learning of an activity such as group participation, and should realize that each child participates in large-group activities as much as he is ready to do so. At no time, therefore, should she expect all the children to participate in such an activity—even if it is eating. The food is available; almost everyone is enjoying it; but no child has to eat, or has to be part of the group at that time, unless he wants to do so. His teacher should make sure that a demurring child is aware of the choice he is making, but in no way penalize him for it. The child who has his refreshment served at play in the sandbox has to learn by experience that it is more fun to have it at the table with the other children and his teacher. "Maybe tomorrow you will join us at the table," says the teacher who earlier invited him to participate in the group activity. But she avoids saying that he has to join the group. He will arrive at self-discipline more

169

surely and successfully if he does so out of choice rather than under adult pressure.

Keeping in mind a child's need for a rhythm of rest and activity, many teachers plan activities of interest to all the children at a time when the children are most rested. One nursery school teacher working with four-year-old children felt that a large-group activity was especially appropriate as the first activity of the morning. She liked to start her preschool group by gathering the children into one large group for a brief talking time in which they planned whatever special activity they wanted to carry out that morning. Another teacher felt that her group of three-year-old children should start their day with their own choices of activity, and should meet as a large group at refreshment time, at which time she often read a story to them or talked with them while they were still together as a group. Each teacher should gather together the entire group of children at whatever time seems most in keeping with the rhythm of rest and activity of that group of children. All teachers should see that no child is forced to participate when the group meets and that it meets only so long as it takes up something of concern to everyone, never to the point of fatigue.

Neighborhood tours, nature walks, and study trips to some point of interest in the larger community are large-group activities which are important as a means of enriching the preschool program. Their success depends on teaching the children to stay together as a group. The "magic rope" is a device for helping them learn to do this. By holding onto the rope each child has a tangible reminder that he is part of the group.

The "magic rope," of course, is a smooth, lightweight cord which the children enjoy holding. After the children have been accustomed to using it, it is replaced by an imaginary rope which likewise keeps them together. Older children can hold hands and go, two by two, along the sidewalk, but younger children like to have their hands by their sides and to use the magic rope.

PLANNING ACTIVITIES FOR SMALL GROUPS

In a well-staffed school, adults are available in sufficient numbers so that the choice of activities for children includes one or more small-group activities. These are of four kinds:

1. An activity that is new to the children (e.g., water coloring, testing objects to see if they float).
2. An activity in which children need assistance frequently (e.g., easel painting, carpentry).
3. Making some object of interest to the children but too difficult for them to do unaided (e.g., putting brads into a movable puppy made from construction paper).
4. Talking with children as they examine objects new to them (e.g., petrified wood, a magnet, a Japanese doll).

In such activities, adult guidance should be continuously available. A calm adult in charge of the activity makes the difference between a good learning situation and one that is unsatisfactory or is terminated too quickly. It is difficult for the teacher to give more than a brief moment to helping with the activity because she must also supervise and enrich the other activities that are interesting other groups of children at that same time. If a child suddenly needs help in settling an argument or going to the bathroom, the teacher must see that he gets it immediately.

Exploration is enriched by adult and peer questions, and by explanations. (Courtesy of St. Louis Park Public Schools, St. Louis Park, Minnesota.)

The small-group activity is essentially one in which each of several children has access to adult guidance in learning at his own rate and at the level of development of which he is capable. Such timing in learning is not possible for all the children in a teacher-centered large-group situation; it is expensively achieved in an individual learning situation. Small-group activities make it possible to pace a child as he learns at his own rate when he is ready for learning.

Perhaps the greatest advantage of a small-group activity is that it provides a learning situation with a simultaneous talking situation. The opportunity to talk as one works is highly important for preschool children who are at ages in which they are developing the use of language.

CREATIVE TEACHING

Through careful planning of an environment that is stimulating when a child is ready for stimulation and restful when he needs to rest, a teacher can teach each child in a preschool group so that he is free to be creative to the best of his ability. Routine that gives him the security of knowing what to anticipate with assurance is combined with opportunity for emotional expression through crafts, music, words, and "body language."[7]

The experienced teacher who has guided learning of many preschool children in many different groups has a fund of alternatives from which to select what is especially appropriate for the individuals and the group with which she is working. Through successful guidance of preschool children, the experienced teacher has developed a feeling of self-confidence about her ability to work effectively with such children. Her confidence and her knowledge of children and how they learn give her freedom to be creative in her teaching. She can pace the learning of a child, knowing that at any moment she can reenforce his learning, divert him to a new activity, help him with the problem he encounters, or otherwise modify his environment to give him the emotional support, stimulation, or tension release he needs.

The not-so-experienced teacher may attempt to be "creative" without having organized the subsystems and set up the routines that are prerequisites to the creative learning of children. The result is often chaos. Freedom beyond what a preschool child is able to use effectively is frustrating to him. Without a controlled environment, he is apt to be out of control.

In this book we describe basic principles and practices that underlie creative teaching. Acquainted with these principles and practices, a teacher can apply, modify, and rearrange them to meet the needs of children creatively. The result should be such evidences as the following that creative learning is taking place in the preschool group:

1. Interest is high—pupils are alert, observing, reacting physically, intellectually, socially, and emotionally, carrying on activities with zest.
2. A pervasive spirit of moving forward toward worthwhile goals is felt, with motivation coming from within the learner.
3. Individuals engage in a variety of activities either alone or in small groups.
4. Interaction between and among learners is not only permitted but en-

[7] Office of Economic Opportunity, *Project Head Start Daily Program I For a Child Development Center* (Washington, D.C.: U.S. Government Printing Office, 1967), p. 29.

couraged. Interaction does not always follow teacher-pupil-pupil-teacher pattern but frequently may be pupil-pupil-pupil-teacher-pupil-pupil or similar pattern.

5. Objective materials are used to elaborate ideas and to make them more concrete—art media, actual objects, study trips, and the like.
6. Learners participate in planning the enterprises in which they engage. Everyone has a chance to participate in decision making.
7. *Good* is not equated with *quiet*. The atmosphere is that of a busy workshop where everyone is pursuing purposes that are of value to him.

The Day for a Preschool Group

The daily program for a preschool group is planned in terms of the needs of the children, especially their need for a rhythm of rest and activity. Children need to experience such a rhythm in order to establish it within their pattern of living. By resting after activity, they learn to recognize their need for such a sequence. They live it and learn it.

MEETING THE NEEDS OF THE CHILDREN

The art of taking a group of children through a day, a morning, or even an hour of activities is based on sensitivity to the behavior of the children in the group. The teacher, at first consciously and presently out of habit, notices diminished interest and other signs of fatigue in the children:

1. The child who usually plays cooperatively with others is at odds with one or more of the group.
2. The child who is skillful in carrying an object suddenly drops something.
3. A child is cut or hurt, when either he or another child is no longer accurate in judging distance.
4. The child who usually shares and takes turns is no longer willing to do so and insists on being possessive.

Such are the signals that tell the teacher to help the group shift to another kind of activity, to remind the children to go to the bathroom, to have a restful activity, to have juice or other refreshment, or, if it is toward the end of the school session, to get ready to go home. The attention span of the children must be taken into account in planning the activities of a preschool day.

Here is a playhouse conversation between Neal, three years and five months of age, and Susan, five years and two months of age. Negative behavior, sudden aggression, and disinterest are all cues for the teacher. Neal responds to the word *honey* by becoming angry. Shortly thereafter Susan becomes angry, expressing her negative feelings by saying that she is going home, a typical expression of an older preschool child.

SUSAN Let's make dinner.
(*Both Neal and Susan busy themselves getting out cups, other dishes, and silverware for setting the table.*)
NEAL (*picking up a cup*) What's this?
SUSAN That's tea. Here (*hands Neal a spoon*). And you have to stir it. That makes it good.
NEAL (*slurps*) That's hot. Mine is hot. It stays hot.
(*A few minutes elapse while the pantomime continues.*)
SUSAN Honey, I'm pouring some tea for you.
NEAL (*angrily*) I am not "*honey*"! I don't want tea! I am going to pour it back on!
(*More time elapses while the play continues.*)
SUSAN (*lying down*) I am going to sleep. Keep quiet!
(*Neal sings.*)
SUSAN I am going home now!
NEAL Why?
SUSAN Because you're not quiet. I want to go to bed.

The teacher observing such play should consider the ages of the children and their usual ways of playing together, then decide whether or not the children will be able to go on with their play or whether the negative feelings will disrupt it. If she feels that the negative feelings are disruptive, she should step into the play situation and provide a change of activity. If the time is close to the usual nap or refreshment time, she may interpret the negative behavior as a sign that the children are growing tired and are ready for rest or refreshments.

HELPING WITH TRANSITIONS

Her experience with individual children should enable a teacher to pre-dict the transitions a child will need and fit them into those the group will need. For instance, she may notice that four-year-old Stanley, a child who learns easily and concentrates well, is doing a puzzle. She must keep in mind that Stanley will keep at the puzzle until he finishes it and, at that point, will go suddenly out of control. She prevents this by working with him, helping him to relax as he works, minimizing his need for a pendulum-swing from deep concentration and control to lack of control. Thus the teacher can anticipate a trouble spot and prevent its erupting into a group disturbance. Then, smoothly, she can accomplish a transition for Stanley within a transition from one group activity to the next, "We're going to have juice now, Stanley. Will you go out to the sandbox and tell Mrs. Jones, please?" The big-muscle activity of running is the contrast that Stanley needs to the small-muscle activity he has had in putting the puzzle pieces together.

When a teacher shares facilities, play areas, or indoor space with other teachers, she often has to observe a time schedule without letting the children become aware of the precise timing of their activities. She should plan an activity which can be finished easily within the time allotted and should allow ample time for cleaning up, the children helping adults pick up and put away playthings. For the two- or three-minute intervals with the more mature children who finish ahead of others she needs a wealth of brief entertainments—a little song, something from the science corner to show the children, a simple finger play, a question, or an explanation to enrich their thinking.

A schedule that is tight can yet allow for the individual child to paint more pictures while his group goes on to another activity and a second group comes into the room. Sympathetic teachers who are interested in children anticipate this occasional situation. The children also accept it casually, knowing that it is possible to choose between rounding out some constructive individual activity and joining the group in its next activity. As long as the individual child has a real sense of belonging to his group, he slips back into it quietly. Thus, individual needs are met within the preschool program while its rhythm of rest and activity helps the children learn to enjoy conforming to a daily schedule.

SAMPLE PROGRAMS

Although the program for each day is created uniquely out of the needs and interests of the children, it is possible to describe the succession of events during a typical session and to assign to them a time sequence such as is likely to occur. The precise timing of each event depends on the reactions of the children that day and how the teacher feels about prolonging or shortening each activity.

In working out its daily program, each preschool group takes into account the patterns of living of its patrons as well as the pattern of living needed by the children. Following is a program used as a basis for daily planning in a child-development center:[8]

Work-Play Period Both planned and spontaneous activity		1–1½ hours
Quieter Group Activities		40–50 minutes
Examples:	washing and toileting music snack story rest	
Outdoor Play		30–50 minutes
	In bad weather, gymnastics, circle games, dancing	
Preparation for going home		10 minutes

[8] Ibid., pp. 20–21.

For an all-day schedule, the basic three-hour schedule can be preceded by "a homelike and interesting flow of childlike activities" that begin a preschool day that starts at 7:00 A.M.: "Breakfast, quiet play, listening to records, helping to get school ready." It can be followed with:[9]

Luncheon	45 minutes
Nap, rest or quiet time	2 hours
Outdoor play	2 hours

    In bad weather, dancing, singing
        games, gymnastics
    Enriched with trips
    Cooking projects, care of pets
    Helping to close school

In operation, these programs are flexible. Actually, each teacher must work out her own general schedule and the daily deviations within it. For instance, a teacher of a group in California plans a morning program in terms of outdoor activities. After she greets each child and quickly notes his state of health, she guides him toward vigorous play with tricycles, swings, climbers, sandbox toys, or rocking boats. During the first part of the morning she brings the children inside in small groups for activities planned in terms of the curriculum. She depends on assistants and a variety of outdoor equipment to keep the other children well occupied in play. Mid-morning, after the children have gone to the bathroom individually or in small groups, she works with the entire group of children while they rest and have juice together. Then, while assistants put away some of the play centers available earlier, or supervise the outdoor play of children leaving the large-group activity, the teacher is indoors helping the children with some simple art activity—making a collage, for instance. The remainder of the morning she spends with the children in their self-chosen activities outdoors, in putting away apparatus, and in helping each child leave happily with his collage, jacket, and other possessions. By leaving the rocking boats and the balls out until everyone has gone, the teacher is left free to talk with parents who have come to take their children home. She depends on assisting mothers and aides to help the remaining children while she talks with a parent briefly or makes an appointment for a later conference.

Teachers differ in the attention that they give from day to day to different kinds of activities. One teacher who is talented and schooled in music provides a great deal of music for the children. One year she had a group mostly of girls, and she spent much time with them in dancing. She considers music so important that she begins the morning with musical activities for the whole group, and sometimes continues with the music for as much as half an hour when she has a group of interested children. Another

[9] Ibid.

At preschool, lunch may provide the principal meal of the child's day. (Courtesy of Chattanooga Public Schools, Chattanooga, Tennessee. Photograph by Fred Miller.)

teacher enjoys being outdoors in the spring, when new leaves are budding and the plants are changing rapidly. At least once a week she takes her group to a nearby wooded area for the latter part of each morning. This variation of program in terms of the special interests of the teacher is highly desirable because it provides the children with rich, full experience shot through with pleasure and enthusiasm. The preschool program is flexible enough to indulge teacher enthusiasms along with a balanced curriculum. The teacher need only be sure that she does not neglect other aspects of a well-rounded curriculum. At least every week or two the wise teacher checks to be sure that the children's activities have given each child opportunity for

- Large-muscle development and small-muscle coordination.
- Furthering good health habits.
- Communication of his ideas to both adults and other children.
- Appreciation of stories.
- Expression in a variety of art media.
- Enjoyment of music.
- Exploration of his physical environment.
- Getting along well with other children.
- Understanding the social order.

177

If any of these curriculum areas has been slighted, the teacher should plan activities involving them.

The teacher should think of the day's program as having two major functions: helping the children develop a routine way of living and providing them with new experience. At first thought, these two functions may seem at variance with each other. But on second thought, it is clear that the day's program may be viewed as a familiar succession of activities with variation from day to day within each kind of activity.

THE FIRST DAY

The first day of school is an important one for the children as well as for their teacher. The children are approaching a new situation—new people, new locality, new activities. If their approach results in happiness, they will be encouraged to try other new situations. A pleasant first day leads them to look forward to other pleasant days with the preschool group. What each child wants is a friendly teacher who is really interested in him, an opportunity to explore his new situation safely, and familiar activities which he enjoys.

Realizing what the children expect, the teacher should plan a simple schedule of activities which will make the children feel at home and should welcome each child individually and warmly. Talking with each child and using his name, she makes the child feel that she is a real friend who knows him: "What a pretty shirt you have, Tommy. You must like red, as I do. See, your shirt and my belt are both red." By using the names of the children, the teacher can quickly learn them and start to know how each child reacts to different situations.

From their first day, the teacher should introduce the children to the simple daily routine on which they can depend. She has rest time and juice time in the middle of the morning. She introduces the routine of putting playthings away at the end of the morning, before lunchtime. Since the children may be tired by the excitement of a novel experience, she requires them to do only what they volunteer to do and is ready to conclude the morning activities somewhat early, if necessary.

During part of the morning the children should have opportunity for free-choice activities outdoors. This enables them to try out the slide, swings, sandbox, climbers, and other apparatus, and to start learning desirable ways of using each. Another period for free-choice activities acquaints the children with the play centers arranged indoors.

A first day should always include a story because story time, a favorite time at home, links home with preschool group, mother with teacher. The story itself may reinforce this link if it is a story such as *Papa Small*.[10] Whatever her choice of a title, the teacher chooses a well-written story that deals with familiar experiences. The story should be relatively short,

---

[10] Lois Lenski, *Papa Small* (New York: Henry Z. Walck, Inc., 1951).

because listening to a story in a group situation may be a new experience for some of the children.

Story time is also a good time to talk briefly about one or two of the important ideas about school. Both individually and in a group, each child needs to be reassured in words about the security he has in his preschool group: "The grownups love you and will help you whenever you need help. The other children are friends too." Singing a friendship song is one way to bring in these ideas in words. Assisting mothers and teachers express their feelings and tell of their role as they start working with the children: "I'm one of the mothers who loves you. May I help you with that shoelace, Stevie?"

The importance of a child's first day in a preschool group, his first day after vacation, or his first day after an illness is apparent in the experience of Jimmy, not yet three years old, very happy much of his first day at nursery school because to him it represented considerable accomplishment. For months he had watched the children at the playground nursery school, and had longed to have the children as his playmates. When he had asked his mother about going to the school, she had explained that the nursery school did not take little boys who wet their pants. So Jimmy learned in two weeks how to keep dry pants by going to the bathroom.

Jimmy was two years nine months old his first day at nursery school. His mother brought him and, after he was introduced to his new surroundings, asked, "Do you want me to stay here with you, or may I go home and do the ironing?" Jimmy said, "Go home." That day was a rainy day in March. No one thought to tell Jimmy's mother that rainy days were short school days, and that she should come for Jimmy at 11:30 instead of 11:45 A.M. By eleven o'clock, Jimmy was tired; by 11:30, very tired. Other mothers came to take children home, but Jimmy's mother did not come. The teacher and her own little boy were busy putting things away while Jimmy sat and waited. Finally his mother came and took him home.

The next morning, and every morning for the rest of the school year, Jimmy's mother asked, "Do you want me to stay here with you, or may I go home?" Every morning Jimmy answered, "Stay here." When his mother had to go for any reason, Jimmy said, "I'll go with you."

When nursery school began the next fall, Jimmy had his mother stay for the first few times. Then one morning he said, "You can go home and do your ironing. I don't need you." His mother, who did not have any ironing to do that morning, went home. She felt that Jimmy's unhappiness the first day of nursery school was finally integrated into a pleasant first year of schooling.

MAINTENANCE ROUTINE

The following examples emphasize the importance of routine in the day of the preschool child.

Neal entered nursery school when he was a sensitive three-and-a-half-year-old. He needed his mother to help him cope with the new children, new activities, and new location. Each morning he had her come with him and stay during the morning. By November he developed a mother-child routine fitting in with the nursery school routine. He and his mother now came with the car-pool. When nursery school began, with all the children gathered together in a circle with their teacher, Neal sat in the circle with his mother beside him. As soon as the "Good morning" song was sung, he turned to his mother and said, "You go now." He then waved goodbye to her in his special way as she left.

The first nursery school morning following Christmas vacation, Neal's mother was with him for the entire morning because she was helping the teacher. The second morning, Neal had her come in the car with him, as usual. But the morning circle was not held as usual. At her usual departure time Neal's mother asked him, "Shall I go now?" "No, not yet," Neal said. When Neal's mother had to leave an hour later for an appointment, Neal went with her.

The next nursery school morning the circle was held as usual at the beginning of the morning. As soon as the "Good morning" song was sung, Neal whispered to his mother, "You go now," and she left. The routine of nursery school made it possible for Neal to feel in command of himself and his situation again. He could give his mother the proper signal at the proper time, and carry on by himself for the rest of the morning.

This kind of experience is familiar to the wise preschool teacher. She is therefore careful to follow the simple routine of the morning—especially at the beginning of the school year, when children are reaching out for stabilizers, whenever school resumes after a holiday, and whenever a sensitive child returns to school after an illness or other extended absence. She knows that the familiarity of routine helps children to feel at home. She knows, too, that children must learn a routine before they are in a position to learn variations on it.

When Neal was three-and-one-half years old, he and his five-year-old brother Stanley were accustomed to walking to a neighbor's house to drive to kindergarten with the neighbor's girl, Susan, and her mother. Neal would ride back with Susan's mother. The morning that Susan's daddy was to take the car to work just at school time, the children were unable to accept the idea of Stanley and Susan driving to kindergarten with Susan's daddy but without Neal. Both boys burst into tears. Neal was speechless, but Stanley said, between his tears: "If you change it, you call us. Then Neal won't come." The tears of both boys disappeared as soon as the original plan was put into operation. As usual, Susan's mother drove Susan, Stanley, and Neal happily to kindergarten, left Susan and Stanley, and returned with Neal, who then walked home.

This incident illustrates the reaction of preschool children to sudden changes in routine. The three-year-old children are learning the routine.

They expect consistency in it. To contemplate change in it suddenly is frustrating to the point of producing tears and other symptoms of an emotional reaction. If the change is not carried out, the three-year-old child returns quickly to the happy stability of the known routine.

The five-year-old also finds change in routine disturbing. He can cope with it, but he needs preparation well in advance. If the need for change is explained and assurance is given that the routine will continue with only the one exception, the change can then be carried through happily.

A WEEKLY HOUR IN A PRESCHOOL GROUP

When children come once every week or two to a preschool group, the program of their day also has a rhythm of activity, but the cycle is shortened. For instance, one teacher plans activities for the first three quarters of the hour, with refreshments during the last fifteen minutes of the hour. She feels that the children are more likely to be quiet on the way home if they have had a quiet refreshment time before leaving.

When her group of three-and-one-half- to four-and-one-half-year-old children was homogeneous with a larger proportion of girls, this teacher found it possible to gather the children together as one large group for ten or fifteen minutes to hear stories. Aides stayed with the one or two children who preferred to play quietly in the doll corner, in some other quiet activity indoors, or in the sandbox on the patio. When her group of children included several vigorous four-and-one-half-year-old boys, the teacher planned a program of physical activity on the patio for them, with story and talking time indoors for the small group of children interested in that.

The teacher planned variety within the program by having variety within the same type of activities each time, for instance:

1. Children needing physical outlets go to patio to play in sandbox, on swing set, on climber, or on walking boards.
   First week: Walking board between low triangle climbers, for bouncing.
   Second week: Walking board fastened into large triangle climber, for balance and climbing.
   Third week: Large wooden box next to triangle climber, for climbing and jumping.
2. Children interested in quiet activities work at tables with.
   First week: Crayons on white paper.
   Second week: Puzzles.
   Third week: Finger painting.
3. Children may choose the housekeeping corner, dress-up clothes, blackboard, blocks or study of:
   First week: A guinea pig.
   Second week: A magnet.
   Third week: A litter of puppies.

Although record keeping is kept to a minimum in the Sunday school or other weekly group, certain records need to be made. It is important to develop simple record-keeping techniques which can be carried out quickly and without interfering with the rapport of preschool children and their teachers, enhancing it if possible. It is better use of adult time to have attention centered on the children than record making.

In a situation where many children are enrolled in comparison with those who attend, a name card can be made out for each enrollee. These are strung on a piece of yarn long enough to hang around the child's neck comfortably. When the child arrives, his name card is given him to wear. When he leaves, it is left with the teacher who later uses it to make a record of attendance.

FLEXIBILITY

How does a teacher achieve flexibility in her planning for teaching? The experienced teacher often has flexibility because she has built up files of resource material, carefully indexed and easily available. However, in addition to the materials and experience in using them, she probably also has a real affection for the children and an interest in providing them with as rich an experience as she can. She anticipates the kinds of event which may occur in their lives, and is prepared on relatively short notice to help them cope with those events.

Miss Grant, the teacher of a group of four-year-old children, knew that Sally's family was considering a job promotion which might involve their moving. The morning that she saw the moving van pulling up to a house within a block of the nursery school, she quickly replaced her plans for the day with plans she had in mind to use when Sally was on the point of moving. How much better, she thought, to help Sally think about families moving before she is actually involved in such a move herself. Furthermore, Miss Grant knew that having friends and neighbors move in and out of the neighborhood was a sufficiently common occurrence that most of the children in her group would encounter its effects sooner or later.

Miss Grant had already collected a file of material on moving. She had assembled several books, including *Moving Day*.[11] The morning that she saw the moving van at a house a block from the school, she quickly glanced through these books and chose *Moving Day* as the principal book to use with the children. Looking further in her file, she found a reference to a resource box, and opened it to find enough cardboard moving vans to give each child one to fold and take home.

In arranging the sandbox toys, Miss Grant carefully featured the large vans, and laid out doll furniture which could be used as furniture for a family moving. Before the first children arrived, Miss Grant also found time to talk with the moving men in order to find out their schedule for

[11] Mildred Comfort, *Moving Day* (Chicago: Rand McNally & Co., 1958).

the morning. She concluded that she could wait until after refreshment time to take the children for a walk that would disclose the moving van and its activities. On their return to the school the children could fold their little vans and play with them a short time before going home.

Miss Grant is a flexible teacher in that she anticipates the needs of her pupils and is well equipped with materials ready and organized for use. Her file includes materials having to do with a concrete mixer, ready to use on whatever day the concrete mixer is in the neighborhood.[12] *Telephone man, New home, Bread truck, Kittens, Puppy, New pet, Birth of a baby, Hospital,* are other entries in her file. She has found occasion to use each of these entries when evidence of the needs of one or more of her children has warranted a change in her planning.

Appraisal of a Preschool Program[13]

A preschool program can be thought of as a system through which changes are brought about in the behavior of the boys and girls who participate in the program. At the conclusion of the program, the children should be able to carry on new activities and to carry on familiar ones at a higher level of proficiency. They should have developed new beliefs and should have re-enforced desirable basic beliefs—for instance, belief in oneself as a person of worth. They should have new interests growing out of new experiences, and many new concepts. Whether such expected changes have been occurring and the extent to which they have been occurring need to be determined. Parents, teachers, and children take satisfaction in knowing that their preschool program is accomplishing what was intended. In areas where change is less than anticipated, perhaps too much has been expected or perhaps some change can be made to realize the objective with preschool groups that follow.

Recognizing that the people who meet preschool group expenses like to know what they are paying for, the teacher is concerned about appraisal of the progress of her preschool group. If she is to be re-employed, she needs to be able to demonstrate the outcomes of her employment. One way to do this is to make anecdotal records at the beginning and ending of the school term. A record for each child will show how he has developed in, for instance, ability to listen to a story, to play the role of shopper at a market, to sing a song, to help put toys away.

---

[12] Helen Heffernan and Vivian Edmiston Todd, *The Kindergarten Teacher* (Boston: D. C. Heath & Company, 1960). Chapter 16 describes reorganizing a kindergarten day to take advantage of a concrete mixer.

[13] An evaluation of a preschool program which resulted in gains in I.Q. scores over a two-year period is described in an article by Jean C. Fuschillo, "Enriching the Preschool Experience of Children from Age 3. II. The Evaluation," *Children,* 15: No. 4, 140–143, July-August, 1968.

Because appraisal of the progress of children in a preschool group is a specialty of education specialists, if possible the appraisal should be put into the hands of such a specialist as soon as the program is planned. The specialist may want to examine each child as he is about to enter the program, and may want to make observations from time to time through the preschool term. To study immediate change in children, the specialist should be able to interact with them at least at the beginning and at the end of the preschool experience. To study long-time effect, the specialist may want to be able to compare first-grade children having preschool experience with earlier first-grade children who did not have such experience.

Appraisal of a preschool program usually includes not only identification of the changes occurring in the preschool children but also determination of the value that people concerned with the program attach to it. What does the teacher think she was able to accomplish? What did parents want for their children? Do they feel satisfied with the development of their children? Do they want younger siblings to have such a program? Do the children want to come to preschool? What do they especially like to do at preschool? Such questions need to be asked and answered in order to facilitate the work of these responsible for the preschool program. Everyone concerned needs to know the goals of the preschool group, the success in attaining them, the plans for improvement, and the extent of satisfaction in what has been accomplished. Children, parents, teachers, advisors, and administrators all take satisfaction in appraising the worth of the preschool group.

Situations for Discussion

A preschool teacher is apt to find herself in situations similar to the four described here. As you think of what to do in each situation, consider whether each course of action suggested is desirable, or not. Use points brought out in the chapter as well as ideas from your own experience to justify your views. Suggest alternative courses of action to supplement those given.

SITUATION 1   As the director of a private nursery school you talk with parents wishing to enroll their children in the school. Whenever a mother comes to see you about enrolling her child, you should guide the conversation into discussion of

- What she expects the school to do for her child.
- Her own interests and activities.
- The members of her family.
- What her preschool child enjoys doing with her.
- The kind of nursery school that you have.

SITUATION 2   At the beginning of the school year, as teacher of a preschool group you meet with the new mothers to discuss the school and answer their questions abut it. In the course of the meeting you plan to show them

- The equipment and facilities of the school.
- The chart of "Expected Behavior" in this book (Table 5-1).
- Some of the arts and crafts items that the children take home.
- What activities a child participates in during the school day.
- What additional equipment is needed.

SITUATION 3   In January the mother of four-year-old Tom withdraws her son from the children's group because she thinks he is bored with its activities. As the teacher you realize that you need to make greater effort to communicate both to parents and children the importance of preschool education. You plan to

- Have the next parents' meeting discuss "Helping Children with Their Problems."
- Help the children be aware of what fun they have in the preschool group.
- Discuss Tom's withdrawal with the mother of Tom's best friend in the group.
- Say nothing to the children about Tom's leaving.
- Each year have an early fall meeting of parents to talk about preschool education for the child who is bored.

SITUATION 4   You have a new position teaching a preschool group which is one of two groups meeting at the same time. The groups share one outdoor play area and such equipment as a piano and painting easels. You feel that your new position will make it necessary for you to

- Move all the group from one activity to another on time.
- Have a repertoire of brief activities such as finger plays and hand-puppet plays.
- Allow ample time for cleaning up after an activity.
- Avoid having creative children express themselves.
- Have clay, punching bags, and other devices which provide emotional outlets.

Current Professional Books and Pamphlets

ALMY, MILLIE, ed. *Early Childhood Play: Selected Readings Related to Cognition and Motivation.* New York: Selected Academic Readings, 1968. [Lawrence Frank, Eveline Omwake, J. McVicker Hunt, and others write about the intellectual content of play.]

Association for Supervision and Curriculum Development. *Perceiving, Behaving, and Becoming,* 1962 Yearbook, ASCD. Washington, D.C.: National Education Association, 1962. [Perception followed by appropriate behavior leads to desirable child development.]

BEYER, EVELYN. *Teaching Young Children.* New York: Pegasus, 1968. [A small book by an experienced and sensitive teacher.]

BIBER, BARBARA. *Nursery School as the Beginning of Education.* Washington, D.C.: National Association for the Education of Young Children, 1960. [The

preschool curriculum includes beginnings of every phase of child development and of each part of the school curriculum.]

BLOOM, BENJAMIN S., ALLISON DAVIS, and ROBERT HESS. *Compensatory Education for Cultural Deprivation.* New York: Holt, Rinehart and Winston,
1965. [Early intervention is desirable to offset cultural deprivation.]

GRAY, SUSAN, R. KLAUS, J. MILLER, and BETTYE FORESTER. *Before First
Grade.* New York: Teachers College Press, Columbia University, 1966.
[Describes an extensive intervention program with less advantaged children.]

HAMILTON, LUCY. *Basic Lessons for Retarded Children.* New York: The John
Day Company, 1965. [Books about teaching retarded children provide a perspective on teaching normal children in the same mental age range.]

Handbook of Research on Teaching. Chicago: Rand McNally & Company,
1963. [In this publication of the American Educational Research Association
edited by N. I. Gage, Chapter 15, "Research on Teaching in the Nursery
School," was written by Pauline S. Sears and Edith M. Dowley.]

HECHINGER, FRED M., ed. *Preschool Education Today; New Approaches to
Teaching 3-, 4-, and 5-year olds.* Garden City, N.Y.: Doubleday & Company, Inc., 1966. [Views of various contributors are presented.]

HEFFERNAN, HELEN, ed. *Guiding the Young Child.* Boston: D. C. Heath &
Company, 1959. [One of the books discussing teaching methods and materials used with children from kindergarten through third grade.]

HEFFERNAN, HELEN, and VIVIAN EDMISTON TODD. *The Kindergarten Teacher.*
Boston: D. C. Heath & Company, 1960. [Chapter 5 discusses the learning
experiences in kindergarten, and subsequent chapters elaborate principles
and practices in each aspect of the curriculum.]

HESS, ROBERT D., and ROBERTA M. BEAR. *Early Education: Current Theory,
Research and Practice.* Chicago: Aldine Publishing Co., 1967. [With a series
of coauthors, Dr. Hess is making available research findings regarding guidance of learning in young children.]

LE SHAN, EDA. *The Conspiracy Against Childhood.* New York: Atheneum,
1967. [The danger of pressure for academic learning by young children is
well documented.]

MACKINTOSH, HELEN K., LILLIAN GORE, and GERTRUDE LEWIS. *Educating
Disadvantaged Children Under Six.* Washington, D.C.: U.S. Government
Printing Office, 1965. [A U.S. Office of Education publication.]

MUKERJI, ROSE and MARGARET YONEMURA. *Schools for Young Disadvantaged
Children.* New York: Teachers College Press, Columbia University, 1968.
[A useful book for preschool teachers working with less advantaged
children.]

National Association for the Education of Young Children. *Teaching the Disadvantaged Young Child.* Washington, D.C.: National Association for the
Education of Young Children, 1966. [Selected articles published originally
in *Young Children.*]

National Education Association of the United States. *Prevention of Failure.*
Washington, D.C.: National Education Association, 1965. [Earl C. Kelley
emphasizes that, "Our task is to build better people"; Donald McNassor
states that "identity in childhood is influenced significantly by school experience"; and so on.]

National Society for the Study of Education. *Sixty-sixth Yearbook,* Part I.

Chicago: University of Chicago Press, 1967. [In Chapter VII, Catherine Brunner discusses "Preschool Experiences for the Disadvantaged."]

Project Head Start. *Daily Program I*. Washington, D.C.: U.S. Government Printing Office, 1967. [0-247-829 and other booklets in the Project Head Start series contain excellent suggestions for guidance of preschool children in a group.]

ROBISON, HELEN F., and BERNARD SPODEK. *New Directions in the Kindergarten*. New York: Teachers College Press, Columbia University, 1965. [One of several good books dealing with the kindergarten or with the nursery school.]

RUDOLPH, MARGUERITA, and DOROTHY H. COHEN. *Kindergarten: A Year of Learning*. New York: Appleton-Century-Crofts, 1964. [Based on the belief that children's needs and interests provide the foundation for the curriculum, with early learning through experimentation, exploration, and manipulation.]

SCHULMAN, A. S. *Absorbed in Living: Children Learn*. Washington, D.C.: National Association for the Education of Young Children, 1967. [Behavioral development is stressed.]

SIGEL, IRVING E., and HOOPER, FRANK H., eds. *Logical Thinking in Children— Research Based on Piaget's Theory*. New York: Holt, Rinehart and Winston, Inc., 1968. [Sigel and others developed a training procedure for acquisition of Piaget's conservation of quantity.]

WANN, K., M. DORN, and E. A. LIDDLE. *Fostering Intellectual Development in Young Children*. New York: Bureau of Publications, Teachers College, 1962. [Describes procedures designed to encourage intellectual development.]

WILLS, CLARICE, and LUCILE LINDBERG. *Kindergarten for Today's Children*. Chicago: Follett Publishing Company, 1967. [A paperback based on the child-development point of view and replete with practical suggestions for appropriate experiences.]

WYLIE, JOANNE. *A Creative Guide for Preschool Teachers*. Racine, Wis.: Western Publishing Company, 1965. [Western Publishing Company is associated with Golden Press, Whitman Publishing Company, and other companies.]

The Young Child—Reviews of Research. Washington, D.C.: National Association for the Education of Young Children, 1967. [Eighteen articles by different authors describe current research about behavioral development in early childhood.]

Films for Teachers and Parents

The Aggressive Child, a Preschool Behavior Problem. New York: Contemporary Films, 1965; twenty-eight minutes, sound, black and white. [A six-year-old who fights is helped through play therapy.]

Betty Sees a Bird. Hartford, Conn.: Information and Education Department, Aetna Life Affiliated Companies, n.d.; sixteen minutes, sound, black and white. [Volunteers, teachers, and nurses test vision of preschool children.]

Blocks. New York: Campus Film Productions, n.d.; sixteen minutes, sound, color or black and white. [This unrehearsed film shows children from five to eleven years of age learning to use blocks.]

Brushing Your Teeth. Chicago, Illinois: American Dental Association, n.d.;

five minutes, sound, color. [Presents methods of brushing teeth approved by most dentists.]

Building Children's Personalities with Creative Dancing. Los Angeles: Bailey Films, 1957; thirty minutes, sound, black and white. [Listening to music, children express feelings in dance movements.]

A Community Nursery School. New York: New York University Film Library, 1966; forty minutes, sound, black and white. [A community defines its goals and provides a nursery school for its children.]

A Day in the Life of a Five-Year-Old. New York: Teachers College, Bureau of Publications, Columbia University, 1949; twenty minutes, sound, black and white. [Activities of a kindergarten group throughout a day.]

Finger Painting Methods. Chicago: Coronet Instructional Films, 1954; eleven minutes, sound, color. [Demonstrates ways of guiding children in finger painting.]

Focus on Behavior: The Conscience of a Child. University Park, Pa.: Audio-Visual Aids Library, Pennsylvania State University, 1963. [Growth and development of emotional expression are studied at Stanford University.]

Food for Freddy. New York: Sterling Educational Films, Inc., 1953; seventeen minutes, sound, black and white or color. [Canadian Department of National Health and Welfare shows the value of an appetizing menu, wise purchase of food, and proper food storage.]

Four- and Five-Year-Olds in School. New York: Modern Talking Pictures Service, Inc., 1954; thirty-seven minutes, sound, black and white. [Four- and five-year-old children work and play at Vassar College Nursery School.]

Frustrating Fours and Fascinating Fives. New York: McGraw-Hill Text Films, 1952; twenty-two minutes, sound, black and white. [Typical behavior of four- and five-year-old children.]

Growth Through a Two-Year Kindergarten. Carbondale, Ill.: Department of Audio-Visual Aids, Southern Illinois University, 1956; seventeen minutes, sound, black and white or color. [Activities are planned and carried through.]

Guiding Behavior. Los Angeles: Churchill Films, 1966; twenty minutes, sound, black and white. [What limits are necessary on the activities of a nursery school child in order to protect him and others?]

It's a Small World. New York: Contemporary Films, 1951; thirty-eight minutes, sound, black and white. [Activities and routines of a day in a London Day Nursery from early morning through late afternoon.]

Pathways Through Nursery School. Chicago: International Film Bureau, Inc., 1964; twenty-five minutes, sound, color. [At Stephens College two students observe and participate in a nursery school.]

Pine School. University Park, Pa.: Pennsylvania State University, 1965; thirty minutes, sound, black and white. [Group experiences for mentally retarded children, ages three to six from underprivileged homes.]

Planning Creative Play Equipment for Young Children. Berkeley, Calif.: Extension Department, Media Center, University of California, 1960; sixteen minutes, sound, color. [Play equipment is devised to stimulate dramatic play.]

Pre-School Incidents No. 1—When Should Grownups Help? New York: New York University Film Library, 1950; fourteen minutes, sound, black and white. [Four episodes in which adults do not intervene.]

Pre-School Incidents No. 3—When Should Grownups Stop Fights? New York:

New York University Film Library, 1950; fifteen minutes, sound, black and white. [Four conflict situations involve children ages two to five years old.]

Principles of Development. New York: McGraw-Hill Text Films, 1950. [Child development is continuous, with both patterns and individual differences.]

Setting the Stage for Learning. Los Angeles: Churchill Films, 1966; twenty-two minutes, sound, black and white. [The nursery school child should have equipment to stimulate his activity, learning, and imagination.]

Techniques of Non-Verbal Psychological Testing. Chicago: International Film Bureau, 1964; twenty minutes, sound, color. [At Children's Hospital in Los Angeles, tests make it possible to identify normal and abnormal children between the ages of six weeks and six months.]

Terrible Twos and Trusting Threes. New York: McGraw-Hill Text-Films, 1951; twenty-one minutes, sound, black and white. [Typical behavior of two- and three-year-olds.]

They Learn from Each Other. Detroit, Mich.: Wayne State University, Audio-Visual Center; twenty-nine minutes, sound, color. [At nursery school much play of preschool children is solitary.]

Time of Their Lives. University Park, Pa.: Pennsylvania State University, 1962; twenty-nine minutes, sound, black and white. [A kindergarten classroom shows interrelationships of children.]

Two- and Three-Year-Olds in Nursery School. New York: New York University Film Library, 1950; thirty-seven, sound, black and white. [Two- and three-year-old nursery school children have a variety of activities within a day and within a season of the year.]

Understanding Children's Drawings. New York: A. F. Films, Inc., 1949; ten minutes, sound, black and white. [Three- to seven-year-old children at the Manhattan Jewish Center progress from scribbles into forms and designs, and into telling stories through pictures.]

Visual Perception and Failure to Learn. Los Angeles: Churchill Films, 1964; twenty minutes, sound, black and white. [Accurate visual perception and eye-motor coordination in tying a shoe may involve difficulties in learning and need for guidance.]

Filmstrips for Teachers and Parents

A Day in a Jerusalem Kindergarten. New York: Pioneer Women, 1958; fifty-eight frames, silent with text, color. [Kindergartens help government, working mothers, and the children themselves.]

A Day in the Kindergarten. Tujunga, Calif.: Herbert M. Elkins Co., 1957; forty frames; silent with captions, black and white. [Shows a typical day in a well-organized and well-equipped kindergarten.]

A Good Day in the Kindergarten. El Cerrito, Calif.: Long Film Service, 1956; twenty minutes, sixty frames, sound, color. [Produced by Helen Heffernan, this filmstrip for California Association for Childhood Education shows groups of parents and teachers what a good kindergarten is like.]

Children and the Church. St. Louis, Mo.: Christian Board of Publication, 1955. [A series of filmstrips and disc recordings for The National Council of Churches includes: "Nursery School and the Church" (seventy-six frames, silent with captions, black and white) and "Kindergarten Child and the Church" (seventy-two frames, silent with captions, black and white).]

Going to School Is Fun. Jamaica, N.Y.: Eye Gate House, Inc., 1959; twenty-nine frames, silent with captions, color. [Shows such school activities as coloring, listening to a story, having lunch, singing songs, and playing in the school yard.]

Kindergarten and Your Child. Detroit, Mich.: Wayne University Audiovisual Materials Consultation Bureau, 1951; forty frames, silent with captions, black and white. [Explains the nature of the kindergarten program and how parents can cooperate with the school.]

Nursery School—A Planned Program for Three- and Four-Year-Old Children. Thousand Oaks, Calif.: Atlantis Productions, Inc., 1963; eighty-two frames, twenty-five minutes, sound, color. [Produced and narrated by Helen Heffernan, this filmstrip shows typical experiences of children in a nursery school program.]

Tommy Goes to Kindergarten. Jamaica, N.Y.: Eye Gate House, Inc., 1954; thirty-eight frames, silent with captions, color. [Tommy is invited to visit kindergarten, observes its activities for a day, and is eager to attend regularly.]

Part Two
THE CURRICULUM
FOR THE GROUP

CHAPTER **6**

Health and Safety

Of the utmost importance to a preschool group as well as a school group are the health and safety of its children. If a child is to learn, he must be well. As soon as possible he must learn the health habits and the safety precautions commensurate with his age level. The preschool or school group can be of help only to children who are present and ready for learning experiences.

Even with the best of precautions, children of the preschool age range are often absent. The child's first venture into a larger world, whether it be for nursery school, kindergarten, or first grade, brings him into contact with more people—and with more hazards to his health. His first year in a group is one in which he builds up immunities to certain diseases; his second year, one in which he builds up immunities to other diseases. One health-minded mother pointed out one of the less-mentioned advantages of a preschool group as she said to the first-grade teacher: "My children never miss a day in the first grade. I send them to nursery school and kindergarten so they are all over the mumps and measles and the other diseases that children usually get when they start school."

The importance of mental and physical health in children is pointed out by Daniel Prescott as follows:

The child's health affects his classroom mood, learning, concept of and feelings about himself, and relationship with parents and with other children.[1]

Certainly, the behavior of a preschool child is related to the maturity level he has reached in his growth and development, his energy output, and his handicaps and limitations. Those who work with preschool children are vitally concerned with the health of the children: good health is

[1] Daniel Prescott, *The Child in the Educative Process* (New York: McGraw-Hill Book Company, Inc., 1957), p. 354.

essential to them now, and to their ability to develop optimally in the future in school.

Maintaining the Health of the Children

Because preschool children are so highly susceptible to illness, several precautions are necessary in order to maintain the health of any such group.[2] When he joins the group, each child should be examined by a physician. Both the doctor's report and a report of the health history of the child should be on file for use as needed.

Each child should be inspected each day to be sure that he is well. At the same time, provision must be made to care for the child who suddenly becomes ill or injures himself.

The preschool group recognizes the importance of good food in helping children to stay well. Careful attention is therefore given to the serving of food and to the sanitation of provisions for handling it.

Records of height and weight show the pattern of growth for each child and are a base against which to view his development.

ENROLLMENT MEDICAL EXAMINATION

When a child enters a preschool group, he should be examined by a competent physician. This examination should determine whether the child is physically ready to participate in the group activities or whether any limitations should be placed on his participation. At the same time, the child should be immunized to such communicable diseases as whooping cough, diphtheria, smallpox, measles, and poliomyelitis. Because he is apt to suffer small cuts in school, the child should also be protected from tetanus.

An increasing number of preschool groups get health information directly from the physician who examines the child. This is done by giving the parents a form to be mailed or taken to the physician. This form is filled out and signed by the physician (usually without charge), and returned directly to the school. Descriptive information regarding the nursery school is helpful to the physician in assaying the child's readiness to participate in the preschool group. At the same time, it gives him the information he needs as a basis for recommending to other families that they give their preschool children group experience.

The assurance that a child is physically ready to participate in activities with other children is so important that many preschool groups which meet only weekly require a medical examination, especially for participation in swimming or dancing classes. Such a requirement is made by teachers sin-

[2] Office of Economic Opportunity, "Project Head Start—Medical." Washington, D.C.: U.S. Government Printing Office, 1967. (Outlines an eight-point medical program for a child development center.)

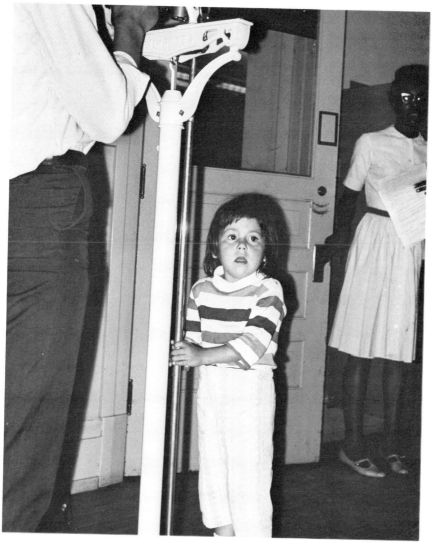

Weight and height records show growth. (Courtesy of Minneapolis Public Schools and Mrs. Mary Jane Higley, Minneapolis, Minnesota.)

cerely interested in the best development of the children. Thoughtful parents of preschool children select group activities which require a medical examination before enrollment.

HEALTH HISTORY

Many preschool groups find it helpful to have a health history on file for each child. In case of contagious illness, the director can look at the health history forms to see what children are immune to the illness by virtue of inoculation or natural or acquired immunity and which children may be vulnerable to it. She can then get in touch with the families of the vulnerable children to warn them that their children have been exposed to a contagious disease.

A typical health record form asks for information such as that given below. It is filled in by a pupil welfare aide, a teacher, or an assistant teacher.

Health Record[3]

1. *Identification*

   Child's Name _____

                 Last   First   Middle

   Address _____

           Street   City   Zip Code

   Birth Date _____ Sex _____

   Parents or Guardian _____

   Address _____

           Street   City   Zip Code

2. *History of family health*

   General Health: Good   Fair   Poor if dead; cause of death

	Good	Fair	Poor	if dead; cause of death
Mother	☐	☐	☐	_____
Father	☐	☐	☐	_____
Sibling	☐	☐	☐	_____
_____	☐	☐	☐	_____
_____	☐	☐	☐	_____

   Check if family history includes:

Allergies	Heart disease	Rheumatic fever
Anemia	Jaundice	Syphilis
Bleeding disorder	Kidney disease	Tuberculosis
Diabetes	Mental disorders	None of above
Epilepsy	Mental retardation	
		_____
		Other

   Does family have a family doctor?   If yes, name: Dr. _____

                                            Address: _____

[3] Adapted from a form of Economic and Youth Opportunities Agency.

3. *Obstetrical and neonatal history of child*

Check if complication occurred; and show month of pregnancy

Anemia	Infections
Bleeding	Kidney disease
German measles	Swelling
High blood pressure	

Duration of pregnancy: _____

Months   Weeks

Duration of labor: _____

Hours

Method of delivery: Vaginal   Caesarean _____

Condition of child at birth?   Good   Fair   Poor

Birth weight: _____ lbs.   Birth length: _____ Inches.

Neonatal complications. Check if complication occurred.

Anemia	Convulsions
Birth defects	Cyanosis
Bleeding	Feeding problems
Breathing difficulty	Jaundice

4. *Development history of child*

At what month did child walk? _____ month
When did he say single words? _____ month
When did he use sentences?   _____ month

5. *Illnesses*

Check if child had illness; and show age at time of illness

Chicken pox	Kidney trouble	Polio
Convulsions	Measles (red, seven-day)	Rheumatic fever
Diabetes	Meningitis	Scarlet fever
Diphtheria	Mumps	Tuberculosis
Heart trouble	Pneumonia	Whooping cough

Check illness that the chid has now:

Asthma	Reaction to medication	Bone or joint disease
Eczema	(Specify) _____	Frequent colds
Hay fever	_____	Frequent ear infections
Other allergies	_____	Frequent sore throats
(Specify) _____	Anemia	Paralysis
_____	Bleeding disorder	

Hospitalization: Reason _____ Age _____
Hospital: _____

Name   Address

Surgeries or operations: _____

6. *Immunizations*

Give dates of immunizations if known

a. DPT: #1_____ #2_____ #3_____   d. Small pox vaccination
   Most recent booster _____   Primary_____
b. POLIO: Most recent booster _____
   A. Shots #1____ #2____ #3____   _____
      Most recent booster_____
   B. Oral type I____ II ____ III ____   e. List any other immunizations
      Trivalent #1___ #2___ #3 ___   _____
      Most recent booster_____
c. Measles   f. Reactions to immunizations
   Killed #1_____   _____
   Killed #2_____   _____
   Live_____   _____

Person taking history given above: _____
                                                    Signature

   Date:_____   _____
                                                    Position

Information about eating and toilet habits is useful to the teachers of the children's groups as they help incoming children with their daily routines. A child is more comfortable in learning to be a member of a group if his personal habits fit in easily with the activities of the group.

Especially for preschool groups which have a family social worker or a parent-education program that includes conferences and group meetings, it is valuable to know parental opinions about the child's health, personality, and care. Such opinions indicate the point at which to start working with parents in supporting or improving their ways of thinking about their children.

DAILY INSPECTION

Personnel of preschool groups are generally agreed that there should be a daily health inspection, but they differ in their ideas as to who should make the inspection and how it should be made. In some groups, a nurse in uniform (for example, from the Visiting Nurse Association) carefully checks each child; she looks into his throat, notes his skin and eye condition, and talks with him briefly to see how he feels. In other groups, the teacher can depend to a considerable extent on daily health checks by parents who have been instructed in how to observe the health of their children and in the importance of sending the child to school only if he is well.

When the child is dressed in the morning, his mother has a chance to notice whether or not he has a fever. Her hug and kiss also provide an opportunity to make sure he is well. She must realize that if he has a temperature he must forego preschool until twenty-four hours after his temperature has returned to normal, and she must be prepared to have him cared for whenever necessary. The mother of preschool children knows from experience that her best-laid personal plans are subject to change at any time.

Since health is of prime importance, even the driver who picks up preschool children and drives them to school also must take responsibility for screening out any sick children. The child who is coming down with a contagious disease may infect the other children in the car. The morning that John is becoming ill with mumps, he may give them to his companions before he ever reaches school. The driver therefore should look closely at each child as he helps him into the car. If any mother expresses concern that her child may become ill during the day, the driver should encourage having the child remain at home or should carefully transmit those fears to the teacher, who will watch for signs of illness during the day.

At the school or center, the **teacher**—or a nurse—should check the state

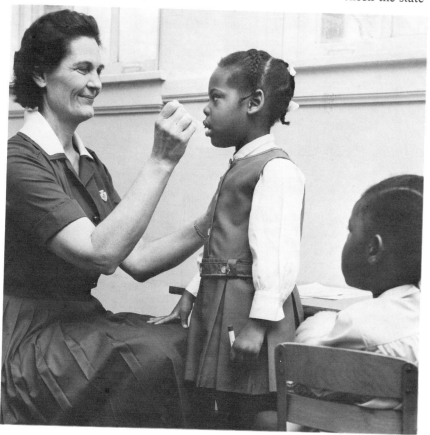

With people you trust, health inspection is a usual part of the preschool day. (Courtesy of Lincoln Public Schools and Nebraska Association for Childhood Education.)

of health of each child quickly but carefully. In most groups, the teacher makes her own health inspection and is conscientious about looking closely at each child as she greets him at the beginning of each session. She notices whether there is any evidence of fever and whether the child deviates in any way from his usual pattern of behavior. If a child has become ill on the way to school, he should be isolated from the other children so that he can play quietly and the others will not be exposed to his illness.

The sensitivity of the teacher to any unusual behavior in a child is probably the best safeguard to the health of each individual child and that of the group. If the teacher notes any change in the way a child acts, she should continue to observe him until she has determined if he is physically ill, emotionally upset, or otherwise in need of unusual attention from her.

PROVISIONS FOR INDIVIDUAL CHILDREN

The preschool child may be well when he comes to the school or center, yet develop a fever within an hour or two. He may be in control of himself one minute and lose control the next. He may be playing happily and suffer a sudden accident. Such rapid changes make it necessary for the school or center to be prepared at all times for helping the individual

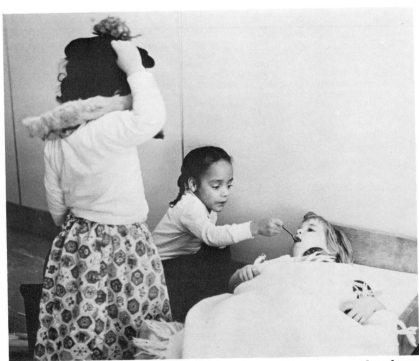

Dramatic play prepares children for roles they suddenly may need to know. (Courtesy of The Merrill-Palmer Institute and Donna J. Harris, Detroit, Michigan.)

child with any emergency. It therefore should have a first-aid kit, a room in which a child may play quietly by himself or rest on a cot, and a file containing the telephone numbers of each child's parents and physician, together with a signed statement permitting the preschool group to obtain medical assistance in an emergency.

The usual first-aid kit for adult or family use is supplemented with supplies suited to preschool children. There are Band-Aids for cuts on tiny fingers, round Band-Aids as well as rectangular ones and colored ones for those who need the distraction of making a simple choice. There is a disinfectant which does not sting (for instance, ST37). The kit of first-aid supplies is kept out of the children's reach, but in a place where it is easily available either indoors or outdoors. Every grownup in the school must know where it is and be prepared to make immediate use of it.

Probably the most important provision for first aid is a calm adult. Preschool personnel are practiced in moving quickly but quietly to where they are needed. They know that their calm and pleasant demeanor is essential to the calm of the children, and that the sight of a shrieking and running adult may be far more upsetting to the child than the usual minor accident. Often a potential accident is avoided because an undisturbed child is able to complete successfully his awkward attempt to regain his balance. Adult calmness is reassuring to children and helps them in having trial-and-success rather than trial-and-error learning.

When a child is hurt, the nearest adult must determine what to do with the child and with the other children. Can the hurt child rest where he is? Can the other children be interested in play at some other spot? As soon as possible, a second adult must be summoned so that one adult can have responsibility for the group of children; the other, for the injured child. Every preschool group must have a second adult available at all times.

All the children—including the hurt child—are interested in what has happened. The calm teacher should realize that the children are curious and take advantage of the educational opportunity at once as well as later. She may explain:

Mary slid down the trunk of the tree the way she usually does. But today she did not have long trousers over her legs, and the rough tree bark scraped some of the skin off her legs. I'm going to get something to put on the scrapes so that they will feel better and any germs on them will be killed. Mary is going to sit here and rest, and everyone else can go on playing. I'll be right back.

The assurance of the teacher and her obvious confidence in the fact that each child will do what he should while she gets the first-aid kit and additional adult help are good examples for the children. If the teacher is unsure about a particular child, she should take him with her instead of leaving him in the children's group during the brief interval she needs to be gone. "Tony, I'll need your help," she may say, and Tony can be important and responsible in bringing something back either for Mary or for the group.

The nursery school or center is also prepared to help the child who has a toilet accident or who slips into a puddle on a rainy day. To be suddenly wet often upsets the poise of a child. Especially if he is a three-year-old he may be unwilling to accept dry clothing or help in changing into it. He is more apt to change his clothes if the teacher has discussed with the group the possibility of such an emergency and has had each child bring a change of clothing to be kept on the top shelf of his locker. The teacher may reassure the wet child: "You need some dry clothes, Russell. Did you know you have some here? Remember you brought extra clothes in case you fell into a puddle. Aren't we lucky, though! We have this nice pair of pants. . . ."

Part of the first-aid provisions for a preschool group is a quiet place where an individual child may rest if he is ill and is about to be taken home. This room may have other uses as well, especially if it adjoins the office of the director. It can be a place for an adult to rest, a place for health examinations, a place for a toddler who has come with a parent, or a place to take an emotionally disturbed child. The room's floor, walls, and furniture should be easy to wash. The room should have a window with an inside screen; a cot or bed which has a plastic mattress cover as well as washable sheets and blanket; modeling clay, a toy hammer, and other indestructible toys within reach of children, with other toys for quiet play easily available on high shelves.

An isolation room is necessary for a child who is emotionally disturbed. It must have physical outlets for the child who feels like hitting and kicking, and soundproofing to take care of his crying. When a child is temporarily out of control, some modeling clay to pound, a hammer toy to hit, or a balloon man to punch gives him an opportunity to release the feelings that adrenalin and other secretions from his endocrine glands have created inside him. Using these emotional releases, the child is able to work out his emotional disturbance to the point at which he is able to rejoin the group.

NUTRITION

Children's centers and other preschool groups that have children during mealtimes are responsible for meeting the nutritional needs of the children and must work with the parents in seeing that each child has the food he should have. Records of changes in the height and weight of preschool children show that children at these ages are growing and developing at a rapid rate. Furthermore they are physically vigorous as they participate in a variety of school activities. To be sure that the children have the energy they need, careful attention must be given to their diet.

The children's center does three things to meet the nutritional needs of the children who attend. First, it provides a noon meal that has about one third of the child's daily food requirements as outlined by the National Research Council, including a protein dish of meat, fish, or eggs, or an occasional meat substitute such as peanut butter, cheese, dried beans, or peas. Second, it informs the parents about what the children will have to eat. This is often done by posting on the bulletin board the menus for the coming week and by sending a copy of them home with each child on the preceding Friday. Third, it provides for any needy child a breakfast, snacks, and dinner which the child might not otherwise have.

In preschool groups that keep children for the day, the personnel responsible for feeding the children should make every effort to serve them wholesome food that is simple but attractive. They may capitalize on the contrast between pink ham and green peas, for instance, and provide other food attractions. But they should avoid such items as the expensive ice cream molded to please adult gourmet tastes. They should make a point of getting acquainted with the nutrition specialist who is responsible for the lunches served in the local public schools, and of consulting her as needed. In short, they must realize the importance of their responsibility and make every effort to carry it out to the best of their ability. This includes the development of sanitary personal habits which help to keep the food free from germs—especially the habit of washing hands before working with food and after going to the bathroom. It also includes proper attention to the washing of dishes and cooking utensils so that they are also free from germs.

In the preschool group for less advantaged children it is important to "establish sound nutritional practices by providing food to program participants as well as educating families in the selection and preparation of food in the home."[4] Good nutrition attempts to assure prevention of impairment of physical growth and mental development. A good physical basis is essential to success in the learning process; the preschool program in nutrition is a major factor in helping a child to be ready for school. It has the further advantage that "learning to think of mealtime as a pleasant occasion for conversation with other children and staff members may represent a significant step in the process of social development."[5]

Suggested patterns for breakfast, snacks, and lunch assume that the impoverished child should be given food at each opportunity, as follows:

A Pattern for Breakfast
    Fruit or fruit juice
    Milk
    Cereal, bread or roll
    Plus one or more of the following:
        piece of cheese

[4] Office of Economic Opportunity, "Nutrition—Better Eating for a Head Start." Washington, D.C.: U.S. Government Printing Office, 1967, p. 2.
[5] Ibid., p. 3.

egg, hard cooked or scrambled
peanut butter

. . . .

The Mid-morning or Mid-afternoon Snack could include one or more of the
following:
Fruit, such as orange sections, apple wedges or peach halves
Raw vegetable pieces . . .
Milk
A piece of cheese
Juice—either fruit or vegetable
A Pattern for Lunch
Meat, poultry, fish, egg, cheese, peanut butter, dried peas or dried
beans (choose one of these)
Bread and butter or margarine
Raw or cooked vegetables
Fruit or cooked dessert
Milk[6]

In the parent-cooperative nursery school, the mothers and the teacher
decide whether juice time is to consist only of juice or of juice and a
cracker. Some groups think that having more than juice keeps the children
from eating a good lunch. Other groups think that a cracker as well as
juice are a desirable midmorning snack for the children. Probably either
method is all right. Certainly the children should have something to eat or
drink to prevent fatigue. Whether they do or do not have a cracker or two
will probably make little difference in what they eat in the course of a week.[7]

Whether children are eating a snack or a noon meal, they should enjoy
it. Pleasantness makes for good digestion; irritability may interfere with it.
Knowing this, the adults who are with the children at mealtimes are calm,
happy, cheerful people who make available to children what there is to eat,
quickly replace and quietly clean up what is spilled, and guide the children
in conversation if they are old enough to eat and converse at the same
time. Attention to several details makes for more pleasant eating times, for
instance:

1. Distribute grownups so that each child may have the adult attention
   he needs.
2. Use dishes that are lightweight and designed for stability (i.e., more
   weighted at the bottom than at the top).
3. Pour liquids up to half or two thirds of the way from the top of the
   glass, rather than to the top.
4. Place liquids in front of children and beyond their other dishes. Explain

[6] Ibid., p. 5.
[7] Research of Dr. Clara Davis showed that over a period of time with a variety
of wholesome food available, children choose a good diet. Dr. Benjamin Spock
reports the research in *Baby and Child Care* (New York: Pocket Books, 1967),
pp. 274–276.

Breaking and tasting a coconut is a delightful new experience. (Courtesy of Seattle Public Schools, Seattle, Washington. Photograph by Royal C. Crooks.)

this placement to the children from time to time as a means of preventing spills from sudden movements of elbows or arms.

5. Serve small portions attractively. Have second servings available for those who want them.

6. Have a fund of finger plays and simple action stories for those children who finish before the others.

7. Let the children participate in the food rituals as much as they can at their age level. Children may take turns in seeing that everyone has a paper napkin before eating and an opportunity to put it in the waste-basket that is passed around after the meal.

Mealtimes in a preschool group should never be made unpleasant by making the children conscious of how they are or are not eating. The teachers should know that each child, when he is ready, takes on the table manners of those who eat with him, but that conscious awareness of table manners is appropriate for children in elementary school, not in a preschool group. The girls are more apt to acquire table manners similar to those their mothers or teachers use before boys of the same age do. Of course the grownup may sometimes teach desirable table manners, but she does not expect the children to learn them. She should praise desirable manners when she observes them, but she does not criticize poor manners or be-moan their absence. She may say: "Do you know where I am going to put my glass of juice? [Holds it up.] Right out here where I can reach it but where I won't hit it with my elbow. [Puts the glass down above her other dishes.]" Or a kindergarten teacher may turn the conversation to how people eat by saying: "Have you ever noticed how grownups hold their spoons? When I hold it this way [demonstrating], my elbow stays down at my side and I don't get in the way of my neighbor"; or by saying: "Jeannie is holding her spoon with her fingers the way grownups do. Good for you, Jeannie."

SANITATION

The nursery school or kindergarten should have provisions for the sani-tary handling of food and be kept in good general condition. Regular cleaning and orderliness are part of the lives of children. "Children don't notice," says the operator of one private nursery school as she hastily dusts before the public health inspector arrives. But she should realize that the children are constantly absorbing and imitating the ways of people around them. The children in every preschool group should have teachers who appreciate the importance of sanitation and incorporate it into the life of the school. Cleaning should be done regularly, not just for the approach of a visitor. Laundering and other housekeeping should be considered im-portant and receive careful thought and attention. Supplies and equipment should be kept in order and maintained in good condition for maximum use. Attention to cleanliness and order makes for a well-functioning pre-school group with happy children and adults at work in it.

MENTAL HEALTH OF THE CHILDREN

An atmosphere of love pervading the preschool group is the best guar-antee that the children will be in good mental health. But the school also needs to know something of the out-of-school conditions in which the child lives. If the school is to help a child with his fears and anxieties and with his relationships to other people, it may find it useful to obtain from parents pertinent facts and opinions about the child's siblings; daily home schedules; ability to dress himself, go to the bathroom, and wash his hands; favorite relatives, friends, games, and toys; and any fears he may have. Such data constitute a starting point from which to determine what additional information should be obtained through observation of the behavior of the child and through conferences with his parents or guardian.

In working with preschool children from less advantaged families, a teacher not only attempts to provide an atmosphere of love and appreciation and to minimize fears, but also endeavors at every possible point to maximize the self-confidence of each child. "Children from disadvantaged families often seem to feel uncertain of who they are, what they look like, and how they fit into their world."[8] The preschool teacher can help such children build a favorable self-image through expanding their awareness of who they are and what they do.

"Good morning, Tom."
"Mary waited for us at the corner. Now we can all cross the street together."
"Sally painted a blue picture this morning. Pedro painted a red one.'
"You did a good job. You should feel good about it."

Besides helping each child develop awareness of himself as a helpful, capable person, a teacher also carefully avoids reenforcing awareness of fears and inadequacies. She helps a child substitute approach for withdrawal; "I need help," for "I'm afraid;" and "I'll try," for "I can't." A teacher's faith in each child may make the difference between his following routes to success and routes to cumulative failure. Some of the concepts for each child to develop are:

"I am_____(name)."   "I am_____."
"It's mine."   first name   last name
"I see it."   "I'll share it."
"I want it."   "I'll show you."
"I say it."   "Give me it?"   "I choose this."
"I_____."   "I tell him."
       familiar activity   "I try to_____."
                                    new activity

[8] Office of Economic Opportunity, "Project Head Start, Daily Program I, For a Child Development Center." Washington, D.C.: U.S. Government Printing Office, 1967, pp. 26, 27.

Health Requirements for Grownups

Realizing the vulnerability of preschool children, the adults who work with them should be careful to maintain their own health at a high level. They must realize, as Dr. Stainbrook has said: "Every emotion of the teacher (fatigue, headache, and other physical manifestations) escapes into the learning situation of the child. . . ."[9] Before they begin work with their preschool group, they should make sure that they are in good physical and mental health and free from contagious illnesses. Not only should they precede their work with a medical examination, and arrange to have an annual chest X-ray examination, but they should also obtain medical assistance whenever they feel the need of it. They should protect themselves, and the children at the same time.

SICK LEAVE

In order to protect the health of its children, the preschool group should encourage its personnel, both grownups and children, to stay at home whenever they are in the early stages of a respiratory illness. Because the first seventy-two hours of a cold are a contagious period, grownups—as well as children—should stay at home during that time. Sick leave without loss of pay for preschool personnel helps them to realize that their responsibility will be carried on while they take care of their health needs. "I didn't feel like coming, but I didn't want the children to miss out on nursery school," expresses an attitude that is not in keeping with the good health of the children. The adult who has sick leave, on the other hand, can say: "I felt as if I might be getting a cold. I stayed home so that I would not expose anyone else to the illness."

Every preschool group, in advance of illness, should make provision for the responsibilities of each member of the staff to be carried on in case that member is not able to be with the group. Assured of these provisions, each staff member is better able to think objectively about her health in relation to the best interests of the children.

Keeping Children Safe

The teacher should plan always so that the children will be safe. When taking them for a walk, for instance, she anticipates the hazard of crossing a street and uses this situation as an opportunity for helping the children to learn how to keep themselves safe. She talks with them about staying

[9] Quoted in *National Association for Nursery Education Convention News,* No. 3, (June 19, 1959).

together. Then she helps them each find a hand-hold on "the magic rope" which keeps them together as they cross the street.

The teacher also should plan activities that will introduce no hazards. If she sets out the carpentry tools and materials, she should check to be sure that the other activities available to the children at that time will be familiar ones which require a minimum of supervision. The teacher should set up the carpentry center at a time when the children will probably not need to go to the bathroom. Thus she can be sure that she will be at the carpentry play center as the children learn the simple rules that keep the activity a safe one:

Tools stay at the carpentry bench (i.e., they are not carried around).
Tools are used only for the job at hand (e.g., a hammer is for hammering nails, not a child's fingers).

Only when the teacher has made certain that the children carry on an activity safely should she lessen her supervision. Carpentry is an activity for which she provides continuous supervision, but some other activities are different. If there is a group of three-year-old children taking turns on the slide, the teacher should first help each child learn how to hold his feet against the sides as a means of slowing his descent. When she knows that each child can stop himself at any point on the slide, she can give the slide a minimum of attention and go on to enrich the program with other activities. However, she should realize that when the children move into the four-year-olds' phase of exploring variations on sliding, she will again need to supervise the slide rather closely. In their eagerness for a turn, the children need to be reminded to go to the end of the line, to keep below the heels of the person above them on the ladder, to have their heads up at the bottom of the slide, and to clear the track for the next person.

The teacher also should remind the children in the outdoor play area that they need to have their hands free to use in the sand, to enjoy the apparatus and equipment, and to examine whatever they wish to pick up. Some children, she realizes, also need to have the security of a favorite toy or some article brought from home. She has to be ingenious in finding solutions for conflicts between these two needs. She learns how to help the little three-year-old child find a safe place for her dolly to sleep while she is busy playing and how to remind the four-year-old boy that guns come to nursery school only for brief showing, not for shooting.

Supervision of Play Activities

The most important factor in having a safe preschool group is not fencing in the play area or limiting the hazards to those that are an integral part of learning activities, but providing the best quality and quantity of supervision for the children. The personnel of the school or center must become acquainted with each child as rapidly as possible so that they can predict what each child is apt to do. Only when a teacher is able to predict behavior accurately is she able to provide each child with the freedom and guidance which enable him to learn safely through experience.

Four-year-old Stanley, a boy with unusual sensitivity to people and a great interest in the world about him, liked to work with the puzzles at nursery school. One morning he came indoors, sat down at the table, and started doing a puzzle. When he had finished it, the adult supervising indoor activities admired his accomplishment and asked, "Would you like to do this one?" Because the puzzle she presented was new to Stanley, he was interested in it and worked hard in putting it back together. When he finished that, the adult started to show him a third puzzle. Stanley said, "No!"—and threw the puzzle down. The adult then attempted to enlist Stanley's help in picking up the pieces; he reacted negatively and more vigorously. The teacher, who had come into the room, diverted him to physical activities outdoors.

Later, the teacher and the adult who had supervised indoor activities that morning discussed what had occurred. The teacher explained that although Stanley was indeed capable of unusual accomplishment and concentration, he was a four-year-old with a four-year-old's ability to conform to the demands of a situation only for a limited period of time. Stanley had stayed too long at a demanding task and had swung to the negative behavior of a tantrum out of sheer fatigue. The teacher pointed out that expecting too much of a child at Stanley's level may lead not only to difficulty for Stanley but also to danger for any person within Stanley's range of throwing. The teacher helped the adult in learning to observe children more closely and in learning at what point to divert them to less demanding activities that they will find relaxing.

The experienced teacher knows that she must be able to predict the behavior of children—for her own safety as well as that of the other children. The child who runs to his mother and hangs on her with his arms around her neck may transfer that mode of expression to his teacher. Or the child who hits his mother when she is not able to give him what he wants may express his frustration toward his teacher in the same way. Because nursery children are in the process of learning to sublimate their emotional reactions, their teachers need to be prepared to cope with direct, physical expressions of them. Fortunately, young children have neither the aim nor the force that they will have later, but their teachers must know how to substitute a rubber figure or some other resilient material for themselves while they help the children to find better ways of expressing their emotions.

Establishing and Maintaining Limits

The way in which the teacher helps children to understand and maintain limits has much to do with their safety. If she gives them no guidance in recognizing limits and behaving in terms of them, she leaves the children to learn by trial and error. The children feel insecure and make repeated efforts to explore limits. In doing so, they are apt to learn by experience of the hazards to their physical safety. The teacher must help the children to learn safely what these hazards are. The teacher who—through ignorance or emotional problems—is unwilling to do this is unfit to teach four-year-old children who are eagerly exploring the limits of beliefs, skills, and ideas that they have been acquiring. The teacher has to help the four-year-old boy who tries jumping from higher and higher places to realize that he can safely jump only from his own height. She has to help him realize that although he is "tough," he is not tough enough to go without his jacket on a cold and windy spring day. In short, whether or not he remains safe and well depends on the teacher's ability to communicate to him what his limits are and the importance of keeping within them.

But if the teacher is too authoritarian in establishing and maintaining limits with preschool children, she may contribute to their becoming prone to accidents. She must help the children to do what they want in such a way that they will see the importance of having limits and will work with her in deciding what limits are necessary and in helping to enforce these limits. The first sand-throwing incident should be the occasion for getting the children together to realize that this is a problem, and that sand must be kept down. From then on she must be ready to remind them: "Sand hurts our eyes." She should be careful to maintain the limit exactly as it was established. When a child asks if he may throw sand at a target he has set up, she may remind him, "We don't throw sand," and add, "The wind might blow it into your eyes." She knows that the children have learned the limits when she hears them reminding each other of them.

In general, a teacher should try to establish with the children only those few limits which are necessary for their protection. An occasional rule is necessary for the protection of the school property, but a few will do if materials and equipment have been carefully selected for durability and smoothness of surface. The teacher should keep the rules to a minimum in order to maintain her role of helping the children to do what they want to do. Too many rules will make her seem like a person who nags and may interfere with the children's learning that rules are one of the ways to help them do what they want to do.

PUPIL-TEACHER RATIO

The number of pupils supervised by one teacher has much to do with the safety of the children. When the teacher has no more than fifteen three- or four-year-old children during a nursery session that is only two and a half hours long, she can—with the help of assistants—find it possible to have a few minutes of intimate rapport with each child. In this way, she can keep each child reminded of her love and appreciation for him as an individual. She can give him a security that makes him feel his self-importance, keep him in sympathy with her suggestions for his safety, and help him to keep himself safe.

But when that same teacher has more than fifteen nursery children in her group, and only one aide, she may no longer be able to give each child the time and attention that he needs. A child who has gotten demonstrations of love and affection whenever he fell or otherwise hurt himself may seek such demonstrations from adults at school. Such a child, if given no help with his problem, soon reaches the point at which he can be accurately described as accident-prone. Another child, feeling outside the love of his teacher, may withdraw into quietness which will become part of an adolescent neurosis. In short, for children with uncertainty in their family relationships, lack of certain affection in relationships within their preschool group may make the difference between a child who has good mental health and one who has not. The pupil-teacher ratio needs to be sufficiently low so that each teacher can be sure she has time during each school session to make each child feel her love and his own importance.

Not only should the pupil-teacher ratio be kept low, but also the number of children supervised by one adult during dangerous activities. An assistant teacher can help two or three children as they learn to saw or hammer, but she must arrange for other children to have turns at a later time. "When Johnny is through using the hammer, he will tell you that it is your turn," she may suggest. Then she can help the waiting child find some intermediary activity by asking, "Is that your favorite tricycle that I see parked near the drinking fountain? Now's your chance to ride it—if you get there before someone else does."

Whenever a new activity is introduced in a preschool group, it is presented to a few children at a time. In this way, the teacher may be sure of what each child has learned. This method takes more time at first, but it is safer and saves time over a period of weeks. The children learn the proper way of carrying out the activity and have no poor habits to correct later. Their interest is higher because it has been enhanced by rapport with their teacher. Furthermore, better initial learning results in more pleasurable and efficient practice later. The children feel more secure in the activity and are less prone to have accidents.

Those who are interested in real preschool experience for children, rather than child care alone, are always in favor of keeping the pupil-teacher ratio at whatever level the teacher thinks best for the children. Teachers differ in their ability to relate to children. Some require a longer period with each child in order to feel satisfied and happy with their relationships. When the pupil-teacher ratio is maintained in terms of the teacher's preference, the teacher—and the pupils as well—have greater satisfaction and better mental hygiene. And they are safer.

HEALTH RECORDS FOR EMERGENCIES

Nursery school and kindergarten personnel have so much to do that they should not be burdened with keeping unnecessary records. At the same time, certain health records are vital to the welfare of the children and essential to the safe operation of the preschool group. For instance, the director of the school or center should have on file in her office, ready for immediate use, those records that enable an injured child to have medical attention at once.

Suppose that a child falls in such a way as to make a large gash on his face. The teacher and the director must keep in mind that stitches may be needed to close the wound and that these must be obtained within half an hour if the child is to have a reasonable chance of avoiding a disfiguring scar to carry through the rest of his life. The teacher stays with the group and the director removes the injured child and puts him to rest quietly for a few minutes while she quickly gets his record from the files. The emergency information form enables her to telephone the child's physician. After describing the injury, she gets his suggestion about where to take the child for help. She gives to another adult the paper with the telephone number of the parent and of a second responsible person who

Children's Center[10]
Consent Form

During the school year beginning _____ 19___ and ending _____
19___ I, _____, who am the father _____, mother
_____, guardian _____ of _____, give permission for:

Dental examination	Yes____ No____
Hearing test	Yes____ No____
Vision testing	Yes____ No____
Medical examination	Yes____ No____
Hemoglobin test	Yes____ No____
Hematocrit test	Yes____ No____
Urinalysis	Yes____ No____
Diphtheria-whooping cough-tetanus immunization	Yes____ No____
Measles immunization	Yes____ No____
Polio immunization by mouth	Yes____ No____
Smallpox vaccination	Yes____ No____
Tuberculin test	Yes____ No____
Study trips	Yes____ No____
Films or photographs	Yes____ No____
Emergency treatment in the event of accident or injury as deemed necessary by the Children's Center	Yes____ No____
Transportation of child for above procedures	Yes____ No____
Transfer of health and other records obtained through above procedures, to public schools	Yes____ No____

Signed _____ Date _____

[10] Adapted from a form of the Economic and Youth Opportunities Agency.

may be contacted in case the parent is not at home. While her assistant is endeavoring to reach the parent or parent substitute, the director puts in her pocketbook the form which has the parent's signature permitting emergency medical care for the child. Ten minutes later, the director is at a medical center with the child. In this way, she is able to obtain medical assistance for the child within half an hour.

Such prompt action in an emergency is possible only if the necessary records are on file in the office of the director. (For families who have religious objections to medical care, the file contains instead a signed statement that no medical care may be given.)

Education for Safety

SAFETY AT HOME OR SCHOOL

The mother of the one-year-old toddler is completely responsible for his safety. Until he is able to take over some of that responsibility, she has to be with him during all his waking hours. She should guide her child toward keeping himself safe. By the time he comes to a nursery group, the child should have learned to respond to adult commands such as a simple, firm, "No. That can hurt you." What else he has learned depends on his level of maturity and on the training he has received.

In the preschool group, the safety-minded teacher should continuously guide the children in ways of being safe. For instance, if she picks up a board with a bent nail in it, she may say to any children within hearing, "That could hurt us. Let's put it in the trash barrel." If she is working with less mature children, she will let a child carry it while she accompanies him to the trash barrel. With more mature children, she will let a child take complete responsibility for putting the hazardous board in the trash. In either case, she rewards this action with justifiable praise, "Good. That board can't hurt anyone now."

As she closes a cupboard door, the teacher may say, "We close the door so no one can bump his head on it. Are you tall enough to bump your head on cupboard doors like this, Jimmy? You soon will be. That's why we always close them. Open the door; close the door."

When a liquid is spilled, the teacher may say, "We need our sponges!" A sponge for the child who spilled the liquid gives him a means of expressing physically any emotional reaction he may have. The teacher gives another child a sponge, and uses one herself, too, to show the children that everyone helps to clean up. As the teacher finishes the cleaning, she should point out to the children that they have all helped to keep everyone safe. "There!" she may say. "Now no one can slip and fall. We all cleaned it up."

When she helps a child to turn on the water faucet, the teacher should ask if he can turn it off when he is through. "Show me how you do it," she may say if he thinks he can. If he succeeds, she says, "That's fine. That's what you will do when you are finished with the water. Okay?" If he cannot turn the water faucet off, she may say, "When you are done with the water, come and get me or another teacher to help you turn it off. Will you do that, please? Good."

If children start a construction project in a passageway, she should help them move it out of the passageway—talking with them, meanwhile, about why they must do this. She may enliven the conversation by pantomiming what might happen to her if she came along that way and stumbled over the blocks, and saying, "You don't want me or anyone else to get hurt like that, so, let's move the castle right now."

The teacher should avoid trying to teach the children things that are beyond their age level. For instance, she may remind them to close the door so the heat will stay inside or so the flies will stay outside. But she does not ask them to close the door quietly. They will have to have several years of experience in opening and closing doors before they will be ready to develop conscious techniques of closing doors quietly. The quiet closing of doors, the conscious use of the handrail on a flight of stairs, and the carrying of chairs safely require techniques beyond the ability of nursery children.

However, the teacher should be consistent in closing doors as they should be closed because many children, learning by imitation, will come to handle the doors as she does. The teacher should illustrate correct form in such matters, but she should not expect that the children will learn them.

The teacher of nursery children should guide them in learning how to handle the problems they have at their own age level. These include the following:

- Bringing broken toys to the teacher.
- Telling the teacher about broken glass.
- Picking up nails or boards with nails in the play area.
- Closing whatever doors they open.
- Turning off faucets they turn on.
- Cleaning up whatever is spilled.
- Playing out of the way of passersby.
- Going slowly, because speed causes accidents.

Older children can learn more safety measures. A five-year-old girl can learn to tie her shoelaces so that she will not trip over them. Kindergarten children can learn to move in a circle, all going in the same direction; they can learn to carry scissors correctly. Both four- and five-year-old children can learn to use carpentry tools only at the workbench and to avoid carrying them around. The more mature the children, the more responsibility they can assume for their own safety. Their parents and their teachers must know how much that responsibility is so they can avoid overprotection, on the one hand, and overexpectation, on the other.

ACCIDENTS

Increasing attention has been given to accidents, the leading cause of death in children from one to four years of age.[11] In 1943, Gesell and Ilg wrote in *Infant and Child in the Culture of Today,*

. . . the incidence of accidents is determined by three sets of interacting factors: (1) the child's physique, (2) his behavior traits, and (3) exposure to risk. These, in turn, are intimately related to the developmental status. Since the 2-year-old leans forward when he runs, falls are likely to bruise the forehead. Later, as the stance becomes more erect, the nose becomes the favorite site of injury. Somewhat later, at 3 or 4 years, the teeth are struck and still later, at 4½ years, the collarbone. . . .[12]

Among nursery school children, boys are more vulnerable than girls and certain children have a tendency toward being injured. Bakwin and Bakwin elaborate both points. Of the difference between boys and girls in accident rates, they say:

The accident rates are much higher for boys than for girls. . . . There are several reasons for this. Boys are more aggressive than girls. They are, in addition, more daring and reckless and are, age for age, less mature. Another consideration is the general biologic inferiority of males.[13]

Of accident-prone individuals, the Bakwins say,

It has been conclusively shown that certain persons are especially prone to have accidents. . . . The characteristic personality pattern of the accident-prone adult is said to be established during childhood in response to parental overauthority. . . .

Some children engage in habitual reckless play which brings repeated injury. They may have fear, unexpressed hatred, and guilt feelings. Injury causes the child to receive attention and sympathy, but there are also indirect benefits, such as avoidance of disagreeable situations and evasion of responsibility. Hurting himself and thus relieving his sense of guilt is probably primary.[14]

The teacher of preschool children can do three things which help to keep accidents to a minimum:

[11] *Accident Facts* (Chicago: National Safety Council, 1965), p. 14.
[12] Arnold Gesell and Frances L. Ilg, *Child Development* (New York: Harper & Row, Publishers, 1949), p. 254.
[13] Harry Bakwin and Ruth M. Bakwin, *Clinical Management of Behavior Disorders in Children* (Philadelphia: W. B. Saunders Co., 1953), p. 454.
[14] Ibid., pp. 454 and 457.

1. She can make the school a friendly, warm place in which each child feels secure and important.
2. She can avoid being an authoritarian figure. She can lead the children by helping them to do what they want to do, rather than by having them do her bidding.
3. She can capitalize on any accidents that do occur by guiding the children toward realizing that behavior is caused.

In these three ways, the teacher can help preschool children to establish nonaccident habits.

The preschool teacher also can help an injured child to talk about his accident. She may listen sympathetically to his fragmentary account and then tell it back to him: "You were running fast and that stool was in your way, so you fell over it." Later, with a larger group of children and her flannelboard, the teacher can bring out the cause-and-effect relationships further, perhaps much as one kindergarten teacher did:

TEACHER Tommy was running fast. One of the stools had been left right in his way. Tommy fell over it. Next time what can we do so we won't have any more accidents like that? What can Tommy do?
(*Group discussion.*)
TEACHER That's right. Next time, walk. Don't run. Going fast causes accidents. And what else can we all do to keep from having such an accident again? Where are we going to leave our stools?
(*Group discussion.*)
TEACHER Yes, we'll put our stools along the wall, not where people walk.

By letting the children talk out their doubts and fears and helping them plan how to avoid future accidents, the teacher is laying the foundation for good mental hygiene and helping the children cope with failures and mistakes as well as successes. When they are seven years old and older, the children, like their teachers, will be able to talk about the cause-and-effect relationships between behavior and accidents.

SAFETY IN THE STREETS

Teachers must appreciate the fact that automobiles are the primary cause of accidental deaths among children from one to fourteen years of age.[15] On excursions, and in school (with the use of flannelboard and toy cars), the preschool teacher should make clear to the children that the street is for cars, not for children. She may say, "Look both up the street and down the street, and listen, to be sure no car is coming. When you are sure no car is using the street, then go across." She also should emphasize the importance of helping the driver of a car see where children are. She

---

[15] Such data are available in pamphlets put out by life insurance companies.

A safe car for future drivers. (Courtesy of Long Beach Day Nursery and Mariam M. Cook, Long Beach, California.)

may say, "When a car is backing away from the curb or coming toward it, stand back so the driver of the car can see you are safely out of the way of the car." Or she may say, "When you want to cross the street, stand on the curb where you can really see both up the street and down the street. Do not stand next to a parked car because it hides you." In the daily routine of school, the teacher should always take time to see that each child practices only safe ways of relating himself to cars and to streets.

It is during the preschool years that children develop the ability to cross a street safely. Gesell and Ilg point out the age characteristics which make these years an auspicious time to teach a child safety habits that he will carry through his life.

It is not until two and a half years that he visually sees and is aware of the danger of a car backing up toward him. At three, he continues to accept his mother's hand as he is crossing a street. At four he is more watchful, more conscious of objects coming from both directions, and longs for the independence of crossing a street absolutely alone. The culture knows that he often overstates his abilities at this age, but responds to his eagerness by allowing him to cross narrow, safe, streets (though not thoroughfares) without holding of hands. By five he is less eager and more self-regulated and accepts the new and helpful control of traffic lights, with his ever-watchful eyes. It is now that he is capable of greater independence. . . .[16]

BEING SAFE IN A BOAT

In a community in which families live or vacation near lakes, rivers, or the seashore, the teacher should help the children learn how to be safe in a boat, especially by sitting on or close to the bottom of the boat. She may dramatize the hazards of a boat as did one teacher who, like several of her four-year-old boys, was sitting in her cardboard box, pretending it was a boat. As the convoy of "boats" went along the edge of the "lake," the teacher helped the children imagine the trip:

TEACHER   We certainly have had a good trip. Let's paddle into shore now, straight onto that lovely beach. Remember to stay sitting toward the back so your boat can go up onto the sand. Sit still until the boat stops moving. (*Suddenly the teacher stands up in the boat, drops her paddle, and falls headlong beside the boat.*)

TEACHER   Oooops! I fell into the water! I stood up too soon. When the boat hit the sand, the jerk threw me out of the boat. (*Continuing her pantomime*) Oh, I'm all wet. Dripping! And I'm all cold. Quick! I'll have to wrap up in my dry coat to get warm. I won't stand up like that again! We have to sit still when the boat is in the water, don't we? Did you sit still until your boat landed, Jimmy?

(*Jimmy nods.*)

TEACHER   Oh, good. You didn't fall in the way I did, did you? How about you Jerry?

On another day when the children are playing with their "boat," the teacher may start to stand up to look at the fishing line, but "remember" the rule in time to avoid falling in. On other imaginary adventures near the water, the teacher should make a point of having each child put on his life preserver, or an empty gallon can slipped into a cloth bag so that it can be tied firmly around the child's waist. Gradually she should help the children incorporate the wearing of a life preserver into all their dramatic games with "boats" and "fishing."

KNIVES? MATCHES?

In every community there are many parents who pride themselves on never letting their young children handle knives or play with matches. In this way they avoid teaching the children safe ways of cutting with a knife or striking a match, and are pleasantly surprised when their children learn these techniques outside their own home.

Knowing the fears and anxieties of parents, the wise nursery school teacher does not avoid the dangerous activities, but makes sure that the parents understand in advance how they are introduced at the school. At

[16] Gesell and Ilg, op. cit., pp. 54–55.

a parents' meeting, prior to the introduction of knife-cutting activities at school, she demonstrates how a teacher works with two or three children at a time, showing them how to hold and use a paring knife properly as they explore cutting some soft media such as sterofoam, apple slices, or soap. She emphasizes the two rules for safe cutting: (1) keep your fingers out of the way of the blade, and (2) always cut away from yourself.

The wise teacher points out that the use of a knife is taught only under adult supervision, and only to four- and five-year-old children who show that they are ready for the activity. She concludes her presentation by saying that knife-cutting activities are offered at school only in the interest of safety. Any parent who prefers teaching his child the danger and the use of the knife himself may ask the teacher to exclude his child from the activities. Learning-to-cut activities should be available at school only for those families who want their children to participate.

The teacher should listen attentively to the parents' discussion after her presentation. If there is considerable negativism expressed directly or indirectly, she should have very little cutting in the preschool program. Later in the year, at another parents' meeting, she can again bring up the question: "Shall we have some more cutting for the children?" If there is little negative comment, she can then provide more opportunity for cutting in the school program.

The teacher should take the same precautions about teaching the use of matches to the children. She discusses with the parents whether or not to have the children learn to light a match under careful supervision. She demonstrates how an adult guides the activity bringing out the following:

- A pan of water is available for putting out the match.
- The safety-match box is carefully closed before the match is struck.
- The match is struck by moving the hand away from oneself.
- The lighted match is blown out and is put into the pan of water.

Whether or not the parents wish their children to have school guidance in handling matches, such a demonstration will make them better able to help their children learn the proper use of matches at home. The teacher can conclude her demonstration by asking each parent whether she wants her child to learn the activity at school or to learn it at home.

In bringing up such questions as whether or not to have knives or matches for the preschool group, the teacher is furthering the safety education of the children. Whether parents decide to take responsibility for such teaching themselves or to share it with the school, they are better able to guide their children after seeing a demonstration and participating in a discussion about it.

A third question for discussion with parents is how to help children in handling toy guns. The number of accidents that children have with real guns is evidence that children need to be taught from the first to point guns at targets and away from people. Even though toy guns are excluded from nursery school and kindergarten equipment, their use should be discussed with parents because they occur so frequently in the toys that children receive as gifts.

Education for Health

Both preschool parent and child should constantly enlarge their understanding of how to maintain good health. A parent education program, especially a program for less advantaged parents, should include education of parents with regard to maintaining their own health and that of their children, making use of community health facilities, and increasing their understanding of usual family health problems. In the health education program for parents in one early childhood education center, topics for each parent meeting were selected on the basis of parent response to an opinionnaire. During one month, weekly meetings with a registered nurse or a pediatrician as speaker dealt with the following topics:

Bed wetting, mental health, sleeping problems, care of the skin.
Health in the schools.
Alcohol and community resources to help the alcoholic.
Family planning.
Menstruation, the birth process, gynecology.
Venereal disease and its control.
Drug abuse.
Smoking, weight control.
Dental health, thumb sucking.
Symptoms of illness in preschool children, communicable disease.

In addition to the general health education program, each children's center in a less advantaged area has a health education program that is an integral part of the program for maintaining the health of the children through physical and dental examinations followed with remedial treatment and immunizations as needed. The effectiveness of the total health education program is apparent in records of children's centers that have been maintained over a period of years. With no change in the program itself, other than variations to make it fit the needs of the current group, the number of health problems per family grows less as the family benefits from its participation in the program of the children's center. Experience with a first child is of benefit to siblings.

Vital to the health of each child is his own education about how to keep himself well. Such learnings are particularly appropriate for the nursery group. First, the sooner these learnings are acquired, the better. Second, the nursery child is highly egocentric: he learns best what concerns himself.

Problems of his own health and safety can be made vivid to him and what he learns will be of use to him throughout his entire life. He should be pleasantly introduced to the importance of eating wholesome food, of seeing, of breathing, and of keeping well. And he should be given favorable impressions of dentists, doctors, nurses, and community aids to health. Such introductions and impressions are the foundation on which subsequent concepts, skills, and beliefs about health will be built.

The preschool child also needs guidance and help as he learns the skills associated with his primary problem in development, namely, the use of the bathroom as a place to relieve himself of the waste products of his body. Throughout the nursery years, he learns to deal with various aspects of the toileting problem. His concern with it is so great that his feelings of success or failure in solving the problem may easily enhance or hinder his learning in other matters. The nursery school adult should be aware of the importance of giving each child the assistance that he needs in solving the problems associated with those of the toilet, including timing in getting to the bathroom; zipping and unzipping and unbuttoning and buttoning clothes; and the cleaning-up and hand-washing routines.

TAKING CARE OF ONESELF

Preschool children must be taught how to care for themselves, especially how to:

- Use the bathroom.
- Get a drink when thirsty.
- Wash hands (using soap) before eating.
- Put on or take off outer clothing as needed, and change to dry clothing when wet.
- Stay at home when ill.

These learnings occur as the child develops appropriate awareness. Use of the bathroom proceeds rapidly after two and one half years of age, as a child notices urination and bowel movement sensations. A child learns to get a drink when he relates getting a drink to the sensations of thirst. Sometimes, five-year-old children still need guidance in recognizing thirst feelings and in making this association. The washing of hands before eating is a habit sequence that can be learned by preschool children through repetition and imitation as well as by older children who associate the procedure logically with having germ-free food.

Putting on or taking off outer clothing according to the temperature is learned by children when they develop awareness of their tactile sense and associate these sensations with the addition or deletion of wraps. Willingness to stay at home when ill also depends on recognizing and interpreting bodily sensations. The following conversation between two four-year-olds illustrates the developing awareness that preschool children have of bodily processes:

SUSAN *(who has returned to school after three days of absence with a cold)*
    I don't got a bad cold.
NEAL[17]   When you blow like that, you got a bad cold.

A preschool child learns when and how to wash. (Courtesy of the Department of Home Economics, University of Utah, Salt Lake City, Utah.)

HELPING A CHILD WITH TOILETING

The nursery teacher must accept toilet accidents as a form of behavior typical of nursery school children. In order to be casual about them, she must attain objectivity about her own toilet training, and put aside any

---

[17] Neal is the preschool boy who was studied in most detail for this book. His behavior is reported in Chaps. 6 to 15 in respect to each area of the curriculum. The anecdotal material about Neal is the kind which can be collected by any preschool teacher wishing to work with a child and his mother in making a study of the behavior of an individual child in preschool group situations.

squeamish reactions to excretory products. Understanding the importance of excretion to the health of the individual, she should be able to share the pleasure of three-year-old children who are proud of their accomplishments in learning different aspects of these toileting processes. She must realize that the child who no longer wears diapers is yet learning how to cope with the clothes he does wear. He must also come to feel at home in bathrooms other than his own, with toilets that feel different from the one at home, with toilet paper placed in a different place. The more acute his sensitivity to spatial details and to interpersonal relationships, the more complicated the child finds the learning process.

Neal, at three and one half years, was only a few months removed from his initial experiences in going to the toilet. He was still learning how to manage his clothing. This problem was complicated by his great admiration for his older brother's trousers that opened down the front, and his insistence on wearing the same kind, complete with belt. Since the belt did not hold the trousers up, Neal also wore suspenders. With colder weather, Neal's problem of going to the toilet was often complicated by outer clothing which he felt had to be removed.

The morning that Neal had an accident at nursery school, the nearest adult hastened to help him. Neal, in his frustration, hit her hard in the face. She retreated and gave her attention to wiping up the puddle. Several minutes later another adult diverted Neal to a group activity.

Neal is an example of a child who is best left alone when he has a toileting accident. His sensitivity was so great that he found it necessary to limit his problems in order to cope with them. Furthermore, he considered toileting a private matter with which only his mother might help him.

A four-year-old child is less apt to have clothing problems. In fact, he is quite nonchalant about the toileting routine. His problem is one of timing: knowing that he can manage the whole affair, he waits until the last possible moment before starting for the bathroom. Of course, among a large number of successes in his learning process, there is an occasional miss.

The teacher should be nonchalant about toilet accidents. If a four-year-old wets his pants, she ignores the matter until the other children are out of hearing distance. Then she may inquire casually of the child: "Say, how about changing to these dry pants? I'll bet you didn't even know that you had another pair of pants at nursery school. Let's put them on in the bathroom, and I'll put your wet ones in a bag for you to take home when you go." In another year, the child will be as independent as five-year-old Susan, who looked on toileting as one of the social events of her day and asked, "Who wants to go BM with me?"

At no time should the teacher tell the child: "Aren't you ashamed of yourself?" Nor does she say. "You should know better than that," or in any way show a negative reaction to the accident. She must keep in mind that such accidents are an important part of developing skill in using the

bathroom. She should be careful to see that no undue attention attaches
to the incident because a child's attention needs to be directed toward his
successes, not his errors. She must have confidence that his future trials will
be increasingly successful. "Start a little sooner, and you'll make it next
time," she may say comfortably to her preschool companion in the
bathroom.

The following excerpt from a teacher's year-end report to parents illustrates the objective, kindly attitude of a mature person toward the toileting
education of preschool children. Reporting on three-year-old Don, she said:

Don's mother hesitated to send him to nursery school sooner because he
had outdoor bathroom habits. It is interesting that I have never once seen him
use the yard instead of the toilet. Of course we have never taken a dim view
of this convenient action of some of our boys—and we have always had one or
another of them who sometimes used this time-saving method of urinating, if
you'll forgive the expression.

In the nursery school that includes among its objectives for the children
the development of skill in urinating and in having a bowel movement, it
is not surprising to find an aide who made the following note early in
December:

I feel that Priscilla and I are becoming good friends. Today she asked me
to take her to the bathroom.

Or to find a child like Cindy who, at the age of three years and four
months, asked, "Can you come and clean my bottom? Or to find a child
like Kimmy who, at the age of about two and one half years, was beginning
to be aware of bathroom procedures and asked her four-year-old sister,
"Do you like to be lonely in da baffoom?" and, at the age of three and one
half years, asked the kitty, "Don't you wish you had a mommy to wipe
you?" and told her sister who was with her in the bathroom, "The next
boomy (BM) is going to be a big one. It's going to be a giant and it will be
friendly to me, but not to you. You will get bited by da giant boomy." As
a more mature four-year-old, Kimmy had the following conversation with
an adult about going to the bathroom at nursery school:

ADULT Kimmy, you went to the bathroom by yourself this morning!
KIMMY Yes, but I'm not big folks any more. I always get iddo [little] in da
middo [middle] of when I'm getting to be big folks.

In such ways the nursery child grows toward the self-sufficiency which
characterizes the five-year-old child.

INTRODUCING NEW FOODS
In the nursery group children have an opportunity to enlarge their list
of "wholesome food I like to eat." Each child comes from a home in which

certain foods are eaten regularly. He is accustomed to this diet and feels at home when familiar items are served to his preschool group. His enthusiasm for an item is an incentive for other children (who may not know the food) to try it. The teacher who appreciates the importance of the children learning from each other can use this imitation method by saying, "Ummm. I like it too."

Children can also be taught to like a food by a favorable introduction followed by practice—at intervals—in eating the food. One nursery school teacher noticed that several children in her group were not used to eating

Familiar foods and sometimes new foods. (Courtesy of Long Beach Day Nursery and Mariam M. Cook, Long Beach, California.)

peanut-butter sandwiches. She found a nearby market where peanuts were ground to make fresh peanut butter. She told the children about it one morning and helped them plan a study trip for the next school morning. After the trip, when the children returned to school, they all enjoyed crackers spread with the fresh peanut butter. The following day, the peanut butter was served again, with enthusiastic review of the trip and of the goodness of the butter. Two days later, the peanut-butter crackers were again served. The next week they were on the menu twice; the following week, once. From then on, peanut butter appeared from time to time as frequently as other items on the menu.

Getting children to enjoy different foods is an important objective during the nursery years. Prior to those years, children enjoy baby foods—which include applesauce and a variety of other processed fruits and vegetables—singly, and in combination with other foods. Between that early period and the time when adolescent growth makes them eager eaters they learn consciously to enjoy different foods. The preschool child is in a period of awareness in which he can be guided to appreciate and, presently, to eat what a beloved adult enjoys eating. His rate of learning is not fast, so he adds new foods only gradually. Even parents who have overexpectations about what their children should eat can realize that with each passing year the child is eating foods that he did not consciously eat before. They need to be aware of such casual remarks as one that Neal made when he was four years and eleven months old: "I want to get stronger than you, Dad. That's why I drank six glasses of milk today."

Making discriminations about foods is something of which a child may well be proud. But the boy who notes that crusts are different from the rest of the slice of bread sometimes may demonstrate his awareness by not eating his crusts. He can get individual attention from his busy mother by insisting that the crusts be cut off the bread he eats. However, at the children's center, he should be able to get attention by eating the crusts first, the way his teacher does because she thinks them so delicious.

Nursery school and kindergarten can help children to enjoy different fruits and vegetables and to learn the value of fruits and vegetables in keeping well. One teacher, who had made a point of having the children enjoy apples in the fall of the year and bananas during the winter, was pleased with her conversation with Stanley (five years and eight months) and Neal (three years and ten months) the morning that Susan (five years and seven months) brought a note of excuse for her absence of the day before:

SUSAN   Read this. (*Hands note to teacher.*)
TEACHER (*reading*)   "Dear Mrs. Teacher. Susan had tonsilitis Friday."
STANLEY   I eat apples every day.
NEAL   I don't get sick.
STANLEY   Neal eats lots of bananas. Neal asks for lots and lots and lots and lots of them.

The teacher was pleased that Stanley and Neal associated the eating of fruit with keeping well. She felt that each year she would continue to provide the children with a series of experiences with each fruit in season—for instance, with apples: eating red apples, eating golden apples, finding a star in the middle of the apple, eating apple slices, eating apple circles, drinking apple juice, and making applesauce. By having such delightful experiences spaced through the fall season, the children come to enjoy apples.

IMPORTANCE OF SEEING

Halloween is a good time to introduce children to the importance of being able to see well. Four- and five-year-old children like to try on a mask. When they have it on, the teacher should help them realize that they cannot see as well as usual.

A teacher who thought it important to prepare her children for going trick-or-treating that evening talked with them just before they went home about how to wear their masks:

TEACHER   We've had a lot of fun today with our costumes and our masks. Raise your hand if you've had fun.

(*All raise hands.*)

TEACHER   Do you know the best place to wear a mask?

JOHN   On your eyes.

JANE   Like yours.

TEACHER   Right up here on our foreheads. That's the best place. Do you know why it's the best place?

(*Various responses.*)

TEACHER   It's the best place because it let's us see. When I wear it down here, I can't see very well and I'm apt to stumble and fall. (*Pantomimes this.*) When you go trick-or-treating tonight with your mother or daddy, where are you going to wear your mask?

CHILDREN   There.

TEACHER   That's right. On your forehead. Then when you're at a friend's house, if you really want to, you can pull it down to scare your friend. But be sure to put your mask right back up on your forehead. Show me where you're going to wear your mask. Put your hand on the place. That's right. Not on your eyes, but above them, on your forehead.

From time to time after Halloween, as the occasion arises, the teacher can remind the children about how glad we are to have eyes that can see. Whenever the children are to cross the street, they can remember with their teacher that they will use their eyes as well as their ears to be sure that no cars are coming. Whenever they are walking on uneven ground, they can remember to watch for gopher holes, old roots, and rocks in the path. In such ways, the teacher can help the children to appreciate the importance of using their eyes to see where they are going.

IMPORTANCE OF BREATHING

A child needs to learn as early as possible that he breathes and has to get air at all times. Only when a child fully appreciates the importance of air is he able to keep himself from such hazards as playing inside old refrigerators with doors that close but do not open or accidentally hanging himself or someone else. It is in the nursery group that he lays the foundation for such appreciation.

The teacher should be careful to teach the importance of getting air without making the children fearful. Knowing what to do and how to do it is what the teacher must emphasize. She can make a point of tying in the idea of getting air with pleasant experiences. One teacher of four-year-old children introduced the idea at the first birthday party of the year.

The children and teacher were seated at the table. Each had a cupcake on which was a candle. Shortly after a grownup had lighted the candles, each person blew his out. When everyone had blown out his candle, the teacher led a brief discussion:

TEACHER We each blew out the candle on our birthday cake. (*Pantomimes blowing.*) Where did we get the air to blow? It came from inside us. We took a deep breath and then we could blow the candle out. Let's all blow. Take a deep breath so you can make a good blow.
(*The children breathe and blow.*)
TEACHER My, we're good blowers! Aren't we glad Johnny has a birthday, and brought us each a birthday cake with a candle to blow out.

The next time that there is a birthday party with candles to blow out, the teacher can carry the discussion a little further.

TEACHER Did you know that we take in air all the time through our nose? We call it "breathing." Everyone breathes all the time. Maybe you can see my hands move out and in while I breathe. (*Places hands one on each side at base of chest and breathes deeply.*) I'm filling my lungs with air. They are right here above my stomach. See if you can feel it when you fill your lungs with air.
(*The children try this: most are unsuccessful. The teacher quiets them down and continues with her explanation.*)
TEACHER There's another way to tell that you're breathing, but it's dangerous. I don't know whether I should show it to you or not. . . . Well, listen very carefully then. Remember we have to get air all the time through our nose. Now watch. (*Pantomimes holding nose for just a second or two, and then gulping air through her mouth.*) It's so important to get air down here in our lungs (*pats lower chest*) that if anything happens to our nose for a second, our mouth has to take in the air. We have to keep filling our lungs with air one way or another. That's part of living.

Whenever she is reminded of breathing or breathing hazards, the teacher should talk with the children about breathing. For instance, when the children are taking a walk on a lovely sunny day, the teacher can stop them for a few minutes and say, "It's such a lovely spring day. Let's fill our lungs with this good fresh air." "Fill your lungs nice and full," she may say, taking deep breaths herself to encourage the children to imitate deep breathing.

The day she read a story about grandmother's old trunk in the attic, one kindergarten teacher mentioned the hazard of getting into a box and closing the lid:

TEACHER   Ted certainly found a lot of interesting things in that old trunk. When the trunk was empty, do you think he got into the trunk?

(*Children say both "yes" and "no".*)

TEACHER   I think he stayed out of the trunk because he knew he might not be able to get air if the lid closed. Remember we always have to have air, so we stay out of boxes that have a lid or a door that might close. We have to be sure we can always breathe. Are we all breathing right now?

(*Pantomimes deep breathing. Smiles as she looks around at everyone*).

We certainly are. Ah, it feels good to breathe.

THE IMPORTANCE OF KEEPING WELL

The shrieking of an ambulance siren occasionally penetrates into the nursery group and demands an explanation. It should be interpreted as the friendly sound of doctors and nurses rushing to help someone who needs them. When a nursery group excursion takes the children past the local hospital, it can be pointed out to them as the place where the doctor helped many of them in coming out of their mother in being born. When one of the nursery group children goes to the hospital to have his tonsils taken out, the whole group can read *Curious George Goes to the Hospital*,[18] and be encouraged to think of the hospital as an interesting place that helps people to become well. In short, whenever the preschool group comes into contact with the health agencies of the community, the teacher should capitalize on the opportunity for making the children familiar with, and glad of, these agencies.

The teacher also should help children to understand that immunizations help them stay well. She should talk with the child who does not like the doctor because "he hurted me." After she listens to the fears of the four-year-old child, she can gently tell how she had to miss lots and lots of school days because she did not have a shot that hurt for only a few minutes but kept her well. She should encourage the four- and five-year-old children in dramatic play as doctors and nurses, knowing that many of their fears and anxieties will thus find expression and that they will come to think of the doctor as their friend.

THE GERM THEORY

It is important for preschool children to learn the simple elements of the germ theory. They watch television with its numerous ads for patent medicines and easily acquire misconceptions unless they are taught otherwise. The teacher should be careful to teach the children what to do and to avoid teaching them fears or anxieties. Here is some feedback that gave one teacher confidence in what she was teaching about germs to the children in a neighborhood play group. Susan (five years and seven months)

---

[18] Margret and H. A. Rey, *Curious George Goes to the Hospital* (Boston: Houghton Mifflin Company, 1966).

and Neal (three years and ten months) were playing with balloons, and Neal wanted to play with the balloon that Susan had been blowing up.

SUSAN   You'd better not give it. It's got my germs.
NEAL   You can wipe them off.
(*An adult comes and gives Neal another balloon, showing him how to stretch it so that he can blow it up. Neal tries, but is not successful.*)
NEAL   Can't do it.
SUSAN   I'll do it.
NEAL   (*hands her the balloon*)   Wipe the germs off.

The children had been taught to wash or wipe off what had been in someone else's mouth. This procedure they followed as a means of keeping well and of helping each other to stay well.

Four-year-old Priscilla was equally considerate when one of the boys took her pastecard during a craft activity. She took it back and found another pastecard for him. She did not want him to have hers; she had been eating it so it had her germs on it.

CLEANING

Children learn the importance of cleaning when they participate in it. Helping to collect the sheets after nap time or the individual washcloths at the end of the day can make the children aware of the necessity for having the sheets and other linens laundered, and may even lead them to the laundry to see what happens to the sheets or washcloths. After a dust storm, each child can have a dustcloth to use in helping the adults with the important activity of having a clean school. If the school windows are within easy reach, the children also can enjoy helping to wash them— especally if it is part of the preparation for having their parents visit school.

Nursery school and kindergarten children should participate in such ways in the operation of their school or center. But their participation should be occasional, not regular. The purpose of the children's activity is not to have them clean the school or center, but to develop their interest and skill in cleaning activities. They will be much older before they are ready to learn to assume responsibility for cleaning. But their occasional participation in the cleaning activities of the school or center is excellent preparation for such later learnings.

CARING FOR TEETH

Those who work with preschool children agree that the children should be encouraged to care for their teeth, but they differ in their expectations of what the children can learn at each age level. Because the care of teeth is of such importance to everyone, most teachers probably teach more about it than the children can learn. They attempt to reinforce the teaching of parents by encouraging the parents to help their children to brush their teeth happily and regularly. At the same time, they must realize that the

Preparing, brushing, and then rinsing. (Courtesy of Alice Public Schools, Alice, Texas.)

mastery of the wrist motions involved in the brushing cannot be expected of children before they are ready to develop such skill, and that girls probably will develop it at an earlier age than boys do. What the nursery group can teach, however, is the belief that it is important to care for one's teeth every day. As the children develop, they will learn that the reason for cleaning the teeth is to keep bacteria from making holes in them.

Three concepts can and should be taught to preschool children:

1. Teeth cut and chew food, making it smaller so that the body can use it. This teaching is an important part of the story of digestion which three-year-old children learn.
2. Foods that give teeth something to do—for instance, apples and carrots —make teeth healthy.

3. Soft drinks and sweets are bad for the teeth. Drinking some water afterward and swishing water through the mouth, helps to get sweets off the teeth.

Teachers in one community feel fortunate that the dentists and a women's group sponsor a clinic which may be visited by groups of preschool children, accompanied by their mothers. While the children listen to a lady who uses a giant toothbrush and set of teeth to show them how to brush their own teeth, the mothers watch a moving picture about the importance of dental care. The rest of the visit is devoted to individual dental examinations by local dentists who volunteer their time. During these examinations, the teacher helps the other children amuse themselves. She brings such transportable materials as a roll of shelf paper and jumbo crayons, together with a simple game such as picture-lotto for the four-year-old children. With the help of some of the mothers, she serves juice and reads stories. She encourages some of the children to take a walk with their mothers—a whisper-walk indoors or an exploratory walk outdoors if the weather permits. Above all, she minimizes the excitement and sets an example of calmness.

Prior to the visit to the dental clinic, the teacher prepares both the children and the mothers' group for the study trip. She makes sure that each group is eager to learn about effective ways of brushing teeth and good foods to keep teeth healthy. She knows that the children must be so interested in what they will see that they will not be disturbed by the new situation. She helps them look forward to seeing the big toothbrush just like their little one and the big teeth just like their own teeth.

Neal, at three years and ten months, was not quite certain that he wanted to go to the dental clinic with the nursery group and his mother. He preferred staying home with his mother. However a conversation with Susan's mother persuaded him to go:

ADULT Neal, do you know what the dental clinic has? A great big toothbrush, this big. (*Uses hands to show the size of it.*) Have you ever seen a toothbrush that big?
(*Neal shakes his head negatively.*)
ADULT Susan remembers seeing that great big toothbrush when she went to the dental clinic with the nursery school. But do you know what? She can't remember the color of the handle—and I can't either. I can't go today because Susan is sick. But maybe you can look carefully, Neal and tell us the color of the handle of that great big toothbrush. Will you do that?
NEAL Okay.

With the important responsibility of finding out the color of the handle of the toothbrush, Neal went happily off to the dental clinic. Upon his return, he reported his finding eagerly:

ADULT Hello, Neal.

NEAL The handle—the handle was blue.

ADULT Blue. Of course. The handle is blue. Thank you so much for finding out. Did the dentist look at your teeth?

NEAL No.

ADULT Oh?

NEAL I sat on mother's lap. I opened my mouth. He looked.

ADULT I see. Thanks so much for telling me about it.

NEAL Okay.

School Policies on Health

The preschool group must have clearly defined health policies. This means that written statements of policy are on file, that every effort is made to have the policy understood, and that every situation involving health is decided in terms of these policies. Because the state of health of the preschool child can change very rapidly, parents and teachers must work together to protect the welfare of each child and to maintain that of the preschool group.

ABSENCE FOR ILLNESS

Parents and teachers must have a common understanding of health rules and regulations and must work together to enforce them. For instance, if a preschool child becomes ill with chicken pox, the parent telephones the teacher to tell her the circumstances of his illness. The director then telephones the local department of health to help her determine

- If the ill child may have exposed other children in the preschool group.
- What can be done to prevent spreading the illness.
- What aid is available for the children exposed to the illness.
- What aid is available for the sick child.
- How long the sick child should remain at home before returning to school.

Understanding how the health regulations apply, the director—with the help of parents—should make sure that each parent knows what the situation is and how it affects her child and herself. By working closely with the parents, the director builds their confidence in her and in her ability to do what is best for their children. She also keeps in mind the dangers that lie in the failure to follow this procedure. Instead of correct information being communicated among parents, fears and suspicions can spread quickly and can result in problems of further illness and increased absence. She therefore should take positive steps to see that correct, authoritative information is spread at once before any misinformation may circulate. In this way she not only maintains the school health at a high level, but also contributes to the better understanding of good health measures by the community at large.

When parents and teachers work together for good health in the pre-school group, they should keep in mind that the first seventy-two hours of an illness are the period when the illness is most apt to be spread. They arrive then at a defined policy: If a child is ill with a common cold or other communicable illness, he will be at home for three days. Under no circumstances will he return to school until at least twenty-four hours after his temperature has subsided. With these rules posted on the bulletin board, written into pamphlet material for parents, and otherwise com-municated repeatedly among the school clientele, a large step is taken toward reducing the total number of absences from the preschool group.

A teacher finds it useful to know some of the health views current among the families with children in her preschool group. A family's point of view about the use of antibiotics will directly affect the attendance of children in her group.

In many families, if a child has a fever, an earache, or other evidence that his body is having difficulty with invading organisms, the family con-sults a physician who is able to prescribe an antibiotic if it is needed. Usually, the child is able to return to school within a few days to profit from the activities of the school.

Families who formed their health concepts when penicillin was the only antibiotic available may retain the point of view that a "wonder drug" is to be used sparingly. They keep a sick child at home without consulting a physician until there is overwhelming evidence of need. By that time, the illness often has progressed to the point where recovery will require several extra days. Thus a child may not be able to return to school for a week or ten days.

Some families still cling to the "weathering through" point of view and use home remedies current in the days before the discovery of antibiotics. Their children are apt to be out of school for weeks at a time.

Parents who find themselves confined at home with sick children for some time may be tempted to send their preschool children back to school when the state of their health does not really warrant it. The return of such a child may result in his becoming ill again and in the succumbing of others in the group. The teacher must check carefully the health status of each child who returns to school after an absence caused by illness.

Whenever a parent discusses health matters, the teacher should listen attentively. The views of the parents are the basis for the educational program they need. Furthermore, the health policies of the school must be developed with the parents so that they understand them and are inter-ested in enforcing them. The teacher, therefore, should work to have health policies in keeping with the current thought of the majority of the parents. At the same time, she should work to improve their understanding of recent developments in the field of pediatrics.

REFUNDS FOR ILLNESS?

Parents whose children are frequently absent from a private nursery group sometimes raise the question of whether or not they should pay for his absence from, as well as his presence in, the group. When they raise the question, they show their need for understanding that the school or center to which their fees contribute must operate to meet the needs of the children who are there each day. Whether or not their child is able to profit from the group is a matter of the child's health, not of the parents' fees.

In one nursery school, an inexperienced teacher responded to the pressure of a parent to refund the monthly fee for her child who was out of school for four weeks because of illness. Immediately, the parents of other children who had been ill asked for refunds for their children's absences. Fortunately, the teacher realized that the refund policy was making for greater absence from nursery school and for insufficient funds to pay her nominal salary. Meeting with the parents, the teacher was able to explain to them the necessity of having a regular monthly fee for each child, regardless of the number of times that he attends. The regular fee provides a school facility and a teacher and the opportunity for each family to have its child attend the school. Whether or not the child does attend is the responsibility of the family.

SHOES AT NAP TIME?

When a preschool group is added to an existing organization, the policies of the organization should be considered carefully to see whether each is applicable to preschool groups. They may or may not be.

For several years, preschool groups connected with one system of public schools had the children keep their shoes on when they lay down on their cots for a nap. The director of the preschool groups thought she should enforce the school district's rule that children must wear shoes. She had never raised the question as to whether or not the rule should apply to preschool as well as elementary school children; she had simply enforced it.

The practice regarding shoes at nap time may reflect any one of several school policies. If the policy of the preschool group is to have a large ratio of children to adults, the numbers of shoes to be tied may require more teacher time than the teacher has to give to this activity. Knowing that three- and four-year-old children are usually not sufficiently mature to tie their own shoelaces, the teacher may think it better to spend time on activities at their level af maturity rather than on tying shoelaces.

If the policy of the group is to have the children experience healthful, desirable ways of living at all times, the teacher will think it important for the children to remove their shoes before lying down on a bed and will work out convenient ways for helping them do this. Perhaps parents can buy shoes with zippers so that the children can easily manage them. Perhaps other school personnel or the parents can take turns in helping the teacher during the postnap period. Perhaps kindergarten children can practice their newly acquired skill in tying shoelaces by helping the nursery school children to tie theirs. In one way or another, the policy of the preschool group will show itself in the practices of the group—even in such details as whether or not the children wear shoes at nap time.

INSURANCE

Each preschool group needs to consider its legal responsibility in case of accidents, and to determine what kind of insurance, if any, it should carry. The practice of preschool groups must be in accord with the laws of the states in which they are located; that of preschool groups connected with public school systems must be in accord with the laws pertaining to the public schools.

In the state of California, private and parent-cooperative nursery groups and kindergartens are asked to comply with the labor code and provide workmen's compensation insurance for their teachers. They are also advised to carry liability insurance.

The question of insurance for parent-cooperative groups is discussed as follows by one council of parent-cooperative nurseries:

Insurance is a question that each cooperative nursery group considers. What risks, if any, should be covered by insurance? What forms of insurance provide maximum protection at minimum cost? Such questions are answered differently by different groups because each group is unique in its personnel, location, and policies.

Since cooperative nurseries are highly selective in their membership, risks are less than in other nursery groups. Member families take responsibility for themselves, and have confidence in others. Many parents carry comprehensive personal liability policies which protect them whether they are at home or elsewhere. Where parents often have nursery children in their car, they make sure that their automobile insurance protects their guest passengers as well as themselves.

In addition to any insurance which cooperative nursery members arrange as families, a comprehensive personal liability policy for the supervisor of children is often paid for by the group. Such insurance protects the children in case of accident or injury which the teacher might feel was attributable to her negligence.[19]

Private and parent-cooperative nursery groups and kindergartens generally are incorporated. Incorporation gives the group a permanent legal status, regardless of changes in personnel, and, in case of an accident fixes liability on the corporation rather than on individual adults who compose the school personnel at the time of the accident.

[19] Vivian Edmiston Todd, ed., *Cooperative Nursery School Handbook* (Long Beach, Calif.: Long Beach Council of Cooperative Nurseries, 1957), p. 5.

Situations for Discussion

A preschool teacher is apt to find herself in situations similar to the four described here. As you think of what to do in each situation, consider whether each course of action suggested is desirable or not. Use points brought out in the chapter as well as ideas from your own experience to justify your views. Suggest alternative courses of action to supplement those given.

SITUATION 1   Teddy is in your class in a state and federally supported children's center. His medical examination revealed a serious hernia requiring surgical correction. His parents are unwilling to permit the necessary surgery. As Teddy's teacher, you should

- Accept the parent decision as final and responsible.
- Visit Teddy's home and explain what can be expected in Teddy's future.
- Arrange a conference with the director of the center, the nursery school teacher, and Teddy's parents.
- Enlist cooperation of the family's minister, priest, or rabbi.
- Inquire about the possibility of excluding Teddy until the correction has been made.

SITUATION 2   Your nursery group is eager to have a Halloween party that will prepare the children for trick-or-treating. As the teacher, you are careful to see that the plans are in accord with the following concepts:

- Overstimulation is fatiguing to children.
- Three-year-old children are easily frightened.
- Except for Halloween refreshments, the activities for the children will be much as usual.
- The party should be before Halloween rather than on that day.
- Costumes complete with masks are to be worn to the party.

SITUATION 3   A mother is concerned about her preschool child who runs across the street to play with his friend without stopping to look for cars. She asks for suggestions about what to do but really wants reassurance that a mother cannot spend all her time watching to see that her child is safe. In talking with her, you should.

- Listen sympathetically to what she says.
- Agree that she has a difficult problem.
- Express confidence in her finding a solution to her problem.
- Explain to her how to train a child to stop on the curb to look and listen for cars.
- Suggest that she get her child a red jacket.

SITUATION 4   Tom's mother talks with you about a birthday present for his fifth birthday. She gave Tom's older sister a bicycle for her fifth birthday and is thinking of such a present for Tom. You point out to her that

- Girls are more mature than boys of the same age.
- Training wheels make a bicycle much like a large tricycle.

- A five-year-old child can master the bicycle but not the safety rules of the street.
- Parents should not thrust a child into dangers he cannot cope with.
- Each child shows in his behavior what he is ready for.

Books for Preschool Children

BEMELMANS, LUDWIG. *Madeline.* New York: Simon and Schuster, Inc., 1954. [In delightful rhyme, Madeline has appendicitis and a trip to the hospital.]

BRANDENBURG, ALIKI. *My Hands.* New York: Thomas Y. Crowell Company, 1962. [The pictures and simple words of this Let's-Read-and-Find-Out book help a child observe and use his hands.]

CHASE, FRANCINE. *A Visit to the Hospital.* New York: Wonder Books, Inc., 1958. [When Stevie goes to the hospital to have his tonsils out, he decides he wants to be a doctor.]

EMBERLEY, ED. *Green Says Go.* Boston: Little, Brown & Co., 1968. [A helpful book for future drivers.]

GREEN, MARY McBURNEY. *Everybody Has a House and Everybody Eats.* New York: William R. Scott, Inc. [Everyone has to get food and shelter, children as well as animals.]

GREENE, CARLA. *I Want to Be a Dentist.* Chicago: Children's Press, 1960. [*I Want to Be a Doctor* also is a beginning reading book with useful pictures.]

GUY, ANNE WELSH. *Gool-bye, Tonsils.* Racine, Wis.: Whitman Publishing Company, 1966. [Mary Ann goes to the doctor and then to the hospital to have her tonsils taken out.]

HOBAN, RUSSELL. *Bread and Jam for Frances.* New York: Harper & Row, Publishers, 1964. [Frances learns to like different kinds of meals and snacks.]

HOLL, ADELAIDE. *The Rain Puddle.* New York: Lothrop, Lee & Shepard Co., Inc., 1966. [When the puddle dries up, each barnyard animal is so glad that the animals he had seen in it had climbed out safely.]

McCLOSKEY, ROBERT. *One Morning in Maine.* New York: The Viking Press, Inc., 1952. [In this preview of what lies ahead for preschool children, a little girl loses a tooth one delightful morning in Maine.]

REY, MARGRET and H. A. *Curious George Goes to the Hospital.* Boston: Houghton Mifflin Co., 1966. [A missing piece of a puzzle leads to an examination by a doctor, X-ray pictures, and both usual and unusual hospital experiences.]

SANDBERG, INGER and LASSE. *When Little Anna Had a Cold.* New York: Lothrop, Lee & Shepard, Inc., 1966. [An imaginative approach to a common experience.]

SEVER, JOSEPHINE A. *Johnny Goes to the Hospital.* Boston: Houghton Mifflin Company, 1953. [A matter-of-fact account of Johnny's trip to the hospital.]

TAMBURINE, JEAN. *I Think I Will Go to the Hospital.* New York: Abingdon Press. 1965. [When Susy visits a hospital and talks with people who have been there, she decides to have her tonsils out.]

WOOLEY, CATHERINE. *Lunch for Lennie.* New York: William Morrow & Co., Inc., 1952. [Lennie explores the roles of several hungry animals before he eats a boy's lunch.]

CHAPTER 7

Furthering Physical Development

In one sense, the entire nursery group and kindergarten program is a program in physical education, planned in terms of helping each child move himself smoothly and safely through space. It guides him as he perfects his ability to walk, run, jump, and climb, and as he develops new skill in movement. It provides much opportunity for development of large muscles and small muscles as the children are ready for such development. It provides apparatus, equipment, and supplies for activities that encourage coordination between different muscles and between eye and muscles. It is not surprising to find that the well-schooled teacher of physical education often becomes a good nursery group teacher when her interests shift to her own and other small children. Nor is it surprising that the preschool child usually continues to have an interest in physical education activities as he goes on into elementary school.

The preschool teacher who appreciates the common ground of preschool and physical education teaching provides equipment and plans activities that will give the children endless opportunity for large-muscle development. Outdoors she makes sure that the playground has ladders and other climbing apparatus, and piles of dirt or sand for digging, so that arm and shoulder as well as other muscles will develop. She sees to it that there is space for running, and she encourages hopping and jumping so that the muscles of legs and the pelvic girdle will develop. Indoors she makes use of trampolines, rockers, and punching balloons as an aid to development of rhythm and coordination. No matter what part of the curriculum she is concerned with, she never fails to provide for physical activities as an integral part of it. She is continuously aware of the desirability of furthering the physical development of the preschool child so that he will have

240

the body structure, the skills, and the interests basic to furthering his physical development in later years.

Curriculum Considerations

VALUES OF PHYSICAL EDUCATION

The value of physical education for the preschool child is readily apparent when the three-year-old child who had swimming instruction is able to survive in a pool until adult help arrives. In preschool groups the child has guidance and patterns of physical skills which may not be available to him elsewhere. He has climbing and other equipment which his own backyard may not afford. Whether in later years he is able to escape from an enemy by climbing a tree or sliding down a pole may be determined by whether he had a chance to learn and enjoy these skills when he was four or five years old.

A preschooler's drive for learning to control his body is so great that he learns many physical skills whether he is in a preschool group or not, but he learns them more easily and with better feelings about himself and his relations to other people if he learns them in the preschool group. The importance of physical education activities for the social and emotional development of children has been pointed out by Prescott:

The ability to manage the body well in a wide variety of activities and the possession of specific game skills are major assets for each child in winning peer-group roles and greatly affect relationships with other children. They also greatly affect the individual's feelings about and concept of himself and therefore play an important part in his emotional adjustment.[1]

The Doctors Bakwin discuss the physical and psychological values of physical education activities in nursery school as follows:

Typically, the young child makes a physical-motor attack on the things in his world, sometimes through manipulating small objects, at other times through putting his large muscles or his whole body into vigorous motion and action. The nursery school is set up to provide ample, varied opportunity for the child to enjoy his physical vigor. . . . Slides, parallel bars, and ladders, jungle gyms, see-saws, wagons, tricycles, scooters, large hollow wooden blocks, kegs, and brooms are part of the standard equipment . . . for an adequate nursery school. Young children in contact with these objects spontaneously engage in a repetitive round of sliding, swinging, climbing, hanging, balancing, rolling, steering, heaving, pushing, stacking, and dragging. The benefits to development of muscular strength are obvious.

There are, in addition, less obvious but more significant psychologic values.

[1] Daniel A. Prescott, *The Child in the Educative Process* (New York: McGraw-Hill Book Company, Inc., 1957), p. 355.

Instructions and restrictions are minimal, and limited to safety needs; the child is thus left free to explore, to experiment, to invent, and to discover. He is free from the host of prohibitions imposed on him at home. . . . He is free from influences to use things in ways manufacturers might conceive, or might seem fascinating to his father. The child, then, has not only the pleasure of varied physical activity but also the delight of making independent discoveries and the experience of impressing his own individual pattern on the environment.[2]

PHYSICAL EDUCATION OBJECTIVES

After each year in a preschool group a child is more skillful in moving his body through space. He has better muscular control and is more skillful in physical activities. He gains increasing mastery of such fundamental activities as walking, running, and climbing, and adds to the list of activities he performs by learning to hop and, later, to skip. Just when he learns each new skill and how rapidly he perfects the familiar ones depends on his individual characteristics. Each child has a different problem in learning to handle his body because each child differs in his physical structure and his ability to develop muscular strength and coordination. Nevertheless several skills are known to be within the ability of most children of a given age level, and are reasonable physical education objectives for children in a preschool group:

Three-year-old children
- Stop or go on the slide.
- Enjoy swinging when helped.
- Do a forward somersault.
- Roll a ball.
- Like being in the water with mother.

Four-year-old children
- Hop.
- Pump in swinging.
- Combine words with movements.
- Do a backward somersault.
- Slide down a pole.
- Fall into a roll.
- Catch and throw a ball.
- Distinguish right from left.
- Dog paddle in water with mother.

Five-year-old children
- Skip.
- Swing without help.
- Walk a rail.

[2] Harry Bakwin and Ruth M. Bakwin, *Clinical Management of Behavior Disorders in Children* (Philadelphia: W. B. Saunders Co., 1966), pp. 83–84.

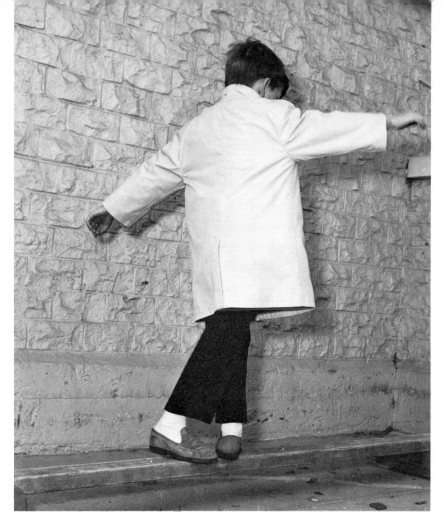

Developing better balance and muscular control. (Courtesy of Riverside Unified School District, Riverside, California.)

- Use an overhead ladder.
- Swim across a pool.

Each year a preschool child becomes more graceful in his movements and has increasing use of the different parts of his body—his arms, legs, and side hinges. Each year his physical development should be well rounded, with shoulders developing as well as hips; arms, as well as legs.

PHYSICAL EDUCATION IN OTHER CURRICULUM AREAS

Because physical education is a concomitant of every other area of the preschool curriculum, it is not often given attention in itself. The view is held that the children will gain a well-rounded physical development incidental to their other activities. The danger in this view is that emphasis may be placed on small-muscle development and the control associated with sedentary activities, without sufficient attention to the activities which

243

further the large-muscle development so essential to children of preschool ages. Table 7-1 lists typical activities in each curriculum area other than physical education, and shows the kinds of physical development which can be expected in relation to each. The wise teacher works out a program of activities with a preponderance of time devoted to large-muscle development.

For example, in considering what literary activities to provide for the children, the teacher may usually read stories to the children, but she may vary this routine occasionally by using a novelty picture book devised for the four- and five-year-old children who have developed sufficient muscular control and coordination to carry on the small-muscle activity which

TABLE 7-1.   Physical Development as an Integral Part of Preschool Activities

Curriculum Area	Typical Activities	Aspects of Physical Development
Social studies	Floor play	Large muscles; coordination; balance
	Sandbox play	
	Playhouse play	Large muscles; coordination
	Dramatic play	
	Study trips	Walking
Science	Gardening	Large muscles; coordination
	Caring for pets	Small muscles
	Nature walks	Walking
	Observing	Muscle control; coordination
Geography	Map making	Large and small muscles
	Using landmarks	Walking
Mathematics	Pouring	Small muscles; coordination
	Measuring with self	Large muscles
Language development	Verbalizing	Aural control
	Dramatizing	Large and small muscles; coordination
Children's literature	Story listening	Muscular control
	Novelty books	Small muscles; coordination
	Dramatizing	Large and small muscles; coordination
Art	Arranging	Large and small muscles; coordination
	Easel painting	Large muscles
	Pasting; crayoning	Small muscles
	Cutting	Small muscles; coordination
Music	Singing	Aural control
	Rhythms	Large and small muscles; coordination
	Dancing	Large muscles
	Listening	Relaxing
Social sensitivity	Hitting a target	Large and small muscles; coordination
	Moving large boxes	Large muscles; coordination
Health and safety	Removing hazards	Large muscles; coordination
	Satisfying physical needs	Walking; coordination; large and small muscles

accompanies the story as it is read by an adult. The child uses a magnet underneath the page to move a figure along the pictured course on the page. A five-year-old child has sufficient muscular control to enjoy a re- cording of a story, played by turning a crank. When he turns the crank evenly, he hears the story.

The teacher who is aware of the importance of providing primarily for large- rather than small-muscle development during the preschool years has the children participate often in dramatic activities. As the children act out a favorite story, they move about and use both their large and small muscles, and they coordinate their physical movements with the words and ideas of the story.

Similarly, in each area of the curriculum, the teacher should plan activi- ties which will give the children opportunity to use the large muscles. She must be ingenious in teaching an important concept through experience that requires gross, not small, movements. She should always choose to have the children do something actively, restricting activities in which they only sit and listen to quiet rest times. She keeps constantly in mind their developmental need for physical activity.

Supervising Outdoor Activities

When a new child comes to a preschool group, the teacher should guide him in learning how to have control of himself as he uses each piece of playground equipment. Whenever a child develops an interest in using equipment that is new to him, or in using it in a new way, the teacher should guide him in handling himself safely. The hazards of the equip- ment are an integral part of the learning opportunity which the equipment affords. She must know how to guide the children in using the equipment safely and in avoiding its dangers.

Swings. The teacher should see that two-year-old children have seat swings which support them and help them learn by feel the upright balance necessary for swinging. She swings each child, not by pushing him, but by bringing the swing to a height then letting it go. Pushing often frightens small children who are thus made to move with more speed than they feel able to handle. The teacher should have the three-year-old child tell her at what height he wants her to let his swing go. By using this method she can help more children enjoy the swings than if she tries to push each one continuously.

For the nursery school and kindergarten children the teacher should see that soft swing seats are provided. A wooden seat may hurt a child if it hits him on the head, but a canvas seat probably will not. As soon as she can, using flannelboard pictures and discussion of accidents that occur, she should help the children understand that they must walk *around* the swing- ing area, not across it.

With the four-year-old children, the adult should encourage dramatic play. The swing is a rocket, and she is the announcer and engineer who guides its takeoff. She may say, for instance: "All aboard for the moon! Loading at Gate Four! All aboard! 5—4—3—2—1—0—Blastoff!" With the five-year-old children, the adult can encourage the children to pump and praise their accomplishments. She also can help them keep their dramatic play within bounds of safety, and may say, "Try jumping from your swing first when it is moving slowly. Then, when you know just how to do that, you can try it going a little faster."

Balls. Ball-handling, which is important to children throughout their years in school, has its beginnings in the preschool activities which are guided by the teacher. Merely having volleyballs or other big, soft balls available is not sufficient incentive for the children to use balls frequently enough to develop any skill with them. But participating in simple games with their teacher is both fun and an aid to developing the coordination of eye and muscle required in ball-handling.

One teacher, motivated by having in her group the son of a good ball player, devised a series of simple games to help the children learn how to catch and throw a ball. In each game she encouraged participation only as long as the children were interested in the activity. She told them: "If you get tired, you can play on the slide or in the sandbox." She had them hold hands with their friends so that they could spread out into a large circle yet be close enough together to catch the ball when she threw it to first one child then another. Next, with their hands ready to catch the ball, she said. "The ball is a friend; you want to catch it. Your arms are a basket. You catch the ball in it and pull it toward your chest." After the child caught the ball, he threw it back to the teacher who kept the attention of the group on catching the ball, and made no comment then about how to throw it. When she went on to give another child a turn at catching the ball, she asked the children: "Is your basket ready?" and then she gently threw the ball to one of them.

On other days the teacher taught the children other ball-throwing skills, one skill at a time. She had them form a circle and get ready for throwing by shaking their hands until their fingers felt relaxed. Then she explained the throw that they were going to use that day, putting both hands on the ball:

- Underhand throw: put the ball just to the right of the hips, and throw from there.
- Side overhand: with the ball on the hand on the shoulder and the other hand to help hold it, throw the ball.
- Underhand pitch: put the ball in a swing between the legs, and throw it.
- Overhead throw: reach as tall as a tree and throw the ball from over the head.

Up the ladder and down the slide. (Courtesy of Long Beach Parent Nursery Schools and Mariam M. Cook, Long Beach, California.)

The fun that the teacher obviously has spreads to the children. They also learn that making mistakes is part of the game even though a person tries to do it right each time. Sometimes the teacher misses the ball, and sometimes a child misses the ball. There is fun in chasing it, then trying the catch or throw again.

Slides. For the two-year-old children, the teacher should provide only a short slide. Two or three steps, a platform with a side railing, and a slide make a delightful combination for the young nursery child. On it he safely explores a variety of balances from which he evolves a good sitting slide. The teacher should guide him in taking turns and in moving out of the way of the next fellow.

When the three-year-old child comes to a nursery group, the teacher should introduce him to the playground slide. She knows the danger of hurtling down a slide out of control, so she puts him on the slide near the lower end and shows him what his controls are. As he holds himself with his hands on the rails, she puts his feet against the rails and may say, "These are your brakes for stopping. Hold them out against the side and

247

It is fun to build large muscles and develop coordination. (Courtesy of Play Garden Nursery, Bakersfield, California. Photograph by Hortense Gordon.)

they stop you. Take them away from the side [she brings the feet together in the center of the slide], and you go fast." Then she lets the child try stopping and starting on the slide, putting him on the slide at a somewhat higher place each time. Finally he feels ready to go up the ladder and try starting and stopping on the slide all the way down it.

Three-year-old children learn to take turns, to stay below the feet of the person above them on the ladder, to wait at the top of the slide until it is completely clear, and to get out of the way of the next person using the slide. The four-year-old child is sure of his balance in a sitting position, and is interested in exploring variations of balance and posture. He needs continuous supervision as he explores the limits of sliding. The teacher points out to him the danger of falling from the top of the slide a distance greater than his own height, the hazard of hitting his head on the end of the slide if he tries to go down head first, and the difficulties at the end of the slide if two or three children try to play they are a series of cars making up a train.

Walking Boards. A three-year-old child is intrigued by walking along a wide board set on top of matched low boxes placed under each end of the board. If the board is high or narrow, he wants an adult to hold his hand. The four-year-old child eagerly walks the board unaided. He may make his own arrangement of the boards and boxes. He sometimes improvises a see-saw arrangement which is past his ability to control safely and necessitates adult supervision continuously. The five-year-old child enjoys walking a narrow board, for instance, a two-by-four set on edge and steadied between pegs driven into the ground. Whatever the age of the preschool child, he profits from the opportunity that walking boards afford for developing muscular control and coordination of eye and leg muscles. He needs this practice in walking, a basic skill important to him throughout his life.

Uneven Ground. Children should learn early from experience the kinesthetic associations which make for good balance and muscular control as they walk over a variety of surfaces. Especially for the children who are accustomed only to the sidewalks of the city, the teacher should plan excursions to parks and vacant lots where the children can learn to walk and run on uneven ground. As they follow the paths and explore this new environment, she may exclaim, "Isn't this fun!" to encourage their pleasure in their activity. Depending on the terrain, she has opportunity for teaching them to

- Cut the edge of the foot into the hill at each step.
- Sidestep up or down a very steep slope.
- Avoid stepping in holes.
- Pick up the feet in stepping over roots and stones.

When a child stumbles over a clod and falls, the teacher laughs with him and says, "Johnny picks himself right up and on he goes." Johnny might have decided to whimper or cry, but instead he accepts the teachers suggestion. Soon he learns how to walk on grassy fields and dirt paths, and enjoys doing it.

Merry-go-round. When the nursery children become interested in the sturdy merry-go-round that is set close to the ground, their teacher should encourage them in learning to control themselves in rotary motion. She guides the timid three-year-old children in sitting at the center and hanging on to the radial bars. As they become familiar with the device, she tells them to try riding it at greater distances from the center. Soon they are able to sit along the edge, always careful to hang on with their hands.

The teacher can guide the experienced four-year-old children in their dramatic play. As they push the merry-go-round to "make the train go fast,' she helps them stop the train for younger children wishing to be passengers or wishing to get off. She may say, "When someone says, 'Stop,' we always stop." When the boys try being train robbers, jumping on the moving train then jumping off again, she reminds them, "Try it slowly first. You can try it faster after you've learned how." When they roll off the train, she says, "Roll out of the way! Roll away from the train!" In view of both the educational opportunities of the merry-go-round and its hazards, the teacher should always have an adult supervising it.

Climbing Apparatus. Young preschool children probably will climb up before they know how to climb down, and need help in learning to face in toward the climber and reach down to feel the step below. Most children are cautious about going high up on a climbing apparatus, and do so only as they feel ready to. Nor will they venture to put the weight of their bodies out into space until their arms are long enough to reach safely to the fireman's pole. When a child wants to reach for the fireman's pole, the teacher guides him in holding himself on the pole with his legs as well as with his hands. She shows him how to swing over to the pole first close to the ground, and then farther up the pole as he gains confidence in his ability to slide down it. The teacher should help each child learn how to handle himself at the times when he reaches out toward new learning.

The merry-go-round stops to let people off or on. (Courtesy of Long Beach Parent Nursery Schools and Mariam M. Cook, Long Beach, California.)

Climbing apparatus offers opportunity for children not only to develop muscles of arms, shoulders, hips, and legs, but also to learn to be considerate of others. A climbing child has to look for stepping places between little hands, not on them. He has to be sure that no person or toy is below him before he turns and jumps off the climber. The adults must watch to see that climbers guide their feet and hands safely for both themselves and others.

Other Apparatus. The exercise bar and the tunnel offer opportunity for

Opportunity for physical development with minimal supervision. (Courtesy of Ontario-Montclair School District, Ontario, California.)

muscular development and coordination at whatever time a child is ready for them. They require only a minimum of supervision, and a periodic inspection to make sure that no toy or tool has been dropped in the sand by the apparatus where a child might trip or fall on it.

Digging and Raking. Gardening, or just digging in the dirt or sand, provides children with the opportunity to learn how to use a tool. Realizing the muscle and eye-muscle coordinations to be learned, the teacher should encourage the children in using tools, that extend what can be done by the hands. However, she must also be aware that the child who still expresses his frustration by hitting is more of a hazard with a tool in his hand. The physical activity of the digging serves as an emotional release, and the hazardous times which need close supervision are the initiation and the conclusion of the activity. The teacher should help the children in starting to work on their digging projects, and watch for the signs of fatigue that are her cues for helping children move on to other activities.

Tree Climbing. The teacher should help children enjoy tree climbing. She stands by ready to give a helping hand to those who learn to climb up before they learn how to climb back down. As she helps them jump off, she reminds them that they can jump safely from a place as high up as they are tall. If they climb higher than that, they climb back down before they jump off. She also helps them learn to hang on with both arms and legs. If bark scratches bare legs or arms, she points out that bark scratches only when we slide across it. But she praises the accomplishment of each child: "John has found a good place from which to drop down." "Linda is hugging the tree carefully." She is quick to echo each child's expression

251

of his own feelings of satisfaction: "I'm high!" "You certainly are!" "Look at this!" "My, look at that!" "I did it!" "Indeed you did!"

The teacher should gain satisfaction in helping a timid and clinging child move out into space and activities away from her. As long as her teacher was standing by, for instance, Linda Sue was willing to be part of the group interested in climbing the tree. While the four- and five-year-old children climbed to the higher branches, three-year-old Linda Sue ventured cautiously into the branches that forked out from the ground or a foot or two above it. By the time she was ready to trust her weight to a branch and reach for a higher one above her, the older children were on their way down. "Watch out! Get out of my way!" said Karla, not wanting to step on Linda Sue's fingers. The teacher smiled reassuringly at Linda Sue as she started at once to retreat. "Here's a climbing place over on this side," the teacher said as she guided Linda Sue's retreat in that direction.

A few minutes later Linda Sue had completed her brief climb up and down. "Oh, isn't this a nice place," she said happily. Again her teacher smiled warmly as she said, "It certainly is." Pointing to the limbs of the tree she continued: "And do you know that you climbed all the way up here and back down?" Encouraged by this praise, Linda Sue started back to the tree. Then she noticed several of the children and another adult over near the cars that had brought the group to the tree place. "They're leaving. See?" she said anxiously. Again the adult calmly reassured her, "They went to the bathroom there next to the cars." Linda Sue's anxious frown disappeared as she again started to climb the tree.

When the children were ready to leave, the teacher talked with them for a minute about the fun they had had together at the tree place: "We all had such fun climbing trees." Smiling at Linda Sue, she added, "When you get home, be sure to tell your mother about how you climbed the tree." Then, talking to the whole group, she said, "We'll come again next week and climb trees some more." The teacher knew that shy Linda Sue as well as the others would be eager to come again because each of them had had a satisfying success in their new activity of climbing trees.

Supervising Indoor Activities

The preschool teacher should plan indoor activities that give children the exercise they need for building large muscles. Especially in a climate that has primarily indoor weather, the teacher must provide daily several centers of interest which will bring large muscles into play and help the children to develop coordination and balance as well as tone in both large and small muscles.

Trampoline. The teacher should supervise children using the trampoline. She sees that an adult is available to hold the hands of the beginner or the three-year-old child while he jumps cautiously, attempting to get the feel of the bouncing. She pays a minimum of attention to the four-year-old who is well practiced and jumps with considerable control. She needs only to praise his accomplishment or remind him to stay in the center of the trampoline. She praises the five-year-old when he performs such tricks as changing from a standing to a sitting position while he jumps.

Parents and others familiar with the trampoline as a piece of apparatus for adolescent gymnasium work are sometimes afraid that it is dangerous for small children. The teacher should reassure them that the trampoline for preschool children is adequately built for their level of development, and does not provide a child with enough force to enable him to injure himself easily. Only one child at a time uses the trampoline. The teacher should also point out that the trampoline is an excellent device for helping children learn to move their bodies rhythmically. It helps them to develop their leg muscles, and the coordination of other muscles.

Balls. Ball handling can be fun indoors as well as outdoors if it is limited to catching and rolling the ball. The children form a circle, sit down on the floor, and spread their legs out so that the ball will stay inside their circle. The teacher starts the ball rolling by sending it to one child who returns it to her. With experienced children she may start the ball rolling and let them roll it back and forth to each other.

Rockers. Rockers and rocking boats are other pieces of apparatus sufficiently quiet for indoor use and excellent in helping the children enjoy rhythmical movement. They require a minimum of supervision.

Boxing Gloves. Boxing gloves are available in a small size that fits preschool children. They are used under the supervision of an adult. One teacher in a parent cooperative nursery school reported on the use of boxing gloves as follows:

Stanley has not yet boxed at school although he introduced us all to the pugilistic art by bringing two pairs of gloves to school. He often brings toys from home and is very generous sharing them with other children.

Florence seemed very eager to box and not at all timid in taking on such a champ as Edmund. It was also pleasant to observe that Edmund, bless his heart, recognized Florence as not quite in his league. He kept giving her tips on how to defend herself from his blows and Florence tried to comply. When she had had enough, without announcement she peeled off the gloves and left Edmund with a left poised in midair. He hadn't hurt her; he hadn't wanted to quit. But Florence did and I guess when you want to quit, you quit.

Punching Balloons. The large "Punch Me" balloons with sand at the bottom are a good means of helping children find release for their emotions, or develop arm muscles and skill in coordinating eye and hand. They require sufficient supervision to see that the children neither try to pick up the whole balloon, nor roll and tumble with it.

Steps-Platform-Slide. Either outdoors or indoors the steps-platform-slide for two- and three-year-old children is useful in developing large muscles and coordination of muscles. It is used quietly and holds the attention of the children. It requires a minimum of attention if only one child at a times uses it, but needs supervision when a group of children want to take turns on it. The children learn to go all in the same direction and to keep moving so that the next children may have a turn, too.

Moving Equipment. One of the activities in which children build muscles and develop coordination is that of getting out or putting away equipment. Working alone or together, they tug and pull, guiding the equipment to a suitable location.

Cleaning Surfaces. Another excellent muscle-building activity which helps to develop coordination is cleaning up the working surfaces, washing windows, or doing other housework at the school. Such activities dignify work and help a child feel important as he takes part in the adult world. The emotionally upset child finds a release in such activities at the same time that he enjoys the physical activity. The adult supervises cleaning activities usually by participating in them, thus setting a good example for the children to imitate and calling their attention to interesting phenomena, such as the kind of spots that come off and the kind that do not.

Physical Transitions

The teacher should know how to capitalize on the child's interest in physical activities, and use her knowledge to help a group of children move from one center of interest to another, or to help an individual child move from one situation to another.

In moving a group of children to a new activity, the teacher should have the equipment and supplies for the activity arranged on location in advance. Then she talks with the children, orienting them with regard to the activity. For instance, she may say to a group of four-year-old children,

Do you know what we are going to do next? Well, first we are going to talk together for just a minute, and then, when I tell you that it is time, we shall put on our jackets and sweaters and go for a walk. What do you think we can find on a day like this, after the rain?

The teacher can move a group of four-year-old children from one part of a room to another for a new activity there. Usually she moves three-year-old children as a group only three or four times within a morning, from the indoors to the outdoors, or from one room to another. Nursery children are learning how to be part of a group and how to move from one group activity to another. Each year the children gain skill in making transitions from situation to situation.

The teacher can also use physical transitions in guiding individual children. When she wants to encourage a reluctant child to go to the bathroom, she may say, "Let's go hopping"; admiring the hopping ability of the child, she leads him to the bathroom. This device is successful because the teacher shares the great interest of the child in one of the physical skills he considers a task of development. He basks in his teacher's appreciation of his skill and feels important about being successful in a new learning. He gets satisfaction out of his ability to control a new movement of his body. He is glad to have his teacher share his satisfaction and is willing to share her interests, too—even to the point of going to the bathroom.

The teacher can also use physical transitions to help a child enter a group activity. His teacher helped three-year-old Neal one day. Neal was hopping on one foot along a crack. The teacher said, "Let's play follow-the-leader. I'll follow you."

Neal went hopping along the cracks of the patio, turning at each corner. The teacher hopped along behind him. When Neal showed signs of getting tired, he was near some other children. The teacher helped Neal enter the new group by saying, "We were playing follow-the-leader. What are you playing?"

These two examples illustrate how to use a physical transition from one activity to another. First the teacher establishes rapport with the child, sharing the physical activity which interests him. Then the teacher guides the physical activity to the location of the next activity. The child responds to the cues of the new situation and moves into the activity associated with it.

Physical activities are used for filling the gaps between longer, more sedentary activities. If a group is to move to another situation not yet ready for them, their teacher may ask, "Can anyone walk on the sides of his feet?" or, "Do you know what I saw Neal doing this morning? He was jumping, and he jumped all the way around a circle." Hopping on the left foot, hopping on the right foot, walking on heels, turning a somersault on the grass, jumping around the room using both feet together, stepping back and forth in place—each of these is an intriguing challenge to the three- or four-year-old child. It will occupy him for several minutes, give him exercise needed for muscular development and control, and help him get ready for his next group activity.

Concomitant Learnings

Especially during the preschool years when children are so physically active, a child's feeling about himself is tied in with his physical skills. As Dr. Prescott points out,

The child continually uses his own body in interacting with objects, persons, and processes in his environment. . . . Thus concepts of self and readiness to attempt things are profoundly influenced by the quality of the child's body and the kinds of skills he develops in using it.[3]

Not only does a child build feelings of self-confidence in connection with his physical activities, he also improves his ability to get along with other children. Using a limited number of pieces of equipment involves taking turns and other forms of sharing. It also may involve problem solving and the learning of relationships, especially those in geography and science which are intimately tied in with nature walks and other forms of physical movement.

BUILDING FEELINGS OF CONFIDENCE THROUGH AWARENESS OF SKILL

Preschool children spend much of their day with people who are more skillful than they. As they become aware of different areas of competence, they often feel frustrated by their lack of skill in each of them. To offset such feelings, the experienced teacher helps them become aware of the competencies that they are building at their own age level.

When three-year-old Neal was playing with five-year-old Susan, he sometimes was unhappy with her expectations that he do what she did. One day when she was jumping from a crossed-leg to an open-leg position, Neal expressed his resentment verbally and asked her why she always wanted him to do what she did. But, as a four-year-old blowing bubbles, Neal showed his awareness of his own development when he volunteered the remark: "Once I didn't make a bubble. Now I could."

Both at home and at nursery school, parents and teachers helped Neal become aware of his physical competence. In this way they felt that the greater competence of his beloved older brother could be made more tolerable. They made a point of telling Neal: "When you are as old as Stanley is now, you will do that, too." Sometimes they reminded him: "You certainly do a lot of things that most three-year-old children can't do yet." They remarked about his competencies and helped him become aware of them, too, for instance, the first time that he hooked train cars together to make a long train, and his ability to walk along a crack in the sidewalk when he was four years and ten months old.

When the teacher has a three-year-old child who needs to be more appreciated by his parents, she can often take time after the school session to jot down in his folder any physical competence the child demonstrated that day. In a few weeks she has a list which she can use in talking with the child's parents and in building their pride in their child. She can also use the list at a meeting of parents to show them the kind of development that is taking place in their children. As parents develop the ability to see specific aspects of child development, they learn to appreciate the development of their own children.

[3] Prescott, op. cit., p. 388.

DEVELOPING PERSISTENCE

The preschool child needs to develop not only self-confidence but also persistence. This he can do in the area of physical development as soon as he is aware of his physical skills. At that point he is ready to make choices between sticking to an activity or abandoning it for the time being, and to exercise conscious control of his behavior in such decision making. He can learn how to "keep at it" even though he has lost his interest in the activity itself.

A teacher can develop a teaching strategy to facilitate the development of persistence. Here is a three-step strategy used by one teacher:

1. Help an individual child develop awareness of some criterion for deciding how long to continue an activity, for instance:
   "I ran until I was tired."
   "I swung until I had enough."
2. Challenge an individual or a small group of children to go beyond the expected limit, for instance:
   "Today you ran until you were tired. Someday see if you can run until you pant like a dog."
   "You have had enough of swinging. Do you want to stop, or do you want to try swinging once or twice more? You can keep on with something a little past having enough of it, you know."
3. When a child does try going beyond his expected limit, praise him for his persistence and accomplishment, for instance by saying:
   "John got tired of jumping. Then he did two more jumps. He went beyond his tired limit. Isn't it good to know that you can go beyond your tired limit if you want to?"

LEARNING TO TAKE TURNS

When the four-and-one-half-year-old children crowded around the new climber each eager for a turn, their skillful teacher gave them time to realize that they had a problem in using it, then gathered them together to discuss the problem of how many children could safely be on the climber at one time. Because each of the children could count to four or five, it was decided that no more than five children should use the climber at any one time and that they should take turns so that they would not get in each other's way.

After the talk five children who had had little time on the climber returned to it. A few minutes later Bobby in his eagerness pushed ahead of the child in front of him. His teacher reminded him to wait for his turn, "You know, Bobby, you're going to have to learn to wait. It's hard, isn't it? But you're learning it." At going-home time the teacher praised the children's accomplishment, "What pleases me is how you used the climber this morning. You stood and waited for your turn!"

PROBLEM SOLVING

Three-year-old Neal discovered the small concrete porch with steps leading up to it on one side and wooden rails on two other sides of it. He climbed from the porch onto the wooden rail, then over it. Then, hanging on to the top rail and walking on the outer edge of the porch floor, he started to climb down to the ground.

"What about the flowers down below you, there?" asked an adult. Without a word Neal changed the direction of his exploration. Hanging on to the top rail, he sidestepped to the corner of the porch rail and came over to the steps. Then he went back up to the porch, climbed over the rail, and lowered himself to the ground, stepping back across the flowers. He had solved the problem he set for himself, as well as the problem defined by the adult's question.

Preparation for School

Because preschool experience precedes school experience that is mandated by law in each state of the nation, it is sometimes looked at as preparation for classroom work, rather than as an experience worthwhile in itself. In fact, Head Start projects assume such a view when they emphasize having each less advantaged child enter first grade of elementary school with experience on which to base learning needed by every future citizen. Underprivileged children are to have their lives so enriched that they will start to school even with or with a head start in advance of middle-class children.

Focus on what lies ahead rather than on learning experiences at hand leads to overexpectations of preschool children, with concomitant frustrations, anxieties, and discomforts on their part. Such expectations may include, for instance:

OVEREXPECTATION	REALISTIC EXPECTATION
Sitting still in a large group	Active learning by doing
Sitting in a special way	Freedom to move around or sit still
Paying attention to a large-group activity	Choosing between individual or large-group activities
Learning a skill right now	Freedom to learn at one's own pace
Participating in reading-readiness activities	Choosing suitable activities from a wide environment that includes readiness activities for reading

However, one aspect of preparing for school is of great importance to preschool children, namely, the identification and removal of any physical barriers that a child may have in learning activities. This objective is so essential to preschool education that every preschool teacher should be trained to diagnose difficulties that a child has in learning, to refer his family or guardian to proper treatment agencies in the community, and to work with both child and family in overcoming deficiencies and minimizing handicaps.

TEACHER DIAGNOSIS

As a teacher works with groups of children in the same age range, she develops expectations about what children of that age range are able to do, about how they behave, and about how much they vary in their behavior. Sometimes, as she observes each child, she will come to identify one as being different from the others. If this difference interferes with his learning, it is the responsibility of the school to work with the parents or guardian of the child in seeing that the difficulty is removed, or at least minimized. Remediation should be completed, if possible, before the child leaves the preschool group.

Newspaper accounts and such books as *Death at an Early Age*[4] are increasing public awareness of the battered child and his difficulties in coping with school and other facets of life. The bruises and the comments of such a child make him easily identifiable in a preschool group.

Bakwin and Bakwin describe the rejected child as follows:

The outstanding personality defect in the rejected child, whether the rejection is overt or concealed, is lack of a feeling of worthiness or a sense of belonging. Anxiety may be prominent. . . .
In all types of rejection the need for affection leads to excessive demands for attention and applause.[5]

Besides identifying a child who has been consistently rejected or battered, a preschool teacher can easily identify children who are compensating for sensory deficiencies—for instance, the child who is not communicating through speech or the child who is not responding to spoken suggestions but is trying hard to move from activity to activity with his friends. Unusual effort on the part of the child day after day may result in early fatigue and lead to identification of an underlying physical difficulty.

In larger school systems, the preschool teacher may be able to report her observations of children who have possible barriers to learning and be assured that the counselor will work with parents in developing a remedial program. The following brief record kept by a school counselor reveals steps taken to assist a teacher in diagnosing a child's problem and in working with both him and his parents to develop a program of remediation.

[4] Jonathan Kozol, *Death at an Early Age* (New York: Bantam Books, Inc., 1968), 242 pp.
[5] Harry Bakwin, M.D., and Ruth M. Bakwin, M.D., *Clinical Management of Behavior Disorders in Children* (Philadelphia: W. B. Saunders Company, 1966), p. 215.

Name: Greg   Parents' Name:_____Phone: _____ School:_____

Age:_____Address:_____ Teacher:_____

March 17. Conference with speech therapist after diagnostic test requested by teacher. Test results as follows:

Spontaneous Speech

Vowel articulation: Deviant.
Consonant articulation: Deviant, with omissions, distortions, and substitutions.
Intelligibility: Unintelligible.
Voice quality: Normal.
Pitch: Normal.
Loudness: Too soft.
Rate: Normal.

Communicative Responsiveness

Responsiveness: Adequate.
Eye contact: Adequate.

Physical Behavior Observed

Gross coordination: Poor.
Fine coordination: Poor.
Drooling, undesirable oral habits: None observed.
Facial grimaces and Tics: None observed.
Hand usage: Left, and ambidextrous.
Foot usage: Right.
Eye usage: Left.

Speech Mechanism

Lips: Adequate.
Teeth: Adequate occlusion.
        Deciduous teeth missing.
Tongue: Adequate.
Hard palate: Adequate.
Soft Palate: Adequate.
Breathing: Adequate for speech.

Speech Correction Articulation Test

Little evidence of speech development.
                              (Will collect medical information.)
April 15. Prekindergarten evaluation: 58
Peabody test: I.Q. score, 88.
                              (Will see parent about enrolling Greg
                              in speech clinic.)
May 8. Home conference with Greg's mother.
Birth: Brain damage indicated.
Infancy: Had convulsions; phenolbarbitol prescribed.
Thirteen months: Convulsions.
Is just five years old now. Wakes up at night with nightmares. Still taking phenolbarbitol twice a day.

May 22. Attendance irregular. If Greg seems to need rest, his mother does not bring him.

June 3. The following report was received from Greg's physician:

> The child had an extremely stormy newborn period with severe seizures associated with periods of apnea. Although the prognosis was extremely poor, Greg has made amazing progress both physically and mentally. It was possible that he might develop a severe cerebral palsy.
>
> The EEG following his last seizure in April found "Focal abnormal electroencephalogram. Paroxysmal 3 to 4 per second sharp and slow wave activity, left cerebral hemisphere."

Summary and recommendations

Greg needs help with development of speech.

He has brain damage from birth. Had convulsions in infancy.

At five years of age now, he takes phenolbarbitol twice a day.

Greg's parents have enrolled him in the Speech Clinic. He enters in September.

Greg will be in kindergarten next fall because his age requires it. If possible, a volunteer or an aide-in-training will be assigned to pace his activity with words, and to interact with him verbally as much as possible.

If kindergarten is overly stimulating for Greg, he will be asked to come to school later than the other children do, or will have opportunity for rest in the nurse's office during the morning.

Situations for Discussion

A preschool teacher is apt to find herself in situations similar to the four described here. As you think of what to do in each situation, consider whether each course of action suggested is desirable, or not. Use points brought out in the chapter as well as ideas from your own experience to justify your views. Suggest alternative courses of action to supplement those given.

SITUATION 1   Your nursery center is two blocks from a small bakery patronized by the families of the children. You plan a succession of activities about the bakery for different days, selecting those activities that aid physical development. You plan to have the children

- Make gingerbread.
- Visit the bakery.
- Listen to a story about a visit to a bakery.
- Talk with a baker who will come to the school.
- Learn to sing "The Muffin-Man."

SITUATION 2   For your newly organized group of three-year-old children, you have an inexperienced assistant teacher. During play outdoors you supervise some of the outdoor activities and have her take responsibility for supervising one of them, for instance:

- Ball-handling.
- The swings.
- The ten-foot slide.
- Tree climbing.

SITUATION 3 As a beginning preschool teacher, you are building a list of physical activities to use in helping a four-year-old child move from one group situation to another. You include in your list the following:

- Walking along a crack.
- Walking a narrow curbing.
- Going tiptoe.
- Hopping on one foot.
- Jumping with both feet.

SITUATION 4 Mary a little girl in your preschool group, arrives each morning when her father leaves her on his way to work. The Monday that Mary has a large black and blue mark on her arm, you telephone her home to ask if Mary should be examined by the doctor. A housekeeper answers the telephone, and tells you that she is employed there. You should

- See if Mary has other bruises.
- Make a record of any days that Mary is bruised.
- Ask Mary if her arm hurts.
- Talk with the counselor about what to do.
- Show Mary's father the mark when he picks her up.

Books for Preschool Children

HAWKINSON, JOHN and LUCY. *Days I Like*. Chicago: Albert Whitman and Company, 1965. [Each month of the year has its activities.]

HUTCHINS, PAT. *Rosie's Walk*. New York: The Macmillan Company, 1968. [Rosie, the hen, safely takes a walk before dinner.]

LENSKI, LOIS. *On a Summer Day*. New York: Henry Z. Walck, Inc., 1953. [Physical activities of children go with the season. *Now It's Fall* (1948), *I Like Winter* (1950), and *Spring Is Here* (1945) are by the same author.]

STEINER, CHARLOTTE. *Kiki Dances*. Garden City, N.Y.: Doubleday & Company, Inc., 1949. [Kiki realizes her ambition of being a dancer.]

WRIGHT, ETHEL. *Saturday Walk*. New York: William R. Scott, Inc., 1954. [A Saturday walk with Daddy is filled with interesting sights.]

YASHIMA, TARO. *The Village Tree*. New York: The Viking Press, Inc., 1953. [In Japan the children of the village swim, climb trees, and enjoy other physical activities.]

CHAPTER 8

Learning to Participate
in the Culture

Preschool groups in Mexico, Japan, the United States, and other countries are alike in many respects but different in others. In all of them the preschool children learn, for instance, how to get along with other children; how to be a boy, or a girl; what mothers and fathers do; what a school is; how to play with toys; how to get acquainted with the community; and how to participate in the national holidays. Yet in each country preschool learning differs in details from preschool learning in another country because the social orders are different. The Mexican child becomes familiar with the community activities that center around the *zocalo,* or plaza. The Japanese child enjoys the importance of being a boy on Boys' Day or of being a girl on Girls' Day. The American child participates in Halloween fun and helps to celebrate other days considered special by the American people. Each child, no matter what the country is in which he lives, must become familiar with the customs, the behavior, and the artifacts of the social order of which he is a part. Preschool groups are invaluable in inducting a child into his culture.

Even children within a single culture learn somewhat different ways, depending on the neighborhood in which they live. For instance, within one California city, a nursery school meeting in a park kept its children reminded that the sidewalks, but not the picnic tables, were for walking on. At the same time at a day-care center in another part of the city, two little boys were playing house. One boy sat down at the table, leaned back in his chair and put his feet up on the table. The other boy said, "I'll get the beer." In both nursery groups the children were learning behavior in accord with that of the neighborhood community in which they lived.

What can the preschool group do to help the children understand and

Through their play, children develop understanding of their culture. (Courtesy of San Marcos Parent Child Workshop, San Marcos High School, Santa Barbara, California.)

participate in the culture of which they are a part? Although the individual teacher must decide about activities especially appropriate for the children in her group, all preschool teachers should provide experiences that help the children learn

- The role of a child, as distinct from that of adults.
- The role of a boy, or of a girl.
- Family roles, including those of father and mother.
- The artifacts of the society and how each is used.
- Roles of different community helpers.
- Differences between city and country.
- The nature of school.
- Relationships of people in the world.
- Basic concepts of the society as exemplified in special days.
- Activities associated with the special holidays.
- Costumes appropriate for a particular activity or occasion, as well as for the weather.

264

It is also important that teachers encourage preschool children to see relationships between people and their environment. They are pleased to hear such conversations as one between five-and-a-half-year-old Stanley and four-year-old Neal:

STANLEY   The fire engines have a siren.
NEAL   Do you know why, Stanley?
STANLEY   Yes. So they can go real fast, and have people get out of the way.

Four-year-old Neal inquired about the reason for having a siren on a fire engine, and five-year-old Stanley replied in terms of relationships between people and fire engines.

Learning Roles

LEARNING TO BE AN INDIVIDUAL CHILD

The preschool child must learn his role as an individual child within the culture. In doing this he must develop an awareness of himself as an individual in his own right and as a child with certain rights and privileges differing from those of adults in the social order.

The three-year-old child often finds it difficult to assume responsibility as an individual child. For instance, three-year-old Neal found it difficult to attend his neighborhood nursery school on days when his mother did not come too. He finally cleared that hurdle when he became four years old. Meanwhile, he gradually learned to differentiate himself from his mother. For instance, when he was three years and seven months of age, he considered the fact that he had short hair and his mother had long hair. "Children have short hair," he announced to his mother, using this difference as a help in learning his role as a child.

The fact that three-year-old Neal liked to direct his mother in her activities also gave her an opportunity to help him to learn his role as a person different from her. When he told her which apron to put on, she chose another apron, explaining to him the basis for her choice. A few minutes later, when he wanted to go out to play, she helped him to realize that he —like any other individual—was free to choose either his sweater or his jacket without regard to her preference.

At nursery school, Neal's teacher was also helping him to learn to express his preferences without expecting them to be followed slavishly. In telling a story to the children she asked, "Which way do you think the chipmunk went? Did he go up to the little girl's house or did he go home?" Some of the children said, "Home," and others said, "Girl's house." Then the teacher told them what the chipmunk in the story did, explaining his reason for doing it: "Well, this time the little chipmunk was very curious, so he went up the steps to the little girl's house."

As a three-year-old, Neal also began to distinguish himself from his older brother. He said, "He rides the bike. I run."

Another hurdle for Neal was that of attending his own Sunday school class while his father attended the church service. First, he and his father spent a morning at the Sunday school, daddy acting as an assistant to the teacher. Next, Neal asked to attend church with his daddy. He sat quietly through the entire service. The next Sunday his father felt that Neal should go to Sunday school while he was at the church service. Neal wanted to go to the church with his daddy. At Sunday school time, his daddy forcibly put Neal, crying loudly, inside the Sunday school room and departed for the nearby auditorium. Neal continued to cry for a few minutes while he absorbed this experience. Then a teacher took him over to the table where children were busy with puzzles. For the rest of the morning hour Neal sat at the table doing puzzles and, later, drinking juice. When his father came for him at the end of the church service, Neal rushed happily to him as he usually did. The next Sunday he was less resistant to the idea of going to Sunday school while his father went to church.

Growing through such experiences that differentiate between children and adults enabled Neal, as a four-year-old, to make discriminations such as those that he made in describing a young man: "He's not a daddy. He's not nothing. He's not a big boy." His teacher at this point helped him by saying, "I think he is what we call 'a young man.'"

LEARNING ABOUT FAMILY RELATIONSHIPS

The preschool child is finding a place for himself within his family, and his teacher—as well as his parents—should watch for every opportunity to help him to develop satisfying relationships with other members of his family and to understand family life as such. She should help him learn that in his family there are different roles associated with different members of the family. For instance, in the morning he may wake up his daddy, but a child who is visiting overnight does not do so; his mother prepares the meals, and his daddy watches television; the baby gets fed whenever it cries, but older children do not.

The wise preschool teacher reads and rereads such favorite books as *Papa Small*.[1] She collects magazine pictures which show pleasant family situations and uses them for flannelboard discussions about what a family does after supper, or on Sunday, or on the forthcoming holiday. She encourages the children in enjoying family celebrations such as birthdays by having them tell the other children about such events during talking time.

Meanwhile, parents are also endeavoring to help the children clarify their ideas about family relationships, as is shown by the following conversations between Neal (three years and nine months) and his mother when Neal was trying to get the attention of his older brother:

---

[1] Lois Lenski, *Papa Small* (New York: Henry Z. Walck Inc., 1966).

MOTHER   Please stop bothering your brother.
NEAL   He is not my brother; I am his brother.
MOTHER   He is your big brother. You are his small brother. You are two brothers.
NEAL   No, we are not. We are two children.

Teachers and parents work together in furthering the children's cooperation in the life of the family. Sometimes parents enroll siblings in the same preschool group because they feel that the children need help in learning how to get along better with others and especially with their siblings. Other parents are eager to enroll siblings—especially identical twins—in separate preschool groups so that each child may develop his individuality in relationships with others. When parents place two or more of the children in a nursery school group, the teacher should encourage the siblings to be considerate of each other as well as of other children. She can also take advantage of their sibling relationship to help all the children appreciate brotherly and sisterly roles. Such books as *Big Sister and Little Sister*[2] are useful to her in doing this.

The teacher should listen for feedback which shows understanding of roles within the family. For instance three-and-one-half-year-old Kimmy said to the playhouse mother: "You're the cook here and you cook such glad things that I like." At a day-care center, the little boy whose father remarried his first wife reported her arrival at home as follows: "I saw the goldfish. I saw the bird. I looked in the closet; it's got her clothes. She's going to stay." A teacher in a nursery school for three- and four-year-old children recorded the following family conversation that took place between four-year-old Lillian and an adult in the playhouse:

LILLIAN   Want a cup of coffee?
ADULT   Yes, please.
LILLIAN   Okay. I'll get it ready. (*Has the table set and pots and pans on the stove.*) My husband came to visit me last night. She's five foot two. My family has gone to visit their grandma. I just got ready for my dolly, but she doesn't eat.
ADULT   Maybe she's sick.
LILLIAN   Oh, no. She just doesn't want any. Here's some candy for your little girl. I'll go out in the mud and bake some cupcakes for you. (*Goes out, and returns in a few minutes.*)
(*Betty Jean, three-year-old, comes in sucking on a triangle. She picks up a doll.*)
LILLIAN   Have some pancakes, Betty Jean.
(*Betty Jean declines. A few minutes later she sits down, eats some sand, and spits it out.*)

[2] Charlotte Zolotow, *Big Sister and Little Sister* (New York: Harper & Row, Publishers, 1966).

LILLIAN   I had a meeting last night. I bought a little cake at the store. It cost thirty dollars. It really did. (*Talks to the doll.*) Baby, do you want to eat?
BETTY JEAN   Yes, she wants to eat.
LILLIAN   No, she wants to sleep.
(*Other children come into the playhouse.*)
BETTY JEAN   I'm finished with my breakfast. (*Gets up from the table.*)

This conversation is essentially a pleasantly cooperative one. Lillian is trying to be a helpful mother. Her observations about her husband reveal the limited understanding that a four-year-old child has about family relationships. The three-year-old girl, who has not yet learned the difference between real eating and pretend-eating, nevertheless is endeavoring to look after her dolly's needs.

The teacher should also appreciate feedback reported to her by parents, for instance, a mother's recording about her conversation with Kimmy, her younger daughter, when the child was two years and three months old:

KIMMY   I'm so gad [glad].
MOTHER   Why are you so glad, Kimmy?
KIMMY   Becus I hab a sisto [sister] in dis house and she hodes my han to cwoss da stweet.

Preschool children need adult guidance in learning about family relationships. Children of nursery school age often ask a neighbor about her husband by inquiring: "Where's your daddy?" They develop concepts of "mother" and "daddy" before those of "husband" and "wife," and before the concept of "grandmother" as the mother of one of their parents. Here are the remarks of Kimmy, Meredy (both three-and-a-half years old), and Neal (three years and nine months old), which reveal thinking about family relationships that can be compared with those at successively older ages:

KIMMY   Daddy, I wish I were a mommy and you were my little boy.
MEREDY   Has Phillips found himself a wife yet?
NEAL   We should have two daddies and one mommy and one child.
NEAL'S DADDY   What shall we call the other daddy?
NEAL   Daddy Neal. I should have two heads and long legs and short legs. When I want to drive the car, I pop out my long legs and when I want to drive the tricycle, I pop out my short legs.

A four-year-old observed Priscilla and Ralph with their arms around each other and said, "Pris and Ralph are going to get married and I'll marry him, too." And one five-year-old girl asked, "Why do ladies always take their husband's name? Why doesn't the husband take the mama's name?"

Children who have grandparents in their home develop a concept of a family which includes grandparents. Neal, for instance, at four years and three months of age, interpreted a picture of a group of different-sized fish as "a baby fish, a mommy fish, a daddy fish, a grandmother fish, a grandfather fish." He also drew a picture of "a mommy with long legs looking over the grandmother."

A wise preschool teacher is glad to find books which help children to understand their relationships to grandparents as well as to other members of the family. A book entitled *Grandfather and I*[3] is a delightful story in

A future mother on the phone. (Courtesy of Modesto City Schools, Modesto, California.)

itself, and also a springboard for talking about grandparents who live with the family or who come to visit it.

Family living is such an important part of the life of a preschool child that his dramatic play often is an expression of what he has been absorbing at home. For instance, three-and-one-half-year-old Marilyn sat down for a moment and noticed a box just at the right spot for putting her feet on. She did so, put her head back against her chair, and pretended to snore. Another day she showed her interest in daddy and what he does at home by

[3] Helen Buckley, *Grandfather and I* (New York: Lothrop, Lee & Shepard Co., Inc. 1959).

picking up a table knife. Putting it to her cheek she said: "I'm shaving."

The way in which children of successive preschool ages absorb the family life of which they are a part is illustrated by their play with dolls. Gesell and Ilg describe this as follows:[4]

Picture a doll, a doll crib, and a chair in the corner of a nursery school:
18-Month-Old toddles over to the crib, seizes the doll by the legs, drags it out, hugs and lugs it a short distance, drops it on the floor.
2-Year-Old picks up the doll more discriminately and holds its head up; he may even restore it to the crib and pull over the cover to keep the doll warm.
3-Year-Old may dress and undress the doll, seat himself in the chair, and say something to the doll.
4-Year-Old dramatizes a complex situation, summons the doctor to the bedside, and takes the patient's temperature.
5-Year-Old may make the crib and doll the center of a yet more complex project, the children's ward of a hospital and may carry the project over imaginatively from one day to the morrow.

LEARNING THE ROLE OF A BOY OR A GIRL

Each child needs to feel important, not only as a person but also as a boy or a girl. The adults who work with him build his confidence as an individual boy or girl, as the case may be. An adult may say to a little girl in slacks: "You are wearing play clothes today. That is what girls wear when they are going to play hard or work hard." Another adult may listen attentively to three-year-old Marilyn vicariously exploring the role of a boy by creating Billy, an imaginary boy who went into the forest to help Smokey the Bear put out fires, and did other boy things that Marilyn as a girl did not plan to do.

In one nursery school the mother of an only child, an adopted girl, initiated an unrealistic labeling which seemed harmless to her and to the nursery school teacher. The days that the mother brought her little girl dressed in a dress, she introduced her as Marie and encouraged her in playing only with the other little girls and girl things. On the days that she brought the girl dressed in cowboy costume, she introduced her as "Roger" and encouraged her to play only with the boys. The other adults in the nursery school overlooked the unreality of this procedure and thought it amusing to go along with what seemed to them to be a game. They would ask the little girl, "Are you Marie or are you Roger today?" They not only failed to help Marie appreciate herself as a girl who plays with other children, either boys or girls, but they also gave her no help in learning the reality of her own sex role. It was not surprising that the little girl by the time she was in first grade, had withdrawn from reality to the point of needing psychiatric help.

How do adults in a preschool group help the children to learn their sex

[4] Arnold Gesell and Frances L. Ilg, *Child Development* (New York: Harper & Row, Publishers, 1959), p. 67.

roles? They encourage them in exploring both masculine and feminine roles, carefully keeping role-playing labeled as such. When a child emerges from the dress-up corner wearing a fireman's hat, the teacher may say, "Good morning, Tommy. I see you are playing fireman. Do you need a fire-engine tricycle to get out to the fire?" Or when the children come out in their long skirts and high heels, she may say, "What lovely ladies! And who is this beautiful senorita? Why, it's Daisy, all dressed up as a Spanish lady wearing a beautifully embroidered shawl!"

The well-deserved compliment also helps children in learning their sex roles. When the adult supervises the playhouse and sees a little girl rocking her dolly to sleep, she may say, "Is your baby almost asleep?" and may add, "You certainly take good care of her, just the way a mother should." The adult likewise encourages the boys in their masculine roles as playhouse daddies, strong and manly helpers, or active boys playing hard on the swings and other apparatus.

When the children arrive in the morning, the teacher finds it easy to help them develop awareness of themselves in their sex roles "What a lovely dress for a lovely girl," she may exclaim, or, "I like your cowboy shirt, Dan." The teacher also capitalizes on story time as a means of teaching the role of boys and the role of girls. For instance, she may read *The Girl Who Was a Cowboy*[5] or may use her flannelboard to show pictures of what mothers and their little girls enjoy doing together and also pictures of what daddy and his son enjoy doing together.

At music time the teacher uses the song that Marcia Berman has recorded about individual boys and girls in the group: "Philip is a boy his daddy loves," and "Susan is a girl her mommy loves." The teacher is delighted whenever she happens to find additional songs, stories, and flannelboard pictures to use in helping the children to learn behavior appropriate for boys and behavior appropriate for girls.

The teacher also listens for feedback which shows that the children are developing pride in their sex roles and their knowledge of the behavior and costumes that go with masculine and feminine roles. She likes to hear an almost-three-year-old little girl say, "I have to wash my dimples," or to hear three-and-one-half-year-old Kimmy say to Ralphie, "Ralphie, you be a rootin-tootin cowboy and I'll be just a plain cowgirl." She enjoys hearing four-year-old Meredy plan what to wear to a birthday party, "I'll just wear my pink puffy dress because that's the fanciest dress I've got." She is especially pleased to hear the mother of one of the four-year-old girls say, "Kay is so full of pretend games with me when we're alone. I am the mother and she is my little girl, Karen, who dances with her loratide [leotard] on."

Preschool children learn to distinguish sex differences in people first by

---

[5] Phyllis Krasilovsky, *The Girl Who Was a Cowboy* (Garden City, N.Y.: Doubleday & Company, Inc., 1965).

noting differences in costume and later by noticing differences in genitalia. The Bakwins summarize these awarenesses as follows:

> The 2-year-old distinguishes sex to some degree by haircut and clothes and thus identifies his own sex. A little later he notices the differences in mode of micturition. By 3 years a child knows his own sex, and this is one of the items in the Binet test for mental age of 3 years.
> Conn found that 50 per cent of the children from 4 to 6 years . . . indicated awareness of the differences in the configuration of the genitals.[6]

The preschool teacher is pleased as she notices the children gaining such information but she is especially pleased by evidence that boys and girls are developing pride and satisfaction in roles of their own sex. For instance, Neal, when he was three years and ten months of age, noticed that the woman who usually guarded the street crossing in front of the school had been replaced by a man. Entering nursery school, he remarked to his teacher: "'s a man crossing guard."

TRYING OUT VOCATIONAL ROLES

By the time children are four years old, the length and complexity of their dramatic play makes it easy to observe their exploration of vocational roles. Three-year-old children also try out such roles, but so briefly that adults are not always aware of the exploration.

When three-year-old Neal visited the airport, he observed not only the airplanes but also the pilots. Telling about it later, he used a few words supplemented by gestures. He described the pilot: "The man had something on his ears [covering an ear with each hand], and here [putting one hand in front of the lower part of his face]." Probably Neal was also exploring the pilot role later, when he made a buzzing sound and ran around the play area.

The four-year-old child puts on a hat and is transformed into the role signified by his hat.[7] When Jerry, four-and-one-half years old, put on a soldier hat, he said, "Look at me. I'm the general." The nursery school teacher knows the value of these vocational impersonations, and sees to it that the dress-up clothes include a nurse's cap as well as ladies' hats, sunbonnets and straw hats, firemen's hats, police caps, pilots' caps, and hats or caps that indicate vocations of men and women in the neighborhood.

By the time a child is five years old, his exploration of various roles may have reached some of the more unusual roles in the social order. Ned, at five and one half, for instance, said to his teacher one morning in February:

NED   Do you know I'm a witch?
TEACHER   Is that so?
NED   I'm a sword fighter also. My sword is right outside.

[6] Harry Bakwin and Ruth M. Bakwin, *Clinical Management of Behavior Disorders in Children* (Philadelphia: W. B. Saunders Co., 1966), p. 114.
[7] Harvey Weiss, *My Closet Full of Hats* (New York: Abelard-Schuman, 1962).

The preschool teacher should make use of appropriate picture books to help the children to form realistic concepts about different vocations. The Lenski books, *Cowboy Small*,[8] *The Little Farm*,[9] *The Little Train*,[10] and *Let's Play House*[11] are examples of simple, descriptive books which are especially useful.

Initial Experiences in the Social Order

GETTING TO KNOW THE ARTIFACTS

Part of a child's induction into the culture is his introduction to its artifacts. In the United States, a child grows up with carpeting, chairs, and beds which a child in Japan does not know. Furthermore, he lives with TV as well as radio, with electric organs as well as pianos, with unbreakable dishes as well as china ones. Electric lights, furnaces, refrigerators, toasters, and other appliances are part of his everyday living. He must be familiar with them and learn how to use them without breaking them. The preschool group and its teacher play a large part in helping a child come to understand the artifacts of his social order.

How does a preschool child become familiar with a telephone? Probably both at home and at school he has a toy one to use. He may use it when the teacher uses hers, or whenever else he wishes to use it. As a two-year-old, he enjoys possessing it, carrying it around with him, dropping it now and then, and pulling off whatever is pullable. As a three-year-old, he uses the play telephone conversationally. He says "Hello" and "Goodbye."

Having two toy telephones available, two boys who were almost four years old carried on a conversation. Russell, who had been playing with one telephone said, "Hello." Paul to whom the teacher had handed the other telephone said, "Hello." Then both boys laughed. Russell put down his receiver. Paul handed his telephone back to the teacher, and went on with riding the rocking horse.

Girls, who are more mature, may carry on such a conversation as that between three-year-old Cindy and her friend, Stephanie:

CINDY   Hello. (*Pause*) No, this isn't Marjorie. It's Cindy. Stephanie, can you come over and play with me? (*Pause*) No, I can't come to your house. You hitted me three times at your house. I won't come. Goodbye.

If school provides a real intercommunication system between the play house and another part of the school, the children begin to use the telephone realistically in their dramatic play. If a mother telephones to the

[8] Lois Lenski, *Cowboy Small* (New York: Henry Z. Walck, Inc., 1949).
[9] Lois Lenski, *The Little Farm* (New York: Henry Z. Walck, Inc., 1942).
[10] Lois Lenski, *The Little Train* (New York: Henry Z. Walck, Inc., 1940).
[11] Lois Lenski, *Let's Play House* (New York: Henry Z. Walck, Inc., 1944).

A busy kitchen. (Courtesy of New Jersey State Department of Education, Trenton, New Jersey.)

nursery school from home or from a public telephone, or if the teacher talks with four-year-old children when they are at home, they have a real experience in using a telephone the way grownup people do. This getting acquainted with the telephone is typical of the process by which preschool children get acquainted with a variety of artifacts. They first become familiar with sturdy models, and then gradually start to use real objects as soon as their interest, their skill, and their size permit. When their interest outruns their skill and size, parents and teacher should make it possible for them to have experience under guidance. A portable step, lightweight and with a handhold, helps them, for instance, to use a real, adult-size washbasin or other bathroom fixture when they are still small.

The nursery school should be equipped with child-size models of the furnishings of a house: stove, sink, refrigerator, table and chairs, dishes and flatware, bed, mirror. As the children play the roles of different members of the family, they become familiar with desirable ways of using these artifacts. A sample of their conversation shows how the material objects of the social order enter into their dramatic play. Neal, three years and five months of age, is the daddy and Susan, five years and two months of age, is the mother. *Garage, closet, crib,* and *car* are an integral part of their conversation. Children in another social order would enjoy house play that includes objects of importance in their society.

Live television for four-year-olds. (Courtesy of New Jersey Department of Education Demonstration Class, Trenton, New Jersey.)

NEAL (*singing*) Go home, go home, go home. We have to have a garage.
SUSAN Here is a closet. Come here, you.
NEAL We have a baby, too.
SUSAN Where is the baby? Where—— Baby goes to sleep with us. You have to make a crib for her. How do you make a crib for her? You have to make a garage.
NEAL How do you make a garage? I don't know how.
SUSAN I know. Here the garage, and here is the closet.
NEAL What do we have to have? We have to have a kitty. Kitty wants some milk. Meow.
SUSAN Where is a car? We made a garage.
NEAL Kitty wants some milk right now!
(*They find a car and a truck.*)
NEAL Now we got it. Dzz, zz zz. (*Drives around.*)

The nursery should also be equipped with dress-up clothes that enable the children to try on a variety of costumes and try out the roles which accompany them. Little girls learn how to handle hats, gloves, pocketbooks, and high heels, as well as long skirts and furs. Little boys learn to feel at home in the costume of a cowboy or a sheriff. These articles of clothing are part of their culture and the children need to be familiar with them.

The following conversation between four-year-old Neal and his mother shows his sensitivity toward having the costume appropriate for the task:

NEAL (*comes in from the sandbox.*) Mom, I want short sleeves.
MOTHER (*selects a shirt from his closet.*) Is this shirt all right?
NEAL Yes, That's my sandy-work one.

Another mother was combing her hair while her son, four years and five months old, talked with her, mostly in a monologue. "Why are you combing your hair? So it will look good in the store?" he asked. Then he answered his own questions by saying, "If you didn't they'd say, 'There's Crazy Lady.'"

When children dress up, they try on not only the clothes that grownups wear, but also some of their ideas. When Cindy (three years and four months) was a lady with a long skirt, high heels, and a fur, she talked with Mary (four years old) who was attired in a beautiful yellow silk housecoat:

CINDY Are you going shopping in your pretty coat?
MARY No. I'm playing house.
CINDY That's too aspensible for shopping.

At three years of age, Cindy was already aware that certain clothes are appropriate for some occasions, but not for others.

The preschool group should have an endless variety of artifacts coming in to enrich the children's play. For the younger children there are sturdy cars, trucks, and planes. For the four-year-old children, the cars and trucks are not only sturdy, they are also of different kinds—the armored truck, the delivery truck, the moving van, the station wagon, and so on. The five-year-old children enjoy the fire engine which has a battery-operated search light. Meanwhile, the little girls enjoy a stove that is little more than a box with knobs on the front. Four-year-old girls want a more realistic model, and five-year-old girls enjoy having a battery-operated eggbeater to go with it.

The preschool teacher who appreciates the importance of actual experience with a variety of artifacts keeps bringing in basic toys as well as the expendable and throw-away materials (see Chapter 4). As each child is ready for new experience, he will enjoy exploring other of the material objects which are a part of his culture. The social value of artifacts has been pointed out by Montagu as follows:

Furthermore, a vast number of inanimate objects, of artifacts, come to assume more or less considerable social significance, in the sense of eliciting social responses. A crucifix, a flag, a book, a painting, apparel, and a thousand and one other things are all, of themselves, capable of eliciting social behavior principally in terms of socially learned responses to socially significant stimuli. . . . The culture artifacts and the objects of the natural environment in vital association with which the person grows up play a very important role in the socialization of the person. These objects are all endowed with value, and it is necessary to understand that this value originates in basic needs which are culturally satisfied in particular ways according to what is traditionally given in any culture.[12]

LEARNING ABOUT FOOD PREPARATION

Industrialization has taken out of home experience several processes of food preparation which young children enjoy. A preschool group makes it possible for a whole group of children to have these experiences with no more arranging than is necessary for one child. The children and their teachers talk together during the process of food preparation and have a pleasant group experience much like that enjoyed by the large family of fifty or more years ago. These processes of food preparation include the following:

- Making ice cream with a hand-operated freezer.
- Shelling and cooking peas.
- Preparing fruit—for instance, making applesauce.
- Squeezing oranges or lemons to make a drink.
- Whipping cream as a topping for crackers or a dessert.
- Making butter from whipping cream.
- Popping corn.
- Decorating cookies or crackers.

[12] M. F. Ashley-Montagu, *The Direction of Human Development* (New York: Harper & Row, Publishers, 1955), pp. 263, 264.

Some modern processes of food preparation are also especially interesting to preschool children, for instance,

- Using frozen juice concentrate to prepare a drink.
- Pouring concentrated fruit juice over ice crushed in a hand-operated crusher.
- Peeling carrots or cucumbers with a hand-peeler.
- Using a blender to purée carrots.
- Making packaged gelatin desserts.
- Making pancakes, cookies, gingerbread, or cakes from a prepared mix.
- Using whipped cream and similar products from aerosol bottles.

In planning for such activities, the teacher should identify those parts of the process to be done by the children and those to be done by adults. She may need to have an extra adult to help with a lengthy process, such as that involved in making homemade ice cream. She may need to have a batch of cookies or applesauce, for instance, already cooked in the event that what was prepared by the children does not get finished or does not turn out as planned.

COMMUNITY UNDERSTANDING

Children in a preschool group acquire a foundation for further understanding of the structure and functions of the community by getting well acquainted with several of the individual workers in the community. Their teacher should encourage them in knowing and in feeling friendly toward those community helpers of most concern to children, especially the fireman and his siren; the policeman who helps lost children and parents; the postman who brings messages, sometimes even to children; and the storekeeper who sells groceries to families.

The teacher should know the resources of the community and help the children to explore them as they get acquainted with each community helper. She should plan a series of experiences which acquaint the children with the fireman, for instance,

First day: When the siren is heard, gather the children together to talk about how firemen blow their siren so that everyone can clear the road to the fire. Then the firemen can get to the fire quickly and put it out.
Second day: Show the children The Big Book of Fire Engines.[13]
Third day: Read The Little Fireman[14] and Little Fire Engine.[15] Have fireman hats for dramatic play.

---

[13] George J. Zaffo, The Big Book of Fire Engines (New York: Grosset & Dunlap, Inc., 1964).
[14] Margaret Wise Brown, The Little Fireman (New York: William R. Scott, Inc., 1932).
[15] Lois Lenski, Little Fire Engine (New York: Henry Z. Walck, Inc., 1956).

Fourth day: Plan to visit the nearby fire station to find out where the siren car comes from and what a fireman does.

Fifth day: Make the trip to the fire station.

Sixth day: Recall the trip to the fire station. Have hoses, fireman hats, raincoats, fire engines, and other properties for dramatic play.

Seventh day: With small groups of children reread *The Little Fireman.* Use the flannelboard in talking about pictures of firemen and fire engines.

At another time during the school year, the teacher might plan a series of experiences to help the children in getting acquainted with their friend the policeman. This acquaintance may begin when a child has just had the experience of getting separated from his parents in a crowd and of being taken home by a policeman. Telling the group about his experience helps the child to gain perspective on the experience, and also helps the group to become sensitive to what a policeman does. The teacher follows up this introduction with such activities as the following:

- Reading *Policeman Small*[16] and talking about what policemen do to help families.
- Having a policeman come to school in his uniform.
- Having policeman caps and badges for dramatic play.
- Reading *Mike's House.*[17]
- Dramatizing how to give one's name and his daddy's name to the policeman.

Through the mailman, the teacher can introduce the children to the flow of mail through the community. If the mailman delivers mail to the school, the children watch for him to come at about the same time each day. When a child is ill, the others make use of the mail service by giving the mailman a card for the sick child. Another day they may receive an answering message brought by the mailman. Meanwhile, the teacher may broaden the children's understanding of what the mailman does by reading *About Postmen.*[18] This may lead to a plan for inviting the mailman to stop in for a few minutes to visit the school and talk with the children.

For Valentine's Day—or Easter, or Mother's Day, or any day, in fact—the children can make a picture message to send home through the mail. The next school day, with the help of an extra adult, each child puts his message into an addressed envelope, puts a stamp on it to pay the postmen for their help, and takes it to the nearest mailbox. Or, if a branch postoffice is near the school, the children enjoy buying a stamp and mailing their letters there. Thus they have a brief introduction to the work of the postoffice as a link between their community and other communities.

[16] Lois Lenski, *Policeman Small* (New York: Henry Z. Walck, Inc., 1962).
[17] Julia L. Sauer, *Mike's House* (New York: The Viking Press, Inc., 1954).
[18] Evelyn Hastings, *About Postmen* (Chicago: Melmont Publishers, 1967).

In developing a study unit about the mailman, the teacher should at times review with the children their experience with the mail and add to it whenever opportunities are available. A letter from a friend or a package of children's books arriving through the mail enlarges the children's appreciation of the mailman. By the end of the school year, each child should feel acquainted with the mailman, and be apt to play the role of mailman as did four-year-old Ned, for instance. He said he was delivering cats and dogs to children.

Almost every preschool child goes to the store with members of his family. He should enlarge on these experiences at school with the help of his teacher and gain a fuller appreciation of the people who work at a store. The children can dramatize store experience with a "store" of their own. It has not only a counter and shelves, but also a cash register, play money, baskets or carts for the shoppers to use, and a supply of packages and canned goods (each carefully emptied from the bottom so that it can look just like the original item on the shelf at the store). Dramatic play goes on for an hour or more, with dressed-up ladies tottering in on high heels to purchase the food for their family. The addition of egg, milk, and cottage cheese cartons to the store goods gives a new impetus to the play and starts the children taking turns again as cashier, salesman, box boy, or delivery man.

The wise teacher often contributes to the store play. Sometimes she is a fellow shopper accompanying a shy customer, a momentary consultant who recommends reducing the price of butter from ten dollars to a more realistic amount. Sometimes, with her flannelboard or a well-chosen book, she helps the children think about the store when it is not actually in operation. She is ingenious in enriching both the store and other activities by relating them to each other. One day she has individual cans of fruit juice and drinking straws for the children to purchase at the store at juice time. Another day, she provides the store with fresh carrots that are sold to feed the guinea pig and also to provide carrot sticks at refreshment time. The day that she reads from *I Want to Be a Store Keeper*[19] the store has boxes of cereals for sale, and the children have refreshments of cereal flakes in a sandwich bag. When she uses the flannelboard to talk about good things to eat, she makes the children aware that their store does not sell candy. In short, she makes the store an integral part of the school program and the roles of store personnel a reality to the children.

In one four-year-old nursery group, the value of the store experience was apparent in helping a boy who was finding that a new town, new school, and new friends were a great deal to absorb. Here are the teacher's brief recordings, which show his coming to feel at home in the new nursery school:

October 3rd: Stanley is not too resourceful yet. He seems happy, pleasant, smiling, and has a nice rapport with teacher.

[19] Carla Greene, *I Want to Be a Store Keeper* (Chicago: Children's Press, 1958).

October 10th: Stanley was glad to drive to Kiddie Town with teacher. He seemed to enjoy the rides, but skipped one of them. His mother says he is not secure yet, and does not go the days we go to the park. . . . Sometimes sucks his thumb, at story time for example.

November 19th: Stanley loves the store, especially the cash register. Has spent an entire morning at it twice.

April 23rd: Stanley has become more sociable as the year has passed. He had a lonely, lost period for a time at first and once in between. But now he often joins another child or a group that is engaged in an activity he enjoys. Even last fall he would join anyone who would play "store" with him, although at that time he wanted to direct the activities. He has leadership qualities in areas which are fascinating to him. A few days ago in an agreeable way he joined a "store" group which Emily was directing. At first he just observed. Presently he was actively engaged in rearranging the furniture. He had to leave a moment later but he called pleasantly to Edward, who was helping: "I'll be back, Edward."

The preschool teacher in the suburban community should help the children to appreciate the garbage collectors as they carry out their important community function. The children watch for their friend the garbage man as eagerly as for the mailman. *Dear Garbage Man*[20] is a book that helps them understand how he feels about his work, even though the title of the book is not in keeping with the account of what he does.

In each preschool community the teacher should consider whether other community helpers are important for the children to know. If the ice cream vendor is part of the community, she arranges for him to come at refreshment time now and then so that each child can have an opportunity to make a real purchase using real money and going to the vendor only when he is right at the curb. She follows up this experience with a flannelboard talk that helps the children to realize why an adult always is with them when they stop the ice cream man, not only to pay for the ice cream but also to help them be safe from cars.

In many communities the preschool teacher can capitalize on the milkman as a community helper. She arranges for him to come in his truck at refreshment time to bring an individual milk carton for each child. She uses the book *The Farmer and His Cows*[21] to help the older children understand where the milk came from. If possible, she makes arrangements for a study trip to a nearby dairy so that the children can see the cows eating hay and being milked, and can have a small carton of milk at the place it comes from. She can emphasize that all the helpers who provide milk make every effort to keep it clean and good to drink.

The preschool teacher should make a point of getting acquainted with the community helpers in the preschool neighborhood. When she meets

[20] Gene Zion, *Dear Garbage Man* (New York: Harper & Row, Publishers, 1957).
[21] Louise Floethe, *The Farmer and His Cows* (New York: Charles Scribner's Sons, 1957).

a friendly person who likes children, she works out with him some plan by which he can show the children his part in the life of the community. In one community the friendly person may be the owner and operator of a small bakery, the man who drives a bakery wagon, an upholsterer of chairs, a tailor, or a dressmaker. Whoever he is, he probably can help the children realize that their community has many workers, each of whom is a helpful and friendly person.

The four-year-old child should become acquainted with what his own daddy does and with what other daddies do—the fireman, the policeman, the grocer, the baker, and others in his own community. This person-to-person acquaintance with the individuals who comprise a neighborhood is a necessary background for the kindergarten and first-grade exploration of relationships within the community, especially the flow of food and other materials through it. The four-year-old child sees the individual community helpers primarily as individuals; the five-year-old begins to see them in relation to each other as well as to families.

The preschool teacher should make sure that each of the many experiences that the children have with workers in the community is a happy one. Pleasant associations with the workers will make the children interested in further interaction with their community. A foundation of pleasant community experience is the best possible introduction to an understanding of the social order. The teacher should also look for feedback that reveals the children's feelings about their experiences. Sometimes the experiences are sufficiently vivid to result in immediate expression through words, through dramatic play, or through the art materials that are always on hand in the school. At other times, a delayed response shows the cumulative effect of several experiences, or a persistent memory of a favorite one, or only delayed opportunity for expression. Whenever she finds evidence that the children are interested in the workers of their community, the teacher can be pleased with having provided the pleasant and educational experiences that gave rise to those interests.

City and Country

The teacher who is aware of the importance of basic understandings in social studies helps the children develop at their own age level an awareness of the contrasts between city and country. On study trips to see farm animals and farm products, she uses the term *country* and relates simple ideas to it: "We are going out to the country to see the cows. Cows live in the country where farmers can grow food for them. It takes a lot of hay to feed a cow."

The teacher should also encourage the four- and five-year-old children in building concepts of the differences between life in the city and life in the country. Several books can help her in doing this. The *Little House*[22]

---

[22] Virginia Lee Burton, *Little House* (Boston: Houghton Mifflin Company, 1942).

tells how a house in the country becomes a house in the city when the city gets so big that it surrounds the little house. She can use *Noisy Book*[23] to contrast the noise of the crowded city with the quiet of the country. *Wake Up, Farm* and *Wake Up, City*[24] also bring out contrasts between city and country life.

PRETEND OUTDOOR EXPERIENCES

Children enjoy gathering small sticks to make a campfire. Then they sit around the fire, warming their hands, listening to stories, singing songs, and sometimes cooking hot dogs or roasting marshmallows. Besides such a real experience, the children also enjoy a pretend camping trip. Through words and pantomine, their teacher can create the experience with them. Especially on a rainy day indoors, in a group having several four-year-old boys, the teacher can find responsive children to play "camping." Gathering together the children not otherwise occupied, she says, "Let's get firewood for a pretend campfire," and starts to arrange some of the blocks in a quiet corner.

Together, the teacher and the children create the fun of a campfire. "Shhhh. Do you hear that little noise?" the teacher asks in a stage whisper. Again she makes a small gnawing noise. "It's a chipmunk cracking a nut. Oh! There he goes scampering along that log." The teacher helps the children to become sensitive to the setting of the campfire. Presently she tells them a story, not a frightening story or cowboy story, but a story suitable to their age—perhaps a simple story about a robin,[25] or other animals,[26] or an outdoor story.[27] Or she sings a ballad[28] as she strums on her guitar or autoharp.

Another day, the teacher can take the children on a pretend fishing trip. Getting out fishing equipment, finding a suitable location, baiting the hook, casting and reeling in, and putting the fish in the bucket or basket comprise a thrilling pantomine for the children. Of course, the teacher has stories to tell while everyone is waiting for the next fish to nibble[29] or watching the birds that fly silently by.[30]

---

[23] Margaret Wise Brown, *Country Noisy Book* (New York: Harper & Row, Publishers, 1940); *Noisy Book* (New York: Harper & Row, Publishers, 1946).

[24] Alvin Tresselt, *Wake Up, Farm* (New York: Lothrop, Lee & Shepard Co., Inc., 1955); *Wake Up, City* (New York: Lothrop, Lee & Shepard Co., Inc., 1957).

[25] Alvin Tresselt, *Hi, Mister Robin* (New York: Lothrop, Lee & Shepard Co., Inc., 1950).

[26] Marie Hall Ets, *Play with Me* (New York: The Viking Press, Inc., 1955).

[27] Robert McCloskey, *One Morning in Maine* (New York: The Viking Press, Inc., 1952).

[28] Ruth Crawford Seeger, *American Folk Songs For Children* (New York: Doubleday & Company, Inc., 1948).

[29] Bernadine Cook, *The Little Fish That Got Away* (New York: William R. Scott, Inc., 1956).

[30] Robert McCloskey, *Make Way for Ducklings* (New York: The Viking Press, Inc., 1941).

The teacher should choose from her own background of outdoor experiences those she has enjoyed most. Through pantomime, story, and song, she can then recreate with the children the action and the fun of such experiences. The imagination of children is stimulated by acting out with their teacher what they have experienced with their own families, or have seen on TV, for instance:

- Climbing a mountain, picking one's way over and around the rocks, seeing the wild flowers, admiring a waterfall, and enjoying the view from the top while resting and listening to a story.
- Hunting with a camera, seeing and hearing different kinds of animals in their many different kinds of homes.
- Paddling a canoe on a lake or a river trip through Indian country.
- Going through a cave which has bats sleeping on the ceiling near the entrance, stalactites and stalagmites that look like many different kinds of things, an underground pool, and an elevator back to the surface.

Of course, the teacher should use all possible aids to stimulate imagination. In preparation for an imaginary outdoor trip, she may show the children pictures of real places similar to those to be visited. A real trip to an actual place in the community is the best prelude to imaginary trips during the following months. Picture-book stories about the outdoors (for instance, *Pip Camps Out*[31]) help the teacher before, during, and after the trips.

The teacher is delighted when the dramatic play of the children includes roles appropriate to country life, as well as those appropriate to city life. Here is an example of the conversation between Russell (four years and two months) and Neal (four years and six months), who are making tricycle excursions around the perimeter of the play area:

RUSSELL   Let's go to the mountains now. (*The boys make another circuit.*)

NEAL   We saw bears and we shot them. I have a giraffe and a bear in my car. Russell has a bear and a lion. (*The boys busy themselves with their tricycles.*)

NEAL   We had to put up our tent on this trip. Last trip we didn't. We put up our tent in the shade.

RUSSELL   We put up our tent. (*The boys again circle the area.*)

NEAL   Hi ya—We got get the animals.

RUSSELL   We went to the office to the man and we said we call him next week. And we said wait a minute. That's all we did to the office.

NEAL   Dingaling. Is that the office man?

RUSSELL   We call him up.

NEAL   He got to call us up.

RUSSELL   (*Leaves again.*)   I goofed. I got to turn around.

---

[31] Myra Berry Brown, *Pip Camps Out* (San Carlos, Calif.: Golden Gate Junior Books, 1966).

GETTING ACQUAINTED WITH SCHOOL

When a child starts to attend a preschool group, he begins an experience which will be an important part of his life for many succeeding years. His initial experiences in his school community should be pleasant and educative, and should make him eager to continue in school. The teacher should help him to gain success in feeling comfortable in the simple routine of the school and in feeling at home in an organized school situation. Whenever an opportunity presents itself, she should remind the children of the fun of going to school, perhaps by saying, "Aren't we glad that we go to school!"

At the end of each preschool year, the teacher should arrange for the children who are going on to grade school to visit it. She and their parents can go with them to visit the kindergarten and to meet the teacher they will have the next school year. Similarly, kindergarten children like to visit the first-grade teacher and to anticipate what school will be like during their next year. This attempt to smooth the transitions from teacher to teacher and from school situation to school situation is one of the ways to help children enjoy going to school.

WORLD CONCEPTS

By the time a child is in a nursery school group of four-year-olds, he has begun to build concepts about himself, not only as a member of a community but also as part of a world of people. His teacher probably has used such books as *Tommy and Dee Dee*[32] to acquaint him with the fact that there are other children in other countries. She has had visitors come to show the costumes, to say a few words, and to tell bits about the lives of the children in that country. She has encouraged the children to share any contacts that they and their families may have with relatives and friends in other countries—telling about telephone or radio conversations and bringing gifts from abroad to show their friends.

Over the years the teacher builds a collection of books and objects which help her to orient the children to the larger world in which they live. Her collection includes such items as the following:

● Simple story books: *Bernadine and the Water Bucket*,[33] *Big World and the Little House*.[34]
● Pictures, such as those in *Children and Their Fathers*.[35]

[32] Yen Liang, *Tommy and Dee Dee* (New York: Henry Z. Walck, Inc., 1953); *The Pot Bank* (Philadelphia; J. B. Lippincott Co., 1956).
[33] Aileen Olsen, *Bernadine and the Water Bucket* (New York: Abelard-Schuman, Limited, 1966).
[34] Ruth Krauss, *Big World and the Little House* (New York: Abelard-Schuman, Limited, 1949).
[35] Eugen Roth, *Children and Their Fathers* (New York: Hill & Wang, 1962). Hanns Reich, *Children and Their Mothers* (New York: Hill & Wang, 1964).

- A child's costume (e.g., a silk kimono or a worker's jacket, child-size, from Japan).
- Dolls in costumes of other lands.
- Simple games and toys enjoyed by children in other countries (e.g., a Christmas *piñata* from Mexico).

With such a collection, the teacher is well prepared to help the children understand that the people of their own countries are from families who have come here from many lands.

The preschool teacher who has emphasized world relationships is pleased to hear remarks such as those made by a highly verbal four-year-old girl, Meredy, who commented on her own home by saying, "All the people in our house are hooma beans [human beings], even sister." At the age of four years and five months, she commented on current military problems by saying, "It would be nice if everyone could live gently and in peace."

THINKING OF OTHER PEOPLE

The nursery child is highly egocentric. When he first comes to a nursery group, he probably has thought mostly about himself and a bit about the other members of his own household. In the nursery group, he is encouraged to think about people from other households. After several months of thinking about people from households much like his own, he is ready to consider people from households quite different from his own. His teacher considers the community and decides on the ethnic group most appropriate for study by the children.

In a California community, a nursery center attended by Mariko and her Nisei family focused its attention on how people live in Japan. *Plenty to Watch*[36] gave the children ideas about what children do in Japan. *Umbrella*[37] told them about the feelings of a child. They were delighted when Mariko brought her Japanese kimono and her brother's and let the children see what it is like to wear a kimono. Mariko also shared with them a Japanese record and a wooden doll from Japan.

In a nursery school where several of the children were from families that had lived in Italy, the teacher spent several days guiding the children in thinking about how children and their families live in Italy. She told the parents about the interest of the children and encouraged the parents in telling their children stories out of their own experience and in sharing these with the nursery school. She read *Little Leo*[38] and soon the children's interest shifted from the distant Italian community to the Italians who were part of their own community.

Preschool children with older brothers and sisters studying about Indians

---

[36] Mitsu Yashima and Taro Yashima, *Plenty to Watch* (New York: The Viking Press, Inc., 1954).

[37] Taro Yashima, *Umbrella* (New York: The Viking Press, Inc., 1958).

[38] Leo Politi, *Little Leo* (New York: Charles Scribner's Sons, 1951).

are interested in studying about them, too, especially if families of Indians are part of their community or come to local celebrations such as county fairs. The preschool teacher encourages her four- and five-year-old children to study Indians through activities such as the following:

1. Like Indians, the children gather nuts and other seed pods in the fall of the year. They plant seeds, too, putting in a bit of plant food the way the Indians did by burying a fish with the corn seed.
2. The children learn to walk and run quietly the way Little Indian and his father did. They also develop their own war dances, first using a record of Indian drums and later their own drum beats. They wear headdresses to enhance such activities.
3. The children enjoy the role of protector of the forest and of its animals, including *Smokey the Bear*.[39]
4. Through craft activities, the children create the objects associated with an Indian tribe:
    a. They make headbands for themselves, perhaps with feathers from the local chicken or turkey shop, or perhaps with paper feathers cut from brightly colored papers and stapled onto a paper headband.
    b. They make teepee models by decorating a precut piece of yellow construction paper, and, with adult guidance, stapling it together.
    c. They make model canoes in the same way, first crayoning and then stapling together precut construction paper of an appropriate light color.
    d. They make a totem pole from egg cartons cut in half. The three-year-old children, for instance, use tempera paints to decorate the sections of the egg cartons. The next day after the paint has dried, they crayon patterns on them. Finally, with adult help, they staple a part of a section across the end of a half-carton to make the completed totem pole.
    e. They string cranberries or rose apples to make necklaces.
5. With grownup help, the children use long but lightweight poles to make the framework for a teepee playhouse. An old nylon parachute, or a discarded bedspread that is light in weight, is fastened to the framework with clothespins, and can be quickly removed in case of rain.
6. With her flannelboard, the teacher introduces the following action story.

Out in the forest is a great big teepee (*stretches both arms upward over head*). Beside the teepee are two big sequoia trees waving in the breeze (*waves arms*). And out of the teepee comes smoke (*twirls hands upward*). And inside the teepee are "One little, two little, three little Indians . . ." (*continues with "Ten Little Indians" song*).

[39] Jane Werner Watson, *True Story of Smokey the Bear* (New York: Golden Press, 1955).

7. The teacher tells the children simple stories about Indian life. One teacher transposes *The Carrot Seed*[40] into the setting of an Indian family. Another teacher beats on a drum as she tells a story about a little Indian boy who talks with his father by drum. She uses different tempos for different messages, and tells how the boy got lost but was able to find his way back home by talking on his drum.

8. Depending upon the resources of her community, the teacher arranges for the children to visit an Indian display, or to have an Indian come in costume to tell the children that Indians are friends and not the kind of people shown as bad men in many moving pictures about the Old West, or to show how Indians weave headbands or make baskets or shape pottery.

Holiday Customs

One third or more of the preschool program centers around the holidays of the social order. Throughout the year, teachers and parents should acquaint the children with each holiday in turn—the meaning of the holiday and the customs and rituals that are part of its celebration. Three-year-old children go along with the activities; they live in a here-and-now world and are delighted to do whatever is being done. Four-year-old children participate more actively in holiday preparation and celebration. They have previous experience which enables them to anticipate the holiday events and to enjoy them—both in prospect and in actuality. Five-year-old children begin to appreciate the meaning of the holiday as well as its activities.

The experienced preschool teacher keeps in mind certain teaching methods that apply to all holiday celebrations. These include the following:

1. Space over two or three weeks the various activities connected with the holiday. This spacing helps the children to anticipate the holiday itself. It also enables them to cope with a single activity at a time and to enjoy each to the full.

2. Plan the final holiday event close to the actual holiday, but not on the same day. Most families have their home celebrations on the date of the holiday, and these celebrations are as much as most children can enjoy in one day.

3. On the day of the school celebration, avoid overstimulation. Plan usual activities and limit the special celebration to one or, at the most one and one-half hours. The period from refreshment time to an early closing time is ample for celebration by a preschool group that meets in the morning for a half-day session.

[40] Ruth Krauss, *The Carrot Seed* (New York: Harper & Row, Publishers, 1955).

4. Remember that the children are more important than the activity. If the holiday activity seems overly stimulating or outside the interest of the children, abandon it in favor of familiar activities.
5. In general, holiday activities for the children should be familiar activities which have been varied in some small way to fit in with the holiday theme. For instance, making a collage is a delightful craft activity which can be varied by using bits of orange and black paper at Halloween time, green and red paper at Christmastime, and yellow and green paper at Eastertime.

HALLOWEEN

Halloween is an evening of play after the work of the fall harvesting. As it has developed in the United States, it is celebrated primarily for school children and young people. The frightening figures of ghosts and witches are inappropriate for preschool children. Realizing this, the preschool teacher should endeavor to bring out the pleasant idea of the fall harvest, and to prepare the children to cope with the imaginary ideas that are beyond their level of maturity.

By enjoying the autumn harvesttime herself, the preschool teacher can have a delightful time helping the children to enjoy it, too. She knows the crops of the community, and she arranges for the children to go out into the farm area to see the harvesting and, if possible, to help in it in a small way. At school she uses story book, flannelboard, and dramatic play to guide the children in reliving their experiences. She provides them with craft and art materials and opportunities for dramatic play of their own creation, so that their feelings about the autumn harvest can find expressions in concrete and verbal form. Here are some of the ideas that teachers have in their file folders under the heading of "Autumn":

1. Visit a farm which has one or more nut trees. Have each child pick up enough nuts to fill a small bag. Back at the school, crack the nuts and eat them at refreshment time.
2. Visit a cider mill and have cider at juice time.
3. Go to an apple orchard to see apples being picked and to an apple-packing plant to see them packed. Use the flannelboard to show how apples come from tree to store to home. Serve apple slices at refreshment time.
4. Have a walk through fallen leaves. Read *Johnny Maple Leaf*[41] and *Now It's Fall*.[42] Gather seed pods of different flowers and weeds. Gather leaves of different shapes and colors. Make a collage of small leaves.
5. Go to see food processing that is done in the neighborhood. Bring the food product back to school for refreshments.

[41] Alvin R. Tresselt, *Johnny Maple Leaf* (New York: Lothrop, Lee & Shepard Co., Inc., 1948).
[42] Lois Lenski, *Now It's Fall* (New York: Henry Z. Walck, Inc., 1948).

6. In cotton-producing localities, show the children how the plant product is made into a thread for use in making cloth.

Each fall the teacher can bring harvesttime displays for bulletin board, library corner, or some other display place where the children may pick up and examine objects and pictures at their leisure after an adult has talked about them. Cornstalks, pumpkins, leaves on a branch, seed pods, nuts, local fruits, and grains can be introduced to the children in this way, or by having an adult talk about the display as the children are looking at the items.

One teacher uses the Halloween pumpkin as a means for teaching children where the greengrocer gets the fruits and vegetables he sells. With the four- and five-year-old children, she develops a sequence of ideas about where the pumpkin comes from. The conversation moves slowly and with elaborations that depend on what the children in the group may say.

TEACHER (*holding up a pumpkin*)   What is this?
CHILDREN   A pumpkin.
TEACHER   Where do we get pumpkins?
CHILDREN   At the store.
TEACHER   Where does the store man get them?
CHILDREN   From the farmer.
TEACHER   Where does the farmer get them?
CHILDREN   He grows them from seed. He grows them in the ground.

Then the teacher makes the pumpkin into a jack o'lantern. She tells a story as she works, shortening it or elaborating it as seems appropriate:

When the farmer first found this pumpkin growing in his field, it was green. The next time he looked at it, he noticed that it was starting to turn orange. He said to himself, "This pumpkin is almost ready to go to the market. When it is all orange in color. I'll send it to the store." The pumpkin started wondering what was going to happen to him.

At the store a boy and a girl with their mother pick out the pumpkin. They say, "That's the one we want, Mommy." Again the pumpkin wonders what is going to happen to him, He thinks, "Oh, dear, I hope they are not going to make a pumpkin pie out of me."

The teacher continues with the story, telling how the mother scoops out seeds and cuts out eyes, nose, and mouth. As she completes each action, she wonders what is going to happen next. She concludes the story by making the pumpkin very proud and happy that he is a jack o'lantern and not a pumpkin pie.

If a pumpkin is not readily available to illustrate the story, the teacher can use a series of paper pumpkins cut from construction paper. Each pumpkin depicts a step in the making of the jack o'lantern.

As Halloween approaches, the teacher should prepare the children for the events which may be frightening to them. She can introduce them to the idea of wearing costumes by reading *Jeffie's Party*[43] if the children are four- and five-year-olds. One day they can make costumes by decorating a large, market-size paper bag which has a hole cut out for the head and a slit on each side for the arms. When their costumes are finished to their satisfaction, they try them on and have the fun of wearing a costume of their own creation. Such activities lead to a day when each child comes to school in costume. The dress-up clothes furnish costumes for children who want one but do not have one. The teacher wears her dress backwards and has fun pretending she is going when she is coming, and vice versa. She helps everyone have fun wearing a costume—or not wearing one, as each chooses.

The wise teacher shows the children what a mask is, and has several masks which they may try on if they wish. As each child tries on the mask, an adult is at hand to help him realize how difficult it is for him to see, but is careful not to frighten him about the dangers of wearing a mask. She develops the conversation casually and objectively in terms of the constructive idea of what to wear and what not to wear as part of a costume. Later, when the children plan their costume day, they decide to wear costumes without masks.

Many three-year-old children and several four-year-old children will have difficulty in absorbing the idea of the differences which costumes seem to create. The teacher should be sympathetic with the reluctance of any child to participate in a costume party and should be understanding about non-participation. She enjoys the costuming herself, and is pleased with sharing the fun with those children who are ready for the experience. She knows that there are sensitive children, like three-year-old Mari, who are afraid of people in masks. When Mari became four years old, she was still more frightened than pleased by masks. She clung to the teacher when her friend, Kathy, came into the nursery school wearing a mask. The teacher reassured her by saying, "Why, Mari, this is your good friend, Kathy. We're not afraid of Kathy." Finally Mari recovered her pose to say, "I like Kathy, but I don't like that!"

To prepare the preschool children for the frightening activities of their older siblings and neighbors, one teacher has successfully used the following finger play:

If you want to scare someone on Halloween (*shaking finger at person*),
   I'll tell you what I'll do.
I'll hide behind a pumpkin head (*putting hands in front of face*),
   And then I'll holler—BOO!

---

[43] Gene Zion, *Jeffie's Party* (New York: Harper & Row, Publishers, 1957).

There is no complete substitute for a firsthand experience. (Courtesy of The Merrill-Palmer Institute and Donna J. Harris, Detroit, Michigan.)

This simple game helps the children understand that Halloween is a time of pretending and of games. *Humbug Witch*[44] helps too.

THANKSGIVING

After Halloween, the teacher should continue to emphasize the fall harvest and also begin to emphasize preparation for winter. Food is harvested and processed so that it will be available all during the winter months. When everything is finally ready for wintertime, the people celebrate with a day of Thanksgiving. They are glad that they have food to last until more food can be grown in the spring. This theme of gladness is especially appropriate for the preschool children. Being glad that there are dried fruits and nuts and other products of the harvest to eat during the winter is a means of helping the children to become aware of these products and their uses.

[44] Lorna Balian, *Humbug Witch* (New York: Abingdon Press, 1965).

Books can help the teacher to develop the idea of the fall season as a time of preparing for winter, and describe the seasonal activities on the farm. Kindergarten children like to hear *Little Bear's Thanksgiving*[45] and *The Thanksgiving Story*.[46]

Because the turkey has come to be an accepted Thanksgiving symbol, the teacher should help the children appreciate it. She can plan craft activities around the turkey theme. She presents the turkey song with its "Gobble, gobble, gobble." If she can arrange a trip to a turkey farm, she does so. After the children have seen a turkey strutting around at a farm or at a zoo, they like to imitate its walk. The teacher can use *Just Me*[47] to enlarge their imitations to include other animals.

At Thanksgivingtime, the teacher can make a point of helping the children to understand that people raise animals to be eaten. Too often the nursery school emphasizes the raising of animals as pets to the exclusion of raising them for food. Sooner or later, children must come to appreciate the fact that animals are raised primarily for food, and only occasionally as pets. Unless the teacher introduces this idea early, children have difficulty with it because they do not want to eat their pets. A story is needed to help children understand that animals are primarily a source of food.

CHRISTMAS

The preschool teacher should know the community and its religious preferences. If some of the children come from homes in which Hebrew customs are observed, she can plan school activities around the Hanukah celebration and use such a book as *Happy Hanukah Everybody*.[48] If some of the children come from Christian homes, she can also plan activities in keeping with the Christmas celebration. When the children are from a variety of ethnic backgrounds, she should emphasize the winter season and the customs that are part of it, the Christmas decorating that is an integral part of American life, and the spirit of giving which underlies all the celebrations of different ethnic groups.

The wise teacher helps the children to find pleasure in the winter season. Instead of thinking of the putting on and taking off of warm clothing as a nuisance, she makes the children aware that "we are glad to have warm clothes to wear." Children like to dress and undress, and to become self-sufficient in taking off and putting on clothing—unzipping and zipping, unbuckling and buckling, unbuttoning and buttoning, untying and tying.

---

[45] Janice, *Little Bear's Thanksgiving* (New York: Lothrop, Lee & Shepard Co., Inc., 1967).

[46] Alice Dalgliesh, *The Thanksgiving Story* (New York: Charles Scribner's Sons, 1954).

[47] Marie Hall Ets, *Just Me* (New York: The Viking Press, 1965).

[48] Hyman and Alice Chanover, *Happy Hanukah Everybody* (New York: United Synagogue Commission on Jewish Education, 1958). Also, Norma Simon, *Hanukah* (New York: Thomas Y. Crowell Company, 1966).

Such activities offer excellent learning opportunities for developing skill in undressing and dressing.

Books such as *I Like Winter*[49] are useful to the teacher in helping the children to be glad of the winter activities that are part of their playground fun. Outdoors, the children learn to lie down on the freshly fallen snow to make an impression of their bodies with "wings" (made by sweeping their arms up and down across the snow). They learn to fashion snow into balls with their hands and to throw them at a target rather than at other people. They learn how to bend their knees as they slide across a patch of ice. They learn to guide a sled by leaning on the corners. Indoors, they make snow taffy which they pour onto snow piled high in a dishpan. Daily they learn new activities to be played in the warm indoors—simple cookery, dramatic play based on experiences from other seasons and other places and other times as well as from the immediate environment.

When a preschool group is located in a warm climate that does not have a winter season marked by snow and ice, the teacher nevertheless should acquaint the children with the kinds of experiences their friends and relatives have in winter climates. She can use ice cubes and frost from the refrigerator to help the children feel coldness. She can read stories which help them to interpret the winter scenes they see on TV.

Especially for four- and five-year-old children who need to have projects that carry over from day to day to give them continuity within their preschool experience, the decorating of a Christmas tree is a delightful series of activities. Furthermore, children enjoy having a Christmas tree that is really their own. Many of them come from homes in which decorating the tree is the responsibility of older members of the family. What a sense of real participation the children have in decorating their school tree! Each child can help in making decorations and in putting them on the tree. Finger paintings are shaped into cornucopia and stapled together. Red cranberries are put on strings. Unbreakable plastic balls and a string of electric lights are all that is needed to make the little tree look more beautiful to everyone.

Many school sessions feature the making of some new kind of decoration, and carry the craft activity over into story time, a musical activity, or dramatic play. Here are some of the ideas that preschool teachers find useful to select from and adapt according to the interests of the children in their group.

1. Have popcorn at refreshment time. Use the leftover popcorn to make strings for the tree.
2. String uncooked cranberries on pipecleaners to make tree decorations. Making cranberry jelly and serve it on crackers at refreshment time.
3. Using the single sections from an egg carton, make little bells to hang

---

[49] Lois Lenski, *I Like Winter* (New York: Henry Z. Walck, Inc., 1950).

on the tree. First, paint the bells with colors. The next day, paint them with glue, and sprinkle glitter on them. When the bells are dry, help each child put a ribbon at the top of the little bell, and hang it wherever he wishes on the tree.

4. Use glue and glitter to make tree decorations out of pine cones collected earlier in the fall. Each child chooses a bright ribbon and the place on the tree for tying the ornament he made.

5. Treat styrofoam balls or stars with glue and glitter, or hang them, undecorated, as little snowballs on the tree.

6. Using strips of gummed paper (preferably green and red in color), make paper chains by putting together the ends of each strip to make a circle as a link for the chain.

7. Cut in half an aluminum-foil pie dish. Flatten it out and convert the half-dish into a cone by stapling one side of the cut piece on top of the other side. Staple a red ribbon at the top to complete the bell for a child to hang wherever he wishes on the tree. Sing "Jingle Bells" to enrich this activity.

In each of these activities the child has an opportunity to be creative. He may choose the colors for his ornament or the ribbon with which to tie it onto the tree. For each decoration he selects an appropriate place on the little tree. His pride in these individual activities gives him a sense of his own importance. At the same time he has a feeling of belonging to the group because, as one of its members, he devises something which contributes to the group project. When he sees the tree with all its decorations, he realizes that many people working together can create something which is greater than that which each can do by himself.

The teacher can use appropriate stories to enrich the children's feelings about the Christmas tree. *The Little Fir Tree*[50] becomes a favorite story for the children and an excellent vehicle for dramatization.

The party on the last school day before Christmas vacation can be simple but thrilling. Santa Claus himself brings a sackful of packages, one for each child. If the Santa Claus is the daddy of one of the children, this "secret" enhances the fun. Santa Claus talks with each child as he gives him a gift.

In addition to Santa's Visit, the Christmas party may have refreshments: milk and a Christmas cookie, or perhaps vanilla ice cream, a cookie, and juice. The refreshments are the usual ones familiar to the children. Shaping ice cream into a gingerbread house or some other unusual form enhances the ice cream for an adult, but not for small children. Until they are more experienced in everyday things, they do not distinguish the unusual and appreciate it as such.

Of course the principal value of the different kinds of celebrations at

[50] Margaret Wise Brown, *The Little Fir Tree* (New York: Thomas Y. Crowell Company, 1954).

the end of the calendar year is their emphasis on giving and on thinking of others. Department stores and other stores have so capitalized on buying and getting presents that teachers need to emphasize giving what we have or can make. The nursery school teacher can introduce the idea of generosity to many children who become ready to take this large step forward from the egocentricism of younger children. The child who has learned to share presently is able to give also. As the teacher talks with parents about some project whereby the children may give outgrown clothes and toys to other children, she should keep in mind that children think in terms of here and now, and in terms of the people and situations they have at hand. Here are some ideas that preschool teachers adapt in accord with the abilities of the children in their group, and find useful in helping the children to be givers as well as receivers of gifts:

1. After the Christmas tree is decorated, the teacher and the children talk together, admiring it and wondering if the tree can make someone else happy between the close of school and Christmas day. Can someone take it home for his family to enjoy? Whose family does not yet have a tree, or plans for getting one? Presently the group decides that a child whose family needs it should take it home. If no child's family needs it, then the teacher's family may be the appreciative receiver of the tree.

2. A visit to an orphanage, or pictures of children living in an orphanage, is a prelude to group conversation in which the children each decide to bring some outgrown article of clothing for an orphan. Something a child has enjoyed wearing can go on to make another child happy. On another day, talking together, the children and their teacher decide to make a picture or a collage, or to bring a plaything for an orphan. A toy that a school child has enjoyed playing with can also go on to make another child happy.

3. After making or decorating cookies at school, the children take them home for members of their family. During one such cookie-making session, a three-and-one-half-year-old girl remarked, "I'm making one treatment after another for Kimmy."

4. Within the school itself, older children may be able to pass on to their younger friends something useful; younger children may pass them on to younger siblings. This handing down can be a delightful experience for both the giver and the receiver. It serves to educate the children in the idea of the flow of resources through a community—a fundamental concept in social studies.

5. Craft or science activities at Christmastime often may lead to some present to take home for mother or for some other member of the family—for instance, a string of macaroni beads, a paper plate painted and decorated with glue and glitter, or a winter bouquet of plants with decorative seed pods.

6. Craft activities with Christmas cards from previous years made the children aware of the Christmas card as a way of saying "Merry Christmas" to friends. Pasting together bits of other cards to make one of their own to take home gives the children practice in saying "Merry Christmas" with a card.
7. Of course Christmastime is enriched by the telling of the legendary stories such as *The Night Before Christmas*[51] and the reading of the fanciful stories produced currently, as well as by the singing of traditional Christmas carols and newer songs such as "Rudolph, the Red-Nosed Reindeer." Special stories are written for Christmas, for instance, *Christmas in the Barn.*[52]

Immediately after Christmas, the teacher may hear conversations among the children which reveal something of what they have absorbed from Christmas activities. An example is this conversation which took place on the fifth of January among Neal (three years and ten months); his brother, Stanley (five years and eight months); and his playmate, Susan (five years and seven months):

NEAL (*playing the part of Santa Claus*)   I found Rudolph.
SUSAN   Get some presents.
NEAL   Rudolph is eating all my raisins.
(*The children munch on their raisins as they play.*)
STANLEY   I see Rudolph.
SUSAN   I found Rudolph at the store. (*talking to Neal*) Go get some presents now. Come on. Go ahead. Go get presents.
NEAL   I am eating my raisins.
SUSAN (*becoming impatient*)   What do you want to do? Sleep with us? Or do you want me to help you?
NEAL   I want someone to help me.
STANLEY   This is part of Santa's village.
SUSAN   Come on. Let's go.
NEAL   I saw Rudolph right there.
(*Neal and Susan go on preparing presents, talking as they work.*)
SUSAN   Come on.
NEAL   Okay. Okay. Okay.
SUSAN   You get some presents for Stanley. Stanley will be happy. (*tying a ribbon around a package*) Put it in the middle every time.
STANLEY   Hurry up, Santa Claus.
SUSAN   Stanley is waiting. Quick.
(*Finally Neal and Susan have the presents prepared.*)
SUSAN (*to Neal*)   Do you want to play Santa Claus?
NEAL   Yeah.

[51] Charles C. Moore, *The Night Before Christmas* (New York: Grosset & Dunlap, Inc., 1949).
[52] Margaret Wise Brown, *Christmas in the Barn* (New York: Thomas Y. Crowell, 1952).

(Susan and Neal sing "Jingle Bells" very loudly as they take the presents over to Stanley.)

VALENTINE'S DAY

Sending and receiving messages of affection are a part of Christmas, but they are the principal activities of Valentine's Day. Of all the holidays, Valentine's Day is especially suitable for young children. It has a single emphasis. Its simplicity makes it easily comprehended by children. Furthermore, although love is abstract, it is expressed in many concrete ways, and is the principal attribute of the life of a preschool child. After the abstractions and complexities of Halloween, Thanksgiving, and Christmas, Valentine's Day comes as a simple and understandable celebration.

It has already been pointed out that many preschool teachers capitalize on the communication aspects of Valentine's Day to acquaint children with the mail facilities and postmen in their local community. Here are activities which teachers adapt to the age level of the children and use to bring out the affectional aspects of the day:

1. Making Valentines for mother, for every other member of the family, and for other beloved people is the featured activity of many school days. With red and white colors, precut hearts, and appropriate stickers, the children use scissors, paper, paste, and crayons to create a variety of Valentines to take home.
2. One nursery school teacher uses the following finger play to enrich Valentine making and giving:

> One little Valentine said, "I love you."
> Tommy made another. Then there were two.
> Two little Valentines, one for me.
> Mary made another. Then there were three.
>
> Johnny made another. Then there were four.
> Four little Valentines, one more to arrive.
> Susan made another, and then there were five.
> Five little Valentines all ready to say:
> Be my Valentine on this happy day.

3. A Valentine's Box at school emphasizes the affectional relations that children have with their teacher and with their friends. By having families participate in preparing Valentines, the teacher enriches the day for both the child and his family. The teacher makes sure that each child participates equally in this activity. She also sees that valentines to take home are distributed just as the children leave. Such precautions assure the pleasure of the children in the activity.
4. A Valentine's party for mother and siblings not yet in school is another way to emphasize happy family relations, and cooperation between fam-

ily and school. Of course, a party gives the children and their teacher opportunity for happy planning as well as a happy party.

EASTER

Eastertime is a delightful time for the preschool child and the teacher who guides him in discovering for himself all the fascinations of the springtime. On walks, she may point out buds which will soon grow into leaves. In the garden, she shares her delight with the little sprouts that soon develop into plants. The everyday world is full of miracles with which the preschool child must become familiar before he will be ready, years later, to understand the stories that are part of the religious lore of his family—stories about such things as Passover, the Resurrection, and the theory of atonement.

Many of the springtime activities of the preschool group are primarily science studies which acquaint the children with plants and animals, and their growth and development. However, along with the science learnings are learnings which help the children, at their own age level, to understand their own relation to such phenomena. For instance:

1. By having his own garden, a child experiences the role of a gardener who selects the seed and tends the plants while they grow. In this way, he gains a sense of his own importance in guiding the events he observes. *Little Farm*[53] is helpful to the teacher in developing the concept of a gardener.
2. Experiences in feeding, caring for, and raising pets are also an important part of preschool activities because they, too, enable the child to develop feelings of importance through responsibility. Books that show pets include *A Puppy for You.*[54]
3. Watching plants and animals grow, the child also learns that he, too, is growing. *The Very Little Girl*[55] and *The Growing Story*[56] are stories that help children to realize the social importance of growing up.
4. The spring, like the fall, is a time when children study how the farms produce the plants and animals that are our food. At refreshment times, the children sometimes have fresh lettuce, strawberries, green peas, or some other fruit or vegetable in season. A trip to a nearby farm shows them where these fruits and vegetables come from, and also introduces them to the baby animals which farmers raise for their food.
5. Four- and five-year-old children are interested in the shearing of sheep to obtain wool for clothing and blankets. Preschool groups in communi-

---

[53] Lois Lenski, *Little Farm* (New York: Henry Z. Walck, Inc., 1942).
[54] Walter Chandoha, *A Puppy for You* (New York: World Publishing Company, 1967). *A Kitten for You* and *A Foal for You* (1967); *A Baby Goose for You* (1968) also have black and white photographs of pets.
[55] Phyllis Krasilovsky, *The Very Little Girl* (Garden City, N.Y.: Doubleday & Company, Inc., 1953), and *The Very Little Boy* (1962).
[56] Ruth Krauss, *The Growing Story* (New York: Harper & Row, Publishers, 1947).

ties that produce and process wool can show the children how wool is obtained and used. Kindergarten groups in any community can use a book such as *Little Lamb's Curls*[57] to introduce the four- and five-year-old children to the use of animal fibers for clothing.

Preschool children enjoy participating at their own age level in the customs that are part of the Easter celebration in their social order.

1. Color hard-boiled eggs with food-dye solutions. Four- and five-year-old children like the two-step process of using a wax crayon and then the dye solution. They also like to use the pictures which will print on the eggs or on the backs of their hands.
2. Enjoy eating hard-boiled Easter eggs, peeling the shells off, and then dipping the egg in a little pile of salt on a plate or napkin.
3. Participate in craft activities that center around the egg, bunny, chicken themes; for instance, pasting paper Easter eggs onto a paper Easter egg tree, a paper plate, or a piece of construction paper.
4. Use glue and bits of brightly colored egg shells instead of glitter to make designs and decorations.
5. Enjoy the imaginative stories about eggs and bunnies; for instance, *The Runaway Bunny,*[58] the *Golden Egg Book,*[59] and *The Bunny Who Found Easter.*[60]

MOTHER'S DAY AND FATHER'S DAY

In a preschool group each day may have many references made to Mother and Father, but when the days officially designated as Mother's Day and Father's Day are at hand, the teacher capitalizes on them to guide the children in expressing their love and appreciation toward each parent. Here are some of the ideas which teachers have adapted and used with their children:

1. Have mothers, or fathers, visit school on a day and at a time that is convenient to them; for instance, Sunday afternoon. This visit enables each child to show his parents what he especially enjoys, and to share his beloved school with his beloved parents.
2. Suggest to the children that each make a picture especially for his mother, or for his father. By taking the picture home and hiding it, four- or five-year-old children can have it for a surprise on the official day.

[57] Polly Miller McMillan, *Little Lamb's Curls* (New York: Lothrop, Lee & Shepard Co., Inc., 1962).
[58] Margaret Wise Brown, *The Runaway Bunny* (New York: Harper & Row, Publishers, 1942).
[59] Margaret Wise Brown, *Golden Egg Book* (New York: Golden Press, 1947).
[60] Charlotte Zolotow, *The Bunny Who Found Easter* (Berkeley, Calif.: Parnassus Press; Eau Claire, Wis.: E. M. Hale & Co., 1959).

3. Plan some craft or science activity which will result in something to take home for a present. In one nursery school the children sprinkled small porous ceramic pieces with perfume to make a sachet for Mother. They used pretty wrapping paper to wrap this present for Mother. In another school near the ocean, the children looked for shells for use as a pin tray for Daddy.

4. With the flannelboard, use pictures showing Mother, or Daddy, with one or more children in activities that the children enjoy. On another day use pictures that show the home activities of Mother or Daddy.

5. Use such books as *Papa Small*[61] to show Daddy as a family man and Mother as a housewife. *Mommies* and *Daddies*[62] are each useful and enjoyable, too.

6. Ask each child what Daddy or Mother does when having fun. Their answers usually include, "Plays with me."

Four- and five-year-old children are interested in the work that daddies do. They like to think of their own daddy, what he does, and what he might do. For instance, when Dan was visiting the fire station with his nursery school group, he told the fireman who was showing them around: "My Daddy is a police." He may have thought that both firemen and policemen had a glamor that his daddy did not have as a skillful builder of houses.

The teacher should help the children to develop pride in what their fathers do and to get as realistic a mental picture as a child can about what Daddy does at work. One teacher asks each child in her nursery school group: "What does Daddy do when he goes to work?" She has found that the four-year-old children have more to talk about than do the three-year-old children, and that both age levels include children who say, "I don't know," or "I don't go." In order to help the children learn about daddies and their work, she reads to them *Daddies, What They Do All Day*[63] and, as they study different community helpers, she guides them in realizing that the helpers are also members of a family.

Such a teacher is pleased to hear a child say, "My daddy works there," when they drive past a factory. She takes satisfaction in the various activities that she has planned for Father's Day when she has a conversation like that with Neal (three years and ten months old):

NEAL   I saw a motorcycle at somebody's house.
TEACHER   Maybe a policeman lives there.
NEAL   Maybe their daddy is a policeman.

---

[61] Lois Lenski, *Papa Small,* op. cit.
[62] Lonnie Carton, *Mommies* (New York: Random House, 1960); *Daddies* (New York: Random House, 1962).
[63] Helen Walker Puner, *Daddies, What They Do All Day* (New York: Lothrop, Lee & Shepard Co., Inc., 1946).

But she also realizes that increasing understanding about the work of daddies goes along with increasing maturity when she has such a conversation as this:

TEACHER   And what does your daddy do, Johnny?
JOHNNY   Takes his teeth out.

THE FOURTH OF JULY

Children who attend summer nursery schools, or day-care and child-care centers which are in session throughout the entire year, celebrate the Fourth of July at school as well as at home. Their teachers can use the

Dramatic play of adult roles is appropriate on any day. (Courtesy of Montgomery County Head Start Program, Maryland.)

holiday primarily as a means of introducing the children to the fact that they live not only in a neighborhood community but also in a larger area called a state, one of the states in the United States of America, and in the world. The teachers should realize, however, that these concepts are beyond the grasp of three-year-old children, and, often, beyond that of many older children.

Sometimes kindergarten teachers have the children recite the Pledge of

Allegiance to the Flag. Those who do so need only listen precisely to what the children say to know that the exercise is primarily one of repeating syllables that are nonsense to the children. However, the children do learn the tonal pattern of the pledge and have that as background for understanding later this part of the patriotic rituals in the social order.

Activities that are more appropriate to the preschool children include waving small flags and marching to well-accented music. The children also enjoy hearing simple poems, such as *A Rocket in My Pocket*,[64] performing craft activities that center around red, white, and blue; and hearing the national anthem.

Situations for Discussion

A preschool teacher is apt to find herself in situations similar to the four described here. As you think of what to do in each situation, consider whether each course of action suggested is desirable, or not. Use points brought out in the chapter as well as ideas from your own experience to justify your views. Suggest alternative courses of action to supplement those given.

SITUATION 1   During a morning at the park, four-year-old Sammy discovers the fun of walking on top of a line of benches attached to tables. As the teacher of the group, you should say

- It's fun to walk on benches. They are like our walking board at school.
- What are benches for?
- Get off the benches, and stay off.
- What will the park attendant think of our doing this?
- Let's all sit down under that lovely tree over there now.

SITUATION 2   You are serving as a consultant for preschool groups in a foreign country. Whenever you visit a preschool group, you review its equipment to see if it has

- Equipment listed in Chapter 4 of *The Years Before School*.
- Dress-up clothing formerly used by mothers and fathers.
- Equipment used in preparing food in the homes of the children.
- Special equipment for use on major holidays.
- Children's books in keeping with basic concepts of the social sciences.

SITUATION 3   You are looking over newly published picture books to select those which are suitable for your nursery group and have beginning concepts of social science in them. You should

- Review the books listed at the end of Chapter 8 in *The Years Before School*.
- Select any book which shows the importance of a river in the lives of people.
- Be careful to stay below the kindergarten age range.
- Select books which emphasize considerate family relationships.
- Include a book about a baker but not about the process of baking.

[64] Carl Withers, *A Rocket in My Pocket* (New York: Holt, Rinehart & Winston, Inc., 1948).

SITUATION 4 You are working with a mature group of kindergarten children, and plan to take up Groundhog Day with them. Your plans include:

- Reading *William's Shadow*.[65]
- Noticing the length and direction of shadows at different times of the day.
- Going to see a sundial.
- Using a flashlight to make shadows.
- Having activities about Groundhog Day on the day itself.

Current Books for Preschool Children

BALIAN, LORNA. *I Love You, Mary Jane*. New York: Abingdon Press, 1967. [Bring a present, say "Happy Birthday," eat ice cream and cake, say, "Thank you."]

BORACK, BARBARA. *Grandpa*. New York: Harper & Row, Publishers, 1967. [A realistic description of what Grandpa and I do.]

BROWN, MARGARET WISE. *The Dead Bird*. New York: William R. Scott, Inc., 1958. [Children bury a dead bird with suitable ritual.]

——, and EDITH THACHER HURD. *Five Little Firemen*. New York: Golden Press, 1949. [Five Little Firemen put out a fire.]

BROWN, MYRA BERRY. *Pip Moves Away*. San Carlos, Calif.: Golden Gate Junior Books, 1967. [Pip finds a new house, new room, and new friend but "same old mom." *Pip Camps Out* (1966) makes a backyard camp-out vividly real.]

CHANDLER, EDNA WALKER. *Five Cent, Five Cent*. Chicago: Albert Whitman and Company, 1967. [In Liberia, Kolu learns how to earn money, and Jack learns that money comes through working, not taking.]

CHANDOHA, WALTER. *A Puppy for You*. New York: The World Publishing Company, 1967. [Photographs develop the concept of a puppy. *A Baby Bunny for You, A Baby Goat for You, A Baby Goose for You* (1968) are by the same author.]

COLONIUS, LILLIAN and GLENN W. SCHROEDER. *At the Airport*. Rev. ed. Chicago: Melmont Publishers, Inc., n.d. [Photographs and accurate descriptions enrich a visit to an airport.]

FOSTER, DORIS VAN LIEW. *A Pocketful of Seasons*. New York: Lothrop, Lee and Shepard Co., Inc., 1961. [Each season Andy picks up something for his pocket.]

HAWKINSON, JOHN and LUCY. *Little Boy Who Lives Up High*. Chicago: Albert Whitman and Company, 1967. [Life high up in an apartment building has a unique point of view.]

HOBAN, RUSSELL. *A Birthday for Frances*. New York: Harper & Row, Publishers, 1968. [Frances gives sister Gloria what she would like to have.]

KRAVETZ, NATHAN. *Two for a Walk*. New York: Oxford University Press, 1954. [On their walk John and Tony visit a grocery store, barber shop, pet shop, a construction job, and a fire station.]

KUSKIN, KARLA. *Just Like Everyone Else*. New York: Harper & Row, Pub-

---

[65] Margot Austin, *William's Shadow* (New York: E. P. Dutton & Co., Inc., 1954).

lishers, 1959. [Jonathan James gets up, gets dressed, eats breakfast and goes to school.]

LENSKI, LOIS. *Big Little Davy.* New York: Henry Z. Walck, Inc., 1956. [Davy grows from a baby who crawls to a little boy who waves to his mother as he starts to school. *Policeman Small* (1962), *Cowboy Small* (1949), *The Little Farm* (1942), *The Little Train* (1940), and *Let's Play House* (1944) are by the same author.]

————. *Davy Goes Places.* New York: Henry Z. Walck, Inc., 1961. [A visit to Grandpa involves rides on many different vehicles.]

LIANG, YEN. *Tommy and Dee Dee.* New York: Henry Z. Walck, Inc., 1953. [Tommy and Dee Dee do the same kinds of things, but in different countries. *The Pot Bank*—Philadelphia: J. B. Lippincott—(1956) tells what Dee Dee and Bao do with the money they save.]

MARINO, DOROTHY. *Goodnight Georgie.* New York: The Dial Press, Inc., 1961. [Georgie visits his grandparents on their farm.]

MARTIN, PATRICIA MILES. *The Rice Bowl Pet.* New York: Thomas Y. Crowell Company, 1962. [A child selects and cares for a pet.]

ORMONDROYD, EDWARD. *Michael the Upstairs Dog.* New York: The Dial Press, Inc., 1967. [Neighbor reactions to Michael and his dog-ladder lead to moving to the country.]

PAPAS, WILLIAM. *No Mules.* New York: Coward-McCann, Inc., 1967. [In Africa, Faan with Golo, his mule, has difficulty in going shopping.]

RADLAUER, RUTH SHAW. *About Men at Work.* Chicago: Melmont Publishers, Inc., 1958. [Brief descriptions of the steam shovel man, the jet flyer, the carpenter, and so on.]

REICH, HANNS. *Children and Their Mothers.* New York: Hill & Wang, 1964. [Pictures of children with their mothers around the world.]

ROTH, EUGEN. *Children and Their Fathers.* New York: Hill and Wang, 1962. [From different countries, pictures of children with their fathers.]

SANDBERG, INGER and LASSE. *Little Anna's Mama Has a Birthday.* New York: Lothrop, Lee & Shepard Co., Inc., 1966. [Ingeniously, Little Anna creates a cake. *What Little Anna Saved* (1965) adds imagining to junk.]

TRESSELT, ALVIN. *Wake Up, Farm.* New York: Lothrop, Lee & Shepard Co., Inc., 1955. [*Follow the Road* (1953), and *Wake Up, City* (1957) are by the same author.]

UDRY, JANICE MAY. *What Mary Jo Shared.* Chicago: Albert Whitman and Company, 1966. [Mary Jo "shares" her father with her group.]

WATTS, MABEL. *My Father Can Fix Anything.* Racine, Wis.: Whitman Publishing Company, 1965.

YASHIMA, TARO. *Umbrella.* New York: The Viking Press, 1958. [On a rainy day, a person carries an umbrella.]

CHAPTER 9

Building Science Concepts

"Late summer is wonderful this year. This morning is cool enough for sparkles of dew on the grass, but the clear sky probably means the day will be hot by early afternoon." Such a remark is made by those who, as preschool children, learned the pleasure of observing the world around them.

Throughout the year, preschool children should be guided to observe seasonal changes in plants and animals in their locality. They need several years of such observations to help them build realistic concepts about each season, more time to build a concept of the succession of the seasons themselves.

Throughout the school year, the preschool teacher should plan a wealth of experiences through which the children will become acquainted with the different aspects of their environment:

- Plants and animals.
- Rocks and physical features of the earth.
- Tools and machinery.
- The sky and its features.

In all these experiences the teacher can guide the children in the fun and fascination of noticing what things are really like. Her own excitement and enthusiasm about each discovery are caught by the children.

Science is an important part of the curriculum of the preschool child. At an age when he is building feelings about himself which will be with him throughout his life, he needs to understand facts and relationships which enable him to interpret and control the world around him. He needs to understand and control his own body. He avoids frustrations and fears through being able, for instance, to turn on a light when he wants to end darkness, to turn water on and off as he needs to use it; and in short, to

Paralleling daddy's work through play with simulated machinery. (Courtesy of Child Study Centre, University of British Columbia, Vancouver, Canada. Photograph by Englefield Studio.)

enjoy safely the new experiences into which his activity and his curiosity lead him.

Much of preschool science teaching has the aim of helping a child develop the concepts which will keep him safe from the hazards of his environment. As soon as possible he needs to know, among other things, that

- A person must have air so he can breathe at all times.
- Spiders help our gardens, but one of the black ones can hurt us.
- Ice on top of water may not be strong enough to hold us.
- The mouth is for food and drink only.
- We keep out of the way of cars and trucks.

At every possible opportunity the teacher should teach and reteach those concepts which a child must have before he can take care of himself. Teachers and parents have the choice of keeping a child safe, or of teaching him how to keep himself safe. Adults can let children have increasing freedom as rapidly as the children gain the understandings which enable them to explore their environment with safety. Furthermore when the children feel safe in their environment, they take pleasure in exploring and understanding it. Safety is an integral part of building science concepts.

Although nature study is an important part of the science program in the nursery group and kindergarten, it is only one part of it. In addition to studying the world they live in, children are eager to know about themselves. The teacher should help them to understand themselves as biological organisms which carry on the processes of digestion, excretion, respiration, sensation, circulation, locomotion, resting, and reproduction. She can help them to understand the span of life and the phenomena of conception, birth, and death.

By the time a child enters the first grade, he should have the basic understandings and interests which will make it possible to enjoy life more completely and to pursue, in a simple way, any branch of science that he has opportunity to study. He should understand the fundamental concepts of each major science as a result of a wealth of realistic experiences in relation to each of them.

Guiding Scientific Thinking

When children are exploring their environment, they should not be hurried. The wise teacher advises the children of a change of activity, but does not demand that the children begin it at once, nor even at the time that she does. She respects the interest a child takes in a sowbug, or in looking for a cloverleaf that has four instead of the usual three leaves. She lets him follow his interest until he is ready for something else. Thus she gives him time to ask questions, observe, see relationships—time for scientific thinking, and time for taking action on the basis of his thinking.

In developing science concepts with the children, the teacher should make use primarily of questions, as did Navarra,[1] and only incidentally of explanatory statements.

The essence of a scientific attitude is curiosity. The teacher should therefore guide the children in learning how to ask simple but significant questions. For instance if she wishes to help the children understand that a snowball and the frost accumulated in a refrigerator are forms of water, she focuses her attention on the questions which lead to that answer: What is snow? Where does it come from? She knows that answering these questions sooner or later will lead the children to know that frost, snow, and ice are just other forms of water.

One mother with a master of science degree recorded the questions that

[1] John G. Navarra, *The Development of Scientific Concepts in a Young Child: A Case Study* (New York: Teachers College, Bureau of Publications, Columbia University, 1955).

her son David asked when he was between the ages of two years two months and two years seven months. The questions of this intelligent boy included the following:

At two years and two months:
What are you doing, Mommy?
Where going, Daddy?
Where is the top?
Where does it turn off?
Where does the window open?
Where does the window close?
How does the Band-Aid go on?
How does the fan turn on?
How does it work?
What's happened here?
How does it fit?
Where does it turn on?
At two years and four months:
How does the baby come out?
At two years and six months:
(*Seeing a new sandwich spread*) Is it a kind of peanut butter?
At two years and seven months:
(*Coming upon something new*) What is it? What does it do?

Within half a year, David moved from using the general question: "Where's this?" and meaning: "What is this?" to using a series of two specific questions; namely: "What is it?" and "What does it do?" Under his parents' guidance, he was developing the beginnings of scientific thinking.

DEVELOPING A SCIENTIFIC ATTITUDE

The scientific attitude stems from interaction of a preschool child with his environment. Grownups can enhance its development by their guidance, or they can interfere with its development. For instance, when construction activities are going on nearby, teachers and parents can express their own interest in the machinery and its use and can share their interest with the children. They can help each child find a safe place from which to watch what is going on, and then can point out first one thing and then another as the work progresses. Their interest and enthusiasm are caught by the child to the point where he will notice similar construction activities and will find an adult to share the experience of watching with him again. Experiences shared with adults are pleasant, and a child endeavors to find more such experiences.

But the child is not always able to find an enthusiastic adult. The little girl who wants to go and watch the gas main being repaired may encounter a negative and discouraging response in her mother or teacher: "Oh, you stay away from those men"; "Little girls don't do that"; "You'll get all dirty there"; We're busy with the housework now." If each attempt by the little girl to satisfy her curiosity about what repair and construction men do leads consistently to such frustrating responses, she is apt to lose interest in them. Instead of learning to observe and think about construction and maintenance, she learns that she can get grownup approval by staying away from such situations. A lack of interest in science situations becomes a satisfying way of life for her.

One of the important things that a preschool child learns is what to be interested in and what not to be interested in. His environment has a wealth of items in it. Those items to which he responds are, in large measure, selected for him by the grownups who can guide him toward certain items and experiences and away from others. Some adults take children to new situations and let them explore those as a means of widening their interests. Other adults do not like to be bothered with their children and leave them with an unequipped backyard or with only a TV screen to watch. They thus give their children only a fifty-fifty chance of discovering

An introduction to use of a microscope. (Courtesy of The Merrill-Palmer Institute and Donna J. Harris, Detroit, Michigan.)

May I feel it? (*Courtesy of Seattle Public Schools, Seattle, Washington. Photograph by Royal C. Crooks.*)

such wonders as the sowbugs and other insects which inhabit the yard. Only with adult assistance and guidance can children become interested in a wide gamut of scientific phenomena.

Especially with four- and five-year-old children can grownups aid the development of a scientific attitude. For instance, consider a child who is building with blocks and attempts a difficult problem such as using cantilevers to support a roof. He adds a block and the structure, off balance, topples. The frustrated child bursts into an emotional tantrum. The nearby adult then has a choice of paying attention to the child and his tantrum, or of considering the problem which initiated it. The adult can calmly say, "Let's get a drink, and then I'll show you what happened." The adult thus takes care of the child's need to relax his concentration at the same time that, with calmness, she shows the child that lack of success is just part of an activity. Adult interest in solving the problem encourages the child in discovering the fun of problem solving.

HELPING A CHILD OBSERVE

When a child notices something, he is delighted to share his interest with someone else who is interested in the same thing. "Come see," says

311

the child, pulling an adult along to enjoy the marvel he has found. If the adult goes eagerly to see, she encourages scientific observation. But if she says, "Just a minute," she is telling the child that his observations are less important than something else she wants to do. On the way to see the worm wiggling in the mud puddle, the adult may find that her interests in keeping her shoes clean or in keeping the child from getting dirty are greater than her interest in sharing the fascination of the worm. However, if she remembers that she can best further the child's scientific interest when he is expressing it, she will enjoy the wiggling of the worm and think about cleanliness later.

The adult who encourages children to observe is the adult who appreciates what they observe and who extends their observations. "Say, it *is* wiggling!" is a comment which appreciates the observation of a child and encourages him to make others. "I wonder if it will wiggle out onto a stick?" is an adult question that may lead to observations beyond those the child would make by himself.

One of the important ways in which adults guide the observations of children is in supplying them with the correct or descriptive word as they are actually making an observation. When a child brings his pet rabbit to share with the other children, the teacher may lead a group of children in observing what the rabbit does: "Do you see his nose wiggling? He is *sniffing*. Let's hold out a piece of lettuce for him to eat. Watch him now. He will *sniff* to be sure it is lettuce before he starts eating it."

"One, two, three. Look and see what is missing," says the experienced teacher in playing a game that helps children become better observers. She has shown them a board with three hooks on which were hung the daddy puppet, the mother puppet, and the little girl puppet. Now she shows them the same board with one of the puppets missing. "What should I put back?" she asks, and the children tell her what she has removed from the board.

In arranging displays for this game, the teacher should be careful to select objects related in the child's world. For three-year-old children she may use the four-piece puzzle of a boy, and remove the piece that is his shirt. For four-year-old children, she may use a six-piece house puzzle and remove one of the roof pieces. The older her group, the greater the number of related objects she can use with them.

A child who has been encouraged to observe the world in which he moves is able to make surprisingly good observations. Neal, when he was three and one half years old, described a kitty in terms of himself by saying, "Kitty curls his tail on me. Kitty likes me." When he was almost four years old, he reported on his trip to the bird sanctuary, "There was a hummingbird with a red neck, and a white tail, and a black head." He also reported that "there was a woodpecker and we saw it woodpeck a tree." When Neal was four years and eleven months old he reported seeing a coot diving into the water, and described the shape of a cat's eyes.

HELPING A CHILD SEE RELATIONSHIPS

Making observations leads naturally into seeing relationships. In the example of the teacher helping children to observe a pet rabbit, the adult relates "wiggling his nose" to "sniffing" and then relates "sniffing his food" to eating. Many people consider this training in seeing relationships as one of the most important parts of scientific thinking. Certainly it is an important way of teaching thinking to preschool children.

Neal, when he was almost four years old, stepped outside the nursery school and observed that it was raining. He said, "It's raining. It's good for our new grass." He remembered the recent planting of the grass and the explanation of how it grows with the sunshine and the rain. When he observed the rain falling, he related his memory to his observation.

The teacher should make a point of helping a child to enlarge each of his observations. When Neal commented on the rain being good for the new grass, his teacher said, "Yes, and it will help the flower seeds grow into plants too." She knew that a child's understanding of the world around him develops by putting one simple idea with others.

With three-year-old children, the teacher must be careful to point out relationships only while the children are actually observing objects. If there are two worms in the puddle, she points out that one is short and the other long. But she does not mention the short worm they saw yesterday, nor even the long worm in another puddle. If she wants to make comparisons, she brings the long worm over to the puddle the three-year-old children are observing.

With four-year-old children, the teacher is able to include a greater variety of relationships. Where she would make only one comparison for three-year-old children, she can make two or three comparisons with older children. Furthermore, she can help the children to recall a past event and to relate it to the present one. "Do you remember the little white rabbit that Stevie brought last time? It was a baby rabbit. This rabbit is a daddy rabbit and is much bigger." Or she may say, "We fed Stevie's rabbit some lettuce. What do you think we should feed this rabbit?"

In helping preschool children to see relationships, it is important to point out the gross relationships rather than the subtle ones which are more appropriate for older children. When a person starts getting acquainted with some new object, he needs to be guided in seeing the attributes of the object as a whole. Relationships among parts and among details come later. The preschool teacher therefore emphasizes such concepts as "big" and "little," "short" and "long," "hard" and "soft," "wet" and "dry"; and descriptive words that apply to objects as a whole—for instance, their colors or their shapes.

HELPING A CHILD INTERPRET HIS FINDINGS

The three-year-old child is busy observing his world and getting names to go with the objects he sees. The four-year-old child goes on to see relationships among the things he observes. With four- and five-year-old children, the adult can feed into their thinking ideas that will enlarge and enrich it. These additional observations and interpretations should be in keeping with science and must be free from superstitions. The wise leader is familiar with the superstitions commonly used in the community, and introduces contrasting science relationships to guide the thinking of the children. Here are examples of common superstitions and desirable science teachings to be used in place of them.

SUPERSTITION	SCIENCE TEACHING
A broken mirror is bad luck.	Broken glass is apt to cut. Use a broom and dust pan to sweep up the broken mirror at once.
A four-leaf clover is good luck.	Each plant is unique. Although most clover has three leaflets an occasional plant may have four.
Walking under a ladder is bad luck.	Keep out of the way of people who are busy. If they are bothered, they may spill something or make some mistake.

Sometimes teachers try to make up stories to go with science relationships. One teacher tried to explain the digestive system to her four-year-old children by making up a story with foxes and other animals. Such embellishments complicate the scientific relationships, and lead children into misunderstandings which must be eradicated sooner or later. It is much better to give the scientific facts alone. Children are fascinated with learning about their physical world and themselves; they need only the facts.

Another way in which the teacher can help children interpret their observations is to have them see how man is able to control his environment. For instance, a child can feel the wind. Then he can put on a jacket to keep himself warm, or he can go inside a manmade shelter out of the wind. Furthermore, people can predict when it is going to rain and can wear raincoats, boots, and caps to keep themselves dry, or can stay inside a house and be sheltered from the rain. The weatherman predicts a storm, and people put their belongings under shelter to protect them from rust or other harm. By having the children observe and participate in such preventive activities, the teacher can help them become aware of man's ability to tell what is going to happen and to prepare himself to be safe and comfortable when it does happen. Children who develop such an understanding are not likely to develop fears about their environment.

Learning About Each Season

Each year the preschool child is taught about each season in succession. Each year he gains a greater understanding of the phenomena of nature that are labeled *fall, winter, spring,* or *summer.* He becomes familiar with what plants and animals do in each season. By the time he is ready for elementary school, he has a background of firsthand experience which enables him to recognize the current season, and even to predict a bit about the forthcoming seasons. His experience in finding out what is happening to the world around him each season leads him to a lifelong interest in and appreciation of the different seasons. His introduction to the seasons is a major part of his preschool experience.

AUTUMN

Throughout the fall months, the teacher should find ways in which to help the children become aware of the outstanding characteristics of autumn:

The days are cooler. We wear more clothing to keep warm. Animals get a heavier coat of fur. Birds fly south to warmer places. The green chlorophyll goes out of the leaves of native plants, and we see the other colors that are in the leaves. Then the leaves become brown, dry, and brittle. Gradually they fall and cover the ground. Autumn is harvest time, when people—as well as animals—gather together the food they need for winter, and when people select the seeds they need for planting in the spring.

The teacher should be careful to see that the children gain only true concepts. For instance, she avoids the usual statements about "leaves turning color." In both the autumn and the early spring, she helps the children notice the many colors that are in the leaves before the chlorophyll develops in them and, in the fall, after the chlorophyll is no longer in them.

In many places, late summer or early fall is a time when caterpillars are found in considerable numbers. The preschool children find them when they go for nature walks, and their teacher can guide them in understanding the life cycle of the butterfly or moth. She also can help them to decide what to do with the animal—whether to watch it, to take it home, or to help it live in its own home area.

What often happens in a preschool group is that one or two children run to the nearest adult to have her "Come, see!" But by the time they return to the group, another child has probably killed the caterpillar, or else grabbed it away from the others. The experienced teacher uses this opportunity to help the children learn the importance of observing before acting. She may come eagerly to the group asking, "What is it?" Upon seeing that the animal is squashed or gone she shows visible disappointment: "But now we can't watch it!" A few minutes later she brightens up with an idea: "Maybe we can find another one, and watch it." Then she tells the children what to do: "If you find one, just watch it. Don't touch it because we all want to see what it does." Later at school the teacher can use the book *Play with Me*[2] to help the children learn the important science concept of being a quiet observer, not a pursuer or a destroyer.

[2] Marie Hall Ets. *Play with Me* (New York: The Viking Press, Inc., 1955). Also on a filmstrip.

When the children gather around a caterpillar that has not been disturbed, the teacher should guide them in making observations. For instance, the color, shape, and markings of the animal make it difficult to find him because he looks like the place where he is. He eats a lot of leaves. With the five-year-old children, the teacher can point out that the mouth structure of the caterpillar is different from ours and makes it possible for him to eat many leaves quickly. He often damages plants and interferes with our food supply.

Knowing that the culture in which children live teaches them to kill a caterpillar or else take it home for a pet, the teacher can use the caterpillar to teach the children something about conservation, or about the care of pets. She can guide the children in deciding to leave the caterpillar where he is, or in taking him back to the school to watch him grow. In either case, she emphasizes that the caterpillar can live only if he has the same kind of leaves to eat and the same kind of environment.

Keeping the caterpillar in a large glass jar with a ventilated lid at school gives the children an opportunity to watch the caterpillar from time to time. By helping him have enough leaves to eat, they can see that he likes to have the same kind of leaf for his food. They can also see that he requires a great many leaves. Through their interest in the caterpillar, the teacher can guide them into finding out more about caterpillars. Together they can enjoy reading *Johnny and the Monarch*.[3] The five-year-old children enjoy *The Sphinx*,[4] especially if they found their caterpillar on a tomato plant and learn that it is a sphinx caterpillar.

If the caterpillar forms a cocoon and later emerges as a moth or a butterfly, the children can actually see the metamorphosis. If the caterpillar dies, they can have an experience in seeing the difference between something that is alive and something that is dead. The teacher should guide them in noticing that the animal no longer eats, breathes, or moves, and is no longer able to take care of waste products (as evidenced by the smell). She can also guide them in learning how to dispose of plant and animal materials that are no longer needed. Talking together, the children and their teacher may decide to flush the caterpillar down the toilet, to put it in the garbage can, or to bury it.

A description of how to capitalize on a caterpillar can be generalized into a plan for teaching about other insects, polywogs, fish, birds, or other small animals.

If some small animal is noticeable at the present time of year, take the children on a nature walk to find it. On the walk, study the animal in relation to his natural habitat. Bring out especially how his coloring serves as camouflage, and how he finds food in the place where he lives. When the animal is brought to school, provide the same living conditions that

---

[3] Margaret Friskey, *Johnny and the Monarch* (Chicago: Children's Press, 1946).

[4] Robert McClung, *The Sphinx: The Story of a Caterpillar* (New York: William Morrow & Co., Inc., 1949).

it had in its home, especially the same food. Have the children take responsibility in providing these. Use appropriate stories to help the children understand the scientific facts.

If the animal does not live, show the children the differences between living and nonliving things. Help them learn how to dispose of dead organisms. Read *The Dead Bird*[5] to them. When children have had experiences with death as well as life, they are able to say as did one preschool child, "My daddy died. It's all right. We got a new one."

During each season of the year but especially in the autumn, the teacher should take the children on nature walks to observe some plant, animal, or scientific phenomenon in its natural setting. Then she also brings back to school whatever it is they have found so that the children can watch it over a period of time and without the distractions found in the natural setting. This use of field trip and laboratory study is begun in nursery school and is continued throughout further scientific study in the years ahead. Here are some examples of field and laboratory study which preschool teachers can use in the fall months in accord with the interests of their children:

FIELD STUDY ON NATURE WALK	LABORATORY STUDY IN SCHOOL
Observe crickets, grasshoppers or other insects in their natural setting.	Put a cricket in a Japanese cage, or other insect in a large glass jar with ventilated lid.
Notice a stray cat or dog; visit a pet kept in a cage near the school.	Bring a pet animal for a brief visit. Put a cat or dog in the middle of a ring of children seated on the floor with their feet touching. Notice what the pet eats, how it moves, and so on.
Watch goldfish or other fish in a pond.	Have fish in an aquarium.
Watch birds flying and feeding.	Have a pet bird. Enjoy pictures of different birds.
Gather leaves of different colors.	Group the leaves according to shape, and compare the colors of the groups. Use the leaves in different craft activities.
Collect seed pods.	Find out how seeds are carried (e.g., burrs stick to cloth; parachutes go in the wind; berries are eaten by birds). Use seed pods in winter bouquets, and in craft activities. Save squash and other seeds to plant.
Help to harvest and process foods.	Notice how good each tastes. Dry popcorn and sunflower seeds for eating later in the winter.

The fall season is also an opportunity to help children come to understand the cycle of growth and deterioration. A few days after the pumpkin

[5] Margaret Wise Brown, *The Dead Bird* (New York: William R. Scott, Inc., 1958).

has had its part as a jack o'lantern, the teacher and the children can enjoy seeing what has happened to it in the warm, moist place where it was left. They notice the gray and white fuzz which looks so soft, and examine the molds with the aid of a magnifying glass. They see that the firm wall of the pumpkin has softened and is going to pieces. The teacher can explain that the pumpkin is going back to earth. She may suggest that they bury it to help make good soil for the garden.

A week or two later, the teacher and the children can plant seeds and bulbs in the garden—some seeds from the pumpkin, but other seeds and bulbs as well. The alert teacher reminds them of the pumpkin that helped to make good soil, and uses other fertilizer as plant food to help enrich the garden. Through such activities the children experience the cyclic sequence of growth, deterioration, and growth.

WINTER

During the winter season, the teacher should help the children to develop an awareness of the characteristics of the season:

Winter is the time of snow, coldness, and ice. We play in the snow and on the ice. We wear more and heavier clothing. Days are shorter. We go to bed by dark instead of daylight. Plants rest. Deciduous trees have no leaves. Many animals rest. Other animals, including people, live on food they collected in the fall. Birds and animals sometimes need help from people to get food throughout the winter.

By getting out in the snow and cold each day, the children can get acquainted with the characteristics of the winter season. By putting on heavy, thick outer clothing they are protected from the cold outdoors. When their mittens get wet, they see that the snow melts to wetness. On warm days, when they play in the little streams running downhill from the snowbanks, the teacher can ask, "Where does the water come from?" and guide them in understanding that the snow is melting to make the water. Sometimes they scoop up a dishpan full of snow to take inside with them. Then they watch the snow melt in the heat of the warm room.

Some days, the children slide on the icy crust formed when the snow melted during the heat of the day and then refroze during the cold of the night. Some days, fresh snow is falling and the children catch the snowflakes on their sleeves to see that each snowflake is unique. The flakes have six sides, but each hexagon differs in some way from the others. Every day the children play outdoors and experience the variation that is an important part of weather. Thus they build an experiential background for later study of meteorology if their interests go in that direction.

It is difficult for the preschool teacher in a warm climate to help the children to build concepts about the winter. A child who had known winter only in Brazil was frightened when he saw his first snowstorm in the mountains in the United States. His crying was more pronounced whenever anyone started toward the outside door. Finally his teacher was able to calm him down to the point where he could talk about his fear. Seeing the snow outside, he thought he was in a cloud. He thought that if anyone stepped outside, he would fall through the cloud and be hurt. This incident emphasizes the need for children to form accurate concepts that are as complete as possible. The preschool teacher makes every effort to provide vivid and realistic experiences that will give the children as complete an idea as possible about weather. Here are experiences and related concepts which are useful with preschool children in any climate, and later will be a basis for understanding the cycle that water follows as it evaporates and condenses:

EXPERIENCE	RELATED CONCEPTS
Hang doll clothes, paintings, on a clothesline to dry. Notice puddles drying up.	Water goes into air.
Notice early morning fog.	A cloud moves down onto the earth and is called *fog* by the people in it.
Make fog by boiling water under a pan of ice water.	When air is cooled, it cannot hold so much water vapor.
See the fog on a cold window pane.	
Put ice into a glass of water; set it aside until water condenses on the glass.	On the cold surface, see the water that came out of the air.
While having a hot bath, notice mirrors and windows. Feel their coldness and dampness. (Use flannelboard and pictures to show this at school.)	Water comes out of the air when the air touches a cold surface.
Visit an ice-making plant, or a cold-storage room. Have the children make little clouds by blowing their warm breath into the cold air of the room.	The water vapor in warm breath turns to drops of water as the breath is cooled.
Notice an early-morning dew.	Water vapor in the warm air comes out of air onto the cold ground and the plants there. These drops of water are called *dew*.
Notice an early-morning frost.	It was so cold in the night that the water vapor came out of the air as frost instead of as drops of water. Snow comes out of the air in the same way when the air is very cold.
Notice rain.	When the air has more water than it can hold, the water comes out of the air, sometimes as rain.

The teacher knows that such experiences as these must be repeated many times and in many different settings before the children acquire the rather abstract concepts related to them. The teacher must be alert to call the attention of the children to such phenomena whenever they occur. At each occurrence, she should put into simple words—and help the children put into simple words—the observable scientific facts.

The winter, when plants are resting outdoors, is a good time to have the contrast of an indoor garden with plants growing where warmth, food, and moisture are available to them. Such plants give the teacher a daily opportunity to help the children realize what plants need for growth. What plants the teacher provides for the children depends on her experience with plants. She should use those plants with which she is familiar. However, she should also select fast-growing plants because she knows that young children lose interest unless they see visible changes frequently. Here are suggestions for indoor gardening projects during the winter months:

1. Each child enjoys having a little bird seed garden in an individual aluminum foil pie plate or paper cup. One teacher described this activity in her parent-cooperative nursery school as follows:

I put wet cotton in small, colorful paper cups. Each child was given one so that he could take it home. I instructed the mother assisting me to let the children feel the seeds and put the seeds in the cup themselves. When each child had his cup, I talked with all of them and said, 'What is it? . . . Yes, It's birdseed, the same kind of seeds that your pet bird likes to eat. . . . I want you to take your cup home and take care of the seeds. Put a few drops of water in your cup each day. In a few days the birdseed will grow like magic. Next week I want you to tell me what happened to your birdseed.'

While the children were waiting for their seeds to sprout, their teacher read them *The Carrot Seed.*[6]
2. Carrots that have started to sprout are cut off and put in a container of water—a discarded juice can or a plastic glass for each child. The child sets the carrot in the sunlight and watches the little sprouts turn green, reach toward the sunlight, and grow taller. Or, like three-year-old Kimmy, have the lack of growth pointed out by another child who may say, as did Meredy: "Kimmy, I've bad news for you. Your carrot died."
3. A sweet potato set in the top of a fish bowl full of water makes roots in the water and vines over the top of the bowl.
4. On an aluminum foil pie plate, a round piece of blotter holds the water to make bean sprouts. Soybean sprouts made in this way can be cooked a few minutes and eaten with either butter or soy sauce. This activity shows how a seed breaks open as the sprout forces its way out, and also demonstrates within the span of a few days that seeds grow into plants for our food.

[6] Ruth Krauss, *The Carrot Seed* (New York: Harper & Row, Publishers, 1945).

5. A flat of earth, sterilized in the oven, is useful for growing seeds of any kind—perhaps radish seeds or seeds of other early spring vegetables or flowers. Picture books, such as *The Flower*[7] and *Up Above and Down Below,*[8] help the children understand what is happening.
6. Bulbs set among rocks in a low bowl sprout, form leaves, and finally blossom. Early spring bulbs, such as daffodils and narcissus, are frequently used for this activity in late winter.

The winter months, when children go to bed when it is dark, are a good time to introduce them to simple astronomical facts. Singing, "Twinkle, twinkle, little star. How I wonder what you are," leads to finding out that most of the stars are other suns, like ours, but very, very far away; and that a very few of the stars are planets like the earth, getting light from our sun. The children enjoy having their teacher use a light for the sun and a ball for the earth to show them how the earth goes around the sun. Sometimes the teacher uses a large grapefruit for the sun and a small ball for the earth. Sometimes the children play "sun and earth" or "earth and moon" with one child circling around another. Sometimes the children hold hands as they circle to show that the sun pulls on the earth and the earth pulls on the sun. Such experiences help the four- and five-year-old children understand the basic relationships among heavenly bodies.

During their preschool years, children move very far in their thinking. This great progress is evident when the understanding of a mature kindergarten child is compared with the understanding that David had when he was an intelligent boy of almost three years. David was playing by himself some distance from the other children. As his teacher came toward him, he was throwing little rocks into the air and saying, " 'way up high." To his teacher he said, "I can't make them stay." She answered, "The earth pulls them back down," and made a mental note that David was ready to learn about the force of gravity. She watched for a time when he was jumping up into the air and asked him, "Do you know what pulled you back down to the earth?" A few days later, she read *All Falling Down*[9] to David and other children, and helped them to learn that the earth pulls on them, on the objects that fall out of their hands, and on everything that is on the earth. She was careful to introduce the children to the idea of "up" as away from the center of the earth, and "down" as toward the center of the earth.

Four-year-old children enjoy the book *Who's Upside Down?*[10] and five-

[7] Mary L. Downer, *The Flower* (New York: William R. Scott, Inc., 1955).

[8] Irma E. Webber, *Up Above and Down Below* (New York: William R. Scott, Inc., 1953).

[9] Gene Zion and M. Graham, *All Falling Down* (New York: Harper & Row, Publishers, 1951).

[10] Crockett Johnson, *Who's Upside Down?* (New York: William R. Scott, Inc., 1952).

year-old children like to think about *You Among the Stars*.[11] Thus they establish themselves in space.

Part of the process of interesting children in the stars and other things to be seen at night is helping them to feel at home in darkness. Especially at three and at five years of age, children are apt to build up fears about what is unknown to them. To obviate such fears the teacher should plan activities such as the following:

1. On a dull day, turn off the room lights and use flashlights or little lanterns which switch on and off easily by a hand squeeze rather than a finger movement. With four- or five-year-old children, expand this activity to include using the lanterns only for a minute or two at a time and letting the dry cells rest in between uses.
2. Take the children to see a display of ultraviolet light or some other entertainment in a darkened room. Encourage the four- and five-year-old children to work out their own dramatic play in a darkened room, perhaps with ghosts or with magic themes.
3. Let the three-year-old children have a dark area where they have two control switches at their height and can make the area light or dark as they wish.
4. Let the four- and five-year-old children have a small dark room with a light switch near the door for use in playing "submarine" after the teacher has introduced them to *The Big Book of Real Submarines*[12] or in playing Mr. Mole when the teacher has read the delightful verse about him in *Where Have You Been?*[13]
5. Have the older preschool children play simple blindfold games for short periods of time; for instance, have them guess which of several objects is the one handed to them.

During the winter season, the teacher should also find opportunity to reteach important concepts developed earlier in the year. For instance, one teacher took advantage of the death of a tiny fish to reteach casually that death is a part of life. She thought the children in her group of three-year-olds should understand what a fish is like when it is dead, and what to do with an animal that has died. When the children were together for their talking time, she brought the fishbowl into the group and asked, "What do you suppose has happened to our little fish?" The children were interested in looking at the fish in the bowl while the teacher guided them in observ-

[11] Herman and Nina Schneider, *You Among the Stars* (New York: William R. Scott, Inc., 1951).

[12] Jack McCoy, *The Big Book of Real Submarines* (New York: Grosset & Dunlap, Inc., 1955).

[13] Margaret Wise Brown, *Where Have You Been?* (New York: Hastings House Publishers, Inc., 1963).

ing what had happened. She said, "Usually he swims in the water. But today he is still on top of the water." After the children had had a minute or two to check this observation themselves, she continued, "Usually his red back is up. Today his white front is up. What has happened to him?" A child who had had his goldfish die at home answered the question. Then the teacher explained the event to the group by saying, "That's right. The fish does not move any more, so we say it is dead." Then she went on to the second concept that she wanted to develop. She said, "The fish is like a broken toy. It is of no use to us now. What do we do with broken toys?" After the children absorbed the idea of getting rid of the dead fish, the teacher talked with them about how to do that. She said, "If a toy is made of wood, or paper, or plastic, we throw it in the wastebasket. But a fish is different; it will make a smell. If it were warm summer time, we could bury the fish outdoors. But with the snow and ice now, we had better flush it down the toilet." So into the toilet went the little fish to be flushed down casually, "Good-bye, dead fish. We don't need you any more."

SPRING

In the spring of the year, the teacher should guide the children in developing an awareness of the spring season. They can notice that the days become warmer, that many days are windy, that other days are rainy, that people wear clothes to keep warm and dry. Such simple facts emerge as concepts in the minds of the children as a result of many, many first-hand experiences. Each rainy day, the children enjoy putting on their rainy-day clothes. Rubber or plastic boots enable a child to go splashing through puddles and yet remain dry. An umbrella or a raincoat and hat keep him dry when it is raining. As an adult helps him put on clothes appropriate for the weather, she can help him understand why he wears the clothes he does. The teacher may say, "The clouds look heavy and dark as if they have lots of water. I think we can wear our rainy-day clothes for our walk. It might rain." Or on another day she may say to the four- and five-year-old children: "The sun has dried up much of the rain, but there are still many puddles. Remember to wear your boots if you want to splash in the puddles. If you don't wear boots, then go around the puddles."

Nature walks in the spring are a delightful means of getting acquainted with the characteristics of the season—the variety of changes in trees and other plants, the development of baby animals, as well as variations in the weather. Here are some of the phenomena that teacher and children can observe on a nature walk in the spring:

1. In early spring, bare branches of deciduous trees get little buds that swell and break open into leaves. Each different kind of tree has a unique kind of bud and leaf.
2. A woods that is leafing out has many colors. These colors are covered up when the green chlorophyll comes into the leaves.

3. Seeds sprout and grow into leafy plants. In fields and gardens are many different kinds of spring flowers.
4. When it rains, earthworms crawl out of the ground. As it becomes warmer, sowbugs, ants, insects, and other small animals are easy to find.
5. Birds fly north to build their nests. They and other animals reproduce.

Every nursery group and every kindergarten should have a garden in the spring, even if it goes no further than preparing the soil and planting seeds. Experience with a garden each spring increases the children's understanding of plants and how they grow, and of the ways in which people help the plants to grow. A garden need not be a successful venture in the adult sense to be highly successful as a learning experience for the children. Adults want the plants to stay in the ground until they have matured to the point of producing flower or fruit or vegetable for adult use. On the other hand, children are interested in the way the plant is each day. They want to pull up radishes every day. Adults need to understand that a child must make these comparisons from day to day, and must also make comparisons from plant to plant on any given day. The experienced nursery teacher provides many seeds of each kind to allow for frequent pulling up of plants. She also has a garden of her own where she can have a few plants grow to fruition to show to the children.

Once the adult has accepted the idea of gardening as a means of daily science experiences rather than a means of producing flowers or fruits or vegetables, she enjoys the garden with the children. If some insect pest comes to the garden, its arrival is not a calamity but an event interesting in itself. The adult guides the children in studying the insect, its behavior, and its response to insecticides. Learning the role of scientific observer is as appropriate to the preschool child as learning the role of gardener. He is interested in his immediate world. His interest shifts readily from one point of view to another. The teacher capitalizes on this short span of attention to acquaint the child with the whole gamut of experiences that arise out of a gardening situation. When the children are older, they will learn the sequence of events which constitute gardening as the adult knows it.

Here are some of the science concepts associated with gardening activities of the children:

GARDENING ACTIVITY	SCIENCE CONCEPTS
Break up the soil of the garden.	Little sprouts must push up through the soil.
Plant seeds in a row, or in one area.	Put the seeds where we will be able to find the plants they grow into.
Cover the seeds with soil.	Plants need soil for food.
Sprinkle water where the seeds are, if it does not rain.	Seeds and plants need water to grow.

GARDENING ACTIVITY	SCIENCE CONCEPTS
Pull out weeds, but not plants.	Plants of one kind are alike, and of a unique pattern.
Pull up one test plant to see how plants of that kind are doing.	A sample gives an idea of what the others may be like. One plant is a good sample; two is a better sample; three, a sufficient sample.
Dig around the plants to loosen the soil.	Roots of plants need loose soil to grow in. Worms help loosen the soil.

The teacher should supplement and consolidate the real experiences that the children have outdoors in their garden and on walks by telling them simple stories with her flannelboard and with a suitable selection of children's picture books. She uses again such books as *The Flower*[14] and *Up Above and Down Below*[15] to reteach the nature of a plant. *Plink, Plink*[16] helps her in teaching about the importance of water for plants and animals.

The teacher should also use books and real experiences to help the children get acquainted with the animals that are grown for food and for pets. She should arrange for the children to visit a nearby farm or a home where baby animals are growing up. If it is not convenient to take the children to see the baby animals, she can arrange to have the animals brought into the school so that the children can see them from time to time as they grow. Such visits with animal families must be planned in advance so that the children know just what they can do or cannot do with the animals. Planning the time for the visit often makes it possible for the children to see the animals being fed, or even to feed them. Planning the length of the visit avoids having the animal mother get nervous about her children, or having the children try out undesirable activities.

Some of the animal families that are interesting to preschool children are chickens, ducks, kittens, puppies. The children also like to go to see baby animals that are as big or bigger than they are, provided they are not in danger of being knocked over by an awkward movement of the big animals. In general, it is better to arrange visits only to those animals that are kept in enclosed areas.

Baby Animals[17] is a large picture book to use in talking with children about baby animals and their mothers. The teacher should use the correct names for the baby animals as a means of helping the children to become familiar with them. The wise teacher notices when some of the children take a special interest in baby animals of all kinds—for instance, the con-

[14] Mary L. Downer, *The Flower* (New York: William R. Scott, Inc., 1955).

[15] Irma E. Webber, *Up Above and Down Below* (New York: William R. Scott, Inc., 1943).

[16] Ethel and Leonard Kessler, *Plink, Plink* (Garden City, N.Y.: Doubleday & Company, Inc., 1954).

[17] *Baby Animals* (New York: Golden Press). Another Great Big Golden Book is entitled *Baby Farm Animals*.

tinuing interest which four-and-one-half-year-old Neal displayed for several months—and times her teaching about baby animals for such periods.

The teacher should not confine her teaching to baby animals, but should encourage the children in learning about the living habits of any animal. For example, she can use a finger play about a bunny and his hole in the ground:

> Here's a bunny (*holds up the first and second fingers of right hand*).
>   With ears so funny (*bends the two fingers forward*),
> And here's his hole in the ground (*uses thumb and first finger on left hand*).
> When a noise he hears
>   He pricks up his ears (*straightens the two fingers*),
> And jumps for his hole in the ground (*puts the right hand into the left*).

One nursery school teacher has a collection of flannelboard pictures of different animals and uses them to acquaint the children with the different characteristics of each animal. Singing "Old MacDonald Had a Farm," she shows the picture of each animal in turn as the children and she imitate the voices of the animals. On another day she uses the pictures of farm animals and asks about each one: "What good are you?" "I give you bacon," says the pig. In this way the teacher brings out the way in which people use each animal.

To acquaint the children with the snake, this teacher makes a model of a snake by stringing together discarded metal tops from soft-drink bottles. With this in her hands she recites a poem that she composed:

> I'm a snake.
>   I'm a snake.
> I wiggle when I walk,
>   Stick out my tongue when I talk.
> I move around like this.
>   I wiggle and I hiss.

Seeing the snake move and watching their teacher, the children are soon saying the poem with her, or moving around the room like snakes. The story of *Crictor*[18] further encourages the children's interest in snakes. If the weather is suitable for gardening, they may decide to have a pet garter snake to help keep insects out of the garden.

SUMMER

The day-care and children's centers and the nursery schools and kindergartens that meet during the summer months give their teachers an opportunity to acquaint the children with concepts of the summer season:

Summer days are long, so long that many children go to bed while it is

---

[18] Tomi Ungerer, *Crictor* (New York: Harper & Row, Publishers, 1958).

still daylight. The sunshine is good for us if we do not get too much of it at one time. Summer days are warm; people wear as few clothes as possible; many animals have lighter coats. People drink a great deal of water, and enjoy playing in water. The baby animals of the spring are big enough to do what their parents do. Plants are green. Many of them are in blossom. Berries and other fruits are ripe. Many vegetables are ready to eat; insects and other animals enjoy them too. Summer storms include lightning, thunder, rain, and sometimes hail.

The teacher is alert for every opportunity to help the children understand these unique attributes of summer. Here are some of the activities that she adapts to the age level of the children and incorporates in the summer program, together with related science concepts:

ACTIVITIES IN SUMMER	RELATED SCIENCE CONCEPTS
Looking at water sprays in sunlight.	Drops of water spread sunlight into its colors.
Running through sprays of water.	Heat from the body makes water drops go into vapor and the body feels cool.
Using a hand fan.	When air moves around us, it takes heat away from our body and makes us feel cool.
Using a small stream of water from a hose.	Water runs downhill; the earth pulls it down.
Getting a drink.	Our bodies need a great deal of water.
Having baby animals visit.	Babies grow up to be like their parents.
Going for a walk to see different kinds of flowers or leaves.	Each kind of plant has a unique kind of leaf and flower.
Visiting a farm, garden, or other place where there are berries, fruits, and vegetables to eat.	Different parts of a plant may be good to eat (e.g., radish, root; celery, stalk; lettuce, leaf; artichoke, flower; berry, seed).
Looking for spiders and insects (e.g., butterflies, grasshoppers).	Spiders, except for instance poisonous black widows, are helpful.
Raising silkworms.	Insects have a life cycle. The life of a silkworm includes egg, larva, cocoon, and moth stages.
Watching a summer storm.	We can tell when a storm is coming.[19]
Listening to thunder; popping a paper bag.	Sudden movement of air causes thunder and other loud noises.
Finding a dead fish on the shore.	Insects and bacteria change dead animals to soil.

Especially during the summer months, construction projects are underway in most communities. These provide an excellent opportunity for pre-

[19] Charlotte S. Zolotow, *The Storm Book* (New York: Harper & Row, Publishers, 1952).

school children to learn what machinery is used in making and repairing roads and in building houses and other structures. When a construction project is within walking distance, the teacher can have the children go to see what is happening each time a new phase of construction is begun. On other days at school, she can use such books as *The Big Book of Real Building and Wrecking Machines*[20] to help the children learn the correct names for different machines and the uses of the major ones.

Adult help is needed for some construction problems. (*Courtesy of The Merrill-Palmer Institute and Donna J. Harris, Detroit, Michigan.*)

Watching the construction of a house gives children some idea about what goes into making a house. They see how concrete is used, and what it is used for. They see wooden boards and beams and see how they are used. They see how windows are set in, how a roof is put on, how electricity and water are provided. At school the children and their teacher can talk about what they have seen and plan what to look for on their next visit.

When children visit construction projects, their dramatic play and their artwork as well as their conversation reflect their experience. Many a sand-

[20] George J. Zaffo, *The Big Book of Real Building and Wrecking Machines* (New York: Grosset & Dunlap, Inc., 1965).

pile has been the place where children made roads similar to those they observed under construction. Kindergarten block-building activities take on greater reality and more meaning after the children have visited a construction project in their neighborhood.

Understanding the Body

Parents who have the legal and moral responsibility for the physical care of their children (and psychiatrists who know well the problems that can spring from faulty or inadequate relationships between parents and children) are eager to help children learn the simple science concepts which they need in order to understand their own bodies. A parent—or a parent substitute—must be with the preschool child every hour of the day to keep the child safe. The parent therefore is eager for the child to learn to take care of himself in an increasing number of ways.

Teachers who are not afraid of biology and who appreciate the importance of enabling children to be as self-sufficient as their level of maturity allows can work with parents to highlight everyday experiences so that children incidentally learn about themselves. If teachers and parents capitalize on the interest that preschool children have in their bodies, they can teach the children the simple concepts needed to understand fundamental biological processes, including digestion, excretion, respiration, sensation, circulation, reproduction, and death. By helping the children to form correct concepts early, they can forestall anxieties, fears, and other difficulties that arise when children pick up misconceptions from their friends or from half-heard conversations.

Of great importance is to help children develop an awareness of their personal growth and development. The preschool child proudly watches his mark on the measuring board rise higher and higher, and gladly gives away his outgrown clothes. The times he notices his growth are the times for adults to mention the relationship between his growth and what he eats: "The good food we eat helps us to grow tall." Casually and from time to time, adults point out simple relationships that gradually help the child to realize, for instance, that eating the meat from animals helps people to grow; that eating fruits and vegetables helps to keep food moving through the body; and that eating certain foods and drinking a certain amount each day helps the process of elimination.

Casually and in very small segments, the preschool child learns simple facts and relationships, not only about digestion and excretion, but also about the other systems of his body. He learns that he must have air at all times. He learns that the blood stream brings food as well as oxygen to each cell, and carries away what the cell does not use. He learns about the sensations called cold and hot. He learns the need for rest as well as for activity. And he learns simple facts about birth and death.

As the child learns about himself, his curiosity and questioning stimulate the adults around him to teach him more and more science concepts. However, the greatest adult incentive for teaching science in the preschool group is the knowledge—confirmed by daily newspaper accounts—that children must have an understanding of science if they are to avoid accidents. The child who suffocates in an old refrigerator or who falls through thin ice is the child who should have had more science teaching, especially about the needs of his body. He had neither parental care nor the ability to care for himself at a crucial moment.

DIGESTION

A two-and-one-half-year-old child who is mastering his elimination processes is ready to understand them as an integral part of the food processing that goes on in his body. When he enters a nursery group as a three-year-old child, the teacher should check to see whether he understands the simple elements of the digestive system:

- Food goes into the mouth (where the teeth bite and chew it into pieces).
- From there little pieces of food go down the red tube to the stomach (where they are made into a solution like gelatin).
- Then the food goes through a long tube (where it may pass through the wall of the intestine into the blood system to be carried to all parts of the body).
- What the body does not need (is dried into solid form, and) goes out the end of the tube as a bowel movement.

The three-year-old child is able to understand these four simple facts (without the detail given in parentheses). His teacher should always present them as an orderly process. Sometimes she uses gestures over her own body to show the location of the processes. Sometimes she uses cut-away pictures of the body or other pictures on her flannelboard. Sometimes she brings out the plastic model of the skeleton to show the children the relation of the digestive system to the bone framework of the body. In such ways and from time to time the teacher can teach or reteach this basic biological process.

As the preschool child grows older, he gradually adds more and more detail to the simple facts he has learned as a three-year-old. It is highly important that these first concepts be accurate in order that they may serve as a foundation to be built upon throughout life.

Through their preschool years, children constantly enlarge their understanding of their digestive system. For instance, when four-year-old Kathy swallowed a large chunk of ice and cried, "It hurts!" she was relieved when an adult reminded her that the warmth of her body was melting the ice to water as it went down the red tube to her stomach.

EXCRETION

When the two-year-old child is sufficiently mature, he concerns himself with developing skill in eliminating wastes through urination and through bowel movements. As he is taking on this responsibility, he needs also to acquire the simple terminology and scientific facts that belong with his new skills. For instance,

- Liquid the body no longer needs is let out through urination.
- Solid food that the body does not need is let out as a bowel movement.
- A body signal tells when to empty each kind of waste.

The teacher of three-year-old children who are entering a nursery group should check to be sure that these simple facts are well understood. With older children parents or teachers can use a model of the human body as well as diagrams to show children more detail about the excretory system. For instance,

- Liquid wastes are accumulated in the kidneys.
- In a boy, a tube from the kidney comes out of the body through the penis.
- In a girl, a tube from the kidney comes out of the body near the vagina.

The parent or teacher can also enlarge the children's understanding of the large intestine as a place where solid wastes accumulate until they are ready to go out of the body.

The teacher of a summer nursery group or kindergarten should make a point of teaching children about the third part of the excretory system, the skin, which keeps the body cool through perspiration. Very simply she mentions the need for drinking much water to replace the water eliminated by saying, for instance, "Our bodies use lots of water when it's hot."

The experienced teacher knows the value of listening to the bathroom conversation of the children. She notices any misconceptions that the children may have and then plans a simple and brief presentation for the children who need to have some part of the excretory system clarified. Sometimes she is able to enter the children's conversation in order to explain what the child needs to know. She may say, "Just BM's come out. Babies come out of another place." Usually she depends on both this immediate, personal teaching and small group teaching as well to be sure that the excretory processes are understood and distinguished from reproduction. Early knowledge about digestion, elimination, and reproduction prevents misconceptions that may interfere with happy and healthy emotional development, and lays a basis for sound marital relations in adulthood.

RESPIRATION

A child needs to learn casually that he must always have plenty of air to breathe. Whenever he climbs into a box, he must be sure that air can come in too. He should always keep his head out of plastic bags and any other nonporous materials that might prevent the air coming into his nose or mouth. He must keep tight things away from his neck so that the air can go down into his body. To be really safe, he must learn the simple facts about the respiratory system, and how to keep it functioning at all times.

In accord with the interest of the children, the teacher should create a variety of pleasant experiences, over a period of time, with which to guide them in understanding their need for air. For instance,

ACTIVITIES	RELATED CONCEPTS
Have the children feel the expansion of the lower part of the lungs with deep breathing.	The lungs get big when air is taken in, and small when it is let out.
Have them run and play a few minutes and then have them feel their breathing again.	When a person runs and plays, he breathes harder in order to give the body the air it needs.
On a country walk, have them take deep breaths.	Fresh air smells good.
Clean a chicken and show the children the lungs and the tube from the lungs, through the neck, to the beak.	The lungs collapse like an empty balloon, or get big with air.
Use "The Visible Man" to show the children the lungs in relation to the bone structure of a person.	The lungs are in the chest.

As the children grow older, they will learn that the blood stream takes the oxygen from the lungs to each cell of the body, and then carries back waste products for the lungs to exhale. The important concept for them to learn as preschool children is that they must always have air coming through their noses down through their necks to their lungs.

SENSATION

The teacher helps the children become aware of the sensations they have from each of five senses, namely: seeing, hearing, touching, tasting, and smelling. Here are preschool activities and science concepts that the experienced teacher can bring out in relation to them.

ACTIVITIES	RELATED CONCEPTS
Use your hand to cover first one eye and then the other.	Each eye is for seeing. Look through a microscope with one eye while the other eye is covered with a hand.
In a shadowy room, look steadily at a lighted window, then at a blank wall.	After-images are first dark and then light. Often they have colors.

ACTIVITIES	RELATED CONCEPTS
Listen to music.	Ears are for hearing.
Listen to an echo from wall to wall.	Ears can hear a sound a second time.
Feel different kinds of fabric.	Fingers feel differences in materials.
Feel metal. Feel the glass in a flashlight that has been in use.	Cold and hot can be felt.
Taste salt, and sugar.	What looks alike may taste different.
Enjoy the flavor of a different food.	"It tastes good."
Smell carnations, other flowers, and perfume on a hankerchief.	The nose is for smelling.

RESTING

The entire program for the preschool group is planned to give the children experience in a rhythm of activity, rest, and activity. Having the children experience this alternation is not enough in itself. They need also to become aware of the need to rest after strenuous activity. The experienced teacher reminds the children, "We played hard. Now our bodies need to rest." By putting rest on the basis of bodily need, she gives the children an impersonal reason for resting and avoids personal conflicts between a child and herself—but more important, she teaches the children an elementary biological concept. She thus helps them toward establishing for themserves rhythms of activity and rest.

When pets are an integral part of preschool experience, the children observe that pets, like people, are active and then must rest. Visits to the zoo, and to see animals at home on the farm, also give an opportunity for the teacher to point out that animals alternate periods of rest and activity.

CIRCULATION

"Is it bleeding?" asks the adult causally when a child has fallen down or gotten a cut. If it is, she applies a disinfectant, and probably a Band-Aid. She also can capitalize on the cut so that the children learn the importance of a scab and of leaving it alone. She should endeavor to make the point that the blood dries to make a scab. A scab is like a Band-Aid: it covers and protects the cut place while new skin grows underneath. When the new skin is ready, the scab drops off all by itself.

During the next few days, the teacher should comment on the scab that protects the new skin. Her interest in the scab makes the child proud to wear it, and prevents the picking off of scabs which often occurs among uninformed children. She may enhance the personal value of a scab by reading to the four- and five-year-old children one of their favorite stories, *Madeline,*[21] the story of a girl who has an appendectomy.

[21] Ludwig Bemelmans, *Madeline* (New York: Simon and Schuster, Inc., 1939, 1954).

Another concept which the preschool teacher should introduce to the children is that the blood goes all over the body in arteries and veins. She can show the children veins that she or they have visible in hands, neck, or legs as evidence that the blood goes through little tubes throughout the whole body.

REPRODUCTION

Three-year-old and five-year-old children are interested in babies and especially in their own babyhood. At these ages of consolidating ideas, they take a step toward maturity by putting into perspective their own early development. These ages, then, are ages at which they come to understand, first, how they were born, and second, how they were conceived. An analyst[22] who has made a study of the importance of the stories of birth and conception to preschool children says that by the age of three and one half, a child should have heard from his mother the lovely and intimate story of how he was born, and from his father by the age of five, the wonderful story of how he was conceived. With this in mind the teacher should talk with mothers of three-year-old children about how to tell the birth story, and with parents of kindergarten children about telling the stories of both birth and conception. She should show them books which are available in the public libraries, for instance *I'm Going to Have a Baby!*[23] and *Johnny Jack and His Beginnings.*[24]

The experienced school teacher sometimes makes use of the expected arrival of a baby to introduce fundamental concepts of reproduction. For instance, four-and-one-half-year-old Billy was well prepared by his family for the expected arrival of a new baby. At nursery school he was eager to share this news with others: "Know what's going to happen soon? Mommy's going to have a baby." When he saw his mother coming to take him home after school, he announced joyously: "Here comes my mommy with her big fat tummy!" During school he liked to talk about the forthcoming event:

BILLY   My mommy's going to have a baby.
ADULT   Yes, she is.
BILLY   Are you going to have a baby?
ADULT   I've already had mine. Timmy is my baby. He's grown into a little boy now.
BILLY   My mommy has a big fat tummy. The baby's getting its food in there.
ADULT   That's right. You got your food in your mommy, too, when you were a baby.

[22] Mrs. Corinne Sturtevant of Los Angeles, an analyst for children and their parents.
[23] Laura Z. Hobson, *I'm Going to Have a Baby!* (New York: The John Day Company, Inc., 1967).
[24] Pearl Buck, *Johnny Jack and His Beginnings* (New York: The John Day Company, Inc., 1954).

With Billy's help it was easy for his teacher to bring out for the group of children that

- A baby grows inside its mother until it is ready to be born.
- Babies get their food from their mother.
- Billy and each of the other children in his family grew inside Billy's mother years ago.
- Billy's mother will go to the hospital when the baby is ready to come out. There the doctor will help the baby to come out and to get started as a baby.
- The baby will do a lot of growing before it will be ready to play with Billy. It will be tiny, and red, and will sleep most of the time.
- It takes both a daddy and a mommy to get a baby started.
- Having a baby is a happy experience for a family.

But Billy had also gotten the idea that a baby grows in its mother's "tummy," and this learning could confuse him later. His teacher talked with all of the mothers about keeping the story of digestion separate from the story of having a baby, and about distinguishing "the special place" inside the mother where the baby grows from the stomach.

The wise teacher listens for feedback which shows what the children understand about the reproduction process. When Neal was three years and seven months old, he often asked his mother about crawling out of her. One day when he and his five-and-one-half-year-old brother, Stanley, were watching a crow, they showed their acceptance of the idea that babies grow inside their mother:

STANLEY Where is her baby?
NEAL Maybe it is inside her.

As a four-year-old, Mari showed her understanding that babies are like their parents when she remarked: "Horses have only horse babies. Cows have only cow babies. Mommies have only child babies." With her mother one day, she summarized their conversations about what a female has inside by saying, "I have everything a lady has except a baby." In another conversation with her mother, about a month later, Mari talked about her pet duck, Stevie, and showed her understanding about male organs. She said, "A duck has everything a boy has, and daddy has everything Stevie has, and daddy has everything a boy has."

The teacher plays an important part in guiding the children to make comparisons among their observations and understandings about babies. For instance, when four-year-old Neal was helping to feed the guppies one morning, his teacher said, "Oh, the mother guppy has had her babies. We must put them into another jar." Neal, who had in mind the little hamsters that had still to be with their mother, said, "No. Babies stay with their mother." His remark gave the teacher an opportunity to explain that baby mammals get food by sucking at the breast of their mother and must stay with her until they can get food for themselves, but baby fish can get food by themselves as soon as they are born, so they do not need to be with their mother.

DEATH

The preschool child copes with the idea that death is something that happens to everyone, including himself. This idea may come as something of a shock to him, or it may come as another in a series of casual experiences with death. Within the preschool program it is important to provide the kind of experiences that every child should have when he is three or five years old:

- Looking at a stuffed bird or animal, and talking about it.
- Talking about pictures of grandparents and great-grandparents.
- Finding a dead bird or mouse and burying it.
- Disposing of a dead guppy, goldfish, or other school pet.

Such incidents are apt to occur in any preschool group. If two or three of them have not occurred, the teacher should set the stage so that the children have opportunity for realizing the incidence of death and talking about it. In this way, she helps them at an early age to acquire a scientific objectivity about an acceptance of death as an integral part of life. Such an objectivity is revealed in the following conversation by Neal (three years and eleven months), driving along with his mother, father, and brother Stanley during a nursery school study trip. The children refer to an earlier conversation about death which had included their playmate, Susie:

NEAL   When we are old men, we are going to die, eh Stanley? Susie cried.
MOTHER   Did Susie cry when you said that?
NEAL   Susie cried.
MOTHER   Maybe Susie had never thought of that before. That's why she cried.
NEAL   Susie is going to die when she is an old, old mommy. Susie is going to be an old, old mommy. I am going to die when I am an old daddy. Stanley is going to die when he is an old daddy. Daddy will be an old daddy. Daddy, are you going to be an old daddy?
DADDY   Yes, Neal.

Several months later when Neal was four and one half years old, he simulated death in his play but was careful not to think of himself as really dead. He said, "I am a dead people but I still move."

By the time children enter school, they should have had several experiences with death as an integral part of life and should understand the basic scientific aspects of death. Through their parents or through participation in a religious-education group, they should also have gained an understanding of some simple religious interpretation of death.

Introduction to Different Sciences

By the time a child is ready for elementary school, his preschool experiences should have provided him with simple concepts basic to each of the sciences. Many of these learnings are a natural concomitant of everyday activities during each of the four seasons. Others must be consciously taught at some time during the preschool years. Beginning experiences in the biological sciences as well as in astronomy have already been discussed in some detail. Attention needs also to be given to teaching preschool children key ideas in such physical sciences as chemistry and physics. Furthermore, bacteriology—which is often left to the home and the advertising agencies—needs careful attention within the science program for the preschool children.

CHEMISTRY

An important question in the study of chemistry is the question, "What is it made of?" The preschool teacher should guide the children in learning to ask this question. She is interested in whether objects are made of wood, metal, plastic, or cement, and she shares this interest with the children. For instance, as she is passing out the paper to the children she may ask, "Do you know what paper is made from?" A minute or two later she answers her own question by saying, "It's made from plants. Most of it is made from trees." Four- and five-year-old children are ready for such incidental learnings. Here are other questions and comments which preschool teachers can make as an integral part of various activities:

ACTIVITY	TEACHER COMMENT
Hammering nails into wood; looking at a picture of a sign nailed to a tree.	How does that sign stay on the tree? Somebody hammered a nail into the sign and the tree the way we hammer nails into wood here at school.
Nailing house numbers onto the playhouse.	How can we put the numbers on our playhouse? We can hammer nails through these little holes in the numbers and into the wood of the house.
Finding toys left out during rain or snow.	What happened to the metal in this car? Metal rusts when water is on it for a day or two. This cup of soft plastic is just the way it was. What happened to this cardboard box? Did anything happen to the concrete sidewalk?

ACTIVITY	TEACHER COMMENT
Having refreshments.	Do you know what our glasses are made of? Are we eating plant things today?

Such simple, everyday attention to what things are made of is part of the foundation that years later will make a child ready for studying the structure of the atom and other complex chemical phenomena.

Through their simple experiences with air, the children should gain an appreciation of it as a substance. On a cold morning, or in a cold room, blow breath out and see it condense into tiny drops of water that look like a cloud. On a sunny day indoors, watch a narrow beam of sunlight coming through a crack illuminate the dust particles moving about in the air. Take in air by breathing and then have it go back out. Blow air into a balloon, making it get bigger. Blow into a soap solution to make pretty bubbles filled with air. With kindergarten children, turn a glass upside down and lower it into a pan of water. When the glass is tipped, bubbles of air come out, and water takes the place of air in the glass. At the service station, put air into tires for a bicycle or a car. Have moving air make a pinwheel or a windmill go around. Float a kite on air.

Through simple, pleasurable experiences with foodstuffs, the children have an introduction to the chemistry of foods. In the course of the school year, the teacher should bring a hotplate and a Pyrex dish to show the children that

- When heated, sugar becomes a liquid which then turns brown and is carmelized.
- When heated, water boils.
- When a salt solution slowly and completely evaporates over a period of several days, crystals are left which are easily seen with a hand lens.
- Water changes into ice when it is put into the freezing compartment of a refrigerator.

Children who have enjoyed cooking in their homes are apt to remark as Neal did, when he was four years and nine month old, "It's fun to watch butter melt."

Another important part of the study of matter is the study of the properties of different substances. The preschool teacher should help the children become aware of different properties of wood, metal, plastic, and concrete, and of everyday objects made of these substances. For instance, at mealtime the teacher may make table conversation about the spoons in this way: "Does your spoon feel cold when you first pick it up? It's made of metal and all metal feels cold when you first touch it. It takes heat away from your hand. Touch the metal edging on the table and see how it feels. If you hold a piece of metal for a while it gets warm from your hand. Is your spoon warm where you are holding it?" During that day and the next several days, the teacher points out metal objects that the children use. Each time she points out the characteristic property of initial coldness. Many experiences with the cold feeling of metal are necessary before a teacher can pick up a coin and say to a mature five-year-old child: "This dime feels cold. What is it made of?" and expect to get the answer that it is made of metal.

The teacher should guide the children in associating only obvious properties with different objects. Usually she calls attention to how some substance feels, or how it looks. However, she also makes a point of introducing the children to another kind of property by helping them find out whether something will burn easily. To do this she can plan a series of experiences with small fires along the following lines:

Let's have a little fire. Where shall we have it? Outside on dirt, away from other things? or inside in a fireplace, or a stove? Fire is dangerous. We must be ready to put it out before we start it. How do we put it out? Let's have the hose, or buckets of water, ready first.

What do we use to make a fire? What things burn? Let's try the things you think we should use, and see which of them burns well. Today we can try two of them, and next time we can try other things.

How do we start a fire? What is a match made of? Yes, it's a piece of wood with some chemicals on the end of it. How do we light the match? Be sure the matchbox is closed so no other matches will start burning. Strike the match away from yourself because you don't want it to burn you. (Teach young children that "only grownups" light matches.)

After the little fire has burned down, make sure it is out by sprinkling water on it. When it is cool, use a stick or a poker to pull out the things put into the fire. Where is the paper? Where is the wood? Where is the rock?

The experienced teacher introduces only one science point at a time. She makes sure that the fire is a safe and happy experience for the children. She knows that during the next fire experience she can teach the children a little bit more, especially if they find the learning situation a pleasant and fascinating one. Both before and after the experiences with small fires, the teacher discusses the science program of the school with the children's parents.

With older preschool children, it is appropriate to do simple demonstrations—for instance, to show them that air is necessary for burning. Here is a teacher's account of how she showed the four-and-one-half-year-old children that a fire cannot burn without air:

This morning I told the four-and-one-half-year-old group that I had a surprise for them. They gathered eagerly around me and watched what I did. I lit a small birthday candle inside a coffee can, and put the lid on immediately. Because of lack of air, the flame went out.

TEACHER Why did the flame go out?

CHILDREN You put the lid on.

TEACHER That's true. But there is another reason.

(*She puts holes in the side of the can, lights the candle, and puts the lid on again. This time the flame does not go out.*)

TEACHER I wonder why the flame didn't go out this time?

TOM You made holes in the can.

KENNETH Air gets in.

TEACHER That's right. Air can get in through the little holes. Fire has to have air to burn; fire cannot burn without air. Do you remember how the fire went out when I put the lid on the can before it had holes in it?

The children seemed to understand the principle, and their attention was very good. It was an excellent opportunity to lead into a safety lesson. I talked about *not* playing with fire or matches.

TEACHER Do you know why you should not play with matches?

CHILDREN Kids don't.

TEACHER Yes, that's one reason. Only grownups use matches. But there's also another reason.

TOM You might get burned.

TEACHER Yes, and burns hurt. (*Uses the word "hurt" because children understand it.*)

This teacher repeats this experiment at Halloween with a candle inside a pumpkin. The children see that the candle flame goes out unless it has enough air coming in through the facial openings or the top. The experiment shows the children the simple relationship between air and burning: no air, no fire.

PHYSICS

The beginnings of physics in the mind of a preschool child, like the beginnings of any other science, are formed out of his firsthand experience when that experience is interpreted for him in terms of basic physical concepts. He must have both the experience and its interpretation. The experience is not sufficient in itself; and the explanation is meaningless without realistic experience at the level of the child.

In the scientific world of today, it is important for the preschool child to develop an elementary understanding of the physical concepts on which he can build further appreciation of physical science. Here are suggestions about teaching preschool children some simple physical concepts concerning mechanics, magnetism, electricity, and light.[25]

MECHANICS

In many neighborhoods today people are constantly making or adding to their homes and community buildings. The child in such a world must be

[25] Sound is discussed in Chapter 14.

able to observe and interpret the activities he sees. He needs also to act out what he has seen, within the resources of the school. His teacher should provide apparatus and equipment with which he can build and rebuild, and with which he can act such roles as those of a workman, an engineer, and a job superintendent. She not only should encourage dramatic play, she also should encourage verbal accounts and expressions through art and craft materials. But, above all, she should help the children to become aware of the scientific concepts that are an essential part of the mechanical operations they observe and imitate in play. Here are preschool experiences with mechanical problems, and science concepts which the teacher can point out in connection with them:

SUPERVISED ACTIVITY	RELATED CONCEPTS
Use a single pulley fastened to the storage house ceiling or a rope over a tree branch to lift a tricycle.	A person can pull down to lift something up.
Push a too-heavy-to-lift box of blocks up an inclined plane made from a walking board.	To raise a heavy object, make a slope.
Put the box of blocks on a wheeled dolly.	With wheels a person can easily push a heavy load.
Use a block and pry pole to lift the box of blocks high enough to slide wheels under it.	A pry pole can pry up a heavy object.
Use a teeter-totter.	A person or weight on one end of a teeter-totter lifts a person at the other end.
Whirl a rope where it can hit only sand or dirt.	The end of a whirling rope goes fast and can hurt.
Whirl a Lazy Susan made of metal or plastic, or one wheel of a turned-over wagon.	Small objects set on a spinning wheel are whirled off.
Stand on the middle, and then on the edge, of a chair on a slippery floor.	Standing on the middle is steady, but on the edge is apt to result in a slip or fall.

Three-year-old children are interested in springs. The "slinky" toys capitalize on this interest with a coil of spring steel which can "walk" down a flight of stairs, and pull-toys in such forms as that of a caterpillar. The jack-in-the-box is an old favorite with small children. Other toys with springs include a variety of heads which move interestingly because they are mounted on a spring neck.

The four-year-old child is interested in how the spring works. He can make a noise with a "cricket" made out of spring steel. If he bends it, it will "chirp" as it springs back into place. A mouse trap has a spring which makes a bar spring back to catch a mouse—or a child's fingers. The springs that hold parts of a flashlight in place, and other household objects made with springs, are also items that the teacher introduces to the four-year-old child. With each experience, the child widens his concept of a spring, its usefulness, and its hazards.

MAGNETISM

Preschool children have a great deal of fun with magnets. Their teacher helps them observe how magnetism functions and enlarges their understanding of it to include the fact that iron, and steels derived from it, have the magnetic property. Here are activities to be enjoyed by the children, three or four at a time, with apparatus for each child and with an adult to see that the little magnets do not get lost or put in a pocket.

Put water in an aluminum foil pie plate or other nonmagnetic dish. Make a tiny boat to carry a steel pin, perhaps from a small piece of cork or half a walnut shell. The child moves the boat, without touching it, by moving his magnet in the direction he wishes the boat to go.

With a small black dog mounted on one magnet and a small white dog mounted on another magnet, have the children see how magnets attract and repel each other when they are free to move around on a smooth surface.

Tie a small horseshoe magnet to the end of a string fastened to a short fishing pole the right size for a child. Make "magnetic fish" by fastening together two fish-shaped pieces of construction paper by a paperclip at the head of the fish. While the children extract the fish from a waterless pail, the supervising adult not only reminds them of the Tommy Tittlemouse nursery rhyme but also explains to the four- and five-year-old children how the magnet on the fishing pole makes the iron paperclip a magnet which it attracts.

Use a magnetic picture book with a few four- and five-year-old children at one time.

On an iron surface, such as that of a stove or a refrigerator, hang a hot mitt, or a pencil, with a magnet in it.

Mount a small paper sail on a paperclip boat. Place such boats on a glass surface. Use a magnet underneath the glass to make the boats move around.

ELECTRICITY

Three- and four-year-old children enjoy switching a light off and on. For several minutes at a time on a dull day they switch the light off and on in their playhouse. When a simple circuit consisting of a battery, a small light bulb in a socket, and a switch is set out for their use, the older children like to manipulate the switch and control the light in the bulb. Their teacher enlarges this experience by telling them that the electricity can light the bulb when it has a path all the way around. Closing the switch makes a path for the electricity; opening the switch breaks the path.

LIGHT

"The dark's turned on," says the three-year-old unwilling to go into the dark room. This awareness of darkness on the part of the child is a challenge to the nursery school teacher. She can work with the parents in providing happy experiences in the dark. For instance, she can show the children objects that glow in the dark. A child goes willingly into a dark closet, first with his teacher and later by himself, to see a ring or a picture or some other object that glows in the dark.

A child also enjoys learning how to use a flashlight to make darkness or light as he wishes. He easily controls the kind of flashlight which has a switch to squeeze in the handle. Armed with this on a rainy day at school, he can make light patterns on the wall and play with moving shadows. Thus he gains a feeling of importance in having control of light and dark, and the gray shadows. "Isn't this fun!" exclaims his teacher. "Fun," echoes the child. His teacher should guide him in his explorations and plan with him so that the light does not shine into people's eyes. Thus the child learns another aspect of consideration of others at the same time that he learns the fun of the dark and how to control light and darkness.

The children also like to play with their shadows in the beam of light from a projector. They observe that their shadows move when they move that the shape of the shadow is the same as their shape. They put up an arm in the light, and they see the shadow of the arm. If they move toward the screen, they get a big arm shadow or an even bigger arm shadow. The teacher can use a white cardboard to show them the circle of light from the projector lens grows larger as the cardboard is carried farther and farther away from the machine. The children see the light spreading out radially from the light source. Many such experiences are necessary to help them realize that light travels in straight lines.

The teacher should also guide the children in observing the difference in length of shadow outdoors. When they come to school in the morning, they see long shadows extending toward the west. At noon they see very short shadows because the sun is directly overhead. In the afternoon they again see longer shadows, but extending toward the east. Indoors, with a dolly and with a flashlight for the sun, the teacher reteaches these concepts by telling the children a simple story about the dolly and her shadow that changed during the day. With younger children she reads *The Shadow Book*[26] and, with older children, *Who Likes the Sun?*[27]

Playing with water sprays outdoors on warm sunny days, the children see the rainbow colors in the spray. The teacher should point out the rainbow and tell them that the drops of water separate sunlight into its colors. When the beveled edge of a mirror spreads sunlight into its colors, the

[26] Beatrice Schenk de Regniers, *The Shadow Book* (New York: Harcourt, Brace & World, Inc., 1960).
[27] Beatrice Schenk de Regniers and Leona Pierce, *Who Likes the Sun?* (New York: Harcourt, Brace & World, Inc., 1961).

teacher again can point this out to the children. If she has a glass prism, she can use it to let the children separate the light into colors themselves. Through such experiences, the children gain satisfaction in controlling light.

The teacher should also help the children observe the light reflections that they see in a mirror. Sometimes she uses the mirror from the dress-up corner, and sometimes she has the children use the mirror made by water in a dark-colored tin or plastic bucket on a sunny day. With skillful questions, she guides them in observing their own reflections, those of their friends, and those of background objects.

The children enjoy a portable mirror as well as a stationary one. The modern plastic materials make it possible for them to have a mirror which they learn to handle carefully without much danger of broken glass. The morning that their teacher brought a round mirror a foot and a half in diameter, the children carried it around, watching themselves in it. "There I am," was soon followed by: "Look! I'm falling!" as they noticed the angle of their reflections. They were fascinated with seeing themselves from many new angles. They even held the mirror above them and saw themselves as if they were standing on their heads. For several days the mirror was an object of great interest. When it became less interesting, their teacher put it away on the shelf of things for occasional use. She knew that it would be enjoyed again later.

The teacher should have other mirror objects on the shelf for occasional use. A plastic Christmas-tree ornament, an unbreakable shaving mirror, and a hand mirror are equipment for helping children to observe and appreciate light reflections. Their experience as preschool children develops their interest in light and provides background for study of it in high school classes in general science and physics.

ROCKETS AND SPACESHIPS

Rockets and spaceships are so commonly talked about that preschool children take them as a part of life. The words take on more meaning as the teacher provides the children with simple experiences related to space objects. For instance, when she starts a child swinging, she asks, "Where do you want to go?" If the child answers, "The moon," the teacher pretends she is an announcer at a rocket-loading station. She may say, "All aboard for the moon. Loading at Gate 1." As the imaginary rocket takes off, she lets the swing go from the high point to which she has raised it. With four-year-old children, she can elaborate the dramatic play of the takeoff, and include a short countdown: "4—3—2—1. Blast off!"

Sometimes the experienced teacher uses long balloons to simulate missiles. Blowing one up, she holds the untied mouth of the balloon down on a flat surface with her fingers pinching the neck of the balloon while she simulates a take-off. At the "blastoff" signal, her fingers release the balloon so that it goes into a brief orbit while the escaping air acts like a jet.

The teacher also can include in the outdoor equipment some of the soft plastic "flying saucers" which help the children imagine spaceships under the guidance of an adult.

Essentially, what the preschool teacher does is to encourage the children to imagine themselves as passengers in rockets or as people helping the rockets take off.

BACTERIOLOGY

Children often get a one-sided view of the microscopic world through watching TV advertisements that advise them only of the germs and of various things to be bought as a means of getting rid of the germs. If mother does not get the things-to-be-bought, the child then may be afraid of germs over which he can exert no control. Realizing this situation, the preschool teacher should teach science concepts which help a child to understand the microscopic world as it is, and his relation to it. Here are activities which help a child know about and control the world of microscopic plants and animals:

ACTIVITIES	RELATED CONCEPTS
Wash hands with soap before eating.	Soap kills germs. Eat with clean hands.
Use a hand lens to see little things (e.g., mold and bacteria colonies on bread or pumpkin; pond scum).	Many tiny plants and animals are too small to see without a lens.
Enjoy eating a mild cheese.	Molds and bacteria make cheese taste good.
Watch the decay process in a pumpkin or some other plant; then bury it in the garden.	Bacteria and other microscopic organisms change plants back into soil. Such soil makes good food for new plants.
Grow bacteria in agar-agar in dishes sterilized in an oven (e.g., Petri dishes).	Bacteria grow only when they have food, moisture, and warmth.

As was pointed out in Chapter 4, the teacher should help the children in understanding how to keep themselves well. If she can find a picture of a child taking his vitamins, she can show this on the flannelboard and talk with the children about taking vitamins to keep in good health. Another day she can talk with them about how we go to the doctor to get vaccinations and other protections against illness, and—when we get an overload of germs—to get medicine that helps our bodies fight the germs. Another day she should talk with the children about going to the dentist as a means of helping us have good teeth. Every time there are opportunities for talking about doctors, dentists, vitamins, and medicines, the teacher should always present these concepts to the children as aids to keeping ourselves well. In this way she encourages them in feeling in control of the microscope world and of themselves.

CONSERVATION

An important concept in science is the conservation of our natural resources. This concept of leaving attractive and irreplaceable resources to be enjoyed later by both ourselves and others must be taught to preschool children if the wild flowers are to remain in the national parks and the stalactite and other formations are to continue to exist in caves open to the public. Preschool children are learning the difference between "mine" and "thine." They learn also the difference between the things to be looked at and the things to be taken.

When the nursery teacher takes the children to the flower gardens in the park, she should tell them about the pretty flowers they will see.

TEACHER   What do we do with the flowers?
CHILDREN   Pick them. See them.
TEACHER   We just look at them. Why don't we pick them? . . . We want to see them again the next day. If we pick them, we can't see them again. Remember: we only look at the flowers. Then we can come again and see them.

Because most groups include at least one child who likes to pick flowers, the teacher usually has opportunity to reteach the conservation concept.

TEACHER   (*to child who has picked some flowers*)   Oh, Tommy, I'm sorry you picked those flowers. We won't see them when we come tomorrow. They are so pretty here, but when you pick them they wilt and are not pretty. Next time, Tommy, will you enjoy the flowers here and not pick them?

The next school day, the teacher should bring the group to the same flower garden to the place where the flowers are missing. She may say, "Do you remember the pretty red flowers that we saw here yesterday? Tommy picked them. They wilted and were not pretty any more. But these flowers that we looked at and did not pick are still here for us all to enjoy. What are we going to do today? . . . Yes, we look at the flowers and leave them here. Tommy and all of us are flower lookers, not flower pickers."

After the children have studied about plants and know that plants need roots to keep on growing, the teacher can have a little crocus, pansy, or other flower to send home in a pot with each child. At Easter, or on Mother's Day, the teacher can use the potted flowers as the culmination of a garden project and as another opportunity to teach the difference between flowers that we take home and flowers that we leave. "We grew these ourselves, so we can take them home to our mothers," she may say. From time to time with her flannelboard she should remind the children to be flower-lookers when they see pretty flowers in other people's gardens.

PETS

So much biology can be learned from pets that no nursery school or kindergarten is complete without them. Watching a hamster enjoy a leaf of lettuce encourages the child to include lettuce in his diet too. Filling the water container for a pet helps a child to realize the importance of water to animals and people. Getting a response from a pet is a thrilling experience for a child. Furthermore, pets at school can help children learn that

A pet affords an opportunity to learn about the rhythm of rest and activity. (Courtesy of The Merrill-Palmer Institute and Donna J. Harris, Detroit, Michigan.)

- Vegetables are good for both pets and us.
- Some animals are grass-eaters and some are meat eaters.
- Pets need care every day—just as we do.
- Pets are active for a while and then rest for a while.
- Pets bite when hurt or frightened.
- A daddy and a mother pet can have babies.

● Pets die when their bodies wear out or when an accident happens to them.

The preschool teacher should realize the practical problems of having pets at school. An older animal that is frightened by the noise and movement of the children may bite. Any animal may confuse a finger with a piece of food. To prevent such happenings, the teacher and the children

What does it eat and drink? (*Courtesy of Seattle Public Schools, Seattle, Washington. Photograph by Royal C. Crooks.*)

probably may think it wise for everyone to keep his hands behind him while he is watching the animals in their cages. To arrive at such a rule through a group discussion is an excellent learning experience for the children. They learn the scientific facts which enable them to decide what is good to do.

When Neal was almost four years old, he brought his hamster to nursery school to show the children the eleven pink wriggling babies born a few days earlier. The children crowded around to see the hamster but they were careful to keep their hands away from the cage because they knew a mother will bite to protect her babies.

The next time Neal brought his baby hamsters to school, they had been weaned and were strong and healthy. They were not old enough to bite hard, and they had been petted so much that they were easy to handle. Neal's mother helped him to explain and demonstrate for the children how to hold a hamster so it would be comfortable. Then each child was given an opportunity to hold a hamster under the supervision of Neal and his mother.

This experience was valuable to Neal, a younger child in a family of two children, and was not harmful to the pets. Neal's teacher was delighted with the explanations that Neal made and with his helpfulness to the other children. He felt important in his role as owner of the pets and decider of turns for holding a hamster.

As soon as each child had enjoyed the hamsters, the teacher put them aside so that the children could give their attention to other activities. The teacher felt that any handling of pets needs to be supervised by an adult at all times.

One Sunday school worked out a pet-lending system much like the lending system of a library or junior museum. On Sunday, a child and his parents could check out the turtle for the week. On the plastic house of the turtle were brief instructions about how to care for him. With the turtle, his house, and his food supply, the child had a week of caring for a pet. The next Sunday, when he returned the pet for someone else to enjoy, the child told what he had observed his pet do. Thinking about the pet each Sunday, each child was eager to have his turn with the class pet.

Here is the kind of learning situation that arises when a pet cat is a continuing part of a nursery group. When three-year-old David came into the room from outdoors, the kitty slipped in, too.

TEACHER   Kitty stays outside. Can you put him out, David, please?
DAVID   No.
TEACHER   Just pick him up under his front legs.
DAVID   He might scratch me.
TEACHER   Not if you pick him up gently—like this. (*Picks up kitty.*)
 I like little kitty,
  Her coat is so warm.
 If I don't hurt her,
  She'll do me no harm.
 Have you ever seen a kitty's feet? (*Holds out a front paw for David to see.*) See the cushions on it?
DAVID   Where are the claws?
TEACHER   Let's see if kitty will put them out for us. Kitty keeps them up above the cushions when he feels safe and happy. But if he feels he might get hurt, he puts them down like this.
DAVID   I don't want to see them.

TEACHER   Kitty won't use his claws because he knows you like him. Kitty
   scratched the little boy the other day because that was the only way
   kitty knew to make him stop hurting him. I think I would scratch to get
   away, too, if someone kept on pinching me. Wouldn't you? Here you go
   outside, kitty. (*Puts kitty outside.*)
DAVID (*goes on indoors*)   "I like little kitty. . . ."

With the guidance of his teacher, David was learning what a cat does
and was replacing his fear of a cat by interest in one.

Situations for Discussion

A preschool teacher is apt to find herself in situations similar to the four
described here. As you think of what to do in each situation, consider whether
each course of action suggested is desirable, or not. Use points brought out in
the chapter as well as ideas from your own experience to justify your views.
Suggest alternative courses of action to supplement those given.

SITUATION 1   One spring morning several children come running to show
you the radishes that each of them has pulled up from the garden. You should

● Tell them that they should have left the radishes alone.
● Help them observe what a plant is like.
● Tell the other chidren what these children have done.
● Talk about how many plants to pull up at one time.
● Make plans about helping the radishes to grow.

SITUATION 2   In teaching science to preschool children it is essential for
the teacher

● To encourage the children to ask questions.
● To answer whatever questions a child asks.
● To teach the superstitions of the community.
● To provide firsthand experience.
● To help children interpret what they observe.

SITUATION 3   You are the teacher for a group of three-year-old children.
One morning as you are walking to school, you notice a dead bird in the
bushes near the sidewalk. You should

● Take it to school to show the children.
● Leave it for the children to find during their walk.
● Tell the children about how you found a dead bird.
● Read *The Dead Bird*.[28]
● Have the children act out finding a dead bird.

SITUATION 4   In planning science experiences to include in the program
for your group of four-year-old children, you should.

● See that they have chemistry or physics activities each month.
● Provide science experiences according to the seasons.

---

[28] Margaret Wise Brown, op. cit.

- Avoid discussing death unless the children ask about it.
- Ask the librarian what picture books she has for science.
- Enlarge your own understanding of science through reading or course work.

Current Books for Preschool Children

ALBERTI, TRUDE. *The Animal's Lullaby*. New York: The World Publishing Company, 1967. [Of the animals, only a baby has mother and father to sing him a lullaby.]

ADELSON, LEONE. *Please Pass the Grass*. New York: David McKay Co., Inc., 1960. ["This meadow looks empty as you look around. Don't be fooled! All the traffic is close to the ground!"]

BASON, LILLIAN. *Pick a Raincoat, Pick a Whistle*. New York: Lothrop, Lee & Shepard, Inc., 1966. [Uses of leaves include making houses, cooking, and making a whistle.]

BATE, NORMAN. *Who Built the Dam?* New York: Charles Scribner's Sons, 1958. [The dam is built and the river tamed. *Who Built the Bridge?* (1954) is by the same author.]

BRANLEY, FRANKLIN M. *Big Tracks, Little Tracks*. New York: Thomas Y. Crowell Company, 1960. [This Let's Read and Find Out book encourages preschool children to look for animal tracks. The same author wrote *What Makes Day and Night* (1961) and *The Moon Seems to Dance* (1960).]

BROWN, MARGARET WISE. *The Diggers*. New York: Harper & Row, Publishers, 1958. [The steam shovel is the great digger among many others.]

BUCKLEY, HELEN E. *Josie and the Snow*. New York: Lothrop, Lee & Shepard Co., 1964. [Josie has a lovely snowy day.]

CONKLIN, GLADYS. *I Caught a Lizard*. New York: Holiday House, 1967. [Lizard, baby bird, grasshopper—I have many pets out of my cage and back in the garden.]

CHANDOHA, WALTER. *A Foal for You*. New York: The World Publishing Company, 1967. [*A Kitten for You* (1967) is by the same author-photographer.]

DE REGNIERS, BEATRICE SCHENK. *The Shadow Book*. New York: Harcourt, Brace & World, Inc., 1960. [Throughout the day a child enjoys shadows.]

DOWNER, MARY L. *The Flower*. New York: William R. Scott, Inc., 1955. [From a tiny seed grows a plant, a flower, and then new seed to go on growing.]

ETS, MARIE HALL. *Play with Me*. New York: The Viking Press, Inc., 1955. [Sitting still is the way to play with animals.]

Gilberto and the Wind (1963) portrays Gilberto's experience with the force of the wind.

FISHER, AILEEN. *Where Does Everyone Go?* New York: Thomas Y. Crowell Company, 1961. [A child wonders where butterflies, frogs and people go as winter approaches.]

FRESCHET, BERNICE. *The Old Bullfrog*. New York: Charles Schribner's Sons, 1968. [When the heron struck downward, the old bullfrog quickly swam away—an early experience with the survival of the most fit.]

GARELICK, MAY. *Where Does the Butterfly Go When It Rains?* New York: William R. Scott, Inc., 1961. [Encourages speculation.]

GAY, ZHENYA. *What's Your Name?* New York: The Viking Press, Inc., 1955. [From a description and a rhyme, guess the name of the animal.]

GOLDIN, AUGUSTA. *Straight Hair, Curly Hair*. New York: Thomas Y. Crowell Co., 1966. [The shape of follicles determines the curl of hair and is not possible to change.]

GOUDEY, ALICE E. *Butterfly Time*. New York: Charles Scribner's Sons, 1964. [Sue and I recognize the butterflies that come into our garden.]

Great Big Animal Book. New York: Simon and Schuster, Inc., 1950. [The Great Big Golden Books for use with a group of children include: *Baby Animals, Baby Farm Animals, The Great Big Car and Truck Book, The Great Big Fire Engine Book*.]

HOBSON, LAURA Z. *I'm Going to Have a Baby*. New York: The John Day Company, Inc., 1967. [Waiting for my baby, I have time to find out where it is and how it got started.]

JARDINE, MAGGIE. *I Need*. New York: Wonder Books, Inc., 1965. ["Birds don't need shoes for walking, but I do."]

JOHNSON, RYERSON. *Let's Walk up the Wall*. New York: Holiday House, 1967. [People can think of new ways to do things that animals do.]

KRAUSS, RUTH. *Monkey Day*. New York: Harper & Row, Publishers, 1957. [The little girl who loves monkeys brings a boy monkey for the girl monkey.]

LENSKI, LOIS. *Animals for Me*. New York: Henry Z. Walck, Inc., 1954. [Hello to the pussy cat, fuzzy sheep, pretty bird, and other animals.]

MILLER, EDNA. *Mousekin Finds a Friend*. Englewood Cliffs, N.J.: Prentice-Hall, Inc., 1967. [Mouskin explores the camouflages of nature until he finds another white-footed mouse like himself.]

ROTHSCHILD, ALICE. *Fruit Is Ripe for Timothy*. New York: William R. Scott, Inc., 1963. [Different kinds of fruit ripen in the summer.]

SAMMIS, KATHY. *The Beginning Knowledge Book of Butterflies*. New York: The Macmillan Company, 1965. [Such well-illustrated books make good reference books for preschool groups.]

SCHWARTZ, JULIUS. *Now I Know*. New York: Whittlesey House, 1955. [Through experience we know about wind, shadow, lightning, and so on. *I Know a Magic House* (1956) is by the same author.]

SHOWERS, PAUL. *Your Skin and Mine*. New York: Thomas Y. Crowell Co., 1965. ["Everybody's skin makes melamin." Freckles are spots of it. *Look at Your Eyes* (1962) is by the same author.]

TRESSELT, ALVIN. *Hide and Seek Fog*. New York: Lothrop, Lee & Shepard Co., 1965. [The fog changes what people do.]

WEBBER, IRMA E. *Up Above and Down Below*. New York: William R. Scott, Inc., 1953. [Plants grow both below and above ground.]

YASHIMA, MITSU and TARO. *Momo's Kitten*. New York: The Viking Press, Inc., 1961. [Momo's kitten becomes a mother cat. *Youngest One* (1962) is by the same author.]

ZAFFO, GEORGE J. *The Big Book of Boats and Ships*. New York: Grosset & Dunlap, Inc., 1951. [The Big Book series includes books about fire engines (1964), trains (1963), trucks (n.d.), and building and wrecking machines (1965). *The Giant Nursery Book of Things that Work* (Doubleday, 1967) is by the same author.]

ZION, GENE, and M. GRAHAM. *All Falling Down*. New York: Harper & Row, Publishers, 1951. [Petals of flowers, water of fountains—all fall down.]

CHAPTER 10

Exploring Time, Space, and Numbers

At first thought, time, space, and number relationships appear outside the ken of nursery children. These are abstract concepts, and three-year-olds are only at the gateway to abstract thinking. But this very fact is what makes the learning of time, space, and number concepts an important part of their preschool experience. These concepts are the foundation for their subsequent study of mathematics,[1] geography, geology, and other sciences. The beginning experiences must be not only correct but also vivid and real. They must stem from concrete experiences which will weld themselves presently into increasingly abstract concepts. From the everyday sensory experiences of the nursery school and the kindergarten comes the basis for arithmetic and geography in the elementary school.

The importance of direct experience as a basis for mastering relationships of time, space, and number was pointed out by Gesell and Ilg, who wrote:

Time, space, number, form, texture, color, and causality—these are the chief elements in the world of things in which the child must find himself.

. . . he acquires his command of these elements by slow degrees, first through his muscles of manipulation and locomotion, through eyes, hands, and feet. In this motor experience he lays the foundation for his later judgments and concepts.[2]

Actual experience enables a preschool child to develop such basic concepts of time as those of the present and the past, or that of intervals of

[1] Jean Piaget et al., *The Child's Conception of Geometry* (London: Routledge and Kegan Paul, Ltd., 1960).

[2] Arnold Gesell and Frances L. Ilg, *Child Development* (New York: Harper & Row, Publishers, 1949), p. 26.

Quick steps to adult height. (Courtesy of The Merrill-Palmer Institute and Donna J. Harris, Detroit, Michigan.)

time. To develop such concepts, a child must establish in his thinking two distinct and separate points in time. This a child does, for instance, when he conceives of himself as he is now in the present and as he was in his past as an infant.

REVIEW OF BABYHOOD

The three-year-old child is much interested in hearing about babyhood in general and about his own babyhood in particular. This interest results in his establishing two separate times in his life, with a time interval between them. He is familiar with the "now" and establishes a "then" in relation to it. Thus he begins to deal with time as something he abstracts from his experience.

Realizing the significance of the child's interest in babyhood, the nursery teacher should create a vivid description of it. She can use a collection of pictures of babies which she has built up over the years, carefully selecting them from current magazines and discarded books. On the flannelboard she may show pictures of babies drinking milk from bottles and eating

354

baby food. She contrasts this infant menu with the favorite foods of the three-year-olds, and helps the children realize how far they have come in acquiring a much more tasty diet than a baby has. They still enjoy some of the same foods—for instance, applesauce—but they are now able to eat many others.

The teacher should bring out the contrast beween the baby, who has to be carried around by an adult, and the three-year-old child, who can run and play and explore a much wider living space. Another point she can mention is that the baby only makes a few sounds and is not yet able to tell people what he needs and wants, whereas a three-year-old can. The teacher also should emphasize that parents love both the baby and the three-year-old child but that they express their affection in different ways because of the differences between the needs of the baby and those of the three-year-old. Of course a major difference between the infant and the child is that the child has the fun and pleasure of going to a nursery group and enjoying all the different kinds of experiences which are a part of nursery school.

In bringing out contrasts between the life of the infant and that of the child, the teacher finds useful such books as *Big Little Davy*,[3] *The Very Little Girl*,[4] and *The Very Little Boy*,[5] which tell what activities babies have and what children do later. She encourages the children in pretending to be babies crawling around, and then in being nursery children who can listen to music and march or run or hop or do other things that the music suggests. All through the variety of activities of the nursery group, the teacher should remind the children that they can do what they were not able to do as little babies at home with mother.

ANOTHER POINT IN TIME

By the time a child is four years old, he is well able to develop some concept of another point in time. For some children, this point may be the era when grandmother, grandfather, or some other older person was a child. Through pictures on the flannelboard and stories about "when Grandmother was a little girl," the child builds up more and more detailed an idea of what the world was like at a time different from the present and different from that of his own babyhood. The preschool teacher can use picture books to help create this understanding. *World Full of Horses*[6] and *Maybelle the Cable Car*[7] are among the well-illustrated picture books

[3] Lois Lenski, *Big Little Davy* (New York: Henry Z. Walck, Inc., 1956).
[4] Phyllis Krasilovsky, *The Very Little Girl* (Garden City, N.Y.: Doubleday & Company, Inc., 1953).
[5] ———, *The Very Little Boy* (Garden City, N.Y.: Doubleday & Company, Inc., 1962).
[6] Dahlov Ipcar, *World Full of Horses* (Garden City, N.Y.: Doubleday & Company, Inc., 1955).
[7] Virginia Lee Burton, *Maybelle the Cable Car* (Boston: Houghton Mifflin Company, 1952).

which the teacher can show to the children and leave in the library corner for them to enjoy further.

Of course what helps most is having a real, long-lived grandmother or great-grandmother to come to school in person. By just being there, the grandmother of a preschool child establishes the reality of another time and gives credence to whatever stories her grandchild may pass on to the other preschool children.

A POINT IN GEOLOGIC TIME

Four- and five-year-old children are able to imagine a world existing in another geologic era. Doing so establishes for them their first experience with geologic time. With *Dinny and Danny*,[8] an excellent resource book, the teacher helps them to create an understanding of what life may have been like for a prehistoric child living among the reptiles of the Age of Reptiles. Reading and rereading *Dinny and Danny*, she helps the children to build a concept of a different point of time. Together they dramatize parts of the story: the slide on the playground is Dinny's backbone; the climber is one of his huge feet; and the treehouse is the cave where Danny and his family lived.

The teacher also uses such authentic pictures as those found in *The World We Live In*[9] to show the children the animal life of the lush Age of Reptiles. She adds dinosaur models, which are available in soft plastic of different sizes, to the sandbox accessories, with another set for use indoors with the blocks. In such ways, the teacher helps the children to conceive of life at a point in time different from the present and completely distinct from it. Thus she helps them to lay a foundation for later study of geologic eras and the succession of events in geologic time.

THE BIRTHDAY

Probably no day of the year is as important for a child as his own birthday. Any day of the year may find him in the sandbox, making a sand cake and decorating it with bits of grass, a twig or two, or shells, or any other reminders of his birthday cake. Especially when he is four years old, he spends much time discussing his birthday and its celebration. When he is five years old, he likes to talk about whether each of his friends is to come to his birthday party. All of this birthday interest is good in that it helps a preschool child to develop the concepts of an event or a special day which recurs annually, and the concept of a calendar year.

At the first of each month during the latter part of the school year, the teacher may ask the older children: "Who has a birthday this month?" Then each child finds out which day on the calendar month is his birth-

[8] Louis Slobodkin, *Dinny and Danny* (New York: The Macmillan Company, 1951).
[9] Lincoln Barnett and the editorial staff of *Life, The World We Live In* (New York: Golden Press, 1955).

day. (The teacher gets this information in advance from the children's enrollment cards.) The teacher guides the children in watching the birthdays get closer. On the day before his fourth birthday, Neal said, "It's very, very, very close to my birthday now." He had been looking at the calendar with his teacher, and was aware that there was less and less space between the current day and his birthday.

When Neal was four years and eight months old, he was interested not only in his own birthday but also in the birthdays of others in his family. With his mother he looked at the calendar and asked, "Where is my birthday?" Then he asked about the birthday of each of the other members of his family. A few weeks later he was sufficiently interested in his mother's birthday to bring his friend Russell to see each of her presents.

The Year

As children experience the succession of birthdays and holidays throughout the year, and as they enjoy activities appropriate to each season, they build up an understanding of the year as a series of recurring events. The three-year-old child understands his birthday as a recurring but infrequent event. The four-year-old appreciates both Christmas and his birthday as events which can be counted on to occur. For instance, when four-and-a-half-year-old Virginia was sorting out and putting in order the important events of the year, she said, "First comes Christmas, then Halloween, and then my birthday."

With each school holiday, the teacher can emphasize that the special event occurs one day each year. Halloween, for instance, comes every fall when the pumpkins ripen. Experiencing the succession of holidays throughout the year is a basis for understanding the year as a large block of time that recurs again and again. Five-year-old children appreciate further the succession of holidays when their teacher reads them *Over and Over*.[10]

Developing a Sense of Time

The teacher should notice how the sense of time develops in her group and help the children to use time concepts. She knows that she helps them to get ready for the next steps when she strengthens each step in its turn. By observing what the children say, she can attempt to increase her awareness of how they make use of time concepts at successive age levels.

The teacher should notice, for example, that the three-year-old child learns the qualitative relationships of time, which will give him a background for learning more precise and even quantitative relationships when he is five years old. As a three-year-old, he is able to use words which show

---

[10] Charlotte Zolotow, *Over and Over* (New York: Harper & Row, Publishers, 1957).

what has happened. For instance, three-and-one-half-year-old Neal said that he had had friends visit last week on Christmas Day by saying, "We already had Christmas time." His remark expresses completion of a past event ("already"), and also shows the use of a specific name for an interval of time ("Christmas time"). At three-and-one-half, Neal had made considerable progress in understanding time relationships.

The three-year-olds learn the meaning of *tonight,* the four-year-olds add to this concept that of *last night.* The five-year-olds learn the meaning of *tomorrow night.* Each is increasing the time distinctions he makes in the sequencing of events. The three-year-old is just beginning to arrange events sequentially. For instance, three-and-one-half-year-old Neal recalled seeing his teacher at the market the day before and said to her, "We went to the market before."

Each child progresses at his own rate in mastering time concepts. For instance, at four years and two months of age, Ned was endeavoring to sort out time concepts and the words associated with them, as follows:

NED   The sun is red.
ADULT   Yes, there's a forest fire. We saw it last night.
NED   I saw the fire from my window tomorrow.
ADULT   Yes, we saw the fire yesterday.
NED   Yesterday.

At the same age as Ned, Neal announced with great care, "The day after today is Stanley's birthday." Probably both boys within six more months will be saying casually, "After I ride this bike, I want to swing."

The fast rate at which time concepts are mastered by four-year-old children is apparent in the contrast between the time concepts of three-year-old and five-year-old children. When the nursery children were talking about *The Shaggy Dog,* a motion picture much advertised on TV, five-year-old Susan, proud to be going to the motion picture, said, "I'm going to see *The Shaggy Dog* on Sunday." Russell, at three and one half, gave some thought as to when he would see it, and then said, "I'm going to see *The Shaggy Dog* one day." Two years later Russell would also be able to define with much greater precision the time at which he would see a current movie. Meanwhile, the teacher should encourage the children to develop a sense of time by listening carefully and appreciatively to their comments and allowing ample time for the children to make them.

The teacher listened sympathetically when Neal (at three years and ten months), who was playing lotto, expressed his awareness of a long time interval by saying, "I did not be a caller a long, long time." She showed her appreciation of his remark by remedying the situation to which he had reacted. In this and other considerate ways the teacher can help children to develop gradually an increasing awareness of time and an ability to express their awareness in words.

Children, as they begin to use time concepts, often make remarks which are appropriate to the general situation but are inexact or incorrect in the specific situation. When four-year-old Robby looks at his toy wrist watch and announces, "It's thirty-nine to seven," the teacher is pleased with his evident awareness that time is reported with numbers. She recalls the description by Gesell and Ilg of the gradual development of a sense of time.

Time words, such as *morning, afternoon, Tuesday, week, two o'clock, year* emerge in the child's speech as he matures. They come in a more or less lawful developmental sequence. They are used in concrete situations long before they are used as abstract notions. At first they are applied on the correct occasions, but without accuracy. There is much dramatic pretense of telling time from a toy wristwatch at four years of age; but a child may be six years old before he can make a discriminating verbal distinction between morning and afternoon.[11]

Because her group of children probably differs from those observed by others, a teacher should make her own observations of their gradual development of a sense of time. Here is the kind of remark that a teacher or a parent should notice because of its significance to the child as well as its significance in his mastery of time concepts.

Kimmy, who would know about waiting and hurrying only when she was years older, said (at two years and three months), "I'm so in a hooey [hurry]"; (at two years and five months), "I'm waiting so fast." Marilyn (three years and five months) endeavored to estimate the time required for bodily changes, "When will I grow up? How long will it take?" and so did blond Meredy (four years old) when she said, "Barbara and I are both four years old. Why doesn't my hair turn brown like Barbara's now that I'm four?" Four-and-one-half-year-old Billy, who was getting used to having a new baby in the family, asked, "How long is the baby going to stay?" Neal (four years and nine months) and his mother talked together as they enjoyed a train ride:

NEAL   Mom, have you been on a train ride before?
MOTHER   Yes, many times.
NEAL   Is this your last one?

Meredy (four years and eleven months) posed a difficult question as she considered the nature of the universe, "Where was everybody when the sun was being built?"

DEVELOPING RELATIONSHIPS FOR DAYS OF THE WEEK

As a child begins to use time concepts, they are noticeable in what he says. Here are records of time concepts expressed by David, a young preschool child just beginning to distinguish sequence of events and the

---

[11] Arnold Gesell and Frances L. Ilg, *Child Development* (New York: Harper & Row, Publishers, 1949), p. 24.

sequence of days of the week: (at two years), "Sun goes down. Stars come out"; (at two years and two months), "After daddy comes home," "Time for lunch," "Wednesday, Thursday. Tomorrow is Thursday. Thursday, trash day"; (at two years and three months), "Yesterday I went to nursery school."

Both the parents and the teacher of the two-and-one-half- and three-year-old child should help him to make associations which distinguish one day from another. For instance, David was encouraged in thinking of the days of the week as follows:

Monday: Daddy goes to work; David goes to nursery school.
Tuesday: Daddy goes to work; David goes to nursery school; garbage day.
Wednesday: Daddy goes to work; no nursery school.
Thursday: Daddy goes to work; David goes to nursery school; trash day.
Friday: Daddy goes to work; no nursery school; garbage day.
Saturday: Daddy is at home.
Sunday: Daddy is at home.

The distinction between the days that Daddy goes to work and the days that Daddy is at home is brought out in *The Daddy Days*.[12] The teacher can use such a book to help the children in discriminating among different days of the week.

ARTIFACTS OF TIME

In the school for preschool children, it is important to have in evidence and in use various devices for measuring time. Clocks, calendars, egg-timers, sundials, and any other simple instruments for measuring time are an integral part of life and, therefore, of the school. If the teacher uses these devices, the child accepts them as part of his world. When he is ready, he will develop various awarenesses of the time aspects of that world. Meanwhile, his teacher should use them audibly, saying for instance to David (two years and four months): "Your mother will be here when the hands of the clock are both straight up. That is ten minutes from now. She will come in ten minutes."

Whenever a child expresses interest in telling or talking about time, his teacher should encourage him. For instance, when four-year-old Bobby stopped for a minute to play with the big cardboard clock face, his teacher came and stood beside him quietly.

BOBBY   I know what time it is when I get up from my nap.
TEACHER   Do you?
(*Bobby arranged the hands so that they read three o'clock.*)

---

[12] Norma Simon, *The Daddy Days* (New York: Abelard-Schuman Limited, 1958). (Not in print at present.)

TEACHER   At three o'clock, you get up from your nap.

(*Bobby considered the clock further, and then made another comparison.*)

BOBBY   The same time's on here as on that clock. (*Points to the large clock on the wall.*)

TEACHER   That's right. Both are clocks to show the time.

CONTINUITY IN PRESCHOOL ACTIVITIES

Because a four-year-old child has a more mature sense of time than a three-year-old, his activities in a nursery group should have greater continuity. He is ready for a project which is begun one day and finished at the next school session. He is no longer adequately challenged by the three-year-old program of activities which are completed within a single session. He is ready for relationships in time from one school session to another.

At three years and ten months of age. Neal had reached the point at which he arranged events of the coming week in sequence. He understood, for instance, that during the next nursery school morning he was to make a valentine for his mother, and that the Valentine Day party would be on the nursery school morning after that.

When the teacher notices this ability of four-year-old children to arrange events on the basis of their sequence in time, she should plan projects that will require two or three days to be completed. Often she plans an activity which can be completed in one day, together with related activities which can be completed within a second or third day. Thus she provides a unified session for the less mature children at the same time that she provides a continuity of experience for the more mature children.

The teacher of four-year-old children should talk with them so that they know what is going to happen at the next school session. The children like to anticipate what they are going to do, and they take satisfaction in seeing that their anticipations are correct. For instance, the four-year-old children were pleased to know that at the next school session they were going to make kites. At the next meeting of the group, the teacher said to the children, "Do you know we're going to make kites today?" Four-and-one-half-year-old Jerry remarked at once, "I heard you say it yesterday." Three-year-old Sandy, sensing that it was appropriate to make remarks, said (at her level of time maturity), "I'm going to get a holster for my birthday."

COMPARISONS IN TIME

One of the ways in which a child grows is in his ability to make comparisons. Teachers and parents help children with this phase of their development when they talk with them, as Neal's mother did with him when he was three years and seven months old. As she was getting breakfast ready, she explained to Neal, "We cannot play with Susie now. Susie's mother is making breakfast in her house. After breakfast we may play with Susie."

When Neal was within a month of his fourth birthday, he was able to make a time comparison at the same time that he made another kind of comparison. When he saw a big collie dog passing by, he said, "That's Lassie," and added, thoughtfully, "I like big dogs. Once I didn't. Now I do. I like little dogs, and big dogs." Thus Neal compared what he thinks now about dogs with what he used to think, and he also classified them into two categories: little dogs, and big dogs.

The parent or the teacher who has a genuine, loving rapport with children can provide an environment in which children are encouraged to develop a sense of time, each at his own rate of development.

Developing Concepts of Space

To develop concepts of space, a preschool child should have direct sensual experience in space, accompanied by verbal comments which help him understand the relationships he feels. The teacher can guide him to make maps, to identify landmarks, to develop contrasting concepts of space (such as *indoors* and *outdoors, small* and *tall, big* and *little*), to develop associations which help him distinguish a particular kind of place, and to develop whatever other concepts help him in coping with the spatial problems of his daily life.

The teacher should be alert to help a child have firsthand experience with unusual as well as usual space relationships. For instance, if she notices a child using a mirror in the dress-up corner, she helps him to expand his knowledgeable experience with it, as she did four-year-old Neal when he wanted very much to wear one of the large sheriff badges. He pointed to the neck of his shirt where he wanted the badge pinned on, and his teacher fastened the badge and then helped Neal appreciate it.

TEACHER It looks very nice. Let's look at it in the mirror.
(*Neal goes over to the mirror.*)
NEAL (*Looks down at himself.*) I can't see it. (*Looks into the mirror.*) But I can like this. (*Admires himself wearing the badge.*)
TEACHER Yes. Mirrors help us see every part of ourselves.

SOME EARLY EXPERIENCES WITH GEOGRAPHY

The nursery teacher should guide the children in her group as they move themselves through the space dimensions of the nursery school and its playground, so that they may learn to understand *indoors* as distinct from *outdoors,* and the interrelationships of windows and doors to the spaces that adjoin them on both the inside and the outside. Literally, she helps her children go "in and out the windows," as they sing the well-known nursery song. "Let's go see" is a familiar phrase which precedes finding out what it feels like to be at the spot one was looking at through the window.

When a child has become familiar with *indoors* as it relates to *outdoors,* and with the interrelationships among indoor rooms and among outdoor spaces, he is ready to conceive of his nursery school as a building constructed within an outdoor space. To make a planned excursion around the nursery school requires careful talking together and affords an opportunity to introduce the idea of a map. This first map is simply a block set on a large piece of paper. This block represents the nursery school building and the land on which it is situated. The teacher should guide the children in envisioning themselves going on the land in such a way as to en-

Constructing a tall, tall tower explores three dimensions. (Courtesy of Montgomery County Head Start Program, Maryland.)

circle the building. They will be able to see all four sides of the building in succession—the front, one side, the back, and the other side. They will be able to see each of several familiar parts of the building with which they are already well acquainted. Thus the children have a first experience in map reading, an essential skill for everyone interested in the study of geography. This map experience is followed by actually making the little circumnavigation trip they have planned, and then— both that day and the next—by rethinking the trip, using the map, and, in fact, remaking the trip itself.

Another map-making trip which the nursery and kindergarten teachers make a point of including in the experience of the four- and five-year-old children is a visit to a house or building on the same street as the school but two or three doors away. The linear nature of the map and the trip makes both easily understood by the children. Furthermore, because the trip is typical of the kind of trip each of them makes in his own neighborhood street, the map is one which a child is apt to incorporate easily into his thinking.

Every simple preschool excursion offers opportunity not only for experience with maps but also for experience with landmarks. During the trip the teacher should guide the children in noticing unusual or large permanent objects which can be used to mark the way. On a second or later trip, she can help the children recall the landmarks they had selected earlier. In this way she helps them to understand what a landmark is and how it is useful. At school she can use the book *Harry by the Sea*[13] to help the children realize how landmarks helped a dog to find his way back to his family. Children should understand and use landmarks because the landmark concept may be of vital importance to some children and the concept enables any child to have greater confidence in his ability to manage his environment.

Children—whether they walk or come by car or bus—should be taken to nursery school or kindergarten by the same route each time until they are familiar with the landmarks along the way. The accompanying adult should help the children to develop an awareness of their route, and may say, "Here we go to school. Down the street to the red house on the corner. Turn the corner. Now we can see the tall trees where our school is. We pass the white house where we went to see the goldfish in the pond. And here we are at school." In a matter of weeks, the children are familiar with the route, and the four-year-old children are pointing out each landmark as they come to it.

When four-year-old children ride to school along the same route, they soon learn to recognize each child's house and then the streets that lead to it. The children talk about them and say, "Here's Tommy house," and later have conversations such as the following:

MARY   Take me home first.
ROBIN   Me first!
ADULT   Well, let's see which way we are going today. I'll turn right here.
ROBIN   That's Linda's way.

---

[13] Gene Zion, *Harry by the Sea* (New York: Harper & Row, Publishers, 1965).

ADULT   Yes, Linda's house is our first stop today.
LINDA (*three years old*)   Me first!

SENSITIVITY TO SPACE RELATIONSHIPS

The beginnings of sensitivity to space relationships are found in a child's interest in how things fit together. The toddler fits colored doughnuts onto a central peg and goes on to master the fitting of a triangular, cylindrical, or rectangular piece into a triangle, circle, or square hole. The two-year-old child likes to find an empty shelf in a low cupboard or some other space that fits him when he crawls into it. Three-year-old Meredy told her mother, "I have a kiss for you that just fits." Three-and-one-half-year-old

Puzzles involve space relationships. (Courtesy of State of Florida Department of Education and Board of Public Instruction, Volusia County, Florida.)

Kimmy pointed out, "Lilla has a spesho ewaso [special eraser] at home, and it fwips [slips] on the pencil and on again"; and she asked about the pregnant cat going into the small opening of its house: "Can the kitty's fatness fit through such a little hole?"

This concern with the fit of things persists throughout the preschool years. Neal, at four and one half, found opportunity at nursery school to go under the table during craft activities. He explored the spaces between the table legs that were not blocked off by children's knees and legs, and presently crawled out from under the table at the point where it touched the wall. "I found a door," he exclaimed, visibly pleased with his exploration of space and its relationships. Neal was fortunate in having an understanding teacher who appreciated his explorations of space and did not discourage him from gaining firsthand experience with it.

In the spring of the school year, when the four-year-old children are well used to exploring their locality on foot and with very simple maps consisting primarily of one straight line, there comes the day when the teacher proposes going around the school by going around the block. Talking together about this enormously exciting idea, the children come to realize the possibility of seeing the back of the building at some point in their expedition around the block. Careful looking at the back of the building and the selection of some identifying bit of it as a landmark is a necessary part of the preparation for the proposed expedition. Presently the expedition is made. Each child is picked up by an adult at the point where he can see for himself the identifying landmark on the back of the school building. Then the walk around the block is concluded by returning to the school from a direction different from the one in which they started out. The children experience the same thrill as did the early mariners in circumnavigating the world. They are pleased with the discovery and with themselves for having made it. For the children to absorb such an adventure completely depends on their being able to repeat it at least once or twice in the course of the ensuing month or two, and to rethink it as they sit together around the simple map (which consists of a block-building set on the rectangular outline of a city block).

The child who has had such preliminary geography experiences as a part of his planned nursery school program is ready, as a four-year-old, for a unique discovery of his own: the grand circle tour which takes him out of his school building in one direction and returns him to it from another direction. The day that four-year-old Billy found his way from the backyard play area to the school entrance, he went at once to his favorite adult, who was preparing the indoor space for the next group activity. Standing in the middle of the room, Billy used his whole arm in explaining his newly found circle tour. "We go this way (*making a sweeping gesture toward the play yard door*), *then this way* (*turning himself around with his arm*), then this way (*more turning and more gesturing*), and this way (*gesturing from the entrance to himself*)!

Billy was pleased and excited with his discovery, and the adult was pleased to interrupt her activity, give Billy her complete attention, and share his great triumph.

Four-year-old Marvin was equally excited the day he found that he could go out the door on one side of the room and come in the door on the other side of the room. "Do you know how I got through there?" he asked an attentive adult. Before the adult could say more than "How?" Marvin went on to explain where he had gone out of the room around to the other side.

BUILDING PLACE ASSOCIATIONS

A preschool child must build an understanding of *indoors* and *indoor activities* as contrasted with *outdoors* and *outdoor activities*. These distinctions are immediately useful to him. He builds a group of associations with the *outdoor* concept, and with the *indoor* concept, including the following:

OUTDOORS	INDOORS
Outdoor voices include noisy ones.	Indoor voices are quiet ones.
Outdoors, additional clothing is often required.	Outer wraps are not worn indoors.
Outdoor activities include using tricycles and wagons.	Indoor activities do not include using tricycles and wagons.
Sand and dirt stay outdoors.	Before coming indoors, sand and dirt are brushed off.

The teacher should patiently and consistently help each child to build such associations in his thinking. She should realize that such associations not only are important to the child in living easily and happily with adults but that they are also important as an initial experience in associating activities with a particular kind of place. These, and similar place associations to be learned subsequently, are useful to a person throughout his life.

Daily, the alert teacher guides the children in developing a sense of location and in thinking of themselves in relation to the place where they are. When she helps the children to remember that the tools stay at the workbench, and when she helps them to put away the toys they have taken out, she lays the foundation for their later understanding of "a place for everything and everything in its place." When she helps the children see that puzzles are put together by placing related parts next to each other, she also furthers their understanding of space relationships.

The morning that Bruce attempted to ride his bicycle indoors during story time, his teacher met him at the doorway and talked kindly but firmly with him:

TEACHER We drive it *outside.*
BRUCE My car drives me in. (*Again drives inside the room.*)
TEACHER I have to take the bike away unless it stays *outside.*
(*Bruce backs up and stays outside with the tricycle.*)

Later that day the teacher found opportunity for sitting down with a group of children which included Bruce and his special friends. Using her flannelboard pictures of children on tricycles, she brought out again the idea that tricycles and such playthings belong outdoors. The four-year-old children laughed with her at the absurdity of a tricycle knocking about in a room filled with people and furniture.

From the standpoint of the adult world, one of the most useful place associations to teach preschool children is that pencils or crayons are used only on paper, not on walls or tables. The teacher should make a point of providing paper whenever she gives a child a pencil or some crayons. If he casually marks on the wall, she can pleasantly remind him at once that "pencils are for paper." Furthermore she can be quite firm about the matter by saying, "If the pencil marks on anything but paper, we shall have to put it way," and by taking back the pencil if this happens.

The children who have parents and teachers that emphasize place associations are able as four-year-olds to make many place associations themselves. Here are examples of place associations made by Neal (four years and one month). He remembered a place he had seen during a walk with his father and described the place in terms of the association he had made with it: "That's where we saw the broken light bulbs. Daddy took us there."

He also remembered a nursery school trip to a park which had a slide in the form of an elephant. When a slide down the trunk of an elephant was mentioned one day at home, he said, " 'Rado Park has one. I went there with my nursery school group."

In the larger community surrounding their homes, Neal and his car-pool friends used a small factory as one of their landmarks. One day Neal discussed the factory with the adult driving the car:

NEAL   Here comes the kut-kut place. Do you hear it?
ADULT   Yes.
NEAL   Kut-kut-kut-kut. Do you hear me do kut-kut?
ADULT   Yes, I do.
NEAL   Kut-kut-kut-kut.
(*Another day, when his car-pool passed the park, Neal noticed the bandstand in it.*)
NEAL   There was a band here. Was.
ADULT   Yes. We all went last spring and heard the band play here in the park.

Another day at nursery school, when Neal was four years and four months old, he gave directions for an imaginary trip. "You go around Australia. Then you go to Camp Rayborn, and then you go up in the sky, and then you fly down, and then you are there." His directions were accompanied by appropriate gestures.

As a kindergarten child, Neal (five years and eight months) showed his thinking about space relationships when he dictated a note for his teacher at the time that she was in the hospital (located on the hill above his home on Stearnlee Avenue): "We eat our lunch on Stearnlee Avenue and you are up on the hill not very far away at all."

The message is interesting because it reflects Neal's awareness of his own street by its name and his awareness of the relationship between his home and the community hospital. As a five-year-old, Neal was beginning to estimate distances and to state qualitative relationships with some precision. His progress with simple geographic concepts is readily apparent when the sureness of his five-year-old dictation is contrasted with the uncertainty shown in his conversation with his teacher and his mother when he was three years and eleven months old:

NEAL   What was my name when I was in Indianapolis?
MOTHER   "Neal." Your name was "Neal" in Indianapolis.
NEAL (*to teacher*)   My name was Neal when I was in Indianapolis.

TEACHING BASIC SHAPES

By the time the child comes to a nursery group he probably has mastered, or soon will master, the postbox toy in which he inserts first the cylindrical packages, then the rectangular ones, and finally (when he is sufficiently mature) the triangular prisms. The teacher can build on this understanding of the circle, the square, and the triangle by providing next a series of such shapes cut out of felt or backed with sandpaper to use on the flannelboard,

Fill a cylinder today, a gas tank later. (Courtesy of The Merrill-Palmer Institute and Donna J. Harris, Detroit, Michigan.)

or cut out of smooth plastic to use on the plastic board. The shapes she provides may be kept in a series of clear plastic bags. Each bag contains one shape cut out of material of several different colors. The contents of the bags are as follows: circles, semicircles, squares, squares cut diagonally in half, diamonds, diamonds cut in half. When a child asks to use the flannel-

Use of two-dimensional space to express concepts and feelings. (Courtesy of Minneapolis Public Schools and Mrs. Mary Jane Higley, Minneapolis, Minnesota.)

board or the plastic board, the teacher should help him choose the shape he wants to use that day. As he makes his choice on the basis of shape, she reminds him of the name of the shape. "You'd like the triangles today," she may say if the child chooses the bag with squares cut in half. Or she may guide his choice in terms of what he had played with before: "Let's see. I think you played with the circles last time. Would you like them again, or would you like the half-circles? You can put half-circles together to make a circle—like this."

For the girls of four-and-one-half years and for the five-year-old children who are ready for conformity, the teacher can have simple patterns on which a child arranges diamond- and square-shaped blocks colored like those in the pattern. She also can have a set of cubes each of which has a white, a red, a blue, and a yellow side, a side divided diagonally between white and red, and a side divided diagonally between white and blue. The children may make their own designs with these blocks, exploring shape in relation to design. An occasional child may wish to follow a simple pattern by placing each block on top of its counterpart in the printed pattern.

As soon as he is familiar with the shape of a circle, the preschool child can develop the concept of the world as a round entity and thus lay a foundation for later study of geography. This he does very simply under the guidance of his teacher who shows him in twilight the rounded shadow of the world he lives on. He can see the rounded shadow and can intuitively sense its relationship to himself. In the school on another day, his teacher enlarges this concept of the round world by making shadows of smaller round objects—sharp shadows and others that verge on the misty quality of the diffused shadow of the earth at twilight.

GUIDING VISUAL OBSERVATIONS OF SPACE

Children have to learn what is and is not associated with some visible cue. For instance, almost-four-year-old Neal needed to learn whether pictures were associated with a telephone the way they were with a TV set. At that time he often ate lunch with Susie at her house and watched a TV program entitled *Sheriff John*. One day, when Neal was ill, his mother telephoned to say that Neal would not come. While his mother was talking on the telephone, Neal whispered to her, "Can you see Sheriff John?" He thought his mother could see over the telephone whether his favorite TV character was on at that time. Discussing this experience, together with planned telephone and television experiences at school and at home, helped Neal understand the space relationships associated with telecommunication devices.

It is important also for a teacher to help children understand how to interpret the space relationships they see in pictures. The interpretations that a child will make from seeing a picture cannot be taken for granted. For instance, one child was sure that his grandmother had lost the part of her arm not shown in the picture she sent to him. Recognizing the possibility of misinterpretation arising through insufficient experience, the teacher may arrange for photographs to be taken at school and help the children to learn from experience that only part of them may show in the pictures. The absence of legs in a picture may be caused by the fact that the person was sitting down. The teacher makes sure that the pictures taken in the course of the school year include a distant, intermediate, and closeup picture of the same scene; a distant and closeup picture of the teacher; and a picture of the teacher which shows only part of her. Pictures taken later in the year can include ones that show only part of some of the children. By seeing themselves in part in a picture, and at the same time feeling themselves in their entirety, four- and five-year-old children come to understand better how to interpret the pictures they see in their books and elsewhere.

CONTRASTING WORDS ABOUT SPACE

As a child develops greater understanding of space, his understanding is revealed in his choice of words regarding space relationships, such as:

| small, tall | front, back | up, down |
| big, little | long, short | in, out |

The teacher who is an attentive listener hears children attempt to use such contrasting words in their speech. At three-and-one-half years of age, Neal stood straight and tall and said, "See how high I am!" Then he sat down on his chair and said, "Now, lower." When he was four years old, he stood on a chair and said, "Now I'm higher than you guys."

When Neal (four years and two months) went on a school trip, he noticed the driver adjusting the seat of the car and commented on the seat adjustments made by members of his family: "Daddy has to have it backwards; Mommy has to have it frontwards." Another child, a five-year-old, noticed Neal's hesitation before choosing the word *frontwards* and said, "Closer up." Neal considered this modification in his statement and then said, "No. Frontwards."

The teacher made no attempt to discuss the matter further at that time. She did not want to detract in any way from Neal's feeling of accomplishment in selecting the right word. But she did make a mental note to plan play experiences at nursery school with Neal in the front as a "driver," and then in the back as a "passenger." She thought of the precise phrases to help Neal learn: *in front* and *in back, front seat* and *back seat,* as well as the directional words, *frontward* and *backward.*

The teacher of preschool children needs to be adept at making up simple games which bring out contrasting descriptions of space and of movement in space. For instance, she squats down with the children, saying, "Sometimes I'm very, very small." Then she stretches up on tiptoe, saying, "Sometimes I'm very, very tall." Then she stands for a moment thoughtfully wondering, "What shall I be now?" Whether she squats down being "small" or stretches up being "tall," she ends the game with gales of laughter, surprised by seeing some children who are "small" and some who are "tall."

The teacher of four- and five-year-old children should appreciate the fact that they are at an age when they enjoy noticing shapes and making verbal comparisons with regard to them. When Neal carefully adds another piece to the giraffe puzzle he is assembling, and remarks, "A baby giraffe has a *little* long neck," she may accept his remark and, giving her full attention to Neal and his puzzle, may enhance his remark by saying, "You think this may be a baby giraffe with a *little* long neck." The repetition of his well-turned phrase encourages Neal to make more of them.

CLASSIFYING

The beginnings of scientific classification are observable in the early and direct experiences of preschool children with actual concrete objects in space. Perhaps the initial classification experience is that of the one-year-old child who, with his color cone, assembles similar colors or graduated shapes along the central rod of the cone. The nursery teacher should provide gradually increasing numbers of similar objects for children to sort and classify, and should encourage them to do so. She should provide many occasions for children to collect objects and should give them an opportunity to play with them in making any arrangement they may desire. These collecting experiences include gathering nuts, seashells, pebbles, rocks, peas, beans, or some other item; or collecting different kinds of seed pods, leaves, flowers, or grasses. The arranging experiences may be with such collections or with precollected arrays, such as samples of wallpaper, suiting, drapery, or other materials. Each item must be free to be moved about, and the working surface must be large enough to provide for large, sweeping arm movements as well as for smaller ones as the children arrange or disarrange the items to their satisfaction.

SPACE RELATIONSHIPS THROUGH WATER PLAY

Children are interested in exploring the space relationships of liquids as well as those of solids. They are glad to spend long intervals of time dabbling in a basin of water and playing with such simple water toys as a cup, a funnel, a rubber bulb, or a squeeze bottle. They persist in using water and gaining control of it. The preschool teacher who recognizes this need for water play provides many opportunities for the children to enjoy it as a phenomenon in space. Here are a few of the activities that she may provide throughout the school year. She should plan each one to give the children an opportunity to handle the water themselves, if possible.

Pouring. In the nursery group—especially on warm, dry days—provide an unbreakable but transparent pitcher of water and two or three glasses of the same kind of material. Encourage the children to pour themselves a drink if they wish, or just to pour. Have other glasses available as needed to provide each person with a clean drinking glass or with an additional container for the water.

For four- and five-year-old children, provide transparent measuring cups and a pitcher with different volumes marked on it.

Floating. With a supervising adult available to help the children interpret what they observe, provide a shallow basin of water and a variety of objects to test for floating, for instance, half of an empty walnut shell, a small pebble, two or three leaves. For kindergarten children, provide a small piece of aluminum foil which can be rolled into a ball, or spread out in the form of a boat.

Water Running Downhill. Start a small stream at the top of a gently sloping concrete area. Watch the water run slowly downhill, making islands and peninsulas as it does so. If the day is warm, let the children go barefooted and enjoy the feel of the water at the same time they watch it go downhill.

The Force of Water. Use a small stream of water to make a plastic toy windmill turn. If the day is a warm one, provide a toy wheel for each child.

Developing Number Concepts

During the preschool years, the child learns to count. Landmarks in this gradual learning process have been pointed out by Gesell and Ilg, and by Piaget, as follows:

A 6-months-old is single-minded when he plays with a block. A 9-months-old child can hold and bring together two blocks and give attention to a third.[14]

. . . at about ten to twelve months, the child is capable of arranging three objects—e.g., three bricks—in order of size, just as he is capable of distinguishing that these three objects constitute "more" than two objects, and this is a beginning of cardination.[15]

At one year he manipulates several cubes one by one in a serial manner, which is the motor rudiment of counting.

At 2 years he distinguishes between "one" and "many."

At 3 years he has a fair command of "two" and is beginning to understand the simple word "both."

At 4 years he can count three objects, pointing correctly.

At 5 years he counts to ten, pointing correctly. He recites numbers in series before he uses them intelligently.[16]

These descriptions of mathematical behavior at different preschool ages show the slowness with which a child learns to count. How can this gradual progress be encouraged by the preschool teacher? Essentially, the answer to this question is that she can aid the child's mathematical development by providing him with interesting and realistic experiences at each successive level of his development. She is eager that he consolidate his learnings at each level and broaden their base of application. She attempts to guide

---

[14] Arnold Gesell and Frances L. Ilg, *Child Development,* op. cit., p. 25.

[15] Jean Piaget, *The Child's Conception of Number* (New York: The Humanities Press, Inc., 1952), p. 125.

[16] Gesell and Ilg, op. cit., p. 25.

Adult interpretation can make pouring an experience in mathematics. (Courtesy of The Merrill-Palmer Institute and Donna J. Harris, Detroit, Michigan.)

his development by means of a variety of qualitative and very simple quantitative experiences. At the same time, she listens for feedback which helps her know how far each child has developed mathematically and gives her a basis for planning further activities for the children. She appreciates a conversation such as that between three-and-a-half-year-old Chris and four-and-a-half-year-old Marie as they rested together for a few minutes at the playground:

MARIE   How old is your daddy, Chris?
CHRIS   I don't know.
MARIE   Is he ten years old?
CHRIS   (*carefully considering the question*)   I'm not sure, but I think so.

Later, the teacher used a measuring tape with Marie and several of the older children in the group. "Do you know how old your mother and your daddy are?" she asked the children. When she thought that each of them had the question well in mind, she unrolled the six-foot measuring tape to its full length. Then she asked the children, "How old are you?" On the measuring tape she showed them where the numbers four and five—that represented their ages—were. Then she showed them the number representing her age, and the numbers that represented the probable ages of their parents. She also showed them the numbers, away out at the end of the tape, representing the ages of their grandparents. She thought that the children would get some feeling for the relative lengths of the tape and would enjoy using it both then and later in elementary school, when they would learn to read the numbers on the tape. At least they could see that, as nursery children, they were just at the beginning of a long interval leading to parenthood and then to grandparenthood.

LEARNING THE SUCCESSION OF NUMBERS

Three-year-old Neal counts, "1, 2, 3, 4, 5, 6, 7, 8, 19 . . . ," and runs to be caught in his mother's arms. He associates the counting with preparation for running and jumping. To him, this counting is a series of verbalizations. A football yell made up of meaningless syllables would do as well for his purposes. Yet the use of counting series prepares him for using it later with real meaning.

The wise teacher always accepts the succession of numbers in the way that the child says it. Usually, the child thinks of the numbers as something he does by himself. He takes pride in this verbalization and does it to his own satisfaction. The teacher does not correct him, although she always uses numbers in their correct sequence herself. She knows that a child hears numbers said in correct sequence often enough to make his own corrections at whatever points he feels a need for them.

CONSOLIDATING THE CHILD'S ABILITY TO COUNT

"I shoot rubberbands today," said four-year-old Neal. He demonstrated his new skill, stretching a rubberband between his thumb and forefinger and letting it pop off. "I have three," he continued. "One in here (*pointing to his mouth*), one in here (*showing his right hand*), and one in here (*opening his left hand*). "Why, so you do," exclaimed his teacher. "One (*pointing to his mouth*), two (*pointing to his right hand*), and three (*pointing to his left hand*)."

By giving her complete attention to Neal, the teacher encouraged him in sharing other counting experiences with her. By reacting favorably to his counting (instead of unfavorably to his chewing a dirty rubberband), she helped him to think of counting as a pleasurable experience. The wise teacher knows the value of such brief but pleasant incidents in helping a child learn to count objects in an endless variety of situations.

The wise teacher also knows the value of finger plays using digits up to, at most, five for nursery children and ten for kindergarten children. One of her favorites is

Clap your hands: 1, 2, 3.
Clap your hands, just like me.
Roll your hands: 1, 2, 3.
Roll your hands, just like me.

TEACHING LESS AS WELL AS MORE

Juice time offers an opportunity to help children learn to observe spatial differences in amount. A four-year-old child can be guided in observing what happens to the level of juice in a transparent pitcher when glasses are filled from it. His teacher may say

Let's see what happens to the amount of juice in the pitcher when I fill your glasses. Where is the juice now in the pitcher? That's right, it's up at the top. Now watch what happens. I pour a glass for Jane (*pours it and hands it to Jane*). And a glass for Tommy (*pours a second glass*). And a glass for Mary (*pours a third glass*). Now let's stop to see what happened to the amount of juice in the pitcher. Is there more juice? Or less? Or just the same?

After the children have observed that there is less juice in the pitcher, the teacher says, "Let's try it again." This time she marks the level of the juice with her finger, holding it there while she pours several more glasses. Again the children guess the amount left and then observe the new level of the liquid. The next time, probably, one of the older children will mark the level of the liquid with a wax pencil. Of course, the last time it is easy for all the children to see that the juice has gone out of the transparent pitcher and to realize that the filling of the glasses has emptied the pitcher of its juice.

Piaget, the French psychologist who studied the development of mathematical concepts in children by presenting them with practical problems (such as that of pouring liquids), reports their use of a single dimension as a criterion for comparison.[17] When a pitcher was emptied into several containers, the children thought there was more in the several small glasses than there had been in the one pitcher. They also thought that there was less liquid when it was poured from a tall thin glass into a squat glass of larger diameter.

Piaget also reports showing a child "two rows of sweets, one containing three that were spread out, and the other four that were close together, the first row thus being longer."

"Where are there more?" the adult asks Boq who is 4 years and 7 months old.
"There," replies Boq, pointing to the row of 3.
"Why?" inquires the adult.
"It's a bigger line."[18]

[17] Piaget, op. cit.
[18] Ibid., p. 75.

The use of a single dimension at a time can also be observed when children make other comparisons. For instance, Billy—a four-year-old boy with a new baby brother—was interested in the size of the baby and was delighted to tell his teacher about it.

TEACHER   Hi, Billy. How big is that new baby of yours?
BILLY (*carefully points to the copper rivet at the top of his pants pocket.*) Up to here.

Billy pointed out a single comparison; namely, the relative height of the baby himself. He measured the baby against himself. An adult might have noted the width or the weight of the baby, as well as its length. Four-year-old Billy noted only the length of the baby and expressed his observation in terms of his own length. He would be many months older before he would want to measure length in the abstract units of a measuring tape and have the ability to count as high as his own height of thirty or forty inches.

Realizing the limits of development in the three- and four-year-old children, the teacher should not expect them to solve problems that are beyond their level of ability. Instead, she should provide them with a variety of realistic problems for their level. She should give them every opportunity to make qualitative comparisons among two or three objects. For instance, she may say:

We need the big ball this morning. Can you bring us the big red ball, Tom, please? It's the biggest ball in the box of balls.
I'm too wide to crawl through that narrow tunnel. Are you just the right size for it?

You know, Ted, when you first came to nursery school, you were so small that I helped you to get a drink at the drinking fountain. Now you have grown so tall that you get a drink by yourself.
John marches with big strides; Sally marches with little steps. Let's all try John's big strides this time, and then Sally's little ones next time.

The wise teacher often guides the children in perceiving similarities and differences by making such comparisons herself. For instance, when his teacher noticed that four-year-old Robby said, "Get some few for me," and "I want some more few grapes," she held up a sprig of two or three grapes in one hand and a bunch of grapes in the other hand and asked him, "Robby, do you want a few grapes or do you want many grapes?"

Whenever she can, the teacher should use with precision the digits up to and including the age of the children, and sometimes she may use the fraction *one-half*. If she used other numbers, she might discourage some children and lead them into unfavorable attitudes toward mathematics. She also should be careful to use numbers only when they have meaning to the children. She may say, for instance

Do you know why our glasses are only half full? . . . We pick them up and
set them down easily.

There are more shovels if we need them. . . . Mary and Donna need shovels.
We'll get two more, then; one for each of you.

Johnny, Billy, and I did not get a cooky. Will you ask Mrs. Greer for—one,
two, three—three more cookies, please, Susan?

SHOWING WHERE NUMBERS ARE USED

The teacher should make a point of showing the children wherever numbers are used. She has a real wall clock as well as play clocks and wrist-

*Five-year-olds see that numbers are bigger when it is hotter. (Courtesy of
DARCEE, George Peabody College of Education, Nashville, Tennessee.)*

watches in the school, and a calendar placed at the eye level of the children. She has play telephones with digits on their realistic dials. In the
course of each school year she can guide the four- and five-year-old children in providing a new house number for their playhouse. Throughout the
year, she may use numbered boxes which have special activity equipment

in them. Thus she provides for the children a world in which numbers are useful and can be seen and talked about.

Whenever the four-year-old or five-year-old children are on a neighborhood walk, the teacher should call their attention to the use of numbers. For instance, on a walk through a residential area, she points out that each house is numbered. "Does your house at home have a number? You look and see when you go home today." She mentions that house numbers help her in finding each of their houses when she goes to visit them. A few minutes later, when they see a postman delivering mail, she explains that he uses the house numbers in getting the right letter to each house.

On another day, on a walk through a residential area, the teacher can start the older children in learning to read numbers. She points out the number that is a straight line, and tells them that it is the number 1. "That's the way we write the number 1," she says. She may also point out the number 0, which is written as a circle. She shows the children how to make these numbers with their fingers, a forefinger extended to make a 1, and a forefinger meeting a thumb to make a 0. At a convenient spot, she takes a stick and draws a 0 and also a 1 in the sand or dirt, and encourages the children to make numbers too. In this way, she can prepare the children for reading numbers—an activity they will be ready for in the primary grades.

At home, preschool children often learn the numbers associated with their favorite TV programs. Neal, for instance, at three years and ten months of age, recognized the numbers associated with the TV channels presenting cartoon programs. "My brother showed me," he said when he was complimented on being able to turn the knob to Channel 5.

In one preschool, a science-minded father prepared a simple electrical device with three electric light bulbs, each of a different color, and each in a socket with a number next to it. He wired the device so that a child could use a separate switch to light each bulb. In this way the child could illuminate the number 1, the number 2, or the number 3 bulb; and a younger child could turn on or off either the red, the blue, or the yellow bulb. In all probability, playing with this electrical device helped the children to build number concepts as well as color concepts and facilitated their learning to count.

THE CONCEPT OF SUBTRACTION

The preschool teacher also should help the children to develop the concept of subtraction. To do this, she uses the well-known game, "1, 2, 3—let us see what is missing," and plays it with the children in simplified form. With the three-year-old children, she uses three closely related objects—for instance, a red, a blue, and a yellow glass. After showing each of the objects and carefully discussing it with the children, she arranges the objects on an open surface. Then each child in the group cups one hand over each eye. While their eyes are hidden, the teacher removes one of the cups and then says, "1, 2, 3—let us see what is missing." With a small group of older children, she can increase the diversity or the number of the objects—for instance, she may try out one additional object and watch to see whether all in the group, not just the more mature children, are responding easily to the game.

Guiding Addition

"I'll take three," says Neal, picking up a favorite book to add to those he is taking to nursery school. Neal, who is three years old, counts to 3 easily. So far, then, he is in a familiar situation with three books. But when he gets to nursery school he may find that he is one of several children who

Find a domino that matches. (Courtesy of Manhasset Public Schools, Manhasset, New York. Photography: W. E. C. Haussler.)

have brought one or more books. The wise parent who helps Neal get off to nursery school and the wise teacher who greets him there both have an opportunity to help Neal experience the process of addition. If the three books he brought are added to those that the others brought, there will be lots of books with lots of stories to read—more stories than there is time to read. Thinking of this with their teacher, the children sense the cumulative nature of addition. As three-year-old children they are able to grasp an abstract concept through actual experience.

Four-year-old children can go beyond the first qualitative abstractions to quantitative precision with the first few digits. When a four-year-old child gets into the car with another child who has brought a book, he can add to know that one book and one book makes two books to be read at nursery school. This simple and actual experience with addition of the first digits is one of many such experiences which, all together, will give him background for arithmetic in school. Realizing the importance of these simple experiences, the teacher should capitalize on the quantitative aspect of everyday situations. She may say, for instance

How many stories shall we read today? Timmy brought a story, and so did I. (*Holds up a book in each hand.*) How many stories?
Jane has her sweater on. Martha has hers on, too. So does Tom. One, two, three. Three children have their sweaters on already.

Guiding Mathematically Gifted Children

It has been suggested that preschool children have collections of pebbles, nuts, shells, or other objects which can be arranged and rearranged endlessly. Essentially, a collection of objects is a mathematical problem. How a child handles it may be rather startling. The day that his teacher gave Neal (four years and three months old) six empty strawberry baskets to play with, he surprised her by doing multiplication he had probably learned from his older brother or his older friends. Moving the strawberry baskets about, he said to his teacher, "This is 2 times 3. I show you. 1, 2, 3, 4, 5, 6—2 times 3."

Such behavior as Neal exhibited is a learning experience which Piaget has described as "logico-mathematical experience," as follows:

. . . there is also logico-mathematical experience. In this case, while the actions are once again carried out on objects, knowledge is derived from the actions which transform the objects, and not from the objects themselves. For example, a child may be surprised to learn that when he counts three groups of two objects he gets the same total as when he counts the groups of three objects. When he learns that the sum is independent of the order of counting he is discovering the properties of the actions of ordering and uniting. He is learning something from these actions themselves, rather than from the objects independent of these actions [p. vi].[19]

Logico-mathematical experience is important to provide for children. When it occurs spontaneously, its occurrence should be noted and recorded in the records transmitted from preschool groups to schools. Aptitude for mathematics can be useful to the world of tomorrow if it is given opportunity for development.

[19] Millie Almy with Edward Chittenden and Paula Miller, *Young Children's Thinking.* New York: Teachers College Press, Teachers College, Columbia University, 1966.

Situations for Discussion

A preschool teacher is apt to find herself in situations similar to the four described here. As you think of what to do in each situation, consider whether each course of action suggested is desirable, or not. Use points brought out in the chapter as well as ideas from your own experience to justify your views. Suggest alternative courses of action to supplement those given.

SITUATION 1   Several of the four-year-old children in your group like to have sugar cookies. One morning, Mrs. Pratt brings a batch of sugar cookies for her son's birthday party. At various times during the morning a child notices the plate of cookies and asks to have one. As their teacher, you should tell each child

● He will have his cookie when it it time.
● The cookies belong to David and Mrs. Pratt.
● The cookies are for refreshment time.
● He has to wait until David has his party.
● To forget about the cookies and go and play.

SITUATION 2   When you give five-year-old Bill a large set of red plastic bricks to play with, he uses them for three or four minutes and then runs to you to come and see what he has built. It is a little house. As the teacher, you should

● Admire the little house.
● Suggest building a big house.
● Give the blocks to another child to play with.
● Talk with Bill about the floor, walls, and roof of the house.
● Ask Bill why he built such a little house.

SITUATION 3   You are the teacher for a three-year-old children's group. At a mother's meeting, the question is raised about teaching the children their home telephone numbers. As the teacher, you should

● Point out that a series of numbers is only nonsense syllables to a three-year-old child.
● Encourage each mother to make up a little tune out of the family telephone number.
● Plan telephone experiences as part of the activities during the next few weeks.
● Point out that teaching a number does not mean that a child learns it.
● Avoid being either "for" or "against" such teaching.

SITUATION 4   You have responsibility for a kindergarten group which includes a quiet, sweet little girl named Mary. One evening Mary's mother telephones you to say, "God has taken Mary's grandmother. Mary will not be at school tomorrow because we are taking her to the funeral." As Mary's teacher, you should

● Ask if you may take care of Mary the next day, and have her at kindergarten.

- Watch to see if Mary is afraid of "God taking me."
- Use a measuring tape to show the children how long they have lived and how long Mary's grandmother lived.
- A week later show Mary and her friends, with a measuring tape, how long they have lived and how long Mary's grandmother lived.
- Mention Mary's grandmother only if Mary talks about her.

Current Books for Preschool Children

Space

BERKLEY, ETHEL S. *Big and Little, Up and Down.* New York: William R. Scott, Inc., 1960. [Beginning concepts of size and direction.]

GOUDEY, ALICE. *The Day We Saw the Sun Come Up.* New York: Charles Scribner's Sons, 1961. [Sue and her brother explore sun and shadow, day and night.]

HENGESBAUGH, JANE. *I Live in So Many Places.* Chicago: Children's Press, 1956. [I live in a house in a town, in a state, in a country, in the world.]

KOHN, BERNICE. *Everything Has a Size.* Englewood Cliffs, N.J.: Prentice-Hall, Inc., 1964. [A small birthday cake with big candles, for instance, or a big cake with small candles.]

SCHLEIN, MIRIAM. *Heavy Is a Hippopotamus.* New York: William R. Scott, Inc., 1954. [Beginning concepts of weight.]

————, *Herman McGregor's World.* Chicago: Albert Whitman and Company, 1958. [Herman's crib-world widened when he took a trip.]

THAYER, JANE. *The Pussy Who Went to the Moon.* New York: William Morrow & Co., Inc., 1960. [The little old man and woman went after their kitty on increasingly long trips.]

WILDSMITH, BRIAN. *The Hare and the Tortoise.* New York: Franklin Watts, Inc., 1967. [The familiar fable.]

ZAFFO, GEORGE J. *The Giant Book of Things in Space.* Garden City, N.Y.: Doubleday and Company, Inc., 1969. [Pictures for expanding ideas of space with more mature children.]

ZION, GENE. *Harry by the Sea.* New York: Harper & Row, Publishers, 1965. [Harry, a white dog with black spots, now has a family beach umbrella of similar description to help him find his way back to his family.]

Numbers

BAUM, ARLINE and JOSEPH. *One Bright Monday Morning.* New York: Random House, 1962. ["One bright Monday morning I saw 1 blade of green grass growing."]

BUDNEY, BLOSSOM. *A Cat Can't Count.* New York: Lothrop, Lee & Shepard Co., Inc., 1962. ["A cat cannot count, but I can."]

KIRN, ANN. *Two Pesos for Catalina.* Chicago: Rand McNally & Co., 1962 (Hale, 1966). [When Catalina has two pesos to spend she buys shoes.]

LANGSTAFF, JOHN. *Over in the Meadow.* New York: Harcourt, Brace & World, Inc., 1956. [This Caldecott Award book is a beautiful counting book.]

McLEOD, EMILIE W. *The Seven Remarkable Polar Bears.* Boston: Houghton

Mifflin Company, 1954. [A hungry polar bear increases his rations with the help of six, but only six, imaginary bears.]

REED, MARY, and EDITH OSSWALD. *Numbers.* New York: Golden Press, 1955. [Look around and find numbers.]

SEIGNOBOSC, FRANCOISE. *Springtime for Jeanne-Marie.* New York: Charles Scribner's Sons, 1951. [Jeanne-Marie and Patapon lose Madelon, the white duck, but find another friend for a fourth. *Jeanne-Marie Counts Her Sheep* (1951) is by the same author.]

SLOBODKIN, E. *The Wonderful Feast.* New York: Lothrop, Lee & Shepard Co., Inc., 1955. [The amount of food for an animal is related to its size.]

SLOBODKIN, LOUIS. *Millions, Millions, Millions.* New York: Vanguard Press, 1955. [The uniqueness of me—and you—is contrasted with millions of other things.]

STANEK, MURIEL. *One, Two, Three for Fun.* Chicago: Albert Whitman & Company, 1967. [Counting from 1 to 5 in familiar settings.]

Time

BUCKLEY, HELEN E. *The Little Boy and the Birthdays.* New York: Lothrop, Lee & Shepard Co., Inc., 1965. [Put circles around calendar days that are birthdays.]

GREEN, MARY MCBURNEY. *Is It Hard? Is It Easy?* New York: William R. Scott, Inc., 1960. [What is hard for one person may be easy for another to do quickly.]

HAWKINSON, JOHN and LUCY. *Days I Like.* Chicago: Albert Whitman and Company, 1965. [Each month of the year has unique activities.]

LENSKI, LOIS. *On a Summer Day.* New York: Henry Z. Walck, Inc., 1953. [*Now It's Fall* (1948), *I Like Winter* (1950), *Spring Is Here* (1945), and this book help children build concepts about the sequence of the seasons each year.]

POLITI, LEO. *The Butterflies Come.* New York: Charles Scribner's Sons, 1957. [A festival is held each year when the monarch butterflies come.]

SCHATZ, LETTA. *When Will My Birthday Be?* New York: McGraw-Hill Book Company, Inc., 1962. [Benjy waits for his birthday through the succession of seasons.]

SCHLEIN, MIRIAM. *Fast Is Not a Ladybug.* New York: William R. Scott, Inc., 1953. [Develops the concepts of "fast" and "slow."]

SEIGNOBOSC, FRANCOISE. *What Time Is It, Jeann-Marie?* New York: Charles Scribner's Sons, 1963. [Simple concepts of time.]

SLOBODKIN, LOUIS. *Dinny and Danny.* New York: The Macmillan Company, 1951. [In the long ago. Danny and his friend the dinosaur helped each other.]

WATSON, NANCY DINGMAN. *When Is Tomorrow?* New York: Alfred A. Knopf, Inc., 1955. [Linda and Peter enjoy the fun of today as they plan for tomorrow.]

ZOLOTOW, CHARLOTTE. *Over and Over.* New York: Harper & Row, Publishers, 1957. [Each year has the same succession of holidays.]

CHAPTER 11

Developing Verbal Communication

One of the major developmental problems of the preschool child is to establish effective verbal communication with the people around him. He must learn the language of his home and its style of life. If the style of life he is in differs from the middle-class style of life of school and business, he must get started learning that language too. This he is well able to do because he is skillful in imitation and uninhibited in practice. At no other period of his life will he be as ready to learn a language through hearing it and practicing until he imitates it as it is spoken by those around him. His doing so, as Susanne K. Langer points out, is an important step in developing explicit thought through guided learning.

Language is, without a doubt, the most momentous and at the same time the most mysterious product of the human mind. Between the clearest animal call of love or warning or anger, and a man's least, trivial *word,* there is a whole day of Creation—or in modern phrase, a whole chapter of evolution. In language we have the free, accomplished use of symbolism, the record of articulate conceptual thinking; without language there seems to be nothing like explicit thought whatever.

. . . Language, though normally learned in infancy without any compulsion of formal training, is nonetheless a product of sheer learning, an art handed down from generation to generation, and where there is no teacher there is no accomplishment.[1]

Language is one of the most effective media for both personal development and adjustment to one's social environment. Through language a

---

[1] Susanne K. Langer, *Philosophy in a New Key* (Cambridge, Mass.: Harvard University Press, 1963), pp. 103, 108.

child comes into a kind of social relationship with his fellows that is impossible without the use of language and is unknown in animals below the level of man. Language is the unmistakable manifestation of intelligence.

Before children ever enter school their speech habits are well established. Most children begin to speak at about fifteen to eighteen months, although some speak a few isolated words earlier and some are apparently delayed in their acquisition of speech. The period which intervenes between the child's first single words and age five are exceedingly important in language development. By the age of five the child has acquired practically all the basic speech forms used among adults. He asks questions, makes long statements, uses phrases and clauses, and employs adjectives, adverbs, pronouns, conjunctions, and interjections as well as nouns and verbs. His grammatical construction is about as good as that of the adults with whom he has been associated and from whom he has learned his language patterns.

Articulation too is well perfected during this preschool period. The average child has discontinued "baby talk" by age five. But his progress in language is very largely determined by the kind and quality of language he hears. Language development constitutes a great argument in favor of nursery school and kindergarten education. Less fortunate children should have opportunity during these important years of linguistic development for contact with excellent speech. Language development is also a great argument for parent education because it is the parents under existing and approaching educational and social organization who largely determine the language patterns of children.

Children imitate the speech about them whether it is good or poor. It is of the utmost importance that they have good models to imitate. If adults desire children to have good articulation, they should not talk "baby talk" in speaking to a child. Not only is language a matter of imitation but it is also a matter of practice, and children must be permitted a full share in the conversation of people whether at home or at school.

The nursery school teacher can help the children in several different ways. For one thing, she can provide them with a clearly spoken pattern which is easy to hear and imitate accurately. She should speak distinctly, calmly, and with only a few well-chosen words at a time. Above all, she should speak pleasantly, so that the child responding to her feels appreciated, capable, and in no way criticized unfavorably. Children learn tonal patterns and then develop words within them, so the teacher should make a point of providing pleasant and happy tonal patterns for them to imitate.

The teacher should also know the value of an atmosphere which favors practice in verbal expression. She may suggest the use of indoor voices so that everyone can better hear what is said, but she should never suggest not talking except when it interferes with listening to what is being said. Then she may say, "This is listening time now. Talking time comes later, after our story." Often she can encourage a shy child by using words or phrases that he has used. For instance, when his teacher handed Neal (three years and ten months old) a white balloon, he asked, "Is this soft?" She responded by asking, "Is it soft? Let's feel it and see if it is soft." This repetition of important words that a child has used is a compliment to his choice of words and encourages him in further communication.

The teacher should stimulate a child to communicate by helping him have vivid experiences, the kind which bubble over into words, as well as into other forms of expression. She can plan each experience in terms of key words which will add to a child's vocabulary and serve as a basis for learning other words. For instance, on a nature walk in the spring, one

Sometimes you paint it and then tell it. (Courtesy of Head Start Program, Minneapolis Public Schools, Minneapolis, Minnesota.)

teacher introduced the children to the jacaranda tree which at that time was laden with beautiful blue blossoms. "Children," she said, "aren't the jacaranda trees pretty! The jacaranda has such pretty blue blossoms." Turning to Neal, she asked, "Can you say *jacaranda?* That's a big word." Neal obliged by saying, "Jacaranda." Then he added softly to himself, "Jackrabbit." Quickly the teacher helped Neal to clarify his association. "Yes, a jackrabbit is an animal, and a jacaranda is a tree." By providing a beautiful sight and relating it to what the children already knew, the teacher was helping them to add to their vocabulary and to their ability to use language.

Above all, the teacher should provide each child with a loving and attentive listener. Whenever a child wishes to communicate with her as an individual (when she is not working with a group of other children), he should know he can have her complete attention. Furthermore, she should make sure that within each school day she has some direct communication with each child.

DEVELOPING A SECOND LANGUAGE

The great facility of the preschool child in learning to communicate verbally makes him an apt pupil in learning a second language at the same time that he is learning his first. Children who have two years of English speaking in nursery school followed by a third year in kindergarten may be ready to learn to read English in the first grade, even though they may have been speaking only another language at home.

The excellence of the language spoken by a child depends not on the number of languages that he is learning but on the quality of the pattern that he has in each. If he hears clear and correct English, he will speak clear and correct English. If he hears broken English, he will speak incorrectly. The fact that he may also be learning a language other than English will not affect the quality of English he acquires in the primary grades of elementary school.

It is important, however, that adults help a preschool child who is learning two languages to distinguish one from another. For instance, if an American child is sent to a Spanish-speaking nursery school, his mother should talk with him in English so that he associates the speaking of English with her. His teacher should always speak to him in Spanish and expect him to communicate with her in Spanish so that he learns to associate the speaking of Spanish with her. He then differentiates between using English and using Spanish as easily as he distinguishes his mother from his teacher.

A child can also build place associations which help him to know when to use one language or another. For instance, he may learn that only English is used at home, and that another language is used exclusively at school. When his mother comes to school, she, too, may speak the language of the school although she speaks another language at home. The consistent association of one language with a particular place or situation helps a child to separate one language from another.

Comparable to the learning problem of a child becoming bilingual is the problem of the less advantaged child who needs to learn the English used in school at the same time that he enlarges his command of the English spoken at home and used by other children on his street. If both home and preschool recognize the importance of his simultaneous command of different communication media, he will be encouraged to focus on learning each of them and on using each as seems appropriate. His school helps him develop academic English, but does not ask him to eradicate other forms of the language. His teacher notes intrusions of street or home versions of

English. "Is that the way you say it at home?" his teacher may ask, and then add a gentle reminder of what is appropriate to say at school.

CHILDREN FROM NON-ENGLISH-SPEAKING FAMILIES

The problem of the non-English-speaking beginner in school is that he will be handicapped in comparison to his English-speaking age mates. It is desirable in his preschool years to orient him to the approaching school situation, to help him interpret his out-of-school experiences, to help him acquire desirable social qualities, and to teach him a new language. The preschool teacher must remember that she is teaching the non-English-speaking child what is to him a "foreign language." Her own speech must be clear, but without exaggeration. She must provide much repetition in an innumerable variety of situations. Simple nursery rhymes and rote songs increase the child's facility and competence in English speech.

The non-English-speaking child should be helped to understand that his "mother tongue" is another language spoken by many people in the world, but that he really needs to speak *two* languages—one to use in speaking to his family and friends at home and another to use in school, where unfortunately his teachers and most of his other friends speak only one language. He should be praised for his accomplishment as he acquires the use of English and should be encouraged also to say rhymes or sing songs he has learned in his native language.

The non-English-speaking child, however, may have the disadvantages caused by poverty, disease, ignorance, and apathy. His lack may not only be a lack of English but a lack of any language. If his speech has not developed between two and four years of age, the years in which speech usually matures rapidly, he may have difficulty in mastering this skill at a later time.

The work of David Ausubel[2] with environmentally disadvantaged children has indicated that retardation in intellectual functioning manifests itself primarily in language. Because language is a learned behavior, its development depends on opportunity to hear and use language and to enjoy experiences that motivate a person to talk and give him something to talk about. The nonverbal environment of the disadvantaged child results in language-deficient children. The children have little or no contact with others who might serve as language models. Theirs is often a physical rather than a verbal world. Children from impoverished language backgrounds are high failure risks in the first grade of school.

The preschool teacher is challenged to find the most effective ways to stimulate the child's language development. He needs a wide variety of firsthand experiences, each with verbal symbols attached. He needs concrete situations in which he can see for himself, be involved, and hear words

---

[2] David P. Ausubel, "The Effect of Cultural Deprivation on Learning Patterns." *Audiovisual Instruction* (January, 1965), pp. 10–12.

that point up his experience. He needs opportunity to communicate ideas and feelings. Oral language must permeate his entire program. He must come to know that "being good" is not the equivalent of "being quiet." Language is a skill and must be used in relation to content. It actually has no content per se. Every area of the child's preschool program must be·mined for its language component.

Understanding Language Development

The teacher of preschool children should attempt to understand the ways in which they communicate with other people. She will be more effective in helping them to communicate if she is aware of the nature of the process

A puzzle may occasion dialog. (Courtesy of Long Beach Parent Nursery Schools and Mariam M. Cook, Long Beach, California.)

at different age levels and in different children. Understanding the nature of their language development should make her better able to help with it, and especially to help with the thought processes it reveals.

To understand the communications of children, the teacher can do two things: she can read the reports of those who have studied the process, and she can validate their observations by making her own observations of the children in her group. In these ways one teacher of a group of three-year-old children developed the following learning device:

Language Behavior of Three-Year-Old Children

REPORTED BEHAVIOR[3]	OBSERVED BEHAVIOR
He likes to compare two objects.	MARI (*to her mother on the day that Jane's mother furnished refreshments that Mari liked*) She's a better cooker than you are.
Likes to make acquaintance with new words . . . [of] phonetic novelty.	NED (*showing off a new shirt*) I'm sweating. It's a sweat shirt.
Uses words with more confidence and with intelligent inflection.	(*Neal and I recall play on the pink concrete animal at the park*) I How is our friend the pink dinosaur? NEAL Different kind of dinosaur. I Is it a different kind of dinosaur? NEAL Anteater.
May not overcome infantile articulations until the age of four or five.	KIMMY I lob [love] you becuz you smiwo [smile] all da time.
Soliloquizes and dramatizes, combining actions and words.	MARILYN (*filling soft plastic milk bottle with water*) I'm going to get water in my bottle. (*Fills bottle and goes to sandbox. Starts filling the bottle with sand*) I filling the water. (*Puts in several shovelfuls of sand*) I finished.
Creates dramatic situations to test out and to apply his words.	As reported at mothers' meeting: Don will talk quite noisily in a small group and brag a bit as is the custom, especially about the fine toys he has at home.
Extends the range and depth of his command of language.	BRUCE (*talking about a proposed trip to the alligator farm*) Except first we're not going for a long days.

After looking for speech situations similar to those described in books, the teacher extended her observations regarding the ways in which children imitate the language used by those around them. She noted that a three-year-old child sometimes murmurs to himself the last phrase spoken by another child leaving a parallel-play situation. Because she also noticed that a child would sometimes repeat a parting remark of her own, she decided to use a key word if possible in her departing remarks to children.

The teacher also observed that the more creative children in her group enjoyed making up words of their own—especially words that were interesting phonetically. Three-year-old Marilyn, playing doctor with her dolly,

[3] Arnold Gesell and Frances L. Ilg, *Child Development* (New York: Harper & Row, Publishers, 1949), p. 203. Verbal behavior of four-year-old children is discussed on pp. 25–26 and 225–228.

said, "Here, take your medicine, Kickee-boy," and four-year-old Susan created the greeting: "Hi, Poopoo Face."

As she observed and recorded language used by the children in her group, the teacher became curious about what others had observed concerning children's language. She read Piaget's report *The Language and*

In communication. (Courtesy of Riverside City Schools, Riverside, California. Photograph by Jim Henderson.)

Thought of the Child,[1] and became more aware of age-level differences such as those she observed between five-year-old Stanley and three-year-old Neal when they were playing with a puppet:

STANLEY (*taking the rubber head off the puppet and pressing it against his cheek*)   Look. This sticks to my cheek.
ADULT   Yes. It's made of rubber and sticks like a suction cup.
NEAL (*squeezing the puppet head against his cheek*)   Look! Sticks! Like it!

[1] Jean Piaget, *The Language and Thought of the Child* (New York: Humanities Press, Inc., 1959).

By the end of the school year, the teacher was able to prepare a report about each child on the basis of the observtions she had made during the year; for instance:

Bobby loves to joke with Dan. He tries to make jokes himself and laughs heartily at Dan's witticisms. Bobby is uninhibited in expressing himself with his schoolmates. He'll cry loudly when enraged and laugh just as loudly (almost) when happy with his friends. He has no shyness and never has had since he arrived so far as I have been able to observe. He is happy a good deal and a great giggler. Life is mostly a lot of laughs to him.

Bobby talks to me sometimes as if his mother had wound him up before school. He is often eager to catch us all up on his private life and talks in his slow, distinct way about current events at home, interrupting anyone when he has something to say. He was almost three when he entered in the fall and, like some others of our younger children, his timing in sharing circle falls a little short of society's prescribed standards. But we all love him dearly and his spontaneity is mighty wholesome. The social graces will come in good time.

Preschool Communication Is Primarily Nonverbal

A brief observation of three-year-old children playing at nursery school is sufficient to demonstrate how much communication is nonverbal. For instance, three-year-old Butchie runs out of the playhouse clutching a pan close to himself. At his heels comes three-year-old Russell, intent on re-trieving the pan. When he sees a book lying in a wagon, he snatches it up and continues the chase. As soon as he gets within range of Butchie, Russell throws the book at him. Butchie stops short and starts crying. The nearest adult puts an arm around each boy and, while using "body language," brings the communication up to the verbal level.

Even at four and five years of age, a child's behavior may be mostly overt, with a minimum of verbal communication. Neal, at four and a half years, carried on a delightful play of changing hats, wearing one and making a tour of the school, then changing to another hat for his next tour. In eight changes of hat, he found it necessary to communicate with the teacher only twice, although she admired his hat each time and made some comment about it. One of his statements was an explanation: "I take off hats." The other statement came at the end of his hat-changing, when his teacher was trying to find out what hat he might be wearing—perhaps an invisible one?

TEACHER Where's your hat?
NEAL No.
TEACHER What hat are you wearing this time?
NEAL I dropped it off.
TEACHER I see. You are wearing *no hat* this time.

Conversation with Activity

Conversation is an integral part of a child's activity. For instance, some children were playing on the swings. One three-and-a-half-year-old leaned against the chains that held the swing and wiggled his extended arms saying, "Look what I can do." "I need a push," said one four-year-old child. "I need a push up to the sky," said another four-year-old. They were echoed by a three-year-old child saying also, "I need a push." Both the three- and the four-year-old children took up the chant, "I need a push." The chant died down presently as the teacher went from swing to swing, helping each child to swing up higher.

The four-and-a-half-year-old children, while swinging, were able at the same time to exchange information unrelated to their swinging. Billy noticed the gun that had slipped out of Jerry's holster and said slowly, "Somebody dropped a gun." Jerry continued swinging while he absorbed Billy's remark and, after an interval, responded to it by saying just as slowly, "It's my gun." The deliberate pace of the boys' conversation was in contrast to the speed of adult conversation during activity, and was in keeping with their age level.

The three-year-old children revealed their age level by limiting their conversation to comments related to their actions and to imitative comments. For the most part they enjoyed the swinging and did not participate in the verbal exchange. When the four-year-old children started to leave the swings, the three-year-olds followed suit, repeating what the older ones had said, "I want to get off." Four-year-old Billy was one of the last to leave. As the teacher helped him out of the swing so he would miss the puddle underneath it, he confided, "I heard the rain last night," and was pleased with his teacher's appreciative response. Three-year-old June followed the lead of the four-year-old. As the teacher helped her out of the swing, she said, "I heard the rain tonight."

Repetition of a word or phrase within a sentence occurs so frequently among preschool children that teachers are not often aware of it unless they are particularly observant. Neal's teacher was observing his group one day when Neal was almost four years old. She noticed that he got quite excited about his accomplishment in blowing up a balloon the way five-year-old Susan did. Then she realized that the evidence of Neal's excitement was his slipping back into the repetition which characterizes early communication and communication with new or difficult words. The words Neal used were not difficult words for him at his age, but the emotional involvement in his success made him use them as if they were:

NEAL (*excited about blowing up his balloon*) I did this, I did this, I did this a little while. I did this, I did this. Susan, I did this, I did this à little while.
SUSAN I know.

CONFUSION WITH PRONOUNS

By repeating phrases they hear, children do surprisingly well with many words. Pronouns, however, are one of the more difficult parts of the language. The pronoun *I* is usually learned first because children are highly egocentric. But correct usage of the different cases of the pronouns is not to be expected from a nursery school group. Four-year-old Rob, for instance, commented on his difficulty in hammering a nail in straight by saying, "I bent she again."

When Marilyn was three-and-one-half years old, she used the pronoun *I*—but without differentiating it from the other pronouns. Her egocentrism resulted in confusion about her birthday. Marilyn's mother told Marilyn: "Today is my birthday." Marilyn was completely delighted and repeated just what her mother had said: "Today is my birthday." When Marilyn visited a restaurant with her mother later in the day, she continued telling everyone: "Today is my birthday." The waitress responded to Marilyn's statement by bringing, with dessert, a birthday cake with a candle on it. Not until they talked together the next day was her mother able to straighten out the confusion in Marilyn's mind to the point where Marilyn belatedly wished her mother a happy birthday. Marilyn will be much older before she understands and uses pronouns with clarity and precision.

Helping a Child Communicate

The nursery school supplements the home by providing the child with loving, sympathetic adults who are interested in whatever he has to say at whatever time he wishes to say it. The teacher routinely does several things to make sure that even a shy or a nonverbal child has an opportunity to talk. These include the following:

- Providing a daily opportunity to tell the teacher about matters of importance to him.
- Scheduling an opportunity for him to show his school to his parents.
- Providing regular opportunities for him to talk with an assistant teacher who takes an interest in him.

The preschool group should provide enough adults to give each child the talking opportunities he needs. A major weakness of a one- or two-adult preschool group is that only a few of the more aggressive children will have regular opportunities for communicating their ideas to their beloved teacher. Every school should have an ample supply of good listeners: volunteers, parents, grandparents, teacher assistants, or student participants. A nursery group or kindergarten should afford the child not only an opportunity to talk with other children (at a relatively low level of conversation), but also an opportunity to talk with adults trained to listen understandingly. Only in this way can children have adequate opportunity for developing their ability to talk.

Preschool children form definite ideas before they are able to communicate them. Teachers who realize this help the children with their communication problem and thus aid not only their verbal progress but also

Communication with an experienced adult. (Courtesy of Metropolitan Public Schools, Nashville–Davidson County, Tennessee.)

their emotional development. A child who is helped to communicate his thoughts feels the importance of his ideas and of himself.[5]

The Sunday morning that three-and-one-half-year-old Neal accompanied his mother—a kindergarten teacher—to class, he happily joined the other children in making stars to hang from the ceiling and green trees to pin to

[5] Over two hundred experiences designed to stimulate language expression are compiled in a teacher-oriented source book: Rose C. Engel, *Language Motivating Experiences for Young Children* (Los Angeles: University of Southern California Book Store, 1968).

the display board. When his star was finished, his mother asked him where he wanted it put. "On the tree," he said. So she pinned it at the top of a green tree on the display board. Neal burst into tears and cried loudly, kicking and shrieking out at anyone who came near him. Removing the star, his mother tried again to find out where he wanted it. "Do you want it on the ceiling with the other stars?" she asked, putting it there. Neal's crying continued. "Maybe you want to keep it?" she suggested. More crying. "Do you want the star on a tree?" she asked. Neal started calming down as his understanding mother fastened his star on a tree. "Do you want the star on the ceiling?" she continued. When she put the star, with its tree attached, among the others on the ceiling, a smile of satisfaction came to Neal's face.

A less patient or less ingenious teacher might have given up trying to understand Neal and would have left him frustrated and disturbed by his inadequacy. But his mother calmly persisted in trying to understand what Neal wanted and succeeded in making his experience complete and satisfying. Furthermore, by letting Neal communicate his idea, she encouraged his creativity in developing an out-of-the-ordinary arrangement. At no point did she evaluate his idea; she only encouraged his expression of it. If Neal wanted to attach trees to stars instead of attaching stars to trees, she accepted his unusual idea as readily as if it were a commonplace.

Hints for Adult Listeners

The adult listener in a preschool group can function in several ways. For one thing, she is a captive listener who enjoys being with the children. As such, she should be a permissive kind of person who accepts what children say, in the way they say it. She should not try to correct what they say because she might inhibit their saying it. The imitation through which they learn will gradually make their imperfect language more and more grammatically correct. She therefore should be willing to have the children speak in whatever way they wish. The children enjoy talking with such a listener, but they should feel no compulsion to talk with her. They must be free to continue or discontinue a conversation as they wish.

NED (*pulling string out of his pocket*) I sure have a lot of string in my pocket.
ADULT (*smiling and interested*) Have you?
NED Yah.

When an adult listener is accepted and loved by the children, they continue to be relaxed and absorbed in what they are doing even while she moves among them. For instance, she can walk by the table where children are busy with books, crayons on paper, or puzzles. As she exchanges smiles with each child, she often exchanges comments, too. A girl may look up from her crayoning and say, "I'm making this and (*pointing to a puzzle*) then I'll do that." Or a boy may sit back in his chair for a moment to admire the puzzle he has just completed to his own satisfaction, "Looka that!"

An adult listener should avoid making evaluative remarks that might inhibit the children in their speaking. She should issue well-deserved praise when it is appropriate, but she should avoid being negatively critical. For instance, when a child has assembled the pieces of a puzzle, she should be pleased with the result—whether the puzzle is completed or not. She should avoid saying, "Aren't you going to finish it?" or, "You certainly got done in a hurry," or, "This piece isn't quite right." But she may say, "That's fine," and ask, "Would you like to play outside now?"

An adult listener needs to keep in mind the differences in egocentrism associated with differences in age level. When a three-year-old child is disconcerted by her appearance, she should know that his reaction may be caused primarily by the nature of the child at a particular age. She should not take the matter personally. A three-year-old child is interested primarily in his own mother. On suddenly seeing someone else's mother, he is apt to cry, "I want my mommy!"

Neal, when he was almost four years old, discovered that he could get a response from an adult by saying, "Hi, dummy," or "Hi, dodo." By making a common label for individuals in this way, the four-year-old child is able to communicate with grownups on a person-to-person basis. Thus the egocentrism of preschool children gradually develops into an increasing interest in the individuals around them.

THREE-YEAR-OLD (*going away, or crying*)   I want my mommy!

FOUR-YEAR-OLD   Hi, dumb dodo! You know what? (*or other direct conversation.*)

FIVE-YEAR-OLD (*settling into a chair next to the growup*)   I know you. You're Susan's mommy.

LISTENING TO INDIVIDUAL REPORTS

Each morning the teacher should listen to what the children have to tell her about their experiences at home. She has prepared the room and planned the activities before the first children arrive. Thus she is ready to give each child her full attention as a means of encouraging him to talk with her. Her interest helps him to recall the happenings of the day before and to communicate his thoughts about them. Furthermore, the opportunity to talk when he first arrives encourages the child to start expressing himself. He thinks of school as a place where he can talk with people.

When he was nearly four years old, Neal delighted his teacher by coming in one morning and—for the first time—bubbling over with something to say, "You know what? Our windows are real clean. We can see real better." The teacher shared his enthusiasm, "Your windows are really clean! You can see better when windows are clean." As another child came in, Neal went on his way, pleased with telling about the windows and muttering, "See better, can see better." He felt he had chosen the right words for telling about what had happened.

In a school in which the adults are always ready to listen to what a child has to say, the children feel free to report what they observe. And by doing so, they gain facility in expressing themselves. For instance, one day on the playground, four-year-old Billy turned to his teacher to say, sniffing the air, "I 'mell weiners." His teacher sniffed thoughtfully. "Why, I smell them, too," she said. "Maybe someone is cooking them for lunch." Billy and his teacher exchanged smiles of mutual appreciation, and Billy went on to another activity.

Showing Mother Around School

Teachers and mothers know that children act differently on the days that Mother comes to school. The teacher therefore uses those days as an opportunity for the child to show off in desirable ways. She may say, "Norman, would you like to show your mother where you like to play?" Four-and-one-half-year-old Norman needs no further persuasion to show his mother the piece of equipment that captivates his interest: a house approached by a ladder and adjacent to a pole for sliding down. He starts talking at once.

NORMAN (*pulling his mother along to the tree house*) I want to show you this. You can climb up there. (*Climbs up the ladder and runs over to the pole.*) Want to see me go down fast? (*Goes down without waiting for an answer. He then picks up a toy fire engine near the base of the ladder, and starts back up the ladder with the toy in his hand.*)

MOTHER I'll hand the car up to you. You need both hands for climbing a ladder, you know.

NORMAN (*climbing*) I don't need two hands to climb. (*Again runs over to the pole.*) Want me to go down fast? Or slow?

MOTHER Can you stop on your way down?

NORMAN (*sliding down the pole without stopping*) I didn't make it stop. (*Climbs the ladder, runs across to the pole, and slides down, stopping in the middle for a moment.*) See? I stopped. (*On the next climb, he stops before sliding down the pole to ask a question.*) Want to see me go down fast?

MOTHER Okay.

NORMAN (*sliding down fast*) Do you want to come up here?

(*When his mother hesitates, Norman urges her to come up by telling her it will only take a minute. His mother climbs up the ladder so that she can see easily into the house.*)

NORMAN (*pointing out the various features of the tree house*) See, these can come off. See that wind thing? (*making it twirl*) (You have to make it go. (*pointing to each of the five windows*) Window, window, window, window, window. See, this is the door. Door, door. (*pointing to the ladder*) This is to climb up (*pointing to the pole*) and go down. (*starting imaginative play*) It's a firehouse up here. Down goes the fireman. (*He slides down the pole, runs over to the merry-go-round nearby, and starts making it go around. He imitates a siren.*) Sometimes we make it slow and sometimes we make it fast. Want me to come back to turn on the belt again? (*Gets off the merry-go-round and climbs the ladder to the treehouse. He then slides down the pole and returns to the merry-go-round.*) This is our fire engine. Want me to make the fire engine go? (*Gets on the merry-go-round and starts it turning.*)

(*When his mother starts to move away, Norman leaves the fireman play and goes back to his original play.*)

NORMAN   Want to see me slide down the pole again?

MOTHER   Okay. Then I must go and get the juice ready.

NORMAN   (*Climbs the ladder and slides down the pole*)   Then I have to get up again and close the door. (*Climbs the ladder and slides down the pole again. Clutches his trousers.*) Everytime I come down my pants get unsnapped.

(*His mother laughs. Norman fixes the snaps on his pants and goes up the ladder again.*)

NORMAN   (*talking from the tree house*)   This time I'll go down it slow. (*Slides down the pole slowly; then, as his mother turns away, Norman follows her.*)

By having his mother at nursery school, Norman had an opportunity for language expression such as he did not often have. His entire conversation was directed toward his mother. When he was sure of her attention, he entered into dramatic play about being a fireman. But when his mother began to edge away, he gave her more direct attention in an attempt to keep her interest. His conversation with her throughout the incident was primarily egocentric and was incidental to his going up the ladder and down the pole again and again. Norman's conversation can be described as a monologue punctuated by an occasional exchange of thought with an adult.

REGULAR OPPORTUNITY FOR TALKING WITH AN ADULT

Three-year-old Neal found it easy to let his five-year-old brother do the talking wth adults whenever the two boys were together. But by himself at nursery school, Neal had opportunity to talk with an adult who was especially interested in him. This adult was an appreciative audience for whatever Neal had to say. In September, communication between the two often consisted of nothing but a smile on Neal's part followed by interest in whatever the adult shared with him. Throughout the fall months his communication was limited to a sentence or two. For instance, "I saw lots of lights last night" was his report about seeing the lighted Christmas trees in neighborhood windows.

One morning in January, when Neal was three years and ten months old, he initiated a conversation about the zoo, although the zoo had not been discussed either in his home or at nursery school for several weeks.

NEAL   We went to the zoo before.
ADULT   Did you?
NEAL   We went once. We saw a monkey, a baby monkey.
ADULT   How big was it? Can you show me?
(*Neal uses both hands to show the size of the monkey.*)
ADULT   Oh, that was really small.
NEAL   The mommy was this big. (*Uses both hands to measure carefully.*)
ADULT   Did the mommy carry the baby around, or did she let it just rest?
NEAL   She carried it.
ADULT   How did she carry it?
NEAL   Under it.
(*The conversation continues with similar discussion about seeing the lion fed.*)
NEAL   I slept in the car.
ADULT   That's a good idea to sleep in the car. Then you wake up and start seeing the animals when you get there.
(*Neal nods his head.*)

When Neal returned home from nursery school that morning, he told his mother—with pride—about his conversation with his adult friend. He pointed out that he ought to have told her about the rattlesnake also. "You can mention it the next time you talk about the zoo," his mother reassured him. "I'm sure she enjoyed your telling her about your trip." Neal nodded as he went happily to other affairs. He had good reason to be happy with his awareness of a new skill: the ability to tell a grownup friend what he had experienced.

HELPING THE CHILD WHO DOES NOT TALK

Joe was a child who did not talk in the nursery group. He knew how to talk, but he did not talk. For two years he attended the parent-cooperative nursery school which his older sister (who had talked) and his older brother (who had not) had attended. When he was leaving the nursery group, his school career was discussed briefly at the mother's meeting as follows:

TEACHER   At the first of the year Joe did not verbalize in the group discussions. I felt that he was not ready to talk. During the year he has interested himself in all the other activities of our nursery school. We all like Joe.
BRIAN'S MOTHER   On the way to school Joe talks with Brian—until we pick up the other children.
JOE'S MOTHER   He likes Billy, too, and had him come for lunch last fall, but I didn't hear him say a word to Billy.
BILLY'S MOTHER   (*laughing*)   Then he came for lunch with Billy and didn't say a word. Everybody else talked and had a good time.
JOE'S MOTHER   The next time he had Billy come for lunch, I told him there was no point in having Billy come if he wasn't going to talk with him. So he did talk with him that time.
BRIAN'S MOTHER   It seems to me that everyone else answers for him. He doesn't have to talk.

JEAN'S MOTHER   We all take it for granted that he doesn't talk, so he doesn't.
MARY'S MOTHER   Don't you think he gains importance by not talking? I know
    Mary admires his not talking—she talks so much.
JOE'S MOTHER   I took him with me to a meeting the other day. The women
    gave him cookies to try to get him to talk.
BILLY'S MOTHER   He's very affectionate. I often have Billy on one knee and
    Joe on the other.

This conversation describes a boy who, at home, has a mother, an older
sister, and an older brother to talk for him; and, in the nursery group, has
others who talk for him. He has no particular incentive for talking. But he
does have incentive for not talking. He has the role of a nontalker to live
up to. He gets attention by not talking, and he does not know whether or
not he might lose that attention if he were to begin talking.

The next fall, his kindergarten teacher realized that Joe needed to have
a new role created for him and that he needed help with talking as he
ventured into his new role. She had the kindergarten group thoroughly
understand that

- Joe is going to talk more and more because he is now ready to talk.
- Joe needs opportunities for talking for himself—until now he has not had
  much practice in talking.

The teacher also had the other children understand their role in playing
with their good friend:

- No one talks for Joe. He can talk for himself.
- We listen while Joe gets ready and talks.

In these ways the teacher and the children helped Joe to communicate
with other people.

SIMPLICITY AIDS COMMUNICATION

Adults who work with young children quickly learn to talk to them as
simply as possible. They come to understand the point of view of children
like Susan who said:

SUSAN   I wanna play.
ADULT   You may go outside if you wish to play.

Susan burst into tears and started to cry in frustration. She wanted to play
with her friends, and this talking adult would not say yes. On the basis
of her previous experiences, Susan thought that grownups meant no whenever they used a lot of words.

Teachers learn that if one word will suffice, they should not use two.
They also learn to use the same word or phrase each time, rather than a

synonym for it. They develop such standardized expressions as, "Do you want to go to the bathroom?" Whenever they give a direction to the children, they say it in the same way each time, for example, "Let's carry our chairs to the table."

BUILDING VOCABULARY

At the same time that they keep their speech simple, teachers should make a point of helping children to improve their communication by adding to their vocabularies.

A brief talking time can use models as well as flannel boards and pictures. (Courtesy of Long Beach Day Nursery and Mariam M. Cook, Long Beach, California.)

ADULT (*picks up a book from the library table*)   This is one of my favorites.
NEAL   Here's my favorite—and this—and this—and this—and this—and this.
   (*Picks up one book after another.*)

The adult made a mental note to explain the meaning of the word *favorite* when she read the book she had selected to a group of children. She knew that three-and-one-half-year-old Neal, having heard her use the word, would notice it the next time that he heard it used. By using the word correctly and explaining later that morning, she could capitalize on Neal's interest in the word before he had time to practice incorrect usage of it. Furthermore, if Neal was sensitive to the word, then the others in his age group were also ready to learn it.

Adult listeners, as well as teachers, should notice occasions when a child needs a word he does not yet have in his vocabulary. For instance, the adult working with Mari (four years and four months) supplied her with the word *pen* when Mari was describing her experiences with the turtle at the home of a friend.

MARI   The turtle was in a little thing that a baby has.
ADULT   Was it in a *playpen?*
MARI   No, a turtle pen, I suppose.

GUIDING GROUP CONVERSATION

Learning how to participate in a group discussion begins in the nursery group. The quiet three-year-old child learns that he can talk too. The talkative four-year-old child learns to shorten his remarks so that others may have their turns.

When every child in a group is eager to say something, the teacher can help them in learning how to take turns. First, she helps them to become aware of the problem, "When we all talk, we can't hear anyone." Then she presents a plan to solve the problem, "We can take turns talking just as we take turns going down the slide. Let's do it this way. When you have something to say, you raise your hand and I'll call on you when it's your turn."

By imitation, the children easily learn to raise their hands when they have something to say. But learning to wait for a turn takes longer. Each day the teacher must pleasantly help the children to remember to take turns. She may say, "I think Bruce is next," or, "Jimmy raised his hand first, so it's his turn."

When group discussions are made a routine part of every day at school, children gradually learn how to participate in them. For instance, on the first school morning after Christmas vacation, one teacher gathered together a small group of three- and four-year-olds to talk about their presents. Each child was to have a turn to tell what he got for Christmas.

"I got a cowboy hat."

"I got a tractor."

"I got a tractor too," said the three-year-old sitting in the next chair.

"Do you know what?" asked a three-and-one-half-year-old boy. "I got some tools."

"Do you know what my brother got for Christmas?" asked four-and-one-half-year-old Jerry, a middle child in a family of three children. "A train! And my baby got a doll."

"I got a turtle," said the last member of the group, concluding the children's discussion.

VERBAL EXPRESSIONS OF AGGRESSION

Grownups guide children in learning to express their feelings of aggression. The biting, hitting, and kicking which accompany the angry cry of the frustrated child are gradually replaced by acceptable physical outlets for his emotions, such as punching the punching bag, washing off the tabletop, or working with clay. The four- and five-year-old children learn to work out in verbal fantasy what they cannot work out in fact. "I'll hit him!" a child may say as he flattens out a chunk of clay.

With more mature preschool children, it is possible to have a verbal interlude to express aggression—much like that which occurred one day when five-year-old Susan had pushed three-year-old Neal and five-year-old Stanley reported her to an adult. The adult's friendly attention to Susan for a few minutes strengthened Susan's feeling of security so that a verbal exchange among the three children and their friend, four-year-old Ned, could release their feelings further:

NEAL (*to Ned, an onlooker in the earlier pushing*)   Do you like Susan?

NED   I don't like Susan. Do you like Susan?

NEAL (*after thinking*)   I like Susan.

NED (*to Susan*)   I was going to take you to the beach. But now I'm not. My mommy is going to take me. I'll take Stanley and Neal, and not you.

SUSAN   I'm going to play with Marie. You can't.

NED   Yes, I can. Huh, Stanley?

NEAL (*to Susan*)   When I'm big, I'll beat up Ned and Stanley. Okay?

SUSAN   Okay.

As five-year-olds, Stanley and Susan are leaders of the children. Stanley exerts a quiet leadership—especially for Ned, who likes to have Stanley's approval (for example, "Huh, Stanley?"). Ned sides with his friend, Neal, and expresses hostility toward Susan. Neal, however, although he was the one who had been pushed, remains friendly with Susan and says, "When I'm big, I'll beat up Ned and Stanley." All four children are sufficiently mature to express their aggressions verbally instead of bursting into tears or taking negative action.

Preventing Speech Disorders

Because children are in the process of learning to speak their native tongue during their entire preschool period, usually any apparent speech defect they may have is only evidence of incomplete learning. When such a defect is marked, however, the child should be examined by a physician. If there is no underlying physical defect, the child should be placed in a nursery group or kindergarten with a teacher who is especially effective in guiding the speech development of children. Such a teacher not only furnishes the child with her example of a clear pattern of speech and helps him with difficult speech sounds, but she also displays much warmth and love so that it is not necessary for him to strive for attention.

Difficulties in learning to talk are not apt to occur in homes where adult speech patterns are adequate and where loving care is given to a child according to his needs. The teacher, therefore, should encourage each parent to spend at least half an hour a day—and preferably a full hour— in doing whatever the child wishes her to do. Many parents are engrossed with other activities, such as housekeeping or shopping, so their child needs a period in which he is the center of attention. Many a parent makes all the decisions and gives all the orders. The child needs a parent who also lets the child play such an ego-building role. Being queen or king for an hour enables a girl or boy to gain the self-confidence needed in learning the difficult problem of talking like adults around them.

Even if the child's home situation does not give him much opportunity for developing self-confidence, his school situation can. The teacher should encourage each child to choose the activities he likes, and she should praise his accomplishments as they occur. Above all, the teacher should make herself available as a loving person who responds to the child whenever he needs her.

Furthermore, a child who is free from physical defect and feels secure in being loved will develop clear speech as rapidly as he is ready to do so. His teacher may reassure his parents by saying, "He will pronounce his *s* sounds clearly when he is ready." This confidence in the child and in his eventual success in speaking well carries over into all teacher relations with both parents and child, and bolsters the confidence of all three.

STUTTERING AND CLUTTERING

Many children stutter or have cluttered speech at some period during their preschool experience. Bakwin and Bakwin discuss the nature of such difficulties:

. . . Stuttering . . . is not known to occur among primitive peoples.
Although stutterers show no specific personality pattern, certain character- istics such as timidity, fear of other children and of new schools and teachers, sleep disturbances, and compulsive behavior, recur frequently. The children are often more restricted and rigid than nonstutterers. . . .
A survey by Brown of over 200 normal preschool children showed that every one of them had repetitions in his speech. The usual type of repetition is repetition of words "Mother, mother, may I have, may I have, some chocolate?" Normal repetition may be mistakenly interpreted as stuttering and lead to unwarranted parental concern and pressure. As a result the child, in a vain effort to improve his speech, becomes tense and anxious, a state which, in turn, increases the frequency and duration of his nonfluencies. About 40 per cent stop their speech repetition before school age.
Between 2 and 4 years of age, when progress in speech is rapid, the child is called upon to make many new adjustments. He is expected to curb his

rapidly emerging desires and abilities, he is being toilet trained, and so on. Often, at this age, he has a new sibling and both jealousy and anxiety disturb him. Children with poor neuromuscular speech equipment show their emotional discomfort by stuttering, whereas others, of different constitution react in other ways.[6]

Realizing the normality of repetition in preschool speech, the nursery teacher should nevertheless see if the children in the nursery group are subjected to any overexpectations or other pressures which can be reduced or removed, or if they need more loving attention. Perhaps a speech repetitive child would like to have his midmorning refreshments brought to him at play instead of having to join the group. Or perhaps he would welcome more attention from a favorite adult while he chooses among different play activities. In every way possible, the teacher should attempt to keep his stuttering period as short as possible in order to avoid the formation of a habit which may be difficult to lose later in school or in life.

INCESSANT TALKING

The parent who said, "First I thought she would never learn to talk. Now I think she will never learn to stop talking," was the mother of a child who, for a time, became an incessant talker. Bakwin and Bakwin describe this disorder as follows:

> Incessant talking is most common between the ages of three and five. Ordinarily, it is the accompaniment of natural inquisitiveness. This is desirable and should be encouraged. . . . Sometimes incessant talking is used to gain attention. Treatment is directed toward the cause of the excessive need for attention.[7]

A talkative child fits into the group very easily and readily as long as the children are free to choose their own activities. But in a teacher-centered group activity, the talkative child and the teacher may seem to be competing for the attention of the group. Realizing this, the teacher should keep such situations to a minimum and help the talkative child to learn when it is appropriate to talk and when it is appropriate to listen.

RETARDATION IN SPEECH

As pointed out by Bakwin and Bakwin, "Speech may be considered to be delayed if recognizable words are not used by 24 months of age and phrases by 36 months."[8] The *Handbook of Research in Teaching* reports a study by Dawes[9] which experimented with methods for offsetting such retardation:

---

[6] Harry Bakwin and Ruth M. Bakwin, *Clinical Managment of Behavior Disorders in Children* (Philadelphia: W. B. Saunders Co., 1966), pp. 371–372.

[7] Ibid., p. 377.

[8] Ibid., p. 367.

Training in language and concepts. To compensate for the meager language environment of a group of orphanage children who have had few conversations with adults, little experience in reading aloud, and low levels of experience outside the orphanage grounds, Dawes[9] instituted a program which included the following types of training:

1. Training in understanding words and concepts.
2. Looking at and discussing pictures.
3. Listening to poems and stories.
4. Going on short excursions.

Emphasis was not on "stuffing" children with words but on real comprehension of the words and concepts. Especial care was taken to see that no direct coaching on test items was included in the training program.

At the end of the training period (about 50 hours), the experimental group had made significantly greater gains than the control group (which had no special training) in vocabulary, information about home living, and general science information. Readiness for reading was significantly better and IQ had increased significantly.[10]

When a nursery teacher has a child whose speech is retarded, she should work with him as she would with a younger child, helping him to learn simpler words as well as those being learned by the other children in his age group. It will take the child time to work through each of the earlier phases of language development, so the teacher must be patient as well as loving as she observes his gradual mastery of speech.

DIFFICULT SOUNDS

F, v, l, r, and *th* are often difficult sounds for preschool children to say, and so are the sibilant sounds the Bakwins mention:

. . . *s, z, sh, zh, ch,* and *j.* These are among the most difficult speech sounds to master and, in the course of normal speech development, are the last sounds to be enunciated clearly. Although many children speak clearly from the beginning, it is not unusual for a child of 5 or even 6 years to form the sibilants incorrectly. This need cause no concern unless an organic defect is present. . . .

The parents should be careful to enunciate correctly. . . . should avoid

[9] Helen C. Dawes, "A Study of the Effect of an Educational Program upon Language Development and Related Mental Functions in Young Children." *Journal of Experimental Education,* 11: 200–209, 1942.
[10] Pauline S. Sears and Edith M. Dowley, "Research in Teaching in the Nursery School," Chapter 15 in *Handbook of Research in Teaching* (Chicago: Rand McNally Company, 1963), p. 845.

correcting the child. Praise for success is a greater incentive to effort than criticism of failure.[11]

The teacher who knows which sounds are difficult makes a point of pronouncing them clearly herself and provides opportunities for the children to say them. For instance, on a day when she feels she can tolerate noise, she may provide each child with a whistle. Pronouncing her *s* sounds distinctly, she introduces them both to the word *whistle* and to the whistles themselves. She may say, "We're going to be noisemakers for a while today. I have a whistle for each of you. You can play with your whistle for a while. Then we will put it away until you are ready to go home. You may each have a whistle to take home." As she passes out the whistles, she says clearly to each child, "*A whistle* for you." While the children are playing with their whistles, she finds occasion to ask each child: "Do you like your *whistle?*" Her stress on the word usually leads each child to say the word himself, imitating her pronunciation. Even a non-English-speaking child of three and one half years can learn to pronounce the word easily and correctly.

The teacher also can use, "Let's see what's missing," as a means of helping children with difficult sounds. She carefully uses objects whose names involve difficult sounds, including *glasses, funnels,* a *flashlight, shells,* a *piece* of *silk,* a *feather,* a *rag, thimbles.* For variation she may use pictures of birds and animals whose names involve difficult sounds, and display them on her flannelboard. She may choose pictures of chickens, ducks, or turkeys at Thanksgiving time. She introduces each picture, carefully pronouncing the words correctly. After she arranges the pictures on the flannelboard, she has the children cover their eyes while she removes one of the pictures. "Let's see what's missing" is their cue to open their eyes to see what has been removed. As they name the missing animal, the teacher notices their pronunciation of the words and identifies those children who need further practice with a particular sound.

The teacher can take advantage of refreshment time to help the children with the word *chocolate.* By giving the children their choice of chocolate or plain milk, chocolate or plain cookies, she can determine which children who select chocolate are able to pronounce the word correctly. For those who select plain milk or cookies, she may have to devise some other situation to determine their mastery of the *ch* sound.

IMPROPER LANGUAGE

According to his parents, five-year-old Rod has been "cussing" for a year or more, and had gained attention by doing so. He used such improper language at school, and got attention there, too. At first, his teacher tried to ignore his cussing in the hope that he would drop it. She tried to help

[11] Bakwin and Bakwin, op. cit., pp. 375–376.

him develop such praiseworthy skills as tricycle riding and clay modeling. When the cussing persisted, she tried to help him understand that such talk is not desirable. One day, after he had been cussing, she talked with him:

TEACHER Do your parents like to hear you talk like that?
ROD Oh, are they here? (*Looks around for them.*)
TEACHER I think they like you to talk without using those words.

On another day Rod came to his teacher to talk further.

ROD Do you know what? A policeman can put you in jail if you say bad words.
TEACHER Is that so?
ROD Yeah. Grandmother told me.

In spite of his grandmother's warning, Rod's use of improper language continued. He heard such talk at a neighbor's house, and he got attention by using it himself. His satisfaction in the attention and his lack of more desirable skills for getting attention made him continue to use this device.

What force can be used to help Rod? What force is greater than that of attention? The wise teacher uses the force of loving rapport between such a child and herself. If Rod really feels his teacher's affection, he will return it by helping her to have the kind of nursery group she thinks they should have. What Rod will not do under pressure, he will do with love. His teacher, therefore, should take immediate steps to get to know Rod better and to give him an opportunity to come to know both her and her love for him. When Rod realizes that he has the loving attention of his teacher, he will no longer need to resort to attention-getting language.

Part of learning the toileting procedures of the culture is learning to talk about them, and then learning when not to talk about them. "Toilet talk" is a normal part of the development of preschool children. However, in the United States, middle-class customs emphasize the individual and private nature of toileting. Many parents become alarmed by the use of "toilet talk" and need help in order to understand that it is only one aspect of preschool language development, particularly evident in four-year-olds. They need to know that a casual attitude toward toileting during the preschool years is a desirable prelude to teaching the children the social customs of the culture and is a sound preparation for a happy adult life.

Enhancing Speech Development

It is well known that association with loving and confidence-building adults enhances the speech development of preschool children. Piaget, in studying language development in children,[12] carefully limited his study to the language children use with other children, rather than the language they use with adults. Prescott pointed out:

> The process of assimilating experience (gaining meanings) is speeded up tremendously when the child communicates with other persons who answer his questions, help him to name things accurately, and show him how to use language in thinking. . . .[13]

The implication to be drawn from such findings is that the nursery group and the kindergarten should provide an opportunity for the children to talk freely—not only with other children, but also with adults. The ratio of adults to children should be high enough for each child to have at least one opportunity for genuine communication with his teacher, and with one or more other adults, during each school session.

It is also reported that the socioeconomic status of the family is associated with the speech development of children. Bakwin and Bakwin point out:

> Of the factors influencing the acquisition of speech, socioeconomic status is one of the most important, children from better environments being consistently more advanced than poor children; in fact, the learning of speech correlates more closely with environmental conditions than with intelligence-test results.[14]

Some families help their preschool children personally, teaching them ways of thinking, ways of expressing their thoughts and feelings, ways of finding humor and pleasure in living. Other families provide preschool group experience for their children. Less advantaged families may be limited in ability to enrich the lives of their children either directly or indirectly. But whatever the ways of the family, its children who participate in preschool groups must be encouraged in the use of language. The desirable ways to guide the development of children are those which further the child's confidence in himself and his ability to use language.

TEACHER-CHILD DIALOGUE

The teacher can think of herself as establishing and developing a dialogue with each of the preschool children in her group. With each child, she is constantly enlarging the dialogue, both by enlarging the scope of objects and activities to talk about and by developing each conversational area in depth through greater precision in observation and in verbal description. For instance, if a child notices the grey cat that visits the pre-

---

[12] Piaget, op. cit.

[13] Daniel A. Prescott, *The Child in the Educative Process* (New York: McGraw-Hill Book Company, Inc., 1957), p. 388.

[14] Bakwin and Bakwin, op. cit., p. 44.

school group, the teacher can use stories and pictures to acquaint the child with other animals such as dogs and horses and bears, and with cats that are black, cats that are white, cats that are known as "Whiskers" because they have whiskers, and so on.

With the preschool child who has had less opportunity to develop communication skills, the teacher may need to work at a very simple level. She arranges for one or more adults in the preschool group to pace the child's activity with words. As the child shares in juice time, for instance, the adult who is pacing him may hold up the pitcher and ask "Juice?" After pouring it, she may say, "Juice," as she sets the glass down in front of him. On subsequent mornings, she may focus on "drink" and "tie" in the drinking activity with the phrase, "Drink juice." By focusing the attention of the child on the object or on the activity, the adult helps him attach words to them.

An adult pacer becomes expert in attentive listening. As a child attempts to use words, the adult does all that he can to give the child the feeling that he is in communication. The adult can think of himself as helping the child experience the normal sequence that a child usually experiences with his mother. From birth, a child and his mother communicate through body language. Out of the diverse sounds that a child emits certain ones become cues to satisfying action on the part of his mother. Gradually verbal cues become the major communication system through which a child makes his wishes known and a mother is able to satisfy them. The adult pacer at nursery school helps a child recapitulate the evolution of attention to verbal cues.

An adult pacer must be sensitive to the fatigue level of the child she paces. Learning is a strenuous activity, and the preschool child who is trying to keep up with the activities of his group and at the same time fill in learning that is compensatory is carrying a double load. If he tires before others do, he may need to have his compensatory communication experience away from his peers or only for short intervals. His optimum work load in the group activities and in the compensatory activities is diagnosed by his pacer and his teacher, often with the help of his parents or guardian.

The dialogue of a teacher and a more mature preschool child is equally significant in his development. If it introduces him to choices, it can lead on into recognition of the consequences of his choices, and it can also lead on into recognition that there usually are alternatives from which one can choose. "Do you want the red or the yellow one?" involves a kind of choice that should be an integral part of the life of every preschool child. It is the kind of question that is an important element in the dialogue of teacher and child.

DICTATION

When the ratio of adults to children is sufficiently high, it is possible for the adults to serve as secretaries for those children who wish to record something they have thought of—perhaps a story or a little tune with words. A child who dictates to an adult feels that what he has to say is important because an adult is interested enough to write it down. His self-confidence expands, and so does his interest in words. Later, in elementary school, he will be interested in how he, too, can learn to make those marks on paper.

Adults in a nursery group should carry little notebooks or pieces of paper in their pockets and write on them frequently, thus encouraging the children to become interested in dictating what is to go on the paper. "What do you want me to write on the paper?" is a question that elicited delightful results from three-year-old Meredy, four-year-old Neal, and three-and-one-half-year-old Tim and Kimmy:

MEREDY (*dictating her "new" name*)   Cinderwawa, Mary Jean, Sister, Denina.
TIM (*composing a story*)   I went up in da sky and dwought [brought] down a cloud fo' you.
KIMMY (*dictating her version of Brahm's Lullaby*)
                    Lullaby and goodnight
                    With roast beef tonight.
NEAL (*dictating his version of a favorite finger play*)
             Little fish puts its head out of the water. (*Puts finger up.*)
             He sees people who was going to catch it;
             So he dives back in the water. (*Puts finger down.*)

Children who have been encouraged to dictate their thoughts in nursery school continue to enjoy doing so. Five-and-a-half-year-old Neal dictated a postcard to a neighborhood friend away on a vacation:

Dear Susie:
    John has a scooter now. When John stops sucking his thumb he will get to ride the scooter. John is a big boy now; he went to the toilet in me and Stanley's house.
    At Bixby Park me and Stanley climbed out the window. Stanley on the grass and Dad was walking and Neal was walking on the cement.
    We saw one dancing. Do you learn dancing there?
    Stanley has a sign. Says "Old Cars for Stanley."
    Neal has new shoes and Neal has new socks.

DEVELOPING A SENSE OF HONOR

Children take on the humor of the people they are with. Within one family, certain incidents evoke humor; within another family, other incidents may be considered amusing. The teacher encourages the children to see humor wherever it exists.

One rainy day, Brian slipped on the sidewalk and fell headlong into the large puddle next to it. The teacher helped him to his feet. "My goodness," she said, "wasn't that a surprise!" Brian, who liked to get surprises, failed to see any connection between a surprise and falling into a puddle. He was negative about the whole matter. He did not like the fall; he did not want to change into dry trousers.

"You know," the teacher continued, "I think we'd better take you home. It's time to go home now, and you can change into dry clothes at home." Brian brightened at this suggestion.

The teacher chuckled and tried once more to help Brian see the humor in his situation. "You aren't the only one who fell into the puddle," she said. "Guess who else did." Brian looked interested. The teacher laughed again, "Russell fell in. You should see him." As the teacher laughed about falling into the puddle, Brian started to laugh too. As others came by, Brian and the teacher shared their amusement with them. "I fell in," said Brian, enjoying the attention he was getting.

In another nursery group, one of the assistant teachers with a good sense of humor helped the children who rode in her car to develop their sense of humor. She pointed out to them a lamp set in a piece of driftwood and chuckled with them over this unusual kind of a light. After that, one of the four-year-old children was apt to say, "There's the funny light," and send the other children into gales of laughter. When humor has been associated with a situation, children remember it and laugh again when the situation recurs.

The group of children in the car also developed a series of humorous remarks describing their route. "Now we pick up Ronny," they would say. A few minutes later someone would add, "Then we pick up Bobby," and chuckle in anticipation of the final line: "Then we pick up nursery school." As each line was added by one of the four-year-old children, all of the group of both three- and four-year-olds enjoyed the humor of the familiar lines.

Another kind of humor that the older children enjoyed was that of saying something that was obviously not true. Virginia, who was almost five years old, liked to point to a house the car was passing and say, "There's my house." Then she would laugh, delighted with her joke.

A teacher should encourage the children in their verbal humor. When four-year-old Ned and his friends played a joke on their teacher, she enjoyed it with them. By doing so she helped Ned add to his active phraseology.

NED   We played a joke. We went one way, and you went another.
ADULT (*laughing*)   And your way was shorter. You got back first.
NED (*softly to himself as he turned away*)   Got back first.

Through her real appreciation of their humor, an adult listener encourages the verbally fluent four-year-old children who attempt to combine activity with their verbal humor:

RUSSELL (*to adult*)   You know what?
ADULT   What?
RUSSELL (*attempts a handspring*).   That's what!

Helping Children to Perceive Relationships

By being both a good listener and a conversationalist, the adult encourages children to explore desirable ways of thinking. By smiling in appreciation, she rewards the child who remembers and expresses a pertinent idea. Whenever she extends the conversation, she increases the probability that the child will express more pertinent memories.

One morning, a nursery group walked over to watch the repairmen fixing the sewer pipe under the street. Three-and-a-half-year-old Neal viewed the open manhole and remembered having seen other workmen at a manhole the day before. "I saw another one over there," he volunteered, pointing down the street. This remark led to conversation about what he had seen, and to exploration of the manhole where he had seen the repairmen. With such satisfying attention, Neal was encouraged to make and express his observations.

One day, four-year-old Marilyn brought her new fan to nursery school. She had a satisfying experience in showing the group—and, later, individual adults—how the fan worked:

MARILYN (*opening her fan*) I'll show you how it gets out. And it puts back in. (*Closes the fan.*)

Her pleasure in such attention-getting situations encouraged Marilyn to bring other objects to nursery school and to explain how they worked.

Four-year-old Neal was encouraged to look for analogies through a conversation that he enjoyed with an adult at the nursery school playground:

ADULT   How fast can we run, Neal?
NEAL   We can run as fast as the merry-go-round.
ADULT (*repeating appreciatively*)   Fast as the merry-go-round.
NEAL   Fast as a doggy.
ADULT   Fast as a doggy—that's *really* fast.

Adults who take an interest in the different words that four-year-old children use encourage them to build their vocabularies and to improve their thinking. An example of vocabulary-building occurred when four-and-one-half-year-old Neal picked up a leaf of a jacaranda tree and presented it to his teacher as a "fern." "It does look like the frond of a fern," she said, thus confirming his use of the word *fern* and making available to him another word, *frond,* if he wanted to use it.

An adult listener is also invaluable in expanding the vocabulary of the four-year-old child who is exploring the rhyming of words. Just by being an appreciative listener, she encourages him in this learning activity. However, if she also plays the game in the role of an admiring helper, she is even more successful in building his self-confidence and encouraging him to explore the game further.

Four-and-one-half-year-old Neal said, "I am cold as bold," and his adult listener asked, "Are you as cold as bold?" Neal responded, "I'm as warm as warm," and went off to play. A few minutes later he was back to say, "I'm as warm as a tharm." That remark called for a delightful laugh, but the adult listener made a point of not enlarging on a conversation that emphasized a nonexistent word.

In all these listening-talking situations between children and adults, the adults keep in mind the importance of building the child's self-confidence, especially by making the situation a pleasant and rewarding one for him. When four-year-old Neal was talking with his mother about his grandmother, she extended the conversation so that he regained his confidence:

NEAL   Who was your mommy when you was a girl?
MOTHER   Grandmother.
NEAL   Oh! (*pause*)   Sometimes I know, sometimes I don't know.
MOTHER (*smiling appreciatively at him*)   So you always ask and find out.

Adult pleasure in children's remarks encourages the children to express the relationships they observe and leads them to further language development.

Situations for Discussion

A preschool teacher is apt to find herself in such situations as the four described here. Thinking of what to do in each situation, consider whether each course of action suggested is desirable, or not. Use points brought out in the chapter as well as ideas from your own experience to justify your views. Suggest alternate courses of action to supplement those that are given.

SITUATION 1   As an observer in a nursery group, you record the following conversation between five-and-a-half-year-old Susan and four-year-old Ned:

SUSAN (*wielding a paintbrush and painting anyone wishing to be painted*)
    When it's dry, you can wash it off—with soap and water.
NED (*looking around at the supplies*)   Where's the soap?
SUSAN (*continuing to paint one of the children*)   It's icky.
NED   Icky. Icky.

The interpretations that you associate with this anecdote include the following:

- Five-year-old children sometimes use a generality.
- Preschool children enjoy the sounds of words.
- Susan made up the word *icky*.
- Ned is concerned with the practicalities of the situation.
- An adult should have stopped the play.

SITUATION 2   You are teaching in a nursery group for three- and four-year-old children, which meets at a church. In your group you have Tommy, a child who has difficulty in talking clearly, especially in making the *ch* sound. You should

- Take Tommy and others on a tour of the church.
- Use flannelboard pictures of children playing.
- Have Tommy help with the baby chickens.
- Ask Tommy, "Can you say *church? Children? Chicken?*"
- Have the children make chains with strips of gummed paper.

SITUATION 3　In the preschool group you are teaching, only Chris has not learned to say *s* words clearly. Within the past few weeks, this difficulty has been augmented by his frequent repetition of words. In talking with Chris's mother, you bring out such ideas as the following

- Chris may become a stutterer.
- Spend time each day following Chris's lead.
- When Chris is ready, he will pronounce his letters correctly.
- Many children in the first grade have not learned to make every sound correctly.
- Chris is a delightful little boy—one to be proud of.

SITUATION 4　One of the boys in your nursery group comes to school with a new word he had learned, *Chrise*—a word that might easily be confused with a swear word. When he greets you, with, "Chrise, howdy," you should

- Say, "Please call me by my real name."
- Say, "We just use pretty names here at nursery school."
- Say, "That sounds like a swear word, and we don't use swear words here."
- Greet Don as usual.
- Pay no attention to Don's attempts to use his new word.

Current Books for Preschool Children

A B C. New York: The Platt and Munk Co., 1966. [From Apple to Zipper through Matthiesen photographs; one of many alphabet books available.]

BEMELMANS, LUDWIG. *Madeline's Rescue.* New York: The Viking Press, Inc., 1953. [In rhyme, Madeline rescues a mongrel and provides a pet for each of twelve girls.]

BRIGGS, RAYMOND. *Ring-a-ring o' Roses.* New York: Coward-McCann, Inc., 1962. [Delightfully illustrated rhymes from Mother Goose.]

BROWN, MARGARET WISE. *Where Have You Been?* New York: Scholastic Book Services, 1966. [Delightful preschool poems available in a paperback.]

DE ANGELI, MARGUERITE. *Book of Nursery and Mother Goose Rhymes.* Garden City, N.Y.: Doubleday & Company, Inc., 1954. [At school, children like to hear the same nursery rhymes they enjoy at home.]

The Green Grass Grows All Around. New York: The Macmillan Company, 1968. [Hilde Hoffman illustrated the traditional folk song.]

GROSSBART, FRANCINE. *A Big City.* New York: Harper & Row, Publishers, 1966. ["Antennas" to "Zigzag outline of the roof tops".]

The House That Jack Built. New York: Lothrop, Lee & Shepard Co., Inc., 1968. [A familiar rhyme.]

KALUSKY, REBECCA. *Is It Blue as a Butterfly?* Englewood Cliffs, N.J.: Prentice-

Hall, Inc., 1965. [When Daddy brings Abigail a present, they play a guessing game about what it is.]

LENSKI, LOIS. *I Like Winter.* New York: Henry Z. Walck, Inc., 1950. [Simple verse about activities of children in different seasons are also in *Spring Is Here* (1945), *On a Summer Day* (1953), and *Now It's Fall* (1948).]

LEWIS, RICHARD, ed. *In a Spring Garden.* New York: The Dial Press, 1965. [Haiku illustrated by Keats include:

> A red morning sky,
> For you snail;
> Are you glad about it?

McGOVERN, ANN. *Zoo Where Are You?* New York: Harper & Row, Publishers, 1964. [When Josh tried to make a zoo, he collected a "zooful of beautiful junk."]

PURDY, SUSAN. *My Little Cabbage.* New York: J. B. Lippincott Company, 1965. [In different countries, grownups have special names for a child.]

REY, H. A. *Anybody at Home?* Boston: Houghton Mifflin Company, 1942. [A brief rhyme with a question and then turning the page to see the answer make this book a favorite of preschool children. *See the Circus* is similar.]

SANDBERG, INGER and LASSE. *Little Anna and the Magic Hat.* New York: Lothrop, Lee & Shepard Co., Inc., 1965. [An imaginative story about everyday things like a shoe and a doll.]

SCHAER, JULIAN and MARVIN BILECK. *Rain Makes Applesauce.* New York: Holiday House, 1964. [Silly talk.]

SHUTTLESWORTH, DOROTHY. *ABC of Buses.* New York: Doubleday & Company, Inc., 1965. [Night bus, School bus, Zoo bus with Motor, Tires and Wheels.]

Sleep, Baby, Sleep. New York: Atheneum, 1967. [Trudi Oberhänsli illustrated the familiar cradle song.]

STEINER, CHARLOTTE, *My Bunny Feels Soft.* New York: Alfred A. Knopf, Inc., 1958. [A first book of definitions. *Littlest Mother Goose* (Random House, 1964) is by the same author.]

TUDOR, TASHA. *"A" Is for Annabelle.* New York: Henry Z. Walck, Inc., 1954. [Through the alphabet with a little girl's doll.]

THOMPSON, JEAN McKEE. *Poems to Grow On.* Boston: Beacon Press, 1957. ["Galoshes," "Now I Am Four," and "Growing" are among the short poems.]

WILDSMITH, BRIAN. *The Wind and the Sun.* New York: Franklin Watts, Inc., Inc., 1965. [Beautifully illustrated familiar fable.]

ZEMACH, HARVE and MARGOT. *Mommy, Buy Me a China Doll.* Chicago: Follett Publishing Co., 1966. [Rhythm with words.]

CHAPTER **12**

Stories for Preschool Children

What kinds of stories precede the wide variety of stories advocated for young children in primary grades? If a child is to enjoy folk tales such as *The Pancake* and *Hansel and Gretel* later, what stories should he hear when he is three, when he is four, and five? Such questions must be answered in terms of the needs and interests of three-, four-, and five-year-old children; not in terms of wishful thinking about them, but in terms of how they actually behave.

Stories to Meet the Needs of the Children

Of course, the reading of any story whatsoever to a child meets one of his basic needs—security. A parent or a parent substitute sits close to the child and shares the words and pictures of the book with him. In this cozy, intimate situation even frightening pictures and stories can be converted into something tolerable, even likable. The delightful, secure experience of storytelling prompts people to recommend a wide variety of stories on the grounds that "I read that story to a child the other day, and I am sure that she liked it." Yet it is clear that some stories are of more worth to a child of three than are other stories, and that stories especially for, say, four-year-old children differ in certain respects from stories for other age levels. It is obvious, too, that some stories more completely meet the needs of a child of five than do other stories. To identify the stories suitable for preprimary children, it is necessary to consider their needs at each successive age level and the kinds of books which help to meet these needs.[1]

---

[1] Chapter 2 of this book and Helen Heffernan and Vivian Edmiston Todd, *The Kindergarten Teacher* (Boston: D. C. Heath & Company, 1960), discuss needs of preschool children. Chapter 12 of *The Kindergarten Teacher* discusses books which meet the needs of five-year-old children.

Mothers, grandmothers, and other volunteers expand story time. (Courtesy of Chattanooga Public Schools, Chattanooga, Tennessee. Photograph by T. Fred Miller.)

Outdoor or indoors, reading a story is fun. (Courtesy of Ontario-Montclair School District, Ontario, California.)

It will be recalled that the needs of the preprimary child include the following:

- The need for a secure, loving, and dependable relationship first with mother, then with father and other members of the family.
- The need for realization of one's own worth.
- The need for adequate achievement.
- The need for belonging to a group.
- The need for freedom from fear, or anxiety, or guilt.
- The need for a variety of experience with the part of the world in which he lives.

BOOKS TO FURTHER SECURITY IN RELATIONSHIPS

The preschool child needs to feel secure in his relationships to each member of his family: his mother, father, and siblings in his home; his grandparents, who are frequently a part of his life; the babysitters who sometimes have responsibility for him. Many of the best-loved books for preschool children further a child's security in these fundamental relationships. For instance, *The Runaway Bunny*[2] is a delight to any preschool child. No matter what the little bunny thinks of doing, his mother plans to be close by. He has the freedom to run away knowing that the loving person he may need is always within reach. Even though he may perhaps seem to reject her, his mother never rejects him. With such a theme, a well-told book such as *The Runaway Bunny* has a place in the book collection of any preschool child or any group of preschool children.

Where's Andy?[3] is another book for the preschool child who is gaining insight into the relationship of a child and his mother. Andy, the hero of the book, plays a delightful game of hide-and-seek with his mother, keeping her attention centered on him throughout the entire game until he concludes it. To the three-year-old, whose interests center on himself, such a plot is most pleasant and satisfying. He easily identifies with Andy, and is eager to play such a game himself.

Books about daddies are also favorites of preschool children. *Papa Small*[4] describes a daddy that is understandable and desirable to a preschool child.

The place of a grandparent in a family is shown in *Grandpa,*[5] a realistic book by Barbara Borack. Nursery children identify with the little girl who enjoys her grandpa and the activities he does with her. Kindergarten children can hear about *Grandfather and I*[6] and about *Grandmother and I,*[7]

---

[2] Margaret Wise Brown, *The Runaway Bunny* (New York: Harper & Row, Publishers, 1942).

[3] Jane Thayer, *Where's Andy?* (New York: William Morrow & Co., Inc., 1954).

[4] Lois Lenski, *Papa Small* (New York: Henry Z. Walck, Inc., 1966).

[5] Barbara Borack, G. *Grandpa* (New York: Harper & Row, Publishers, 1967).

[6] Helen E. Buckley, *Grandfather and I* (New York: Lothrop, Lee & Shepard Co., Inc., 1959).

[7] Helen E. Buckley, *Grandmother and I* (New York: Lothrop, Lee & Shepard Co., Inc., 1961).

and thus further their understanding of the roles of grandparents in relation to themselves.

Desirable relationships among the children within a family are also interpreted to preschool children through books to be read to them. For older preschool children the role of *Big Brother*[8] is presented in terms of a big brother who teases his little sister, but then enjoys coloring with her. A book dear to the heart of a preschooler is *The Carrot Seed*[9] which portrays the interest of each member of the family in the carrot-growing project of their preschool child and ends with his triumphant success. A preschool child who endures kindly discouragement from other members of his family looks forward to having his virtues thus rewarded in the end.

Relating to a new member of the family is a delicate problem for a preschool child, one with which he needs help. Charlotte Zolotow provides this, for instance, by saying, "One day a little girl said to her little brother . . . 'Do you know what I'll do when I grow up and am married? I'll bring you my baby to hug. Like this.' "[10] More direct help in relating to a new baby is provided by Nancy Langstaff in a realistic book[11] illustrated with photographs that show Johnny and his mother with their new baby. *Big Sister, Little Sister*[12] describes the role of a girl who has a younger sister. With realistic illustrations, it tells how an older child can play with and care for a younger child so that both enjoy the activities.

Books which help preschool children to understand their relationships to other members of their family are a basis for understanding later the organization of a family, for instance, as it is presented in *My Family*.[13] But of more importance is the fact that these books, together with others about human relationships,[14] constitute the core of the curriculum for preschool children. Such books help the preschool child in feeling and understanding relationships to other people as he grows older.

BOOKS FOR SELF-CONFIDENCE

The preschool child can enjoy at each age level several books that help him appreciate his own worth. The child who is imaginative and follows *Harold and the Purple Crayon*[15] on adventures can identify with Harold as an important person. He also can enjoy *Tommy and Dee Dee*,[16] a book

---

[8] Charlotte Zolotow, *Big Brother* (New York: Harper & Row, Publishers, 1960).

[9] Ruth Krauss, *The Carrot Seed* (New York: Harper & Row, Publishers, 1945).

[10] Charlotte S. Zolotow, *Do You Know What I'll Do?* (New York: Harper & Row, Publishers, 1958).

[11] Nancy Langstaff, *A Tiny Baby for You* (New York: Brace & World, Inc., 1955).

[12] Charlotte Zolotow, *Big Sister and Little Sister* (New York: Harper & Row, Publishers, 1966).

[13] Miriam Schlein, *My Family* (New York: Abelard-Schuman, Limited, 1960).

[14] See the bibliography at the end of this chapter and Chapter 15.

[15] Crockett Johnson, *Harold and the Purple Crayon* (New York: Harper & Row, Publishers; Scholastic Book Services, 1955).

[16] Yen Liang, *Tommy and Dee Dee* (New York: Henry Z. Walck, Inc., 1953).

about two little boys each in a different social order. The two boys are much alike in many important ways, such as having parents who love and appreciate them.

Several children's books use the setting of the animal world to bring out the importance of young to their parents. *Which Horse Is William?*[17] develops the idea that Mrs. Short is always able to identify her son, William. One of the "surprise" books which H. A. Rey designed for "turning the page and finding out" is entitled *Where's My Baby?*[18] This delightful book shows mother animals and their babies, and concludes with a picture of a mother getting ready to read this very book to her children.

The four- and five-year-old children who identify with a pet animal that is well taken care of enjoy *The Pussy Who Went to the Moon.*[19] This book tells about an elderly couple who have a pussy that likes to wander. They rescue it not only from the top of a tree but even from the moon. Another book which combines the imaginative with a matter-of-fact portrayal of the importance of Emily is entitled *Emily Emerson's Moon.*[20] It tells about Emily, who finally gets a moon with the help of her devoted father.

The four-year-old child is often verbal about his self-importance. When Neal was four years old, he would sometimes contrast his ways with those of his mother or brother. When he was especially involved with developing an idea of the rights and privileges of being Neal, hardly a day passed without his saying, "I'm Neal!" This great discovery of the four-year-old, the importance of it and the excitement of it, and the possibility of catching it in words to show to other children and their parents and teachers, is a challenge to the authors of children's books.

BOOKS TO MEET THE NEED FOR ACHIEVEMENT

The theme of the hero who is able to overcome difficulty and gain recognition is found even in books for three-year-old children. A book with such a theme is *The Carrot Seed,*[21] which is also available in record form. *Down, Down the Mountain*[22] brings out the heroism of Hetty and Hank of the Blue Ridge Mountains who initiate a gardening project and valiantly continue to believe in its success. Their efforts are rewarded with a prize winning turnip that enables them to buy shoes.

Harold and the Purple Crayon[23] also portrays a hero overcoming diffi-

---

[17] Karla Kuskin, *Which Horse Is William?* (New York: Harper & Row, Publishers, 1959).

[18] H. A. Rey, *Where's My Baby?* (Boston: Houghton Mifflin Company, 1956).

[19] Jane Thayer, *The Pussy Who Went to the Moon* (New York: William Morrow & Co., Inc., 1960).

[20] Jean Merrill and Ronni Solbert, *Emily Emerson's Moon* (Boston: Little, Brown & Co., 1960).

[21] Krauss, op. cit.

[22] Ellis Credle, *Down, Down the Mountain* (New York: Thomas Nelson & Sons, 1961).

[23] Johnson, op. cit.

culty and controlling his environment. Harold gets into difficult situations with his purple crayon, but because he has control of the crayon he can stop, back up, or proceed as is necessary to solve his problem. This demonstration of the ability to create and control a world gives the child a vicarious experience in a role of achievement.

The Little Engine That Could[24] is the story of a little locomotive which presently solves its problem of getting over the mountain with its load of toys and goodies for the good little boys and girls who live on the other side. Preschool children, down through the years, have been delighted with this story of achievement. A child catches its positive thinking when he, too, says, "I think I can."

Several stories show a young child taking on a real responsibility that is important in the adult world. For instance, *The Very Little Girl*[25] was small, but presently became big enough to help with the baby. The book is a favorite with nursery children, especially with those who have a new baby at home to help take care of. A book that kindergarten children enjoy is *Country Snowplow,*[26] a book that tells how Tom was able to ride the snowplow and help guide it over roads no longer visible under new-fallen snow. The children identify with Tom and think of themselves as similarly able to contribute to activities important in the community. Vicariously they enjoy thinking of being responsible and of being admired, not only for themselves but also for what they can do.[27]

BOOKS FOR MEETING THE NEED TO BELONG TO A GROUP

A basic need of preschool children is to have a feeling of belonging to the preschool group as well as to the family. How their need for security within the family is met is interpreted for them through many picture books, but as yet few books interpret for them the human relationships within their preschool group. To date, books about a preschool group have focused attention on the new activities and new environment that the child encounters. *My Daddy's Visiting Our School Today*[28] carries the security of family relationships into the preschool group situation, and *Kathy's First School*[29] includes relationships between children. The book has not yet been written that captures the quality of feeling that develops between a child and his teacher and reassures the preschool child that there are other mothers besides his own who love him. Also not yet written is a book that brings out the beginnings of friendships which are to be found in the

[24] Watty Piper, *The Little Engine That Could* (New York: The Platt & Munk Co., Inc., 1954).

[25] Phyllis Krasilovsky, *The Very Little Girl* (Garden City: N.Y.: Doubleday & Company, Inc., 1953).

[26] Leonard Shortall, *Country Snowplow* (New York: William Morrow & Co., Inc., 1960).

[27] Lois Lenski, *Cowboy Small* (New York: Henry Z. Walck, Inc., 1949).

[28] Myra B. Brown, *My Daddy's Visiting Our School Today* (New York: Franklin Watts, Inc., 1961).

[29] Betty Katzoff, *Kathy's First School* (New York: Alfred A. Knopf, Inc., 1964).

preschool group. The abstract quality of *A Friend Is Someone Who Likes You*[30] is appropriate for older children. Could not a book be written to help three-year-old children become aware of friendship experiences within their nursery?

BOOKS TO MEET THE NEED FOR SAFETY

A child must not only *be* safe, he must also *feel* safe. The preschool child, going into first experiences outside the safety and security of his own

Cowboy Small rides again. (Courtesy of Long Beach Day Nursery and Mariam M. Cook, Long Beach, California.)

home, needs to have those early experiences free of fears, anxieties, and feelings of guilt. A picture-story book which contains words or pictures to provoke such feelings is not suitable for a nursery child and should be considered very carefully by a teacher of kindergarten. As a general rule, books that deal with elements that make for insecurity and fear should be left for school-age children, and should be introduced to them only as the children display readiness for handling such elements.

Several delightful picture books bring the preschool child an opportunity to think of situations which bring him the pleasure of safety and security.

[30] Joan Walsh Anglund, *A Friend Is Someone Who Likes You* (New York: Harcourt, Brace & World, Inc., 1958).

Bedtime for Frances[31] is a book that helps a three-year-old child in developing comfortable feelings with regard to bedtime. *Benjie's Blanket*[32] helps put into perspective the security toy that a young preschool child often carries with him as he ventures out into the world.

The older preschool child who is becoming aware of fears enjoys the story of *Terrible Terrifying Toby*[33] who frightened himself until he discovered he was looking in a mirror. Identifying with Toby, a child realizes that something frightening can happen to anyone, and can be a small matter in reality.

BOOKS FOR EXPERIENCE

The preschool child is at the doorway of the new and exciting world that opens to him outside his home, and also is finding his way into the new and fascinating dimensions that open to him as he continues to mature. Guides through these adventures, and means for putting them into perspective, are the picture books for preschool children. Outstanding current ones are listed at the end of each of Chapters 6 to 15.[34]

Examples of books that bring new ideas to preschool children are numerous. *Stories and Poems to Enjoy* by Frances Horwich,[35] for instance, bring many new ideas a few at a time to nursery children, and in terms of an everyday world which they understand. Such books introduce new labels for the child to use in talking about his experiences. They also present relationships which are new but understandable to the child. Sometimes they organize relationships as a child would not be able to organize them for himself.

Every preschool child is familiar with what mothers do, yet few if any four-year-old children would organize their ideas about mothers as they are presented in the book entitled *Mommies*.[36] Children thoroughly enjoy this book. Another delightful book for preschool children is *A Tree Is Nice*.[37] It helps a child in organizing his many pleasant experiences with trees and in appreciating them more completely.

SELECTING BOOKS IN TERMS OF NEEDS

The parent, the teacher, and the librarian who helps them select books should be able to identify one or two books which fit in with the interest or the need of a particular preschool child. This is not always easy, but it

[31] Russell Hoban, *Bedtime for Frances* (New York: Harper & Row, Publishers, 1960).

[32] Myra Berry Brown, *Benjie's Blanket* (New York: Franklin Watts, Inc., 1962).

[33] Crockett Johnson, *Terrible Terrifying Toby* (New York: Harper & Row, Publishers, 1957).

[34] Similar bibliographies of books to use with kindergarten children are given at the ends of Chaps. 6–15 in *The Kindergarten Teacher*, op. cit.

[35] Frances Horwich, *Stories and Poems to Enjoy* (Garden City, N.Y.: Doubleday & Company, Inc., n.d.).

[36] Lonnie C. Carton, *Mommies* (New York: Random House, 1960).

[37] Janice M. Udry, *A Tree Is Nice* (New York: Harper & Row, Publishers, 1956).

can usually be done by considering what basic needs of the child should be met.

The teacher of one preschool group, Mrs. MacKinnon, was looking forward to the arrival of a new girl, Yoko. After three and one half years as an orphan in Japan, Yoko was flying over to be adopted by an American family. She was going to belong to the same nursery group that her older brothers had enjoyed. Mrs. MacKinnon wanted to prepare the group for the arrival of a girl who would look different than they and would not speak their language.

When the teacher discussed her problem with the librarian, the librarian thought of two books: *Two Is a Team*[38] and *Home for a Bunny*.[39]

Mrs. MacKinnon thought that the concept of team play in the Beim book was better suited to children older than those in her group, but she selected and used the Brown book. It is a large book, and she could show it to the group as a whole. She could use it when they were talking about the little girl who was coming to her new home and to their nursery group.

The next year Mrs. MacKinnon was again talking with the librarian, this time about simple, realistic books appropriate to Yoko's language development. Although the librarian and Mrs. MacKinnon found the usual books for three-year-olds good choices, they were surprised that what became Yoko's favorite book was one that had been brought to the nursery group: *Baby Susan's Chicken*.[40] This is the story of a little chicken different in appearance from Nancy's and Bobby's chickens. It did not have shiny black feathers or beautiful brown feathers when it grew up, but it did something neither of the other chickens could do: it laid an egg.

Mrs. MacKinnon wondered if Yoko's choice of a story was related to a feeling of being different. Perhaps, the librarian suggested, Yoko found satisfaction in the idea that what a person does is more important than how he looks. A story about being different probably is a story which helps a child in his experiences with people of backgrounds different from his own.

The following year, when Yoko was in kindergarten, her mother asked the librarian about a book to help Yoko in thinking about differences in skin pigmentation. Yoko's mother recounted the following incident to the librarian:

(Yoko is playing near the sidewalk when Karen rides by on her tricycle and stops to talk.)
KAREN   You're brown.
(Yoko responds by pushing Karen over. Yoko's mother comes and picks up Karen, and then puts an arm around Yoko.)

[38] Jerrold and Lorraine Beim, *Two Is a Team* (New York: Harcourt, Brace & World, Inc., 1945).

[39] Margaret Wise Brown, *Home for a Bunny* (New York: Simon and Schuster, Inc., 1956).

[40] Jean Horton Berg, *Baby Susan's Chicken* (New York: Wonder Books, Inc., 1951).

MOTHER (*to Yoko*)   What happened?

YOKO   She said I'm brown.

MOTHER   Yes, you are a lovely shade of brown. (*Puts her arm beside Yoko's.*) In fact I think the sun has tanned your skin even darker than mine.

(*Bert, a blond six-year-old boy, joins the group.*)

BERT (*holding up his shirttail*)   See my tan.

MOTHER   Say, you're tanned too. (*to all the children*) You know, when we get tanned like that it means that we have been getting the sunshine that keeps us healthy.

The librarian, not able to suggest an appropriate book, concluded her conversation with Yoko's mother by saying, "Maybe one of these years someone will write the book we need about looking different."

Stories for Each Age Level

Stories should be selected not only in terms of the needs of preschool children, but also in terms of the interests and the maturity reached at each age level. Preschool children develop at a rapid rate in some respects, gradually in other respects. The teacher who wants to have books suitable for the children she teaches and the parent who wants to pace his child's development should look for books that are especially appropriate to a child at a particular age level.

STORIES FOR THE THREE-YEAR-OLD CHILD

In selecting books for the three-year-old child, the wise teacher takes into account a very important fact: at the age of three, a child is only at the threshold of abstraction. He must build a wide base of realistic experience and he must see relationships among these realistic experiences before he can go on to even the simplest abstraction. For instance, he needs both actual and vicarious experience with individual kittens and cats before he can enjoy generalized experiences with cats. As a nursery child he enjoys hearing about *Momo's Kittens*,[41] but he will probably be close to kindergarten age before he is likely to enjoy *Millions of Cats*.[42]

Hearing about the kind of everyday experiences he has had, the three-year-old child can put them into focus; hearing about experiences which he may not yet have had prepares him for widening his activities. Having understandable accounts read to him from books awakens his interest in books and stories. The child who attends a nursery group or visits the office of a pediatrician which has good books for preschool children profits from hearing them read and from looking at their clear illustrations.

The book interests characteristic of the mature three-year-old children

[41] Mitsu Yashima, *Momo's Kittens* (New York: The Viking Press, Inc., 1961).

[42] Wanda Gag, *Millions of Cats* (New York: Coward-McCann, Inc., 1938). A black and white film strip is also available.

who attended the nursery group affiliated with the Clinic of Child Development at Yale University are described by Gesell and Ilg as follows:

1. Increasing span of interest in listening to stories.
2. Can be held longer when stories are read to small groups.
3. Continued enjoyment of familiar experiences with repetition and more detail. . . .
4. Likes information about nature, transportation, etc., woven into story form. . . .
5. Likes imaginative stories based on real people and real animals, such as *Caps for Sale.*[43]
6. Enjoyment of riddles and guessing, such as *The Noisy Book.*[44]
7. Enjoys widening of horizon through information books. . . .
8. Makes relevant comments during stories, especially about materials or experiences at home.
9. Some insist on stories being retold and reread word-for-word without changes.
10. Likes to look at books and may "read" to others or explain pictures.[45]

The way that the three-year-old child thinks in concrete rather than abstract terms is observable in what he says. The following excerpt from a three-year-old's monologue shows associations that a mature child makes between a book and her experiences. Kimmy, age three and one half, picked up a book and turned its pages while she "read" as follows:

While he was there they wondered when their pop was going to come back. "When will our pop come back?" And they did have a horse. And everyday Connie ate so much honey she got sick. So every morning she went to the doctor. And they were so happy. They went out and got radishes for their mother. And their mother was going to make jam. And they said, "Thanks, mother." And Connie said, "Oh, mother we found a baby kitten." "Did you bring him home?" "Yes, in a pack of potatoes." Isn't that silly? I could hardly knock your block off if I was a clown. One day the birds runned around. And the squirrel started to crawl. And Kachy the wabbit chased one butterfly.
(*Singing*)   "Snow, snow, roe the doe.
           Hi, ho. Off we go."

STORIES FOR THE FOUR-YEAR-OLD CHILD

A good picture book which interests a three-year-old child also interests a four-year-old child, but for a shorter period. A four-year-old has more breadth of experience than a three-year-old, and is able to assimilate ideas more rapidly. He is ready for somewhat longer realistic stories. He is also eager for new experiences beyond those that he had as a three-year-old. His interest in stories widens until, as a mature four-year-old, his book interests

[43] E. Slobodkina, *Caps for Sale* (New York: William R. Scott, Inc., 1957).
[44] Margaret Wise Brown, *The Noisy Book* (New York: Harper & Row, Publishers, 1939).
[45] Arnold Gesell and Frances L. Ilg, *Child Development* (New York: Harper & Row, Publishers, 1949), pp. 211–212.

may be much the same as those of the four-year-old children studied by Gesell and Ilg:

1. Much more control in listening to stories in larger groups over longer periods.
2. High interest in words, creating stories with silly language and play on words.
3. Enjoyment of nonsense rhymes. . . .
4. High interest in poetry, especially rhyming.
5. Delight in the humorous in stories. . . .
6. Enjoys exaggeration, as in *Millions of Cats.*
7. Interest in alphabet books. . . .
8. Interest in stories telling the function and growth of things. . . .
9. Particularly enjoys information books answering his "Why?" about everything in the environment.
10. Awakening interest in religious books. . . .[46]

The four-year-old child continues to enlarge his understanding of real situations by enjoying longer stories and those which bring him more relationships than he could appreciate as a three-year-old child. *The Real Hole*[47] is typical of realistic stories that four-year-old children appreciate. They also gain a greater understanding of realistic stories by learning to contrast them with imaginative stories. They learn to differentiate between *real* and *pretend* and to cope with accounts that are "just a story." *Do Baby Bears Sit in Chairs?*[48] is a delightful book to help a four-year-old draw a distinction between fact and fancy.

STORIES FOR THE FIVE-YEAR-OLD CHILD[49]

As a five-year-old, a child continues to enlarge his understanding of the widening world in which he lives. He can reach out to ideas like those ably presented in *The Day We Saw the Sun Come Up,*[50] and he can linger over the pleasurable thought that *I'm Hiding.*[51] He can also venture far into the world of make-believe with *Magic-Boy,*[52] appreciate the reality of *Herman the Loser,*[53] and identify with Hetty and Hank of the Blue Ridge Mountains as he reads *Down, Down the Mountain.*[54] He has come a long way as a

[46] Ibid., pp. 234–235.

[47] Beverly Cleary, *The Real Hole* (New York: William Morrow & Co., Inc., 1960).

[48] Ethel and Leonard Kessler, *Do Baby Bears Sit in Chairs?* (New York: Doubleday & Company, Inc., 1961).

[49] Chapter 12 of *The Kindergarten Teacher,* op. cit., discusses such stories and suggests picture books especially suitable for five-year-old children.

[50] Alice Goudey, *The Day We Saw the Sun Come Up* (New York: Charles Scribner's Sons, 1961).

[51] Myra Livingstone, *I'm Hiding* (New York: Harcourt, Brace & World, Inc., 1961).

[52] Mike Thaler, *Magic Boy* (New York: Harper & Row, Publishers, 1961).

[53] Russell Hoban, *Herman the Loser* (New York: Harper & Row, Publishers, 1961).

[54] Ellis Credle, op. cit.

preschool child. At five he consolidates his learnings and widens his horizons so that he will be ready for new activity in first grade.

TEACHING ABOUT FACT AND FANCY

One of the objectives of the preschool teacher, especially the teacher of four- or five-year-old children, is to teach differentiation of what is real and what is imagined. She should be careful to label each story as a story, and to help the children in understanding that what a person makes up as a

Preparing to understand Pinocchio and Moby Dick at later times. (Courtesy of Jacksonville Schools and Florida State Department of Education, Tallahassee, Florida.)

story is what *could* happen—maybe. What actually *did* happen may be quite different. She can use *Lady Bird, Quickly*,[55] to illustrate her point.

That children learn ways in which people relate imaginings and reality is apparent in incidents such as the following. Ann, a four-and-a-half-year-old girl was putting together a puzzle in which a round piece representing a round balloon was missing. The teacher suggested to Ann that perhaps

[55] Juliet Kepes, *Lady Bird, Quickly* (Boston: Little, Brown & Co., 1964; "Your house is on fire" really meant the fireflies were visiting.)

the balloon had popped. Ann replied quite literally that a puzzle piece cannot pop.

Four-year-old Neal, whose father introduces imagination into many different situations, responded differently to an imaginative situation. When Neal was four years and three months old, his father told him that eating a hole in a slice of bread might make him sick. Neal promptly responded, "If you eat a hole, that won't make you sick. Daddy is just fooling. I will eat mine. That won't make me sick. I have a hole in mine."

When Neal was four years and seven months old, he told about pretending that olives are cranberries. He and other children in his Sunday school group picked up olives that had fallen from the olive tree in the churchyard. The next day Neal said, "You know what my Sunday school children call olives? 'Chili beans,' no—'cranberries.' Only my teacher's boy and I know they are really olives, but we like to pretend they are cranberries."

Sometimes parents and teachers who enjoy such delightful imagining as the Santa Claus legend are loath to tell children that Santa Claus is an imaginary character, or that the Easter Bunny story is only a story. If a child asks, "How big is the Easter Bunny?" the adult has an opportunity for helping him understand the difference between story and fact. She can say, "The Easter Bunny is as big as you, or any other storyteller, wants to make him." Then she can help the child make up an Easter Bunny story. He has the fun of having an Easter Bunny made just the way he wants him, one that does just what he wants an Easter Bunny to do. In this way the child can experience the thrill of storytelling and gain satisfaction in controlling the story.

One nursery teacher described her experience in telling a four-and-a-half year-old boy that the Easter Bunny legend is only a story.

Tommy asked me at great length about the Easter Bunny. I told him it was a delightful legend and game that we make for our children. I hated, in a way, to be the one to dissipate his faith in the story. But ten minutes later it appeared that he had accepted only what he wanted to believe. He said, "But how big is the Easter Bunny?"

STORIES INAPPROPRIATE TO PRESCHOOL AGE LEVELS

When a child is three, he needs realistic books which are suitable for a child of his age. When he is four or five, he needs books that are more sophisticated and more dramatic, books suitable for his advancing age. The books which he reads at these early ages prepare him step by step for enjoying books for older children. But if he is given books beyond his age level, he will be disinterested, will resort to other activities, or will otherwise express rejection of the unsuitable books. If the secure relationship of reading stories is highly important to him, he may suffer through the unsuitable books and keep his dislike inside himself. Then his inability to assimilate the stories may express itself in dreams, in hiding the book, or in some other obscure way.

When children are highly verbal and feel free to express their feelings, their questions are a cue to the unsuitability of certain stories. *Epaminondas and His Auntie,*[56] is a troublesome story to the preschool child who asks, "Why didn't his mommy help him better?" Identifying with Epaminondas, the small child is as bewildered as he was. *The 500 Hats of Bartholomew Cubbins,*[57] an enchanting story for older children, is an unhappy story for the nursery child, who interprets it realistically and is as uncomfortable as Bartholomew Cubbins. Such a book should be saved until children have matured to the point of appreciating its humor. An unfortunate reading of the story at an early age may interfere with a child's enjoyment of it later.

The following summary lists desirable and undesirable elements in books for nursery and kindergarten children.

ELEMENTS DESIRABLE IN BOOKS FOR PRESCHOOL CHILDREN	RELATED FACTS ABOUT PRESCHOOL CHILDREN	ELEMENTS TO BE AVOIDED IN BOOKS FOR PRESCHOOL CHILDREN
Happiness Beginnings of plot and dramatic action	A child should know a friendly, helpful world as a basis for exploring difficulties later.	Unhappiness Folk tales which have suspense and much drama
One main character understandable to a preschool child	A child gradually increases the number of units he can handle at one time.	Several important characters
Understandable ideas with a small proportion of new ideas	As a three-year-old, a child moves into the beginnings of abstract thinking.	Abstract or other concepts outside the child's experience, in any large number
Short length	A child learns to enjoy listening for an increasing length of time.	A long story such as a series of four or more incidents not closely related
A small number of new words explainable to the preschool child	The vocabulary of a child increases each year.	A large number of unfamiliar words
Detail such as a child of a particular age is apt to notice	A child becomes acquainted with things as wholes and builds on ideas about their details.	Books with considerable detail beyond that which a child notices
Books that teach only desirable attitudes and ideas	Racial prejudice, autocratic ways, and other undesirable attitudes are easily absorbed at preschool ages.	Books which have to do with undesirable behavior
Number-concepts at the age level of the child	At three, a child understands *three* at four, *four*.	Books with number concepts beyond the age level of the child

[56] Sara Cone Bryant, *Epaminondas and His Auntie* (Boston: Houghton Mifflin Company, 1938).
[57] Theodore Seuss Geisel, *The 500 Hats of Bartholomew Cubbins* (Eau Claire, Wis.: E. M. Hale and Company, 1938).

Illustrations for Preschool Children

Illustrations for stories should parallel the development of children in much the same way that the stories do. The child needs pictures as well as stories to further his development. A three-year-old is becoming aware that the real world around him is described in books. He hears stories about familiar, homey happenings. At the same time, he enjoys the real-

A child likes to look at a book by himself too. (Courtesy of Long Beach Parent Nursery Schools and Mariam M. Cook, Long Beach, California.)

istic, happy pictures which remind him of other happenings like those in the story. This trust in the veracity of pictures enables the older preschool child to depend on them to show him the world beyond his familiar neighborhood.

As the preschool child becomes ready to branch out into the world of imagination, he enjoys pictures by artists such as Crockett Johnson, who can pilot his pretending skillfully. In *Harold and the Purple Crayon,*[58]

[58] Johnson, op. cit.

the child has the simplicity of a single color and of line drawings to guide, but not interfere with, his imagining. He will be much older before he can enjoy the pictures of a book such as *Why?—Because*.[59]

HELPING CHILDREN TO "READ" PICTURES

The nursery child learns to "read" pictures. He often needs help with some of these learnings. He needs to be told that the lady in the picture does have a second arm even though the picture shows only one. If the text mentions two chickens but the picture shows only one of them, he needs to be told that there is still a second chicken. Of course he likes to count each of the baby ducks which Robert McCloskey skillfully puts into the realistic and beautiful pictures in *Make Way for Ducklings*,[60] and to feel that he can depend on the pictures to show him what happened.

When Neal was four years and five months old, his older brother helped him learn one of the conventions about pictures that are taken for granted by adults but which must be taught to preschool children. As the two boys looked through a comic book together, Neal learned that a comic book shows the same character in each of several pictures.

NEAL (*pointing to two pictures in the comic book*) How come he is running and he is looking?

STANLEY They are both the same.

NEAL That means this is this guy?

STANLEY Yes.

SELECTING PICTURES APPROPRIATE TO PRESCHOOL CHILDREN

As more becomes known about how preschool children react at each age level to different kinds of pictures, it should be possible to have picture books which are highly appropriate for them. Until more elaborate studies are made, the experience of teachers and parents with small groups and individuals of preschool age should be a basis for avoiding the selection of pictures which are not suitable to a sensitive preschool child.

One child received *Black and White*[61] as a gift when he was three years old. As his mother read it to him, he reacted sharply to the stark contrast between the white figures and the black backgrounds. Tied into this reaction was his introduction to the word *fire* in connection with a picture showing a little fire of handwarming size.

When his mother and his nursery school teacher became aware of his fear of *fire,* they attempted to provide him with many pleasant and interesting experiences with fire. Yet his fear continued, and the only clue to its basis was that he had seen *fire* in a book. Both his mother and his

---

[59] Jo Ann Stover, *Why?—Because* (New York: David McKay & Co., Inc., 1961).
[60] Robert McCloskey, *Make Way for Ducklings* (New York: The Viking Press, Inc., 1941).
[61] Margaret Wise Brown, *Black and White* (New York: Harper & Row, Publishers, 1944).

teacher read to him pleasant books for small children dealing with fire but made little impression on his problem.

Years later, when the boy was in secondary school, he found the book *Black* and *White* among his childhood things. "Here is the book that made me afraid of fire," he said. When his mother asked him to draw what he had been afraid of, he drew a simple, very small, childlike picture that was on contrast to the detailed and elaborate drawing he was then doing. The relation of his simple picture to those in the book was readily apparent.

Many such accounts of individual and group reactions to different kinds of illustrations should be collected and analyzed as a means of determining what is desirable in the way of illustrations for picture books for preschool children. Until such research findings are available, teachers and parents may well extend what is known about story interests of the children at each age level. They may surmise, for instance, that children who are three years old should have first books which have pictures of things colored as they actually are colored. The pictures should be realistic in their general outlines and be free of confusing detail. Children who are four and five years old can branch out gradually into the world of imagination with pictures that have more details, that show what is possible but not probable, that have colors which might but usually do not occur.

Books to Avoid

Publishers, authors, and illustrators annually provide so many excellent books for preschool children that it is not necessary for a parent or a teacher to select a book that she questions using. Even cutting a long story to make it suitable for younger children is not often necessary, now. But it is still necessary to eliminate the snarling big bad wolf which is apt to be frightening to the young child, although fascinating to older children. Eliminating books that may inspire fear in nursery children is a step towards helping them develop favorable reactions toward books. A book which causes a child to have bad dreams or a book which a child rejects should be put aside in favor of the many delightful books which he can enjoy at his age level.

Matching Pictures and Story

To encourage better illustrations in children's books, the Caldecott Medal is awarded annually "for the most distinguished American picture book for children." Since the first award was made in 1938, there has been increasing awareness of the importance of artistic quality, and of the compatibility of text and illustration. In 1962 the award was won by *The Snowy Day,*[62] a book for younger children by Ezra Jack Keats. This book, illustrated with simple pictures in gently contrasting colors, recounts in simple words the adventures of Peter and a friend playing in the snow.

[62] Ezra Jack Keats, *The Snowy Day* (New York: The Viking Press, Inc., 1962).

Many books for preschool children are written and illustrated by the same person. In this way text and pictures are unified. *Umbrella,*[63] by Taro Yashima, presents both in words and pictures a preschool child waiting to use her rainy-day things. Having as author and illustrator one and the same person usually avoids a manuscript written for children of one age level with illustrations designed for children of another; for instance, the discrepancy between text about "your very own mommy" and illustrations presented with the sophistication of contrasting purple and yellow, black and white; or the discrepancy between text gently contrasting baby with adult animals and illustrations boldly emphasizing the power and fierceness of full-grown animals.

SELECTING A PRESCHOOL BOOK

The preschool teacher should take into account both illustrations and story in selecting a picture book to use with a particular group of children. For example, a teacher of a group of four-year-old children sought the help of a children's librarian in finding books to increase the sensitivity of the children to the sounds in their environment. She had used the books of Margaret Wise Brown and the recordings devised to accompany them. Now she wondered if current books for preschool children had anything further to offer.

The librarian immediately thought of two books, and helped the teacher find them. They were *The Listening Walk*[64] and *Do You Hear What I Hear?*[65]

With the two books in her hand, the teacher now thought about her group of four-year-old children and wondered whether either, neither, or both of the books were suitable for them. Here are some of her thoughts as she looked through first one book and then the other.

About *The Listening Walk:*
- Are the pictures out of the everyday life of the children? Do the people in the pictures look like people the children feel at home with?[66] Can I show the pictures to the children easily as I read?
- Are the ideas of the book understandable to four-year-old children? Can the children participate in the telling and learn to imitate sounds? Does the book help the children to listen for new sounds? If the telling is long, can I cut it short if I need to do so?

[63] Taro Yashima, *Umbrella* (New York: The Viking Press, Inc., 1958).
[64] Paul Showers, *The Listening Walk* (New York: Thomas Y. Crowell Company, 1961).
[65] Helen Borten, *Do You Hear What I Hear?* (New York: Abelard-Schuman, Limited, 1960; Eau Claire, Wis.: E. M. Hale & Co., 1966).
[66] Marilyn Jasik, "A Look at Black Faces in Children's Picture Books, *Young Children,* Vol. 24, No. 1, pp. 43–54 (October, 1968). This article contains two bibliographies of "Black Faces in Children's Picture Books."

About *Do You Hear What I Hear?*

● Will the children like the illustrations? Is the intensity of contrast between the black and bright yellow apt to frighten a sensitive child like Ronny? Will the green snake be frightening?

● Will the children understand all but a few of the ideas presented? "Mysterious as a secret," "haunting as a church bell," "combination of sounds in rhythm," "symphony of sound"—are these phrases incidental to the story or important to it? Is the level of abstraction beyond four-year-old children? Can I explain the abstract concepts simply, or omit them, without spoiling the story?

The teacher thanked the librarian for her help and checked out both books. She planned to use *The Listening Walk* with her four-year-old group, and to show the other book to the kindergarten teacher at her preschool center.

LIBRARY STORY HOURS

Librarians are increasingly sensitive to the importance of helping children enjoy books and the library at an early age. In many instances, children's librarians are familiar with the picture books for preschool children and offer a series of story hours especially for preschool children while their older brothers and sisters are in school. The children who attend the story hours enjoy hearing familiar stories with familiar illustrations, and enjoy getting acquainted with new ones, too. Their mothers not only extend their acquaintance with stories and illustrations suitable for their children, they also find out about techniques which enhance their own storytelling. A children's librarian points out values of a story hour for preschool children:

The children are learning many things by coming together in the library. They are learning to concentrate and how to behave in a group. They are being gently led to conform to accepted library behavior such as no running and playing tag in the Children's Room, and most important, they are becoming small library users. For at the tender age of three they are choosing their own books and they can be very vocal in their likes and dislikes too. By making them book lovers first, they are becoming library users of the future. . . . It seems that there has been a long awaited need for some specialized library service to these potential young library borrowers.[67]

Many libraries like to have organized groups of preschool children visit them and enjoy a special story hour in the library. This kind of visit is another way to acquaint preschool children with the library as well as with children's books. If their schedules permit, children's librarians are also

[67] Beth Caples, "Story Hour for the Three- to Five-Year-Old" (Baltimore, Md.: Enoch Pratt Free Library, April, 1958).

glad to visit children's and parents' groups as a means of making them familiar with suitable books.

Presenting Stories to Preschool Children

In presenting a story to a preschool child or a group of preschool children, an adult should communicate with them as completely as possible. She should talk directly with the children, going from conversation into telling a story. To enrich the telling, she can pantomime action, show pictures on a flannelboard, or use a puppet. She can "read" a picture book, showing each picture as she reads. But in each of these situations she should be so familiar with the story that she and the children have excellent rapport with each other and communication is maximized. Frequently she should let the children dramatize one of their favorite stories.

At the same time, the storyteller should avoid overexpectations about the attention of her audience and should keep in mind that the preschool child is learning to listen to stories. His learning is a gradual process. A child beginning to listen to stories may do well to hear one short story all the way through. A year or two later he may enjoy hearing two, even three stories at one time. An understanding teacher described the behavior of a three-year-old boy in the story group situation as follows:

In our story circle Bobby is easily distracted by any horseplay in his vicinity and sometimes promotes such shenanigans himself. He'll burst in with commentary whenever the spirit moves him. Or he will leave us flat for more interesting business outdoors. I am unable yet to stem the flow of his chatter at story time, and sometimes in the interest of moving onto the next episode, I tenderly ask Bobby if he would like to play outside. Sometimes he does and often he doesn't. He just feels like talking to someone, I think.

But a preschool group has Allisons as well as Bobby and its teacher should encourage the Allisons by trying to make each story an experience in vicarious living, sufficiently vivid that its thought spills over into children's words, or overt action, or expressions in art media.

When Allison's teacher finished reading a story about a little girl who needed a star for her Christmas tree, Allison, who was three-going-on-four, was completely sympathetic toward the heroine. "I'll give her a star," she said. "Good," said the teacher, "she will like that." Allison went to the science corner of the room, got a chair, and climbed up until she could reach the fishnet decoration. From it she extracted the starfish. Then she climbed down and ran across to the library table on which the teacher had laid the story book. Carefully Allison laid the starfish on top of the book. With a satisfied glance at her completed project, she went on to another activity.

Such spontaneous movement from story to action is apt to occur in the family or in the preschool group which moves from story to dramatic play and from dramatic play, conversation, or happening to a story. A good preschool group has a teacher who is apt at any point to be reminded of a story, and has dramatic play in keeping with the stories she has been reading.

One teacher of a Sunday school group of five-year-old children was pleased with the attentive way in which the group listened to *The Dead Bird.*[68] When the children went outdoors to play, they too found a dead bird. With Jane as their leader, they decided to dig a hole and bury the bird. Quietly they stood around the open grave while Jane led them in a short but suitable service modeled on what she had heard in church. As the body went into the grave, she concluded the service by saying, "Praise God, the Father, the Son, and here it goes!"

READING A STORY

After a teacher has selected a story appropriate for her group of children, she should read and reread it until she feels that she knows the story well enough to read it to the children in much the same way that she talks with them. In fact, if she is just beginning to read stories to a new group of three-year-old children, she should be especially careful to speak naturally as she reads to them. She can use a few simple gestures, as she does in talking. But neither the gestures nor the inflections of her voice should be distracting. As the children become accustomed to hearing stories, she will be able to introduce more voice inflections into her reading. She can use slow, measured words as the elephant walks heavily; fast, light words with the patter of the mouse's feet; her voice can slow down as the train pulls into the station. But she should avoid the inflections, the facial expressions, and the gestures that the reader uses for elementary school children who enjoy suspense and other dramatic situations.

The principal objective of the reader should be to have the children learn to like stories. She can help them in being comfortable on the rug and in seeing the pictures. As she reads she can help them in being attentive so that they will be more apt to understand the story and be interested in it. If a child's interest wanders, she might regain it by saying, "And then, Joan, the chipmunk came right up to the log." Or she may personalize the story by saying, "The birthday cake looked just like the one we had for Jimmy's birthday last week." Whenever she thinks it appropriate, she should encourage the children in helping with the story by putting in the sound effects. If the children's participation reaches the point of detracting from the story, the reader might bring the children back to their role of listeners by saying, "Yes, that's the way it was. But now something else is going to happen. Listen. . . ."

[68] Margaret Wise Brown, *The Dead Bird* (New York: Young Scott Books, 1958).

One skillful preschool teacher describes how she read stories and noted the reaction of children to them as follows:

This morning I chose two books because they have "child appeal"—not too many words, good illustrations, and some dramatic activity so that the children can feel that part of the story or act it out. The first book was about *The Choo Choo Train.* I made my voice deep for the engine, and the children and I made the sounds for the little black engine as it began to huff and puff and call out: "Choo." Then in sequence each yellow, blue, or green car called out to the engine: "Take me with you!" Each time, the engine said in a deep voice: "Hook on."

At the very end of the train was the little red caboose. I paused without saying the word *caboose,* and let the children say it as I pointed to its picture. The children continued filling in words as I continued the story: "The little train went over a *bridge;* through a *tunnel;* up a big high *hill;* past a great big *city;* and right back to where it started."

After the story seemed to be a perfect time to add music, so we sang "The Train Song" and "The Little Red Caboose." I sang them and did the motions while the children all joined in with the rhythms and some of the words. We sang loudly at first, as if the train were close, right in the station. The next time we sang very softly because the train was going far away from us down the track. In this way I set the stage for the next book, *The Quiet Book.*

For the first ten pages, with only two lines on each page, the children joined in, making the various animal and toy sounds as I pointed to the pictures: quack like a duck; roar like a lion; whistle like a boat, bang like a gun, and so on. The last ten pages are quiet things such as flowers growing; stars twinkling in the night, smoke curling out of sight, and finally *you,* when you're sleeping in bed.

I said, "I like to go to bed. Do you?" Most of the children said they like to go to bed too. Steve said, "I cry when I go to bed." When I asked him, "Why do you cry, Steve?" he said, "It's ghostly when Mommy shuts the door." This conversation was important, not only because Steve expressed his fears, but also because he volunteered a remark for the first time. From then on he has talked more and joined in group play. I spoke to his mother about his fear and she has been leaving his door open with a hall light on. It is a very satisfying experience to be able to help a child.

After children are familiar with a story, they like to have it read again in such a way that they can participate in telling the story. If the reader wonders what is going to happen next, the children are delighted to tell her. The four- and five-year-old children become so skillful in telling the story that they need little more than the introduction, the succession of pictures, and an occasional reminder such as, "I wonder what the little dog will do now?" in order to tell the entire story.

SIZE OF GROUP

A parent or anyone else using picture books with only one or two children at a time need not be concerned about the size of the book. She can use a large, middle-sized, or small book. Several small books are especially appropriate for preschool children; for instance *The Little Book,*[69] with its simple story about the little girl who greets each of several different animals and then plays with the little boy whom she meets. The dramatic action of *The Little Dog*[70] and the imaginative story of the *Magic Boy*[71] are appreciated by older preschool children who are ready for each of them. *Big Brother*[72] is appreciated by younger children in a family with older brothers who tease.

However, the teacher of a preschool group needs to use books appropriate to the size of the group with which she is working. She should keep on hand small books to use with a child or two, and should encourage participating students and mother assistants in reading them, especially to children with a particular interest that could be served by the book. The teacher should also have a collection of books whose pictures can easily be seen by a large group of children gathered together around her on the rug. Several series of large books include books especially suitable for preschool groups.[73] Furthermore, publishers of children's books sometimes offer large-size books suitable for kindergarten as well as primary grades; for instance, *Madeline.*[74]

DRAMATIZING A STORY

When a group of preschool children is familiar with a story, the children like to participate in telling it with pantomime. As the teacher tells the story, the children who have been selected that morning for each part act out the story. Children who are not "on stage" are the audience for the performance. Having suitable properties enhances the performance.

One parent-cooperative nursery group of three- and four-year-old children enjoyed acting out *Caps for Sale.*[75] The mothers cooperated in the project by providing a cap for each child and by making other properties which they thought might enhance the fun of presenting the story. The play was staged on the playground, with the climbing apparatus serving as the tree into which the monkeys climbed. The part of the cap salesman was played at first by an adult, while the children developed their roles as monkeys. Later, one of the older children played the part of the cap salesman. In each practice session, the teacher served as reader and director.

At the start of the year the teacher can encourage the beginnings of dramatic expression in a group of three-year-old children by using a book

---

[69] Beatrice S. de Regniers, *The Little Book* (New York: Henry Z. Walck, Inc., 1961).

[70] Denise and Alain Trez, *The Little Dog* (New York: Harcourt, Brace & World, Inc., 1961). This is also available in Spanish as *El Perrito.*

[71] Mike Thaler, *Magic Boy* (New York: Harper & Row, Publishers, 1961).

[72] Charlotte Zolotow, *Big Brother,* op. cit.

[73] For instance, The Great Big Book series (Western Publishing Co., Inc., Racine, Wisconsin) includes *Baby Farm Animals.*

[74] Ludwig Bemelmans, *Madeline* (New York: The Viking Press, Inc., 1939).

[75] Esphyr Slobodkina, *Caps for Sale* (New York: William R. Scott, Inc., 1957). Both a film strip and a movie are available.

such as *Do You Move as I Do?*[76] Later in the year, the children will enjoy dramatizing a scene such as that presented in the story of *Theodore Turtle.*[77] As each child has a turn trying to help Theodore Turtle get off his back, he gains a satisfying relationship to the story.

Four-year-old children who enjoy dramatic play much of the time are enthusiastic about showing each other how a story goes. At Christmas time a group that has come to know *The Little Fir Tree*[78] likes to act it out. In fact, in each season the children like to act out the activities appropriate to that season. *The Snowy Day,*[79] *Mud! Mud! Mud!,*[80] and *On a Summer's Day*[81] are guides to this kind of dramatization.

Many teachers feel that nursery rhymes and nursery stories are an essential part of the cultural heritage to be taught to preschool children. Dramatizing "Jack and Jill,"[82] and "The Three Bears," and other such simple folk tales is fun for kindergarten children.

Dramatizing a story is a creative activity. The dramatic presentation is kept within the channel of the original story; properties may vary from performance to performance, and the interpretation of a particular role is whatever each performer makes it. With preschool children, the teacher structures the presentation as she guides the children in their roles. A first attempt to dramatize a story should be very close to the story as read. It should include spontaneous dramatic play situations that the teacher has observed, and should introduce other situations at a comparable level of maturity. It should at all times be a happy experience, and no standards of performance should interfere with the children's feeling of success in their roles.

USING THE FLANNELBOARD

The flannelboard is as useful in telling stories as it is in teaching science concepts or other ideas. It is equally useful with three-, four-, or five-year-old children. The length and complexity of the story increases with the increase in age of the children.

One story for a teacher to work out on her flannelboard is that of Kitty Whiskers, a kitten who found out what food was best for him by trying the foods of other animals. The teacher prepares in advance the pictures needed for the story: a kitten, a pig, apples, a squirrel, nuts, a rabbit, carrots, and a bowl of milk. On the back of each picture she puts strips of

---

[76]Helen Borten, *Do You Move as I Do?* (Eau Claire, Wis.: E. M. Hale & Co., 1966).

[77]Ellen MacGregor, *Theodore Turtle* (New York: McGraw-Hill Book Co., 1954).

[78]Margaret Wise Brown, *The Little Fir Tree* (New York: Thomas Y. Crowell, Company, 1954).

[79]Keats, *The Snowy Day,* op. cit.

[80]Leonore Klein, *Mud! Mud! Mud!* (New York: Alfred A. Knopf, Inc., 1962).

[81]Lois Lenski, *On a Summer's Day* (New York: Henry Z. Walck, Inc., 1953).

[82]Marguerite De Angeli, *Book of Nursery and Mother Goose Rhymes* (Garden City, N.Y.: Doubleday & Company, Inc., 1954).

sandpaper to make the picture stick to the flannelboard. She also makes an apple tree and another tree to use as the setting for the story.

With the flannelboard set up and a picture given to each child, the teacher explains to the children what they will do. As she tells the story, each child listens for her to mention the picture he has. When she does he takes it up to the flannelboard and presses it onto the board. He goes back to where he is sitting and listens to the rest of the story.

When the children are comfortable and ready to listen, the teacher begins to tell the story: "Kitty Whiskers is a little kitten, a very hungry little kitten. . . ." Often the teacher interrupts the story to remind a child what he is to do: "Who has the kitten?"

When the kitten is in place, the teacher continues. "Here is Kitty Whiskers, a hungry kitten who is looking for some food. He looks all around under the apple tree— "Who has the apple tree?" When the apple tree is in place, the teacher continues, "Under the apple tree he finds Mr. Pig. . . ." Sometimes the teacher has to remind the children to sit back until it is time for each to put his piece on the board.

Kitty Whiskers finds that the apple Mr. Pig considers so juicy and delicious is too sour; the nuts Mr. Squirrel likes, too hard; the carrots Mr. Rabbit enjoys, too tough. But the bowl of milk is just right for him. With the bowl of milk in place on the flannelboard, the children and their teacher conclude the story with "And he wasn't hungry any more."

TEACHING HUMOR

Preschool children need help in learning what is to be thought humorous. The teacher who makes a point of showing them the humor in a picture of a monkey reading a book can expect to hear a conversation such as one that took place between Neal and Ronnie.

NEAL (*looking at the picture of a monkey reading a book*)   A monkey can't read!

RONNIE (*also looking at the picture, and laughing*)   Yeah, a monkey can't read and he was reading!

At Easter time, one nursery teacher taught her children an amusing song about "I had a little bunny with some jelly-bean shoes." She sang it to the tune of "Buffalo gal, won't you come out tonight?" and repeated a sentence throughout the tune. After singing about "My doggy caught the bunny with the jelly-bean shoes" and "My doggy kissed the bunny with the jelly-bean shoes," she concluded the song with "My doggy ate the bunny with the jelly-bean shoes." When she asked, "Why did the doggy eat the bunny?" the children laughed and chuckled with her about the bunny being a cooky.

Each preschool teacher should select stories which she considers amusing and thinks she can use to show amusing situations to children. Stories that have an element of surprise are usually a good kind to select. A teacher can try reading such stories as *Where's Andy?*[83] and *Edward and the Boxes,*[84] anticipating, then laughing at the amusing situations, and explaining to the children the amusing factor in each of them. She may say, for instance, "Now here comes a funny part. . . . Isn't that funny! His mother thinks the box is empty, but it isn't. Out jumps a frog! What would you do? You'd laugh, just the way Edward's mother did."

PRESENTING POETRY

The adult who is eager to introduce the small child to the realm of poetry is often discouraged by the brevity of the child's interest, and his failure to react to poems selected for him. Actually, the adult who has observed such disinterest is in a favorable situation for learning to select those poems of genuine interest to a preschool child—the brief poems within his world of action and concrete experience.

The adult who picks up a book of poems for children must be prepared to pass over the pages involving abstractions beyond those of nursery children. In the collection titled *Laughing Time,*[85] for instance, "The King of Hearts," accompanied by a picture of a king laughing is probably worth trying out on children who use hearts on Valentine's Day and can learn what a king is. "Laughing Time," the next poem in the book, may have a couplet or two which can be related to the experience of the children; for instance,

> It was laughing time, and the tall giraffe
> Lifted his head, and began to laugh:
> Ha! Ha! Ha! Ha!

may be useful if the children are going to the zoo. The adult who knows that rules are of interest to five-year-old children, but that *law* is a concept built up after experience with rules, probably will postpone using "It's certainly not against the law." "Why" may also be a poem for more mature children. "Hats," with the help of illustrative hats that are "round or square or tall or flat" is comprehensible to the four-year-old child who knows from his experience that "people love to wear hats."

Leafing on through this poem collection, the adult finds the brief poem, "The Mirror," and plans to use it with a child to enlarge and enrich his experience with a mirror.

Most of the poems, however should be put aside until the child is older. The wealth of implied and actual comparisons that enrich poetry are enjoyed when a child has greater maturity. However, the simple and brief

---

[83] Jane Thayer, op. cit.

[84] Dorothy Marino, *Edward and the Boxes* (Philadelphia: J. B. Lippincott Co., 1957).

[85] William Jay Smith, *Laughing Time* (Boston: Little, Brown & Co., 1955).

beginnings of poetic expression and poetic comparison[86] may be presented vividly and enjoyably to the nursery child as an integral part of his experience with the world around him.

The mother of a gifted child describes the benefits of incidental poetry as follows:

I have made no effort to teach my little girl, Meredy, to memorize poems, but there is a stick-to-it-iveness about poetical expression that holds on to the mind. At a tender age, Meredy said, unprompted:

> "Little Jack Horner sat in the corner,
> Eating his Christmas tree."

And I was proud. I contend that a slight misquote often lends freshness to well-worn phrases. She improved on "Mary had a little lamb," too, by saying: "It made the children laugh and play with their toys . . . ." And she censored Wee Willie Winkie as "Naughty Wee Willie Winkie" for rapping at the windows and waking up the babies.

So many poems and jingles have become part of everyday life. We say "Rain, rain, go away," and we invent games, such as jumping over an improvised candlestick, as did our friend Nimble Jack. Meredy, age three, thought she should teach our baby, age eleven months, to go in a circle to "Ring Around the Rosy" and finish with all-tumble-down.

There are numerous valuable byproducts of teaching poetry to children. New words are easily remembered if they are learned in verse. Poetry is a tremendous vocabulary builder, perhaps because it is a colorful kind of expression. Terms like *scalawag, topsy-turvy, chatter-chin,* or *jig, jog, and jump,* for example, have come from poems into common and appropriate use. Poetry seems to prompt a euphonious kind of terminology, too. Meredy's doll has the original and rhythmical name, "Heggity-Dug," which is a variation on the expression *fluggity dug,* quoted from a jingle her daddy recites.

Early tunes are frequently invented to known rhymes. And, of course, rhythmical meter finds a ready response in very young children. My baby smiles and listens attentively to the poems I recite. The vocabulary is beyond her, but not the rhythm and poetical expression.

Meredy's recognition of letters of the alphabet has been incidental to reading of poems based on the letters of the alphabet. A is for *Alice,* but we see A in many other places, too. A little snake is an *S* and it stands for Suzy. The counting rhymes also brought the number concept without any explanatory remarks from me.

These early years are indeed the time to introduce poetry. In my own experience I remember that one of the earlist philosophical ideas came to me by way of poetry:

> "The world is so full of a number of things,
> I'm sure we should all be as happy as kings."

---

[86] Richard Lewis, ed. *In a Spring Garden* (New York: The Dial Press, 1965). This includes haiku within the experience of a preschool child.

Working early on the child mind will make it fertile ground for great ideas, poetically expressed.

The four-year-old child who is greatly attuned to the sounds of words likes to create his own alliteration and rhymes. He likes to talk about "cereal—bereal—mereal—dereal—," repeating his play on words for any appreciative audience. In one nursery group of three-year-old children, the teacher helped the children in creating their own action play, a poem:

> Turn the handle;
> Open the door;
> And people will come
> And walk on the floor.

Indeed poetry has an important place in the preschool group. Bits of rhyme and brief poetic couplets punctuate the day of the preschool child delightfully.

Situations for Discussion

A preschool teacher is apt to find herself in situations similar to the four described here. As you think of what to do in each situation, consider whether each course of action suggested is desirable, or not. Use points brought out in the chapter as well as ideas from your own experience to justify your views. Suggest alternative courses of action to supplement those given.

SITUATION 1   You are selecting books to use with your group of preschool children. You should keep in mind the importance of

- Beauty in illustrations.
- Beauty in the sound patterns of words.
- Age level as it relates to content.
- Age level in relation to words used.
- Human relationships.

SITUATION 2   As director of a nursery, you are asking each teacher to list new books to be considered for purchase. You suggest that they include

- Books recommended by a children's librarian as "outstanding children's books."
- Two or three books of poetry.
- Books from those listed at the end of this chapter.
- Well-known folk tales such as "Hansel and Gretel."
- Caldecott Medal books.

SITUATION 3   In May you visit the local library to ask the librarian about current books to use with preschool children. She shows you the April issue of the American Library Association Bulletin with its list of "Notable Children's Books" for the year. Checking over the list, you should consider books

- Written by an author of books your children enjoy.
- Illustrated by an artist who has illustrated books your children like.

- Obtained by the library for its collection.
- With titles that have simple and familiar words like those the children use.
- Recommended for the age level you teach.

SITUATION 4 Among books outgrown by families with older children, you find one entitled *A Day with Daddy*. Written by a well-known author of children's books, it is illustrated with photographs, and is published by a company of good reputation. The book deals with Daddy, rather than Mother, in the role of homemaker—putting his child to bed, helping him with breakfast in the morning. You wonder whether or not to use the book in the parent-cooperative nursery. You should

- Keep the books for individual, but not group use.
- Show the book to mothers and get their recommendation about using it.
- Ask other preschool teachers whether they use the book.
- Ask the children's librarian if the book is recommended.
- Find another book about the role of daddy.

Current Books for Preschool Children

Association for Childhood Education International. *Bibliography of Books for Children.* Washington, D.C.: Association for Childhood Education International, 1968.

BAUM, ARLINE and JOSEPH. *Know What? No, What?* New York: Parents Magazine Press, 1964. [From apple tree to Christmas tree, and other imaginings.]

BROWN, MARGARET WISE. *The Dead Bird.* New York: William R. Scott, Inc., 1958. A childhood experience recounted beautifully. [*The Little Fir Tree* and many other books by this outstanding author are also favorites for children.]

BUCKLEY, HELEN E. *The Little Boy and the Birthdays.* New York: Lothrop, Lee & Shepard Co., Inc., 1965. [Remembering birthdays leads a boy to being remembered on his birthday.]

DE REGNIERS, BEATRICE S. *May I Bring a Friend?* New York: Atheneum, 1964. [The king and queen are most gracious about bringing a friend. *The Little Book* (Walck, 1961), *The Giant Story* (Doubleday, 1953) and *Who Likes the Sun?* (Harcourt, Brace & World, Inc., 1961) are by the same author.]

ECONOMAKIS, OLGA. *Oasis of the Stars.* New York: Coward-McCann, Inc., 1965. [Abie keeps digging until damp earth makes it possible for his tent family to build a more permanent home.]

ETS, MARIE HALL. *Just Me.* New York: The Viking Press, 1965. [I walked like different animals, but I ran "like nobody else, just me" to go with Daddy. *Gilberto and the Wind* (1963) and *Play with Me* (1955) are also excellent.]

HOBAN, RUSSELL. *A Baby Sister for Frances.* New York: Harper & Row, Publishers, 1964. [When Baby Gloria arrives, Frances runs away—until she realizes her importance in her family. *Bedtime for Frances* (Harper & Row, 1960) and *I'm Going to Have a Baby* (John Day Co., 1967) are by the same author.]

HORWICH, FRANCES R. *Stories and Poems to Enjoy.* Garden City, N.Y.:

Doubleday & Company, Inc., 1962. [A collection of writing for young children.]

KEATS, EZRA JACK. *Peter's Chair*. New York: Harper & Row, Publishers, 1966. [When he realized he had outgrown his chair, Peter helped his father paint it pink for Baby Susie. *Whistle for Willie* (Viking, 1964), *The Snowy Day* (Viking, 1962), *Jennie's Hat* (Harper & Row, 1966), and *A Letter to Amy* (Harper & Row, 1968) are by the same author.]

KRASILOVSKY, PHYLLIS. *The Girl Who was a Cowboy*. Garden City, N.Y.: Doubleday & Company, Inc., 1965. [Margaret now wears two hats, a cowboy hat and a girl's hat.]

LENSKI, LOIS. *Davy Goes Places*. New York: Henry Z. Walck, Inc., 1961. [Earlier books by this outstanding author include *Big Little Davy* (1956), *On a Summer's Day* (1953), and *Let's Play House* (1944).]

LOCKE, EDITH RAYMOND. *The Red Door*. New York: The Vanguard Press, Inc., 1965. [When Peter's house is replaced by a tall apartment house, Peter is able to have his red door again.]

KEMPNER, CAROL. *Nicholas*. New York: Simon and Schuster, Inc., 1968. [A balloon man helps Nicholas find his way home while his mother is at work.]

KESSLER, ETHEL, and LEONARD. *Do Baby Bears Sit in Chairs?* New York: Doubleday & Company, Inc., 1961. ["No, but they roll down hill—just as I do."]

MINARIK, ELSE HOLMELUND. *A Kiss for Little Bear*. New York: Harper & Row, Publishers, 1968. [The kiss from his grandmother is brought by friends. *Little Bear's Visit* (1961) and *Little Bear's Friend* (1960) also recount simple, everyday adventures.]

POLITI, LEO. *Piccolo's Prank*. New York: Charles Scribner's Sons, 1965. [Piccolo, Luigi's tiny monkey, explored the cable car.]

SCHLEIN, MIRIAM. *The Best Place*. Chicago: Albert Whitman and Company, 1967. [In which place is it best to hide? To ride? To rest?]

YASHIMA, MITSU, and TARO. *Momo's Kitten*. New York: The Viking Press, Inc., 1961. [Momo's cat becomes a mother. Taro Yashimo also wrote and illustrated *Umbrella* (1958) and *Youngest One* (1962).]

ZOLOTOW, CHARLOTTE. *Big Sister and Little Sister*. Harper & Row, Publishers, 1966. [Big sister and little sister learn about taking care of each other. *If It Weren't for You* (1966) also helps to build mutual appreciation in a family, and *My Friend John* (Abelard-Schuman, 1966) outside the family.]

CHAPTER 13

Arts and Crafts for a Preschool Group

Arts and crafts activities for a preschool group serve to introduce the children to a variety of art media. Sometimes the children use their hands directly with such materials as clay, dough, paste, finger paints, flowers, and materials of different textures. At other times, they use brushes, scissors, and carpentry tools, and gradually develop some skill in manipulation. Through these experiences they begin to perceive relationships of color and differences or similarities in texture and they develop an appreciation of balance in line, color, and mass as they arrange and rearrange the materials with which they work. They also experience the satisfaction of controlling their use of materials and of finding acceptable outlets for their emotions. Furthermore, they enjoy the social aspects of working with others on craft projects.

The preschool teacher should not make realistic representation the objective. The formless scribble of the three-year-old presently will develop a shape as he grows into a four-year-old. The five-year-old may or may not react to the pressure of the social order by drawing representations of its different aspects as he sees them. The teacher should not press the child for realism, not even by praising it above other art expressions. She should value whatever expression the child happens to make.

Children at different age levels express themselves with different degrees of skill in different media. Three-year-old Lynn described the playsuit that she was wearing as "pedal pushers with arms." Her verbal ability was thus sufficient to express an interesting mental image of her clothing. But, as a three-year-old, she did not have the ability to express this same concept in any other medium. To model a playsuit in clay or to paint a picture of a playsuit would require years of experience with such art media. Realizing

451

this difference between a child's ideas and his ability to express them, the preschool teacher should expect only that the children will enjoy the variety of art media to which she introduces them.

As she shares a child's satisfaction with some completed painting or model, the teacher can point out the artistic relationships that she observes, introduce appropriate terms, or encourage the use of some bit of technical skill. Her praise serves to guide the child toward further artistic expression. Only if the child develops sufficient interest and satisfaction in expressing himself through art media will he continue to attempt such expression to the point of achieving technical competence.

The preschool teacher, as well as the parent, should help a preschool child to appreciate beauty in everyday life. Each day affords at least one opportunity to call attention to something beautiful—clouds against the sky; the lovely form and color of a tree or a leaf; the feel of grass, or sand, or a rug. For instance, the teacher may say, "Aren't we glad that we have beautiful flowers!" Or she may point out what she enjoys perhaps by saying, "Oh, what lovely colors in your dress."

ART AS ARRANGEMENT

It is often said that all art is essentially arrangement. Certainly, the arrangement of different objects is the essence of art experience for preschool children. The making of collages is their fundamental art activity. In the course of the school year, they make collages out of many many things, including dry weeds gathered in the fall, pieces of discarded Christmas cards, bits of colored papers, and stickers of spring flowers. They arrange such materials and paste them on background sheets of various colors and textures. Each collage is different from every other, but they all provide the opportunity for the child to express his own ideas about arrangements. The preschool child enjoys such expression.

The nursery school teacher should see that the children have daily opportunities to arrange different objects. At the table where books and puzzles and crayons are available, she can place a child-sized flannelboard, together with dots, dashes, and other shapes cut out of felt of different colors. On other days, she can place there a plastic-covered board with a collection of bits of plastic in different shapes and colors. Sometimes she may provide pop beads for the children to arrange and to wear as bracelets or necklaces. For table use on sunny days outdoors, she may have a collection of large samples of plastic upholstery materials in different textures and colors. Because the pieces are large, the children—in arranging them—use large- as well as small-muscle movements, and there is not much possibility of the pieces getting lost.

For the homemaking child, the teacher can provide a plastic vase and some artificial flowers to be used in the playhouse or on the tea table, as the child desires. She can also provide washable plastic tablemats or tablecloth, which the child can use if she wishes. The five-year-old girl who is going to learn to enjoy arranging an attractive table must have suitable materials with which to work.

Not only in the playhouse, but also outdoors, the teacher should encourage realistic and functional arrangements of objects. She can provide a collection of smooth rocks for the children to use in making a small rock

Pasting and painting can contribute to either an individual or a group project. (Courtesy of Riverside Unified School District, Riverside, California. Photograph by Jim Henderson.)

garden. The sandbox and its accessories also afford endless opportunity for arranging such things as birthday cakes decorated with colored pebbles or weeds.

In encouraging a child to arrange materials, the teacher should restrict herself to providing the materials and—when the project is completed to the child's satisfaction—to admiring what has been created. She should encourage each child to express himself in whatever way he wishes with the materials he has.[1] This awareness of individual differences is evident in one teacher's description of the use of gummed crepe paper by a group of four-year-olds:

My group of older prekindergarten children enjoy "scrap" pasting because they can do it independently, without adult assistance. They can cut gummed crepe paper by themselves because it is a good weight for cutting. I choose colors that are more vivid and consequently more interesting to the children. Sometimes I cut gummed crepe paper with pinking shears to make the collage-making more interesting to them.

For moistening the gummed paper, I provide sponges cut in two-by-three-inch oblongs. The sponges are wet and put in small pie tins. The children touch the gummed side of the colored paper to the wet sponge and apply the gummed paper to a piece of construction paper that each has chosen.

This morning the favorite color of construction paper was yellow. Some children did a collage on both sides, and some made two sheets. One child was methodical in that every little bit of his black construction paper had to be covered with a color. One boy covered one half of one side of his sheet and was finished. Another child put colors all around the edge of his paper but not in the center. One boy chose mostly brown and dark-blue gummed paper, colors least popular with the other children.

Some children rapidly did four sides and were off to other activities while other children were slower and more painstaking in their work. Some showed their aggressiveness by getting all the colors they wanted first before they started pasting. By contrast, one child sat quietly waiting whenever she ran out of colors until an adult noticed her need for more materials. Another girl obviously enjoyed the activity and remarked, "Gee, it's magic!"

This craft activity is creative in that each child picks his own colors, and applies his selection of paper bits in the design he wants. Each child shows his individuality and expresses himself according to his own personality not only in the colors he chooses but also in his dexterity, rapidity, design, attention span, and even aggressiveness.

Children enjoy not only the freedom of arrangement in making collages but also the channeled arrangement of putting together jigsaw puzzle pieces to conform to a preconceived form. However, in the latter activity, they are able to handle only a relatively small number of pieces. For instance, a three-year-old child first puts together a three-piece puzzle—perhaps that of a little boy. Furthermore, he needs help from a supervising adult who guides him in starting the puzzle by putting the head up at the top "since people's heads seem to be at the top," or by putting the shoes at the bottom "where they can walk on the floor."

The adult supervising the puzzle table should guide the children pri-

---

[1] Natalie Robinson Cole, *Children's Arts from Deep Down Inside* (New York: The John Day Company, 1966).

marily by praising what they do. She may say, "You have a red sweater on the little boy. That's fine," or "Good. You have his sweater on top of his pants. That's the way boys wear them." Thus she can call the child's attention to the color of the sweater that the boy in the puzzle is wearing, or to the relation between his sweater and pants. By such directional comments, the teacher helps to prepare the child for later selection of clothing in socially desirable forms and color arrangements.

With four- and five-year-old children who are achieving competence in assembling puzzles of more pieces, the supervising adult can guide the child in recognizing different masses of color and the extension of particular lines. For instance, she may say, "Can you find a piece that has this same line on it? Or she may say, "Maybe there are some more pieces to make the blue car. See if you can find some pieces with that blue color on them." By making such discriminations as to form and color, she prepares the child for other visual discriminations he will need to make.

DEVELOPING A FEELING FOR TEXTURE

Adults gain pleasure from the materials used in a Japanese garden or a modern patio and in the blend of color in a flower garden. They also enjoy the variety of textiles worn by the women at a party, and the various surfaces used to furnish a room. The development of such cultivated tastes begins in the preschool group, where the teacher provides not only finger paints, clay, and dough to squeeze through fingers but also such supplies as the following:

- A collection of suit materials obtained when daddy's trousers had cuffs made.
- A boxful of samples of dress materials: silk, satin, velvet, cotton, orlon, and so on.
- A sample book of wall papers.
- A sample book of yardgoods or drapery materials from a mail-order house.

The teacher should encourage the children to feel the different samples and to tell her about those they especially like. With four-year-olds, she can pretend she is a tailor helping Daddy to select material for a suit, or a dressmaker helping Mother to select material for a dress, or an interior decorator helping Mother choose the furnishings for her home.

The teacher can also provide bits of cloth, rickrack, braid, and other trimmings for the children to use in making a collage on colored paper. She can guide them in noticing texture as well as color and design. "Mmmm, that feels good," she may say as she runs her finger slowly over a bit of silk. "It's so smooth," she may add, giving the child a word to go along with the feel that he enjoys. "Feel the smooth silk," she may suggest as she encourages the child to imitate this way of enjoying the material.

Whenever she can obtain discarded materials from a stationery store, the teacher can bring the children a collection of different kinds of paper for cutting. By using scissors, the children learn from experience that some papers are hard and tough; others, fragile to look at but hard to cut; still others, easy to tear. Tissue-, typing-, and wrapping papers and newsprint furnish a simple variety of textures and help the children to notice the feel of the materials they work with.

In a small group, each five-year-old learns concepts of color, shape, and number. (Courtesy of DARCEE, George Peabody College of Education, Nashville, Tennessee.)

ENJOYING COLOR

In nursery and kindergarten groups, children have opportunities for exploring and enjoying the use of color. They like colors and they like being able to choose among them. Each day they should be provided with one or more situations in which they can gain control of color: easels supplied with large sheets of paper and several cans, each with a brush and a different color paint; table or easels supplied with paper and a box of crayons of a size comfortable to small hands; bits of colored paper for making a collage; felt pieces in different colors to use on a feltboard, or plastic pieces in different colors to use on a plastic board. In short, children should have a daily opportunity to arrange materials and work with colors.

Experiences with color should be selected according to the age level of the children. The child who is free of inhibitions enjoys putting on an apron or a smock and immersing his hands in the thick starch mixture used for finger painting.[2] When his teacher sprinkles blue tempera paint onto the mixture, he moves his hand to make blue patterns. If his teacher adds yellow tempera, he can make some yellow patterns—and green ones, too. Finger painting is an appropriate way to provide experience with color for the nursery school child.

When the ratio of adults to children is high enough to provide for suitable guidance, preschool children should be allowed to experiment with color through using watercolors of the semimoist variety. The activity is especially attractive when it can be conducted outdoors at a table with a washable surface. The children should feel free to experiment with colors, mixing them on their papers, on the lid of their color box, or in the water provided for washing their brushes. If they enjoy the coloring activity and are guided by encouraging praise rather than restrictive prohibitions, they gradually develop control of the watercolor process.

By the time children are in kindergarten, they can distinguish among a variety of colors and are ready to distinguish among the tints and shades of particular colors. To help them make such distinctions, the kindergarten teacher can use easels and solutions of powder paints in the three primary colors: red, yellow, and blue. She should make solutions of each of the colors at full intensity, solutions of their tints, and solutions of their shades —nine solutions in all. Tints are easily made by adding white to the solutions of the primary colors; shades by adding black. The addition of a small amount of oil of clove or oil of wintergreen to the solutions keeps them from spoiling, making it possible to mix large batches at a time so as to have them always on hand.

The kindergarten child who is free to choose colors of full intensity or of various tints and shades can explore the degrees of intensity of a single color. He can also experiment with the use of tints or shades of several colors and thus explore color hues within tints, or within shades. The whole world of color is open to him.

---

[2] A teacher may prepare starch for finger painting as follows:

1 cup laundry starch	3 tbsp. talcum powder
2 qts. boiling water	1 tsp. oil of cloves or peppermint
½ cup soap flakes	

Make a thick, creamy mixture of starch with cold water. Pour boiling water over mixture and cook until clear, stirring continuously. Remove from heat. Add soap flakes, talcum powder, and oil of cloves or peppermint.

GAINING EMOTIONAL CONTROL

By expressing an idea, a person gains a measure of control over his relationship to the situations and personalities connected with the idea. For some people, verbal expression serves this purpose; for others, physical expression—especially through art media of one or more kinds—is more satisfying. For children this sublimation of experience first through physical movement and then through art media is highly important. The child who is less verbal than other children is one who most needs to express himself through art media.

"Mommy!" says the child as he makes a digging-in kind of scribble. By hitting the paper, or crumpling it, he is probably also getting rid of considerable aggression toward his mother. Maybe all that he needed at that moment was to dig in as he scribbled in order to express his frustrations against the worldly pressures channeled into his life through his mother.

The means for emotional release selected by children at nursery school include not only pounding with hammers and hitting a punching bag, but also pounding clay, crayoning or finger painting aggressively, or making sweeping strokes with a paintbrush. One morning, Don expressed his feelings of aggression by using crayons. He selected red and yellow and used them vigorously in long strokes across the paper. After he had crayoned for some time, his pressure on the crayon broke it. He stopped then, as if the breaking of the crayon were the period at the end of his sentence of expression.

Another morning he worked at the easel, taking a long turn. Using large strokes, he covered the entire paper with red paint. Then he used the blue paint available at the easel. Finally, he painted over the entire paper in the third color that was available: white. The completion of his painting left Don in an agreeable mood which carried through the rest of the morning.

DEVELOPING A FEELING FOR FORM

Many young children develop creatively through the use of such plastic materials as modeling clay, which is kept moist and is always accessible. The child works with it on a board that is at least 12 by 12 inches. Articles that he fashions and wishes to keep can be dried and then painted with tempera paint to which starch has been added.

Children also enjoy exploring forms they fashion from manipulative dough. This plastic material is made by mixing three cups of flour, one cup of salt, and one cup of water. It can be colored with tempera colors and can be kept in an airtight container for use in the variety of ways that the material will suggest to the children.

To print on newspaper, children use tempera paint and a variety of shapes: carrots or potatoes carved at one end into an interesting shape; cardboard tubes; small and hollow boxes that are square or rectangular. As they work, older children are encouraged to talk about the shapes, colors, and interesting designs they work with.

The use of papier-mâché contributes to a feeling for three-dimensional objects. Crumpling a small piece of newspaper into an egg-shaped form creates a core around which to wrap strips of newspaper about 1 inch wide and 12 inches long dipped one at a time into a thin paste mixture. Eggs, fruits, and vegetables can be shaped in this way, colored with paint after

A small group of kindergarten children enjoys creating a design. (Courtesy of the University of Connecticut and Mansfield Public Schools, Mansfield, Connecticut.)

they are dry, and made available to the children to handle in the nursery school store.

SOCIAL BENEFITS

Getting acquainted with different art media may be a solitary exploration of what can be done with paint at an easel, or it may consist of pounding clay flat on a table as an emotional release. More often, it is a social experience which takes place in a small group, with children enjoying a variety of activities; or in a large group, with almost all the children using much the same kind of materials.

Children like to come to a table where other children are quietly using crayons or arranging colorful pieces of plastic or felt. They also like to work with others, crayoning together on wide shelfpaper unrolled across a smooth floor. It is relaxing to create something with such materials when friends are there and it does not matter what product is created or how much or how little is done.

Children also like to sit down at a small table at which an adult has interesting new materials to work with and is helping children to learn to use them. Such a small-group introduction to modeling clay, stringing beads, cutting with scissors, applying stickers, or pasting together links for a chain is a happy one for a child. It is a necessary one for more complex activities such as using watercolors, frosting cakes, or decorating cookies. In fact, for three- and four-year-old children, such complex activities should always be supervised by an adult, working with a small group of children. For five-year-old children experienced in these activities, only minimum supervision is required.

After children have been introduced in small groups to some simple craft technique, they are ready to use the technique in a large-group situation. Usually such craft groups are begun after two or three weeks of school, when the children have been inducted into other large-group activities: brief planning sessions and such routine activities as resting, having refreshments or meals, and listening to stories. As in all other large-group activities, the children are encouraged to participate but are free to choose other activities if they wish.

A teacher in one parent-cooperative nursery school described to parents the social benefits of the large-group art period:

> Our planned community activity in arts or crafts provides each child with a different set of neighbors, and often is the occasion for increasing sociability. Don, for instance, is very attentive to his work but is willing to discuss it with a neighbor. Some children show the same courage with neighbors during art period as they show in parallel play. For the shy children, easy spontaneous bits of talk help to promote a nice group feeling and sense of belonging. Thus the organized but flexible art period gives the less aggressive, resourceful children the help they need. Even the boys who are eager for the things outdoors like to work with others at the art table and stay with the group after refreshments to take part in the planned art activity.

In both large- and small-group situations, the teacher has an opportunity to help the children to learn to share the craft materials with which they work. When the children are using crayons from a box shared by two or three others, she may help a child get started by asking, "What color do you want to use?" Then, after he has made his selection, she can say,

"When you want another color, put that one back in the box for someone else to use, and choose your next color."

The teacher should also help the children by appreciating their pleasure in the social situation. When they are working along well, she may say, "Isn't this fun, coloring together? It feels good to work with others in a group." Her pleasure in the group situation, expressed through such statements, helps the children to develop an awareness of their own pleasure in both the craft activity and the group situation.

Arts and Crafts in the Curriculum

An arts and crafts activity may be either complete within itself or integrated into other parts of the curriculum. The teacher should be familiar with both uses of arts and crafts activities, and should have one or more of them each day.

The children learn the use of each new medium and each new tool as a separate arts and crafts activity. After a skill has been introduced as a separate activity, the teacher should plan an activity which makes use of the skill in relation to a simple project. Although the project may be related to other aspects of the curriculum, it may also be an activity which is fun to do or which helps the children to develop an appreciation of some aspect of art. Simple projects of this nature include the following:

- Stringing (and eating) Cheerios or some other cereal of similar shape to make a bracelet with a pipecleaner base.
- Dipping a string in tempera paint; then pulling the string through a folded piece of paper; opening the sheet to reveal the design created.
- Putting spots of paint on a piece of paper; folding the paper over and pressing the halves of it together; opening the sheet to see the design created.
- Blowing bubbles in the sunlight to enjoy their form and colors.
- Modeling a ball of clay or dough which has been put inside a paper bag; opening the bag to see the new form of the clay or dough.

CRAFT ACTIVITIES AND THE CURRICULUM

The teacher can use craft activities to enhance projects that are developed primarily within other areas of the curriculum. Craft activities can be used because of their relation to health, physical development, social understanding, science, space relationships, mathematics, favorite stories, or music. Many other examples could be given. The preschool teacher should be ingenious in adapting the usual art and craft activities to the particular theme she is emphasizing with her group of preschool children.

Health. On a rainy day, when she has talked with the children about keeping dry, the teacher can have little half-circles or umbrella shapes for the children to paste on a sheet of paper. Sometimes these pieces are cut from gummed paper and can be moistened by touching them to a wet sponge; sometimes they are to paste on with school paste.

Physical Education. In the spring, the children can enjoy making kites with which to run in the wind. Their teacher provides them with pieces of construction paper which have holes punched in one corner and a length of string tied through each hole. In a three-year-old group, each child decorates his kite as he wishes and then flies it outdoors. Four-year-olds like the realism of kite tails and fashion them by pasting an inch-wide strip of brightly colored crepe paper to their kites. Then they run with their kites, getting practice in running as they try to keep the kite in the air.

Social Understanding. When children study about how clothes are made, they become interested in sewing. Their teacher can provide them with cards having a picture of a boy whose sweater and trousers are outlined with holes to be used in guiding a cord or shoelace in and out, or of a girl whose dress is to be "sewed" in the same way.

Science. When the children watch caterpillars eat leaves, they can make a caterpillar out of egg cartons cut in half lengthwise. One day they color the series of humps. Another day they paste large colored dots on them as they wish. With adult help as needed, each colorful caterpillar gets two pipecleaner antennae and is ready to take home at the end of the session.

When the caterpillars observed by the preschool group emerge from their cocoon stage as butterflies, the teacher can provide each child with a large butterfly cut out of construction paper. On this the child pastes bits of colored paper. Then, with a string attached to the middle of his "butterfly," he runs to make it fly up in the air.

Space. Paper folding gives the children experience with space relation-ships. Four- or five-year-old children like to make soldier hats from sheets of newspaper.

Mathematics. Questions of "How many?" are an integral part of a craft project. A three-year-old child may make a Halloween collage using three pieces of orange and two pieces of black. A four-year-old child may paste as many cherries on his George Washington tree as he is able to count.

Favorite Stories. The day that the teacher reads *The Little Fish That Got Away,*[3] she can give the children precut fish which they paste on pieces of construction paper.

Music. The children may also paint paper plates, which are subsequently made into rhythm instruments. On another day, the children use crayons to decorate the plates further. Two decorated plates are stapled together (by an adult), with some small beans inside and gay ribbons hanging outside.

---

[3] Bernadine Cook, *The Little Fish That Got Away* (New York: William R. Scott, Inc., 1956).

SEASONAL CRAFT ACTIVITIES

The preschool curriculum should help the children to enjoy each of the seasons and to understand the meaning of the principal holidays. The craft activities associated with each season and each holiday are, therefore, an essential part of the curriculum. The teacher should have in mind special activities appropriate for each holiday. For instance, when Halloween is at hand, she can get out lipsticks and eyebrow pencils for the

Making indoor snow balls. (Courtesy of The Merrill-Palmer Institute and Donna J. Harris, Detroit, Michigan.)

children to use in making up their faces. She also should know how to adapt each simple craft activity so as to help the children increase their understanding of each holiday and the customs associated with it. Some examples of such adaptations are shown in Table 13-1 on the next page.

GETTING READY FOR CHRISTMAS

As Christmas approaches, the usual preschool craft activities take on the colors of the season. The children have a variety of shapes cut from green paper to paste on red paper, or bits of red paper to paste on green paper. Often they make colorful decorations to hang on their Christmas tree.

In one nursery group, the teacher cut a boot from red construction paper for each child. With bits of cotton, and paste for applying the cotton, each child decorated his boot as he saw fit. Meanwhile, the teacher put a loop of red ribbon on a tree branch for each child. Then, when a child brought her his completed boot, she asked him to select the branch on which he wanted it to hang. As soon as he made his choice, she took the stapler out of her pocket and quickly stapled the corner of the boot onto the ribbon.

TABLE 13-1. Adaptations of Craft Activities to Major Holidays

CRAFT ACTIVITY	HALLOWEEN	CHRISTMAS	EASTER
Applying stickers	Put pumpkin stickers on black paper	Put Christmas seals on green-paper tree	Put flower seals on yellow paper
Cutting	Cut orange paper	Cut used Christmas cards	Cut green paper to put in baskets
Making collages	Put black bits cut with pinking sheers on orange paper	Put short lengths of colored yarns on white paper	Put bits of Easter-egg shells on gold paper
Arranging and pasting on paper	Use fall leaves	Use parts of Christmas cards	Use small flowers or new leaves
Stringing	Put orange macaroni on pipecleaners	Put tree decoration on a ribbon	Make necklace from cellophane straw pieces strung on dental floss
Making chains	Paste together links of orange and black paper	Make chains to decorate the tree	Make necklace of pastel links
Frosting cakes	Frost a doughnut	Decorate Christmas cookies	Frost cupcakes

In this way, the child could identify his boot by where it hung, as well as by the name written on it.

The teacher of a group of four-year-old children cut a simple doll figure out of red paper for each child. She found a jolly Santa Claus head packaged as a Christmas seal and gave one to each child to put on his doll figure. She also provided bits of cotton for the children to use in making beards and eyebrows for their Santa figures if they wished. Each completed Santa figure could either be hung on the Christmas tree or be taken home by its maker.

A brightly colored cornucopia is another tree decoration that children like to make. The teacher prepares in advance a semicircle of white paper for each child to decorate by using paint sticks, or crayons, or whatever coloring medium is appropriate to the paper. When a design is completed and dry, the teacher staples the two sides of the paper together to make the cone for each child to hang on the tree.

EASTERTIME

At Eastertime, pastel colors are popular and craft work has pinks, apple-greens, and yellows in greater profusion. Easter eggs have different sizes and a variety of decoration. One day the teacher may have for each child a large egg cut out of white paper. This the child paints or colors, making an Easter "egg" to take home. Another day, the teacher may provide smaller "eggs" and shakers filled with glitter. The resulting "eggs" may be so pretty that the teacher suggests hanging them on the twigs of a bare branch to make an Easter-egg tree.

When the children are modeling clay or dough, the older ones enjoy making baskets. Usually a four-year-old child can get as far as making a pancake. Then his tactful teacher can show him how to fold the edges up so that eggs will not fall out easily. A five-year-old child can make a long roll to use as a handle on his basket.

Another kind of Easter basket is made from an egg carton. A square of four egg cups, painted and decorated, makes a basket for four Easter eggs. One egg cup, covered with aluminum foil and having two pipe cleaners to make a handle, makes a smaller basket.

Another part of Eastertime craft activities is the traditional coloring of hardboiled eggs by dipping in solutions of food coloring. As the children roll their eggs, one at a time, in a small aluminum foil dish containing dye solution, they enjoy the colors and designs they obtain.

"Here Comes Peter Cottontail," a delightful Eastertime song, inspires some teachers to help the four- or five-year-old children in making hand-puppet bunnies out of a brown-paper lunchbag. The children work on their puppets on each of three successive days, as follows:

First day: Make a bunny face on the bottom of the bag. This can be done by pasting on circle eyes, triangle nose, and semicircle mouth.
Second day: Paste two pre-cut ears on the two bottom corners of the bag.
Third day: Paste a piece of cotton on the back of the bag as a tail.

Each day the children have fun working as their puppets near completion.

In one parent-cooperative nursery school before Easter, the teacher planned a craft activity using a half-sheet of yellow construction paper, shaped like half an egg, and a pre-cut little duck. A brad through the duck and the half-egg made an illustration for a story[4] about a little duck hatching out of an egg. The teacher described this craft activity:

[4] Margaret Wise Brown, *Golden Egg Book* (New York: Simon and Schuster, Inc., 1947).

In the group of eighteen children we had already read the *Golden Egg Book*. Today we talked about the story while we colored the eggs of yellow paper to make them look like Easter eggs. Coloring a large cracked egg out of which the duck pops is an activity that the children could all take part in at the same time without any assistance or waiting. One mother helped by seeing that each child had crayons, by putting the children's names on their work, and by attaching the ducks to the half-eggs with brads. We worked with half the children while the others were resting. All the children in both groups made the duck popping out of his cracked shell.

Some children colored the half-egg fully and wanted to make another one. A few children, with short attention spans for art work, colored just a little and were ready to play with the duck. These I encouraged to color just a little more by saying, "I wonder what color this crayon makes?" And then the children would try it on their egg. Another suggestion I made was: "This empty space on your egg needs some pretty colors." Each child followed through on these suggestions. However, I knew when each of the children had reached his capacity and I did not try to push a child beyond his limits.

The children seemed pleased with what they accomplished. Artwork in hand, they went around hopping and quacking like ducks. One child, popping his duck out of the half-egg as he played with it, said, "My duck is cracking out of his egg." This action may have been a dramatic enactment of the story he had heard earlier.

Guiding Art and Craft Activities

The adult who is helping children with art and craft work often wonders about her role. How should she supervise the work? Should she participate in the activity? Should she demonstrate desirable techniques? Should she point out better techniques than those being used by the children? The answers to such questions all bear on the point that children must first learn to do something before they can learn *how* to do it. Preschool children need experience in a variety of craft activities. Not until they are in elementary school will they be ready to concern themselves with techniques.

When a teacher introduces preschool children to some new art or craft activity, she gives them only a very brief explanation and emphasizes only the one point which is crucial to achieving initial success. Her explanation may include a very brief demonstration, but only if it contributes toward the one point she is attempting to make. She knows the children will learn partly by doing and partly by imitating.

In order to give the children the benefit of an example they may imitate, the teacher may continue her activity for a moment or two after introducing it. Then she begins to move around among the children, getting them well started in doing it. Whenever an adult participates in an activity with children, she should be careful to do so only at their level of ability. If she forgets this child-like role, she will find that the children stop what they

An artist likes to have his work on display and to show it to friends. (Courtesy of Lincoln Public Schools and Nebraska Association for Children Education.)

are doing. It is easier for them to watch a beloved adult perform a new activity than to do it themselves. But, as watchers, they do not build the muscles needed in the skill and they do not learn the activity to any great extent. At the same time, unfortunately, they learn to be watchers rather than doers. Realizing this, the skillful teacher is careful to limit her leadership to a level only slightly above that of the children and well within their range of achievement.

Every adult supervising children's art and craft activities needs to be impervious to the children's requests to "make me a house" or "draw me a cat." It is no kindness to show a child something impossible for him to achieve for years to come and thus to rob him of the opportunity of doing something himself. When an adult is asked to "draw me a picture" or to do something else a child can do for himself, she reassures him of her interest and her confidence in him. She may say, "You can do it yourself," or she may make a suggestion about how to start the activity. When the child completes what he is doing to his own satisfaction, she should be careful to praise his accomplishment realistically, pointing out some one feature which would be desirable for him to incorporate in subsequent work.

A PERMISSIVE ATTITUDE

Especially with art activities, the teacher should be permissive, constructively encouraging the children in what they want to do and tolerating their occasional disinterest. One teacher's description of a mature boy in a four-year-old group shows this permissive attitude:

Stanley, who is almost five years old now, is good at arts and crafts. He cuts well, and when we have some material that is especially attractive, he asks me for some to take home. Several times this year he has gone home with a bit of clay or paper or colored dough. These donations are part of our design to endear him, or any other child, to our school.

On one occasion, Stanley refused to finger paint, perhaps simply through indisposition. At other times he has slopped along with the others contentedly. He doesn't feel compelled to conform with our organized program, and I think that is all right. His nonparticipation is not caused by timidity as it may have been when he came last fall. He has an easy attitude toward doing or not doing what there is to do. In some things he has a keen interest; in others, none at all.

LIMITS TO FREEDOM OF EXPRESSION

The teacher, along with the parents, determines the limits to be set on freedom of expression. In some groups, children attend dressed in attractive but nonserviceable clothing. The teacher is expected to return the children to their parents in the same condition in which they arrived. However, in most preschool groups, the children wear playclothes, and the teacher feels free to have them use water-soluble paints and other materials which do not stain clothing.

In one backyard group, after Susan had used bright red paint and had gone on to paint the other children, the parents and the teacher decided on certain limits of expression. While five-year-old Susan painted, three-year-old Sally was an admiring on-looker, Neal (three years and ten months) was a participant, and Ned (four years and four months) was a delighted and more vocal participant:

SUSAN (*painting her fingernails*) When it's dry, you can wash it off—with soap and water.

NED Where's the soap?

SUSAN (*finishing her fingernails and admiring them*) It's icky.

NED Icky, icky.

SUSAN Who wants to have some on his forehead?

NED I do! I do!

NEAL I do!

(*Susan obligingly paints the foreheads of each boy. Each dances around happily crying, "Yippee! Yippee!"*)

SUSAN Who wants to have some on his ear?

ADULT (*moving in and out of the group on her way to someplace else.*) The paint is all right on the skin, but don't get it on clothes.

SUSAN All right, teacher. Who wants to have some on his ear?

NEAL   I do! I do!

NED   I do!

(*Susan again decorates the boys, who then dance around with "Yippee! Yippee!" The conversation and artwork continue as Susan asks about a new place and then decorates each child with the paints. Soon the children have red spots on their ears, back of their necks and arms.*)

SUSAN   Who wants to have some on her foot?

NEAL (*taking off his shoe*)   I do!

(*Sally quietly takes off her shoe and stocking, as does Ned.*)

TEACHER (*joining the group*)   In the fall we keep our shoes on because the sidewalks are cold. You can feel their coldness with your hand. (*She puts her hand on the sidewalk.*)

(*The children feel the sidewalk and realize its coldness.*)

TEACHER   Let me help you with your shoes and stockings. (*Quietly puts on Sally's stockings and shoes.*)

(*Ned starts putting on his shoes, and the teacher ties his shoelaces.*)

SUSAN (*having painted everyone's feet but her own, runs off with Ned.*) Sticky! Sticky!

When the mothers picked up their children at the conclusion of the session, they reacted in different ways to their children's red spots. Neal's mother picked him up happily and said to the teacher, smilingly: "I can see the children really had fun this morning." Sally's mother frowned on seeing Sally and spoke sharply before they were out of earshot: "Look at you! And look at your dress!" Ned's mother said, "Well, I think we'd better have a bath when we get home," and Ned replied, "I want to leave it on!"

Aware of these conversations, the teacher made a note to have the next parents' meeting include a discussion of the benefits and limits of expressing oneself through various art media. She felt that the parents would profit from knowing what other parents considered to be the proper limits of such expression, and that she should be aware of the variation in their views. Whether children limit their painting to paper, or to paper and skin, is a matter of group policy.

GUIDANCE ACCORDING TO AGE LEVEL

In planning craft projects for her preschool children, the teacher should take into account their age level. With three-year-old children she should be careful to present only one idea each day. If the children are putting stickers or green tree-shaped construction paper in order to hang it on their own Christmas tree, she may plan to have them decorate their little tree on one day, and hang it on the tree the next day. In this way they can enjoy two different activities: the making of the decoration, and the arranging of the decorations on the tree.

The adults who work with the children must be careful to write the name of each child on the back of his work so that he can use his own decoration for the next step. They must also provide a few extra decorations so that a child who was absent the day they were made or who took his home by mistake can go on with the group activity the next day.

With four-year-old children, the teacher often plans projects which carry over from one day to another. The four-year-old is able to plan ahead and likes to know what is going to happen "next time." He enjoys decorating something as complicated as a box. One day he paints the box itself. The next day, when the paint is dry, he decorates the box further—perhaps with crayons, or perhaps with stickers, or perhaps with paper bits pasted on it. Then, on yet another day, he eagerly gets adult help in folding the box into a rectanguler shape to take home.

The teacher is able to plan somewhat more varied activities for each successive age level. Three-year-old children keep busy getting acquainted with the basic activities of using paste, paints, crayons, scissors, clay, dough and carpentry tools. Four-year-olds are intrigued by variations on these simple processes. They like to paint with a sponge as well as with different kinds of brushes; to use flat crayons on paper that covers surfaces of different texture such as tile, ribbon, wire, or corrugated paper; to work with chalk on butcher paper dipped in buttermilk; or to make interesting shapes out of plaster of Paris poured into sand tunnels and hollows. Five-year-olds show the benefits of past experience with a variety of media and are able to paint a picture or to cut and paste a valentine with considerable skill and a minimum of supervision.

Developing Skill with Tools

Experience with a tool starts with the simple use of the tool. A preschool child starts using a brush, scissors, a hammer, or another tool by devoting his attention to the process of using it rather than to the product to be achieved through its use. As he gains skill in using the tool, his attention will gradually shift to the product he has in mind. Some more mature four- and five-year-old children can produce simple but creditable products. However, most preschool children are attentive to processes. The teacher guides them primarily by encouraging their interest in the process and by praising their increasing skill. The children gain satisfaction by their sense of achievement in having increased their mastery over the materials with which they work. A feeling of success accompanies the structuring of the materials even though the structure itself evolves by chance and without easily recognizable form.

USING A BRUSH

Every day preschool children should be given the opportunity to paint at an easel with large paintbrushes which feel comfortable in children's hands and also encourage large arm movements. Each child should know that he can paint when he wants to do so. An adult should be available to help him into the costume appropriate for painting and to supply him with paper as he needs it.

The adult who supervises easel painting can notice when a child is ready to learn simple techniques—using or not using drips, covering part or all of the paper, or making dots and lines. "Mix the colors on your paper," she may suggest when a child starts to combine two containers of paint. Or she may remind him that the brush goes with the container. Primarily, the adult should encourage each child in his painting and assist him in getting the materials he needs for it.

When four-year-old Tommy had his turn at the easel, he chose the can of red paint and brushed red paint onto the paper. When one side was well covered, he stepped over to the other side in order to cover that side well too. The adult standing near the easels noticed that Tommy's brush came out of the can loaded with so much paint that it dripped as he brushed with it.

ADULT   Tommy, do you want to make drips?
(*Tommy pauses in his painting, brush uplifted.*)
ADULT   When you have a lot of paint on your brush, it runs down your hand the way it is doing now and it runs down the paper the way it did here. (*points out drip marks*) If you don't want drips, take the extra paint off your brush as you take it out of the can. (*Shows him how.*)
TOMMY   I want 'em.
ADULT   (*smiles*)   Sometimes you want them, and sometimes you don't. Now you know how to make them or not make them.

While the adult helped another child into his painting costume, Tommy continued covering the paper with red paint. He experimented a bit with dripping or not dripping, but primarily he concentrated on painting the paper red.

When the paper was all red, Tommy announced that he was through. The teacher heard his announcement and came over to admire his production. "You've made the paper all red, every bit of it!" she exclaimed. After standing back to admire the painting, she continued, "I wonder what it would look like if you used another color, too. Do you know how to make a dot with your brush?" On another piece of paper she showed him how to make a dot, a thin line, and a thick line. As she went away, she said, "You might use another color and make some dots on that pretty red paper."

Tommy took the brush out of the can of orange paint and made some large irregular dots with it. Then he added blue ones and finished his composition. This time when he announced that he was through, the adult standing nearby helped him out of his painting costume. Together, Tommy and the adult took his painting over to where it could dry until the end of the day.

Cutting with Scissors

One of the skills developed in a preschool group is that of cutting. The scissors, blunt but sharp enough to cut well, are an important tool for the nursery child to master. He needs much opportunity for the practice which helps him to develop skill. Such practice consists of three steps. First, free cutting of paper enables the child to get used to handling the scissors and helps him to develop the hand and finger muscles necessary for keeping the blades of the scissors close together in cutting. Second, cutting out forms of his own devising enables him to express with scissors some of the ideas he has in his mind. Third, cutting along straight and curving lines (marked for him in advance) makes it possible for a child to cut out paper dolls and other objects of interest to him. When he has acquired skill in cutting along a line, he has considerable coordination.

The three-year-old child enjoys cutting a variety of different kinds of paper. Newspaper cuts easily. Construction paper is attractive because of its color but is difficult to cut because of its thickness. Other colored papers which are thinner are probably better for the beginning cutter to use. A teacher can often obtain discarded papers of a quality desirable for easy cutting.

The four- or five-year-old child is ready on occasion to cut out something that he is thinking about. His teacher can sit down at the table where children are cutting and join the activity for a few minutes. First, she cuts freely—as the children are cutting. Presently she may say, "I'm going to cut out a worm," and proceed to cut a strip along an edge of a sheet of paper. When she is done, she holds it up for the children to see, and she may say, "Maybe some of you would like to cut worms." Then she moves around and enjoys watching the children cutting. If she sees that a child has cut a worm quite crookedly, she praises him for cutting such a wiggly kind of worm. Soon the children are cutting straight worms and wiggly worms as well as cutting freely.

The teacher who occasionally participates in the children's activity at their level of skill can easily determine when they are ready for cutting out forms or for cutting along a line. When the teacher points out that her cutting made a triangle, children who are mature enough to be interested in exercising some control of the cutting process will also attempt to cut out a triangle. When the teacher shows the children that, in cutting newspaper, one can either cut across the lines or along them, children who are mature enough to start cutting along a line are easily identified.

If some of the more mature children are ready for cutting along a line, the wise kindergarten teacher is careful not to overemphasize the use of this skill. She provides opportunity for such cutting from time to time, but in the main she attempts to help the children to develop their skill in cutting by using it in free cutting. Four- and five-year-old children like to cut up folded pieces of paper and open them to find surprising patterns.

CONSTRUCTION

Nursery school children are most interested in construction. Boys especially are eager to hammer and saw the way their fathers do. The preschool years sometimes mark the start of what may be a lifelong hobby or even a vocation.

Even though construction is a highly desirable activity, it should be provided in a nursery group only when it can be supervised continuously by an adult who does nothing else at the time. If the adult must leave the carpentry bench, she does so only after removing all the working tools. The tools are real tools, not toys, and the sharp blade of a saw or the weight of a small hammer can cause serious injuries. Furthermore, a child who concentrates too long on a fascinating new experience in construction may suddenly recoil from his work and hit anyone or anything within reach. A strong four-year-old boy can hit hard with a hammer, or make a considerable cut with a sharp saw. He must be closely supervised.

Three-year-old children learn the coordination required for driving in a nail. They take considerable pride in their visible accomplishment of

A hammer can "take out" as well as "put in." (*Courtesy of The Merrill-Palmer Institute and Donna J. Harris, Detroit, Michigan.*)

hitting a nail hard enough and long enough to make it stick in a board—at least temporarily. They like to take home a block of soft wood into which they have driven large-headed nails to make a pretty design.

Three-year-old children also like to see quick results of their sawing. Their teacher can provide for this satisfaction by giving them styrofoam and, later, soft wood to saw. She can firmly fasten the material in a vise, and then show them how to pull the saw back and forth across it. The child follows the indentation the teacher started for him and soon saws through the board. Then he is ready to be praised for making two pieces out of one —a proud achievement in both construction and mathematics.

Four- and five-year-old children have enough construction skill to use it in making some simple object, such as a boat. The teacher should provide them not only with the carpentry tools and the lightweight blocks of wood that are easily worked but also with a box of scrap materials: a bit of cloth for making a sail, an empty spool to use as a funnel, and bits of plastic or large-headed nails to put on as decoration. She also should provide them with the vivid experiences with boats, trains, cars, or planes which lead children into making models of them. She can help them in planning and executing some simple design, such as using two crossed boards to make a plane, or using a pointed block to make a boat.

Over a period of time, kindergarten children become capable of making and painting model planes or boats that bear considerable resemblance to real ones. Younger children do not often achieve such a result. But no matter what their level of accomplishment, the teacher should remember that her prime objective is to help the children to enjoy construction work and to develop an interest in doing more of it. The wise teacher, therefore, accepts what satisfies the child, and helps him to appreciate one or two good points about his work. She knows that his next attempt will be more successful and she encourages him in going on to such other attempts.

WHITTLING

Whittling is a useful skill to teach to four- and five-year-old children if their parents agree and if the number of adults in the nursery school or kindergarten makes it possible to supervise each child's work at all times. The paring knives for whittling are real knives, sharp enough to cut a child as easily as they cut the soft material (usually styrofoam) used in the activity.

At first, as in other craft activities, the children are encouraged to explore the process itself. They cut the styrofoam in whatever way their knives seem to go—but always cutting away from themselves, as the teacher has explained. Whenever they start using their tools with strokes that might endanger either themselves or someone else, the teacher helps them learn how to move their hands safely, in a direction away from their bodies. On occasion she may put her hand over the child's hand and move it in the desired fashion.

After the children have enjoyed free cutting on several occasions, the teacher may look for pieces they have cut with some recognizable shape to them. She may pick up a triangular piece, saying, "You've cut a triangle!" or asking, "Did you know that you have cut a triangle? Here it is. A triangle." The child, pleased with having done so, will attempt to make other such pieces. If he succeeds, he is ready for whittling shapes he has thought of. The preschool teacher need not take him further in his development of whittling skill, but she can continue to provide him with whittling materials and with opportunities to practice under supervision. These opportunities enable him to build the muscles necessary for developing his skill at a later time if he wants to do so.

Situations for Discussion

A preschool teacher is apt to find herself in situations similar to the four described here. As you think of what to do in each situation, consider whether each course of action suggested is desirable, or not. Use points brought out in the chapter as well as ideas from your own experience to justify your views. Suggest alternative courses of action to supplement those given.

SITUATION 1   Jeannie is a pretty little four-year-old who is brought to your nursery group each morning by one of her grandmothers. Many of the activities are new to her. You are endeavoring to get the children started working with clay, but she seems reluctant to get her hands into the "sticky stuff." When she says, with her most endearing smile: "You show me," you should

● Put a bit of clay in her hands to have her see how nice it feels.
● Tell her: "Do whatever you like with it."
● Have her wait until you help the other children get started.
● Tell her that she will like working with clay.
● Start working the clay for her as she asks.

SITUATION 2   You are assisting the teacher of a group of four-year-old children who are seated at a large table, working with crayons. After seeing that each child has paper and crayons, you move quietly around the group, interacting with each child. You make such remarks as

● You have the sky here, don't you?
● Tell me about your picture.
● That looks like a cat.
● Don't you want to use your red crayon?
● Do you like blue?

SITUATION 3   You are participating in a parent-discussion group which has been listening to a talk about the teaching of art in nursery school. One of the mothers tells about her practice of bringing along crayons and coloring book for her preschool child whenever she takes him to a meeting of grown-ups. You should

● Make no comment.
● Point out the importance of free drawing at the nursery level.

- Mention that coloring books are useful with children beginning to read.
- Suggest a roll of shelf paper and a box of jumbo crayons as portable art material for either an individual child or a group of children.
- Thank Mrs. Smith for bringing up the question of what parents can take for preschool children when it is necessary to have them in a place planned for grownups but not for children.

SITUATION 4   You plan to have each child in your group of four-year-olds make a box for jewelry as a gift for Mother on Mother's Day. You should

- Obtain a white cardboard box for each child to decorate.
- Collect egg cartons until you have one for every three children.
- Have the children decorate their jewelry boxes with oil paints.
- Plan one day for decorating the boxes.
- Have the children use two or three colors that are pretty together.

Current Books for Preschool Children

BORTEN, HELEN. *Do You See What I See?* New York: Abelard-Schuman, Limited, 1959. [Line, shape, and color give a person ideas and feelings.]

BRIGHT, ROBERT. *I Like Red.* New York: Doubleday & Company, Inc., 1959. [The little girl who likes red has red hair.]

BROWN, MARGARET WISE. *The Color Kittens.* New York: Golden Press, 1958. [Two kittens mix and match colors.]

BUDNEY, BLOSSOM. *A Kiss Is Round.* New York: Lothrop, Lee & Shepard Co., Inc., 1954. [A ring is round, the world is round, and so on.]

JOHNSON, CROCKETT. *Harold and the Purple Crayon.* New York: Scholastic Book Services, 1955. [With his purple crayon, Harold solves problems that arise. *Harold at the North Pole* (Harper & Row, 1957) is by the same author.]

KALUSKY, REBECCA. *Is It Blue as a Butterfly?* Englewood Cliffs, N. J.: Prentice-Hall, Inc., 1965. [Abigail and her daddy play a guessing game about her blue present.]

LOCKE, EDITH RAYMOND. *The Red Door.* New York: The Vanguard Press, Inc., 1965. [His red door was of great importance to Peter.]

MYRUS, DONALD, and ALBERT SQUILLACE. *Story in the Sand.* New York: The Macmillan Company, 1963. [Sand can be shaped to tell a story to a good observer.]

SANDBERG, INGER, and LASSE. *Nicholas's Red Day.* New York: Delacorte Press, 1967. [Adventures with red lights and other red things culminates in breaking out with red measles.]

SHAPUR, FREDUN. *Round and Round and Square.* New York: Abelard-Schuman, 1965. [A circle and a square can even make a little boy and a little girl.]

SPILKA, ARNOLD. *Paint All Kinds of Pictures.* New York: Henry Z. Walck, Inc., 1963. [Pictures can be whatever the artist wants them to be.]

STEINER, CHARLOTTE. *My Bunny Feels Soft.* New York: Alfred A. Knopf, Inc., 1958. [Twelve words, such as *soft,* are defined.]

———. *My Slippers Are Red.* New York: Alfred A. Knopf, Inc., 1957. [Colors are taught with brightly colored pictures of familiar objects.]

TRESSELT, ALVIN. *Hide and Seek Fog.* New York: Lothrop, Lee & Shepard, Inc., 1965. [Beautiful description such as this book exemplifies encourages children in being good observers.]

UNGERER, TOMI. *Snail, Where Are You?* New York: Harper and Row, Publishers, 1962. [If you look, you see a snail-like spiral in many places.]

VILLAREJO, MARY. *Art Fair.* Alfred A. Knopf, Inc., 1960. [This story can encourage children to enjoy a local art fair.]

WEZEL, PETER. *The Good Bird.* New York: Harper & Row, Publishers, 1964. [This book illustrates that a story can be told using only pictures.]

Wolff, Robert J. *Seeing Red.* New York: Charles Scribner's Sons, 1968. [Enlarges a child's concept of red through experience with it.]

ZOLOTOW, CHARLOTTE. *Big Brother.* New York: Harper & Row, Publishers, 1960. [Little sister and big brother who teases are happy coloring together.]

CHAPTER 14

Enjoying Musical Sounds

Music is an integral part of the preschool program because it is an integral part of children. Often a child learns the tonal pattern of a phrase before he articulates the words within it. Children are so sensitive to tones of voice that they will react to the tonal pattern of what is said sometimes more than to the words that are said. When a mother's voice becomes stern, a child is apt to say, "You don't like me!"—a reaction to the sternness, rather than to the comment. Fortunately a child also reacts to pleasant tones of voice; feeling caressed by a pleasant voice, he cooperates with what is suggested.

Throughout his preschool years a child makes amazing progress within the world of sound. Usually, by the time he enters elementary school he has learned to distinguish and use each of the sounds which comprise the English language. With encouragement, he can learn to identify a great many of the sounds occurring repeatedly in the world about him, and to imitate at least a few of them. He can find out that sound is vibration and can explore different means of producing sound. He can learn to distinguish among sounds, to differentiate music and noise, and among musical sounds, high tones from low, soft sounds from loud. Depending upon his special talents, he may make considerable progress in getting acquainted with the realm of music within the world of sound. He may even compose music. But no matter what his talents, he can learn to enjoy the various kinds of experience with melody and rhythm which are part of his culture. He can become acquainted with singing, with moving to music, with using musical instruments, and with listening to different kinds of music. Music is an essential, enjoyable part of his preschool experience.

The most important thing for a teacher to do about music is to encourage it. When a parent wonders about providing more music for the children, the teacher should avoid reacting defensively and encourage the parent by suggesting how to provide more music. Perhaps the parent plays

Sometimes musical experiences are led by the teacher and sometimes by others. (Courtesy of New Jersey Department of Education Demonstration Class for Four-Year-Olds, Trenton, New Jersey.)

the piano or some other instrument and would be happy to come and play for the group selections her own children enjoy. Or perhaps the parent knows someone else who could enrich the program for the children, or could bring phonograph records to be played during rest time. Whatever is suggested is a welcome addition to the children's program.

Children of nursery age do not, as a general rule, discriminate among different kinds of music. Classical, jazz, popular, European, Oriental, or other adult classifications of music are outside their understanding. Their teacher need not make these adult discriminations either. She should welcome a blues record or a record of African drums as enthusiastically as Brahms' "Lullaby." She can use each of them with the children, but at different times in the day's activities. The discriminations that she endeavors to teach the children are those appropriate to their age level—soft and loud, high and low, fast and slow. These can be taught with any of an infinite variety of music.

One teacher said that she thought of music as a golden thread woven into each part of the day, binding together and enlivening the whole pattern of the preschool group session. In her preschool group, music was to be expected at any time. Whenever a child or a grownup was reminded of a song, he shared it with the others around him. Whenever a child or a grownup wanted music, the teacher responded at once.

In addition to spontaneous music, this teacher provided musical interludes tied in with the routine for meeting the needs of the children. For instance, she began their group activities by singing their "Good morning" song with them. She always had new musical experiences, or those requiring rather careful attention, when the children were fresh. First thing in the morning was her time for teaching a new song, playing a new record to listen to and dance with, or practicing rhythm-band accompaniments in preparation for the next time that parents were coming to visit. At refreshment time the teacher led the children in singing a "Thank you" song before they started to eat. When rest time began she sang "Resting time has come for the children," and when it was over she would inquire, in song, "Are you sleeping?" or suggest that "Ho, Every Sleeper Waken." At the end of the session, the teacher enhanced departure time by leading the children in singing "Now It's Time to Say Goodbye," or some song to which she had put simple words about leaving now to come back another day.

The teacher should encourage the interest of each child in music activities of his choice and tolerate disinterest in other musical activities. This permissive attitude is observable in the following anecdote concerning a mature boy in a four-year-old nursery group:

One day Stanley (almost five years old) brought from home a toy trumpet. He said that he wanted us to have a parade: "I'll be the leader with my trumpet." We had a wonderful parade with at least a dozen children participating.

Stanley sings loudly when he chooses. In fact, his rendition of "Ho, Every Sleeper Waken" is something to hear. He gets stuck on the "cuckoo" part out of sheer love for the sound and sometimes just "cuckoo's" on and on until I manage to stop him in the interests of singing some other song.

Stanley plays the phonograph now and then, but does not dance.

To help children enjoy and learn more about music and other aspects of sound, the preschool teacher should be as relaxed and comfortable as she is in helping the children enjoy and learn about other facets of their world. She should share with the children the music that she knows and enjoys, because her pleasure in it will make it a pleasurable experience for the children too. A teacher who had grown up in Germany hesitated to use the folksongs that she had learned as a child. One day she made up a little verse to go with one of her favorite German songs. When she sang it to her nursery group, the children liked it as much as she did. She was able to make it seem delightful to them, as it was to her.

This incident is repeated over and over with teachers who have been overlooking the music that they know as they search for music suitable for preschool children. Music for preschool groups is like the bluebird of happiness—it is to be found at home. The young teacher who loves to listen to and dance to popular tunes should share her selection of such music with the children. The teacher who enjoys a quiet hour of classical music within her day should select from such music what she thinks the children would like.

Every teacher should seek to enlarge her musical repertoire[1] as a means of enlarging the musical experience she can provide for the children. As a teacher enjoys more music, she can put more music into her teaching and find it increasingly pleasurable and rewarding.

Helping Children Listen

The preschool teacher who is aware of the importance of helping children learn to listen capitalizes on every listening situation that presents itself. If a plane flies over, she does not consider it an interruption but an opportunity to have the children listen to the roar and try to make their toy planes roar realistically. If a bird is singing, she helps the children become aware of its song and answer the bird in its language of sounds. Any unusual sound that her ear notices becomes something to share with the children as a means of helping them understand and enjoy their audio-environment—the squishsquash of boots on a rainy day, for instance; the squeak of a rusty wheel, the crunching sound of celery being eaten.

The teacher who is always ready to listen to the song a child has made up or has learned sets a good example which the children are apt to follow as they learn to enjoy the role of listener. The good teacher hears a child's song, sings it back to him, and helps him share it with listeners and singers around him.

---

[1] The following are good books for accomplishing that purpose:

Satis M. Coleman, *Another Dancing Time* (New York: The John Day Company, 1954). *Singing Time* (1929), *Little Singing Time* (1940), and *Another Singing Time* (1937) are by the same author and Alice G. Thorn.

A. M. Ashton Dalton and E. Young, *My Picture Book of Songs* (Chicago: M. A. Donahue & Co., 1947).

Helen Jill Fletcher, *Children's Dances Around the World* (Darien, Conn.: The Educational Publishing Corporation, 1961).

Evelyn Hunt, *Music Time* (New York: The Viking Press, Inc., 1947).

Beatrice Landeck, *Children and Music: an Informal Guide for Parents and Teachers* (New York: William Sloane Associates, Inc., 1952). *Songs to Grow On* (1950) and *More Songs to Grow On* (1954) are by the same author.

L. Pendleton MacCartney, *Songs for the Nursery School* (Cincinnati, Ohio: The Willis Music Company).

Muriel Mandell and Robert E. Wood, *Make Your Own Musical Instruments* (New York: Sterling Publishing Company, Inc., 1957).

Mary Miller and Zajan Paulson, *Finger Plays, Songs for Little Fingers*. (New York: Schirmer Music Company, 1955).

Ruth Norman, *Sing and Do* (New York: Mills Music, Inc., 1953).

Emma Sheehy, *There's Music in Children* (New York: Holt, Rinehart & Winston, 1947).

Katherine T. Wessells, *The Golden Song Book* (New York: Golden Press, Inc., 1945).

By reading such stories as the *Indoor Noisy Book,*[2] written by an author sensitive to sounds, and by playing such records as "Muffin in the Country" and "Muffin in the City," the teacher can help the children in hearing and identifying sounds that they hear. She can also help them become aware of the sounds which can tell them what is to happen next; for instance, the kitchen sounds that announce time for eating; the footsteps of a parent or a friend coming to the group; the clock-sounds which announce the time for leaving.

One morning Randy came into the room chanting " 'It's raining. It's pouring. The old man is snoring. Bumped his head on the side of the bed, and couldn't get up in the morning.' That's my song. My sister taught me," he said proudly, and proceeded to sing the verse all over again. His teacher, interested in teaching the children to be good listeners, made the most of this opportunity. "That's a good song," she said to Randy. "When we are all together at juice time, will you sing it for all of us?" Then at juice time she said, "We are going to listen while Randy sings," and reminded them that, "When you sing for us, we listen quietly to you. Now it's your turn to listen while Randy sings."

Communicating Feelings with Music

Music can be used to communicate ideas, but with preschool children it is primarily a medium for communicating feeling. Children who view TV absorb musical stereotypes as they watch cartoons and listen to the musical accompaniment for the action portrayed. Children whose mother sings lullabies to them at bedtime relate their pleasant feelings about their mother to the lullabies they hear her sing.

The teacher of a preschool group should consider what relationships her children have with music. If she consistently sings, "Now it's time for juice," do they associate singing with refreshment time? If the children's, "You can't come in," is followed by the teacher's singing, "You can come in," do the children build a pleasant association with the singing? Do they learn to associate soft and melodious music with relaxing at rest time? Does music heighten a variety of experiences in the course of the day, making them more joyous? If, each day, music is an integral part of the pleasant activities of the preschool group, the children come to enjoy it and to think of music as one of the pleasant things in life.

The teacher who orients her preschool group toward religion can use a song of thanks in much the same way that other teachers use the expression "Isn't this fun!" to help the children appreciate the joy inherent in most group activities. At refreshment time the teacher can use "Thanks for

---

[2] Margaret Wise Brown, *Indoor Noisy Book* (New York: Harper & Row, Publishers, 1946). *Country Noisy Book* (1940) and *Seashore Noisy Book* (1941) are by the same author.

juice" as a grace; at other times she can use the same simple song with different words. She may say, "Children, let's give thanks for this wonderful chance to play here at nursery school," and then lead them in singing "Thanks for play."

Enjoying Musical Games

The musical games of the preschool group are only simple beginnings of games. The degree of game organization increases with increasing maturity of the children. The three-year-old child who has had his sawing experience elaborated by having others sing a simple sawing-song enjoys this experience so much that later, during the quiet minutes following refreshments, he may say, "Let's saw!" Then his teacher can lead the group in the short action song "Saw-ing, saw-ing, see how I can saw." The back-and-forth motion of the saw is reflected in the high-low sequence of the notes of the song.

Three-year-old children can learn to enjoy the more formal and more extended game of "Train to the Zoo." With a row of chairs for their train, and the "Train to the Zoo" record on the phonograph, the children play first the role of train passenger, then the role of visitor to the zoo. The music enhances and structures their dramatic play, and their dramatic play enlarges their musical experience. "Let's do it again," shout the children at the end of the record. When their teacher asks, "Last time?" and the children agree to do it only once again, the teacher can finish the record and the dramatic play by saying, "Let's wave goodbye to the train."

The teacher who is good at suiting action to song and song to action can build a collection of musical games to bring a rainy day spent indoors up to the level of a delightful experience. For instance, she can bounce a ball to a child and sing. "Bounce and catch my pretty blue ball." Thus she provides large- and small-muscle exercise together with musical experience. With four- and five-year-old children she can also use the jumprope, swinging it gently back and forth for a child to have his turn, sometimes swinging it all the way over for an older child. This jumping activity becomes a simple musical game when the teacher leads the children in a musical chant describing what the jumper is doing; for instance, "Back and forth, I'm jumping now. When I miss, you have a turn." The rhythm for the chant is picked up from the rhythm of the jumper.

Quieting Down with Music

The teacher should know how to stimulate children so that they eagerly participate in musical activities. She should also know how to use music in helping them to move from activity into rest. The spontaneity which is a part of musical creativity can become exciting to the point at which it is desirable for the teacher to introduce formality, perhaps by having the children take turns. Thus she helps them regain self-control through an accustomed procedure. If the children have been responding to music creatively and individually to the point where they have become fatigued, the teacher needs to draw them back together by having them work with her and with each other in some group activity that is not highly structured. For instance, a four-year-old group that enjoys doing the "Hokey-Pokey" will respond to hearing the familiar record and seeing their teacher start doing it. From such a group activity led by the teacher the children are easily moved into a quiet interlude.

One teacher moved her group into quiet rest time by playing her favorite lullaby on the piano. Her verbal invitation to rest presently became unnecessary; the children learned to recognize the lullaby in much the same way that they learn to recognize the music of a commercial advertisement for a TV program they like to watch.

The teacher who enjoys playing restful music while the children relax on their cots or mattresses often makes a selection of a recording by a pianist and plays it at low volume. If she enjoys listening to chamber music while she relaxes, she may choose a recording of a string quartet, or perhaps a violin duet. Whatever is restful for her is a good choice of music for the children because they are apt to respond imitatively to her yawning and relaxing.

For brief relaxation between more vigorous activities, the teacher may like to sing, or to strum on an autoharp. To enlarge her repertoire of songs for such quiet times she can get such record albums as "Activity Songs" or "Activity Songs for Kids," sung by Marcia Berman. By playing the record and using the printed sheet enclosed with it, the teacher can familiarize herself with both the melody and the words of each song. Then she is ready to use one of the songs with the children, either to help them relax or to help them learn the song. "I Sing My Dolly a Song" is apt to become a favorite song to use for relaxation.

ABSORBING SADNESS IN MUSIC

Although the preschool group experience is composed primarily of joyous events, it can swing down into sadness, on occasion, and needs at that point the widening and deepening of emotion which music can provide. The ballads composed by the sad and lonely cowboy on the range deal gently and realistically with such vital events as the loss of a loved one, or the last run made by a locomotive. They are part of the folklore which the preschool child absorbs in small amounts from time to time. So also are the repetitive chorus parts of Negro spirituals and old English ballads. Only complex and heavy music is to be avoided. Simple rhythmic, melodic compositions are sufficiently numerous to supply the music for preschool children.

With or without an autoharp, the preschool teacher can teach the children some refrain, such as "Old Joe Clark," which has both a simple melody and simple words. When this has become familiar to the children, she can use short verses—sometimes sad, sometimes gay—which she sings between the refrains which the children sing with her. Thus she helps them learn to listen for the point at which the music tells *them* to start singing. Of course, she can also help them learn to enjoy ballad music in other ways —perhaps by pushing holes in the air or clapping as they feel the pulsing accent of the music, or by improvising other words to substitute in the refrain.

Expanding Activities with Musical Experience

FROM ACTION INTO SONG

When children model clay, one of them may start pounding it. Presently he may develop a rhythmic pounding which others soon imitate. As the rhythm of the pounding pervades the place, the teacher may wonder what to do. Should she ignore the pounding and let the children continue with it? Should she have the children put the clay away until they agree to use it only for modeling? Or should she expand the pounding into musical fun for the children?

Probably the teacher will pick up the rhythm and fit some such phrase to it as, "Pound the clay, pound the clay," or, with younger children, "Pound it, pound it." Presently she or someone else may suggest another phrase in the same rhythm, perhaps rhyming with the first phrase. Then she can put the two phrases together and lead the children in singing "Pound the clay, hear us play." With four- or five-year-old children, she should elaborate the song in that way. However, with young preschool children, less skilled both with words and with paying attention to more than one kind of activity at a time, she probably should lead the children into using the second phrase for awhile, then move them back into more modeling activity.

The teacher who likes to enrich activities with music will find many rhythmic motions which she can emphasize by composing a simple song on the spot. The motion of the swings may make her think of "Up in the sky" or, "Make me go high," or may lead her to turn some child's expressions into a chant. When she needs to move her group from one activity to another, she can develop such spontaneous chants as "Juice time, juice time," or, "I see our bus."

A STORY AND A SONG

A story can lead into a song and, especially with four- and five-year-old children, a song can lead into a story. Often a teacher tells a story and then introduces the song that tells the same story in music. For instance, she may read *The Carrot Seed*.[3] After the children are familiar with it, she may play the recorded musical version of the story as a means of helping the children learn to enjoy listening to music. They can follow along by looking at the pictures in the book as they hear the music.

[3] Ruth Krauss, *The Carrot Seed* (New York: Harper & Row, Publishers, 1945).

The preschool teacher who helps the children enjoy each of the holidays throughout the year can enhance each one with songs. From a story about trimming a Christmas tree, the children can go on to learning the song "Come and dance with me, 'round the Christmas tree," or they can make up their own song, perhaps elaborated out of the greeting "A Merry Christmas to you!" or, "Let's trim the Christmas tree!"

FROM SINGING INTO MOVEMENT AND MORE MUSIC

A song is most apt to lead into movement and more music. A group of four- or five-year-old children who have just sung "Oh Where, Oh Where Has My Little Dog Gone?" are delighted to look for him as the music continues. Later in the year they like to look for him in the garden, "in New York," or "on the moon," for instance. If the children want to look for their little dog in the garden, the music may change and take them into the nursery song about "Mistress Mary, Quite Contrary,"[4] and may go on to helping them pretend to be flowers swaying in the breeze. If the children want to look for their dog in New York or on the moon, their teacher can ask, "How do we get there?" Using the children's answers, she leads the group in moving their bodies like a train, singing a folksong about the train, or imitating the sounds that a train makes. The children's answers may lead the group into dramatizing the takeoff of a rocket complete with appropriate sound effects. In short, a song can lead any place that the teacher and the children want it to go.

With three-year-old children the teacher should keep a song within closer limits. If the children are singing a familiar song such as "Oh, Do You Know the Muffin Man?" she may help them vary it a little by substituting someone else whom they might know, perhaps the letter man or the parcel man. This substitution of another phrase introduces variation at the same time that the children have practice in repeating the melody of the song. Then, listening to the melody played at the tempo of their walking, the children can pretend to go from house to house, suiting a simple movement to familiar music.

"Johnny, Get Your Haircut"[5] is an example of a simple, melodic folk song which can have an infinite number of improvisations of both words and dramatic action. Every teacher should have a repertoire of several such songs which she can use to enhance an experience and build it musically and emotionally into a pleasantly vivid occasion which may spill over into expression in words, art media, or more music.

A teacher who had taught her group "The Bear Went Over the Mountain," and used it with many variations, was delighted to hear the melody

---

[4] Katharine T. Wessells, *The Golden Song Book* (New York: Golden Press, 1945), p. 16.

[5] Ruth Seeger, *American Folk Songs For Children* (New York: Doubleday & Company, Inc., 1948).

of it sung in excellent rhythm by Peter as he played in the sandbox with his dump truck. Jerry who was playing there with him joined in the song:

Dumpty, dumpty, dumpy.
Dumpty, dumpty, dumpy.
Dumpty, dumpty, dumpy.
Dumpty, dumpty, dum.

She was pleased also when Neal's mother repeated the song that he had sung at home one day about his nursery school activities:

We like to play with the teeter-totter,
Up and down, up and down.
We like to swing. We like to clap.
We like to live in houses.

Getting Acquainted with Instruments

Through a variety of experiences with different instruments, the children can learn that sound is a result of vibration. They can have a simple introduction to the different groups of instruments which constitute an orchestra: the violins and other string instruments, the flutes and other woodwind instruments, the horns, drums and cymbals and other percussion instruments. Four-year-old children especially can learn that there are limits in using an instrument, and five-year-old children can start learning the rules for playing each instrument. Such learnings will occur more rapidly and for more of the children if some of the instruments are available in a music corner for the children to use at all times.

The music corner should have a piano with which the children can explore sound, melody, and harmony. It should have drums with which the children can explore tone and rhythm, and at least one or two sturdy xylophones on which the children can compose tiny tunes or just have the fun of changing motion into sound. During part of the day, other instruments, perhaps relatively inexpensive band or orchestra instruments that can be replaced, can be put out for brief exploration under adult supervision. Other interesting additions to a music corner include two or three pans that make harmonizing tones, and coconut shells that make sounds like those of horse's hoofs.

The high shelves from which the teacher brings down additional musical devices hold the teacher's phonograph and the boxes of instruments for the rhythm band. The shelves also hold the plastic versions of orchestra instruments that are brought out when a parent or friend comes to show the children a musician's instrument. A real Stradivarius violin stays in the hands of its owner, but a plastic toy violin can give a child a beginning experience with a violin as a means of producing sound. In a preschool group, the plastic toy instrument is useful in much the same way that the plastic toy telephone is—as a toy counterpart of an expensive device for adult use.

Four-year-old Russell picked up the toy banjo from the music corner and asked the supervising adult to play a record for him. As she got out the phonograph and selected a medley, Russell said, "Do you know what I'm doing? Getting ready." With the toy banjo under one arm, he stood poised, ready for the music to begin. As soon as it started, he strummed the banjo. With each succeeding tune, he chose some appropriate musical expression, sometimes a stepping kind of dance, sometimes a bit of strumming, sometimes just listening. He enjoyed the entire record, and at the end reminded the supervising adult to "take care" of the phonograph.

LEARNING ABOUT VIBRATION

To learn that sound is vibration, each child can stretch a rubberband around the top of the back of his chair, or around an open and sturdy box, to make a one-string violin. He can pluck it, then hear its tone and see it vibrate. He can pluck it, then stop its vibration by touching it. He can stretch it tauter and hear a higher sound. In these ways he can make and control sound. With a pot lid that has a knob for a handle, a child can have an introduction to the percussion instruments. Striking the lid starts it vibrating, producing a sound. Touching the vibrating lid enables the child to feel the vibration at the same time that he stops it and ends the tone. With several lids, a child can hear that there is a range of tones, some higher and some lower in pitch.

With simple whistles the teacher can help the children have experience basic to understanding both woodwind instruments and horns. Blowing across the end of a bullet shell makes the column of air in the shell vibrate to the point of producing a sound. A preschool child can have as many different experiences as there are different varieties of whistles—wood, cardboard, plastic, or metal; the kind that unrolls a tube of paper; plain or a slide whistle, which has a movable piston inside the cylinder—all kinds of whistles are useful for exploring the production of sound, and all are fun in themselves.

SUGGESTIONS FOR USING DIFFERENT INSTRUMENTS

Although instruments should be available to children, they should not be abused. They are available as a means of helping children to appreciate their musical qualities, and should be used for making music and for exploring the nature of sound. The child who wants to make noise, attract attention to himself, or express strong feelings should be guided into other activities or into making such noise outdoors rather than indoors.

Piano. Encourage each child to explore playing the piano. If his exploration becomes distracting to others, suggest that he try using just the black keys. If several children want to enjoy the piano at the same time, the

A child likes to play the instrument too. (Courtesy of Western Washington State College, Bellingham, Washington. Photograph by Joffre T. Clarke.)

output of sound can be lessened by having them take turns in using it. Show the children the inside of the piano when they ask about it.

Autoharp. Children accustomed to having their teacher use an autoharp are eager to use one too; they can learn to make pleasing chords on it. A parent singing with or strumming on an autoharp is an excellent center of interest during the time that children choose their own activities. One child at a time can help the parent, the child playing on one side of the autoharp, the parent on the other.

Ukulele. A ukulele, like the autoharp, provides a portable accompaniment to singing and permits music to be either an indoors or outdoors activity. The inexpensive plastic versions of the ukulele enable an adult to feel comfortable in letting the children produce sounds on it.

Phonograph. For listening times the teacher should have a phonograph that produces beautiful sound. To keep the instrument in good condition, the teacher should store it on a high shelf.

Because preschool children are highly imitative, the teacher should provide them with a phonograph for their own use. An old phonograph and some discarded 78 rpm records enable a three-year-old child to produce sound and learn how scratches make the sound repeat. A better instrument and expendable records without scratches can be used by an older child to play music by himself.

Voice. Guide the children in feeling the vibrations made in the larynx when they talk or sing, and in hearing the difference between speech and song. Children can learn to distinguish soft indoor voices from the loud ones used only outdoors.

Drums. Make different kinds of drums available to the children. From the branch of a tree suspend a large Indian drum or a round Oriental hanging drum so that a child can hit it with a large drumstick and feel its vibration when he stops its sound by touching it. Have sturdy wooden drums which the children can play with their hands or the teacher can use when she wishes to pick up the rhythm of a child's action for a group rhythmic activity. Encourage parents to stretch rubber from automobile inner tubes over the ends of empty oatmeal cartons to make inexpensive drums for use in a rhythm band or other rhythmic activity.

Instruments That Parents Play. The younger preschool child who does not like to share his parents' attention with an instrument should not be asked to share his parent with both the instrument and other children. But most preschool groups have at least one child who likes to have his daddy or mother bring his instrument to school. The daddy who brought his guitar and helped the children sing "Mary Had a Little Lamb," "Go Tell Aunt Rhody," and "She'll be Comin' 'Round the Mountain" gave pleasure to all the children and added to his own child's prestige within the group.

Rhythm Instruments. A variety of simple devices for producing rhythm have been collected from folk groups in different countries, and new ones have been developed. Many of these rhythm instruments can be easily made by parents or teachers. The following simple instruments can be supplemented with local favorites.

- *Triangle.* Its lovely tone justifies the purchase of this instrument. To prevent the loss of its accessory parts, use a nylon thread to tie the hitter and the holder to the triangle at its corners. Keep the triangle handy so that it can be used to emphasize a rhythm or to play the part of a bell.
- *Maracas.* These shakers are made from gourds. They are shaken separately, not hit together. If the handle separates from the gourd, show the children what makes the noise in the shaker, then glue it back together. Several shakers are desirable for a rhythm band.
- *Finger cymbals.* For the child who wants to hit two things together, this instrument gives a sound that is less apt to drown out others than that of a larger cymbal.

- *Clappers.* Smooth wooden blocks hit together give interesting sound as well as rhythm. A rhythm band can have several clappers.
- *Wooden sticks.* Children like to hear about the Japanese man who reminds the families in his community to put out their fires before going to bed. Nightly he makes his rounds each hour, hitting together wooden sticks as he walks.
- *Sand blocks.* A piece of sandpaper glued around a wooden block makes a sand block. Rubbed against one another, two such blocks make an interesting sound.
- *Wrist bells.* Sleighbells between half an inch and one inch in diameter are sewed to a cloth wristband which has an elastic insert. The child shakes his arm to make sounds in rhythm.
- *Tambourine.* Older preschool children like to shake or hit this instrument; a younger child does more hitting than shaking. Children can make tambourines by putting metal bottle caps between the edges of two pie-sized paper plates.

Music as a Group Experience

One of the important objectives of a preschool is to help children learn to be part of a group. The preschool child learns to play by himself, with one or two others, with a small group, and with a larger group. Musical activities are a vehicle for helping him with each of these situations. Alone, or with a friend or two, he can explore the creation of sound by an instrument; with other children, sometimes in a small group and sometimes in a group that includes almost all of the children, he can experience the pleasure of sharing a song, of moving to music, or of participating in a rhythm band. The child who learns to enjoy music comes into more group experience than does the child who participates only in the sequence of group activities that are part of the daily routine for meeting bodily needs.

The preschool child is learning to be part of a group. He is invited and encouraged to participate in a group activity, but is not expected to do so until he is ready. The child who plays with blocks or clay at the side of the room sometimes stops his play to listen to and watch what the group does. Later he may come closer to the group and watch it for a longer time. From that point on, he can gradually be drawn into the group activity— first by helping the teacher to pass out materials, later by engaging in some of the musical activities in which the teacher and the children are involved.

Costuming enriches group experience with music. Many a girl has been enticed into dancing activities out of a desire to wear one of the "stick-out" skirts. The four-year-old who can dramatize a role takes on the accompanying music as easily as he wears the cap that goes with his role. A preschool child who likes the feel of a silk scarf enjoys the fun of playing with it with music in the background.

TEACHING RHYTHMIC MOVEMENT

The kindergarten teacher can say, "Let's walk the way our dolly walks," then help the children in thinking about how a dolly might walk. But the nursery teacher should avoid such structuring. Instead, she should encourage the children to move as they wish to when they hear the music: "Let's listen to the music and dance." Listening for a moment, the teacher starts moving quickly or slowly in accord with the music. The children do as they wish while the music is played. Frequently they try to do what their teacher does. If she turns around, they try making turns. If she puts her arms up, they put their arms up in the air, too. As a child tries some new movement, his teacher should smile and imitate his movement. Imitation is a high compliment to the child, and encourages him to continue to practice the movements that his teacher praises in this way.

With preschool children attention should be given to moving as the music suggests, not to the learning of specific dance steps or to structuring of the child's movements into dance movements. The child's forms of expression are molded into formal dance movements only as the child is ready for such molding. The teacher should introduce new movements whenever she sees that the children are ready to imitate additional movements. Watching and imitating their movements make it possible for her instruction to pace their development.

Depending on their capacity for imitation, the teacher should help young preschool children learn to associate particular kinds of movements with different kinds of music. When she plays a march, she listens for a moment, then marches off around the room with the children doing likewise. When she plays a Hungarian dance, the children get the feel of the music both by hearing it and by seeing how she reacts to it. Records are available to help the children learn to clap, walk, run, jump, or hop—older children to gallop and skip as well—to music.

With four- and five-year-old children, the teacher can capitalize on dramatic play by adding music, costumes, and story to enhance it. For instance, children who have just watched frost scrapings from a refrigerator melt down into a puddle of water, or watched snowflakes float down through the air to melt on the ground, can wear a paper snowflake and pretend to be one as they listen to soft, swaying music. Children who have listened to an adventure of Raggedy Ann follow the lead of their teacher as she dances a few simple steps, makes some floppy jumps, and collapses on the floor in relaxation. Children listening to a repetitive drumbeat and wearing a feather headband become Indians walking quietly through the forest, the way Little Indian and his daddy did.

The teacher should encourage the older preschool children in listening to the music themselves, and in associating verbal instructions and ideas with it. When the kindergarten teacher plays a march, she may ask the children, "What does the music make you want to do? Show what the music tells you to do." If Mary is marching especially well, the teacher may say, "Mary is marching to the music. Let's *all* march with Mary to the

Properties enhance musical experience. (Courtesy of Long Beach Parent Nursery Schools and Mariam M. Cook, Long Beach, California.)

music." Next she may play a Hungarian dance and ask the children, "What would you like to do to this music? Will a silk scarf help you?" The children soon learn to identify and differentiate marching and dancing, running and walking, music to play and music for resting.

With nursery or kindergarten children, the teacher is especially eager to have them really dancing, the way Bobby's preschool group did.

One day Bobby said that he would play Stanley's trumpet and I would play the piano for his older sister and the other girls to dance. And that we did. I said, "Bobby, let's play 'Farewell to Thee' for the Hawaiian dances," and we played it. Then we played the "Valse Poupée" for the dollies to dance. And on and on with Bobby sitting on a high stool playing like Louis Armstrong. He was so pleased with playing that we did not quit until both the teacher and the dancers gave out.

The spontaneous, imitative, and cooperative rhythmic play of children is reported in the following observation of Neal (about three years and six months old), Karen (about four years and six months old), and Susan (about five years and six months). The initiator of the activity was Susan. "Let's do this," she said as she started jumping, moving in a circle. Immediately Neal and Karen began jumping in the same way, facing each other in a circle. Without further conversation, Susan added circular arm movements to her jumping. At once Neal and Karen imitated her, with

493

differing degrees of success, according to age. For several minutes the children carried on rhythmic movements with Susan as their leader. They had no conversation but communication was continuous as they exchanged glances of mutual approval.

Here, then, for the teacher are the essentials of guiding preschool children in rhythmic movements:

1. A leader who moves from one kind of movement to another pacing the interest of the children.
2. A minimum of spoken suggestion.
3. A feeling of mutual appreciation.

The mature teacher adds music and one other technique: she notices when a child begins a new movement and imitates it.

The importance of adequate space in which to express one's feelings about the music cannot be overemphasized. A child is not free to express his feelings if he feels that he is apt to bump into another person or a wall. A supervisor of music recalled the difficulty she had in moving in time to music when she was a five-year-old child in a kindergarten group in which each child was expected to stay in line as he skipped to music. As the largest child in the group, she was placed at the end of the line and had no room for more than one or two skips before she had to stop or else hit the person in front of her. The experience was frustrating to her because she liked to move freely to music; it was disappointing to her teacher, who concluded that this girl, the daughter of a musician, was not musical. All that was needed to remedy the situation was freedom to use the space available.

TEACHING A SONG

The short and simple songs of the preschool group are easily learned as whole units by the children. In fact, the ease with which children acquire a song is evident in their ready learning of commercial advertisement songs on TV programs. When an appealing song is presented in its entirety repeatedly, they hear others singing it, and they soon sing it, too. In other words, they learn readily through imitation and by hearing a song in its entirety.

The teaching of a new song should be scheduled for a time when the children are eager for new activities. Teachers who appreciate the importance of teaching music often present a new song as the first group activity of the day, just after the children arrive and have had health inspection. Other teachers like to have the children enjoy a new song just after they have rested and had refreshments. A familiar song can be sung at the end of the day, but a new song should be sung when the children are active learners.

The teacher should be ready to present the new song. She may learn it from a record, playing the song over and over until she has heard and memorized each word of it. If no word sheet accompanies the record, she can write down the words by listening carefully to the singer. The teacher who likes to sing with an autoharp or guitar accompaniment should practice the song the way she will play and sing it for the children. She should be able to play her instrument well enough that it adds to her rapport with the children and does not interfere with it by taking her attention away from them as she sings with them. When she uses an autoharp or piano accompaniment, the teacher should keep the accompaniment so soft that it does not drown out the light voices of the children.

To say, "We're going to have a new song—let's listen to it," is abrupt. Preschool children require more time for orientation to a new activity, and respond more fully when their teacher creates a background for introducing a new song. One teacher prepared her group for learning the song, "The Farmer Plants His Corn," by reading to the children about Farmer Small.[6] Then she suggested that Farmer Small might be planting his corn on such a nice spring day and led them into singing about "The Farmer Plants His Corn." On a later day the children sang the song again and dramatized it as well.

A teacher who consistently made a point of relating songs to other activities of the children felt rewarded the day that Bobby, three years and seven months old, climbed to the top of the ladder of the slide, paused there high above the playground, and sang the fireman's song—"Bong! Bong!"—before descending on the slide.

When she presents a song to the children, the preschool teacher should sing all of it. Depending upon the age and musical experience of the children, the song may be a brief two lines for a new group of three-year-old children, or a four-line stanza for older preschool children. The teacher helps the children hear the melody as a whole. She teaches the song on several successive days, singing it once or twice each day. As soon as the children have most of the melody in mind, she may help them hear and sing a part of the song more musically. She may say, "Listen, children. This part of the song goes like this: . . . ." Whenever she sings with the children, the teacher should use an open throat tone which the children can imitate. The vibrato and falsetto qualities admired in some adult singing should be avoided in the beginning song experiences of children.

The preschool teacher should select only very simple songs with which to enrich the lives of the children. For instance, she should choose carefully among folk songs, selecting two to four lines from songs that are simple and repetitive. The *piñata* song, sung in Mexico and other Spanish-speaking countries to encourage the child trying to break the *piñata* with a stick is an example of a song especially suitable for four- or five-year-old children. To introduce the song, the teacher may explain how each child has a role

[6] Lois Lenski, *The Little Farm* (New York: Henry Z. Walck, Inc., 1942).

in the *piñata* game: a child who is blindfolded tries to hit the *piñata* with a stick while other children as well as the grownups encourage him in his hitting. "What shall we say to the boy trying to hit the *piñata* and break it open for all of us?" she may ask. "Hit it!" will probably be suggested as

Indians drum and sing with their chief. (Courtesy of Long Beach Parent Nursery Schools and Mariam M. Cook, Long Beach, California.)

words of encouragement. Then the teacher can tell the children how Spanish-speaking children sing "Hit it": *"Dale!"* [dá-lay]. She can then enlarge this bit of advice into the Spanish folk song:

Dale, dale, dale!	Hit it, hit it, hit it!
Dale, dale dura!	Hit it, hit it hard!
Dale, dale, dale!	Hit it, hit it, hit it!
Dale mas y mas!	Hit it more and more!

If the children are not accustomed to learning songs, the teacher should probably limit this song to its first two lines the day that she introduces it. But if the children learn the first lines easily, she may feel that they are ready for the second half of the song, too. As in telling stories, the wise teacher watches for signs of fatigue in deciding how long the song activity should be continued. Since the words of a folk song in another language are usually new to most of the chidren, the teacher is more apt to shorten than to lengthen the teaching of such a song.

ENCOURAGING PERFORMERS

One of the things that parents of gifted children do for them is to act as an audience. The children get used to performing well while people watch them. The nursery child profits from a similar opportunity. His teacher can provide it when children are gathered together as a group. For instance, after they have been singing their greeting song, "Hi-ho, hi-ho, good morning," she may ask, "Who would like to sing it for us?" If no one volunteers, she continues by asking, "Would you like to sing it for us, Jean? Come over here by me." When Jean finishes, the teacher expresses appreciation of her performance, "Thank you, Jean." She may also lead the children in clapping: "Let's clap for Jean. Two or three claps." She reminds the children that each of them will have an opportunity to sing when he is ready, "Maybe some others will sing for us tomorrow just the way Jean did this morning."

PANTOMIME SONGS

A teacher should have a repertoire of short, entertaining, and educational activities which she can use at any time or in any place whenever she needs to collect children into a working group, or to keep them as a group for a brief time while waiting to gear into the schedule of others. She should include in her repertoire pantomime songs that are favorites of the children. These she can glean from records, books,[7] and other preschool teachers.

The teacher of three-year-old children should select short and simple action songs with simple arm movements; for instance, "Here's a ball." The teacher of four- and five-year-old children can select longer, more dramatic songs, such as "Little Cottage in the Wood." Songs the motions to which are made with large muscles are appropriate for younger preschool children; with small muscles, for older children. A song such as "Eeensy-weensy spider" can have simple finger motions for use with four-year-old children, more complicated finger movements with older children. The songs which have counting as part of them should be selected with reference to the numbers that children understand at a particular age. However, a song such as "Five eggs, five eggs—that makes ten" can be learned by

[7] An example of such a book is Lucille Wood's *Songs for Singing Fun* (St. Louis, Mo.: Webster Publications). *More Singing Fun* is another paperback book by the same author. 78 rpm records with the same titles are available.

older preschool children just as syllables that fit into a pleasant tonal pattern. In general, it is best to use those pantomime songs especially appropriate to children at a given age and leave until later other songs appropriate to subsequent age levels.

A teacher of four-year-old children tells of a favorite pantomime song of her group as follows:

We sing the "Shoemaker's Dance." It is a lilting, happy, repetitive tune that the children love. While we sing the words, we wind the thread for the shoemaker, and pound the hammer. We "make" shoes for ourselves, Daddy, Mommy, Baby; and we even make great big giant shoes. We sing the song over six or seven times.

HAVING A RHYTHM BAND

Children who are sufficiently mature and experienced in being members of a group enjoy participating in a rhythm band. They hear stories about a band[8] and they talk about being in a band until they are eager to have one themselves.

In having a rhythm band, the teacher must be sure that there is a rhythm instrument for each child, and that an adult is available for playing suitable music on either the piano or the record player. When she gathers the children together to form the rhythm band, she should talk with them briefly so that each child knows that playing an instrument in the band is fun; that each child will have an instrument to play; that a child who is busy with another activity may finish that activity and join the band when he is ready to do so; and that everyone in the band is going to watch for the signals to begin playing and to stop playing. Then she quickly passes out the instruments. As she does so, she may say, "Have you played the triangle? This is the way to hold it." "You're going to have a lovely time with these bells." "Is the cymbal a loud or a soft instrument? That's right, it's a very loud instrument, so we have to play it softly." "Children, please keep your instruments quiet until I give the signal to play them." The instruments should be distributed quickly, with only as much choice on the part of each child as is consistent with rapid preparation for the rhythm band.

After the children have played several times in unison, their teacher may say, "We shall start by all playing together. Then each instrument is going to have a turn to play. When I say *triangle,* then John and Rose have their turn to play. When I say *clappers,* then Mary, Tom, and Bobby have their turn. . . ." Through this activity the children can learn the names of the instruments and that each kind of instrument has its own individual sound.

To help the children learn about differences in rhythms, the teacher may say, "You are going to have to listen well with your sharp ears because

---

[8] One such story is Margaret Wise Brown's *The Little Brass Band* (New York: Harper & Row, Publishers, 1955).

the music is going to sound a little different and you want to keep right with it." Before long the rhythm band is able to keep the rhythm of a march, then shift to that of a waltz, thus learning to respond to gross differences in rhythm.

The teacher should lead the rhythm band at first. But soon the imitative children are eager to take turns playing the role of conductor. The conductor role is not only an experience in leadership, it is also an experience in listening to the rhythm of the music and emphasizing it by making a strong downbeat at the first of each measure.

The teacher can conclude the rhythm band activity by having the children put away their instruments. Those who want to try another instrument are reminded that they can choose it next time, and can use the one in the music corner whenever they wish. A nonparticipant who has been listening to the band is asked to help the teacher pass around the box in which the instruments are kept. In this way he begins to have a feeling of belonging to the band. If the teacher exclaims enthusiastically, "We really make music!" she helps the children to appreciate their rhythm band.

The first day of a rhythm band consists of passing out instruments; playing one selection, or two if the children are fairly mature; and collecting the instruments. The period of time allotted for the rhythm band gradually lengthens, but never to the point of inducing fatigue. This fact, together with the fact that this activity—like any other musical activity—is optional, also helps to make the rhythm band an enjoyable experience for the children.

Absorbing More Music to Teach

MAKING A COLLECTION OF RECORDS

Each preschool teacher should have an increasing collection of records suitable for use with her group. With planning she can do this quite easily, especiallly if the parents of the children help with the project and appoint a committee to work with her in selecting two or three good records for the group. If such a selection is made each year by the parents, the group soon has a useful record collection.

One council of parent-cooperative nurseries allocated fifty dollars of its budget to buy records to be lent to each nursery as a temporary supplement to its own records. When the teachers of the nurseries met each month, they each checked out one or two records to use until the next meeting. Thus, at each meeting, each teacher could return records she had been using and obtain other records for the children to enjoy. The records in this collection included the following titles:

Amahl and the Night Visitors
A Visit to My Little Friend
Captain Jinks
Folk Songs for Orchestra

Music for New Music Horizons, Series I
My Playful Scarf
Pinocchio

Indoors When It Rains
Let's Play Together
Little Puppet
Lullabies from Around the
   World
Manners Can Be Fun
Mary Poodle
Merry Toy Shop
Music for Early Childhood

Puss'n Boots
Put Your Finger in the Air
Ride 'em Cowboy
Rhythm Instruments
Sing Along
Songs to Grow On
Train to the Farm
Train to the Zoo
When I Grow Up[9]

The teacher of a preschool group should be a member of any committee selecting records for the children because she is the person who will use the record. If she has ideas about how to use it, she is apt to use it frequently. But if she does not think about its use with the children, it will probably remain on the shelf.

In any community there are various agencies which can help a teacher to learn about records useful for children of the age of those she teaches. Many public libraries have a record collection which includes records for use with preschool children. By talking with the librarian in charge of such a collection, the preschool teacher can borrow records for her group and can find out ones which the children enjoy so much that their group should own the record. Librarians can also lend to a teacher or parent books about teaching music to preschool children. These in some instances contain selected bibliographies which can help a teacher in selecting records especially suitable to the level she is teaching.[10]

A music shop or the music section of a department store lets the preschool teacher listen to records before making a selection. The shop is glad to put the name of the teacher on its mailing list, and will send her notices about new records as they become available.

Phoebe James[11] has developed a set of creative rhythm records for young children, together with books for teacher use. Records especially useful with preschool children include the following:

Animal Rhythms
Favorite Action Songs
Free Rhythms
Fundamental Rhythms

Christmas Rhythms
Nursery School Rhythms
Warm Ups

LEARNING FROM OTHER TEACHERS

The teacher needs suggestions not only about *what* to teach preschool children but about *how* to teach them. Having the same kind of musical

[9] A teacher committee with Mrs. Bertram McGarrity as chairman selected these records for the Long Beach Council of Parent Participation Nursery Schools.
[10] An example of such a book is by Helen Heffernan and Vivian Edmiston Todd, *The Kindergarten Teacher*. Boston: D. C. Heath and Company, 1960. Pages 302–304 have a "Suggested Record Bibliography."
[11] Phoebe James, *Creative Rhythms and Accompaniments*. Verdugo City, Calif.: Phoebe James, Box 286, California 91046.

experience that children have is a good method for her to learn teaching techniques. She can visit the preschool group of an experienced teacher who enjoys music and incorporates a great deal of it into the children's activities. If she visits an experienced teacher in a parent-cooperative group, she can participate with the children in their musical activities just as if she were one of the mothers assisting the teacher. As a member of the group, she can experience the melody and the rhythm of the music and get a feel for the timing of its presentation. She has a fuller learning experience than if she had just sat and listened to a talk about how to teach music. When the children have left, she can talk with the experienced teacher and get more suggestions about ways of working with the children musically.

Another realistic way of learning music-teaching techniques is to participate in a workshop conducted by a preschool teacher who has developed particularly effective ways of teaching music to preschool children. Such a teacher prepares for the workshop by duplicating lists of suitable songs and records for each participant to take home, and by selecting records and songs to use in the workshop. The day of the workshop she brings her own collection of rhythm instruments, her record player and selected records, and her songbooks, containing the songs she plans to use with the participants. If possible, she arranges with her favorite music shop to borrow autoharps that the participants in the workshop can use to accompany themselves as they sing and compose songs for preschool children.

When the participants assemble, they begin at once a series of activities each of which they might use subsequently with their own group of children. They feel the music. They respond to the teacher's comments, such as: "Now we're going to enjoy this lovely, relaxing music"; or, putting her hands over her ears: "That is so loud that it hurts my ears"; or: "You have such marvelous rhythm." As they work with the experienced teacher, the participating teachers and parents can learn effective ways of working with preschool children in enjoying and creating music.

The teacher or parent who eagerly reaches out to learn, create, and teach new songs has the satisfaction of hearing remarks such as the one Neal made when he was four years and nine months old. He said, "I know the most songs. Some I make up, and some I learn."

Conclusion

It does not matter whether a teacher provides experiences with music that is primarily classical, modern, folk, or some other kind of music. But it is highly important that these experiences become increasingly more musical. The child who is interested in exploring a drum should be encouraged to use it for creating rhythm or a musical sound, not just noise. The child who is interested in singing a song should be encouraged to produce a pleasing musical version of it, not just yelling without regard either to amplitude, quality of tone, or the composer's intent to produce melody. The child who is interested in moving to music should be encouraged to listen to the time and texture of the music and to bring his movements into relationship with them, not just to move about aimlessly or without purposeful control. Whatever the child's immediate interest in the music around him, he should be guided into enlarging that interest in the direction of increasingly beautiful music.

A music supervisor tells of her three-year-old niece whom she had helped to enjoy music. Whenever the niece visited her, they spent some time in singing little songs. As a three-year-old, the niece had a considerable repertoire of songs which she sang as she had heard them—in tune, and with a singing voice. That summer, because she was occupied in attending a nursery school, the niece did not visit her aunt for three weeks. On her next visit, the niece told her aunt about her nursery school activities, including singing. She demonstrated what she had learned by yelling loudly and off-key what she called a "song." Her aunt recognized what her niece was attempting to sing and helped her in singing it as it was originally intended to be sung. Thus the aunt provided the child with an experience with real music.

Situations for Discussion

A preschool teacher is apt to find herself in situations similar to the four described here. As you think of what to do in each situation, consider whether each course of action suggested is desirable, or not. Use points brought out in the chapter as well as ideas from your own experience to justify your views. Suggest alternative courses of action to supplement those that are given.

SITUATION 1　You are to lead half of the children in some action songs while they wait for the other group of children to finish clay-modeling. You should prepare for this responsibility by

- Writing out the words of the action songs on a card.
- Memorizing the action songs.
- Arranging for the use of a suitable record.
- Planning to repeat one action song until most of the children know it.
- Reviewing the action songs the children have had.

SITUATION 2　When the children are seated around the table at refreshment time, four-year-old Tommy starts pounding on the table. His simple rhythm is picked up by another child, and juice cups wobble dangerously. As the teacher of the group, you should say

- Let's drink our juice now and have rhythms later.
- I like Tommy's rhythm.
- I have a new song for you today—If you know it already, help me sing it.
- We don't play games while we are eating.
- You are going to spill your juice if you are not careful.

SITUATION 3　You want to teach a small group of four-year-old children a new song. One child in the group, Sandy, keeps watching some other children playing with blocks instead of watching you. You should

- Say, "Look at me, Sandy, I'm going to sing a song."
- Tell Sandy that he can play with the blocks later if he wants to.
- Ask the children: "Are you ready to listen?"
- Start singing the song.
- Tell the children a story leading up to the song.

SITUATION 4   You are interested in having more music for the children in your preschool group. You should

- Send home with the children copies of the songs that you teach them.
- Visit a preschool group taught by a former music teacher.
- Arrange for a music workshop for the teacher group you attend.
- Visit a music store that specializes in children's records.
- Ask a librarian to help you.

Current Books for Preschool Children

BORTEN, HELEN. *Do You Hear What I Hear?* New York: Abelard-Schuman, Limited, 1960 (Hale, 1966). [Listen, and you will hear many sounds.]

BROWN, MARGARET WISE. *The Little Brass Band.* New York: Harper & Row, Publishers, 1955. [The band with trumpet, drum, bassoon, horn, flute, clarinet, and oboe come into the town. They play, and then go to their homes. Earlier books by the same author, published by William R. Scott, Inc., New York, include *Country Noisy Book* (1940), *Indoor Noisy Book* (1946), and *Seashore Noisy Book* (1941), and *The Quiet Noisy Book* (1950).]

GAEDDERT, LOU ANN. *Noisy Nancy Norris.* Garden City, N.Y.: Doubleday & Company, Inc., 1965. [Nancy learns to control the noise that she makes.]

GREEN, DIANE HUSS. *Lenny's Surprise Piano.* San Carlos, Calif.: Golden Gate Junior Books, 1963. [The beginning of Leonard Bernstein's musicianship.]

GRIFALCONI, ANN. *City Rhythms.* Indianapolis: The Bobs-Merrill Company, 1965. [Jimmy listens for the rhythm of the city and gets in harmony with it.]

HOBAN, RUSSELL. *Henry and the Monstrous DIN.* New York: Harper & Row, Publishers, 1966. [Henry gains control of the monstrous din he created. *The Song in My Drum* (1962) is by the same author.]

HORVATH, BETTY. *Jasper Makes Music.* New York: Franklin Watts, Inc., 1967. [Jasper finds a way to earn money for the guitar he wants.]

LENSKI, LOIS. *When I Grow Up.* New York: Henry Z. Walck, Inc., 1960. [Through both words and songs, a boy and a girl explore what each may do as an adult.]

SHOWERS, PAUL. *The Listening Walk.* New York: Thomas Y. Crowell Company, 1961. [Imitating sounds that one hears is part of the fun of listening to this book.]

SLOBODKINA, ESPHYR. *Boris and His Balalaika.* New York: Abelard-Schuman, Limited, 1964. [Boris serves his country as a player of the balalaika.]

STEINER, CHARLOTTE. *Listen to My Seashell.* New York: Alfred A. Knopf, Inc., 1959. [The delight of holding a seashell to your ear.]

ZEMACH, HARVE. *Mommy, Buy Me a China Doll.* Chicago: Follett Publishing Co., 1966. [An example of the well-illustrated books portraying a familiar folk song.]

CHAPTER 15

Guiding Emotional Development

During their preschool years, children do a great deal toward forming the emotional basis for their lives. They explore a wide emotional gamut, and—from the adult reactions to their emotional expressions—they find satisfaction in relating certain kinds of situations with certain kinds of emotional expressions. They learn which emotional reaction to use with a particular situation. They also learn what kinds of emotional reactions are to be avoided. Also, during the period of the preschool years, they learn to internalize many emotions. They develop consciences. They are able to initiate desirable mental-health habits, such as enjoying activities, expressing feelings of love and affection, helping others individually and in a group, sharing the use of toys by taking turns with them, and building realistic mental concepts about the world they live in. They can learn to enjoy finding out what they do not know and thus minimize the fear of the unknown. And they are able to develop an awareness of their emotional reactions and to choose socially acceptable outlets for strong emotions.

The teacher of the preschool group and the parents of the preschool child need to understand the nature of emotions and the various ways of helping children to handle their strong emotions and to learn to use mild emotions constructively. The wise adult continually reminds children of the fun that they are experiencing in what they are doing and encourages them to feel the mild, pleasurable emotions which enhance their learning. The wise adult is able to use a child's mild frustration to give him an added sense of pleasure in overcoming it. But the wise adult also helps the child to avoid frustration which evokes strong emotions that the child may not yet be able to handle within the limits of social acceptance.

Probably the most important way in which an adult helps a preschool child is in helping him establish an identity for himself and, as he matures, in encouraging him to establish a concept of his own importance. The preschool child who is really able to develop self-confidence probably is more apt to withstand frustrations and to be successful.

Children from less advantaged families sometimes need to learn their name. "Hey, you!" may be as close as they have come to an identity of their own. At preschool they learn that their name belongs uniquely to them. Each day they can count on being called by name, on having their belongings recognized as theirs alone, and on having their drawings and other productions marked so that they can each have their own to take home. The fact that their teacher knows each of them and that each of them is important to her gives each child a sense of his own importance. Being valued, he is valuable, and he feels valuable.

The teacher is the principal agent for helping each child develop a sense of his own worth. She greets each child by name when he arrives and is genuinely delighted to see him. In the course of the day she has at least one activity for the group that enables her to establish rapport briefly with each child. One day she may use snack time as a time for sitting and talking with the children in such a way as to include each of them individually. Another day she may use a free-play time as an opportunity for interacting with each child. Sometimes she tells a story in such a way that she draws each child into dialogue. If the first story was long enough to involve only part of the group, she sees that the next story affords opportunity to talk individually with each of the other children. She concludes the day for each child with a personal "Good-bye." In such ways she helps each child realize that he is important to her and therefore important himself.

A teacher can think of herself carrying on a dialogue with each child in her group. Often she is explaining to him, giving directions, and otherwise taking the initiative in the dialogue. But she needs to encourage each child to take the initiative too. He must learn that what he says is meaningful to others.

One day when he was four years old, Neal, who lived near the nursery school which he attended, decided that his mother (an assistant teacher at the nursery school) should take him home so that he could wash his hands there. His mother patiently discussed the problem with him and identified the following ideas in Neal's mind: he was willing to wash his own hands; he would wash them at home and then would return for the rest of the nursery school activities.

Presently Neal's mother said to his teacher, "Neal wants to wash his hands at home and then come back for juice time." The understanding teacher nodded, and smiled appreciatively at Neal. A slow smile of success crossed his face as he went, not toward the gate, but toward the nursery bathroom to wash his hands. He had established the point that he could go home to wash his hands if he wanted to do so. With this confidence, he could choose to conform with the group procedure.

The Teacher Uses Mild Emotions

Each of the chapters in Part II of *The Years Before School* has many suggestions about how adults can work with children to help them to learn

Successful completion of a project builds self-confidence. (Courtesy of Minneapolis Public Schools and Mrs. Mary Jane Higley, Minneapolis, Minnesota.)

readily, to overcome their difficulties and solve their problems successfully, and to enjoy the fun and satisfaction of a variety of new experiences and the repetition of familiar ones. These suggestions should enable the teacher to help the children to experience the stimulation of mild emotions that will enhance their learning.

Prescott, in discussing the physical aspects of emotions, advocates greater use of mild emotions by teachers as well as parents:

Mild emotion, whether it is pleasant or unpleasant, produces modest increases in the rate at which all processes involved in the ingestion, digestion, distribution, assimilation, and metabolism of energy-releasing materials are carried on. . . . In other words, the effect of mild emotion, both pleasant and unpleasant, is generally tonic to all normal body processes. . . .

If more people realized the tonic effect of mild emotions, we might well use them more in the educative process both at home and at school.[1]

Some of the ways in which a preschool teacher uses mild emotions can be pointed out by considering such important aspects of teaching as expressing affection, being realistic, encouraging cooperation, stimulating the development of a conscience, furthering desirable peer relationships, and listening for feedback.

A Teacher Is Affectionate

Teachers should create a warm, affectionate atmosphere in the preschool group so that the children are supported by an emotional climate favorable to active learning. They should express their genuine affection for the children in the group. Teachers of young children in nursery schools and centers are apt to express their affection through hugs and by holding the child who needs reassurance, because young children communicate primarily through physical contacts while they are learning to communicate through words and new kinds of action.

When her teacher had held her for a moment, one three-year-old girl presently said comfortably, "My mommy's at home."

Preschool teachers differ in their methods of expressing affection for the children in their group. One teacher may respond to all hugs and kisses initiated by the children and put her arm around an insecure child, but she may not initiate kisses herself. She mirrors back to the children the affection which each displays. Another teacher may consider a hug and a kiss an integral part of her daily greeting of each child and is pleased when mothers tell her how their children look in the mirror for the tell-tale lipsticks marks on their foreheads or their cheeks. Such a teacher takes the lead in displaying affection.

Probably the way in which affection is displayed by a teacher is less important than whether or not she is consistent in her display. If a hug is part of her morning greeting, she must be sure that each child has such a greeting so that no child feels left our or rejected. Each teacher should be aware of how completely she is meeting the children's needs for physical expression of her affection.

One teacher who had a warm and friendly atmosphere in her nursery group revealed it in her written reports, such as the one about a four-year-old boy in her group:

---

[1] Daniel A. Prescott, *The Child in the Educative Process* (New York: McGraw-Hill Book Company, Inc., 1957), p. 396.

Stanley always seeks me out when he arrives. He'll talk about any number of things if he finds me available. He enjoys telling the things he knows or discovers.

Stanley, I think, comes to me when he needs me or feels I can help him. But I do keep an eye on him because it does not always occur to him to make demands in a dull moment.

Stanley's mother says he is now ready to visit me on a Tuesday noon as have most of the children. He was not "ready" the first time I asked him to come but he has agreed now to come next week. I suppose he has progressed both in his relationship to me and in his relationship to the other children. He knows another child or two will also come along on Tuesday.

Stanley always lets me hug or kiss him. He smiles sweetly and on request will give me a hug almost any time.

Knowing that teaching is a matter of establishing affectionate human relations, the wise preschool teacher gives her entire attention to the children. When she presents some activity that is new to her, she is always careful to have practiced it in advance to the point where she can do it easily. If she is helping the children to make ice cream, for instance, she arranges to have had sufficient practice in making the ice cream so that she can guide them in the process with a minimum of attention to the ice cream and a maximum of attention to their pleasurable experience in making it. Thus she makes sure that the activities of the preschool group enhance, rather than interfere, with the rapport between the children and herself.

The teacher should avoid any situation which may take her attention away from the children. She schedules parent or student conferences for times when she is not working with children. She makes it clear that school hours are solely for the purpose of helping the children. It is not a time for adults to converse or to carry on any other activity that distracts their attention from the children. It is a time for creating a warm emotional climate favorable to the maximum development of the children.

THE TEACHER IS REALISTIC

The teacher affectionately and realistically respects the wishes of each child. If he asks for something, she makes sure that she understands what he wants and that he knows that she understands. Then she either provides him with what he wants, or explains why he cannot have it and diverts his attention to something else. For instance:

(*Four-year-old Teddy sees the cookies to be served at refreshment time. He selects one to eat.*)

TEACHER   Is that the cookie you want? I'll save it for you for juice time. (*Takes cookie and puts both it and the plate of cookies up on a high shelf out of both sight and reach of children.*) The cookies are a surprise for today. Our other surprise today is a new tricycle. You can have a ride on it right now.

(The day that four-year-old Roger's mother brought ice cream for the nursery group, both Roger and his four-and-a-half-year-old friend Neal were interested in having some.)

ROGER *(to a mother assistant)*   I want some ice cream.

MOTHER-ASSISTANT   The ice cream is a surprise for juice time. You have to wait quite a while until juice time.

NEAL *(to the mother asisstant)*   I told him that.

The mother assistant enhanced Roger's and Neal's pleasure in the ice cream by having them wait for it. She also helped the boys to be realistic about the group schedule and reinforced the concept that Neal had already formed about waiting for the proper time to have the ice cream.

The child who gets a considerate and realistic response to his demands soon learns what to ask for and what to do for himself. The attention seeker is often the child who has not been getting a considerate and consistent response from the adults around him. For instance, if a child is kept waiting in the car while his mother and teacher talk, he is apt to honk the horn. His next action depends upon the response he gets. If the adults ignore the honking, he will continue it. If they firmly tell him to stop and then return to their talking, he will find opportunity to continue at the earliest possible moment or will seek attention in some other, probably more annoying, way. But if an adult responds realistically to his signal, he will understand that he has signaled and will learn to use honking only that way.

(Mike, sitting in the driver's seat and grinning broadly and teasingly, honks the horn.)

TEACHER *(running over to the car)*   What's the matter? Are you hurt?

(Mike continues grinning in embarrassment. His mother comes over to the car.)

TEACHER *(to Mike's mother)*   Mike honked the horn, so I thought he needed help. *(to Mike)* You see, Mike, the horn is a signal. A driver uses it when he needs help. He tries not to use it unless he really needs to have people come.

When two children are putting frustrations in each other's way, the teacher helps them to resolve their differences realistically, and in such a way that they experience desirable kinds of behavior. Their early frustration and their subsequent satisfaction in socially approved behavior help them to learn it.

Bruce and Sally were two of the children helping an assistant teacher take the wooden boxes and walking boards out of the play house:

ADULT   We can put the end of the board on top of the box.

SALLY   I want to do it my way.

BRUCE   I want this way.

ADULT   Let's do it Sally's way for a few minutes, and then Bruce's way.

Sally put the second board across the first one and then led the children, Bruce included, across it. The board teetered, one edge just missing Bruce's chin. The adult picked up the board, saying to Bruce, "Whew! The end of that almost hit you!" Bruce then helped the adult to set the second board so that it made the second side of a steady triangle.

SALLY   Let's do it my way.
BRUCE   This way. (*He helps the adult place the boards safely on the boxes.*)
ADULT   We did it your way, Sally. Now it's Bruce's turn to try his way.

In need of help in coping with a problem. (Courtesy of the Merrill-Palmer Institute and Donna J. Harris, Detroit, Michigan.)

The children walked happily on the boards with Sally leading them around the triangle.

THE TEACHER ENCOURAGES HELPERS

Children do not become helpful to others as a matter of chance, but as the result of teaching which makes use of mildly pleasant emotions. When a child helps another, his teacher should notice his action and be quick to commend it. "Did you see that, children? I dropped one of the books I was carrying and Johnny picked it up. Johnny is a helper, and that's what we want to be, helpers!" Johnny appreciates getting attention in this way and is apt to look for other occasions to be helpful. Of course, most often he will get less conspicuous attention. An appreciative smile or a quiet "Thank you" soon gives him that same feeling of having done something worthwhile. But while Johnny is learning the role of helper, and while the teacher is developing in children an awareness of the helper role, she should make her praise obvious.

When an experienced teacher visited his nursery group several times, Billy, who was almost five year old, asked her, "What's your name?" The visiting teacher replied, "My name is Molly, and your name is Billy. I remember your name because you're such a good helper."

In the middle of the morning, when the children are together having refreshments, and at the end of the session, when they gather at the gate, the teacher has an excellent opportunity for remembering with the children how many wonderful things happened during the morning to make it a happy one. Talking together at juice time, they can mention the children and mothers who helped to prepare the refreshments; just before leaving, they can mention those who helped to put away toys and equipment. "And now," the teacher can conclude, "we have one more way to show that we are all helpers. How do we go to the cars?" Soon each child feels that he is a helper as he walks, not runs, to the car that takes him home.

"It feels good to help another person," is a teacher's praise that helps a child to learn to be a helper. "It feels good to help the group," makes a child aware that what he did was desirable. His pleasure in hearing deserved praise will lead him to repeat his helpful behavior at the earliest opportunity.

FORMING A CONSCIENCE

Children of preschool age form ideas of what to do and what not to do. They take on the behavior patterns of their intimate associates and are influenced by verbal statements about desirable and undesirable actions. For instance, three-year-old Lynn noticed a little boy whose mother was trying to persuade him to stop kicking and shouting. Lynn talked the matter over with the adult who was near her:

ADULT   That little boy is trying to act smart.
LYNN   Why doesn't his mama take him home?
ADULT   He certainly should not act smart like that.
LYNN   Mama doesn't want me smart.
ADULT   Your mama likes you to be smart, but not to act smarty. That boy is acting smarty.

Such brief conversations between adult and child are excellent for direct moral teaching in the home as well as in the preschool group. The evaluative remarks of a parent or a teacher about behavior that the child observes give the child his views about right and wrong. Often the adult's tone of voice as much as her words help the child to understand if the behavior is considered "good" or "bad."

The preschool teacher who realizes the importance of direct teaching uses her flannelboard and her pantomimes to show the children familiar situations and to stimulate their thinking about what to do and what not to do in such situations. For instance, the teacher shows a picture of a child and a dog and leads a discussion about being kind to friendly animals. Or she shows a picture of a crying baby and talks with the children about ways in which to make a baby happy. Such brief talks help the children to know how to behave in out-of-school situations. Also important are the brief talks which help them to learn how to behave in the preschool group. If children have been crowding together to use the slide, the teacher can get out her file of pictures which show some children using the slide safely and considerately and other selfishly crowding.

Of course, what is essential is the direct teaching of children in an actual situation. The teacher should always be alert to help children interpret their individual experience. But she should also be alert to help children learn from the experience of others. The flannelboard and pantomimed reenactment of an observed incident helps all the children learn what to do and what not to do.

Furthermore, children's books can help the teacher to guide the development of consciences in children. Peter Wezel has drawn pictures to show children both *The Good Bird*[2] and *The Naughty Bird*.[3] The skillful teacher can use these as a basis for telling stories that show good behavior, and then, later, a contrasting story that helps children be aware of less desirable behavior. The kindergarten child can develop conscious awareness of behavior that makes friends and behavior that interferes with friendship.

The casual conversation between teacher and child in the course of a preschool day can also be an effective aid in helping children to develop guides to good behavior. For instance, the teacher's conversation with three-year-old Marilyn began as an imaginative account about "Billy," the boy counterpart whom Marilyn had invented as a means of exploring the role of a boy, but ended with a decision about Marilyn's own behavior.

One morning, three-year-old Marilyn told her teacher that Billy was a naughty boy. He pulled the wallpaper off at his house. The understanding teacher accepted the report and tried to find out more about what had happened. "Did a lot of paper get pulled off?" Gestures on the part of both child and teacher showed how much paper had come off. "Can daddy fix it?" the teacher asked. Marilyn was reassured that the paper could be

---

[2] Peter Wezel, *The Good Bird* (New York: Harper & Row, Publishers, 1966).
[3] ———, *The Naughty Bird* (Chicago: Follett Publishing Company, 1967).

fixed. "Next time Marilyn will leave the paper alone, won't she?" the teacher concluded, with an affectionate hug. Then Marilyn went off happily to play. She realized that her teacher knew it was she who had torn off the wallpaper, and that her teacher still loved her. Meanwhile, her teacher felt that she had helped Marilyn both in developing a conscience and in taking responsibility herself without the crutch of an alter ego.

Helping Children with Peer Relationships

Whenever she can, a teacher of preschool children should help them to achieve the pleasant satisfaction which derives from establishing happy relationships with other children. She should help preschool children of all

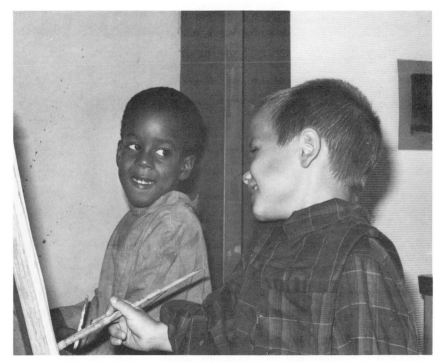

Painting can be a pleasant social experience. (Courtesy of Minneapolis Public Schools and Mrs. Mary Jane Higley, Minneapolis, Minnesota.)

ages to form such relationships, and she should help the older preschool children to become aware of what they can do in order to have happy play with others.

An experienced teacher described a nursery group situation in which she assigned roles as a means of helping the children play together more effectively:

After rest period the children came bounding outdoors, ready for action. Although other large-muscle equipment was available, all the children wanted to ride the tricycle. I diverted some of the boys and girls by saying, "If you wait here in the station (i.e., the bench), I'll help you get a turn." Everyone followed instructions except one boy. Jerry held on tightly to the handle bars of the tricycle he wanted to ride and would not let the other child ride it.

I said, "Jerry, we need a gas-station man. All these cars are out of gas." Jerry loosened the death grip he had on the trike and ran to the gas hose. He became very busy and officious in his role as gas station man. I felt that this was a good outlet after his disappointment in not getting a tricycle to ride. He had a feeling of importance as he told the drivers when they could come in for gas and as he collected their imaginary money.

In a few minutes, the boy who was riding the tricycle that Jerry had wanted to ride came up to Jerry and changed places with him. Meanwhile, I helped the children who were waiting at the station to get a turn on the tricycles.

A few minutes later, Jerry was again aggressive. He grabbed the red "Stop" sign from the boy who was the policeman directing traffic. I said, "We don't take things from our friends. But I think this policeman is going to lunch pretty soon and I'll help you get a turn being the policeman." He accepted this suggestion and went back to riding the tricycle. I felt he needed the tricycle until I could help him get the job as policeman.

Both at home and at nursery school, where her mother was a teacher, four-year-old Mari lived in an environment of love. She received love, and she expressed it. When she was four years and four months old, she said of a friend, "I love her, I love her, I love her as big as the world!" But she was perplexed by another of her friends who said to her, "I hate you!" She asked her mother about what the girl had said, "Menny says she hates me, Mommy. What does *hate* mean?" Her mother tried to explain that hate sometimes gets mixed up with love, and that good friends sometimes say, "I hate you," when they are unhappy for the moment, but really go on loving their friends all the time. Mari listened carefully and then said, "A little she doesn't like me, and a little she does like me."

Another day Mari and her mother talked about Mari's remark to another girl at nursery school. "Ha, ha. I have a new dress, and you don't." Mari listened to her mother's explanation about what to say and what not to say. Then she explained it back to her by saying, "If I say 'Ha, Ha! I have a new dress and you don't!' it's not a good thing to say. But if I say, 'Ha, ha!' it is a good thing to say."

In another nursery group when four-and-a-half-year-old Jan came crying to her teacher, Mrs. Jones put her arm around Jan and asked, "What's the matter?"

JAN She . . . (*Dissolves in tears.*)

MRS. JONES You have to tell me what happened before I can help you.

JAN She hit me! (*Reaches up to touch the top of her head.*)

MRS. JONES She did! Well, I'm sorry she hit you. Was it right here? (*Feels the top of Jan's head.*) A little bump. No blood. Suppose we dampen my clean handkerchief and you hold that on it until it feels better.

Having identified with Jan and taken her part, Mrs. Jones knew she was now in a position to help her with whatever had caused the hitting.

MRS. JONES   Who hit you?
(*Jan mumbles indistinguishably and points in a general direction.*)
MRS. JONES   Let's go find the girl who hit you.

Hand in hand, Mrs. Jones and Jan walked across the playground to the sandbox where Betty was playing.

JAN   She hit me.
(*Betty looks up from her play, but says nothing.*)
MRS. JONES (*to Jan with her arm around her comfortingly*)   What did you do to her?
JAN   Nothing.
MRS. JONES   What did you say to her?
JAN (*hesitantly*)   "I don't like you."
MRS. JONES (*to Jan*)   "I don't like you." How does that make you feel? Does it make you feel like hitting? You told Betty, "I don't like you," and Betty hit you. If you say, "I like you," I think both Betty and you will have fun together. You try it now.

As Mrs. Jones left Jan and Betty to their sandbox play, she made a mental note to watch for other occasions when Jan would say, "I don't like you." Mrs. Jones knew that more than one on-the-spot explanation would be needed before Jan had completed exploring the use of the phrase, "I don't like you." Probably the next two or three occasions would require detailed analysis, and then subsequent ones might require only a gentle reminder that the "I like you" game is better than the "I don't like you" one.

The nursery group provides daily experience with such well-known rules of conduct as taking turns and sharing crayons or toys with others. The kindergarten extends the concept of taking turns to include the idea of waiting for one's turn, and extends the concept of sharing to include the idea of letting a friend use the toy for as long a time as the child himself used it. Meanwhile, other rules of conduct are learned less obviously. For instance, four- and five-year-old children have a great sensitivity to other people which can be guided either into unselfishness or into selfishness. When Mary shares her toy with Velma, Velma may do one of several things: start playing with the toy, ignoring Mary or say, "Thanks," and smile appreciatively at Mary. If a nearby adult notices the incident, she may expand it so that both Mary and Velma develop ways of expressing feelings. If the adult says to Mary appreciatively: "It was nice of you to share your toy," she helps Mary to feel good about sharing. If this pattern of sharing is repeated frequently, Mary will probably become a little girl who shares her things with others.

If the adult ignores Velma's reaction, Velma may be started on her way to becoming the kind of person who takes the kindness of others for granted. However, the adult may say to Velma: "Wasn't that nice of Mary to share her toy with you?" Velma shares the adult's pleasure in the situation and is receptive to the idea of saying, "Thank you," as the adult suggests.

In much the same way, the four- or five-year-old child who has hit another child can be guided into saying thoughtfully "I'm sorry you're hurt" (but not "I'm sorry I hit you."). He can learn to express sympathy and to offer help to a child who is hurt.

It is from the everyday situations described that nursery children take on the basic attitudes of the people around them. If the teacher is a kindly and considerate person, the nursery children will imitate her ways and grow toward being kindly and considerate people.

The preschool years are a time for guiding children toward the ways they will have as an adult. Parents and preschool teachers need to be aware of whether they are guiding children toward

- Leadership, or followership, or some of both.
- Social sensitivity, or social insensitivity.
- Sympathy, or lack of sympathy, or cruelty.
- Unthinking obedience to authority, or self-sufficiency, or some of both.
- Doing what is fun, doing what is one's duty, or doing what gets attention.
- Hitting back, defending oneself as a means of helping the hitter learn better ways, or running away from the hitter.
- Expressing feelings in socially acceptable ways.

The teacher should be aware of the children who relate to each other in leadership-followership roles. She helps the younger child, the follower, to grow in independence. She reminds him, "You don't have to do what Susan says, unless you want to." Or she may enter their play and ask the younger child: "Neal, do you want to do that? You don't have to, you know. You can play with Johnny if you want to."

Three-year-old Neal and five-year-old Susan played together, with Susan suggesting activities and Neal agreeing to them, or ignoring them. When Neal reached the age of four, he was able to question this relationship verbally:

SUSAN   Here's scissors for you, Neal.
NEAL   Why do you always want me to have what you have?
SUSAN   I want you to.
NEAL   I don't want to.

When Susan saved the seat next to her for him, Neal, as a four-year-old, could question her beneficent paternalism:

NEAL   I don't want to sit by you today. I want to sit by Tommy. (*Goes over to the seat that was still vacant next to Tommy.*)

Neal could even express awareness of Susan's wanting to be a leader, and say "No" to that:

SUSAN (*starting a game of follow the leader*) Let's be a leader.
NEAL   Why do you always want to be a leader?
SUSAN   'Cause I want to.
NEAL   I don't want to.

The teacher should also help a leader to accept the leadership of others: "Susan, you have been a leader. Now let Neal be leader and you follow what he does for a while." The teacher should also help Susan to learn how to play with children who are more nearly her equals. "Susan, Neal does not want to follow you now. Why don't you help Johnny build his castle? Maybe you could build a garage for the castle."

Because most children have the opportunity to follow the lead of their parents, their teachers, and older children, they are more apt to need help in assuming leadership roles. The experienced teacher watches for appropriate opportunities.

If a child brings something to share with the others, she encourages him to show it to the group, to demonstrate its use, and to have one or two playmates help him use it. The child who brings boxing gloves shows the others how to box. The child who brings his pet tells the children how he got his pet and shows them how he feeds it.

If a child asks for an activity, the teacher helps him to organize it. For instance, the child who wants to arrange chairs to make a train needs another child or two as assistants. Then he needs help in getting the passengers aboard. The teacher lets him do as much as he can by himself, but is quick to add assistance whenever it is needed.

The teacher encourages a shy child to interact with the other children. If she is passing out materials to use, she has the shy child distribute some of them. If she needs someone to help her show the group some object of interest, she gets the shy child in front of the group with her.

The teacher should realize that a continuing dominant-submissive relationship between two children is evidence of their need for new social techniques. As each child finds satisfaction in playing with others on a basis of equality, he widens his repertoire of roles and is no longer dependent on the single role of leader or follower. The teacher should help each child to widen his social skills. A single role may represent a considerable achievement for a three-year-old, but a four-year-old should have more to choose from.

An older preschool child sometimes tries to go further than controlling his own behavior; he may insist on trying to control the behavior of another child, his mother, or his teacher. Then it is necessary to help him understand that each person determines his own behavior in terms of what he believes to be best for the whole group and the whole situation. For instance, on an excursion a child who does not understand that one road leads to a particular place may attempt to tell the driver where to turn. The wise teacher knows that such behavior indicates readiness for learning and she patiently and affectionately helps the child to consider the situation realistically and in terms of others.

LISTENING FOR FEEDBACK

The teacher who is interested in providing mild and favorable emotional experiences for the development of preschool children is delighted with evidence that they are considerate of each other, helpful, and able to withstand mild frustration. She is pleased to observe a little girl helping another put on her wraps while she explains, "I'm sharing," and to hear an older girl say to an older boy pushing toy cars over the floor, "You ride this fire engine and I'll ride this one," or to hear Neal, at four years and seven months, say in his dramatic play, "This is a rescue boat. I am rescuing this child."

One teacher, who was a considerate person herself, recorded her observation of a three-year-old girl at play in the playhouse corner of her nursery center:

A little girl was in the housekeeping area, imitating a very busy housewife— cooking, cleaning, putting dishes in the sink and then on the table. A little boy with her was her "dog." "Here, doggy," she said, "I've got some food for you." She put a dish down on the floor for him, and he pretended to lap it up. All the while he kept his "traveling" piece of shirt in his mouth [a symbol of his need for security].

As they left the housekeeping area, the boy dropped the piece of shirt out of his mouth. He did not seem to miss it. This is probably a first step away from his need for the piece of shirt; the need is being satisfied or replaced with good play experience.

Another boy recognized the piece of shirt on the floor, picked it up, and ran over to give it to the younger boy. I noticed this same consideration in other children. Whenever the boy dropped his piece of shirt, they recognized that he needed it.

In another nursery group, the teacher felt that her emphasis on helping each other contributed to the following incident:

One morning, Neal, almost four years old, and four-and-one-half-year-old Norman were each attempting to put a box on the high shelf in the playhouse. Presently, Neal, who could not quite reach the shelf, said, "I can't do it." Norman put his box up and, without comment, reached over and pushed Neal's on to the shelf.

Their teacher felt that both Neal and Norman were trying to be helpful by putting away playthings on the shelf. Furthermore, Norman saw where help was needed and willingly provided it. She also noted that Neal was able to distinguish between what he could and could not do, and to comment on it. This, she felt, was in keeping with the matter-of-fact realism she attempted to encourage in the nursery group.

Handling Unpleasant Emotions

By providing a calm, pleasant atmosphere, the preschool teacher cultivates the mild emotions favorable to learning. She should try in every way to help the children to be successful and to maintain their self-control. If she notices that a four-year-old child is interested in sliding down the fireman's pole, but withdraws from any suggestion that he try it, she should not put him at the top of the pole and insist that he go down. Doing so would put the child into a situation probably beyond his control at that time. The teacher who realizes the importance of pleasant feelings as an aid to learning therefore helps the child to master simple activities that are connected with sliding down the pole but that also are within his powers— for instance, climbing to the top of the pole and climbing back down or sliding from a point near the foot of the pole at first and then from points successively higher. At the same time, the teacher helps him to maintain and to further his self-confidence by reminding him that he will slide down the pole when he is ready to do so. Thus the wise teacher avoids the sink-or-swim situation which may arouse strong emotional reactions. Instead she selects those hurdles that will provide only enough frustration to evoke mild emotions of satisfaction as the child overcomes them.

At the same time that the teacher uses mild emotions, she must be aware of the possibility of unpleasant emotions, and she must know how to help the children to cope with such emotions. She should realize the nature of unpleasant emotion and the fact that "unpleasant emotion is experienced when the individual's processes of becoming, or of realizing himself through action, are blocked or threatened."[4] She must know at what points to look for unpleasant emotional outbursts, what the warning signals are, what techniques and devices will help the child regain his composure, and how to ward off recurrences of such disturbances, if possible.

Children do not want to lose their self-control, but their nervous systems are not sufficiently mature to make control possible under all circumstances. Overstimulation may give rise to hyperactivity, or to a tantrum, or to some other sign of fatigue. The sensitive teacher tries to avoid overstimulation. However, with a new group of children, she cannot always predict what may be over-exciting for each child. She is prepared, therefore, to help each child with his emotional outbursts, no matter what their nature.

WHAT ARE SIGNS OF LOSS OF CONTROL?

By the time a child comes to a preschool group, he already has learned to react emotionally to many kinds of situations. For instance, he may

[4] Prescott, op. cit., p. 394.

react to a surprise by jumping up and down happily and reaching for it. Or he may react to a severe tone of voice by bursting into tears. The teacher must find out as soon as possible what these reactions are and what situational factors are associated with their occurrence. When she can predict their occurrence, she is in a position to decide whether a program of re-education is necessary. She may feel that she can provide a series of re-educative experiences for the child within the preschool group situation, and that she should work with his parents to help him improve his patterns of emotional response.

The teacher should realize when a child is not in good control of himself. She may notice that a usually amiable child comes into the room

Meeting an emotional crisis. (Courtesy of Head Start Eljoa and Rosella Lipson, Beverly Hills, California. Photograph by Fitzgerald Whitney.)

hitting at things and other children. He feels like hitting, and she must help him in finding some socially acceptable means of expressing this feeling. Or she may notice that a child avoids her to play by himself. He feels like withdrawing and she must reassure him and help him to regain his self-confidence. Or, as she listens to the sounds made by the children at play in activities of their own choosing, she may hear one child's voice rise above its usual pitch. This change in sound is apt to accompany the muscular tension in the child as he attempts to maintain control of himself or of a situation. The teacher should immediately move closer to the play group and try to identify the disturbing element in the situation.

If she thinks the disturbing element is one with which the children are able to cope successfully, she simply stands by. But if she thinks the disturbing element is unfamiliar to the children, or lies beyond their ability to resolve, she probably should enter their play in order to help them solve the problem.

WATCHING FOR SITUATIONS INVOLVING PRESSURE

A child's emotional reactions are evident when he is under pressure. The adult who is sensitive to a child's emotional responses therefore finds it desirable to observe how he reacts to the pressures of new situations. How does the child relate himself to a new toy in a known environment? to a new toy in a new environment? to a new child in a known environment? to a new child in a new environment? to a new adult in a known environment? to a new adult in a new environment?

As the preschool child goes out from his familiar home environment into the new environment of his preschool group and his neighborhood, he should be helped to enjoy the satisfaction of exploring new horizons and to avoid the fears and frustrations that might arise from situations that seem to him to be threatening. The wise teacher plans ahead so that a child has the techniques he needs to deal with new situations and is able to find satisfaction in them when they occur.

Not all the emotional reactions of children in a preschool group are caused by situations arising there. For instance, emotional problems occurring at the start of the school session may be carried over from home. As Prescott points out:

Every teacher knows that the child "brings his family to school with him." That is, the emotional climate in which he lives at home constantly influences his mood, susceptibility to emotional disturbance, and feelings in the classroom. . . . Every child has a need for emotional security based on the assurance that he is loved and valued by those who are responsible for him. If this need is met, his feelings of security can carry him through many difficulties and failures. Lacking it, he has a persisting adjustment problem that gives rise to continuing anxiety and self-doubt or to hostility and aggressive demands for notice.[5]

A child who is rejected or treated inconsistently at home must be helped to find suitable emotional releases for his early-morning play in the preschool group. One teacher guided a boy who was rejected by his mother into early-morning use of the record player. Another teacher helped an aggressive boy whose parents were having marital problems by providing him with a daily supply of tin cans from which she had removed the top and bottom. He flattened these cans by jumping up and down on them until he felt he could join the group without wanting to hit other children.

A teacher in a parent-cooperative group was able to help three-year-old

---

[5] Ibid., p. 400.

Ralph, a boy with an eye difficulty, a baby brother, and an aggressive pattern of behavior. She kept brief notes about his progress in learning how to play with other children:

September: Ralph seems happy to be with the group. On the second day it is evident that he is very aggressive. He pushes and hits without provocation. He is only three now and has to learn about playing in a large group.

October 11th: Today was Ralph's birthday. He has improved greatly, and does not do nearly as much pushing, and so on. He displays a little aggressiveness, but it is not extreme or frequent.

October 12th: In accord with the plan developed with Ralph's mother, he was isolated for a few minutes for pushing. Later there was another pushing episode with Diane. When I spoke to both of them, Ralph seemed to feel less unhappy at being "jointly" in the wrong. I try to keep encouraging him and loving him a lot in between incidents.

November: I have not observed any of the pushing, and so on, in several sessions. I know it has not ceased entirely because I have heard of an occasional incident. But it does appear that Ralph is much less violent in expressing himself.

February: Ralph *occasionally* will be aggressive but not often. When he had a "bad" morning recently. I had the impression that he was not feeling well.

April: Ralph has from the start been loving and affectionate. He often kisses me. He was most provoked recently at being "admonished." I think this may be indicative of a greater awareness of standards of behavior. From the mothers in Ralph's car-pool I hear of occasional dissension, but two of the mothers are proud to report that no permanent enemies result. In fact, a really forgiving and loving attitude is evident on occasion.

May: Ralph plays with many of the children. Today he had nice play with Linda at one time, and again with the boys in his car-pool. He played in harmony and complete silence with Danny as together they filled one truck after another with sand.

Even the usual activities of the preschool group may seem overly demanding to a child whose margin of control has worn thin. The child who is tired at the end of an activity which required a high degree of attention; the child who needs rest, or a trip to the bathroom, or refreshments; the child whose fatigue has accumulated throughout the preschool session— these are the children whom the teacher must watch carefully if she is to help them avoid going out of control with an emotional display that is disturbing to them and to the other members of their group. Her watching of children who have a narrow margin of control is part of her supporting affection for them. With such children, the teacher should watch closely for opportunities to give deserved praise and to remind four- and five-year-olds of their past and future successes. She should become expert in guiding the tired child into a quiet place near an understanding adult—a situation in which his tension can be released (perhaps into a far corner where he can splash or dabble his hands in a bowl of sudsy water, or perhaps into a place where he can listen to restful music, or perhaps into an attractive room with a place to stretch out and rest comfortably, or perhaps to a corner table where he can pound or model clay if he wants to). The teacher should also become expert at moving the group into less demanding activities and at replacing the stimulation of new and exciting activities with the satisfaction of reassuringly familiar activities (with adult admiration at hand)—especially relaxing activities with unstructured media, such as finger painting, or digging in the dirt, or playing with dough or clay.

Sometimes a teacher becomes aware of a new maturity in a child when his new sensitivity leads him into an emotional display. When Neal was three and one half years old, he went beyond the limits of his self-control. This happened the morning that he suddenly found himself in a leadership role. It was thrilling to discover leadership. He left his three friends doing what he told them to, and stepped over to the adult nearby. "Fix my belt," he said, continuing in his dominating role. The adult sensed Neal's newly found majesty and obligingly fastened his belt. Thus properly equipped and morally supported, Neal returned to his playmates. For the rest of the morning he suggested and they agreed. It was a wonderful and exhilarating experience. But when the morning was over and his friends went home, Neal greeted his mother with a temper tantrum. It took fifteen minutes of his mother's complete attention and support before he regained control of himself and could start counteracting his fatigue with food.

How Does a Teacher Help a Child with a Tantrum?

The child who has gone as far as he can by himself in a situation needs immediate help. When he throws himself to the floor, kicking and screaming, he is out of control and is asking for adult control until he can regain his own. The teacher should respond at once to this appeal, turning her responsibility for the children over to another adult, perhaps by saying to the children, "Johnny needs me. Marie is here to help you in case you need her." By removing Johnny to another room, she lessens his problem: he no longer has an audience to respond to; he has only himself, and a loving helper who will stay with him while he solves his problem.

If Johnny tries to throw things, the teacher can provide him with bean bags and a box to throw them into. If he wants to kick, she can give him a kickball. If he wants to hit, she can help him to pound clay or a punching bag or some other suitable material, until he is all done with the need to hit. Thus she can help him to learn that it is all right to throw, kick, or to hit—if it does not hurt someone else. She can teach him a very important concept that he will use throughout his life: it is all right to feel angry and to express anger in some physical manner that is socially acceptable. If Johnny tries to leave the quiet place, the teacher can reassure him: "When you are ready, we will go back to the others." Thus she can help him learn that a person must have control of himself before he can be part of a group. In short, the teacher can help Johnny

An old pair of jeans for a target can be a means for emotional release. (Courtesy of Long Beach Parent Nursery Schools and Mariam M. Cook.)

learn how to handle himself. His tantrum gives his teacher the opportunity to help him when he is most in need of help.

The methods by which the loving nursery teacher helps Johnny are in contrast to methods formerly in vogue. Under the old method of isolation, for instance, the teacher would have put Johnny in a room by himself and left him there to struggle with his problems alone. Today the teacher realizes that Johnny needs guidance in finding one or more emotional outlets suitable to his personality. But, more important, she realizes that Johnny needs to be reassured that he is loved even when his behavior is most objectionable; the more unlovable a child is, the more he needs loving. The rejection of Johnny's behavior must be distinguished

524

from a rejection of Johnny, if he is to be helped to make the distinction between what is and what is not socially acceptable behavior.

Another outmoded method is that of spanking. Johnny hits; the teacher spanks. Why is it all right for the teacher to hit, if it is not all right for Johnny to do so? The modern teacher avoids confusing Johnny in this way. She remains completely in character, endeavoring to help Johnny help himself. It may be necessary for her to hold his wrists so that he cannot inflict damage on her, himself, or someone else, but she does so in love, not in anger.

The teacher should handle the child's emotional disturbance as calmly as she handles any other kind of disturbance. If a child cuts himself, vomits, wets his pants, or has other difficulty, she removes him from the group and helps him to resolve his problem. At all times she gives him the loving support that he needs.

The calmness with which the teacher handles the emotional outburst of one child is reassuring to the whole group. Each member of the group feels that he, too, is loved by the teacher and will be given the same help at any time that he needs it.

When Johnny again has control of himself, his teacher should make sure that any underlying physical factor is taken care of. If the day is warm or if Johnny has been playing hard, he may be thirsty. Does he need to go to the bathroom? Is he hungry? If Johnny is hungry, the teacher should be careful to provide him with a cooky or cracker in such a way that he does not think of it as a reward for his tantrum. She may say, "You know, Johnny, I think I would like a cracker. Would you like one?" If Johnny is not hungry, the teacher may say, "I should really wait until lunchtime too," as she puts the crackers away. If Johnny is hungry, she should talk with Johnny's mother to determine whether Johnny needs additional food. If Johnny is thirsty, or in need of toileting, she makes a mental note to see that he has the needed attention regularly each morning. In this way she provides for improvements in the morning routine that may help Johnny to avoid further emotional upsets.

When Johnny is ready to find a place in the group again, he and the teacher return to the other children. As they enter, the teacher should notice a play situation that is a favorite of Johnny's and direct his attention to it: "Mary is playing a record. Shall we listen to it with her?"

If any of the children have noticed Johnny's tantrum, the teacher can talk casually with them about it:

MARIE   Johnny had a tantrum.

TEACHER   Yes. He was thirsty. He got a drink and is happy now. Do you get a drink when you are thirsty?

MARIE   Yes.

TEACHER   That's good. When you get a drink, maybe you can ask Johnny to go with you to get one. That will help him.

When a teacher has more demands for her attention than she can meet at that moment, she has to separate the child from the group until she can give him her full attention. She does this not as punishment for the child's behavior but as a means of helping him learn how to fit better into the group. If the child is hyperactive, the quiet interval may be a welcome relief from stimulation. Whenever the teacher isolates a child for a few minutes, she is careful not to interfere with the child's feeling of belonging to the group nor with his need for activity. She may say, for instance, "Susan, do your pasting over here (*helping her move her things*). Now you have plenty of room and can keep your hands to yourself."

Discouraging Destruction

In general, the teacher should emphasize construction and see to it that destruction is not rewarded by undue attention. The morning that five-year-old Mickey quietly worked with building blocks and created an elaborate structure, his kindergarten teacher called all the children together to admire his handiwork:

TEACHER   Children, I want you to see something special. Come and see what Mickey built while we were busy doing other things this morning. Let's listen while he tells us about it. What did you tell me you built, Mickey?
MICKEY   Disneyland.
TEACHER   Disneyland! Think of that! Mickey built Disneyland. It's very well done, Mickey. We're glad you made it.

But when the four-year-old boy knocks down a block structure just built by someone else, his teacher may calmly say to him, "Next time we feel like hitting something, let's hit the clay. Everyone will be happier." Thus the teacher encourages the four-year-old to become aware of his feelings, and to find outlets that are in keeping with a happy group situation.

The catharsis of destruction may be used in constructive activities. A child who feels like hitting and kicking also feels like tearing up newspaper to make papier mâché, or crumpling it to make stuffing for a punching bag made from a pair of old trousers. His tendency toward action is thus channeled into a project helpful to the group. Or, if adults have washed out and removed the ends of tin cans, a frustrated child can jump on each open-ended cylinder. As he flattens the can, his feelings of frustration are replaced by a feeling of accomplishment as he sees the bulk of the tin can become a small and compact pile of metal.

Are Disappointments Necessary?

Sometimes children experience disappointment that is more severe than it need be. Such disappointment, with its concomitant strong emotions, has no place in a preschool group. The understanding teacher should know how to plan with children so that they can learn to accept changes in plans with a minimum of frustration. For instance, when a movie and TV hero caught the fancy of children in every community across the land, one teacher of four-year-old children bought the hat and insignia that characterized the hero, for use with her group. Then she made sure that each child understood he would have a turn at wearing one of the hero outfits. Each morning, the teacher reminded the children of those who had had a turn already, and arranged for others to take turns throughout the morning. Thus each child had a satisfying experience in waiting for his turn. He also experienced a series of turns in which, as the weeks passed, he had one eagerly awaited, then another, and presently one that he really did not care much about having.

Knowing that weather may cause disappointment, the wise teacher plans with the children for a study trip "on the first sunny day," rather than "next time." It is good to have special rainy-day plans so that the children come to look forward to rainy days, when they not only can wear their rainy-day clothes but also have a surprise activity at school. Children who have discovered that worms are to be found on rainy days, or who have enjoyed catching snowflakes on their sleeves look forward to stormy days as days of fun.

Adults who work with young children plan with them in terms of the weather and help them to associate certain kinds of activities with certain kinds of weather. Children need to learn not how to endure frustration, but how to plan so as to avoid it. The skillful teacher does not rely on a single plan; she has several plans from which to choose one especially appropriate for the day.

The Role of the Teacher in Furthering Emotional Development

UNDERSTANDING THE NATURE OF EMOTIONS

In order to further the emotional development of preschool children, the teacher or parent must understand not only how to use the desirable mild emotions and how to channel displays of strong emotions into desirable outlets, but also how to deal with the physical changes that are an integral part of emotions. The teacher should keep in mind the necessity of helping children to convert their strong emotions into physical activity—and, if possible, into socially acceptable and constructive activity.

Prescott, after mentioning that the strong emotions may be either active or depressive, points out that both types involve extensive bodily changes:

The general effect of the changes in organic processes that occur during strong active emotions is to mobilize the body for immediate intense mental and physical activity. . . . Then comes the maximum stepping-up of functions favorable to rapid and sustained energy release. These include increased rates of heartbeat, blood pressure, oxygen supply and carbon-dioxide elimination through respiration, and adrenalin production, and immediate release into the bloodstream of red blood cells stored in the spleen and sugar stored in the liver.

. . . These adaptive changes are made with terrific speed, and the body is immediately ready for whatever action may be implied by the situation. The emotions producing such an adjustment seem almost to require some form of action to utilize the energy so dramatically released. . . . These details of what goes on in the body during strong active emotions may help teachers realize what the child is up against during such experiences and enable them to help him find socially acceptable ways of using the energy that is generated.

. . . The general effect of the changes in organic processes that occur during strong depressive emotion is to reduce action to a minimum by reducing the rate of all body processes involved in energy transmutation and release. . . . In contrast to active emotions, depressive emotions reduce the capacity and need of the body to spend energy.[6]

The child who expresses his feelings about frustration actively is attempting to solve his problems himself. His activity is desirable in that it shows others how he feels and provides behavior which can be gradually diverted into more socially acceptable forms. But the child who reacts to frustrations by withdrawing from them must first be helped into activity itself. For him, any activity—socially acceptable or not—is desirable. After he learns to express his feelings in action, he can then be helped to express them in socially acceptable ways. The four-year-old child who does not talk has made great progress when he says his first word, even though it be a swear word.

The teacher of preschool children should take every opportunity to encourage the children to keep their fears and anxieties out in the open. One understanding teacher tells about her part in helping a child to express her fears and anxieties about a witch:

Of five children making sand castles, four dug windows in the sides of their structures while Cathy made hers without either doors or windows. As she piled the sand higher on it and punched and patted it, her voice kept getting louder and more shrill: "There, you old witch! I got you in there and you can't get out!" She kept up such a running monologue about the bad witch that I knew this was more than ordinary dramatic play, and I felt compelled to talk out her concern with her. As I knelt beside her, she carefully stuck one finger into the castle, made a very small hole, and yelled in: "Are you in there, witch?" Then she quickly covered up the little opening.

I smiled at Cathy and then asked, "What witch do you have in there?" Cathy replied, "That awful witch in *Sleeping Beauty*. I got her in there. She can't get out."

I explained that *Sleeping Beauty* is a "pretend story." "Did you see it on television?" I asked. She nodded. Then I said, "Sometimes in stories the mean old witch turns into a good fairy."

Cathy looked at me thoughtfully, and then went back to patting the castle.

[6] Ibid., pp. 397–98.

In a short while Cathy dug a doorway into the castle, and put her hand in. Then she threw her hands high in the air and said, "Look! The mean old witch is good now. I let her fly away." I smiled and shared the pleasure of the moment with her.

The next day Cathy molded sand again but this time she made a wide swimming pool. As I stopped beside her for a moment, I asked, "No witches today?" "No," she replied, "there's no such thing as witches. They're just to scare kids anyway." It seemed to me that she had probably been told this but had not fully accepted the idea until now.

When Cathy's mother read these notes, she said, "My goodness! Is she still talking about that witch? I thought she got over that months ago!"

The principal tools for helping the child who expresses strong emotions frequently are the ones that further his learning under other circumstances as well. They include suitable reminders of the affection of his teachers and parents, opportunities for seeing his own achievements and for having them appreciated by others, pointers to help him develop techniques for getting along well with other children, and visible confidence in his eventual success.

A Sunday school teacher used these and other techniques one December morning when four-year-old Evelyn explored the limits of acceptable behavior in a crowded room where there were only three inexperienced mother-assistants to help the teacher of the forty children in the four-year-old group.

OBSERVATION	REMARKS
Four-year-old Evelyn had had her hand whitened so that she could make a print of it on a green star. She had used the cooky cutter in printing a sheetful of trees. She looked around for some vigorous activity. The doll corner? No. The blocks? No. Listening to a story? No. The teacher helped by playing "Ring Around the Rosy" but there really was not enough room for it.	Both activities required attention to detail and conformity to adult expectations. Did the mother-assistant help Evelyn appreciate her achievements?
Suddenly Evelyn dashed for the basin of sudsy water where she had washed after making her handprint. Plunging in both hands, she slopped the sudsy water well over the nearby table and chairs, and onto the floor. A mother dashed to mop up the mess while Evelyn grabbed the handy tin of red paint and turned it over. Another mother started to clean up that mess while Evelyn reached for another tin of paint. The teacher reached her at the same time that another mother started to sponge off Evelyn's hands. "I'll take her to the bathroom," she said to the nearest mother-assistant.	The teacher uses a familiar physical activity as an emotional release. Evelyn chose water play. The teacher works with the child and leaves the environmental problems to others or until later. She must have assistants to work with the group while she works with an individual child.

OBSERVATION	REMARKS
In the bathroom, Evelyn said, "I don't need to go. I'll wash my hands." Evelyn enjoyed washing while she remembered the commotion she had caused and smiled with satisfaction. Then she grabbed up the soap and ran around the bathroom with it. When she slowed down, the teacher said, "Keep on going, Evelyn, until you feel ready to be part of a group again."	The teacher helps Evelyn in helping herself. The physical activity provided some emotional release. Evelyn must take responsibility for being ready to join the group.
A few minutes later Evelyn and the teacher returned to the room. Evelyn dived for the sudsy bowl to do it all over again. The teacher lifted her bodily from the bowl and back to the bathroom. "You weren't ready to be part of the group again," she said, and talked with her about individual limits.	Evelyn needs to learn more about taking responsibility. The teacher reminds Evelyn about her responsibility to the group.
After being reminded of what the limits are, Evelyn fitted better into the group—for a few minutes. But now it was nearly noon; Evelyn was tired and hungry. She picked up a pencil and starting drawing on the tabletop. "We draw only on paper," said the teacher, putting a large piece of paper under Evelyn's pencil.	Fatigue lowers the level of self-control a child can maintain.
A few minutes later Evelyn had covered most of the paper with circular scribbles, and had enlarged her arm movement to mark broadly partly on paper and partly on the tabletop. "We mark only on the paper," said the teacher. "Here's a sponge for cleaning it up."	The teacher remains calm, firm, and affectionate.
Evelyn started scrubbing with the sponge. This was fun—just the vigorous arm movement she needed. She scrubbed with a will. "It's easy to make the marks, but hard to get them off," the teacher remarked.	Evelyn now has a constructive physical activity as an emotional outlet.
Other children watched Evelyn and asked to help. The teacher encouraged them to share Evelyn's activity. Soon a group of children, each with a sponge, were scrubbing the table, cleaning it up.	The teacher helps Evelyn in her relation to the other children. Evelyn is getting attention through being helpful, not destructive.
Twenty minutes later, when Evelyn's mother came for her, the teacher explained to her: "Evelyn is going to mark only on paper after this. It's hard to get pencil marks off the table."	The teacher helps Evelyn continue cleaning until the table is free from pencil marks. Evelyn is expected to be responsible for cleaning up her markings. The teacher works with Evelyn's parents in helping her.
Later, the teacher telephoned Evelyn's mother and arranged for her to be with Evelyn at Sunday school.	

GUIDING THE INDIVIDUAL CHILD IN THE GROUP SITUATION

The teacher sometimes wonders about how much attention she can give an individual child without neglecting the group. For instance, one morning Mrs. Oswald was helping the group to plan a study trip when she noticed that Jim had stayed outdoors to throw more mudballs. The mother who was helping Mrs. Oswald was not sufficiently experienced in teaching the group to be able to lead it in planning. So Mrs. Oswald qiuckly instructed her to keep Jim throwing mudballs at a target until he was completely finished with his desire to throw.

If Mrs. Oswald had been the only adult present, she would have had to bring the group planning session to an end and move the group to familiar activities—modeling clay, for instance. Then, as soon as the children were well started with their modeling, she might say to their leader, "I'll be back as soon as I can help Jim get himself ready to join the group."

The teacher should know each child so well that she can anticipate when one is apt to need an unusual amount of attention. A child whose family is involved in financial difficulties or other stress, a child faced with competition within his family group, a child who has just lost a member of his family—these are the children apt to have emotional problems that interfere with their feelings of belonging to any group. A child who has been absent from the preschool group is also a child who needs the teacher's help in regaining his sense of importance and his feeling of belonging. When she has such a child in her group, the teacher should try to arrange for additional adult assistance so that she may, if necessary, leave the group under adequate supervision while she helps an individual child.

In general, even if adult assistance is available, the teacher should try to avoid having to choose between working with the group and working with the individual child. Instead, she should try to attend to the individual child within the group situation. Both the individual and the group need the help of a beloved teacher who knows them and loves them. She may keep a lonely three-year-old physically close to her as she talks with other children. She may talk with a four-year-old while glancing briefly from child to child. She can help an unsure child by entering a dramatic play situation with other children and letting the child transfer his attention from her to the other children before she withdraws from the play. In short, she can work with an individual child at the same time that she works with the group.

If a teacher feels that she is not reaching a particular child emotionally, she may plan with his parents for the child to be with her outside the preschool group. If the group meets in the morning, she may invite each of the children—one, two, or a few at a time—to bring their lunch and eat with her. If the school meets all day, she may arrange a special time alone with a child within the school schedule. She can use this special individual time as play-therapy time or just as a happy time together, depending upon the needs of the child.

The morning that one of the fathers brought the triangular climber to the four-year-old group, Mrs. Baker knew that it would be the center of interest—especially for Billy, an aggressive and older member of the group. During the free choice of activities, Billy and the other "just five" boys were climbing all the way up the six boards of the climber to its six-foot high top. Watching them jump out from the third and fourth boards, Mrs. Baker noticed that they were landing dangerously close to where smaller children were playing. When she heard Billy remark, "I'm going to jump from the top," she decided that limits should be set to avoid having an accident. "Climb down now, Billy," she said. "It's time for juice."

When the children were toileted and gathered together, drinking their juice, Mrs. Baker said, "While we are all together, we had better talk about our climber. Jimmy's daddy made it for us, and we are all enjoying it very much. What should we tell Jimmy's daddy?"

"Thank you," said several small voices.

"Yes, indeed. Jimmy, will you tell your daddy 'Thank you' for us please?"

Jimmy nodded as he took on this responsibility.

"You know," Mrs. Baker continued, "we need to have a rule about how to use our climber. Do you know how high a person can jump safely?"

"From the top," said Billy.

"Not that high, Billy," said Mrs. Baker. "A person can jump safely only from a place that is no higher than he is. Jumping from places higher than that is apt to hurt us. Let's see, Billy, how high you should go on the climber."

Mrs. Baker helped Billy measure himself against the side of the climber. Together they concluded that Billy should jump only from the fourth board. Then Mrs. Baker finished the group discussion by reminding the children that Mrs. James was at the climber to help them climb or to measure how far up to go.

A few minutes later, when half the group went inside for a story while the rest modeled blue dough at a table outdoors, Billy did not go inside with his group. Instead he ran to the climber and quickly climbed to the top. "I'm going to jump from the top," he said to Mrs. Baker who had quietly followed him.

Mrs. Baker knew that the new rule had to be enforced, for the good of the group, and for Billy to learn about limits. "Billy," she said, in her kindest way, "we have a rule about how to use the climber. If you want to come here and use the climber, you have to follow the rule. You may jump from your own height, but not from the top because it is higher than you are. Jump from here, Billy," she concluded, putting her hand on the fourth board.

When Billy was on the ground beside her, Mrs. Baker took up the other point that she felt Billy needed to learn. "That was a good jump, Billy, but you are missing the story. Mary's mother is reading a new story about polar bears. It's a good story. But you're going to miss it because you came over to the climber when you were supposed to go inside with the other children. You keep on jumping now, but next time go with your group so you don't miss out."

After Billy had modeled the blue dough with his group, it was time to put away the materials and go home. As children and mothers moved toward the gate, Mrs. Baker saw Billy make one more attempt to run to the top of the climber. Catching his attention, she said in a voice all could hear, "I know the children can walk to the gate." Billy changed his pace from a run to a walk, and headed toward the gate.

"Who can tell me why we walk to the cars?" Mrs. Baker asked the children.

Billy responded. "I know," he said. "Because the cars go so fast. I'm going to walk to the car," he added.

Mrs. Baker was quick to praise Billy's desirable behavior. "That's what I like to hear," she said. "It makes me feel good all over to have you say that."

Billy swaggered off in an exaggerated walk toward the car while Mrs. Baker started planning for the next week, and for a time when Billy could stay alone with her for lunch and for a climb to the top of the climber.

TEACHING PROPERTY RIGHTS

Somehow the wise teacher has to steer her preschool group between the Scylla of oversubmission and the Charybdis of overaggression. She may have children in her group like four-year-old Cindy, who gave up the toy she was playing with and said, "Let's not have fights. I like you and all the children in the world." She is apt to have children like five-year-old Ned, who, with a large star-shaped pin on his chest, felt himself to be a sheriff. He found a stick and, in his capacity of sheriff, hit Susan on the head:

SUSAN   Ned hit me! (*Runs to the nearest adult, the teacher.*)
TEACHER (*smiling sympathetically and wondering what may have preceded the hitting she saw*)   What did you do to him?
SUSAN   Nothing!
TEACHER (*smiles at Ned*)   Did you hit Susan?
NED   Yes, I'm the sheriff!
TEACHER   I don't think sheriffs hit people, my dear.
NED   I saw it. On TV.
TEACHER (*sensing that home and school may differ in what is taught*)   Oh, that's just a pretend story on TV. But real sheriffs don't go around hitting people.
NED   Sheriffs hit people. Daddy said so.
TEACHER   Well, we don't use sticks that way at nursery school. I'll take it now and give it back to you when you go home. How about the sheriff and Susan riding their horses now? Here's one for each of you.

When the teacher recounted the incident to Ned's mother, she found her to be emotionally involved in it. Ned's mother said, "Susan has hit Ned many times. Now he's big enough to hit her back. People remember, and sooner or later a person gets what he deserves."

Should the preschool teacher go along with this an eye for an eye a tooth for a tooth philosophy? Or should she further the idea of, "I will not hurt others, nor let them hurt me"?

One preschool teacher reported several incidents which are in keeping with the policy of replacing blows with words, and of getting and keeping what a person needs to use at that time:

Penny was very sweet with Roger one day when I said we could use our arms to hug but not to hit. She turned to Roger who was next to her and put her arms around him. He was pleased and full of smiles.

We had one problem with Don, as with Bobby and Edmund, who are also three-year-old boys. Don would appropriate any toy by force, if necessary, if he wanted it. He would forcefully evict another child from a trike, for example, and my explanations about this behavior were futile. Don, like Bobby or Edmund, would have a tantrum on being denied the toy.

In these situations I always see that Don has his turn as soon as the toy is not in use. My intention is to teach him that all things come to him who waits. I have been uniformly unsuccessful in selling this lovely thought as a substitute for appropriating the coveted toy, so we have had some tears.

But I have seen many a child come in good time to understand such a reason. Already with Don, things are vastly improved. Don is a dear, solid little citizen here and we love him.

One particular kind of incident was repeated again and again through the year, with only minor variations. Bobby, like Edmund or Don, would see a toy in someone else's possession. When it caught his momentary fancy, he had a standard approach to acquiring it—the most direct approach: he took it, or tried to, sometimes successfully, sometimes not. A tense moment ensued in which Bobby, or his victim, would begin to protest. If Bobby succeeded in getting the toy by force, I would try to return it and then explain to Bobby how it is in these matters. Whereupon Bobby, according to pattern, would howl or, in some instances, have a tantrum from which he slowly emerged. Then we would try reasoning again.

As time passed, Bobby became easier to deal with in these perilous incidents. I have not seen a tantrum in a long time. About a month ago, when I had to evict him from Sammy's wagon which he was trying to take, a glorious object lesson followed a short time later. I evicted Edmund from Bobby's wagon, and explained to Bobby that rules are often protective and not just frustrating. He could observe that in the second incident the law operated to his advantage.

Bobby is a lovable child and I wish I had a boy just like him.

The teacher of preschool children should help each of them to hang on to a toy that he is using; to take a toy that is not in use; to hang on only to what he can use; to wait for his turn for a toy that is in use; to say that he wants a turn; to say, "Let's share" and to talk about turns; to give up equipment at the end of his turn and to line up for his next turn; to provide a toy for another child while he keeps one for himself; to ask, "May I have it next?" and to say, "Here you are. I'll use it again later." Thus the teacher helps preschool children to develop basic concepts of their property rights.

RECOGNIZING EFFECTS OF PARENTAL ATTITUDES

Anyone working with preschool children must appreciate the fact that "The attitudes of the parents are of great importance for the development of personality during early childhood."[7] When parental attitudes are loving ones that help a child toward self-realization, the preschool teacher is able to help the child grow through the curricular activities that she plans. But when parental attitudes include overprotection, overindulgence, or over-authority, she has to help the child with his emotional problems before she can help him with educational ones.

How does a teacher help the child who is often emotionally upset? For one thing, she tries to steer his parents to social workers, religious-education workers, or pediatricians who can work with them directly and can advise them of any need for psychiatric assistance. People who have studied both normal and abnormal psychology are in a position to identify the needs of the adults; the work of a teacher is with the preschool children in the family.

The Doctors Bakwin mention problems of children with overprotective parents and recommend preschool group experience for them.

The problems presented by the children of dominating, overprotective mothers are principally shyness, anxieties, fears, and submissive behavior. . . . The nursery school, play groups, outings with other children . . . are used in order to separate the child as much as possible from the mother.[8]

Whether the parents are receiving assistance with their emotional problems or not, the teacher must help their preschool child with his. She should understand the nature of his problems and the kind of help that the preschool group can give him.[9]

In some communities, parents put a high social value in "good manners" and exert considerable pressure to have their children learn particular customs for eating, using the bathroom, "obeying," and speaking—or not speaking—on certain topics. The teacher who knows that emotional problems arise when children are subjected to excessive pressure should be aware of what these pressures are and should work with the parents to see that each child is able to cope with his pressures successfully or—if he is not—to see that the pressures are reduced to the point where he is not unduly frustrated by them. No matter what the home pressures are, the teacher should provide each child with a preschool group situation in which he is free from over- or under-expectation and has to cope only with expectations appropriate to his level of development. After a teacher understands the effect of unfavorable parental attitudes, she should learn to understand when a child is apt to need help with his emotional problems and what kind of help the group situation can provide for him.

[7] Harry Bakwin, M.D., and Ruth M. Bakwin, M.D., *Clinical Management of Behavior Disorders in Children* (Philadelphia: W. B. Saunders Co., 1966), p. 204.
[8] Ibid., pp. 210 and 211.
[9] See Chapter 7, p. 247, for instance.

A teacher accidentally overheard a conversation which revealed the relationship between a child in her group and his overly authoritarian mother. This information gave her a greater understanding of his problems and of the kind of support the preschool group could give him. The teacher was in a toilet cubicle when Michael and his mother went into an adjoining one. Presently Michael attempted to go out.

MOTHER   Close that door!
(*Michael attempts to crawl out under the door.*)
MOTHER   Stay in here!
(*In a few moments, Michael again attempts to crawl under the door.*)
MOTHER   You do what I say! Stay in here!
MICHAEL   I don't like the smell.
MOTHER   You do what I say! You stay here!

Michael started crying, and his mother continued yelling at him until she finished and opened the door for him to escape. Her nagging stopped as she came out where other people were, and Michael's crying stopped shortly thereafter.

The next morning Michael came to his nursery group in a competitive mood. There, however, he encountered cooperation, absence of pressure, and calm. For the first half-hour Michael was aggressive. He started taking cars out of the red wagon pulled by another child. An aide helped him to find a wagon of his own. He knocked around the play centers, grabbing whatever he wanted. About an hour after his arrival, he found a place at the pasting table for a few minutes. Then he was off again.

Presently, Michael noticed a volunteer reading stories, and joined her group. A few minutes later, the children who had heard the story went away and Michael was left with *Tootle*[10] and the volunteer. Michael turned pages and looked at pictures. He started talking out loud. "What happens here? I don't want to read! . . ." The adult sat calmly, entering into his conversation as he permitted her to. After having enjoyed her complete attention for awhile, Michael was able to go to the paint table and work quietly. He could now take suggestions about painting on his paper and not on his neighbor's paper. He had entered the cooperative world of the nursery group.

GUIDING DOLL PLAY

In guiding doll play, a teacher should be ready to help the children to learn housekeeping, family and school relationships, and the role each will play as a boy or a girl, a daddy or a mother. But, at the same time, because a child may have emotional reactions toward his family or toward the school situation,[11] the teacher should also be prepared to help each child to get

[10] Gertrude Crampton, *Tootle* (New York: Golden Press, 1946).
[11] Edith Lesser Atkin, *Aggressiveness in Children*, 48104 (Ann Arbor, Mich.: University Microfilms, 1950).

emotionally ready for future events and to express his feelings about past events. For instance, the teacher may read a book that describes a day in a preschool group and, in this way, prepare the children for future days at school. Another effective preparation is to use dolls, puppets, or a dramatic skit to preview some future event, such as a study trip. The children identify with the dolls, puppets, or people and learn what to do. Then, in the actual situation, the children handle themselves well, even though the situation may be an exciting one.

The wise teacher uses such anticipatory guidance and desensitizes the children to anxieties which may arise in new situations. One teacher, on the first day with her nursery group, used the doll technique to enact the saying of "Goodbye" to mother. She knew that the child who is busy waving to Mother, greeting his teacher, and getting started with nursery play is not the child who bursts into tears. By having the doll demonstrate the happy fun of desirable behavior, the teacher helped the children toward such behavior themselves.

Play with dolls may proceed pleasantly for a while and then a child may become emotionally involved with his own problems of relationships and, while working them through, become highly destructive. The teacher who observes such emotional involvement must recognize it as such and provide more suitable emotional releases on subsequent occasions.

One day in the early fall, Mrs. O'Neill gathered the three- and four-year-old children together for a quiet song and a story during the fifteen minutes before departure. She noticed that Jimmy, four and one half, was missing. She looked around for his current best friend, four-year-old Clyde. He too was missing. As she led the group of children, she heard noise from the playhouse and surmised that Jimmy and Clyde were playing there. Since Jimmy had been a boy who stayed close to his mother and acceded to her suggestions about how to behave, Mrs. O'Neill let the boys play until after most of the children had left.

As she went to get the boys, they emerged from the playhouse, and went off happily with Jimmy's mother. Then Mrs. O'Neill started to put away the apparatus stored overnight in the playhouse. When she opened the playhouse door, she saw that the place was a shambles. The sturdy furniture was overturned and whatever could be thrown down on the floor, had been.

Mrs. O'Neill remembered the high standard of housekeeping in Jimmy's home, the day he was absent from school because he was cleaning up the eggs he had thrown on the livingroom rug, and his three-year-old's timidity in staying at the nursery unless his mother was there too. Mrs. O'Neill was delighted with the mess in the playhouse because it was evidence of Jimmy's emotional rebellion against the restrictions of his home—a rebellion he was able to terminate when it was time to go home.

Mrs. O'Neill heard an involuntary gasp behind her. Three-year-old Linda had followed her teacher and was appalled at the appearance of her beloved playhouse. Mrs. O'Neill put her arms around Linda, agreed that no one should do that to the playhouse, and assured her that when she came next time the playhouse would be all ready for her to play in.

Mrs. O'Neill, after all the children had left, made plans for discussing the playhouse and ways of keeping it tidy and beautiful. She also made plans about having Jimmy for lunch and a play-therapy hour with her.

The next day, Mrs. O'Neill talked with Jimmy about the playhouse when they had a few minutes alone. "Did you have fun wrecking the playhouse yesterday?" she asked. Then she said, "When you want to do that again, let's do it when the other children are not here. You see, the playhouse belongs to all of us, and we help each other keep it looking nice during nursery time."

The guiding of doll play requires not one but a variety of skills. The experienced teacher should be able to identify several types of doll-play situations and to guide children in each of them.

TYPE OF DOLL PLAY	GUIDANCE NEEDED
Child learns and practices housekeeping skills, such as:	Teacher observes skills and plans further experiences to help the child learn and practice housekeeping
putting dishes for each person arranging flowers sweeping floor wrapping up baby in blanket making bed	Teacher praises desirable outcomes Teacher may step in to demonstrate briefly
Child constructively plays out relationships of	Teacher observes relationships expressed and plans further experiences for the children as needed
family play group nursery or kindergarten	Teacher occasionally enters play to encourage better relationships
Child destructively plays out relationships he has in his	Teacher observes relationships expressed Teacher plans play therapy for child by himself
family play group nursery or kindergarten	In group situation teacher helps children understand desirable relationships and behavior limits

THE TEACHER ROLE HAS ITS LIMITS

Although preschool children must have a considerable area of freedom in which to develop their own self-discipline, they must also have limits to define the area in which they do not have freedom. An important objective of a preschool group is to help the children learn the limits which are essential in life—for instance, it is all right to hit a target, but it is not all right to hit a person. The wise preschool teacher emphasizes this limit daily by saying, "Sand hurts eyes. We do not throw it"; or by saying, "If you feel like hitting, you may pound the clay," or, "We hit the balloon man, but not people." Thus, by helping the children to stay within the cultural bounds, the teacher helps them to avoid feelings of guilt and shame.

Some children may come from homes in which the limits are at variance with those of the preschool group and of the larger community. If such individuals receive play therapy, under the competent guidance of a child psychologist, they will have wide limits in which to work out their problems of relationship to other people. Perhaps they will tear apart or bury doll figures which represent to them people who bother them. But even in the play-therapy situation they will be expected to keep from attacking the adult in charge.[12]

To help children learn their role as children in relation to parents and teachers and to help them learn the respect for adults characteristic of the social order, the teacher must maintain her role as a responsible adult who lets the children express their feelings only to the point at which they are still able to handle them. In one preschool situation, an unwise adult let the children shoot and bury her in dramatic play. In this way, she deprived them of adult support in finding acceptable limits to their behavior and left them to cope with their guilt feelings by themselves.

The teacher must keep in mind her role as a teacher. She may participate briefly in dramatic play situations but only to enhance their educational value, or to make a transition to other learning situations, or otherwise to use them for the good of the children. At no time does she abdicate her position as a responsible adult who is there to help the children in growing toward responsible maturity without feelings of guilt or shame.

The role of a teacher differs from that of a psychologist who may come to visit a preschool group. The difference in roles is apparent in a comparison of two accounts: one, by a psychologist visiting a nursery group; the other, by a teacher showing her understanding and permissive relationship with a highly intelligent boy in her group of four-year-old children.

The psychologist visited a nursery group in connection with her interest in four-year-old Don, who was having a difficult time in his family situation. His mother had more housework than she could accomplish easily and preferred to spend her time in caring for Don's little sister. Don's older brother was his mother's constant companion in his out-of-school hours, and sometimes even when he should have been in school. Don, as the middle child in a family of three children, found it difficult to compete with the other members of his family for his mother's attention.

The morning that his psychologist friend came to visit his nursery group for an hour, four-year-old Don welcomed having such personal attention. He felt that she liked him, and he proceeded to test the limits of this affection. He went through his entire repertoire of things-mothers-do-not-like. He threw clods of dirt at selected targets and, occasionally, at her feet. He got a drink of water, held it in his mouth as he came toward her, and then spat it out at her feet. He clung to her ankles so that she could not

[12] Clark E. Moustakas, *Children in Play Therapy* (New York: McGraw-Hill Book Company, Inc., 1953).

go away. He touched her skirt in back, saying, "I see your fanny." The understanding psychologist kept Don away from the nursery group and let him go through his attention-getting routine while she made sure that he was not thirsty. She knew he was hungry because it was close to lunchtime. When she felt that he had expressed his need for attention in all the undesirable ways, she talked with him, telling him that she liked him but did not like to play the games they had played that morning. She made plans with Don for more constructive activities the next time she visited the nursery group.

The limits that the psychologist permitted during her hour with Don in the setting of his nursery are much wider than those a teacher can permit. In her report on the behavior of a boy of high intelligence in her group of four-year-olds, one teacher mentions the unusual activities which the boy introduced on occasion into the nursery activities:

Stanley is a bright boy and loves to talk about many things in a way that is mighty adult.

On occasion Stanley is a tease and Susan is sometimes his target. She responds in such ideal form that it only serves to egg him on. When I say, "Stanley, I guess she doesn't want to be teased any more," I think Stanley feels that the fun is just beginning. But he is not difficult to persuade and is soon busy with some other activity.

Stanley has sometimes teased me by crawling under our rickety tables, or by getting under the oilcloth on the table, or by howling like a wolf at resting time. I have never failed to forgive him and, in fact, rejoiced to see such comfortable deviltry. From Stanley, it was a good sign.

The teacher who is skillful in guiding the emotional development of preschool children is a firm and affectionate person who furthers the development of each child within a setting of love. Her teaching should be based on an understanding of the bodily processes which enables a person actively to overcome his frustrations or keep him protectively immobile until he can be helped back to attacking his problems actively again.

The teacher should appreciate her role as a person schooled in methods of working with each individual child in her group whenever he encounters upsetting frustrations. She should arrange for someone else to handle the group if she is needed by a disturbed child. She must also provide for a room in which she can work with an individual child away from the other children and adults, because an upset child is helped if the situation is simplified and pressures are minimized. She learns when and how to use play therapy with children who have emotional problems or finds out where such help is available in her community and refers the child to it, if necessary.

In general, the teacher who studies children's emotions tries to provide each day those activities which give them an opportunity to release their feelings constructively. She appreciates the importance of having a period of rest and relaxation alternated with periods of stimulation and activity. Her schedule provides refreshments, toileting, and less demanding activities as the children need them. She decreases the probability of an emotional upset by seeing to it that each child has the space he needs to react physically to frustration, is free from pressures to internalize rather than express his emotions, and receives as much attention and affection from a beloved adult as he needs. In short, the preschool teacher sees to it that the preschool group has the physical facilities, equipment, program, and personnel that make it possible to further the emotional development of

*Fun, fellowship, and **emotional release**. (Courtesy of Daily Preschool, First Presbyterian Church, Garden Grove, California. Photograph by McKeon.)*

each child in the group. But especially she sees to it that each child has the love which three-year-old Carlos knew he should have:

ADULT (*suddenly stepping in front of Carlos*)   Boo!
CARLOS   You scared me.
ADULT   I meant to scare you.
CARLOS   I am not meant to be scared. I am meant to be loved.

Situations for Discussion

A preschool teacher is apt to find herself in situations similar to the four described here. As you think of what to do in each situation, consider whether each course of action suggested is desirable, or not. Use points brought out in the chapter as well as ideas from your own experience to justify your views. Suggest alternative courses of action to supplement those that are given.

SITUATION 1   For the first three weekly child-care hours, Janey's mother stayed with the group for the entire hour. The fourth morning she left as soon as Janey began playing on the slide. Presently Janey stopped playing, sat quietly for a few moments, and then started crying. As the teacher for the group, you went over to Janey and, with your arm around her, asked. "What's the matter, Janey?" A mumbled "Mummy" was the only answer distinguishable from the sobs. You should comfort Janey by saying

- Mummies always come back. Your mommy will come when the others do.
- Do you know why Ellen is happy playing? She knows that she plays here for a while and then her mother will come for her.
- Let's find a puzzle to play with.
- I'm a mommy, too, and I'll take care of you until your own mommy comes back.
- Let me tell you a story about the mother doll and the little baby doll.

SITUATION 2   David had quietly gathered all his favorite toys around him in the sandbox. As other children came to the sandbox, he defended his stockpile from them. He was so busy doing this that he had no time to play with the toys. All he could do was try to hang on to them. As David's teacher, you should

- Arrange for a time when David can play with the toys by himself.
- Point out that he can play with only one or two toys at a time.
- Ask him which of the two trucks his friend Billy can use.
- Quietly remove one of the trucks for another child to play with.
- Remind David that "we share the sandbox toys at nursery school."

SITUATION 3   One muddy day after a rainy period, four-year-old Ned enjoyed wading through the puddles in his overshoes. Then he wanted to ride a tricycle and tried to take one away from Ruth by hitting her. Unsuccessful, he comes indoors where you are busy and says, "I told her I was sorry but she keeps on crying and crying and crying." You should say

- I'm glad you are learning to say, "I'm sorry."
- Next time instead of hitting her, ask her to let you have the tricycle.
- We're going to read a story now; come and hear about Judy and Billy.
- Let's take off our overshoes before we come inside.
- Let's go see if we can make her happy again.

SITUATION 4   In your group of four-year-old children, Jack has been quietly working on puzzles. About ten minutes before refreshment time, he suddenly starts throwing the pieces of the puzzle in every direction. You should

- Remove Jack to another room.
- Start picking up the puzzle pieces so they will not get lost.
- Ask Jack to help you find the puzzle pieces.
- Serve refreshments at once.
- Get Jack bean bags to throw into a box.

Current Books for Preschool Children

BROWN, MARGARET WISE. *Runaway Bunny*. New York. Harper & Row, Publishers, 1942. [Mother Bunny finds her runaway.]

BROWNSTONE, CECILY. *All Kinds of Mothers*. New York: David McKay Company, Inc., 1969. [Mothers have variety.]

BUCKLEY, HELEN E. *The Little Boy and the Birthdays*. New York: Lothrop, Lee & Shepard, Inc., 1965. [The boy who remembered birthdays of others had his birthday remembered too.]

FRESCHET, BERNICE. *The Old Bullfrog*. New York: Charles Scribner's Sons, 1968. [When the heron struck downward, the old bullfrog jumped and swam away ahead of the strike.]

HOBAN, RUSSELL. *A Baby Sister for Frances*. New York: Harper & Row, Publishers, 1964. [Frances copes with the competition of a baby sister for parental attention.]

————. *Herman the Loser*. New York: Harper & Row, Publishers, 1961. [With help from his father and sister, Herman learns to be a finder.]

————. *The Stone Doll of Sister Brute*. New York: The Macmillan Company, 1968. [Sister Brute learned to love members of her family as well as stone dolls. *The Little Brute Family* (1966) introduced a series of books.]

KEATS, EZRA JACK. *Whistle for Willie*. New York: The Viking Press, 1964. [Finally Peter learns to whistle and is able to call Willie, his dog. In *Peter's Chair* (1967), Peter helps to paint his chair for his little sister.]

LEXAU, JOAN M. *Everyday a Dragon*. New York: Harper & Row, Publishers, 1967. [Father plays dragon with me.]

MAYER, MERCER. *There's a Nightmare in My Closet*. New York: The Dial Press, 1968. [A little boy of the tricycle set copes with nightmares.]

MINARIK, ELSE HOLMELUND. *Little Bear's Friend*. New York: Harper & Row, Publishers, 1960. [*Little Bear* (1957) began a series of books which portray relationships of Little Bear to his mother and a friend.]

ORMONDROYD, EDWARD. *Theodore*. Berkeley, Calif.: Parnassus Press, 1966. [Although Lucy was careless with Theodore, her beloved bear, they loved and understood each other.]

SCHLEIN, MIRIAM. *Billy the Littlest One*. Chicago: Albert Whitman & Company, 1966. [Billy the Littlest One knows he will not always be the littlest one.]

SCOTT, ANN HERBERT. *Sam*. New York: McGraw-Hill Book Company, 1967. [What Sam tries to do results in a series of "Don'ts!" until his mother helps him find what he can do.]

ZOLOTOW, CHARLOTTE. *My Friend John*. New York: Harper & Row, Publishers, 1968. [John and I like "everything that's important about each other." *I Want to Be Little* (Abelard-Schuman, 1966) is by the same author.]

Professional Books and Pamphlets

AXLINE, VIRGINIA. *Dibs: In Search of Self*. Boston: Houghton Mifflin Company, 1964. [Response of a disturbed five-year-old child to play therapy. *Play*

Therapy: the Inner Dynamics of Childhood is by the same author.]

Bettelheim, Bruno. *The Empty Fortress.* New York: The Free Press, 1967. [What is done with an autistic child in an orthogenic school has implications for helping any child with his human venture. *Love Is Not Enough* is an earlier book by the same author.]

————. *Paul and Mary.* New York: Doubleday & Company, Inc., 1961. [Two case histories of truants from life.]

Child Study Association. *When Children Need Special Help with Emotional Problems.* New York: Child Study Association, 1961. [Helpful suggestions about working with a child under stress. Also available is *Some Special Problems of Children Aged Two to Five years* (1966).]

Doll, Ronald C., and Rorert S. Fleming, eds. *Children Under Pressure.* Columbus, Ohio: Charles E. Merrill Books, Inc., 1966. [A collection of readings about how pressure originates, how children and parents react to pressure, what medical and educational specialists say about what can be done to relieve pressures.]

Ginott, Haim G. *Group Psychotherapy with Children.* New York: McGraw-Hill Book Company, Inc. 1961. [Theory and practice of play therapy is useful to those who work with preschool children.]

Hymes, James L., Jr. *The Child Under Six.* Englewood Cliffs, N.J.: Prentice-Hall, Inc., 1963. [Good guidance of children minimizes disruptive emotions.]

Janis, Marjorie G. *A 2-year-old Goes to Nursery School: A Case Study of Separation Reactions.* New York: National Association for the Education of Young Children. 1965. [Learning that mother returns may involve emotional reactions.]

Murphy, Lois B., and associates. *Personality in Young Children.* New York: Basic Books, Inc., 1966. [This two volume work includes a case study of Colin in nursery school and kindergarten.]

Murphy, Lois B. *The Widening World of Childhood.* New York: Basic Books, Inc., 1962. [Study of thirty-two normal children dealt with their ways of coping with stress as well as daily routine.]

Moustakas, Clark E. *Psychotherapy with Children.* New York: Harper & Row, Publishers, 1959. [Reports of preschool and other cases show that relationship therapy deals directly with the feelings of a child rather than his symptoms.]

Prescott, Daniel A. *The Child in the Educative Process.* New York: McGraw-Hill Book Company, Inc., 1957. [Extensive study of emotions underlies this significant book.]

Rubin, Albert I. *Projective Techniques with Children.* New York: Grune & Stratton, Inc., 1960. [A collection of articles about the use of such techniques as free play, Rohrsach, and others are applicable to preschool children as well as older ones.]

Taylor, Katharine Whiteside. *Parents and Children Learn Together.* New York: Bureau of Publications, Teachers College, Columbia University, 1968. [Joy and sympathy are part of learning during preschool years.]

Torrance, E. Paul. *Mental Health and Constructive Behavior.* Belmont, Calif.: Wadsworth Publishing Company, 1965. [An authority on creative talent discusses mental health, personality, group resources, and mental resources in response to stress.]

Part Three
PARTICIPATION IN THE PRESCHOOL GROUP

CHAPTER **16**

Parent Education

Parent education is a major challenge to those who work in preschool and adult education. Whether the life of a child will be better outside the hours he is in a preschool group, and in the years after his preschool group experience, depends on the extent to which parent education is part of that experience. Preschool groups influence the out-of-school life of a child through his parents.

Parent education is valuable at each educational level, but it is especially valuable when the oldest child in the family is at the preschool level. What parents learn at that time may influence their relationships not only with their preschool child but also with other children they may have.

Parent education is important not only for individual children but also for the preschool group itself. The statements parents make about the group, influence the parents of younger children who are considering enrolling them. Parents who understand and appreciate the contribution of the preschool group to their children and family spread their enthusiasm to other parents and help to assure the future of the group. Parent education is a factor which offsets the family instability that may arise in the parent-cooperative group from the mobility of the junior executive; in the children's center, from unemployment; and in private schools, from alterations in family income.

Many children remain in a preschool group for only one year or a part of it; a lesser number, for two years; and relatively few, for three (two years of nursery school and one year of kindergarten). This continuing change in enrollments implies that there is a continuing need to educate parents. What was understood by the parents of four years ago often is unknown or distorted in the minds of this term's parents. The nursery school and kindergarten cannot take it for granted that parents know; they must help them to learn what they need to know, especially

- What children are like at preschool ages.
- How parents can help children develop.
- How group experiences can help children develop.

In children's centers and in private nursery schools, parents must learn to have confidence in what the school does for their children. Through interviews, conferences, meetings, and written communications, teachers should try to help parents understand the basic philosophy of the preschool group. When teachers and parents both emphasize the same basic values—especially love and democracy—it is easier for the child to develop as a good member of home and social order. But to hope that parent education will make it possible for the child to have the same kind of handling at home as he has at school is not always realistic. Many children who get along with one set of values in their home and another in school are fortunate in spending at least part of their lives in the wholesome environment of the preschool group.

Parent education is especially important in the groups where the teacher has parents as assistants. Assisting parents should have the same basic philosophy and handle the children in essentially the same ways as the teacher. The team of adults must really function as a team. Many groups, in order to have such uniformity of teaching methods, require mothers of entering families to take a course in "Guiding Children's Growth." When it is not possible to arrange for such a course, the mothers can regularly study together *The Years Before School* and related books. An essential part of the preschool group is the mother's development through learning more effective ways of guiding child development.

Some of the attitudes, skills, and concepts that can be brought out in a course for mothers are important for mothers to use both at school and at home. As mothers extend their study of children and their work with them, they should broaden their understandings of such basic attitudes, skills, and concepts as the following:

Attitudes and Beliefs
- A child learns when he is ready.
- It is fun to be with children.
- The role of a mother is an important one, and a rewarding one.
- A child should have a feeling of success and of belonging whenever possible.
- Each child is an important person.
- Limits of the environment, aggressive behavior, and accidents give opportunity for learning.

Skills
- Express affection and personal regard for each child.
- Let a child do what he wants to as long as he is safe and is constructive.
- Point out limits pleasantly.

- Realize when a child has a problem.
- Give a child assistance when he has gone as far as he can by himself.
- Help a child find suitable emotional outlets.
- Find out how a child behaves at a given age level.
- Observe behavior objectively and record these observations.

Concepts
- Praise and other pleasant stimuli facilitate learning.
- Negative criticism may interfere with learning.
- Learning something in a variety of situations is better than identical repetition of it.
- Cause-and-effect relationships determine behavior.

Parent understanding develops through being a visitor. (Courtesy of Long Beach Parent Nursery Schools and Mariam M. Cook, Long Beach, California.)

Means for Educating Parents

When parents enroll a child in a preschool group, they assume responsibility not only for providing and labeling clothing as needed, facilitating transportation to and from school, and reporting illness or absence of the child, but also for reading the bulletins issued by the school or posted on the bulletin board, visiting the school as often as seems desirable for the child, and attending group and individual conferences. Of these responsibilities, the last three are especially useful means for parent education.

Parent education proceeds as parents read about, observe, and participate in the activities of the preschool group, and enter into parent-teacher interviews, conferences, and group discussions. The more the parent takes part in these various activities, the more he can learn from them. The most active form of parent education—the participation of parents in preschool groups—is the most important. (See Chapter 18.)

The choice of means for educating parents depends on the objectives to be accomplished. For instance, when parents need to feel more comfortable with a group of children, opportunities must be provided for the parents to be with groups of children. Furthermore, these opportunities must be pleasant and relaxing situations. Accordingly, first experiences are provided in which the parents can enjoy some activity with the children—perhaps sitting with some of them during story time. When parents learn to feel comfortable participating with the children in such simple activities as moving to music or looking for wild flowers during a walk in the fields, they can move forward in the parent role by assuming responsibility gradually for helping to guide and instruct a group of children.

To generalize, then, about how to select some suitable means for parent education.

- Decide on what skill, attitude, or understanding is desirable to encourage in the parents.
- Plan a series of experiences which gradually involve the parents more and more in actively using what they are learning.

Usually such a series of experiences should move quickly from passive listening as a member of an audience to active discussing and, presently, to active doing in a realistic situation.

As parents develop the skills, attitudes, and concepts which make them better parents, they should become more confident in their role as parents. This, then, is a criterion for selecting and evaluating methods suitable for parent education: a good method is one which helps parents to develop confidence in themselves as parents. By the same token, any method which makes parents feel ill at ease in their role as parents should be scrutinized carefully in order to determine how it may be improved upon. In general, parent education should be positive and constructive, with emphasis on what is good for parents to do rather than on what is to be avoided by them in their relationships to children. As they learn more and more about what to do, parents should reach the point of being able to distinguish desirable methods of working with children from methods which are undesirable in themselves or which have undesirable side effects.

BULLETINS, HANDBOOKS, AND BULLETIN BOARDS

Parents who enroll their child in a preschool group need answers to such questions as, "What are our roles as parents?" "What responsibilities does the school assume and what does it expect us to assume?" Bulletins are an excellent means for giving the parents, briefly and clearly, the information they desire. If bulletins are used only to convey important information, parents are more apt to read them than if the bulletins are frequent and trivial. Information important for parents in most preschool groups includes the following:

- Schedule for the children.
- Health and safety policies.
- Financial arrangements, if parents pay all or any portion of the costs.

In children's centers and parent-cooperative groups where mothers take turns in helping the teachers, bulletins must be more numerous and must deal with such additional topics as the following:

- Location of equipment.
- Schedule of turns for each mother to assist the teacher.
- Responsibilities of each adult as an assistant to the teacher.
- Suggestions for mothers to use in assisting the teacher.

In fact, many parent-cooperative groups find it desirable to provide a handbook of information for each family who enters the group. The handbook can be easily referred to at any time during the school year and can be a basis for study in meetings of the parent group.

To make needed information easily available to the parents, the preschool teacher should put any bulletin into their hands as directly as possible. She may give the bus or car-pool drivers one bulletin for each family and ask that the bulletin be given to each mother as she greets her child. A word to the parent at that time helps to assure that the parent will read the bulletin. The driver may say, "The bulletin answers the questions parents have been asking about school holidays."

Of course, to know whether a bulletin has been read, the director of the preschool group needs to provide some arrangement for having the parents show that they have indeed read it. The mother may be asked to sign the slip at the bottom of the page, tear it off, and return to the school within a specified period. For instance, one preschool group used such a slip as part of a bulletin on safety and asked that each parent bring the slip to the parent meeting scheduled for two days later. The slip said:

I have read the "Safety Bulletin" and have talked with my children about waiting for a grownup to open or close the car door.

_____   _____
Parent's Signature   Child's Name

By checking the returned slips against the list of enrollments, the director knew which families had read the bulletins. She then needed to discuss the safety rules personally only with those families who had not returned the slip. By receiving the signed slips at the start of the parents' meeting, she

*By helping at preschool, **parents learn how to teach safe practices.** (Courtesy of Long Beach Parent Nursery Schools and Mariam M. Cook, Long Beach, California.)*

could decide whether meeting time was needed to discuss the safety bulletin or whether she should discuss it briefly during the social hour.

A bulletin board can make important information available to anyone who comes to the school. Current bulletins, schedules, announcements of forthcoming events for parents and children, and brief reviews of books of interest to parents can be posted on the bulletin board. Thus the bulletin board dispenses valuable information and encourages desirable attitudes that further the education of parents.

The bulletin board can also be used to help parents to develop such parental skills as that of helping children to form desirable health habits. In one community the teachers at the municipal day nurseries make a point of talking with parents when they come for their children and of showing them what good food their children had to eat that day. Such bulletin-board conversation can be used to help the parents improve the home diet, with the teachers and parents working together to provide the child with the food that he needs for good health and maximum growth. In a similar way the bulletin board can be used to show the amount of rest that each child had in the course of the day, thus helping parents to determine the amount of sleep the child needs at home. A bulletin-board record of toileting incidents can also be useful to teachers and parents in helping each child to establish good habits of excretion. When parents and teachers work together to determine what kinds of information are to be placed on the bulletin board, the board is apt to be consulted frequently.

In the educational program for the parents, the director and teachers of the preschool group should make good use of written materials. Bulletins, a handbook, bulletin-board records and announcements are visual aids for keeping parents and school personnel aware of the policies and objectives of the group.

PARENT INTERVIEWS

The parent interview is a means of educating parents in a face-to-face situation. It has the advantage of dealing with an individual child in a particular family, but it has the disadvantage of requiring a great deal of time. Yet the quality of human relationships formed and the greater motivation made possible through the interview are thought to more than offset the cost of providing additional time for parents and teachers to confer. These benefits may be derived at lower cost by using the group conference for discussing problems and questions which occur in most families and the private interview only for discussing the problems of an individual family.

A parent interview can be initiated by any parent who has a question about her child or herself in relation to the preschool group. Such interviews are to be encouraged in every way by those responsible for parent education, but they should not be relied upon as a means for educating all parents. Often the parents most in need of an interview are apt not to ask for one. It is therefore necessary for the teacher to take the initiative in scheduling an interview with the parents of each child in the preschool group. At the beginning of the school year, she can use this interview for getting acquainted with each family; and, at any time of the year, she can use it for evaluating the progress the child has made in the preschool group.

The parent interview is an opportunity for parents and teacher to share their understanding of the child. Parents tell about the child's activities outside the preschool group, his likes and dislikes, his interests, his feelings, his problems, and the help he needs. The teacher describes how the child gets along with others, both children and grownups; how he participates in different phases of the activities; how changes in his skills, attitudes, and ideas are revealed by changes in his behavior. The teacher also describes the program of activities and the reasons for having such activities in terms of the needs of the children. She is also willing to discuss such problems as the dropout of the child's best friend from the group, his illness, or his being hurt by other children in the group. By sharing experiences with the child derived from two different situations, the parents and the teacher have an excellent basis for planning for his continuing development.

In order to work toward having such an ideally smooth interview, the teacher should keep in mind such suggestions as the following:

- Remember that a parent is apt to be as sensitive about her child as about herself.
- Avoid being defensive or putting the parent on the defensive.
- Sit on the same, not opposite sides of the desk.
- Be friendly and relaxed.
- Avoid talking in the presence of the child.
- Avoid having any interruptions.
- Avoid discussing other children or making comparisons between children.
- Be a good listener and encourage the parent in talking.
- Find out how the parent feels about the child.
- Accept the parent's plan of action insofar as is possible.

The discussion of real, emotionalized problems of individual children and their families sometimes serves as a cathartic for getting rid of emotional tensions which may tend to be disruptive. Such emotional forces must be carefully handled by the interviewer if the discussion is to keep within the realm of objectivity. The interviewer must avoid becoming a target or getting personally involved. The interviewer should learn to sidestep the what-would-*you*-do question and make some pleasant remark such as, "It is difficult to know what to do," which can lead into an objective discussion of the experience of others in similar situations. The interviewer should also learn to listen calmly and sympathetically to a personalized criticism about what has happened in the preschool group and to thank the critical parent sincerely for telling about how he feels. Judicious use of humor, the able interviewer knows, can often relieve emotional tension and help to keep an interview on a constructive and pleasant level.

VISITING THE PRESHOOL GROUP

Parental visits to the preschool group are a valuable factor in parent education, especially in developing favorable attitudes toward the group and some understanding of its activities. Furthermore, the relationships between parents and child are enriched through the sharing of a day in the preschool group, and parents are often motivated to learn more about the education of preschool children.

The practical problems involved in arranging for parents to visit the preschool group are easily resolved if the teacher keeps in mind that the

A welcome visitor. (*Courtesy of Oklahoma City Public Schools, Oklahoma City, Oklahoma.*)

arrangements—even if they must be quite different from the usual—must be convenient for the parents. Many situations lend themselves to visits by groups of parents; others, to individual visits. Here are some general plans for visiting preschools:

1. On a Saturday morning or a Sunday afternoon, have a preschool group session for the children and their fathers who work during the times that the group usually meets.
2. Provide care for preschool siblings so that mothers can visit the preschool group during a usual session.
3. For mothers who have a younger preschool child and no babysitter,

arrange for one mother at a time to visit the preschool group with her younger child. The success of such a visit depends upon the inter-dependencies of the mother and her children.

4. Invite mothers and preschool siblings to come to a preschool group party for an hour or, at most, two hours.

5. Encourage working mothers to plan for a half-day of vacation, perhaps as a birthday present for their child, and to spend it in a visit to the child's preschool group.

Parents' visits to the preschool group can be extended into the use of the preschool group as a laboratory situation in which parents may observe the children. For instance, in some localities parents regularly observe their children's groups and discuss their observations with the adult education instructor and with the teacher and her assistants. Thus parents have an excellent opportunity to learn effective ways of working with preschool children in general and with their own children in particular. They can try out at home the techniques they observe, and can compare the effects they obtain with those obtained in the preschool group by other parents, and can discuss any questions they have about their findings.

In assisting the preschool teacher, a parent has opportunity to improve her understanding and guidance of her child. She can gain perspective on the behavior of the child by observing him among his peers. She can develop skill in working with a group of children, and become more capable of helping neighborhood children and her own child play together more fruitfully. As her parental understanding and skill increases, her pride in her mother role will increase.

From the point of view of parent education, it is indeed desirable to provide opportunity for parents to participate in teaching the preschool groups their children attend. Those parents who are interested in their children and have the time to attend their children's preschool group regularly enjoy the role of mother-assistant, and they learn a great deal from the experience. Chapter 18 describes such participation.

In one preschool group, each mother assistant selected one of the children to observe throughout the school year. On the day she worked with the children's group, she stayed for a few minutes to record her observations on the child for that day. Twice during the year the mother assistants brought their record booklets to a meeting in which they discussed briefly the progress being made by each child. However, lacking guidance in how to improve their observations, the mothers only continued to make the same kind of limited observations and soon tired of the recording activity. At a final meeting, devoted to discussion of the children on the basis of the observations, the mother assistants were still giving reports such as the following:

Ned is such an attractive boy. Each morning he is neatly dressed. He always has a smile for everyone, and is so agreeable about doing what a person tells him to do. I certainly wish my Don were like him.

Although such observations have limited usefulness as records of child behavior, they are not without a social value. The mother assistant reporting on Ned's behavior was reassured by the other mothers that her Don had his own charms, and that she was indeed successful in her role as his mother.

In prechool groups where mothers act as assistants to the teacher, some time is set aside for the recording activity, and suggestions are made about recording actual incidents rather than personal opinions. In addition to the days she works assisting the teacher, each mother assistant comes to the preschool group one day each month solely to observe and record. This recording process sharpens observations, and a recording made on the spot at the time of a happening captures the exact wordings of children and adults. The resultant recordings are much more useful than those made after a lapse of even a short interval of time. The recorded observations can be used at meetings of mother assistants and teacher as a basis for discussion and interpretation. Through their use, the mother assistants improve their understanding of individual children and of methods by which to guide them.

Evaluating Pupil Progress

Although the demands on children as future citizens are not yet felt at the preschool level, it is nevertheless important to have parents working with the teacher of the preschool group to appraise pupil progesss. Appraisal is a means of parent education. The parents and teacher who have considered together the progress of an individual child have not only a better understanding of the child, of other children of his age level, and of the process of appraisal, but also more confidence in themselves as parents and teacher.

What kind of evaluation procedure is desirable for parent education? The procedure will differ from group to group, according to the needs and interests of the parents and the extent of their participation in preschool group activities. For example, in a group not yet familiar with the process, pupil appraisal may consist of a brief, encouraging note at the end of the year to bolster parental pride, increase parental appreciation of the child, and encourage further participation in preschool group activities. Here is such a note about three-year-old Kimmy:

Kimmy is a very affectionate, volatile little girl. She loves and seeks affection and gets it from all of us at the nursery school. She is, I believe, trying to be less dependent on her older sister. Her next year with us should be of great help in this respect.

Kimmy has an admirable independence about her abilities. She certainly should prove to be even more capable of taking care of herself in all situations next year.

In a preschool group in which mothers assist the teacher, an effective evaluation procedure involves devoting one or two meetings at the end of the year to brief group evaluations of the progress of each child. A short statement by the teacher can be supplemented by discussion of the progress noted by different mothers, especially those who know the child as a neighbor. The child's mother, as one of the group, is free to make any statement or to ask any questions. The general tone of the meeting is one of mutual appreciation and planning for the coming year.

With experience in evaluation, the teacher soon learns the value of keeping anecdotal records and using them as a basis for evaluative remarks. The teacher and the parents can work together with records of observed incidents and arrive at a better understanding of the child. Furthermore, the teacher can use anecdotal records to make an evaluative statement, such as the following one about three-and-one-half-year-old Chris:

Relationships to teacher: When Chris arrives at school in the morning, he answers my greeting with a grin. He and his neighbors sometimes come yipping in, full of good spirits. Chris often shows me what he has brought or tells me the news. He seems to feel completely comfortable about communicating with me and he'll let me know if he has "insurmountable" troubles. I can joke with Chris and he enjoys it. Mostly he is pretty busy but he seems to enjoy some direct attention and likes to have me listen to what he has to say.

Relationship to children: Chris feels glad with the gang around him. I observed him at work one day during our art activities. Chris sang while he worked and from time to time announced in a loud voice the state of his progress at cutting. He seemed sure everyone was interested in a blow-by-blow account of his work. When he resumed singing, Rodney asked, "What are you singing, Chris?" And Chris replied, not unkindly, "Never you mind, Rodney." The song title just was not important. Meanwhile, Danny, off to one side, giggled at Chris's boisterousness. He admires the noisy person who sort of dances around while pasting, using no chair, working on his feet so he can move freely while he cuts and pastes. Presently Chris announced, "I'm making this for my Mommy."

Special interests: Chris participates in all our activities except dancing, which is definitely a predominantly female pursuit this year. He participates in our musical games and will be a galloping gray pony with the others. He joined the parade that Stanley organized one day. He's interested in arts and crafts. He is often in the sandbox. He's a climber and proud to show me his prowess. He goes along with imaginative play. He was fearless with our gopher friend at the park the other day.

Progress: Although Chris is young, he acts like a seasoned member of our community. He knows his way around, is outgoing and resourceful. He is affectionate and sociable. I think he will be quite a leader here next year. It will be a fine experience to be a senior member of the group, a "big-shot" and "man-about school."

Evaluation at the preschool level should not be made in great detail. Neither the teacher responsible for a group of children nor the parent with limited experience in observing children objectively is able to comment on more than a few aspects of behavior. Nor can the teachers comment validly on behavior more apt to occur at home than in the preschool group. Most preschool teachers do well to limit their evaluative comments to only three of four aspects of behavior.

The teacher who wrote the evaluative statement about Chris arrived at that kind of four-paragraph statement through her frustration in attempting to use a three-page outline of topics dealing with detailed aspects of the physical, intellectual, social, and emotional development of the individual child. She felt that such items as *concentration* and *motor control* were not easily observable in the social situation of the nursery group. She also felt that an attempt to report in detail would result in general statements rather than in meaningful descriptions of behavior. The simple, four-part form she developed is quite different from the more detailed outline she wisely discarded. It is noteworthy that the more interesting parts of the original evaluative statement are the anecdotal records:

Physical vigor: Chris has plenty of it, I would say. He sometimes engages in really boisterous games. He has been able to sustain energetic activities with vitality throughout the morning very well.

Motor control:

Intellectual development:

Concentration:

Language ability: Chris is very capable of communicating with us and he has not been shy about talking. He ventures to tell us things in our sharing circle.

Response to stories: This is good. He likes stories and sometimes brings something to be read. (Most recently he brought a comic book.)

Response to arts and crafts: He often has asked, "Make mine for me." But, in spite of the insecurity he feels in the necessary techniques, he always joins us at the art table, wanting to make something.

Curiosity: He pesters me to tell my secrets and reveal my surprises. Chris seemed fascinated with my account of the kittens being born. When I finished telling the children how the kittens came out of the mama cat, Chris said, "Now let's see the kittens go *back* into the mommy."

GROUP MEETINGS FOR PARENTS

Probably the most frequently used device for parent education is the group meeting. This takes a variety of forms, and its chief aim may be either educational or social. A lecture on child development, a film with sound accompaniment, or a panel discussion followed by opportunity for questions from the audience are some of the techniques commonly used by preschool groups as a means for helping parents to acquire a better understanding of preschool children and their group experience. Such educational meetings may be scheduled as single events or a series of events, as a workshop or conference, or even as an adult education or college course.

The group meeting may be primarily social—an occasion to foster group feeling (perhaps a monthly Saturday-night potluck supper for families of children in the preschool group). Such a meeting has educational value because it brings together people with similar interests in bringing up their children, and gives them an opportunity to discuss their mutual interests and common problems—for instance, the eating or sleeping habits of children, appropriate TV programs, activities of the preschool group, or the behavior of individual children.

As preschool groups recognize the parents' need for social as well as educational opportunities, they plan group meetings which offer parents both kinds of experience. For instance, when a parent counselor at a day nursery worked with a committee of parents in developing a program for the nursery parents, the committee decided to have not only two large evening meetings but also a series of smaller coffee-hour discussions throughout the year. These coffee-hour discussions, led by the parent counselor, proved so popular that the parent committee thought it desirable to have two smaller coffee-hour groups in place of each large one. The parents were separated into two groups, on the basis of the number of children in their family. The guests at the first coffee hour were parents of only one child; at the second coffee hour, parents of two or more children. The attendance, as well as the expressed appreciation for the meetings, was evidence that the meetings were enjoyable and educational.

Pointers for Educational Programs for Parents

Programs for parents and preschool teachers must take into account the important role of the teacher as well as the responsibilities and importance of the parents as parents. Both teachers and parents should contribute to the planning of the program, to the program itself, and to the follow-up action which implements the thought of the group. As teachers and parents work together, the respect of each for the other should deepen.

The good teacher, by virtue of her experience and study, is expert in working effectively with preschool children of a particular age level. She has observed children and thought about them so that she understands well how they behave and can predict what they are apt to do. She also has become skilled in working with the children in the social situations appropriate to their level of development. She knows how to work with groups of children as well as with individual children.

The role of the teacher of preschool children is important and unique. So also is the role of the parent—the expert on growth and development of the individual child. The mother knows her preschool child as no one else can because she has had responsibility for him twenty-four hours a day, day after day. She has had to cope with her child when he was sleepy, hungry, irritable, emotionally upset, and physically ill. She continues to cope with an emotional range far wider than that usually apparent at school. She must also react to her child both when he is well in command of himself and when he is tired or ill. Parent and child attain a unique intimacy, an intimacy different from that usually attained by the child and his teacher.

When teachers and parents appreciate each other, they can work smoothly together for the best interest of the children. Their mutual respect should be constantly enhanced by leaders in parent education because an awareness of their importance in both teachers and parents adds to their self-confidence and helps them in carrying out their roles.

The determination of a suitable time for a parent group to meet illustrates the importance of parent participation in planning for the meeting. Only parents know the answers to such questions as the following:

Do the fathers enjoy babysitting so that mother can occasionally attend an evening meeting?

Are the fathers enrolled in evening courses? Or do they work during the evening hours?

If both parents are to attend the meeting, how much notice do they need for making suitable babysitting arrangements? Is the babysitter's fee within family means? Are there volunteer adults available to act as babysitters?

Are the preschool children old enough to participate in a noon picnic at a recreation center where they can play while mothers and teachers have a meeting?

PARENTS PARTICIPATE IN PLANNING PARENT-EDUCATION PROGRAMS

Parent education should not be something arranged *for* parents or done *to* parents; it should be an activity planned and carried out *with* parents. Plans may be initiated by sensitive parents who are aware of their need to develop some skill or understanding; or they may be initiated by a wise teacher who identifies some attitude, skill, or understanding that is important for the parents to develop. Further planning then must be done by parents and teachers, working together.

The family counselor at a children's center found that her ideas about a suitable program for a meeting differed from those of the parents, and that the meetings were better attended when the program was planned by a parent committee working with her. In planning the program for the first meeting of the year, the counselor pointed out to the committee the excellent films available to parent groups and suggested that one be shown as a springboard for discussion. However, the parents thought that most parents wanted to know what their children did at the nursery center. This parental idea was developed into a laboratory program during which the parents took part in some of the activities that their children took part in at the center. They painted, modeled in clay, and cut and pasted as they wished. The parents were glad to experience their children's activities.

When the parent committee met with the counselor to plan the next meeting, the parents said that they wanted to know more about what their children did at nursery school. They liked to talk with the children about nursery school and they needed to know what the children did all day. Again this idea was developed into a parent program for an evening meeting. With explanation, pantomime, and pictures, the parents were taken through "a day at nursery school."

The experience of the family counselor in planning programs for parents emphasizes the focus of parent attention: "I want to know what my child does at nursery school." This interest is an excellent starting point for parents' programs in any kind of preschool group—nursery school or kindergarten, children's center, private nursery school, parent-cooperative group, or laboratory school. Even mothers who take turns in assisting the teacher of a preschool group welcome an opportunity to help other parents learn what each child does in the preschool group, and often are eager to put on such a program for fathers and mothers not yet acquainted with the group's activities.

THE PARENTAL POINT OF VIEW

The point which parents have reached in coming to understand preschool children, the values of the preschool group, and themselves as parents is the starting point of any parent education program. At the same time, the program must take into account such basic parental responsibilities as the responsibility for keeping the children safe and well and for passing on to them the cultural heritage. Parents must be concerned with such health and safety questions as the following:

How shall I keep my child from running out into the street?
How can I encourage my child to be friendly yet cautious with strangers?
What shall I feed my child? How do I help him get the rest he needs?
How can I help him be healthy?

And with such questions regarding the cultural heritage as the following:

How do I teach my child good manners?
How can I help my child to speak correctly?
How can I see that my child acquires good bathroom habits?
What shall I teach my child about fighting?
How shall I help my child to be good?

Often parents are so concerned with their own immediate parental problems that they must work out solutions to these problems before they can go on to more fundamental considerations about children. A parent education program that starts with problems of concern to parents makes it possible to reassure parents about their success in the parental role while helping them to learn more and more about children and about their development through preschool group experience.

The self-interest of parents must not be underestimated. Parents wonder if their methods are gaining them social approval. If not, what should they do differently? Parents like to get attention in their role as parents. If people say to a mother, "What a sweet little girl! She looks like a doll," the mother is apt to continue dressing the little girl so that people will admire her. The mother basks in the reflected glory, and reaches out for more. Likewise, if people say to a mother, "Your little boy bites!" the mother may enjoy the role of being the mother of an aggressive male. This may be the best role she has ever played, from the standpoint of giving her the attention she craves.

Parents who are primarily concerned about themselves are eager for suggestions about what to do with their children because they look on these suggestions as a means of enhancing their own parental roles. This egocentric view is recognized by the teacher, who helps parents to understand that the first thing to do is to look at any problem they may have from the viewpoint of the child. It may take the mother a long time to be able to shift the focus of her attention from herself to her child. An occasional mother may not be able to do this without psychiatric help. But most mothers will presently focus their attention on the child if the teacher often leads them in discussing anecdotal material from the standpoint of the child.

As parents become child-oriented, they develop readiness for further understanding about children. The adult educator can develop a program of parent education around the following points:

Concept: Each child needs to be loved, and to be made to realize that he has his own special place in the affections of his parents and his teacher.
Discussion: How can I help my child get along with our new baby?
Concept: A child benefits from nursery or kindergarten experience according to his age and personality.
Discussion: How is my child doing in the preschool group?
Concept: A child matures at his own rate. His development is noticeable sometimes in one area, sometimes in another. He solves his developmental problems at his own rates.
Discussion: When is a child ready to share his toys? To wait for his turn? And so on.
Concept: As a child grows, he alternates between outgoing, exploratory periods and more quiet, withdrawing periods of assimilation.
Discussion: What activities are appropriate for a four-year-old child? For a three-year-old child? For a five-year-old child?
Concept: Cause-and-effect relationships are evident in a child's behavior. What a child does depends in large part on how members of his family and his teacher react to him.
Discussion: Does hitting behavior in the preschool group have any relation to policies at home?

PARENT DISCUSSIONS

An important objective of parent education is for parents to learn to discuss their problems and to express more objectively their feelings and ideas about their children. This is such an important objective that meetings should regularly allot to it a certain amount of time (often known as the discussion hour and conducted by a chairman).

If time is not set aside for discussion, talking is apt to pervade the whole meeting and may prevent it from starting or ending on time. In a parent group, talking may mix with business to the point that people are distracted from considering the matters needing decision. It is well, therefore, to limit discussion to the first hour of the meeting. Groups that follow this plan find that their members are eager to come—and they arrive promptly. Parents do not want to miss the educational program because it enables them to bring up any question or misgiving they may have and to take part in discussions which concern their children and themselves. When the educational part of the program is over, business matters can receive their proper attention because feelings have been expressed, egos have been satisfied, and pertinent basic ideas have been thoroughly discussed.

In order to foster the communication of ideas among the members of a discussion group, seats should be arranged in a circle, so that no one is shunted to one side or to the rear. This physical setting creates an atmosphere of equality. Furthermore, the opportunity to see faces rather than backs of necks is conducive to the expression of ideas. By stimulating sympathy and friendliness, the circle arrangement encourages members to express their feelings and beliefs.

Learning to talk professionally about children will help nursery school parents now and later, when their children are in elementary or high schools. Talking objectively, reporting actual happenings briefly, re-creating an incident that occurred in the preschool group, presenting a puzzling question—all these experiences are an integral part of an educational discussion hour.

Through experience, parents can learn that any preschool problem can be discussed—even as drastic a problem as the child who has moved into a phase of hitting, withdrawing, clinging, or dominating. Each question is considered from the point of view of the person who is a problem to himself, and the group sincerely attempts to arrive at the best solution for everyone concerned.

WHAT TO DISCUSS

The educational program for a parents group should deal with the group's immediate problems, rather than problems of a general nature. A program centered around questions current in the minds of the parents holds their interest and encourages their participation. A general program is less apt to lead either to discussion or to action.

In organizing such a program, the chairman of education may choose from all resources available: panel discussions, symposia, films, speakers, anecdotal material, book reviews, and conference reports. However, she usually makes use of the resources of the group, insofar as is possible, and devotes at least part of the program to a discussion centered around one or two key questions. Here is a typical list of topics for a series of monthly meetings to be held throughout the school year:

MONTH	PROGRAM TOPIC
September	Our School—Children, Schedule, and Equipment
October	What I Want My Child to Get Out of His Preschool Experience This Year
November	How We Try to Help the Group
December	Christmas Activities and January Fatigue
January	What I Saw Happen in the Preschool Group
February	How to Help Preschool Children Develop
March	Daddies are Parents Too
April	How Our Children are Developing in the Preschool Group
May	Are the Children Ready for Their Next Year in a Group?
June	Summer Activities

CONFERENCES AND WORKSHOPS FOR PARENTS AND TEACHERS

In addition to its regular meetings, a preschool parent group should have its parents and teachers benefit from meetings with parents and teachers of other preschool groups. These conferences or workshops provide an opportunity to learn additional ways of working effectively with children, other techniques useful in parent education, and new ways of thinking about the recurring problems of the preschool group.

When an area group of the National Association for the Education of Young Children cooperated with the Council of Parent-Participation Nursery Schools in the same area in conducting a workshop for people interested in preschool education, the program-planning committee consisted of teachers and parents from each subgroup within both associations. The general focus of interest for their conference was the question: How well are we fulfilling our objectives, especially in relation to the four- and five-year-old children who will be in kindergarten the following year? The conference title was "Perking Up Our Preschool Program." The planning committee identified thirteen general topics of interest and then developed titles for the correponding discussion groups:

GENERAL TOPIC	TITLE FOR DISCUSSION GROUP
Art	From Experimenting to Expression
Literature	Mother Goose to Dr. Seuss
Music	Making Merry with Music
Science	Bus, Beasts, and Buzzer Boards
Dramatic Play	I'll Be You and You Be Me
Creative Free Play	A Bird Can Fly; So Can I
Rainy-Day and Quiet Activities	A Mouse in Your House
Sharing and Showing	A Shell, a Story, a Song
Parent-Teacher Relationships	One Is Good, but Two Are Better

GENERAL TOPIC	TITLE FOR DISCUSSION GROUP
Child-Teacher Relationships	We're Pals
Discipline	Taming of the Shrewd
Puppets	Knock, Knock, Knock; Talk, Talk, Talk
The Physical Setup	How Does the Physical Setup Affect the Children?

The committee felt that one carefully planned intensive session on a Saturday afternoon was more suitable for the parents and teachers than a one- or two-day session. The schedule planned for the afternoon was as follows:

1:00 We see together the Vassar Child Study movie *The Fours and Fives.*
2:00 We scatter for discussion groups on different facets of the preschool program, with resource people in each group.
3:00 We come together for a brief summary of the discussion sessions.

The committee thought this schedule would give participants a rapid orientation, an opportunity for discussion within a defined area, and a means of finding out what notable ideas had emerged in other groups.

The planning committee also recognized its responsibility for developing trained leaders who could take responsibility in their own preschool groups and in subsequent conferences. The committee obtained lists of potential leaders among the teachers and parents in local preschool groups and used the lists in designating a chairman, a co-chairman, a recorder, and an alternate recorder for each small group discussion of the conference. Each of these designated people—and anyone else who was interested in leadership—was invited to attend an evening meeting for training leaders. At that meeting the function and responsibility of each position was explained, and the meeting itself was used as a laboratory experience in democratic leadership. A mimeographed sheet of suggestions helped the participants in the meeting to carry home such concepts as the importance of appreciating each idea contributed by members of a discussion group, of avoiding evaluative remarks concerning those contributions, and of encouraging a variety of opinions. Through this training meeting, several members of each conference discussion group began thinking about the discussion and were well prepared for it before the conference began.

The other function of the program committee was to plan exhibits to be viewed both before and after the discussions. These visual aids to parent education were solicited from the private nurseries, the day- and child-care centers, the parent-cooperative groups, the child-development center, and the parent education classes in the area. Like the other facets of the workshop, the exhibits facilitated an interchange of ideas among the parents and teachers who attended.

USING ANECDOTAL RECORDS

Anecdotal material recorded by teachers and other observers during the weeks preceding a meeting provides parents with an excellent basis for discussion. For example, in a group for three- and four-year-old children, the chairman of education interviewed both the teacher and her assistants in order to obtain information on the happenings of the month. From her notes concerning these happenings and from anecdotal records kept by the teacher and her assistants in connection with their teaching, the chairman of education constructed a series of brief descriptions of situations that might arise in the children's group. She entitled these described situations "What would you do?" and had copies to put in the hands of each parent attending the next monthly meeting.

With the mothers eager to talk about the children, the discussion hour of the meeting started promptly. The chairman explained that everyone would work on a committee with two or three other people. During the first ten minutes of the hour, each committee was to read over the situation assigned to it and plan a desirable way to utilize the situation for the good of the child. Then each group was to read its problem, and act out both the described nursery situation and its proposed solution to the problem. A brief discussion period would follow: questions about the problem, suggestions for alternate courses of action, and additional comments.

The chairman passed out numbered slips for each committee group, as follows:

What Would You Do?

1. In the nursery group on a rainy day, you are helping a child pull the block box to a place suitable for play. Suddenly, a three-year-old boy goes shrieking past, chasing another child. What do you do?
2. As you turn a corner and come into the dress-up area, you see a four-year-old girl pounding another girl on the back. What do you do?
3. A four-year-old girl says to the other girls in the bus, "I'm wearing my new dress. You don't have a new dress." A few minutes later she turns to the shy four-year-old girl beside her and says, "Your hair is messy." Then, addressing other girls, she says, "We don't like messy hair, do we?" How can you help this four-year-old girl to be cooperative instead of competitive?
4. While you are supervising the painting group, a three-year-old girl comes over to you for help in untying her apron. She is slow in speaking and stutters a bit when she does speak. How can you help her to communicate?
5. You are helping a group of children to cross the wide street safely. While you wait with them on the curb, four-year-old Mary runs out into the street. You remind the others to stay on the curb until no more cars are coming. Then you pick up Mary and carry her back to the sidewalk. As you do so, she bites you. What do you do?

The fun of working in a small group and acting out and discussing each of the situations made the parents' meeting one of active learning. The mothers, who had been assisting the teacher two or three times a month and studying about preschool children, were able to remind each other of such fundamental concepts as trying to see the situation from the point of view of the child and trying to help children learn through their own activity. The teacher felt free to comment whenever the mothers' discussion did not include points she deemed important, but she kept her participation to a minimum. She was interested primarily in listening to the contributions made by different mothers so that she could help each of them to develop her understanding further in the laboratory situation of the preschool group.

Fathers, grandparents and friends who were babysitting at home, also benefitted from the meeting because the chairman gave each of the mothers a copy of the five "What would you do?" situations to take home and discuss with them.

USING ANECDOTAL RECORDS IN SOLVING THE FATHER PROBLEM

In actual practice, most parent education programs are designed for mothers. With special efforts on the part of the teachers, the mothers, and the fathers themselves, the fathers may attend one or two meetings each year. Their nonattendance is often based on the belief that it is more important for the mother to attend meetings for parents because she is the one who has a continuing daily responsibility for the child. The father may have a very real interest in learning to be a good parent, but his responsibility for the economic welfare of the family may make it difficult for him to do much about this interest. To devote two or three hours to a meeting for parents is not always possible. In most families it is more difficult for both parents to attend than it is for just the mother. How, then, can a father as well as a mother be educated in the parental role?

One good way is to provide him with anecdotal records to interpret. He can read through such a record in a rather short time. Then both parents can interpret the record. What one sees in the record of behavior supplements what the other sees. As parents use anecdotal materials together, they can enjoy sharing their understandings about children and continue to develop as parents.

ENRICHING PROGRAMS FOR LESS ADVANTAGED

As programs for the less advantaged have multiplied, they have brought in their wake the realization that broadening the preschool experience of a child is greatly facilitated by broadening the experience of his family. The memory of shared events enriches family life. What has been experienced by parent and child can be recalled later by the parent to help the child remember. What the child recalls can be reinforced at once by parental pleasure both in remembering the original happening and in having the child refer back to it. Furthermore, the parent who has been there is in a position to elaborate what the child recalls.

Experimental programs with families of preschool children have involved both parents alone and parents with their children. In the program of one children's center for a metropolitan school district, parents have bus trips which take them from one place to another within the city. Within an hour the parent group can visit two or three places, each accessible by public transportation. At each place the parents think about what will be interesting for them to show to their children when they return with their family at their leisure. In group discussions they talk with other parents in planning a family experience, and later in recounting the actual adventure. They compare what they noticed on the initial parent excursion with what they saw when they returned with their children to the same place. Thus they gain skill in observing and in teaching their children to observe significant patterns and details.

Whenever possible, mothers of children in the group should be encouraged to attend the children's group regularly in the role of mother assistant to the teacher. In assisting the teacher a parent has opportunity to improve her understanding and guidance of her child. She can gain perspective on his behavior by observing him among his peers. She can develop skill in working with a group of children and become more capable of helping neighborhood children and her own child play together more fruitfully. As her parental understanding and skill increase, her pride in them increases. From the point of view of parent education it is indeed desirable to provide opportunity for parents to participate in teaching the preschool groups their children attend. Chapter 18 describes such participation.

Preschool parent education groups can work with parent-teacher groups for the primary grades of elementary school in arranging a series of parent education programs, perhaps with a certificate available for those attending all but one of the meetings. Such early childhood education parent meetings often deal with and discuss such topics as the following:

TOPIC SUGGESTED BY SCHOOL NURSE	TOPIC SUGGESTED BY PARENT COMMITTEE	TOPIC SUGGESTED BY NUTRITIONIST
Bed Wetting; Mental Health; Sleeping Problems; Care of the Skin	Personal Grooming for Children Thumb Sucking	Keeping a Grip on Our Dollars
Dental Health; Thumb Sucking	Sex Education for Children	Nutrition Principles and Menu Planning
Family Planning Drug Abuse; Alcohol	How Can I Help My Child Be More Responsible?	Comparing Meat Costs Stretching Your Food Dollar

The Preschool-Group Experience and Parental Development

One summer Mrs. Osman and Mrs. Lane agreed to take responsibility for the preschool children of the families attending a one-week family camp. With only six mornings in which to give group experience to the children, they felt that careful advance planning was necessary in order to achieve their purposes, which were to have a nursery that would meet the needs of the children and at the same time demonstrate the worth of group experience with their peers.

Mrs. Osman and Mrs. Lane thought that the parents should know about the plan for the nursery group early, and especially about parental participation in it. The teachers therefore prepared a letter which they mailed to the parents two weeks before their departures for camp. The letter followed the general camp publicity, which mentioned the camp's parent-participation nursery group. The letters bore the return addresses of both teachers so that a parent could write to either teacher, if he wished. The letter and the request for equipment enclosed with it, are shown on pages 570–71 and 571–72.

By asking the parents to help in equipping the nursery group, the teachers encouraged them to begin at once to participate in the preschool group. The teachers also specified the time and place for the first meeting of parents, a planning meeting a day before the start of the actual group program for the children, and an opportunity for both parent and preschool child to explore the situation of the preschool group. Thus further participation was provided for, and participation in the preshool group itself was introduced as one of the responsibilities of the parents: "Please sign up . . . on the parent-participation schedule. . . ."

Furthermore, the role of the parents in the preschool group was stated plainly. With the teachers, parents were to provide "a really worthwhile experience for the preschool children." In the last paragraph of the letter their role was defined further: "to give personal attention to children when required," to meet "the needs of our particular group of children," and to make any suggestions that might improve the nursery group.

By including in the letter a daily schedule for the nursery group, its teachers helped the parents in thinking about the activities the nursery children would have—the activities to which the parents would contribute as teacher-assistants. With the parents set to thinking about the nursery group, the teachers now turned their attention to preparations for the group itself. Each phase of preparation was completed with some channel for communication with the parents, usually an exhibit to be placed on the bulletin board.

Announcements for Nursery School Parents was the title of the bulletin

June 3, 19—

Dear Parents,

We are writing to you because you will be coming to camp with a preschool child. We are looking forward to meeting you and your preschooler and to providing together a really worthwhile experience for the preschool children. As you know, the nursery school is operated on a parent participation basis and can operate only with your dedicated help. The mother or the father of each preschooler enrolled in the program is expected to give at least one, maybe two, three-hour periods of his or her time to this program. Please sign up, as soon as possible upon arrival, on the parent participation schedule which will be posted on a bulletin board near the outdoor area to be used by the nursery school.

Our program is planned for children 2½ to 4½ years old. Children between 2½ and 3 years old will be cared for by Elaine Dunn after juice time at 10:30 A.M. A brief outline of our daily schedule is attached. Please note that the preschool program ends at 11:45 A.M. and not at noon.

The preschool group is planning to meet in an outdoor location this year. We plan to locate ourselves between the parking lot and upper toilet house. Please plan to meet us there at 5 P.M. on Saturday so that we may begin our acquaintance and so that your preschooler may see where his school will be.

We want this to be a rewarding experience for your child. If he or she is not ready to stay at school without a parent at first, please be prepared to give him or her some more of your time. A favorite toy helps some children in making the transition to a new situation.

Above all, we wish to create a relaxed, loving atmosphere in which the children can explore and feel secure. There should be sufficient adults present at all times to give personal attention to children when required. We will need to be flexible in meeting the needs of our particular group of children. We welcome and encourage your suggestions, and we are sure that this will be a rewarding experience for all of us.

Sincerely yours,
Betty Lane and Ursula Osman

board, a large sheet of wallboard into which thumbtacks could easily be inserted. At the top was the "Parent-Participation Schedule," with blanks to be filled in with parents' signatures for each of the six mornings (Sunday through Friday) the group was to meet, and for the Friday afternoon clean up time at the conclusion of the week.

The bulletin board had familier communications across the bottom of it: both pages of the letter mailed to each family, and two quotations which the teachers thought expressed well the philosophy of a nursery group, and of parents who think constructively and realistically about their children. It also had space for any communications that parents might like to post, and for clippings from the camp newspaper. The long-term education of parents was the reason for having a sign-out sheet to be used by parents checking out parent education books for themselves or picture books for

Equipment You May Lend or Donate to the Preschool Program

Sand toys, especially shovels
Dump truck or other road-building truck, cars, boats
Wagon
Large ball
Stick-type hobbyhorse

Tarpaulin or blanket for sitting on the ground
Smocks for painting
Cigar boxes
Worthwhile books for the children
We need plenty of all of the above items.

Outline of Daily Schedule

9:00	Free Play, includes: Housekeeping Sand-and-water play Easel painting Spontaneous music and nature activities Play on a variety of equipment
10:30	Juice time (after juice two-and-one-half and three-year-olds leave this group)
10:40	Quiet time with stories
11:00	Special activity such as a walk or special craft
11:30	Music
11:45	Parents pick up children. Note this is 15 minutes earlier than end of morning for older children, but necessary because the morning is very long for preschoolers.

their children. The sheet had four columns to be filled out: author, title of book, name of borrower, date of return. A note reminded borrowers that all books were to be returned on Friday. Information to be read daily by parent-assistants and teachers was also posted on the bulletin board—two sheets, each written in large print which could be seen at a glance, one a list of names of the children, the other a daily schedule of activities.

Three hooks along the edge of the bulletin board held items in daily use. On one hook were hung plain white three-by-five cards, each strung on red yarn so that it could be worn around the neck. There was a card for each child, bearing his name and age, to be worn by the children to help the adults identify the children personally as they worked with them. The cards served as a means of noting or recording absentees quickly at any convenient time during the morning. Another hook had hung on it a little booklet[1] in which an adult could find a list of suggestions about guiding the activities commonly used in a parent-cooperative nursery group. From the third hook hung a second set of cards bearing schedule information used by each adult working with the children.

The nursery teachers had worked out the general schedule for the nursery group in enough detail to make up sets of cards for themselves and the parents assisting them in working with the children's group. From the Master Schedule (Table 16-1) they copied off the separate schedules for each of the four adults. The schedule for each parent involved the super-

[1] Elizabeth Page and Betty Garlick, *Guides for Teaching in a Cooperative Nursery School* (East Lansing, Mich.: Michigan State College).

TABLE 16-1. Master Schedule for a Preschool Group

Time	Parent-Helper A	Betty	Ursula	Parent-Helper B*	Elaine
Before 9:00		Set up equipment for special free-play activity Welcome parent-helpers	Set up equipment for activities other than dirt-and-water play; special, and paint activity		
9:00	Set out easels, paints and paper Supervise painting	Welcome children Supervise free choice of activities	Welcome children Supervise free choice of play activities	Set up equipment for dirt-and-water play Supervise these activities	
10:20	Put away easels		Supervise hand-washing	Put away dirt-and-water play equipment	Take less-than-three year-olds for rest and quiet play
10:30		Serve juice		Help with hand-washing Help with juice	
10:40	Put away other equipment with Betty	Help with equipment or story as needed	Tell story Supervise quiet time	Assist with story and quiet time	
11:00	Help with special activity	Help with special activity, or, on alternate days, introduce it	Introduce special activity, or on alternate days, help with it	Help with special activity	
11:30	Assist with music	Take charge of music time	Put away equipment or help with music	Quietly put away equipment	
11:45	Help end the day	Say "goodbye" to children and parents	Say "goodbye" to children and parents	Help end the day	

* When Parent-Helper B is the mother of a less-than-three-year-old child, she helps Elaine with the young children, leaving the two teachers and Parent-Helper A to complete the morning session for the older children.

573

vision of an entire activity: putting out the necessary materials and equipment, helping to supervise the activity itself, and putting away the equipment after use.

With their advance preparations made, the teachers were eager to meet the children and parents. The knowledge that they were well prepared for the nursery group gave the teachers confidence and enabled them to give their attention to building the self-confidence of the children, and that of the parents in their parental role. As the teachers met each child they had in mind their major objectives for the week: to have each child begin to realize that a nursery group is fun, and that other mothers loved them. As the teachers met each parent they had in mind the goal of helping the parents to understand and appreciate the values of a preschool group. The teachers made sure that each parent had an opportunity to sign the schedule sheet for helping with the children, and had received a page of suggestions which might help him to be successful as an assistant to the teachers. The written suggestions follow.

Suggestions for Parents for Their Workday

The children come first: Help each child know that he has worth and dignity, that you trust him and have faith in him. Some of the ways you can do this are:
1. Let the children take initiative whenever possible.
2. Avoid interrupting a child's activity; encourage him to finish what he wants to do.
3. Listen carefully when a child has something to tell you. Get down to his level by squatting or sitting. Mirror or enlarge what he says, but do not evaluate it.
4. Be generous in giving deserved praise.
5. Laugh with the children, not at them.
6. Use positive suggestions. Avoid "don'ts."
7. Talk with other adults only when necessary.
8. Discuss the children with other adults only in conferences, never in front of the children.

During easel painting: Display an interest in the children's work, but do not ask what they have made. They may not know!
1. Have only one child at each side of an easel at one time.
2. Encourage each child to put on a smock as a proper costume for painting. Some children may not paint if they have to wear a smock, so do not force this.
3. Encourage the child to replace the brushes in the correct cans.
4. Tell the child, "We paint on the paper."
5. Write the child's name on a corner of the paper. Add any interesting comments and the date.
6. Hang paintings to dry with clothespins on a rope between posts.
7. Let children who wish to, take paintings to their cabins; others may be saved for end-of-camp display.

During sand-and-water play: Provide sand or dirt and a dishpan filled with water for many kinds of activity much enjoyed by small children.

1. Provide small cans, boats, trucks, and shovels.
2. Allow children to explore as they choose, but help them stay within a limited area.
3. Encourage children to keep their clothes dry. Help them change clothes in case they get wet.
4. Join in their digging or be their guest to "eat" the cake they make.
5. Teach children that they may not throw sand or dirt at other children. You may say, "Keep the sand low," or "Sand hurts eyes."

During story time:
1. Join the group of children and show interest in the story.
2. Let a child who is disturbing others sit in your lap. If this is not enough, take him to a quiet place where you may read or look at a book with him, or just give him your attention in conversation.

During music time:
1. Feel free to participate with the children in singing, finger plays, and other musical activities.
2. Help children enjoy responding to music by enjoying it yourself.
3. Let some children respond with their whole bodies with rolling, swimming, or hopping movements; other children prefer to watch until they are ready to participate. Those who participate actively at some times may prefer to watch at other times.
4. Give a child disturbing the group your special attention with another activity in a different location. (See item 2 under "During story time.")

About your own child: It is not always easy for him to share you when you are working in his group. He needs your particular understanding attention as he gradually learns independence of you.

The Saturday afternoon meeting and the before-school conversations with parents made the teachers aware of differences among the parents and gave the teachers opportunity to start helping parents with their problems. The teachers recognized as mature people the father and mother who brought their youngest child, their fourth girl, and asked that each of them have a morning with the nursery group. The teachers knew it would be a pleasure to help these parents to observe in more detail the behavior of children the age of their own child. The teachers recognized the need for an out-of-school conference with the mother who came by herself to say that her child was the problem of the cooperative nursery school he had been attending, and that she would welcome suggestions about how she could help him.

The teachers found it difficult to arrange an appointment with the mother of two little girls whom she described as "inseparable." The mother wanted her two-year-old as well as her three-year-old to be in the nursery group while she spent her morning at adult meetings. She revealed her awareness of the two-year-old child's need for individual attention by bringing a ten-year-old girl who, she said, would stay with the children as a baby-sitter. The teachers were able to schedule a parent conference with this mother only as a condition of the arrangements worked out with the mother by the camp director. The teachers also referred to the camp director other requests concerning admission of two-year-old children, knowing that the director would encourage parents of two-year-old children to organize their own group of mothers and children.

The teachers planned their afternoon schedules to include time for conferences with parents who wanted to talk about their preschool children. The teachers knew that parents who would not be ready for direct help would nonetheless profit from seeing how other parents, and especially the teachers, worked with the children. One mother, whose preschool child was the youngest of three children, seemed particularly intent on having her child stay clean; she was relatively insensitive to the child's social and emotional needs. The teachers planned to work with the mother in the nursery group situation, pointing out from time to time the children's responses to the environment and the values of the nursery group activities.

As the week progressed, the teachers were pleased with the ways in which parents showed their increasing awareness of the values of the nursery group. The teachers knew that the week was not long enough for getting feedback from every parent, nor for revealing the changes in attitudes which would continue to develop in parents through successive contacts with preschool groups. They took satisfaction in the increased tolerance of the parents who had said to their child, "Oh! You're all dirty!" but now asked, "Are you making a nice mudpie for me?"

In evaluating the nursery group they had provided, the teachers concluded that

The over-all impression is that the program proved successful. Most parents and children seemed satisfied. For some children and parents this was a first nursery school experience. This fact points to the vital importance for parents to have even a one-week parent-participation preschool program. The school affords many opportunities for helping parents understand what a good preschool program is, and for helping parents to be good teaching-parents.

The teachers also took pride in having introduced several families to preschool group experience. They reported the eager father who came to the group in the middle of the morning to ask his child, "Have you painted yet?" and the mother assistant who profited from seeing that her question—"Shall I make a painting for you?"—interfered with the children's learning. They also mentioned the father assistant who kept replacing the water in the children's large dishpan whenever he noticed that it became dirty. By the end of the morning, however, he had concluded that this was a futile activity. He had learned something about when to let children carry on an activity without adult interference.

OUTCOMES OF PARENT PARTICIPATION

It is generally agreed that parents who have participated in preschool groups as assistants to the teacher have profited from the experience: as a result of it, their attitudes, their skills in working with children, and their ideas about children, families, and preschool group experience changed.

A major objective of teachers working with them is to help mother-assistants understand, appreciate, and make use of the child's point of view. The abilities of parents to see the world as a child sees it vary, but a mother should steadily progress toward understanding what a child observes and how he reacts. The mother who has been a mother assistant should become more and more interested in children, and less and less self-conscious.

When it involves parent participation in the activities of a children's group, parent education is an active learning process. Such participation should bring about more changes in parental attitudes, skills, and concepts than do less active phases of parent education. Many teachers who work with mother assistants report evidence indicative that such changes do occur, over a period of time.

In one preschool group, two mothers expected their children to obey by responding at once to any command that the mother issued. After four months of taking turns as mother-assistants, each of the mothers became aware that the teacher did not expect such obedience of the children. When the mother asked the teacher to have their children obey her—for instance, by coming at once when refreshments were served—the teacher explained that the children were learning to move with the group in its activities, and that they were developing a self-discipline which made it no longer necessary for her to tell them what to do about having refreshments. As the mothers continued to act as mother assistants, their negative awareness of the difference between their expectations and those of the teacher gradually changed to questioning of their own behavior. They observed and began to understand that a child who is absorbed in what he is doing needs an opportunity to finish his project more than he needs to wash as soon as refreshments are served to the group.

Just how far a mother is able to move from an unrealistic expectation of obedience depends upon circumstances other than her experiences as a mother assistant. For instance, it may be that her feelings about herself are bolstered by puppetlike behavior from her child. Or it may be that feelings of rebellion against domination by her own parents reinforce her wish to have a child who relies on himself. At any rate, the fact that mother assistants move from unrealistic expectations of obedience from preschool children through negative and questioning phases of learning toward more realistic child-centered expectations indicates that even basic attitudes can be modified through experience in working with a group of children in a parent education laboratory situation.

Research is needed to test the hypotheses that can be made about the occurrence of changes in parents who serve as mother assistants. As a result of experience with children, can parents acquire the skill to give directions that are positive, not negative? To remain outwardly calm when a child appears apt to fall, or be hurt? To perceive accurately times when

Preschool makes it possible to observe what children do at different ages. (Courtesy of California State College at Long Beach and Mariam M. Cook, Long Beach, California.)

a child needs help and times when he is self-sufficient? To help a child solve the problem that he faces? The investigation of such questions awaits the attention of those who are interested in helping parents become more skillful and more assured in their parental role through participation in teaching a group of preschool children.

Appraisal of Progress in Parent Education

When parents study about preschool children and have experience with them, their attitudes concerning them change; they develop new skills in working with them, and they modify their ideas about the children and about their own relation to the preschool group. The more the parents participate in parent education, the greater the changes to be expected in their behavior. Parents who participate in a course on guiding children's growth while participating in a preschool group situation probably change their attitudes, skills, and concepts more than do parents attending only an occasional parent meeting.

Instructors who teach a course for parents and also supervise the parents in observing and participating in the preschool group can identify changes that occur in the parents. They are not surprised to have a mother remark

578

at the start of the school year, "I don't expect anyone to put up with my child crying," or to see a mother hurrying along a child who tries to stop and explore the world around him. But at the end of the school year they expect these same mothers to recognize their children as persons, too, and to explain the child's point of view to other adults by saying, for instance, "I'll get there in a few minutes. Tommy found a sow-bug." Furthermore, parent education instructors expect parents to develop pride in their parental responsibility and instead of saying, "Oh, I'm just a housewife," to explain proudly what she does in her role of mother.

It is easy to observe differences between parents who have just joined a parent education program and parents who have been participating in the program for some time. The new parents are concerned with keeping their child quiet, the experienced parents, with having him enjoy his environment. The new parents are quick to turn off the water; the experienced parents help their child extend his use of it. New parents may be astonished by the idea of seeking help for their children or for themselves from professional services in the medical or social fields; experienced parents view such services as important to use as needed.

It is also easy to observe ways in which parents gain skill in working with children. The mother who was only an onlooker at the start of the school year may be reading a story to a group of children or accompanying them on a nature walk by the end of the year. The mother who could only pour juice in the kitchen may have learned how to sit and talk comfortably with the children while they drink their juice. Or the mother who tried to help the children by performing the activity for them may have learned to watch and to give help only when it is needed or requested.

As the parents continue their study, their strains and tensions as parents should lessen. Their adherence to rigid schedules for their children is gradually replaced by relaxed confidence in their ability to meet the children's real needs. The parents who bring up problems about "Am I doing it right?" or about having their children "do the right thing," should have fewer problems. Conflicts between parents and children should also decrease.

When certain parent education programs were studied, it was found[2] that the parents in the second year of the program had wider interests than those in the first year, and that the parents in their third year of study had the widest interests of all—in children, in problems of the family, and in the societal impact of families.

A study was made in Santa Monica of parents' attitudes toward help given by parent education classes. A majority of parents responded affirmatively to a questionnaire asking if the classes had enabled them

● To understand themselves and the reasons for their behavior in dealing with their children.

[2] Reported by a parent education teacher participating in the study.

- To understand better their children's patterns of behavior, growth, and development.
- To develop within the home a greater degree of harmony and cooperation among all members.
- To have more of a feeling of confidence in dealing with their children.
- To achieve improved relations between themselves and their children.[3]

One of the most important changes that can occur in parents who participate in a parent-education program is that they develop the ability to observe child behavior objectively. The parents who develop this skill have an important tool which should enable them to continue to develop in their role as parents. The ability to discuss objectively what children do and say is another important skill which parents should acquire early.

Especially for less advantaged parents who have had limited opportunity to be graduated from school programs, it is satisfying to receive a diploma at the completion of a parent education program. They have concrete evidence of their accomplishment and are encouraged in enrolling for additional parent education programs. Having a visible symbol of their status as a parent who studies to improve his parental skill also encourages them to recruit additional parents for the program. The cost of providing certificates of completion of the program is small in relation to the resulting improvement in public relations for the program.

Today the appraisal of programs of parent education has only begun to receive attention. As the programs expand, it is to be expected that their objectives will be clarified and that the programs themselves will be evaluated to determine the progress already made and possible directions for further development.

Situations for Discussion

A preschool teacher is apt to find herself in situations similar to the four described here. As you think of what to do in each situation, consider whether each course of action suggested is desirable, or not. Use points brought out in the chapter as well as ideas from your own experience to justify your views. Suggest alternative courses of action to supplement those given.

SITUATION 1 You have responsibility for the parent education program in connection with the Community Nursery School. You should

- Work with a committee of parents and teachers.
- Use a parent questionnaire to decide whether to have panel discussions, films, or a speaker.
- Plan to have four evening meetings for fathers as well as mothers.
- Arrange for parents to observe the preschool group in session.
- Develop a handbook for parents.

[3] Charles E. Johnson, "A Survey of the Public Schools' Parent Education Program in Santa Monica, California." Master's thesis, University of California at Los Angeles, 1948.

SITUATION 2   At the children's center you are chairman of the committee on evaluation of pupil progress. When your committee discusses whether or not to report pupil progress to parents, you should point out that parents need to learn

- Ways of working with teachers for the good of their children.
- How to interpret anecdotal records.
- Skills in observing child behavior.
- How to record their observations of their child.
- How to talk objectively about children.

SITUATION 3   You are the instructor for an adult education course in which parents bring their three-year-old children and observe them at play in a group situation. You should use the time

- For parent discussion.
- For mothers to be with their own child.
- As a laboratory in which mothers help you guide the children.
- For free choice of play activities for the children.
- As a demonstration of how an adult guides different group activities of children.

SITUATION 4   As a teacher-director of a children's center in a less advantaged community, you request paper for use with parents and plan on sending each of them

- A questionnaire about topics they want to discuss at meetings.
- Menus for each week for the children in the preschool groups.
- Invitations to each meeting of parents.
- A list of community places worth a family visit.
- A letter about adult education courses offered.

Current Professional Books

AUERBACH, ALINE B., and Child Study Association of America. *Parents Learn Through Discussion: Principles and Practices of Parent Group Education.* New York: John Wiley & Sons, Inc., 1968. [Through their discussion group, parents can learn, each at his own pace, how to be more effective parents.]

ARNSTEIN, HELENE S. *What to Tell Your Child.* New York: The Child Study Association of America, 1960. [Suggests what to say to a child about birth, divorce, illness, and other unusual family events.]

ATKINS, EDITH LESSER. *Aggressiveness in Children.* New York: The Child Study Association of America, 1950. [An example of excellent material for parents available in inexpensive pamphlets.]

AUERBACH, ALINE "Group Education for Child Rearing," *Helping the Family in Urban Society.* New York: Columbia University Press, 1963, pp. 98–108. [Parent education helps the urban family.]

BABITZ, MILTON. *Parent Education—Curriculum, Methods and Materials.* Bulletin, California State Department of Education, Vol. XXX, No. 2 (May, 1961), pp. 4–39. [Practical suggestions about parent education programs.]

582 PARTICIPATION IN THE PRESCHOOL GROUP

BETTELHEIM, BRUNO. *Dialogues with Mothers*. New York: The Macmillan Company, 1962. [Direct discussions about topics of concern to parents.]

BEYER, EVELYN. *Sharing—A New Level in Teacher-Parent Relationship*. Washington, D.C.: National Association for Education of Young Children, 1968. [Other NAEYC pamphlets are also useful in parent education.]

BRECKENRIDGE, MARIAN E., and MARGARET N. MURPHY. *Growth and Development of the Young Child*, 7th ed. Philadelphia: W. B. Saunders Company, 1963. [Development of the child through age five with emphasis on physical development, psychological development and family relationships.]

BURNETT, DOROTHY KIRK. *Your Preschool Child*. New York: Holt, Rinehart & Winston, Inc., 1961. [Out of experience with her own two children, a creative mother makes suggestions for parents of children from ages two to seven.]

Children's Bureau. *Your Child from 1 to 6*. Washington, D.C.: U.S. Government Printing Office, 1962. [One of a list of inexpensive government publications in English and in Spanish to help parents and others concerned with preschool children.]

CHRISTIANSON, HELEN M., MARY M. ROGERS, and BLANCHE A. LUDLUM. *The Nursery School: Adventure in Living and Learning*. Boston: Houghton Mifflin Company, 1961. [Chapter 4 is especially pertinent to the education of parents.]

GINOTT, HAIM G. *Between Parent and Child, New Solutions to Old Problems*. New York: The Macmillan Company, 1965. [Improvement of parent and child relationships.]

HEFFERNAN, HELEN, and VIVIAN EDMISTON TODD. *Elementary Teacher's Guide to Working with Parents*. West Nyack, N.Y.: Parker Publishing Co., Inc., 1969. [Suggestions for working with parents of various styles of life.]

HELFER, RAY, M.D., and HENRY C. KEMPE, M.D. *The Battered Child*. Chicago: University of Chicago Press, 1968. [Each year tens of thousands of children are severly battered or killed.]

HYMES, JAMES L., JR. *Three to Six: Your Child Starts to School*. New York: Public Affairs Committee, Inc., 1963. [Besides Public Affairs Pamphlet No. 163 are such other pamphlets as No. 141 entitled "Enjoy Your Child—Ages 1, 2, and 3."]

ISAACS, SUSAN. *Intellectual Growth in Your Children*. New York: Schocken Books, Inc., 1966. [A readable book to help parents understand intellectual development in children.]

KIRK, SAMUEL A., and others. *You and Your Retarded Child: A Manual for Parents of Retarded Children*. Palo Alto, Calif.: Pacific Books, 1967. [Books about how to work with exceptional children are interesting to parents of children in the same mental age range.]

LIFTON, WALTER M. *Working with Groups: Group Process and Individual Growth*. New York: John Wiley and Sons, Inc., 1966. [Such books about group dynamics emphasize that groups can free their members as individuals and help them deal with social pressures.]

MARTIN, E. A. *Nutrition in Action*. 2nd ed. New York: Holt, Rinehart and Winston, Inc., 1965. [A basic textbook dealing with nutrition and child health.]

MOK, PAUL P. *Pushbutton Parents and the Schools*. New York: Dell Publishing Co., Inc., 1964. [This paperback deals with learning begins at home, parent-child communication, learning to look at things and people, home and school rapport.]

National School Public Relations Association, and others. *The First Big Step.* Washington, D.C.: National School Public Relations Association, 1966. [Department of Classroom Teachers, National Education Association, and National Congress of Parents and Teachers cooperated in preparing a handbook for parents whose child will soon enter school.]

Project Head Start—Parents Are Needed. Washington, D.C.: U.S. Government Printing Office, 1967. [Suggestions about parent involvement in a child-development center.]

Project Head Start—Points for Parents. Washington, D.C.: U.S. Government Printing Office, 1967. [Fifty suggestions about how parents can participate, and a list of films for parent education programs.]

WILLS, CLARICE, and LUCILE LINDBERG. *Kindergarten for Today's Children.* Chicago: Follett Publishing Company, 1966. [Chapters 25 and 26 offer many practical suggestions for effective work with parents of the kindergarten-age child that are applicable to younger children as well.]

WOLF, ANNA W. M. "Parent Education: Reminiscence and Comment," *Modern Perspectives in Child Development.* New York: International Universities Press, 1963, pp. 612–626.

Sources of Materials Useful in Preschool and Parent Education

American Public Health Association, Inc., New York 10019.

Association for Childhood Education International, Washington, D.C. 20016. ["Bits and Pieces," "Housing for Early Childhood Education," and other booklets; *Childhood Education,* published eight times a year.]

Bank Street College of Education, New York 10014.

Child Study Association of America, New York 10028. [In 1966, published "Recommended Reading about Children and Family Life," an annotated bibliography, for instance.]

Child Welfare League of America, Inc., New York 10010. [*Child Welfare,* a monthly publication.]

Children's Bureau, Washington, D.C. 20402. [*Children* is published six times a year.]

Early Childhood Education Council of New York, Flushing, N.Y. 11355. [College and university departments of child development, family relationships, education, home economics, and psychology.]

ERIC Clearinghouse on Early Childhood Education, Urbana, Illinois 61801. [Bibliographies on topics such as the culturally disadvantaged, language development.]

Family Service Association of America, New York 10010.

Life insurance companies.

Local nursery school associations.

Medical groups.

Merrill Palmer Institute, Detroit, Mich. 48202.

National Association for the Education of Young Children, Washington, D.C. 20009. [Books, pamphlets, and a periodical entitled *Young Children*.]

National Association for Retarded Children, Inc., New York 10016.

National Committee for Day Care of Children, Inc., New York 10010.

National Congress of Parents and Teachers, Chicago 60611.

National Council of Churches of Christ in the U.S.A., New York 10027.

National Council on Family Relations. [*Journal of Marriage and the Family*, a quarterly.]

National Education Association, Washington, D.C. 20036. [Pamphlets such as "What Research Says to the Teacher-Nursery School and Kindergarten," and *Today's Education* published nine times a year.]

National Kindergarten Association, New York 10018.

National Safety Council, Chicago 60611.

National Society for Mental Health, New York 10019.

Office of Economic Opportunity, Washington, D.C. [Project Head Start booklets about such topics as "Food Buying Guide and Recipes," "Project Head Start, Daily Program III," "Project Head Start, Points for Parents."]

Parent Cooperative Preschools International. Montreal, Canada. [*Offspring* is published twice a year.]

Play School Association, Inc., New York 10019.

Public Affairs Committee, New York 10017. [Publishes Public Affairs Pamphlets, including one entitled "How to Choose a Nursery School."]

Parents' Magazine, New York 10017. [Publishes *Parents' Magazine* and has a Group Service Bureau to help parent groups use articles published in monthly issues of the magazine.]

Science Research Associates, Inc., Chicago 60611. [Publishes the Better Living Booklets, a series of booklets for parent education; and materials for teacher use.]

State Departments of Education (of any state). [For instance, Bulletin No. 2, 30 (1961), State Departments of Education, is entitled "Handbook on Parent Education."]

Today's Child News Magazine. New York 10001. [A monthly news publication for parents.]

U.S. Department of Labor. Washington, D.C. [Children's Bureau publication #461—1968 is entitled "Child Care Arrangements of Working Mothers in the United States," for instance.]

U.S. Department of Health, Education, and Welfare. Washington D.C. [U.S. Office of Education publication, OE-87021, is entitled "Child Care and Guidance—A Suggested Post High School curriculum," for instance.]

Films for Parents

Answering the Child's Why. Wilmette, Ill.: Encyclopedia Britannica Films, Inc., 1951, thirteen minutes, sound, black and white. [Child behavior is affected by parental attitudes.]

Becky. Falls Church, Va. 22041: Stuart Finly, 1967, fifteen minutes, sound, color. [Slow-learning five-and-one-half-year-old Becky needs extra care and attention.]

Child Care and Development. New York 10036: McGraw-Hill Textfilms, 1950; sixteen minutes, sound, black and white. [Good parent and child attitudes help to establish good habits of eating, sleeping, and bathing.]

Children Growing Up with Other People. New York 10001: Contemporary Films, 1948; thirty minutes, sound, black and white. [During the first four years of life, narcissistic attitudes become increasingly social.]

Children in the Hospital. Chicago: International Film Bureau, Inc., 1961; forty-four minutes, sound, black and white. [The feelings as well as the pains of a child should be dealt with.]

Children Learning by Experience. New York: 10001: Contemporary Films, 1948; forty minutes, sound, black and white. [Through planning and imagination, children learn work and play activities which differ from age level to age level.]

Children of Change. Chicago: International Film Bureau Inc., 1960; thirty-one minutes, sound, black and white. [Sponsored by the U.S. Department of Health, Education, and Welfare and the Pennsylvania State Department of Public Welfare, this film shows the value of a day-care center with qualified teachers and a social worker for mothers who work.]

Children's Emotions. New York: McGraw-Hill Book Company, Inc., 1950; twenty-two minutes, sound, black and white. [Parents can recognize such emotions as fear, jealousy, and joy and can further happiness in their children.]

Children's Play. New York: McGraw-Hill Book Company, Inc., 1956; twenty-seven minutes, sound, black and white. [Parents help children have healthy play at different age levels.]

A Child Went Forth. San Francisco: Grandon-Western Cinema Guild, 1942; twenty minutes, sound, black and white. [At a summer camp, children from two to seven years of age explore a new environment, work out new social relationships, and work on new problems.]

Family Circus. Chicago: International Film Bureau, 1956; ten minutes, sound, color.[Sibling rivalry occurs when a parent favors one child over another.]

Fears of Children. Chicago: International Film Bureau, 1951; thirty minutes, sound, black and white. [Either overprotection or overexpectation can add to a child's fears.]

Feeling of Rejection. New York: McGraw-Hill Textfilms, 1947; twenty minutes, sound, black and white. [Shows early childhood overprotection and subsequent immaturity of a twenty-three-year-old young woman.]

Food as Children See It. Minneapolis: General Mills Film Library, 1952; eighteen minutes, color. [Feeding problems often disappear when the child's point of view is considered.]

Frustrating Fours and Fascinating Fives. New York: McGraw-Hill Book Company, Inc., 1952, twenty-two minutes, sound, black and white. [Shows typical behavior of the four-year-old child and of the five-year-old child.]

He Acts His Age. New York: McGraw-Hill Book Company, Inc., 1951, fifteen minutes, sound, black and white or color. [At a picnic children from ages one to fifteen reveal behavior typical of their ages.]

Helping the Child to Accept the Do's. Wilmette, Ill.: Encyclopedia Britannica Films, Inc., 1948; eleven minutes, sound, black and white. [This and a companion film, *Helping the Child Accept the Don'ts,* show ways of helping a child in his relationships with other people.]

Helping Your Child Feel Emotionally Secure. New York: Seminar Films, 1953, thirty minutes, sound, color. [In fifteen incidents, parents demonstrate desirable and undesirable ways of working with children.]

He Who Dares to Teach. Los Angeles 29, Calif.: Moulin & Associates, 1955, eighteen minutes, sound, color. [Shows the nursery school and its once-a-week evening class in parent education in a California community.]

Johnny's New World. New York: National Society for Prevention of Blindness, 1954, sixteen and one half minutes, sound, color. [Nature, symptoms, and treatment of strabismus which causes vision loss in thousands of children.]

Journey in Health. Chicago: Smart Family Foundation; 1960, twenty-two minutes, sound, color or black and white. [The well-being of a child should be maintained under the supervision of a family doctor.]

Palmour Street. New York: Modern Talking Pictures Service, Inc., 1951; twenty-seven minutes, sound, black and white. [Parents influence life patterns of confidence and trust.]

Planning Creative Play Equipment for Young Children. Berkeley, Calif.: University of California, Extension Media Center, 1960; sixteen minutes, sound, color. [Parents pool their resources and talents to have play materials for preschool children.]

Preface to a Life. New York: United World Films, Inc., 1950; twenty-nine minutes, sound, black and white. [The views and values of parents influence the behavior of their children.]

Right from the Start. New York 10016: Public Affairs Committee, 1964; 16 mm., twenty-two and one half minutes, sound, color. [Territorial Directors of Public Health Education developed this film to show the importance of a child having a good start in life.]

Roots of Happiness. Chicago: International Film Bureau, 1953; twenty-five minutes, sound, black and white. [Feelings of parents affect the emotional life of their children, as shown by homelife of a Puerto Rican family.]

The School that Learned to Eat. Minneapolis: General Mills Film Library, 1948; twenty-two minutes, sound, color. [In a small Georgia grade school, children and teachers work for higher health standards in their community.]

Shyness. New York: McGraw-Hill Book Company, Inc., 1953; twenty-three minutes, sound, black and white. [Three shy children respond to three different methods of working with them.]

Sibling Rivalries and Parents. New York 10001: McGraw-Hill Textfilms, 1956; eleven minutes, sound, black and white. [Shows conflict situations in a family of five children, and how to work off hostility and develop mutual respect.]

Starting Nursery School: Patterns of Beginning. New York: University Film Library, 1959; twenty-three minutes, sound, black and white. [In the Vassar Nursery School, the plan for starting nursery school reduces the stress and anxiety associated with a child leaving home and mother for the school.]

Study of Twins, Part IV. State College, Pa.: Psychological Cinema Register, Pennsylvania State College, 1950; nineteen minutes, silent, black and white. [Shows development in coordination, cooperation, and self-sufficiency at ages three, four, and five.]

The Terrible Two's and the Trusting Three's. New York: McGraw-Hill Book Company, Inc., 1950; twenty-two minutes, sound, color. [Shows typical behavior of the two-year-old child and of the three-year-old child.]

A Two-Year-Old Goes to the Hospital. New York: New York University Film

Library, 1953; fifty minutes, sound, color. [At two years and five months, an eight-day separation from his family for hospitalization affected a child's individual play and his interaction with hospital personnel and with family visitors.]

Understanding the Child. Bloomington, Ind.: NET Film Service, Audio-Visual Center, Indiana University, 1955; thirty minutes, sound, black and white. [A series of seven films dealing with intellectual, social, physical, and emotional development.]

The Volunteer. Nashville, Tenn.: Methodist Publishing House, 1958; fourteen minutes, sound, black and white. [Because she feels neglected, a retired school teacher does not make her much needed talents available to the nursery school.]

When Should Grownups Help? New York: New York University Film Library, 1951; thirteen minutes, sound, black and white. [At nursery school, grownups often let children solve their problems for themselves.]

When Should Grownups Stop Fights? New York: New York University Film Library, 1951; fifteen minutes, sound, black and white. [Shows decisions made in four problem situations arising in a nursery school.]

Who Cares about Jamie? Chicago: Smart Family Foundation, 1963. [A family recognizes emotional problems their son encounters and helps to promote his good mental health.]

Your Children's Play. New York: McGraw-Hill Book Company, Inc., 1952; twenty-one minutes, sound, black and white. [Adults can either help or hinder children in learning through play.]

CHAPTER **17**

The Preschool Group as a
School Laboratory

Sooner or later, everyone must establish a relationship with children of preschool age. The pupil in the upper grades of elementary school learns either to ignore the younger children in his neighborhood or to play with them and help them with their problems. In junior high school, students may either reject the role of babysitter, or explore it. They may either overlook or take advantage of opportunities to gain greater understanding of preschool children. Usually in senior high school, and no later than junior college, students should have sufficient knowledge of and experience with preschool children to make realistic decisions about marrying and about having one, two, or more children. Study units about preschool children and laboratory situations for working with them must be provided for prospective parents.

The preschool group laboratory situation can be useful not only to prospective and actual parents but also to prospective and actual workers with preschool children, especially their teachers, pediatricians and other specialists. Colleges and universities must provide laboratory courses for students who choose vocations involving work with children.

A children's center, a private nursery school or kindergarten, or a parent-cooperative preschool group can be used as a laboratory until a specially planned laboratory center can be developed. Administrative sympathy and understanding for the laboratory project are essential factors in making it a successful experience for students, parents, and children.

Values of the Preschool Group as a Laboratory

The preschool group is valuable as a laboratory situation for students in the fifth and sixth grades of elementary school, in junior high school, in senior high school, in junior college, in senior college, and in university graduate schools. As yet, the attitudes, skills, and concepts especially desirable for each of these grade levels have not been clearly defined. Different teachers emphasize different objectives and teach in terms of the unique characteristics of their classes. This adaptation to individual differences is highly desirable. At the same time it can be expected that the variety of experiences to be derived from the preschool laboratory should presently give rise to some definition of the kinds of participation especially appropriate for students at a particular grade level. It is already possible to point out in general terms the values of preschool laboratory experience for student groups.

As soon as students have sufficient writing skill, they should be encouraged to record their observations of preschool children and to use these records as a basis for discussing the behavior of children in relation to that of their teacher and to objects in their environment. The ability to observe accurately and to record objectively what children say and do is essential to understanding the child's point of view, and is an important objective for students at every grade level. A person who really appreciates the point of view of a child can become a good parent, a good teacher, or a good consultant about children.

Values for Pupils in Fifth or Sixth Grade

By the time they have reached the upper elementary grades, children need to have learned that younger children are important individuals, too, and should have developed effective social techniques which allow them to feel comfortable with preschool children. One or two study units about preschool children, together with opportunities to be with such children, will help elementary-school students to come to appreciate younger children more fully. Experience in a laboratory situation is especially important for those students who do not have younger brothers and sisters at home. They need to interact with preschool children at least until they reach the point at which they are not uncomfortable about being with them.

One upper-grade group of students had an opportunity to assess and to improve their thinking about younger children by using their responses to an evaluation device as a basis for class discussion.

Manners with Young Children

Directions:
   1. Put a checkmark ($\sqrt{}$) in front of each statement about what is desirable to do.

Helping preschool children helps a fifth-grade pupil gain self-confidence.
(Courtesy of Ontario-Montclair School District, Ontario, California.)

2. Put an X in front of each statement about what is rude to do.
3. Write in other statements about what is desirable to do.
4. With your classmates discuss the choices that you make. Point out
   a. how Marian felt.
   b. how the other persons felt.

Situation: Twelve-year-old Marian is on a trip with her older sister. They are visiting their aunt and her two children: eight-year-old Don and five-year-old Susan. Various incidents come up in which Marian must decide what to do.

Incident 1. Marian saves her apple from lunch to eat later. In the middle of the afternoon she remembers it and gets it out. Susan who had her apple at lunchtime, says, "Please give me some." Marian says,

_____ It's mine and I'm going to eat it.
_____ You should have saved yours, too.
_____ I'll share it with you.
_____ Ask your mother for one.

_____ . . . .

Incident 2. Marian and her sister decide to play cards. Don and Susan want to play, too. Marian says,

_____ You don't know how to play our game.
_____ Go away. Don't bother us.
_____ What game do you want to play?
_____ Here's a deck of cards for you to play with.

_____ . . . .

Incident 3. On a ride in the nine-passenger stationwagon, Marian wants to reserve the seat next to hers so that she and her sister may sit next to each other. Marian chooses to sit in the middle seat and puts her jacket on the jump seat, which is next to hers.

    Don, intent on getting into the seat at the back of the wagon, climbs over the jump seat and steps on the corner of Marian's jacket. Marian says,

_____ Don't step on my jacket!
_____ Can't you look where you're going! You've ruined my jacket!
_____ Wait! Let me fold back the seat for you.
_____ Why don't you sit in the front seat with your mother?

_____ . . . .

Incident 4. During the ride, Susan needs to go to the bathroom. Marian's aunt drives into a service station to get gas and make the restrooms available. Marian, who does not need to go to the restroom, says,

_____ [*To her aunt*] Do you want me to take Susan to the restroom?
_____ [*To her aunt*] You don't expect me to take Susan, do you?
_____ [*To her aunt*] I'll take care of Susan while you take care of the car.
_____ [*To Susan*]   Susan, your restroom is the second one.

_____ . . . .

Incident 5. Towards the end of the ride, everyone is tired. Marian puts her head in her sister's lap and settles down for a nap. Five-year-old Susan, sitting next to Marian, leans over against her to make a comfortable place for herself. Marian says,

_____ Don't lean against me.
_____ Leave me alone. I want to sleep.
_____ Let me help you stretch out on the back seat.
_____ Lean against the door if you are sleepy.

_____ . . . .

Incident 6. One afternoon Marian's aunt gives Don, Susan, and Marian each a dime to get an ice cream cone at the corner drugstore. At the drugstore, Marian remembers how much she enjoys a banana split, and decides to have one. She uses money she has earned for babysitting to pay for it.

When Marian is served her banana split, Susan immediately wants one, too. Marian tells her,

_____ You eat your cone, and I'll eat my banana split.
_____ This is mine. I paid for it with money I earned.
_____ I'll let you have some of mine.
_____ We'll get you one next time.

_____ . . . .

After the students had reacted to the evaluation instrument, their teacher helped them discuss their responses. She wanted them to be able to identify different courses of action, as follows:

1. A statement or question which calls attention to the problem. This kind of statement accentuates the problem, and does nothing to aid its solution. Whether the statement is rude or not usually depends on the tone of voice used.
2. A statement or question which is rude in its implications. This may reject the other person, call him names, or be personally negative toward him.
3. A suggestion which is helpful. This may be only enlightened self-interest, but it is constructive.
4. A suggestion which may sound helpful but really is not because it involves a lack of realism about sources of frustration for the other person. These statements include overly long postponement of satisfaction, not as much help as the other person needs, or a hazardous solution (e.g., leaning against a car door).

VALUES FOR JUNIOR HIGH SCHOOL STUDENTS

For junior high school students, experience with a preschool group can aid in understanding human relations in general, particularly those which exist between themselves and other members of their families. The students can clarify their own feelings about themselves, and arrive at a more complete understanding of the family relationship. For them, experience with a preschool group can serve as an introduction to adult responsibilities.

At each succeeding age level, students should gain a deeper understanding of themselves, at the same time that they learn the skills and techniques of working with preschool children and gain an understanding of human relationships. Junior high school students, who are maturing physiologically, often gain a new perspective on their own development when they hear preschool teachers answering the questions of preschool children about growing up, getting married, and having babies. The student notices the direct, casual answer and is encouraged to think directly about his own problems of maturation, rather than to be overly concerned about them or to avoid considering them.

The junior high school student often has a high interest in babysitting as a way of earning money by doing real work in the community. Observing and participating in the preschool group, he can learn how to meet the needs of the preschool child and how to get along with the child's parents and teachers. Thus the student can lay a basis for success as a babysitter and become increasingly eager for further relationships with young children and with the adults who work with them. Through these experiences outside his own home, the student can gain the skills, attitudes, and understandings that will help to make him more successful as a member of his own family. By learning to understand relationships between

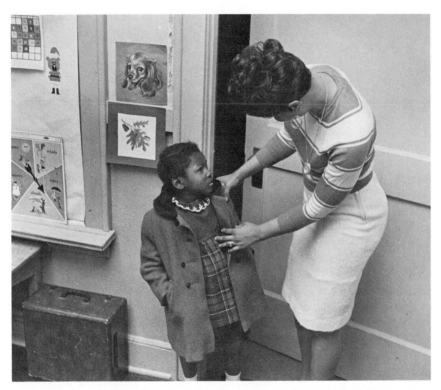

An aide helps a child who arrives with a problem. (Courtesy of Chattanooga Public Schools, Chattanooga, Tennessee. Photograph by T. Fred Miller.)

parents and preschool children, he should come to a greater understanding of parent-child relationships in general and those in his own life in particular.

VALUES FOR SENIOR HIGH SCHOOL STUDENTS

Experience with a preschool group may be of even more worth to the senior high school student, who usually has a great awareness of himself in relation to other people. He faces several of the most important developmental problems of his whole life: How shall I find a mate? How shall I earn a living? How shall I establish myself in the adult community?

Participation in preschool groups can help him to understand how to work out solutions to these problems. For instance, as he observes preschool children solving the developmental problems of their age levels, he can become aware of problem solving as a technique. He can see that the children work directly at their problems, whether these concern communication with others or the mastery of some physical skill, such as hopping on one foot. He can see how children react to frustration, how others help them to overcome their hurdles, and how the children develop in the process. While he is thinking about the children, the student is also thinking about himself: How do I meet frustration? What kind of help do I need? How do I get help? As he observes the relationships of child to child and child to adult in the preschool group, he also thinks about his relationships to others: How do I get along with others in my age group? How do I get along with the adults in my family? What makes for good relationships? What makes for a happy home life? The sensitivity of the senior high school student should make his experience in a preschool group a rich source of help as he moves toward solving his own developmental problems.

The senior high school student is often very close to becoming a parent himself. Preschool group experience can help him to develop the attitudes, skills, and understandings which will be helpful in his experience as a parent. He can get practice in handling children consistently, in trying to help them solve their problems successfully, and in seeing the world from their point of view. He can learn how to guide them through love and understanding rather than by force and frustration. The senior high school student will find his participation in a preschool group a valuable experience that serves to prepare him for marriage and parenthood.

By the time a student is in senior high school, he is skilled enough in writing to begin to develop skill in recording observations of what a preschool child says and does. The ability to observe and think in terms of other people is one of the major tools of the adult world and is a key to understanding in the behavioral sciences. The development of this skill in high school students is important to them as future citizens and parents.

VALUES FOR JUNIOR COLLEGE STUDENTS

Junior college students also benefit from observing and participating in a preschool group. If they are not already parents, they probably realize that they will soon assume the task of creating homes and families of their own. In the nursery school and kindergarten, they can find the key concepts and simple techniques they will need to learn in order to function with love, democracy, and realism. They, too, can use the preschool group experience to clarify their thinking about themselves and about family relationships, and as an introduction to the responsibilities of adulthood.

The students, as well as their teachers, can evaluate the progress they are making in working with children if they keep diary records, such as

Responsibilities Taken in a Preschool Group

Name _____ Date: From _____ to _____

Type of Activity	WHAT I DID			HOW I FELT	
	Helped with the activity	*Responsible for the activity*	*Description*	*Felt comfortable*	*Need more experience*
Supervising a small-group activity, when children choose activities	10/1 10/3	10/8	Easels Finger paint		
Serving refreshments					
Supervising rest time					
Supervising an educational activity (e.g., crafts, music, science, dramatic play)					
Arranging and conducting a study trip					

that on the form entitled "Responsibilities Taken in a Preschool Group" (see this page). They can see their growth toward teaching their own or other children.

TOWARD A GENERAL EDUCATION

When a preschool group is an integral part of a college, it can enrich the education of the students, especially their study of child development and psychology, education, health and physical education, home economics, philosophy, and behavioral sciences generally. By observing the preschool group activities and participating in them, students can gain insight into the concepts emphasized by their instructors—such concepts, for instance, as the following:

Child development and psychology

1. Within a group, individuals differ markedly with respect to any particular characteristic (e.g., body build, skin tone, speed of reaction, emotional response).
2. Each person is unique in the rate and pattern of his development, and in his level of maturation and readiness for learning (e.g., readiness for learning to read or to toilet himself).

A student enjoys participating in a preschool group activity. (Courtesy of The Merrill-Palmer Institute and Donna J. Harris, Detroit, Michigan.)

3. A person gains maturity through solving the problems related to his development.
4. Each person needs to have a rhythm of rest and activity, with routine in his living, and freedom of choice in his activities.

Education
1. Programs for children are planned in terms of the needs of society and the needs and abilities observed in children.
2. Desirable teaching techniques are those that promote expected changes in behavior, and self-confidence.

3. Pleasure reinforces what is learned; displeasure may interfere with learning.
4. Unsolved personal problems may interfere with learning. A child who is emotionally disturbed must find a physical outlet for his emotion before he can continue to learn.

Health and Physical Education
1. Each person must learn how to keep himself safe and well.
2. Each person learns how to move his body through space in everyday activities and in games and sports.
3. Skill develops through interest in an activity, understanding of and experience in it, and the building of endurance in performing it.
4. Arm control develops before leg control does.
5. A greater proportion of positive rather than negative comments fosters mental health. Cooperation furthers accomplishment.

Home Economics
1. Family planning should help each member of the family to develop.
2. For women, the roles of wife and mother are highly important.
3. In the management of family and preschool groups, economic as well as educational and social factors must be considered.
4. Provisions for children grow out of family needs in the community, and the sense of responsibility felt by the community.

Philosophy
1. Self-consideration is a basic concept on which to build a code of ethics. Helping others is a way of helping oneself.
2. The good man is the fundamental element of the good society.
3. Every person should consider his relationship to the universe.

Behavioral Sciences
1. The preschool group attempts to meet family needs and to preserve the family.
2. Family participation in preschool groups is related to its style of life.
3. Child behavior is typical of personal behavior in human relationships.
4. The child in a preschool group is introduced to many facets of his culture, including:

Property rights	The succession of holidays and special events
Democracy	Artifacts of the society
Cooperation	Toileting and other customs

The preschool group laboratory situation is especially valuable to the college student because it is a laboratory in human relationships, and the college student needs to develop skill in the objective observation of what people do and say, and in the exploration of various hypotheses proposed as possible interpretations of the behavior observed. He needs to perfect a skill which will be especially useful to him as he goes out from college

Observation: Watches activity. Remark: Preparing to do it too. (Courtesy of Montgomery County Head Start Program, Maryland.)

into new situations of work and recreation: the ability to observe and interpret behavior accurately.

By using and making observational records, the student can learn what constitutes a clear and useful record. Through experience, he can see the necessity for keeping separate records of what he observes and what he thinks about the observations. He will also come to appreciate the usefulness of observational records by participating in professional conferences of teachers and parents who try to enlarge their understanding of the individuals and groups of preschool children with whom they work. Through using simple case records, he will come to see the value of such records and the value of adding his own observations to them.

Observation records are useful to college students in helping them to understand the important concept of individual differences. For instance, when students observe the reactions of a group of preschool children to a new climbing apparatus, they can see the variety of individual responses to a simple situation. The observation records show how each child reacted differently to what seemed to be one and the same situation.

In advanced courses, college students can utilize the preschool group situations by conducting research projects on the development and guidance of children individually and in groups. The opportunity to observe and to participate in the activities of the children can usually be supplemented by opportunities to work with parents individually and in groups. The preschool laboratory can lead to research projects in adult education, in pediatrics, in home economics, in education, or in behavioral science, according to the interests of the students and the ingenuity of the professors who advise them.

TOWARD PROFESSIONAL PREPARATION

Senior college students can use the preschool group experience as an introduction to the vocation of their choice, especially teaching, nursing, pediatrics, the ministry, social work, and other fields which deal with preschool children and their families. As an observer in a preschool group, the college student can learn what is important to observe in children, and how to record and to interpret his observations. As a participant in the

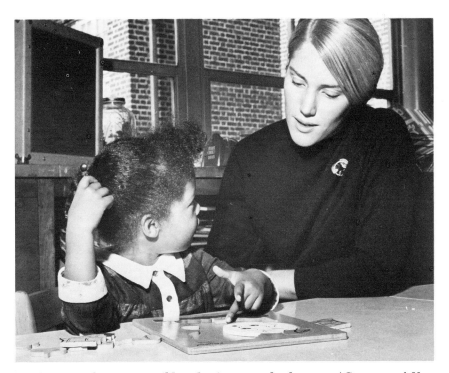

Students can have responsible roles in a preschool group. (Courtesy of New Jersey Department of Education Demonstration Class for Four-year-olds, Trenton, N.J.)

teaching of the preschool group, he can learn how to guide children, how to plan suitable activities for them, and how to provide nursery school and kindergarten opportunities for them. If he chooses a vocation that involves preschool children, he can go on to more specialized work with them. He can study in detail the behavior to be expected at each successive age level, the reactions of children to various educational techniques and materials, and the methods of planning and directing preschool group activities on a continuing basis. And he can also study how to work with the parents of preschool children—both as individuals and as members of parent study groups. The advanced college student can prepare himself for participation in a preschool group as a teacher, a program director, or an advisor to those participating in it.

As students prepare for vocations involving work with preschool children, their attitudes, skills, and concepts are modified by their experiences with children and their study about them. They are especially eager to acquire the skills they will need in their future professions. They can evaluate their progress by using a checklist such as the one shown on pages 600 and 601.

Checklist of Teaching Skills for Assistants in a Preschool Group

Directions: Use the following list of skills to record the skills shown by another person, or yourself, in a preschool group situation.
1. At the top of the first set of columns, record the date of your evaluation.
2. In the column entitled "Did," put a checkmark after each of the skills the person used that day.

After the preschool session is concluded, the person you observed completes the evaluation by showing how she felt about each of the skills used, as follows:
1. She puts a checkmark in the column entitled "Comfortable" if she felt comfortable in the skill.
2. She puts a checkmark in the column entitled "Need" if she feels she needs more experience in order to feel comfortable in the skill.

The second set of columns is to be used after an interval of experience with preschool children. Make the second evaluation in the same way as the first. The differences between the two evaluations are evidence of increased skill in working with preschool children.

SKILLS   EVALUATIONS

	Date:			Date:		
	Did	Com-fortable	Need	Did	Com-fortable	Need
1.1 Takes out equipment as requested						
1.2 Takes out equipment as planned						
1.3 Prepares materials for next activity						
1.4 Places related equipment together						
1.5 Prearranges equipment so it is attractive to children						

SKILLS   EVALUATIONS

	Date:			Date:		
	Did	*Com-fortable*	*Need*	*Did*	*Com-fortable*	*Need*
2.1 Takes a child to bathroom when asked by teacher						
2.2 Invites to the bathroom the child who needs to go						
2.3 Toilets children before refreshments or after art activity						
3.1 Puts equipment away as asked						
3.2 Puts away equipment when children leave it						
3.3 Helps children finish their activity and put away their things						
4.1 Helps serve refreshments						
4.2 Guides one or more children in helping to serve or to clean up						
4.3 Leads children in conversation and finger plays at table						
4.4 Takes responsibility for refreshment time						
5.1 Answers a child's question						
5.2 Talks with child as long as he is interested						
5.3 Notes interest of child, and asks questions to guide his thinking						
5.4 Plans further activities in terms of interests expressed by children						
6.1 Reminds children of limits when necessary						
6.2 Helps individual children overcome frustration						
6.3 Identifies group problem and explains what to do about it						
6.4 Gathers children together to discuss a group problem						

The progress of college students is also observable in the quality of the observations they make about preschool children. The following observations show that the student is relating actual classroom happenings to the theory of child development; that she is observing teacher behavior (and her own) in relation to child behavior; and that she shows insight in observing a considerable variety of behavior.

Observations of a Group of Four- and Five-year-old Children[1]

OBSERVATION	INTERPRETATION
Janet was near Becky in the painting area. BECKY I'm making a donkey. JANET It dosen't look like a donkey. BECKY It's a donkey. JANET I'm making a map. I suggested that there were many ways to make a donkey and that that was Becky's way of making a donkey. I said to Janet: "Your map has many pretty colors in it."	Becky was not easily influenced. She is secure in her own feelings about herself.
In the sandbox, Jeff threw sand. Linda standing nearby called out, "He's throwing sand." Mrs. M. went over and said, "Do you need more water?" Children didn't answer but went on with their play. No more sand was thrown.	
Jeff was at the pegboard with Janet. Linda went over and wanted a turn. Jeff and Janet told her to go away. When she continued to stay, Jeff got up and struck at the air near her.	Jeff is able to play cooperatively with Janet, but doesn't seem to be ready to take in others yet.
Kit played alone putting puzzles together. He looked for shape and sizes. After he put it together, he took it apart and did it again. At the peg table, Kit stood watching for a time. Didn't seem to want to join in.	Kit needs a special friend—it is easier to begin with one friend before trying out the group. He discriminates between colors, sizes and shapes. Children like to do what they know how to do.
At the dough table, all the children except Kit shared the large piece of dough. I asked them about seeing fireworks. Kit quickly volunteered that he had seen the fireworks. I asked: What did they do? KIT They burst. I asked: What colors were there? Kit didn't answer.	Pushing children into sharing before they are ready will not result in sound learning. Kit will learn to share with people he knows and likes. Then he can broaden his sharing ability.

[1] Muriel Johnson, in paper prepared for a summer workshop entitled "Child Development Techniques," conducted by Mrs. Molly Morganroth. California State College at Long Beach, Long Beach, Calif.

A Preschool Laboratory for High School Students

In order to discuss the kinds of administrative and teaching problems which arise in the use of a preschool group as a laboratory by high school students, consider the use of a preschool group as a child development laboratory in a home economics course on homemaking. Such a laboratory can help the students to learn how to observe objectively what preschool children do and say, how to work comfortably with children, how to plan activities for them as individuals and as a group, and how to identify the characteristics of each age and stage of their development.

The content of a high school laboratory course in homemaking is as varied as the objectives of the teachers teaching them. Some teachers emphasize the development of human relationships; others, the preparation for parenthood; others, the care, selection, preparation, use, and repair of toys; still others, the organization and management of a group. Such breadth in emphasis is desirable because of the variations from community to community, from class to class, and from teacher to teacher. The child-development laboratory can enrich a wide variety of classes in homemaking.

PROVIDING A PRESCHOOL GROUP SITUATION

The chairman of the home economics department should discuss with the school principal the idea of having students learn about preschool children by actually working with them. The principal and the teacher will probably agree that if the students have actual experience in observing and working with children their attitudes toward children will change and they will acquire a more complete understanding of how children behave and develop. How can the students be in a preschool group at the time their homemaking class is scheduled?

First, the principal and the department chairman should consider whether some preschool group now serving the community might be used by the high school students. Is there a children's center, or a parent-cooperative group near the high school? If such a group is too distant from the school for the students to get to it easily and quickly, perhaps the group and its equipment can be moved to some suitable location on the high school campus. Often a public school system has day-care, parent-education, kindergarten, or other preschool groups already under its supervision, and can easily arrange for one of the groups to be housed on the high school campus rather than on an elementary school campus.

If there is no existing preschool group nearby, the principal and the department chairman should consider whether the preschool children in the immediate neighborhood of the high school need a nursery or kindergarten group; and whether adult education instructors or children's center personnel of the school system, parent leaders, or social service workers can develop a preschool group, utilizing facilities on the high school campus. In order to make use of the preschool group for the benefit of the high school students, it may be desirable for a high school homemaking teacher to be responsible for the children so that she can either be with them or, when she needs to be a resource person for a student class, can exchange places with their teacher.

If it is not possible to arrange for a continuing preschool group in which students can observe and work with children, the principal and the department chairman may decide to have the students plan and operate a play school[2] during a two- to four-week period of the school term. The rough plans for the play school project can be developed in detail, an estimate of costs obtained, and even a request for funds to be used in equipping the play school.

Whatever plans are made to develop a preschool group as a laboratory for the high school students, both the principal and the department chairman should make every effort to have the plans favorably publicized and understood within the community. Continuing success of such an enterprise depends on continuing publicity regarding it. As the preschool laboratory program gets underway, its community advisory committee, the parents of students who have participated in the program, the students themselves, and the parents of the preschool children constitute the nucleus of an expanding group of enlightened people favorably disposed to child-development laboratories for high school students.

SCHEDULING

The nature of the preschool group clientele and the scheduling of the high school classes determine the hours of the child-development laboratory. If most of the children come from one-parent families or from families in which both parents work, the children will need care throughout the working day and will be available for high school students at any time of the school day. If most of the children are from two-parent families, each group will need only an enrichment program for a few hours of the day, two, three, four, or five times a week, depending on the age level of the children.

When the class needs of high school and college students are such as to require having preschool children available every day of the week, it is often possible to have several preschool groups use the same facilities at different times of the day. This arrangement makes it possible for any class of students to have access to the same laboratory group or to laboratory

---

[2] *The Play School in the High School: Homemaking Education in Oregon Secondary Schools* (Salem, Ore.: Oregon State Department of Education, 1952); Mildred Weigley Wood, *Observation of Children in the Home Economics Program* (Phoenix: Arizona State Department of Vocational Education, 1963).

groups of different age levels, or to have laboratory days interspersed with days of classroom discussions. This arrangement also makes it possible for more families in the community to benefit directly from the preschool groups, and thus provides an opportunity to increase the understanding and appreciation of the community for both the preschool groups and the sponsoring high school or college.

The number of possible combinations or permutations in scheduling preschool children as laboratory groups for students is limited only by the needs of the children and the ingenuity of the administrator who makes the schedule. One administrator devised the following schedule for six preschool groups using two sets of facilities:

PRESCHOOL GROUPS: A: Three-year-old children   O: Four-year-old children
B: Three-year-old children   P: Five-year-old children
N: Four-year-old children   Q: Five-year-old children

	MONDAY	TUESDAY	WEDNESDAY	THURSDAY	FRIDAY
MORNING	N—Set 1	N—Set 1	A—Set 1	N—Set 1	A—Set 1
	O—Set 2	O—Set 2	B—Set 2	O—Set 2	B—Set 2
AFTERNOON	P—Set 1	P—Set 1	P—Set 1	P—Set 1	P—Set 1
	Q—Set 2	Q—Set 2	Q—Set 2	Q—Set 2	Q—Set 2

Recognizing the needs of students should not conflict with meeting the needs of preschool children. In each laboratory situation, adaptations should be made as seems best.

MULTIPLE USE OF LABORATORY SITUATIONS

If parents and different groups of students are to benefit from the preschool group laboratory, administrative ingenuity must be exercised in scheduling observers of and participants in the preschool program. Those responsible for a nursery or kindergarten can determine whether its preschool groups are to be for preschool children only; for parents as well as for children; for students and children; or for students, parents, and preschool children. In almost every situation the preschool program is enriched by student and parent participation at the same time that such participation enriches the education of both parents and students.

A Unified School District in California has a parent education program that illustrates some of the arrangements that can be made in utilizing preschool laboratory situations for multiple purposes. The General Adult Division of the Unified School District maintains a Child Development Center for the campus of the local city college. This center is designed primarily for nursery school children whose parents wish to enroll in courses offered by the college. The mothers who have preschool children in the center attend eight or nine two-hour evening meetings each semester. In addition, they and their husbands are encouraged to attend workshops dealing with problems of toys and equipment, health and safety, and other topics of interest to parents; and forum meetings which present leaders in parent education. Thus the parents have an opportunity to discuss child development and family relations and to learn the views of resource people. They also have four out of five half-days a week in which they may pursue their education at the college while their preschool children are in the preschool groups nearby.

Children may be enrolled in the center when they are thirty months old and may remain until they are old enough to enter kindergarten. They are assigned to one of ten groups according to their age, and attend five days a week, either in the morning or in the afternoon. Each mother acts as an assistant to her child's teacher for one session a week, forty minutes of which she spends with the codirector of the preschool group, discussing school and home events.

At the same time that the center furthers the development of parents and their children, it is useful to high school and college students of the Unified School District. Classes of students are encouraged to arrange for visits at any time during the school term. Someone from the center comes to the class before the visit in order to help the students plan good use of their observation time. The same person accompanies the students during their visit to different preschool groups, and comes to class again afterwards to discuss any questions the students may have in regard to observations made.

The center also enriches the city college program that prepares teachers of preschool groups. Certain lectures and discussions are presented in connection with laboratory experience at the center. Opportunity to observe children and participate in their group activities is an integral part of the program.

The preschool groups at the center are an important part of programs which continuously educate a succession of prospective parents, parents with children of preschool age, and women who teach or are preparing to teach, preschool groups.

In one Arizona city, a nursery school of twenty to twenty-five children between the ages of two and five serves as a laboratory situation for high school students and as an observation situation for the parents of the children. The students participate in the nursery school, each concentrating her efforts on one particular child and conferring with the mother of that child once every three weeks.

This arrangement has several advantages for the high school student: it enlarges her understanding of the child at nursery school with information about the child at home; it gives her opportunity to be with children under supervision and with real responsibility; it provides, in her relation to the parent and to the child, an experience in relationships much like those involved in babysitting.

These arrangements also have advantages for each mother. She can see how others handle her child and children of similar ages. She can observe her child in relation to children of other preschool ages. She has an opportunity to discuss what she observes and the problems arising out of family living both with other, like-minded parents, and with an experienced and well-educated family-living teacher. She can talk with a high school student and learn from experience how to work pleasantly and effectively with young babysitters.

LEARNING TO OBSERVE CHILDREN

A primary objective for high school students is to learn how to observe children. This they can accomplish, not by filling in observation record forms, but by recording the child behavior they see and hear. As they use these records of what children do and say, the students can see that simple and accurate records are useful in learning, for instance, what children of a given age level do, or what reactions a grownup can expect to get to what she says or does. They can see that the three-year-olds use a piece of equipment differently than four-year-olds do, that a three-year-old child needs a push in swinging but a four-year-old child needs only a starting push and a five-year-old child needs no physical help at all. The students can also learn to identify the aspects of development involved in their recordings of child behavior. They may note unusual use of language or some other aspect of intellectual, emotional, social, or physical development.

When their records are used in class discussion, students feel their observations serve a real purpose. Furthermore, they can see that some aspects of child behavior are more significant than others, and more important to record and discuss. Thus students are encouraged to improve their recording technique.

Before students go into a nursery or kindergarten to observe children, they need to be sensitized to the situation so that anxieties about themselves and how they are doing will not interfere with their work. By going over written directions, students can be helped to anticipate the actual observation situation. In addition to learning how to record what they observe, they can learn how to

- Walk through a room without disturbing its occupants.
- Sit quietly.
- React to a curious child.
- Leave without attracting attention.

Here are suggestions given to high school students in one child-development center:

In planning for student visits we have tried to make sure that the children's program can be carried on without disruption, and that students can observe a typical nursery school situation. . . . This is only possible if visitors remain fairly inconspicuous, so that the children are not distracted from their usual activities.

1. If you have a cold or are not feeling well, please postpone your visit until a later time.
2. Enter quietly, report to the coordinator or the nursery school director, who will assign you to a group.
3. Sit down as much as possible. Choose a place in the background, but near enough to hear and see the children.
4. One or two students sitting together are less conspicuous than a group of three or four. Please try to avoid talking together.
5. Do not initiate conversation or play with the children, as this takes them away from their own activities. Do not hesitate, however, to respond briefly to a child's friendliness. If it continues, you might say, "Now I have to do my work," and begin to write, or move away to another location.
6. Avoid commenting on the children, or laughing about their activities in their presence.
7. Do not step into situations with the children unless there seems to be real danger. Situations which need handling are the teacher's responsibility.
8. Make a note of questions which you may have. There will be opportunities to discuss these with the coordinator, the director, or your classroom teacher. Teachers working with children cannot leave them for long enough to be helpful with questions. Please try not to divert them.[3]

For any and all observations, it is important to help students focus their attention first on recording what children do and say, and then on interpreting their behavior. This sequence of student thinking is developed by having students first record their observations and then discuss their interpretations. It is interfered with by having students use forms to direct their observations or having them look for certain kinds of behavior (e.g., "What seems to frustrate the child?" or, "What is the child afraid of?"). It is encouraged by having students observe what a child does and says in each of several different kinds of situations; for instance, going into a new place, having a new toy to play with, responding to teacher directions, watching another child use the toy he wants.

STARTING TO WORK WITH PRESCHOOL CHILDREN

When a student is scheduled to work with preschool children, he should visit the preschool group first and talk with its teacher. He needs information about the children and their activities and equipment, but even more he needs help in getting acquainted with his own role and reassurance about his eventual success in it. Explanations and specific suggestions are an aid to the beginning student assistant in the preschool group.

It takes time for young children to know new people well enough to be sure of them. When they are not sure, they show this in different ways. Some

[3] Mary Alice Mallum, *Child Development Center* (Santa Monica, Calif.: Santa Monica Unified School District, 1959), p. 6.

may be shy and not want you to help them; others may be "silly" and look for teasing ways to get attention. . . . Students can make it easier for children to know them when they . . .

1. Remember that the child who cannot accept you has no personal feeling against you. He simply needs more time to know you.
2. Show the children that you are really interested in what they are doing by how you look at them and by what you say.
3. Be friendly. Smile; use names as soon as you can; say "Hello" when you come each day.
4. Look for helpful things you can do for children. This is one of the best ways to make friends with them:
   (a) Tie an untied shoestring.
   (b) Help put on a doll dress.
   (c) Offer to read a story.
   (d) Find something a child wants.
5. In the beginning, work mostly with the children who are ready to be friendly with you. After a few days all of the children will know you well enough to be comfortable with you.[4]

If the student is to be helpful to the children in a child development laboratory, he must know the rudiments about how to keep them safe. Here are written suggestions used by students working in a child development center:

The physical safety of children is a first concern at all times. . . . Move quickly but calmly to stop dangerous behavior. For example:

1. Remove the child who is about to push others on a piece of high equipment.
2. Move quickly to the child who is about to throw something which can hurt others.
3. Stop the tricycle or wagon which is moving too fast.

The best way to keep children safe is to look ahead to possible danger and plan ways of avoiding it. Some important ways to avoid hazards are:

1. Know what every child in your group is doing at all times. Do not let your attention to one or two children keep you from knowing what the rest of your group is doing.
2. Never stop to talk unnecessarily with teachers or other students while supervising children. When conversation is necessary, continue to watch your group as you talk.
3. Always stand near high climbing equipment being used by your group so that you are ready to help a child who may have difficulty.
4. Help the children with wheel-toy traffic problems; stop drivers and remind them of wheel-toy rules.
5. Watch for unsteady equipment which may fall, such as climbing boxes, ladders, boards, block building.

[4] Ibid., pp. 4, 5.

6. Remove and put out of sight any sharp or broken objects which children may be using.
7. Watch woodwork and gardening activities closely. Never leave the children alone with these activities. If you must leave, and no teacher can take your place, put the tools away and offer a different type of activity to the children.
8. In all play activities, keep the size of your group small.
9. Always tell the group teacher when it is necessary for you to leave your group.[5]

UNDERSTANDING ONESELF BETTER

As students work with preschool children and discuss with their teachers and fellow students what they have observed and experienced, they gain considerable insight into their own problems in relating to other people. Preschool group experience can help high school students who need and want to know how to find a place within a social group. Their social sensitivity as adolescents makes them eager to acquire the skills which enable them to move easily into and out of group situations. Their problems in doing this can be put in perspective as they tackle the problem of finding their role in the preschool group as assistants to the teacher. Each day they must enter the children's group. Each day they can observe the skill of other students and of their teacher in doing this. And each day they can watch children entering and leaving a group or remaining apart from it. With their own teacher they can discuss the succession of social experiences: individual play, parallel play, and cooperative play which gradually increases in frequency and duration. They can also draw up suggestions for helping students to feel at home with a preschool group. For instance,

1. If you feel quite inadequate your first day with the children, remember that this feeling is normal.
2. When you try to help a child, ignore the fact that he may reject you at first.
3. Notice where children are playing with little or no guidance, and take charge of that area. Or, if many children are crowding into one place, see if you can interest some of them in moving to another area.
4. Listen carefully to what the children say. If you need more information as a basis for guiding them, ask them what you need to know.

One student observed and identified with a child who kept trying to find a place, first in one play group of children and then another. The student came to realize that the child would be accepted into a group as soon as he learned techniques for approaching it. As the student worked

---

[5] Ibid., pp. 7, 8.

with the child, helping him enter the playhouse group or some other group, she saw ways of improving her own skill in joining a group.

Developing rules of conduct to be used with the preschool children is one way of helping students to become aware of the rules that govern their own conduct. For instance, students should discuss the importance of giving positive, not negative, directions. They should be encouraged to practice using "do's" instead of "don'ts" with their families and their friends, even prior to their participation in the children's group. Then, when they come into the children's group, they can notice how many times they say, "Don't do that!" Under the pressure of the new situation of being an assistant teacher, the students are apt to revert to methods by which they were brought up and to forget the methods they have since learned to consider more desirable. They should develop awareness of such regression, and come to a better understanding of their individual behavior in this regard.

Learning to Take Responsibility

Participation in a child-development laboratory gives junior and senior high school students opportunity to assume responsibility. For instance, in one homemaking course the teacher in charge of the nursery group advised the students about fitting into its routine. She provided each student with a mimeographed manual and discussed with them what it said about their responsibilities, including the following:

1. Come directly to the nursery school each day at your regular class time. Check off your attendance on the attendance record sheet posted in the nursery school office. Leave your books and purses in the office.
2. Plan to be in attendance every day that you are scheduled to work in the nursery school. The teacher needs your assistance, and you need the opportunity to be with the children.
3. If you are unable to attend, call the nursery school teacher at her home before 8:00 A.M.
4. At least once a week make conference appointments with the nursery school teacher and keep these appointments.
5. Read your nursery school manual *before* coming to participate in the nursery school. Refer to it from time to time as you think about your work with the children. Turn it in to the nursery school teacher on the last day of your work as a student assistant.

With records of attendance and appointments, the teacher and the student together could consider the evidence of responsibility taken by the student. They could talk objectively about what had or had not been done and make plans for further responsibilities in the future.

In the child-development laboratory, students should have an opportunity to help preschool children assume responsibility for themselves. A student assisting the teacher can encourage the children to take off their jackets and sweaters and put them in their lockers when they come indoors. A student can help the children to put away toys that have been played with.

In some instances a requirement for junior or senior girls in an advanced homemaking course is to plan and carry out a project with a group of children in the preschool group. These projects may include making cookies, planting a garden, enjoying a craft or musical activity, or going on a study trip. The projects may be planned by one student, working alone, or by two students, working together. Projects are submitted to the teacher of the preschool group. If she approves them, she schedules time for each project to be fitted into the program of activities for the children.

PREPARING FOR PARENTHOOD

Participation in the activities of a preschool group is especially desirable for high school students as preparation for marriage. Prospective mothers—and prospective fathers, too—should have ample opportunity to preview their roles as parents. They need to develop favorable attitudes toward parenthood, and to see the importance of preschool group experience for children. They need to know the resources of the community for helping them when they have children of their own: How can parents find preschool groups suitable for their family situation? Where can they have experience with children under the guidance of well-trained preschool teachers? What counseling services are available for parents?

Through participation in preschool group activities, students can develop the attitudes, skills, and concepts they will need as parents. Their active participation enables them to learn more fully and vividly what they might have learned only intellectually in a classroom situation. It is one thing to know that an adult can redirect, ignore, praise, or isolate a child who has taken off a shoe and is using it to beat out a musical rhythm. But it is another thing for an adult to carry out immediately a plan of action appropriate to a preschool group situation in which one child is hitting another.

By assisting the teacher of a preschool group, a student can learn from experience what a child, intent on play, feels when the adults in charge want him to put away his toys. The student can see the difference between letting the child complete his activity and then happily put his things away, or frustrating him by removing his toys before he has rounded out his experience. And the high school girl can lay a foundation for her later experience as a mother by learning the importance of taking care of the needs of her children before she goes on to the problems of housekeeping. Through participation in a preschool group, she can come closer to understanding love, with all that it implies about recognizing the needs of the individuals in her family as well as her own needs as a person.

PREPARING FOR EMPLOYMENT AS AN AIDE

High school or junior college students in some localities are able to enroll for a home economics course designed to prepare them for initial employment as an aide to a teacher of an early-childhood or a special-education group for educable younger children. One such high school course is designed especially for less advantaged students who feel the need for employment, either full or part time. Through preparation to be an aide for a preschool group, a student can look forward to working during the morning or afternoon while attending high school or junior college classes in the evening or in the remainder of the day.

The senior high school class in occupational home economics begins with opportunity for the students to meet as a classroom study and discussion group. They learn from their teacher, from each other, and from their textbook, which is well illustrated and uses a simplified vocabulary.[6] They recall experiences each has had with young children, and they develop simple generalizations about young children and how to work with them.

When the students are ready to work in laboratory situations and when selected preschool and primary-grade groups are ready for aides to work with their teacher, the students begin a series of four assignments as aides to teachers in a variety of preschool and primary-grade groups. Each assignment involves four mornings or afternoons with the children and a fifth morning or afternoon with other students for workshop, lecture, and discussion activities. Each is long enough for the student to become acquainted with the physical arrangements of supplies and equipment, to learn the names of all the preschool children, and to understand the day-by-day behavior of several of them in detail, and to start learning how to guide preschool children in each of their many activities. By their fourth laboratory experience the students have become accustomed to moving quickly into their responsibilities as aide and have considerable competence in carrying out such responsibility as the following:

Is on time ready to work as scheduled, or has telephoned in time for other arrangements to be made.

Is appropriately dressed for her role.

Helps individual children as requested by the teacher. For the preschool child, this includes helping him in:

Removing outer clothing when he comes indoors.

Going to the bathroom.

Doing an activity new to him.

Quietly cleaning up what spills.

Finding a quite place away from the group when he is out of control.

Staying with his group on a walk or study trip.

[6] Baker, Katherine Read and Fanez, *Understanding and Guiding Young Children.* Englewood Cliffs, N.J.: Prentice-Hall, Inc., 1967.

Putting away equipment when through with it.

Marking his project or collection for latter retrieval.

Finding his clothing, collections, and craft products to take home.

For the elementary school child in the primary grades, this includes:

Working quietly at his seat.

Practising number and other drills with flash cards, and so on.

Finding out whether written work was done correctly.

At her request helps the teacher to:

Prepare a bulletin board display for parents and public.

Lay out supplies and equipment in advance of an activity.

Prepare materials needed for a craft project.

Run a mimeograph to prepare materials for parents and more mature children.

Take attendance.

Operate a tape recorder with listening posts, record player, overhead and other projectors, microscope, and other classroom equipment.

Prepare and serve food as needed for snacks and meals.

Put away equipment so it is clean and ready for use.

By the end of the school year more capable students are beginning to take initiative in seeing what help a child or a group needs and in supplying it before it is requested by the teacher. Their study and work with the children has done a great deal in building their self-confidence and in developing competence in handling human relationships at home, at school, and in their laboratory situations. They should be better parents and better people as a consequence of their course.

The students who should be encouraged in thinking of an extended career in working with preschool children are those who identify with the teacher and are especially competent in establishing rapport with individual children and in helping with the management of small groups. But every student has her notebook containing finger plays, songs, lists of records and suitable books, and other aids to providing a wealth of activities for the children. Each student also has her collection of puppets, music rhythm toys, and other equipment she devised in construction workshop hours. Each student is ready for at least summer positions, part- or full-time responsibility, as an aide to a teacher or director at a camp, children's center, play ground, church, hospital, or museum having preschool children participating in its programs.

APPRAISING STUDENT PROGRESS

Teachers vary in what they expect of students as a result of their experience in a child-development laboratory and concomitant study. Some teachers emphasize the acquisition of skill in observing children or in working with them. Other teachers are more concerned that the students learn to enjoy the children and to be comfortable with them. Such a change in attitude may be taken for granted by other teachers, who concentrate on having the students understand such concepts as the differences in child behavior from one age level to another. Whatever skills, attitudes, and concepts are emphasized in the teaching of the course, these are the changes which should be evaluated in appraising student progress.

In the Child Development Center at Santa Monica, California, a series of pictures was assembled as a device for evaluating student progress in interpreting and dealing with child behavior. The pictures depicted family situations with preschool children, such as that of a little boy pinching

How does a student interpret this picture? (*Courtesy of Santa Monica Unified School District, Santa Monica, California.*)

his baby brother's toe, painting on a wall, or having a tantrum; nursery group situations, such as that of a crying child wanting a tricycle ridden by another child, or that of a child sucking his thumb instead of playing with his toys. For each situation pictured, the student described what was happening, what feelings were shown, and what the adult should do. Now the opinionaire[7] is developed for use as a pre- and post-test for evaluating student progress with the respondent selecting from eight courses

[7] "Child Development Opinionaire." Santa Monica, Calif.: Santa Monica Unified School District, 1960.

of action the three he considers most desirable and the three he considers least desirable.

In another situation, a homemaking teacher appraised the progress senior high school girls had made during the two-week period in which they had assisted the nursery school teacher and after eight weeks of class study and discussion about young children. Her appraisal of their progress was an integral part of their activities. The teacher identified six major objectives of the unit of study, and listed the kinds of behavior observable in students attaining those objectives. Whenever she noted evidence of a student attaining one of the objectives during the unit of study, she recorded it. Her records then provided a basis for appraising the progress made by each of the students.

Here are the changes the teacher expected to be able to observe in her students:

CHANGE EXPECTED IN EACH STUDENT	EVIDENCE OF SUCH CHANGE
1. Learns to observe children	
Appreciates that each child is unique	Does not treat each child alike
Observes how a child reacts to different people	Records anecdotes showing such observations
Observes how a child reacts to different situations	
2. Feels secure with children	Is aware of how secure she feels
Understands what frightens a child	Records anecdotes showing such understanding
Observes good timing in others	Records anecdotes showing such timing
Does not retreat from children	Is able to help a child needing help
3. Is able to guide group play	Takes charge of a group activity (e.g., nature table, block play, sand play, dress-up corner, puzzle table)
4. Is able to apply underlying principles	In interpreting records of observations, notes the application of such principles as: (a) Use praise, not blame (b) Let the child do it himself if he can (c) Have guidance available as needed (d) Encourage taking turns (e) Encourage care of equipment (f) Talk it out without any hitting
5. Becomes increasingly interested in children	Spends more time with them
6. Is able to identify methods of guiding a child	In interpreting observation records, correctly labels the method used

Multiple Challenges of the Preschool Group

Those who understand the rapidity of development in the preschool child are challenged to make available to him the group experiences which facilitate and broaden his development: the three-year-old coming into a nursery group moves into a social experience highly suitable to his age level; the four-year-old plunges into the many activities of a nursery group and expands his world immeasurably; the five-year-old enters kindergarten and consolidates his preschool experiences in preparation for the intellectual challenges of elementary school. A realization of what can be accomplished at each age level encourages expansion of preschool groups.

The laboratory situation of the preschool group is a continuing challenge to those who work with future citizens and future parents. The preschool group is indispensable in helping prospective citizens to become objective viewers of human behavior, and in helping prospective parents to learn effective and comfortable ways of working with preschool children.

Those who use the preschool group as an integral part of adult education know its value in helping parents to develop the skills, attitudes, and concepts which they, as parents, should have. Hope for continuing improvement in family relations rests on the premise that parents can be educated. Effective parent education can be achieved through the use of the preschool group as a laboratory in which parents may observe and work with their own and other children.

The challenge of the preschool group for those who work with students in the liberal arts is to use the nursery school and kindergarten as laboratories in human behavior. Students in the fields that involve behavioral science, medicine and education for instance, especially benefit from actual experience with preschool children.

For advanced students in vocational fields involving work with preschool children, the preschool laboratory is an excellent place to learn how to observe objectively what people do and say, and how to work easily and well with children and with adults interested in children.

The challenge lies in using the preschool group for the good of preschool children and—at the same time—for the good of prospective and actual parents, pediatricians, teachers, and others who study human relationships in general and child-adult and child-child relationships in particular.

Situations for Discussion

A preschool teacher is apt to find herself in situations similar to the four described here. As you think of what to do in each situation, consider whether each course of action suggested is desirable, or not. Use points brought out in the chapter as well as ideas from your experience to justify your views. Suggest alternative courses of action to supplement those that are given.

SITUATION 1   As a student you are assisting the teacher of a group of four-year-old children. At their rest time, when first one child and then another endeavor to get your attention you should

- Ask the teacher to help you.
- Plan to play soft music the next time you are in charge of rest time.
- Ask the children to listen to the bubbles in the aquarium.
- Yawn and relax as you want the children to do.
- Tell any attention-seeking child that you will help him later and that now is rest time.

SITUATION 2 Janet, the young woman who is assisting you with a group of three-year-old children while they are free to choose their own activities, has been reading stories to a small group of the children. She is intent on holding the book so that the pictures are easily visible to the children and the print is visible to her. She does not notice that the children are becoming more restless, more interested in each other and less interested in the story. When Janet picks up a third book to read, you should say

- To the children, "Remember, we cross our legs. We put our hands in our laps."
- To Janet, "Do you think maybe the children have had enough stories for now?"
- To Janet, "Here are some puzzles the children like to do."
- To the children, "Isn't it nice to have Janet read us stories today!"
- To the children, "Who is going to be the first one down the slide today?"

SITUATION 3 You have a contract for teaching homemaking in a high school that has offered foods and clothing courses. You feel that the high school students should study child care and development. During the school year, you should

- Fit into the program as it is now presented.
- Talk with fellow teachers about the desirability of a child-development laboratory.
- Discuss with the high school principal plans for having a unit on child development the following year.
- Through local women's organizations, try to develop community interest in a child-development laboratory.

SITUATION 4 When a preschool group is proposed for the local high school, you find opportunity to discuss it with members of different women's organizations. You bring out the point that

- Future parents need actual experience with children.
- The way preschool children get along with each other has elements identical with the way high school students get along with other people.
- Preschool children in families living near the high school can join the preschool group.
- Baby sitters should have nursery experience.
- Many young people marry when they are in high school.

Current Professional Books and Pamphlets

Arlington County Schools. *Child Develpment and Training for Employment in Day Care Centers.* Arlington, Va.: Arlington County Schools, 1964. [Content, learnings, and experiences for an occupationally oriented course for high school students in child development.]

BAKER, KATHERINE READ and FANEZ. *Understanding and Guiding Your Children*. Englewood Cliffs, N.J.: Prentice-Hall, Inc., 1967. [Written at the high school level.]

BRISBANE, HOLLY, and A. P. RIKER. *The Developing Child*. Peoria, Ill.: Bennett Publishing Company, 1965. [One of several texts for junior college and high school students of child development.]

CHRISTIANSON, HELEN M., MARY M. ROGERS, and BLANCHE A. LUDLUM. *The Nursery School: Adventure in Living and Learning*. Boston: Houghton Mifflin Company, 1961. [Chapter 3 is entitled "Participation in a Laboratory University School."]

City Federation of Women's Organizations of Ithaca, New York. *Taking Care of a Pre-school Child*. Ithaca, N.Y.: Child Care Booklets. [*Taking Care of a Baby* is also clearly and simply written for students.]

Department of Public Instruction Commonwealth of Pennsylvania. *Preparing for Employment in Child Care Services in Pennsylvania Schools*. Harrisburg, Pa.: Commonwealth of Pennsylvania, 1965. [In this curriculum guide for a course "leading to employment in occupations of less than professional level in child care services," key concepts are to be built on generalizations and experiences, and student progress is to be evaluated.]

HILLE, HELEN M. *Food for Groups of Young Children Cared for During the Day*. Washington, D.C.: U.S. Children's Bureau, U.S. Department of Health, Education, and Welfare. [One of many government bulletins useful with students.]

HOFFMAN, LOIS W. and MARTIN L. *Review of Child Development*, Vols. I and II. New York: Russell Sage Foundation. Vol. I, 1964; Vol. II, 1966. [Prepared under the auspices of the Society for Research in Child Development, many chapters are useful to introduce students to the great volume of significant research on the development of young children.]

Home Economics Education, University of Kentucky. *Suggested Guide—Training Program for Child Care Aides*. Lexington, Ky.: Wage Earning Program, Home Economics Education, University of Kentucky. [University pamphlets; and publications by state, national, commercial, and professional organizations are useful for students.]

JENKINS, GLADYS G., HELEN S. SHACTER, and WILLIAM W. BAUER. *These Are Your Children*. Fair Lawn, N.J.: Scott, Foresman, and Company, 1966. [Prospective as well as actual parents enjoy this book.]

LANGFORD, LOUIS M. *Guidance of the Young Child*. New York: John Wiley and Sons, Inc., 1960. [The book talks about different aspects of preschool programs.]

MALLUM, MARY ALICE. *Child Development Center*. Santa Monica, Calif.: Santa Monica Unified School District, 1959. [This handbook was prepared for secondary students who observe or work with children in the Child Development Center at Santa Monica.]

PRESCOTT, DANIEL A. *The Child in the Educative Process*. New York: McGraw-Hill Book Company, Inc. 1957. [Chapter 13, "The Child-Study Program," describes in-service development of teachers through making case studies of pupils and participating in professional discussions of case materials.]

READ, KATHERINE H. *The Nursery School, a Human Relationships Laboratory.* Philadelphia: W. B. Saunders Co., 1966. [A new edition by an early author.]

RUDOLF, MARGUERITA, and DOROTHY H. COHEN. *Kindergarten: a Year of Learning.* New York: Appleton-Century-Crofts, Inc., 1964. [One of several useful books for those who work with five-year-olds.]

SHUEY, REBEKAH M. *Learning about Children.* Philadelphia, Pa.: J. B. Lippincott Co., 1964. [Play groups in high school are useful in learning about children.]

U.S. Office of Education, Division of Vocational and Technical Education. *Child Care and Guidance—A Suggested Post High School Curriculum.* Washington, D.C.: U.S. Government Printing Office, 1967. [Practical suggestions for the post high school program include suggestions for evaluation of student progress, as well as bibliography, equipment list, floor plan, and other curriculum essentials.]

WARING, ETHEL B. *Principles for Child Guidance,* Cornell Extension Bulletin 420. Ithaca, N.Y.: New York State College of Home Economics, 1939. [Affection, respect, help, and approval contribute to security and adequacy of a child, to his interest in experience, and to his self-confidence.]

WOOD, MILDRED WEIGLEY. *Observations of Children in the Home Economics Program.* Phoenix, Ariz.: Arizona Association of Future Homemakers, 1963. [Deals specifically with the use of the play school in high school classes in a homemaking program.]

CHAPTER **18**

Participation in Teaching Preschool Groups

Teaching is generally recognized as an aid to understanding and guiding the behavior of children. Parents and prospective parents, prospective teachers of young children and other teacher aides, and other students and volunteers who work with or are preparing to work with preschool children should participate in teaching preschool groups. Through interaction with preschool children under supervision, they come to understand the behavior of the preschool child and to realize how to guide his development effectively.

Participants in teaching a preschool group assist the teacher sometimes in one way and sometimes in another, depending upon the teacher, the participant, and especially the needs of the children in general and at that time. However, in general, their roles are definable in terms of the functions that they are apt to perform with the preschool children, as follows:

PARTICIPANT ROLE	FUNCTION
Observer	Observes individual behavior, and responses of members of a group; records his observations; develops anecdotal and case material as feedback for planning how to guide children, parents, and other adults working with children.
Aide	Assists teacher with supplies and equipment, and with individual and group activities of children; assists children in their activities as needed, under supervision.
Assistant teacher	Guides an individual child or a small group of children as needed; and is prepared to take over direction of and responsibility for the entire group in the event of an emergency.

A volunteer can help a beginning carpenter and supervise a more experienced one. (Courtesy of Chattanooga Public Schools, Chattanooga, Tennessee. Photograph by T. Fred Miller.)

Additional adults means additional firsthand experience. (Courtesy of The Merrill-Palmer Institute and Donna J. Harris, Detroit, Michigan.)

A parent, a student, or a volunteer may participate in teaching a preschool group in any of these three ways. As he assists the teacher, his understanding of the behavior of preschool children and effective ways of meeting their needs increases. With increased skill, he gains confidence in himself as an aide.[1]

Making and Using Observations of a Child

Whenever groups of preschool children are available for adult education purposes, participants should have an opportunity to use observation records and to learn how to make them. Even though preschool groups are designed to benefit the children rather than the adults, those who are interested in understanding children and in improving their ability to work with them effectively should be encouraged to make and use observation records. Such activities sharpen awareness of child behavior, adult behavior, and the relations between the two. The written records can also be useful in helping participants and others who spend less time with the children, to understand them better.

The recording of observations is so important that the participant should give the process her complete attention. The experienced teacher can record during those brief moments when the children are playing happily and assistant teachers are available to help them. The adult who is a beginner as an observer should record her observations during a preschool session when she is not helping the teacher. The participant who assists the teacher and then attempts to record her observations immediately after the children have left is apt to have difficulty in remembering the precise words used by the preschool child. In general it is best for her to arrange time to record her observations when the children's activities are in progress and she has no responsibility which might distract from her observing.

Making and Using an Observation Record

In order to improve her understanding of a particular child, the participant can make a direct record of what the child says and does. Such a record is useful in itself and also when used in connection with a record of her impressions of the child's behavior. What a child actually does, when compared with what a participant thinks he does, is useful as a basis for helping her to develop attitudes, skills, and understandings that she needs in working with children.

The following record of Stanley's behavior when he was twenty-five months old was made on blank sheets of paper—the first observational record his participating mother had made of any child. Stanley's mother recorded precisely the words chosen by both Stanley and herself and de-

[1] Jeanne W. Quill, *One Giant Step, A Guide for Head Start Aides* (Washington, D.C.: National Association for the Education of Young Children, 1969).

scribed the actions of both. Her interpretations were made afterwards. The record is useful in studying any aspect of child behavior, in making a case study of Stanley, in studying the behavior characteristic of a particular age level, or in studying the interaction of a mother and her child.

STANLEY   Mummy doing? [What is mummy doing?]
MOTHER   Writing at the desk.
STANLEY   Dishes all washed?
MOTHER   Yes, the dishes are all washed now.
(*Mother writes at the desk. Stanley brings over his own small chair, stands on it, watches what Mother is doing, and looks out the window over the desk.*)
STANLEY   Look. Man. Look at!
MOTHER   Yes, he is talking to Mrs. Henshaw.
STANLEY   Daddy doing?
MOTHER   Daddy is at work.
STANLEY   (*seeing a robin on the front lawn*)   Robin doing?
MOTHER   (*looking up*)   Flew away.
STANLEY   Hunt's? [Did it fly to Hunt's yard?]
MOTHER   Maybe.
STANLEY   (*noticing a coffee cup on the desk*)   Mummy's coffee?
MOTHER   Yes, Mummy had coffee.
(*Stanley starts to play with things on the desk. He finds a pad of telephone numbers and snaps it open.*)
STANLEY   (*proudly*)   Look at! (*Pulls out a page.*) Came apart. (*Pauses.*) 'Nanley geta telephone.
MOTHER   Are you going to get your own telephone?
STANLEY   (*pointing across the room*)   Mummy's telephone 'way back.
(*Stanley runs to his own room, brings his own telephone, and places it on the desk beside his mother.*)
STANLEY   (*carefully adjusting his telephone to get it into just the right position*)   Telephone. Table. (*Makes his telephone ring, and picks up its receiver.*) Hello. Hello!

*   *   *

STANLEY   Where's the book? (*Looks around for it.*)
MOTHER   Where did you put it?
STANLEY   (*proudly remembering*)   In there! (*Points to couch.*) Me get it.
MOTHER   (*knowing that help will be needed in opening the sofa bed*)   Just a minute.
STANLEY   Me get it too! (*Stamps feet. Tries whining. Gets impatient. Starts to play with telephone pad again. Tries to close it.*) Hard, Mummy! Hard! (*Struggles with it more.*) Look! Closed it!
MOTHER   Fine! And shall we get the book now?
STANLEY   Ehem!
(*Mother opens the sofa bed. Stanley shrieks with delight at seeing the book.*)
STANLEY   Me get it! Me get it! (*Refuses any help in getting the book*) Look at! Book! Me sit down. Look at! (*Pauses.*) Look at! Beaver book in there too! Come here! Look! Me take it out!
(*Stanley places the book in its place on a shelf nearby. Mother attempts to close the sofa bed.*)

STANLEY   Leave it open.
(*Mother leaves the sofa bed open and returns to her writing. Stanley goes to front door and looks out through the screen.*)
STANLEY   Look at! Robin!
MOTHER   What's it doing?
STANLEY   Getting worms!
MOTHER   Getting worms?
STANLEY   Ehem!
(*Stanley stands quietly for a few seconds. Then he tries to open the front screendoor which generally is fastened with a hook. He first pushes the door with his hips. Then he hits it hard. It opens.*)
STANLEY   Bang! Door! 'Nanley hit it! Open! 'Nanley opened it! (*Closes the screendoor again.*) Flies coming in.

* * *

STANLEY   Where's daddy?
MOTHER   At work.
(*Standing in his chair by the desk, Stanley leans over affectionately and bumps Mummy's head with his forehead.*)
STANLEY   Mummy! Mummy, hi! (*suddenly*) Daddy opened hook!
MOTHER   Which?
(*Stanley points to front door in answer.*)
MOTHER   No, daddy didn't open it. He wasn't here.
(*Stanley goes out, then comes back to the livingroom. Sees sofa bed is still open. Tries to close it and has difficulty.*)
STANLEY   Mummy helpa 'Nanley!
MOTHER   Shall I come and help you?.
STANLEY   Ehem! (*With an extra-hard effort, succeeds in closing the sofa bed before mother gets there to help.*)
MOTHER   Oh! Stanley did it all by himself.
STANLEY   (*satisfied with himself*)   'Nanley closed it. (*Goes to front door and looks out quietly for a while.*)

Comments of Observer

Since Mother was busy writing, her comments to Stanley were necessarily brief. His interest span was therefore short because he had no encouragement for continuing his interest in any one thing for long. Many different aspects of child behavior are illustrated, some with more than one example:

Sense of accomplishment and of power	In opening and closing the telephone pad
	In opening the door
	In closing the sofa bed
Attempt to gain understanding	By asking what each person is doing
	By asking what the robin is doing
	By proposing that Daddy unhooked the screendoor
Expression of joy	At the robin getting a worm
	At seeing the book in the sofa bed

Creativity	Getting his toy telephone
	Opening the screendoor
	Explaining why he closes the screendoor
	Explaining why the screendoor was not fastened
Attempts to get attention	Asks questions
	Does unpermitted things (e.g., tears page out of telephone pad)
Expression of affection	Leans over to say "Hi" to Mummy, and bumps her forehead
Doing what is socially acceptable	Returns book to shelf
	Closes screendoor to keep out flies
Expression of autonomy	Gets the book from the sofa bed himself
	Tries to close sofa bed by himself

A recorded observation such as this is much more useful for understanding the behavior of a child than the information asked for on a standard form. The observational record of two-year-old Stanley can be compared with excerpts from another record—a detailed two-page form dealing with motor, intellectual, social, and emotional development, and developed for use in an adult education class for mothers.

Recorder's Name: *Stanley's mother*   Child's Name: *Stanley*

A. Description of child	1. Age: 2 years 8 months
	2. General build: Slender
	3. General health: Excellent
	4. Energy and tendency to fatigue: Plenty of energy. Does not nap during daytime.
B. Motor development	1. Large muscle:
	2. Small muscle:
	(a) Dressing and undressing: Not at all, except perhaps one sleeve of a sweater
	(b) Handling materials such as hammer, nails, scissors, balls, and paints: Enjoys all these.
C. Intellectual development	1. Memory:
	(a) Remembering procedures and routines: Very little memory of events more than a few months passed but does remember routines of weekly or daily activities
	(b) Recalling songs and stories: . . .
	2. Concentration:
	(a) Length of attention span: Generally short, but quite long over a puzzle or dramatic play

(b) Is child easily distracted from activity?:
Not as easily as his brother
3. Curiosity: Asks many questions and investigates
4. Reasoning: Very little

This second record about Stanley is greatly influenced by the opinions of the observer, and is therefore useful only in terms of these. It can be used by a preschool or an adult education instructor in conjunction with the first direct record as a basis for a personal conference with Stanley's mother, and can be the basis for raising such questions as the following:

- Do you think Stanley should be more independent in dressing and undressing, or do you think that he is not ready yet for such responsibility?
- Is Stanley's memory typical of that expected at his age level?
- How do Stanley and his brother compare?
- Do you know what psychologists have found out about the age at which children begin to display the ability to reason?

By discussing such questions with a parent in a private interview, the preschool teacher or the adult education instructor can help the parent to understand her child and the characteristics of most children of his age level.

Students, parents, and teachers of preschool children should make a direct record of a child's behavior as a means of increasing their understanding of children. The experienced teacher of preschool children, who has perfected her ability to record child behavior accurately and objectively, can work with record forms herself but she should encourage students, parents, and assistant teachers to make only direct records. If she also makes direct records of the behavior of each child, she can use these records in group as well as individual situations to help students, parents, and assistant teachers to understand the children and to become better observers, and to help staff members to improve their ability to guide preschool children effectively.

SEPARATING OBSERVATIONS FROM EVALUATIONS

Both Chapter 2 and this chapter have emphasized the importance of keeping observations of child behavior entirely separate from interpretations of that behavior. Observations are recorded while the child is active; interpretations are made later, on the basis of what was recorded. This separation of observation and interpretation helps the observer to separate herself from her usual role as teacher or parent—a role which emphasizes the ultimate goal of education, far removed from its beginnings in the preschool group. Both teachers and parents are adults with responsibility for maintaining the mores and passing on the cultural heritage. Often they are eager to have children grow up more rapidly than is possible, and their feelings of frustration at a "slow" pace give rise to negative interpretations of child behavior and such derogatory labels as "bad," and "failure." The overexpectations of teachers and parents can easily slip into their reports about preschool children unless they develop an awareness of this tendency. One mother observer reported that Timmy's older sister, Mary, had tried to teach him how to write his name and the number *1*. But when Timmy made the *1* crooked, "Mary thought that it was bad that he couldn't make it straight." This report was in keeping with her subsequent comment, "I'm afraid Timmy isn't as far along as the other nursery children. Robert's mother was telling me that he reads and writes now."

To help Timmy's mother and other mothers to appreciate their children's development and to feel confident in their roles as mothers, the teachers should encourage them to observe their own children and other children of the same age. But the observations must be objective recordings of what the child said and did, not slanted in terms of what the observer might expect of someone older.

Here are some examples of statements that may occur in observation records when the adult's point of view rather than the child's is uppermost in the thinking of the observer:

He does not tussle for play but makes moves to hurt.
Dianne is such a sweet child. She was so cute the way she said, "Come see."
Tommy grabbed my shirt and practically tore it off.
He deliberately left the wagon right where someone could trip over it.

As participants continue to observe children, trying to record objectively and vividly what the children say and do, such statements gradually disappear from their records, and they become more skillful in seeing what the children are doing and saying, and subsequently in comparing that behavior with their own expectations about what it ought to be. During this learning process, participants should have many opportunities to use good records that are free from editorial comment and to use the records which they themselves have been making. The observer whose records are not used is apt to find some more satisfying activity. But the observer who finds her records of interest to the teacher and to other observers is encouraged to continue her recording. The use of observational records as material for discussions in parent education groups stimulates further recording, promotes improvement in recording technique, and leads to greater use of the records themselves.

Making Anecdotal and Time Recordings

When participants begin to record their observations of children, they usually are asked both to make a time record of what an individual child does and says, and also to make a record of significant anecdotes. The following excerpt from a handbook for parents in cooperative nurseries[2] gives suggestions about how to make such records:

> . . . observations may be recorded either as brief but significant anecdotes, or as a running account of what was done over a given time interval—for instance, twenty minutes. The anecdotal observations are especially appropriate for studying social and emotional development; the time recording, for studying physical and mental development. When made over several weeks, such observations and recordings are easily developed into a mini-case study of a child. . . .

Anecdotal Observations

Suggestions for making anecdotal observations:
1. Write descriptively and vividly what actually happens.
   (a) Record conversations.
   (b) Note social contacts.
   (c) Record signs of emotional reactions. Include negative expressions of hostility, aggression, resentment, anger, guilt, as well as expressions of joy, pleasure, sympathy, affection, and so on.
2. Record the age of each child, and give the setting of the situation.
3. Use as expressive and specific words as possible—e.g., "Diana *patted* the clay," rather than: "Diana *played* with the clay."
4. Report *what* the child does and *how* he does it—e.g., "With a big smile, Tommy rode the hobby horse."
5. Separate descriptions of what was said and done from interpretations.
Example of an anecdotal observation:

What Child Says and Does	*What Teacher Says and Does*	*Interpretation*
Tommy, age 3, tried to push Peggy, age 2½ off the Cal's Colt. Peggy screamed in anger.	Teacher said to Tommy: "You go ride the steamroller until Peggy is ready to give you a turn."	Tommy is learning to accept substitute activities. Such learning is usual at his age, . . . and happens once or twice a day now for Tommy.
Tommy got on the steamroller cheerfully.		

Time Recordings

Suggestions for making time recordings:
1. Record everything that the child does and says for at least 20 or 30 minutes, in order to obtain an accurate picture of a child's behavior pattern.
2. Give the age of the child, and the setting for the child's activities.

[2] Vivian Edmiston Todd, ed., *Cooperative Nursery School Handbook* (Long Beach, Calif.: Long Beach Council of Cooperative Nurseries, 1957), pp. 27–30.

3. Report vividly and specifically both what the child does and how he does it. Put any interpretations in a separate column.

EXAMPLE:

Child: Laura, age 2 years and 7 months, a second child whose brother is 4 years old. She is small for her age and young for the cooperative nursery group. She is just beginning to play alongside other children and takes little part in cooperative play. She is most happy playing alone, especially in the doll corner where she enjoys a richly imaginative play.

Situation: The beginning twenty minutes of nursery school on a Monday morning in March.

What Child Does and Says	*Interpretation*
Laura arrives at nursery school carrying a soft doll. She runs in merrily and makes straight for the doll corner. She puts the doll in a chair at the play table; then goes to the stove and fetches a cup and saucer and bangs the cup over the doll's mouth. On her way back to the stove with the cup and saucer, she finds the stethoscope, and puts it into her ears and sounds her doll's chest. Then she makes for the ironing board and goes back and forth with the iron for a few brief moments. Then Laura dances off and gets the Taylor Tot, puts her doll in it, wraps a blanket around, and wheels it in. Next she takes the sweeper and sweeps back and forth for a few seconds. Then she spies the baby buggy a little way off beside the blocks. She piles several blocks into the doll buggy and wheels them over to the Taylor Tot. She tries awkwardly to pile the blocks on the Taylor Tot. Then she runs off to get the ball. She runs with the ball toward the sandpile where Alan is digging. She finds 3 pie plates which she fills with sand. After patting them out, she puts them in the wheelbarrow and wheels them away a short distance. Knowing it is time for the train to pass, the other children run to the net. Laura goes too, wedges herself in and waves, "Bye-bye." She discovers Neil busy painting wood. "Me paint," she exclaims. She goes to the woodbox for a piece of wood. She dons a painting apron, gets some blue paint, paints side of the wood, turns it over and paints the reverse side and then runs to get another piece of	Laura is well adjusted to nursery school; is ready and eager to come

Imaginative and imitative play

Motor activity

Parallel play (a little)

Made social contacts

Parallel play

Creative play
Learning to use paint on wood |

What Child Does and Says	*Interpretation*

wood. She finds the hammer in the woodbox and hammers the painted piece 2 or 3 times: then puts it back in the box and starts painting again. Neil, who is busy painting, stops and turns over her wood: "You forgot this side, Laura." She says nothing but goes on painting her second piece of wood. Then gets another and another which she paints rapidly and sketchily. Neil remarks, "I'm busy painting." She says, "I was painting too." She finds the hammer again and hammers the wood several times. Neil says, "I'm all through, Laura." She says, "I'm all through. too." They take off their painting aprons and go inside to wash their hands.

Self-absorption of a typical two-year-old
Independence and initiative
Conversation
Beginnings of three-year-old self-awareness
Parallel play

CONDUCTING A GROUP OBSERVATION

Participants who are learning how to observe a children's group should have guidance in what to observe. This guidance can be given before, during and after the observation both by the teacher of the children's group and by the adult education leader. Before the observation, the observers can discuss what they will look for and prepare to focus their attention on particular kinds of child or teacher behavior. After the observation, they can describe what they were able to observe and plan how better to use their next observation period. During the observation, the teacher may encourage them to notice particular behavior as she calls attention to a problem or to a praiseworthy deed. Or the observers may be guided by their own adult education leader, perhaps by comments written quickly and quietly on a chalkboard or on large sheets of paper, or flashed on cards prepared in advance.

When participants are observing a teacher who is working with a group of preschool children, their observations are influenced not only by their adult education leader but also by the teacher herself. How a teacher may modify her plans in terms of the needs of the observers is illustrated by the following description a teacher wrote about an incident which occurred at the conclusion of her demonstration of musical activities for a group of four-year-old children:

The children had used musical instruments, marched around the room, and sung songs of their own composition. At that point, one of the boys left the group in order to play with the interlocking blocks at the side of the room.

The boy's mother, one of the observers of the demonstration, seemed disturbed that her boy was not participating in the children's group activity. She went over to him to ask him to please come back into the circle. He said, "No."

At this point, the teacher had to choose among several alternative courses of action. Should she enforce the rule that children either participate in the music circle or play outdoors? Should she continue with the group activity and plan to use the adult discussion period later for explaining her choice between giving attention to the group or the individual child? Or should she go over and talk with the boy, or let him and his mother work out their own solution?

In terms of the greatest good of the greatest number of people, her choice was clear. She continued with the group musical activity, but, noting the fatigue of the one child, she went on quickly to the final action song she had planned to use that morning.

Later, with the group of observers, the demonstration teacher was able to capitalize on the incident to bring out several points about children, including the following:

A child shifts to a familiar activity when he has had enough of an adult-centered activity. His doing so is one evidence of fatigue.

A child can play quietly and without adult direction when he carries on a familiar activity such as block building for a four-year-old child.

The teacher was also able to remind the observers of the rule that a child plays outdoors unless he is participating in the group activity, and that the responsibility for enforcing that rule has to be in the hands of those assisting the teacher.

Another time, the demonstration teacher might choose to work briefly with the individual boy in order to demonstrate that an adult-centered children's group will continue to function as a group only so long as the adult is giving the group her complete attention, although five-year-old children can continue with a substitute leader for a time.

In such ways the teacher helps to provide a clearcut situation for participants to observe. By being aware of the needs of the observers as well as those of the children, the teacher can handle the children's group for both the good of the parents and that of the children. Through the choices that she makes about what to do with the children, she can illustrate for the observers fundamental principles and rules about working with a group of children.

In the group discussion following an observation period, an adult education leader often takes charge of guiding the discussion. She may review briefly the succession of observed events in order to be sure that everyone has noticed important points, but she should keep in mind that a long listening period for the observers is apt to interfere with the spontaneity of their subsequent discussion. She should encourage the observers to feel that their questions and other contributions to the discussion are respected and appreciated.

The leader of the observer group, as well as the teacher of the children's group, should avoid labeling behavior as "good" or "bad," and should emphasize stimulus-and-response relationships. Each should describe with precision the behavior that occurred, and then point out possible explanations for it. Each should be sensitive to comments and questions that indicate an unfavorable evaluation of children. When someone says, for instance: "That little boy with the dirty face was shoving other children around," the leader can call attention to the importance of trying to understand a child's behavior from the point of view of the child rather than from the standpoint of adult standards of cleanliness and acceptable behavior.

A teenager and a preschool child can relate to each other. (Courtesy of San Marcos High School, Santa Barbara, California.)

Initial Experience as a Participant

Getting acquainted with a preschool group in order to help with the teaching of it requires considerable time. The prospective assistant or aide must learn the location of supplies and equipment, the usual daily program and its major variations, and the names and personalities of the children and their teacher. Until an assistant feels sufficiently at home with the physical and social aspects of the nursery school or kindergarten, she is not ready to give her fullest attention to learning the techniques of working effectively with individual children and with small groups of them.

BEGINNING HURDLES

Admiring the skill with which a well-trained teacher handles a preschool group, one is tempted to inquire about her initial experience as an aide or assistant. In one parent-cooperative nursery group, the competent teacher in charge had been, six years before, the new mother-assistant who consistently teetered into the school on high heels, dressed as if she were going out to an afternoon tea. The other mother-assistants had usually done part of her work as well as their own. At the mothers' meetings they did the talking while she sat quietly listening. Yet her minimal experience as a mother assistant was sufficient to interest the new mother in becoming the leader of a preschool group in another community.

Another leader in preschool education describes her early experiences as an assistant this way:

My memory of my first day at nursery school is simply a memory of chaos in which the calm figure of the teacher offered the only measure of stability. Little children darted here and there in all directions.

I soon learned that an assistant can take refuge in the kitchen. Only adults are permitted in the kitchen. From this vantage point she can peer out from time to time to see what is happening. Whenever an adult enters, she can putter busily with refreshments or the inevitable cutting of paper for craft projects.

By the middle of the year my peerings had made me aware that the chaos was taking on some evidences of organization. Furthermore, I had located a few other places besides the kitchen where I could go from time to time and give the impression of being a helpful assistant putting equipment away.

But my temporary security with things was not to last long. It was decided that each aide would provide an activity for the children as she had her turn in assisting the teacher. Two weeks later, armed with a slinky steel spring, I gathered together my first small group of children. As I was about to start showing them how the spring worked, one of them grabbed it. It went quickly from small hands to small hands. By the time I managed to retrieve it, it was hopelessly entangled. I beat a hasty and ignominious retreat while the sympathetic teacher took the group into more appropriate activities.

From such beginning experiences it is clear that the assistant has as her initial hurdles the tasks of

- Learning to feel at home with a group of preschool children.
- Becoming acquainted with the supplies, equipment, and activities of a nursery school or kindergarten.
- Developing interest in the growth and development of preschool children, especially through group experience.

Later in the year she should be able to help the teacher, not only with the care of the children, but with their development, too. Gradually she should acquire skill in guiding activities of small groups of children as well as those of individual children. The extent to which she develops the interests, skills, and understandings desirable in working with preschool children will depend on her individual abilities.

Supervision of Assistants to the Teacher

In the parent-cooperative nursery school or kindergarten, the teacher of the children and the chairman of the mothers usually take responsibility for helping parents to be assistants to the teacher. In adult education or collegiate programs, the supervisor for the teacher assistants may or may not also be the teacher of the children. The advantage of having one person work with the parents and another with the children is that each needs to be expert at working with one age level only. Very few teachers are expert with two age levels. Working at the calm, slow pace desirable for preschool children is very different from working at the pace required for eager adults. To be expert in working both with preschool children and with adults of differing expertness requires much practice in each pace, and in changing pace too. It is easier to work either with preschool children or with adults of one maturity level than with both.

When the supervisor of teacher assistants is a person other than the teacher, both persons must work together closely so that the assistants are not confused by differences of opinion.

Both the teacher of the children and the supervisor will find that clarity is the result when each explains his views to the other members of the parent group in terms of the needs of children and effective ways of meeting those needs. Differences of opinion lead to difficulties in human relationships, when they are expressed and supported in terms of personal preferences rather than objectivity about children's problems.

The person supervising the work of assistants must keep it in mind that many young people are themselves still resolving personal problems of rebellion against parents and other figures of authority. She should therefore avoid making suggestions on the basis of her authority as a teacher; rather, she should point out to her assistants the cause-and-effect relationships observable in the children's behavior. As often as possible, she should realistically praise what they do. She should encourage them in assuming responsibility as rapidly as they feel ready for it.

Here are suggestions the supervisor of assistants can follow to help them develop a pleasant working atmosphere.

1. Confer individually with each assistant teacher or student aide at least once every two weeks. This gives each of them a chance to air her ideas or her problems and gives you feedback on their progress as well as that of the preschool children.

2. Identify what children in the preschool group need to learn and what the assistants, or aides, need to learn.
3. At the next meeting of assistants, or aides, present the problem that underlies what is to be learned. Analyze the problem objectively. If possible, arrive at a policy for the group.
4. Feel free to call the advisor for the preschool program. (If possible, a preschool program should have an advisor—a specialist in child growth and development, group dynamics, and preschool education.)
5. Do not rush to solve the problem. Give it much thought, much discussion, and consideration. Take it up from all sides. After a path of action has been agreed upon by the group, stand by the group decision. Do not expect immediate operation of the new policy; setbacks often occur during adult as well as child learning.

The person supervising assistants must know how to help each one use whatever talents she has for the good of the group. The supervisor must be able to work with new assistants who come into the preschool group for the first time, as well as with experienced volunteers. She must be able to enjoy working with assistants who have given little or no prior thought to the problems of preschool children as well as with those who may have spent years in the study of child development and psychology.

Inducting New Assistants

The new assistant coming into the preschool group often finds her first security in using her housekeeping skills. Later she moves on to using and enlarging her skill with children as individuals interacting with one or two other children; gradually she acquires skill in working effectively with larger groups of children. If she is interested in becoming a teacher, she must become highly skilled in working with groups of a few children and with all the children as a large group. But if her interests are only those of a parent, practising or prospective, she need only come to a fuller understanding of individual children, acquiring skill in guiding individual development. The important aim, then, of the person supervising the work of assistants is less the improvement of their skills in handling large groups of children than the improvement of their skills in working with children as individuals and small groups of, say, two or three.

To get assistants quickly over the initial hurdles of becoming acquainted with the physical arrangements of the preschool group and with the members of the group, the supervisor takes these steps:

1. Acquaints the new assistants with the purposes of preschool education, especially those for the age level with which they will work.
2. Becomes both personally acquainted and friendly with each new assistant so that she will feel comfortable in discussing any problem she may encounter.

3 Discusses the importance of a course (e.g., Guiding Children's Growth) that will enrich and interpret the experiences each assistant will have with the children. If necessary, helps plan transportation to attend the course.

A participant does name writing but not painting. (Courtesy of San Marcos Parent Child Workshop, San Marcos High School, Santa Barbara, California.)

4. Plans for regular meetings of the assistants. Decides on the time and place of meetings. If necessary, helps plan transportation for each mother to attend the first meeting.
5. Introduces the new assistants to the experienced mother-assistants. Arranges for each new mother-assistant to have an experienced mother-assistant as a "big sister."

An assistant learns when a child does and does not need help. (Courtesy of California State College at Long Beach and Mariam M. Cook, Long Beach, California.)

6. Helps the new assistant to schedule her first two visits to the preschool group: the first, by herself for the purpose of getting acquainted with the program of activities and the methods used by the teacher, and with the personnel of the children's group; a subsequent visit for the purpose of observing at least one child in relation to the group, and for reviewing and enlarging her earlier observations.
7. Arranges to be at the school on the day that each new assistant helps the teacher with the children for the first time. Makes sure that the assistant is familiar with the locations of supplies and equipment, is familiar with the bulletin board and the postings on it concerning the program and activities of the children, and knows the names of the children in the group.

CAPITALIZING ON EXPERIENCED ASSISTANTS

Experienced assistants are a valuable resource, especially in helping new assistants to learn their role and in assisting the teacher during the time that new assistants are developing the skills of their job.

During the first weeks of the school term, an experienced assistant probably will act as a "big sister" to an incoming mother. She may go with her to the school to show her where equipment and supplies are kept, to help her learn the names of the children, and to explain the routine operation of the school and the responsibilities of assistants. The day the new aides or assistant is scheduled to assist the teacher, her "big sister" should be one of the team of experienced assistants that day. When the "big sister–new assistant" combinations are a mutual selection, both find the experience rewarding—the new assistant or aide receives help which she needs; the experienced assistant has the satisfaction of contributing to the development of a new assistant or aide.

Sometimes the volunteer who has several children may have had so much preschool experience that she will seem to be only going through the motions unless the teacher can reawaken her to the delights of watching a small child learn, and of working with others in helping the preschool group. The wise teacher is sensitive to the interests of such a mother. She gives her opportunity to make use of her understandings, but avoids loading her with what she may regard as drudgery.

When the participant has developed skill in working with individual children and is ready to explore the handling of children in large as well as small groups, the wise teacher helps her to become sensitive to the importance of group techniques. The teacher gives her opportunity to read and tell stories to a group of children, and presently to carry a group of children through a transition period between one group activity and another—perhaps with finger plays, simple physical stunts, or a song. As the participant gains skill in handling groups, the teacher helps her to plan and carry through educational projects— perhaps a nature walk, or a craft activity. When the participant has also taken responsibilities for the period of rest and refreshments and the putting-away period at the end of school, she probably feels ready to be recognized as an assistant capable of taking the group through an entire school session.

The teacher who works well with experienced assistants should know how to step out of her teacher role while the assistant assumes the responsibility of being the teacher. The regular teacher of a group of children may say to them, "Today Lorna is going to take you on a nature walk while I help the State Supervisor, who is visiting us today. Lorna is going to be your teacher today." The teacher then refers any child who comes to her to Lorna, perhaps by saying, "Lorna will help you. She is your teacher today." Thus the regular teacher releases the children so that they will respond to their teacher-of-the-day.

An experienced assistant and one of the new aides took responsibility for the rest period of a newly formed nursery school group while the regular teacher and assistants discussed activities of the children. The assistant described this experience as follows:

Neither of us knew any of the children's names, nor where the blankets for the cots were kept. I said to the children, "I need a helper. Can you help me find your blankets?" The children all knew where to get their blankets and brought them to me. Soon the children were all resting on their cots.

Someone came in, turned on the record player, and then left. The music was the wrong kind for resting, and the children were up again in half a minute. I turned the record player off. I told the children to lie down and I would sing them a "birdie" song.

After I sang the song about "the little birds sleeping," I went to each child (my "birds"), rubbed his back and quietly commented about something he was wearing or said, "Johnny-bird is resting." The children who were not yet on their cots lay down voluntarily so that I would come around to them, too. (This device usually works, but not always.) I sang two other resting songs, and everyone was quiet temporarily. One boy went to sleep. My voice is not very good, but the children did not seem to notice that.

Ten minutes later a little girl said, "I have to go potty," and a little boy added, "Me, too." Another boy said he wanted to go. The three children and I tiptoed into the bathroom "quiet as little mice." One boy and girl took care of themselves, but the other boy looked at me without any expression and said, "It's a trap." I interpreted this to mean that his clothes were too difficult for him to unfasten by himself. I asked him if I could help him. He nodded his head "yes." The other boy said, "I wet my pants, but not today." He was proud of the fact that he was able to take care of his own needs. I told him I thought he did a fine job today.

The rest period was about a half-hour long. Then many of the children were eager for some activity. They helped us put away their blankets. Then we helped them put on their sweaters and jackets and go outdoors to play.

This description shows how an experienced assistant expects and gets help from the children at the same time that she helps them. Her confidence enables her to go ahead with what must be done, even though what she needs is not at hand or the wrong equipment has been brought for her use.

SCHEDULES FOR ASSISTANTS

The teacher should give assistants written suggestions in addition to the verbal suggestions she makes during the school session. Written suggestions given in advance of the session help the assistants in making the mental map and schedules which will help them to assist as needed. Such written suggestions also reduce the suggestions that need to be made in the course of a session, and increase the adult attention given to the children.

Each teacher should plan her schedules of activities to be congenial for the children, for her assistants, and for herself. At the outset of the school year she writes out a more detailed schedule than she will prepare after the assistants have become familiar with the school, the children, and her ways of working with them.

Mrs. McNeil was the teacher for a group of three- and four-year-old children. Because fifteen children were enrolled in the group, she had two assistants each day. Before the first meeting of the children, she prepared a tentative draft of the schedule for each of the assistants and herself (shown in Table 18-1). At the meeting held prior to the opening of school,

TABLE 18-1. Schedule of Community Cooperative Nursery

TIME	ACTIVITY OF:			
	Children	Teacher	First Assistant	Second Assistant
8:45		Prepare room and playground	Put juice in refrigerator Put out cups and napkins Put towels, soap in both bathrooms Open windows Start children on play activities Supervise paints	Open playhouse (Sweep if needed) Put toys in playground Get out hammers and paints
9:00	Arrival, greetings Health inspection Toileting	Greet people Make health inspection Supervise play Initiate games		Supervise carpentry
9:40			Put away toys.............................	
9:50	Toileting, handwashing Refreshments	Supervise refreshments	Help children with toileting and handwashing Help with juice	Get out blankets
10:10	Rest	Supervise rest	Clean up after refreshments	Get out equipment for quiet play (e.g., clay, puzzles, crayons, beads)
10:30	Rhythms	Supervise rhythms	Assist teacher	Supervise quiet play
10:45	Story time	Tell stories	Prepare craft materials (e.g., finger paint, clay, paper and scissors, crayons)	Get out children's aprons
11:00	Creative craft activity	Supervise craft activity	Talk nondirectively with each child	
11:20	Put toys away Prepare to go	Supervise departure	Put toys away	Help children wash hands
11:30		Supervise cleanup	Clean up	

Cleanup: Sweep the floors; wash tables; clean up kitchen (if not already done); arrange chairs; close windows; clean bathrooms; put away soap and towels; remove finger marks from woodwork.

641

she went over the schedule in detail with the assistants and incorporated into it revisions favored by the group.

Although the original schedule developed in the fall of the year continued to be posted on the bulletin board, the assistants gradually became independent of it. Their mental maps and schedules were sufficient reminders of what to do. Every morning the first of the two assistants to arrive made her choice of roles, then discussed her choice with the other assistant. She might say, "Hello, Jane. I've started with the kitchen work. Would you like to supervise outdoors while I supervise indoors?" As the

Understanding child behavior develops through participation in child projects. (Courtesy of the Minneapolis Public Schools and Mrs. Mary Jane Higley.)

assistants and teacher worked during the morning, they helped each other. Sometimes they worked together, moving heavy equipment or quickly completing necessary preparations. At the end of the morning, they usually expressed their mutual appreciation: "I enjoyed working with you," "We were a good team today," or, "We certainly had a good day."

How Assistants Work with Individual Children

In an ongoing preschool group, an assistant who has visited the school, observed the children, and worked as assistant to the teacher three or four times usually has become familiar with the locations of supplies and equipment and with the usual sequence of activities. She should know the name of each child; she should be acquainted with several of the children individually. Next she should focus her attention on the skills that the teacher and experienced assistants use in meeting the needs of individual children. As she gradually develops these skills herself, she will further her understanding of the behavior of the children with whom she works. With increased understanding she will be able to expand her skill further.

GENERAL SUGGESTIONS

Assistants should first learn those techniques which are useful in working with most children most of the time. If such techniques are provided in written form, they can refer to them from time to time. Here are suggestions formulated out of the experience of assistants for one or more years:

1. Make positive suggestions; e.g.: "Sand hurts our eyes," "We play over here," "We climb on the jungle gym."
2. In making a suggestion, enter the mood and the imaginative play of the child. Give the child time to respond. For example: "After Mother finishes tucking dolly in bed, she goes to the bathroom."
3. Be calm, quiet, and relaxed; speak in a low tone of voice. Avoid quick or hurried movements.
4. Be cheerful. Cultivate a sense of humor. Cultivate a warm, sympathetic attitude.
5. Be on the job at all times. Talk with other adults only when absolutely necessary.
6. Be alert to potential physical hazards, such as nails lying on cement or sticking out of boxes.
7. Anticipate and prevent difficulties. Try to forsee what a child is going to do. When necessary, give constructive and preventive directions.
8. Avoid punishing a child; do not make him feel guilty.
9. Observe how the children are affected by what the teacher does and says.[3]

Assistants should have an initial meeting with the teacher to discuss how to work with the children. In order to encourage them in relating theory to practical situations, the teacher in one nursery prefaced an initial discussion with these remarks:

I should like to discuss "The Assistant in the Nursery School," with a view to preparing ourselves for the challenging job of creating for our children an enriching group experience.

[3] Todd, op. cit., p. 23.

Briefly, and in a very general way, we must first define our objectives, and then we may proceed from there in our discussion to explore the ways in which each of you, as an assistant, can help to accomplish these objectives.

First, then, our school places major emphasis on the individual. It is our aim to provide a climate that is conducive to the healthful growth of each child, emotionally, socially, mentally, and physically.

Second, it is our aim to help him fit his individual development in with his first large-group experience, without pressure to mold him. The conformity or limitations imposed by this new social experience are flexible and gentle, allowing each child to integrate and relate with the group *when* he is ready and in his own way.

Third, we desire that each child have an opportunity to develop confidence in himself as an individual by playing and working in a situation geared specifically to his capacity and potential. Your suggestions to a child should keep in mind his level of development.

Fourth, we desire to make the nursery group experience one of warmth and love and mutual understanding.

Fifth, we will provide opportunity and environment to encourage the development of some skills, but we have no aim to hurry. When Johnny or Suzy has a taste or inclination to learn to cut, or build, or paint, the material will be there. These skills, which the children will develop will be of service to them, will help to give them some sense of fulfillment, and will contribute to their feeling of self-confidence, but there will be no pressure brought to bear on developing techniques. When the child is ready, the opportunity and help are given.

Now, how does the assistant help to achieve these things in our school?

Helping an Aggressive Child

As the assistant continues working with preschool children, she has to cope with the aggressive child whose activity requires immediate adult guidance, both for his own good and for the good of the group. When an assistant starts remarking about how aggressive behavior was handled by the teacher, or asks about what to do when a child grabs a toy away from another child, or takes his turn ahead of time, the assistant is ready to make use of written suggestions about helping the child who is aggressive, and to discuss anecdotal material about adult responses to aggressive child behavior. Here are some suggestions formulated by experienced mothers and teachers to help assistants as they react to aggressive child behavior.[4]

1. Accept the child as he is. Help him find a suitable outlet for his hostility. For example: "You feel like hitting something. We don't hit people. What is there for you to hit?"
2. Interpret aggressive behavior to the child attacked. For instance: "Johnny did not mean to push you. He was trying to catch the ball."
3. Encourage the children to tell each other how they felt. Do not force them to say they are sorry.

[4] Ibid., pp. 23–25.

4. Encourage older children to be sympathetic and to help the other child become happy again.
5. Help hostile children to play in small groups if they need to exclude others.

Illustrative Anecdotes

WHAT HAPPENED	INTERPRETATION
Andrea, age two years and four months, aggressively attempts to take doll away from Linda, age two years. Adult steps in and says to Andrea, "Let's go find another doll for you. Linda needs her dolly."	Aggresive child was helped to find a satisfactory substitute, and to respect property rights of others.
Bobby, age three, stick in hand, runs after Peggy, age three and one-half, who has taken a doll away from the play-house corner where they had been playing. Adult steps in and says to Bobby, "I know you're angry because Peggy took the doll away. It's all right for her to hold the doll for awhile. Let's go find the drum and pound it with the stick you have in your hand."	Adult accepted child's feelings, and helped him channel them in a releasing manner. The aggressive child drained off his feelings of hostility in an acceptable activity.
Tommy, age four, Linda, age four, and another child are sitting in the sandpile when Tommy takes Linda's shovel. Linda throws sand at Tommy, and he throws sand back at her. Adult says, "Sand hurts our eyes. Would you like to stay in the sandpile?" The children reply, "Yes." The adult says, "Then you will need to stop throwing sand. I shall help you get another shovel, Linda."	The adult accepted the children's aggressiveness, and helped them to understand the situation.

HELPING THE SHY CHILD

The assistant who observes a child behaving with shyness in the nursery or kindergarten situation is apt to seek advice about how to help him. Her interest can yield suggestions, such as the following, and anecdotal material about shy behavior for discussion.[5]

1. Help the shy child interpret the behavior of other children.
2. Help him form a close friendship with another child.
3. Have him come earlier to school, so that he can get used to the equipment without the complicating presence of other children.
4. Let him watch as long as he needs to.
5. Protect his dependence on a particular piece of equipment for his security: "Let Tommy have the doll. He *needs* it."
6. Encourage him to stand up for his rights.

---

[5] Ibid., pp. 25 and 26.

Illustrative Anecdotes

INTERPRETATION	WHAT HAPPENED
Dick, age two years and four months, is riding on a large Cal's Colt when Tommy, age three, comes over and attempts to push him off. Adult steps over and says to Dick. "Hold on. Don't let Tommy push you off." To Tommy the adult says, "When Dick has finished taking his turn, he will let you have a turn!"	The adult protected the shy child from an aggresor, giving him a boost and helping him stand up for his rights.
Joan, a timid three-year-old, is clutching a doll she has brought from home. Dick, age 3-and-one-half, tries to take it away from her. Adult says, "Joan needs this dolly. I'll help you find another one that you may hold."	The adult helped the shy child by protecting her exclusive rights to her "security" toy.
Susan, age four years, is in the sandpile putting sand in the tin pie plates by herself. She is a shy, reserved child who has not made many social contacts with the children. Adult says, "Would you like to choose a friend to help you bake your cakes?" Susan says "Yes," and suggests that she would like Gale to help her. Adult asks Gale to come help Susan bake her cakes.	The adult helped the shy child in forming a closer relationship with a child she likes.
Tommy, age four, greets the adult enthusiastically and then goes to music corner to play records. He stays there all alone. After awhile, the adult suggests, "Over here are some blocks just for you. Would you like to have someone help you build something?"	Tommy was helped to play with equipment along with another child. The adult recognized Tommy's need for companionship and helped him find it.

WHAT SHOULD AN ASSISTANT SAY?

The teacher or assistant should endeavor to establish rapport with as many of the children as possible each day. As soon as she can, she wants to have a bond of affection and understanding develop with each child. She therefore spends a few minutes entering the play of each child and sharing his experience with him. Here are situations which are apt to occur the first day that a child comes to a preschool group, together with examples of comments which an adult could make to reassure the child.

CHILD BEHAVIOR	ADULT REMARK
Actively explores situation after situation, going from one center of interest to another.	"Is that your special house? You just fit into it." "It's fun to ride a horse like that."
Stays in the place to which he was first taken until he is taken to a new center of interest.	"You've put the pieces all together. Would you like to try the slide now? I'll show you how."

CHILD BEHAVIOR	ADULT REMARK
Stands or sits in one play center, moving things around with his hands but watching what others are doing.	"What a lovely picture you have made. It's an all red one. Would you like to make another picture to take home?"
Plays with his parents as he would in a home situation with similar centers of interest.	"Would you and your mother like to read a story?"
Clings to his parent but watches what others are doing.	"Peek-a-boo. Where's Tommy? I don't see Tommy. Oh, there he is!"
Clings to parent and cries from time to time.	"What a pretty dress you have. It's yellow, just like your mother's."

Each adult in the preschool group, especially during the early meetings of the group, should try to help each child learn; for instance, that

- Our preschool group has many fascinating activities.
- Other mommies love me and help me the way my own mother does.
- Our mothers bring us and always come back for us to take us home.
- In a preschool group there is always water for drinks, juice time, bathrooms, and another mother to help us with them.
- Each time we come, the same toys are here—we can leave them, knowing that they will be here when we come back.

A new assistant to the teacher of a three-year-old group prepared for this responsibility by rereading "Three Years Old," Chapter 18 of *Infant and Child in the Culture of Today,* by Arnold Gesell and Frances Ilg. As she studied the material she organized it for her immediate use as shown below. She put down precise wordings, not because she expected to use them verbatim, but because they helped her in imagining what to do in the situations which might arise.

CHILD BEHAVIOR	ADULT REMARK
A child is slow about coming indoors.	"Do you want to come in the front door or the side door?"
Everyone but Mary has taken off his wraps.	"Is your dress a pink one?" or in a whisper, "Where do you put your sweater?"
A child is slow in finding a place to sit.	"You may sit here, next to John."
A group is slow in starting an activity.	"When we are all listening, I have a surprise for you."
A child is slow about choosing a crayon.	"Do you want blue or red?"
A boy wants to join the grocery store staff but is not welcomed.	"Here comes the deliveryman," or "Maybe John could be the box boy."
A child is watching others.	"You may help, too."
Two children want the same toy.	"Tom is using it now. Here is one for you to use."
A child becomes emotionally upset when asked to choose what to do.	"Let me tell you what we are going to do later this morning."

CHILD BEHAVIOR	ADULT REMARK
A child sprays water over the floor.	On the next day, remind the children about what to do: "Remember, we are going to keep the water in the basin."
A child hurts his finger.	"Next time we shall keep our hands to ourselves, won't we?"
A child says, "I'm hungry."	Look at watch or clock and say, "It's time to wash our hands and get ready for juice."
The children in the playhouse get into negative talk or conflict behavior.	"Is dinner ready?"
A child crawls under the table at which other children are sitting.	"We sit at the table."
The child persists in crawling over the legs of other children.	Remove the child, taking him to a place by himself. Explain that "You're bothering the other children."

WHEN SHOULD AN ASSISTANT OFFER HELP?

An assistant should quickly learn the obvious times to assist the teacher. The teacher tells her in advance the points at which certain supplies or equipment and assistance will be needed. The teacher makes it clear that a child leaving a group needs the attention and possibly the guidance of an assistant. But an assistant finds it more difficult to learn when to help an individual child, and when to move into a group of children at play. Learning to identify situations in which an adult is needed takes practice. Gradually an assistant becomes successful more often in catalyzing learning, and is less apt to be an interference to a child or a group working on their own problems.

The new assistant is likely to be self-conscious. Feeling that she should be actively doing something, she may busy herself awkwardly or take attention away from the children by asking the teacher, "What shall I do now?" As she feels more at home in the preschool group situation, her attention shifts from herself to the children. She learns to observe the children's play, listen to its hum, and calmly move into action when the movement or sound changes to a frequency that indicates loss of control.

In supervising play that the children choose, the assistant must learn that children are most apt to need supervision at the critical points—the beginning and termination—of an activity. She watches for those children who are nearing the end of an activity or have been engaged in one activity for a considerable time. She does not interrupt their play. She merely moves over within hearing range of the activity, and listens for indications that the children are tired of the activity. If voices rise to a higher pitch, if personal, negative remarks are made with force, or if an aggressive move is made, she is prepared to step into the play to help one or more of the children move on to other activities, or to needed rest or refreshments.

IMPROVING THE GUIDANCE OF INDIVIDUAL CHILDREN

During the school year the teacher should constantly encourage each assistant to share her problems with her and with the group of assistants.

The teacher should see that at least one or two problems are presented at the regular meetings of assistants and teacher. She should encourage these presentations to be made in the form of an anecdote—a brief account of what was said and what was done by a child, his playmates, and the adult nearest to the child. When no one has an actual incident to discuss, the teacher can present anecdotal material that she has accumulated from previous years. Usually, and especially at the beginning of the year, she should present only anecdotes recounting desirable adult behavior. During the discussion she should encourage the assistants to suggest alternate adult behavior. She should also encourage them to note any sequence of behavior such as the negative behavior of Don after his play had been interrupted by an older child:

Randy and Dale, four-and-one-half years old, were playing in the lovely wet sand in the sandbox, shaping and molding. Three-year-old Don, only a few months removed from early toilet training and still given to relieving himself out-of-doors, was playing with a cab and trailer, loading and carrying sand from one place to another. Randy tried to draw Don into play with Dale and him by saying, "Have some cake." Don went on silently with his own play, avoiding Randy's advances. Then Randy molded a little brown ball, and tried to get a reaction from Don by saying, "Have a BM." Don resented this, and started a fight. When Randy pressed sand against Don's lips, a mother-assistant intervened, saying, "Don does not want to play your games, Randy. He wants to play with the truck." She helped Don go and wash the sand out of his mouth. As he resumed his play of loading and unloading the truck and trailer, she seated herself on a bench near the sandbox.

Randy and Dale continued their sand-molding. Randy made a nice brown pie in a pie tin and brought it to the mother-assistant, saying, "Have some pie." She responded appreciatively: "Doesn't it smell *good.* though! My favorite pie!" and made appropriate eating motions.

Randy again tried to draw Don into the play. "Want some?" he asked Don, holding out a closed fist. Don pushed him away. Randy opened his hand and said, "See what it is? Nothing!"

Randy and Dale molded and "ate" pies enjoyably. Then Randy made one more attempt to play with Don. He showed Don how to pretend to eat. Presently he overplayed his part and got some sand in his mouth. The mother-assistant helped him go to the water fountain and rinse out his mouth.

When refreshments were announced, Randy and Dale left the sandbox, but Don insisted on staying longer. About five minutes later he arrived at the door with a load of sand in the truck trailer.

ASSISTANT   Oh, here's Don just in time for juice.

DON (*retreating*)   Don't want juice.

ASSISTANT   Your truck made the trip away over here. That was a good long trip. Now the driver is going to have a good rest and some juice. (*Don goes in with her for refreshments.*)

When assistants have acquired some skill in working with individual children, they should have occasional opportunity to discuss anecdotes which recount adult behavior that was not adequate to meeting the needs of the children, and to suggest alternative courses of action which might have prevented an accident like that reported in the following anecdote:

Florence joined the group in the sandbox. Presently the other children drifted away, leaving Florence and Sammy. These two four-year-old children were facing each other. Florence started throwing sand at Sammy. The assistant sitting on the bench nearby noticed that Sammy did not like the sand-throwing and that he said, "Quit!" When his repeated "Quit!" went ignored, the assistant stepped in front of Florence in such a way that Florence had to look at her directly. Then the assistant explained to Florence that when one person asks another to quit, he quits.

A few minutes later the assistant went over to the swings to help the children who had been asking for her help. Florence resumed the sand-throwing. Sammy again said, "Quit!" When Florence ignored Sammy's request and threw more sand, Sammy threw the metal toy in his hand. It hit Florence on the forehead, cut a gash, and made her cry.

Achieving Depth of Understanding of Children

An assistant establishes better rapport with individual children and comes to understand them more fully in proportion to the time she spends with the group. The assistant must understand that the depth of her relationship with a child depends on the frequency and the quality of her interaction with him.

RAPPORT THROUGH CARING FOR CHILDREN

When a new mother-assistant asks how to get started knowing a child, she is often told to try tying his shoelaces for him. This specific suggestion illustrates the broader concept that rapport with a child grows out of helping him with his problem. "Caring for a child" has a dual meaning: providing for his needs, especially his physical ones, and having an emotional tie with him. Parental love is in large measure the outgrowth of parental responsibility. Those who work as assistants in a preschool group should come to appreciate the fact that the children they especially like are the children they help most.

When an aide confides in the teacher that she "can't stand that little Smith boy with the runny nose," the teacher should make a point of helping the aide learn more about the Smith boy and his allergy problems. She also should provide opportunities for the aide to help Tommy Smith and praise her success in working well with him and winning his affection.

After several assistants have experienced a change in their attitude toward a child as a result of working with him and coming to know him better, the group of assistants can share their experiences with each other and come to realize the relationship between helping a child and loving him. This experience can help them to understand one of their great values as parents, caring for their own children and providing a secure affection within the family. Some may also realize that helping one's mate carry out projects of importance to him leads to increasing love between husband and wife.

Observing Individual Children

Assistants improve their understanding of children as they observe the behavior of a child and try to determine the factors associated with the behavior. Their understanding is aided by the recording of their observations. A recorded observation can be studied later by the assistant and her colleagues. Scrutiny of a sequence of observations recorded for one child makes it possible to broaden one's understanding of that child; under the guidance of someone who has studied child development in detail, such scrutiny is a springboard for interesting and educational discussions.

Regular Staff Meetings

Regular staff meetings of assistants and the teacher give the opportunity to learn new ideas to try out with the children, to appraise their own progress, and to report on what they have been learning. By sharing her experience with the others each assistant helps to accelerate the learning of the whole group.

One new assistant who confidently volunteered to take charge of finger painting reported on her experience this way:

I had the finger painting materials all ready for the children to use as soon as they came in from their play outdoors. As they entered, I helped each to find a place at the craft table.

Now, I should have had sense enough to leave them alone to explore a new medium of expression. But I felt that I was in charge and that I ought to be doing something. So I made the mistake of asking, "What are you going to paint? Why don't you paint a house?"

Marlene looked at me for a minute, and then said, "I don't know how."

Well, I missed that cue, but I plunged on, trying to be helpful. I started painting a house for Marlene. In a matter of minutes every child at the table had stopped his own painting and was watching me or was whining, "I don't know how to paint a house."

I don't know what I would have done if Mrs. McNab hadn't rescued me. She came up beside me and said quietly: "You're frustrating them." Well, I certainly could see that, so I let her take over.

Calmly she got the children started using the finger paints again. While they were busy covering paper and getting the feel of the painting, she reassured me and explained that preschool children don't paint "something." They just paint.

Next time I am to say to the children: "You may paint on the paper anyway that you want," and then let them alone to do just that.

Such a report helps the assistant making it as well as those hearing it: all are reminded of the importance of letting the children learn to do something by doing it themselves.

As a means of helping a group of assistants learn to report their experiences, an evaluative instrument, such as the one following, may be used as a basis for a staff-meeting discussion.

How to Help Billy

Here are four incidents out of Billy's experience in a nursery group. As an adult helping Billy's teacher, you are to do two things after reading each incident and the courses of action suggested for it:
1. Choose the one course of action that seems *best* to you. Put a checkmark in *front* of it.
2. Identify each course of action that seems *acceptable* to you. Put a checkmark *after* each such course of action.

Billy, an only child, is in the three-year-old nursery group. He is a tall, strong, husky youngster, well developed for his age. He lives a few blocks from the nursery. During the first week that Billy came to the nursery group, he explored the equipment, raced around on the tricycles whenever he could, and followed along with the group activities.

Monday of the second week you observed that Billy became more and more restless during story time. As you were helping with the preparations for the next and last activity of the morning, you saw Billy streaking across the street in the direction of his home. You should

_____	1. See that some adult slips out to catch Billy.	1. _____
_____	2. Call out that you are going after Billy, and run after him.	2. _____
_____	3. Ignore Billy's departure.	3. _____
_____	4. Tell the children that Billy is naughty to leave early.	4. _____
_____	5. Next day tell the children that no one is to run away.	5. _____

As Billy became more familiar with the nursery group, he started to play with other children, often hitting them. The morning you were on the playground during the time for children to choose their own activities, Billy and another boy started toward the favorite red tricycle at the same time. Billy pushed the other boy down and got on the tricycle. You should

_____	6. Tell Billy we hit the push bag but do not push people.	6. _____
_____	7. Get Billy started hitting the push bag.	7. _____
_____	8. Take the tricycle from Billy and give it to the other boy.	8. _____
_____	9. Send Billy to the "bad-boy" corner.	9. _____
_____	10. Put the red tricycle away for the rest of the morning.	10. _____

Billy continued pushing his way around the nursery group. Usually he was agreeable about it, but one morning in the third month of school his anger mounted as he tried unsuccessfully to become a part of the playhouse family. As you reached the playhouse door, Billy was pushing a tearful little girl out of it. You should

_____ 11. Have Billy see what he can do to make the little girl   11. _____
happy.

_____ 12. Tell Billy that he has made the little girl cry.   12. _____

_____ 13. Ask Billy why he did that.   13. _____

_____ 14. Tell the playhouse family not to let Billy play with   14. _____
them.

_____ 15. Tell Billy you are tired of having him push people   15. _____
around.

As the weeks passed, he fitted more and more smoothly into it. In his own way he tried to be helpful. One morning, as the group shifted from rest period to a craft activity, Billy noticed that Jimmy was slow in getting to his feet. Billy went over to him and started pulling him up by the head, choking him in the process. You should

_____ 16. Show Billy how to help a person get up.   16. _____

_____ 17. While Jimmy lies down, have Billy and others fan   17. _____
him.

_____ 18. Tell Billy: "Stop that!"   18. _____

_____ 19. Tell the children they will have the craft activity   19. _____
another day.

_____ 20. Tell Billy never to do such a thing.   20. _____

Discussion of the responses they have made on the evaluative instrument should help the assistants to distinguish those courses of action which are helpful both to Billy and to the other children; those helpful to Billy but affecting the other children little, if at all; those inimical to Billy's well-being in the group; those which are more in accord with adult than children's views; and those typical of the responses made by adults who have not studied child development.

IN-SERVICE EDUCATION OF TEACHERS AND CONSULTANTS

Of what value is a preschool laboratory situation in a workshop or college course for experienced preschool teachers and consultants? Clearly those who work with preschool children are not greatly in need of further experience in the skills of caring for children and working with them as individuals and in groups. Their time can be better spent than in getting a group of preschool children organized and functioning as a group. What they do need however, is an opportunity to check their thinking about children against the latest psychological and educational theories and against the thinking of others who work with preschool children. They have had much laboratory experience with preschool children; they need to interpret that experience with the help of resource people as well as with that of their fellow workers.

Of course, teachers and consultants should have records of their experiences in order to share them with their professors and classmates. If they have not developed skill in the observing and recording of significant behavior or in the recording of their interpretations of this behavior, they will need to develop these essential skills at once. An ongoing preschool laboratory situation is highly valuable, then, so that workshop and other students can practice the objective recording of what children do and say, and can use their own records to supplement the existing records. By making and using records of child behavior, they can come to increase their understanding of children and to learn more effective ways of working with them.

The following record of observations was made by a preschool teacher when she became aware of her need to develop skill in recording observations. With the record are listed some of the comments or questions which can be used by an adult education teacher or by a supervisor of teachers to help his students to progress as teachers.

OBSERVATIONS	LEADS FOR FURTHER STUDY
March 14. Twenty-two children present. Indian hats made; side decoration for Janet, Ann. Finger painting—Ann, Janet, Sharon, Rose.	
Crayons—Judy. Judy said Alice and Susan made fun of her. Alice, Susan cut hearts and pasted them on paper; Robert, a pumpkin.	Observations such as these are a basis for planning subsequent craft activities
Two easel paintings.	Is this observation worth recording?
Puzzles by John, Sandy. Block-building of a zoo with reindeer, other animals—Jay, Doug.	How is creativity encouraged in children?
Susie and Randy played well in playhouse until cleanup, when they fought over a stuffed doll. Both wanted to put it away. Randy took the doll from Susie. Susie objected, followed Randy, and hurt him in the drum corner.	This paragraph is useful material for making a study of Susie
Randy cried hard but after sitting in the kitchen was ready to help sponge the tables. The doll was taken from Susie—she didn't cooperate well—no juice, and rest alone—didn't want to dress for outdoors, but finally did want to go outside before her mother left. (Susie's parents were gone Sunday for more than twelve hours to take an examination. Susie said she didn't want the babysitter again; pouted when mother said she'd have to have her Tuesday.)	Would you like to know more about emotions in children? What is cooperation?
Little Bear story enjoyed, although many children had extraneous comments. Alice and Susan both broke in with comments, loudly. Betty Jane drew	Children's reactions to stories are the basis for developing a list of stories suitable for each age level.

OBSERVATIONS	LEADS FOR FURTHER STUDY
close as she heard the story progress.	
Snack and rest followed a quick washup in basement. Susie, Betty both refused snack. Susie wanted to take cookies home.	More material about Susie.
Rest was quiet through *Liebestraum*. Interest in "In the Hall of the Mountain King" was great. Noise at end was not great enough to suit Brian.	Such observations can lead to a list of music suitable for resting, a list for music appreciation.

Usually, anecdotal and time observations of children are collected in folders under the name of each child in the laboratory group. These collections are useful to experienced teachers and consultants in learning how to make a case study of a child. They can see the various types of behavior to be observed in getting acquainted with the many facets of a child's personality. They can see the necessity of observing a particular facet at successive intervals in order to evaluate growth and development. They see from experience that several divergent interpretations can be made about a child's personality on the basis of observations of what he does and says. In short, recorded observations can be used in helping experienced workers to increase their understanding of children through case studies.

Recorded observations can also be used by experienced teachers and consultants to study the effectiveness of different methods of teaching. For instance, if the teacher of a preschool group is consistently using some technique, such as singing in a minor key, when a child is exploring boundaries between socially acceptable and unacceptable behavior, observers of that group can assemble all their records dealing with child behavior at the time when the teacher sang in a minor key. Careful study of such records will show the kinds of child behavior associated with the teacher's singing in a minor key. Were the children kept from undesirable behavior in some instances? If so, what—if anything—did those children have in common? Or, what was common to the situations in which the children were deterred? to those in which they were not? By attempting to answer such questions through the use of observational feedback, the experienced workers actually use a technique which they can continue using in order to continue improving in service. At the same time, they become aware of techniques which are effective with preschool children and techniques which are thought to be useful but probably are not.

A third way in which recorded observations may be useful to experienced teachers and consultants is in helping them to develop increased awareness of the characteristics of children at particular age levels and to use their awareness as a basis for improving the curriculum for the children. For instance, a workshop of experienced teachers can assemble anecdotes, collected over the years, which show how preschool children think about their families, or about the concept of numbers, or about some aspect of the preschool curriculum. By grouping these observational records according to the age levels of the children, the teachers can arrive at a description of—for instance—the development of time concepts in preschool children, and can go on to plan activities which will enrich these concepts at each age level.

Situations for Discussion

A preschool teacher is apt to find herself in situations similar to the four described here. As you think of what to do in each situation, consider whether each course of action suggested is desirable, or not. Use points brought out in the chapter as well as ideas from your own experience to justify your views. Suggest alternative courses of action to supplement those given.

SITUATION 1   As a teacher of a nursery group, you have three assistants to help you with a group of twenty children. While one assistant works indoors, the other two help supervise outdoor activities. One morning you observe that the assistants working outdoors have divided the outdoor space between them and each is trying to entice children to play in her area. You should

- Remind the assistants to support, not interfere with, the children's play activities.
- Withhold comments until the assistants learn how to pace children's activities.
- Encourage the assistants to make written observations of a child.
- Devote the next meeting to a discussion of desirable and undesirable ways of supervising childen's activities.
- Supervise the outdoor area yourself.

SITUATION 2   Janet, one of the assistants, takes little or no initiative in helping the children. She asks you for specific directions about what she should do, and avoids making any decisions herself. As the teacher you should

- Have her supervise an outdoor area at a distance from other adults.
- Encourage her to do more of the housekeeping activities instead of activities with children.
- Make brief comments to Janet about what you are doing with individual children.
- Whenever you can, make such remarks as "Children, when you finish coloring your puppy, Janet will help you put him together with brads."
- Have an experienced but quiet assistant work whenever Janet does.

SITUATION 3   You have a new assistant who, on her third working day, offers to read stories to the children. As the teacher, you should

- Advise her to observe you during story time before trying it herself.
- Let her read to the children, then praise what she does.
- Help her to select stories that are favorites of the children.
- Have her read to a small group of children.
- Introduce her to the group of children before she starts reading to them.

SITUATION 4   One of the assistants is of little help to the other children because her own three-year-old demands her attention constantly. As the teacher, you should suggest that the assistant

- Spend at least half an hour daily at home following the lead of her child.
- Be patient until this phase of her child's behavior has passed.
- Bring her problem to the regular staff meeting for discussion.
- Talk with the child about sharing her mother with other children.
- Consider having her child in another preschool group.

Current Professional Books and Pamphlets

Association for Childhood Education International. *Toward Better Kindergartens.* Washington, D.C.: Association for Childhood Education International, 1966. [ACEI makes an excellent series of publications available to preschool teachers, both prospective and in service.]

COHEN, DOROTHY H., and VIRGINIA STERN. *Observing and Recording the Behavior of Young Children.* New York: Bank Street College of Education. [This one of the many booklets handled by Bank Street College Bookstore encourages teachers to learn more about children though using and recording anecdotal material.]

FOURACRE, MAURICE A., and others. *The Effects of a Preschool Prgram upon Young Educable Mentally Retarded Children.* New York: Teachers College, Columbia University, 1962. [Through appraisal of programs, teachers are able to improve the programs.]

GEORGE, A. E., tr. *The Montessori Method.* Cambridge, Mass.: Robert Bentley, Inc., 1965. [Such books making methods developed by Montessori available to teachers in this country are worthy of study by the preschool staff.]

GOULD, JOSEPHINE T. *Growing with Nursery and Kindergarten Children.* Boston: Beacon Press, 1960. [This adult guide for the Martin and Judy series for children suggests ways of teaching such topics as disappointment on a rainy day, fears, and dreams.]

HEFFERNAN, HELEN, and VIVIAN EDMISTON TODD. *The Kindergarten Teacher.* Boston: D. C. Heath & Company, 1960. [Pages 378–84 give practical suggestions about how interested parents may assist the teacher, and the last chapter, about development of teachers in service.]

Project Head Start—The Staff for a Child Development Center. Washington, D.C.: U.S. Government Printing Office, 1969. [A child-development center is a community facility to which contributions are made by volunteers, parents, and other supplements to the teaching staff.]

Project Head Start—Volunteers in the Child Development Center Program. Washington, D.C.: U.S. Government Printing Office. [Volunteers enrich the program of a center, bring problems with them, and gain satisfaction through their contributions.]

SPODEK, BERNARD. *Preparing Teachers of Disadvantaged Young Children.* New York: National Association for the Education of Young Children, 1966. [Summarizes thinking of directors of National Defense Education Act Institutes for teachers of disadvantaged children, expressed at a conference at the University of Wisconsin-Milwaukee.]

STOTT, LELAND H., and RACHEL S. BALL. *Infant and Preschool Mental Tests, Review and Evaluation.* Chicago: University of Chicago Press, 1965. [Society for Research in Child Development helped to make this available.]

TAYLOR, KATHARINE WHITESIDE. *Parents and Children Learn Together.* New York: Bureau of Publications, Teachers College, Columbia University, 1968. [Parent-cooperative preschool groups have mothers as assistants to the teacher, learning to be better guides of child learning at the same time that they enrich the program for the children.]

Teaching the Disadvantaged Young Child. New York: National Association for the Education of Young Children, 1966. [Fifteen articles selected from *Young Children,* a regular publication of the NAEYC. and one of its series of publications to help preschool teachers.]

Index

Accidents in the preschool group, 216–17

Adults, reaction of, to age characteristics of preschool child, 50–55

Adults associated with preschool group, 73–105. *See also* Teaching in preschool group
business responsibilities of, 75–76
calmness of, when dealing with emergencies, 201–202
contribution of, to emotional climate, 82–85
employer, 84
parents, 84–85
teacher, 83–84
cooperation among adults, 87–92
education aides, students as, 93
preparing for employment, 613–14
facilities and equipment needed by, 109 *t.*, 110
father, the, 78–79, 568
getting started as a teacher, 92–97
housekeeping responsibilities of, 76
number of, 79–81
in parent-cooperatives, 76–78
parent education assistant, 94–95

parents. *See also* Parent education; Parents in preschool group
responsibilities of, 6–7, 87–88
professional responsibilities of, 75
in Project Head Start, 81–82
teacher. *See* Teacher, the

Age of entrance into a nursery group, 149

Art
as an arrangement, 452–55
concepts of, developed by preschool curriculum, 165 *t.*
physical development, as an integral part of, 244 *t.*

Arts and crafts, 451–77. *See also* Art
developing a feeling for form, 458–59
developing a feeling for texture, 455–56
developing skill with tools, 470–75
construction, 473–74
cutting with scissors, 472
using a brush, 470–71
whittling, 474–75
enjoying color, 456–57
guiding activities in, 466–70
according to age level, 469–70

661

Arts and crafts (*Cont'd*)
  limits to freedom of expression, 468–69
  permissive attitude, 468
  in other curriculum areas, 461–62
  seasonal activities, 463–66
    Christmas, 463–65, 464 *t.*
    Easter, 464 *t.*, 465–66
    Halloween, 464 *t.*
  social benefits, 459–61

Behavior of preschool child
  gifted and handicapped, 57, 58 *t.*, 59
  how to interpret, 35–38
  need of adults to understand negative behavior, 52–54
  skills, attitudes, and concepts developed by preschool curriculum, 163, 164–65 *t.*
Books and pamphlets, professional
  on guiding emotional development, 543–44
  on parent education, 581–83
  on preschool group, 27–28, 71–72, 105, 143–44, 185–87
    as a school laboratory, 618–20
  on teaching in preschool group, 657–58
Books for preschool children
  arts and crafts, 476–77
  emotional development, 543
  health and safety, 239
  language development, 418–19
  music, 503
  number, 384–85
  physical development, 262
  science, 351–52
  social development, 304–305
  space, 384
  stories, 422–39, 449–50
  time, 385

Child Development Center, 9–10
Children, preschool
  adult reactions to age characteristics of, 50–55
  behavior of. *See* Behavior of preschool child

characteristic behavior of, 30–31
  development of. *See* Development of preschool child
  effect of home environment on, 32
  how to observe, 32–35
  individual differences in, 55–63
    between boys and girls, 60–61
    body build, 59–60
    dexterity, 59
  meeting needs of, 63–69
    adequacy, 67–68
    belonging, 67
    development of a healthy personality, 64–66
    integrity, 69
    physical needs, 64
    safety, 66
    security, 67
    self-realization, 68
Children in the preschool group, 145–60
  development of self-discipline, 153–54
  factors deciding whether or not to enroll child, 145–51
    age, 149
    exceptional child, 149–51
    family readiness, 146–48
    toileting question, 148–49
  parental release of children, 154–57
  ways to prevent "dropouts," 152–59
Creative teaching, 172
Culture, the
  learning to participate in. *See* Social understanding
Curriculum, preschool, 160–67
  arts and crafts. *See* Arts and crafts
  compared to elementary school curriculum, 160–63
  emotional development. *See* Emotional development, guidance of
  exploring time, space, and number. *See* Time; Space; Number
  health and safety. *See* Health and safety
  music. *See* Music

physical development. *See* Physical development

of a religious nature, 166–67

science. *See* Science

skills, attitudes, and concepts developed by, 163, 164–65 *t*.

social understanding. *See* Social understanding

stories for preschool children. *See* Stories for preschool children

verbal communication. *See* Language development

Day nurseries, 8–9, 78

Development of preschool child, 20–26, 36 *ff*.

adults and, 82–85

aspects of, 36–37 *t*.

creative, 26

developmental problems, 43–44, 45–46 *t*.

emotional, 25, 36–37 *t*.

identifying stages of, 42–43

intellectual, 25, 36–37 *t*.

knowing level of, 39–49

importance for parents, 41–42

importance for teachers, 39–41

as a person, 23

physical, 25, 36–37 *t*.

readiness for learning, 44, 46–49

social, 23–25, 36–37 *t*.

Education aides, 93

preparing for employment as, 613–14

Elementary school, the

curriculum of, compared to preschool curriculum, 160–63

getting acquainted with, 285

preparation for, 258–61

teacher diagnosis of development of child, 259–61

Emotional development, guidance of, 504–544

establishing an identity, 505–506

limit to teacher's role in, 538–41

teacher uses mild emotions, 506–519

affectionate, 507–508

encourages helpers, 510–11

helps children with peer relationships, 513–18

listens for feedback, 518–19

realistic, 508–510

stimulates development of a conscience, 511–13

teacher's handling of unpleasant emotions, 519–27

avoiding severe disappointments, 526–27

discouraging destruction, 526

helping a child with a tantrum, 523–26

watching for signs of loss of control, 519–21

watching for situations involving pressure, 521–23

teacher's role in furthering emotional development, 527–38

guiding doll play, 536–38

guiding individual child in the group situation, 530–33

recognizing effects of parental attitudes, 535–36

teaching property rights, 533–34

understanding nature of emotions, 527–29

Employer in the preschool group

contribution of, to emotional climate, 84

Equipment and supplies of preschool group, 125–42

adapted equipment, 137–38

basic equipment, 126–27

care of equipment, 137

equipment for the teacher, 141–42

indoor equipment, 132–37

junk, 138–39

outdoor equipment, 129–32

portable equipment, 139–41

unstructured media, 128–29

Exceptional child and the preschool group, 149–51

Films

for parents, 584–87

for teachers and parents, 187–89

Filmstrips for teachers and parents, 189–90

Geography. *See also* Space
  concepts of, developed by pre-
    school curriculum, 164 *t.*
  physical development, as an inte-
    gral part of, 244 *t.*

Head Start programs. *See* Project
  Head Start
Health and safety, 193–239
  concepts of, developed by pre-
    school curriculum, 164 *t.*
  health education, 221–34
    arts and crafts, as an integral
      part of, 461–62
    caring for teeth, 231–34
    cleaning, 231
    germ theory, 230–31
    helping child with toileting, 223–
      25
    importance of breathing, 228–30
    importance of keeping well, 230
    importance of seeing well, 228
    introducing new foods, 225–27
  health maintenance, 194–207
    daily inspection, 198–200
    enrollment medical examination,
      194–95
    health history, 195–98
    mental health of children, 206–
      207
    nutrition, 202–206
    provision for individual children
      in any emergency, 200–202
    sanitation, 206
    sick leave, 208
  keeping children safe, 208–221
    establishing and maintaining lim-
      its, 210–11
    health records for emergencies,
      212–14
    pupil-teacher ratio, 211–12
    supervision of play activities,
      209–210
    taking care of oneself, 222–23
  physical development, as an inte-
    gral part of, 244 *t.*

safety education, 214–221
  accidents, 216–17
  knives and matches, 219–21
  safety in boats, 219
  safety at home or school, 214–16
  safety in the streets, 217–19
  school policy, 234–37
  on absence for illness, 234–35
  on insurance, 237
  on refunds for illness, 236
  on shoes at nap time, 236–37
Holiday customs, 288–303

Indoor activities, teacher's supervision
  of, 252–54
Indoor equipment, 132–37

Kindergartens, 8, 12
  curriculum for, 161 *ff.*

Laboratory schools, 8, 10. *See also*
  School laboratory, preschool
  group as
Language development, 386–419
  children from non-English-speaking
    families, 390–391
  concepts of, developed by pre-
    school curriculum, 165 *t.*
  enhancing speech development,
    411–17
    developing a sense of humor,
      414–15
    dictation, 413–14
    helping children to perceive rela-
      tionships, 416–17
    teacher-child dialogue, 412–13
  helping a child communicate, 396–
    406
    building vocabulary, 404–405
    guiding group conversation, 405
    helping the child who does not
      talk, 402–403
    hints for adult listeners, 398–99
    listening to individual reports,
      399–400
    regular opportunity for talking
      with an adult, 401–402
    showing mother around school,
      400–401

simplicity aids communication, 403–404

verbal expressions of aggression, 406

physical development, as an integral part of, 244 *t.*

preventing speech disorders, 406–411

difficult sounds, 409–410

improper language, 410–11

incessant talking, 408

retardation in speech, 408–409

stuttering and cluttering, 407–408

second language, development of, 389

understanding language development, 391–96

confusion with pronouns, 395–96

conversation with activity, 394–95

preschool communication is primarily nonverbal, 394

Learning, readiness for, 44, 46–49

Love, as the basic element of a preschool group, 14–17, 85–86

Mathematics. *See also* Number

arts and crafts, as an integral part of, 462

concepts of, developed by preschool curriculum, 164 *t.*

physical development, as an integral part of, 244 *t.*

Montessori system, 166

Music, 478–503

arts and crafts, as an integral part of, 462

communicating feelings with, 482–85

absorbing sadness in music, 484–85

enjoying musical games, 483

quieting down with music, 483–84

concepts of, developed by preschool curriculum, 165 *t.*

expanding activities with musical experience, 485–87

as a group experience, 491–99

encouraging performers, 497

having a rhythm band, 498–99

pantomime songs, 497–98

teaching rhythmic movement, 492–94

teaching a song, 494–97

helping children to listen to sounds, 481–82

instruments, getting acquainted with, 487–91

autoharp, 489

drums, 490

learning about vibration, 488

phonograph, 489–90

piano, 488–89

rhythm instruments, 490–91

ukulele, 489

voice, 490

as an integral part of the preschool program, 478

learning from other teachers, 500–501

making a collection of records, 499–500

physical development, as an integral part of, 244 *t.*

Nature walks, 316, 317, 323

Number

developing concepts of, 374–82

addition, 381–82

consolidating child's ability to count, 376

guiding mathematically gifted children, 382

learning the succession of numbers, 376

showing where numbers are used, 379–80

subtraction, 380–81

teaching less as well as more, 377–79

Nursery groups, 8, 12

age of entrance into, 149

curriculum for, 161 *ff.*

Office of Economic Opportunity. *See* Project Head Start
Outdoor activities, teacher's supervision of, 245–52
Outdoor equipment, 129–32

Parent-cooperatives, 13–14, 99
functions of parent in, 76–78
Parent education, 547–87
appraisal of progress in, 578–80
educational programs, 560–69
conferences and workshops for parents and teachers, 565–66
enriching programs for less advantaged, 568–69
parental discussions, 564
parental point of view, 562–63
parents participation in, 561–62
using anecdotal records, 566–68
what to discuss, 564–65
preschool group experience and parental development, 569–78
outcomes of parent participation, 576–78
ways of educating parents, 549–60
bulletins, handbooks, and bulletin board, 551–53
evaluating pupil progress, 557–59
group meetings for parents, 559–60
parent interviews, 553–54
visiting the preschool group, 555–57
Parent education assistant, 94–95
Parental attitudes
teacher's recognition of, when guiding emotional development, 535–36
Parental release of children, 154–57
Parents in preschool group. *See also* Parent education
contribution of, to emotional climate, 84–85
father, the, 78–79, 568
functions of, in parent-cooperative, 76–78
health education for parents, 221
responsibilities of, 6–7, 87–88

Parents and teachers
conferences and workshops for, 565–66
Physical development, 240–62
arts and crafts, as an integral part of, 462
concepts of, developed by preschool curriculum, 164 *t*.
concomitant learnings, 255–58
building confidence through awareness of skill, 256
developing persistence, 257
learning to take turns, 257
problem solving, 258
curriculum considerations, 241–45
physical education as an integral part of preschool activities, 243–45
physical education objectives, 242–43
values of physical education, 241–42
indoor activities, supervision of, 252–54
ball handling, 253
boxing gloves, 253
cleaning surfaces, 254
moving equipment, 254
punching balloons, 253
trampoline, 252–53
outdoor activities, supervision of, 245–52
ball-handling, 246–47
climbing apparatus, 249–50
digging and raking, 251
merry-go-round, 249, 250
slides, 247–48
swings, 245
tree climbing, 251–52
walking boards, 248–49
physical transitions, 254–55
preparation for elementary school, 258–61
teacher diagnosis on development of child, 259–61
Planning committee of preschool group
considering basic needs of children, 107–109

considering needs of adults, 109–110

preparation of facilities by, 115–25

selection of location by, 110–14

Preschool children. *See* Children, preschool

Preschool education

parental responsibility in, 6–7

rationale for, 3 *ff.*

Preschool group

adults in. *See* Adults associated with preschool group

children in. *See* Children in the preschool group

curriculum for. *See* Curriculum, preschool

daily program for. *See* Program, daily

development of child in, 20–26. *See also* Development of preschool child

creative, 26

expected changes, 20–23

equipment and supplies. *See* Equipment and supplies of preschool group

first day of school, importance of, 178–79

getting the school ready, 106–144. *See also* School, preparation of

love, as the basic element of, 14–17, 85–86

organization of, 73–105. *See also* Adults associated with preschool group

planning committee, 107–110

preparation of facilities

indoor, 115–18

outdoor, 118–22

storage, 122–25

as a school laboratory. *See* School laboratory, preschool group as

selection of location, 110–14

teacher in. *See* Teacher, the; Teaching in preschool group

types of, 8–14

backyard groups, 14

church-sponsored, 12

day nurseries, 8–9, 78

Head Start projects, 4, 9–10, 81–82

laboratory schools, 8, 10. *See also* School laboratory, preschool group as

parent cooperatives, 13–14, 76, 99

private nurseries and kindergartens, 12, 78. *See also* Kindergartens; Nursery groups

school-affiliated, 10–11

Preschool program, appraisal of, 183–84

Professional books and pamphlets

on guiding emotional development, 543–44

on parent education, 581–83

on preschool group, 27–28, 71–72, 105, 143–44, 185–87

as a school laboratory, 618–20

on teaching in preschool group, 657–58

Program, daily, 173–83

flexibility in, 182–83

importance of routine in, 179–81

samples of, 175–76

Project Head Start, 4, 9–10

personnel in, 81–82

preparation for elementary school, 258

Pupil-teacher ratio, 211–12

Readiness for learning, 44, 46–49

Relating to others. *See also* Emotional development, guidance of

concepts of, developed by preschool curriculum, 165 *t.*

Safety. *See* Health and safety

School, preparation of

equipment and supplies, 125–42

planning committee, 107–110

preparation of facilities, 115–25

selection of location, 110–14

School facilities, preparation of, 115–25

indoor, 115–18

School facilities (*Cont'd*)
  outdoor, 118–22
  storage, 122–25
School laboratory, preschool group as, 588–620
  checklist of teaching skills for assistants, 600–601
  for high school students, 603–616
    appraising student progress, 614–16
    learning to observe children, 607–608
    learning to take responsibility, 611–12
    multiple use of laboratory situations, 605–607
    preparing for employment as an aide, 613–14. *See also* Education aides
    preparing for parenthood, 612
    providing a preschool group situation, 603–604
    scheduling, 604
    starting to work with preschool children, 608–610
    understanding oneself better, 610–11
    value of, 593–94
  values of, 589–602
    for fifth- or sixth-grade students, 589–92
    for junior high school students, 592–93
    for junior college students, 594–95
    for senior high school students, 593–94
    toward a general education, 595–99
    toward professional preparation, 599–600
School location, factors in selection of, 110–14
Science, 306–352
  arts and crafts, as an integral part of, 462
  concepts of, developed by preschool curriculum, 164 *t.*
  guiding scientific thinking, 308–314
    developing a scientific attitude, 309–311
    helping a child interpret his findings, 313–14
    helping a child observe, 311–13
  introduction to different sciences, 337–50
    bacteriology, 345
    biology (pets), 347–50
    chemistry, 337–40
    conservation, 346
    electricity, 342
    light, 343–44
    magnetism, 342
    mechanics, 340–42
    physics, 340
    rockets and spaceships, 344–45
  learning about each season, 314–29
    autumn, 315–18
    spring, 323–26
    summer, 326–29
    winter, 318–23
  nature walks, 316, 317, 323
  physical development, as an integral part of, 244 *t.*
  preparing a garden, 324–25
  simple astronomical facts, 321
  understanding the body, 329–37
    circulation, 333–34
    death, 336–37
    digestion, 330
    excretion, 331
    reproduction, 334–36
    respiration, 332
    resting, 333
    sensation, 332–33
Situations for discussion
  arts and crafts, 475–76
  emotional development, 541–42
  health and safety, 238–39
  language development, 417–18
  music, 502–503
  parent education, 580–81
  physical development, 261–62
  preschool group, 26–27, 69–70, 103–104, 142–43, 184–85
    as a school laboratory, 617–18
  science, 350

social understanding, 303–304

stories for preschool children, 448–49

teaching in preschool groups, 656–57

time, space, and number, 383–84

Skills, attitudes, and concepts developed by preschool curriculum, 163, 164–65 t.

Social studies

physical development, as an integral part of, 244 t.

Social understanding, 263–305

arts and crafts, as an integral part of, 462

concepts of, developed by preschool curriculum, 164 t.

holiday customs, 288–303

Christmas, 293–98

Easter, 299–300

Fourth of July, 302–303

Halloween, 289–92

Mother's Day and Father's Day, 300–302

Thanksgiving, 292–93

Valentine's Day, 298–99

initial experiences in the social order, 273–88

community understanding, 278–82

contrasts between city and country, 282–83

getting acquainted with the elementary school, 285

getting to know the artifacts, 273–77

learning about food preparation, 277–78

pretend outdoor experiences, 283–84

thinking of other people, 286–88

world concepts, 285–86

learning roles, 275–73

learning about family relationships, 266–70

learning to be an individual child, 265–66

learning the role of a boy or a girl, 270–72

trying out vocational roles, 272–73

Space

arts and crafts, as an integral part of, 462

developing concepts of, 362–74

classifying, 373

contrasting words about space, 372–73

geography, early experiences with, 362–65

guiding visual observations of space, 371–72

place associations, 367–69

sensitivity to space relationships, 365–67

space relationships through water play, 373–74

teaching basic shapes, 369–71

Staff meetings, 651–52

Stories for preschool children, 420–50

arts and crafts, as an integral part of, 462

books to meet needs of children, 420–29

in belonging to a group, 425–26

for experience, 427

to further security in relationships, 422–23

for safety, 426–27

selection of, 427–29

for self-confidence, 423–24

concepts of, developed by preschool curriculum, 165 t.

for each age level, 429–34

five-year-old child, 431–32

four-year-old child, 430–31

inappropriate stories, 433–34

teaching about fact and fancy, 433

three-year-old child, 429–30

illustrations for stories, 435–39

books to avoid, 437

helping children to "read" pictures, 436

matching pictures and story, 437–38

selecting appropriate pictures, 436–37

Stories for preschool children (*Cont'd*)
  library story hours, 439–40
  physical development, as an integral part of, 244 *t.*
  poetry, 446–48
  presentation of, 440–48
    dramatizing a story, 443–44
    reading a story, 441–42
    size of group, 442–43
    teaching humor, 445–46
    using the flannelboard, 444–45
  selecting a preschool book, 438–39

Teaching, the. *See also* Adults associated with preschool group
  attributes of, 85–87
    love, 85–86
    maturity, 86
    understanding how to teach, 86–87
  calmness of, when dealing with emergencies, 201–202
  contribution of, to emotional climate, 83–84
  decisions of, about selection of equipment and supplies, 125 *ff.*
  equipment for, 141–42
  helping the children learn, 167–73
    creative teaching, 172
    planning for a free choice of activities, 168
    planning large group activities, 168–69
    planning small group activities, 170–72
  pupil-teacher ratio, 211–12
  role of, 18–20
    in guiding emotional development. *See* Emotional development
  selection of, 97–103
    qualifications, 97, 100
  sick leave, 208
  supervising indoor activities, 252–54
  supervising outdoor activities, 245–52

understanding preschool children, 29 *ff.*
Teachers and parents
  conferences and workshops for, 565–66
Teaching in preschool group, 621–58
  achieving depth of understanding of children, 650–53
    observing individual children, 32–35, 651
    rapport through caring for children, 650–51
    regular staff meetings, 651–52
  how assistants work with individual children, 642–53
    general suggestions, 643–44
    helping an aggressive child, 644–45
    helping the shy child, 645–46
    improving guidance of individual children, 648–50
    what should an assistant say?, 646–48
    when should an assistant offer help?, 648–50
  in-service education of teachers and consultants, 653–56
  initial experience as a participant, 633–35
  observation of child, 623–33
    conducting a group observation, 631–33
    making anecdotal and time recordings, 628–31
    making and using observation record, 623–26
    separating observations from evaluations, 627–28
  participants and their functions, 621–23
  supervision of assistants to the teacher, 635–42
    capitalizing on experienced assistants, 638–40
    inducting new assistants, 636–38
    schedules for assistants, 640–42
Time
  developing a sense of time, 357–62

artifacts of time, 360
comparisons in time, 361–62
continuity in preschool activities,
   361
developing relationships for days
   of week, 359–60

establishing concept of points in
   time, 354–57
Toileting
   helping child with, 223–25
   readiness for school and, 148–49